More praise for
The Purina™ Encyclopedia of Dog Care

"Canine alphabet soup has never been so easy going down: a mix of practical information with a dose of helpful training tips and a dash of hot news. *The Purina™ Encyclopedia of Dog Care* is a user-friendly, one-stop guide for sharing your life with a four-legged best friend. Amy Shojai is one bulldog of a journalist; you can be sure to find the lastest in cutting-edge medical news [in here]."

— STEVE DALE
> Syndicated columnist, "My Pet World," Tribune Media Services
> Host, "Pet Central," WGN Radio
> Senior columnist, *Pet Life* magazine

"Shojai provides a plethora of up-to-date information on the A–Z topics of dogdom. If you've got a dog, you'll have questions—if you've got this book, you'll have answers."

— CHERYL S. SMITH
> Author of *The Trick Is in the Training* and
> *The Complete Idiot's Guide to Showing Your Dog*

"Amy Shojai is one of the very best when it comes to writing about pet health. Her name on the cover is a guarantee of top-quality information inside."

— GINA SPADAFORI
> Pet columnist, Universal Press Syndicate
> Author of *Dogs for Dummies*

"With *The Purina™ Encyclopedia of Dog Care*, Amy Shojai has crafted the perfect companion to her *The Purina™ Encyclopedia of Cat Care*. This comprehensive volume deserves a place in every dog owner's library."

— DARLENE ARDEN
> Author of *The Irrepressible Toy Dog*

ALSO BY AMY D. SHOJAI

The Purina™ Encyclopedia of Cat Care

THE PURINA™
ENCYCLOPEDIA
OF DOG CARE

AMY D. SHOJAI

Ballantine Books · New York

A Ballantine Book
Published by The Ballantine Publishing Group

www.randomhouse.com/BB/

LIBRARY OF CONGRESS CATALOGING-IN-PUBLICATION DATA
Shojai, Amy, 1956–
    The Purina encyclopedia of dog care / Amy D. Shojai.—1st ed.
    p.   cm.
    Includes index.
    ISBN 0-345-41286-9 (hc : alk. paper)
    1. Dogs—Encyclopedias.   2. Dogs—Diseases—Encyclopedias.
3. Dogs—Health—Encyclopedias.   I. Ralston Purina Company.
II. Title.
SF422.S55   1999
636.7'0893—dc21   99-10800

Text design by Holly Johnson

Cover design by Min Choi
Cover photo © Ron Kimball Studios

Manufactured in the United States of America

First Edition: June 1999
10   9   8   7   6   5   4   3   2   1

For all the dogs
of our lives—

from the past, who touch our souls;
of the present, who fill our hearts;
and in the future, who renew our joy.

Especially for Fafnir, my furry muse—
This one's for you.

Contents

Acknowledgments

This book would not have been possible without the help of many people—and dogs, like Dixie, Sandy, Toby, Lady, Pickles, Fafnir, Skye, and others—who offered their expertise, help, and inspiration along the way. Huge thanks go to my parents—Mom, who urged me to write down my "pet experiences," and Dad, who has always been my cheerleader.

The unfailing support and humor of my husband, Mahmoud, has sustained me from the beginning. Thanks to my writing buddies—of the pet persuasion and otherwise—who endlessly inspire me with their professionalism and willingness to lend a hand. Special thanks to Moira Anderson Allen for encouraging my earliest efforts, the "pet press" for recognizing them, and the Dog Writers Association of America and the Cat Writers Association for reminding me what's important.

Countless veterinary teachers and researchers across the nation have given freely of their expertise to answer my questions over the years. In particular, I must thank the veterinary professionals at: Auburn University, Cornell University, Ohio State, Texas A&M, Tufts University, University of California at Davis, University of Florida, University of Minnesota, and University of Pennsylvania. I'd particularly like to thank Ken L. Lawrence, D.V.M., for his expert help and advice over the years.

Grateful thanks to Kerry Lyman at Purina, who believed in the book before it was ever written—and championed my cause at all turns; to my editors Joanne Wyckoff who had the vision to choose the book, and Elizabeth Zack who makes me look good; to Jane Popham, Fran Pennock Shaw, and Betsy Stowe whose photos so eloquently illustrate my text; to my brother Laird Monteith who brings my own photos to life; and especially to my agent Meredith Bernstein, who does all the really hard stuff so I can live my writing dream.

Finally, thanks be to the dogs—to those who live in our past, our present, and in our future. Without you, this book would never have been written.

Foreword

If you are reading this foreword, you want to be a responsible pet owner, and being a responsible pet owner requires one thing: information.

In order for it to be useful, the information must be good and solid: not opinions or theories, but correct information. And it is not enough for the information to be just excellent and proven; it must also be delivered in an understandable, readable fashion. This is a tall order in any field of knowledge, but it is an order that this encyclopedia fills with ease.

The Purina Encyclopedia of Dog Care enables dog lovers to not only raise a healthy, well-behaved family dog but also to become ambassadors, sources of correct, understandable, and useful knowledge about their canines.

The information in *The Purina Encyclopedia of Dog Care* is complete. Amy Shojai takes you effortlessly through the complex subject of dog care, from selecting a breed to raising a puppy, from learning canine body language to understanding the dangers ticks pose to your pet. This is one comprehensive book.

But perhaps more important than its extensive information is the fact that it is honest. Amy Shojai clearly writes with both you and your pet's best interests firmly in mind, giving ethical information on cropping and docking, as well as complete information on dog breeds.

This is one of the most thorough and easy-to-understand books on everything you might want to know about your dog that I have ever had the pleasure to read, and I have read a few in my many years in this field.

While many books claim to be "of interest to the novice and experienced dog person alike," this book truly is. Inside its covers you will find detailed information on housebreaking a new puppy or how to deskunk a dog as well as clear, up-to-date details on such problems as ketoacidosis or babesiosis.

The appendices are a delight. There you can locate almost any phone number a dog owner might need, or refer to the "at a glance" symptom assessment chart, as well as specific care guidelines for common health problems.

This is a book I will purchase for every dog person I know—whether they've been winning in the show ring for years or just recently won the heart of a stray. Every dog lover should have a copy at their fingertips at all times.

This will be a cherished, dog-eared resource here at the Kilcommons's household. Enjoy!

— BRIAN KILCOMMONS
Director of Animal Behavior and Training
City of New York Center for Animal Care and Control

THE PURINA™
ENCYCLOPEDIA
OF DOG CARE

Abscess

Abscess refers to the body's attempt to wall off infection. The fight against infection results in an accumulation of white blood cells and other blood components, commonly called *pus*. This liquid collects in a fleshy pocket beneath the skin, which swells and becomes very painful. The swelling is called an *abscess*.

Almost anything, like a bite wound, splinter, or even an INSECT STING, can result in an abscess if the surface of the skin is penetrated. When the skin surface heals over the wound, bacteria is sealed inside, the body's IMMUNE SYSTEM is activated, and a pocket of infection may form.

Signs of abscess include a soft swelling and/or draining of purulent material at the site, pain, fever above 102.5 degrees, lethargy, loss of appetite, and reluctance to move the affected area. Bite wounds that plant infectious organisms deep into the tissue are prime causes of abscesses. Abscesses commonly are found in the head and neck region but may appear anywhere on the body. They can also result from chewing an inappropriate object that splinters. Dogs also can suffer from abscessed teeth (see PERIODONTAL DISEASE). Head, neck, and teeth abscesses typically cause one side of the neck to swell, and your dog may drool and refuse food. Dogs also commonly suffer from ANAL GLAND abscesses, in which the area surrounding the rectum becomes red, swollen, and tender.

The diagnosis of an abscess is generally made from the signs. If your dog has a heavy coat, the injury may be hidden from view and the problem not noticed until the dog is in pain and flinches from your touch, or the abscess begins to drain. As the injury swells with pus, the skin stretches and becomes

a

ABSCESS

SYMPTOMS
Painful skin swelling, or draining sore; fever; loss of appetite; lethargy

HOME CARE
Moist, warm compresses; clean with damp cloths; supportive nutrition

VET CARE
Surgical lancing and draining; usually antibiotic therapy

PREVENTION
Prevent fights by neutering and spaying, and confining dogs to fenced yards; regular anal gland care and dental care

thin until it ultimately ruptures. The smelly fluid is white to greenish with tinges of blood, and it may soak the surrounding fur.

Abscesses should be treated as soon as they're noticed to prevent further damage to the surrounding area. The infection can spread until nearby tissue dies, muscle or nerves are damaged, and/or the resulting massive wound is difficult to heal.

In most cases, the abscess is so painful your dog must be anesthetized before the veterinarian can treat him. The fur around the swelling is clipped, and the area disinfected with a surgical scrub solution like Betadine. Then the wound is lanced, the infection drained, and the abscess flushed with a solution like peroxide and water. Antibiotics are often prescribed as well.

When the abscess is very deep or intrusive, a drain or "wick" may be surgically stitched into place to keep the area draining as the surface skin heals and to prevent the abscess from recurring. When the surgical site is within reach of the dog's teeth, an ELIZABETHAN COLLAR prevents the dog from bothering the healing wound.

If an abscess ruptures on its own, and if your dog will allow you, use a fifty-fifty solution of hydrogen peroxide and water to clean the area. When the wound is shallow, simply keep the area clean over the course of a week by flushing the area with this solution once or twice a day until it heals. Usually, though, it's best to have your veterinarian evaluate the sore, especially if it's a deep sore.

Prevent abscesses by reducing your dog's chances of injury. NEUTERING or SPAYING your dog will greatly diminish AGGRESSION and subsequent bite wounds. Supervise chew objects and make sure only safe alternatives are offered (see CHEWING). Good dental hygiene and routine care of anal glands will help reduce the chance of abscesses in these areas.

a

Acanthosis Nigricans

This unusual disease in its primary form most commonly affects Dachshunds; its name literally means *thickened, black skin.* Typically, Dachshunds develop the disease prior to age two. However, it is commonly seen as a secondary disorder in any age or breed dog due to atopy (see ALLERGY), chronic DERMATITIS, HYPOTHYROIDISM, CUSHING'S DISEASE, or certain CANCERS—and can be managed by removing the underlying cause and providing topical therapy.

Primary disease is recognized as the skin of the dog's armpits and groin darken to black, and a greasy, rancid discharge forms, which is often accompanied by a bacterial skin infection. The disease slowly spreads to affect more and more of the body until it may encompass the legs, chest, abdomen, and lower back.

The cause of the primary form is unknown, and there is no specific treatment. Diagnosis is based on clinical signs and sometimes a skin biopsy, in which a sample is removed and examined microscopically.

Current management aims at keeping the dog as comfortable as possible by using canine SEBORRHEA shampoos that remove bacteria and excess oil. Oral antibiotics are helpful when infection is present, and sometimes cortisone preparations may soothe skin irritation. Oral corticosteroids and vitamin E may be effective; ask your veterinarian for a recommendation.

ACANTHOSIS NIGRICANS
SYMPTOMS
Thickened, blackened skin and greasy, rancid skin discharge beginning at groin and armpits, spreading over body
HOME CARE
Seborrhea shampoos
VET CARE
Same as home care; also antibiotics for skin infection, sometimes cortisone to soothe irritation
PREVENTION
None

a

There is no way to predict or prevent the condition. However, it is recommended that dogs suffering from the disease not be bred, to prevent their passing the condition on to puppies in the event that it is inheritable.

Acne

Canine acne results from the plugging of hair follicles and is common in adolescent dogs, particularly short-coated breeds, like Doberman Pinschers, Great Danes, and Boxers.

The cause of canine acne is thought to be similar to the condition that arises in human adolescents. The sensitivity of the sebaceous glands and hair follicles is increased by sexual hormones that are present at puberty, which in dogs is between the ages of five to twelve months. An increased production of sebum, the oily material that helps lubricate the skin and hair coat, may promote inflammation of these areas and result in skin problems.

The diagnosis is based on clinical signs. Acne primarily affects the skin of the dog's chin, and sometimes lips and muzzle. Signs primarily are unsightly blackheads, pimples, and crusty sores. There is rarely any itchiness involved. Most dogs—like most humans—outgrow the problem. The condition is primarily a cosmetic concern.

Canine acne rarely requires treatment and usually resolves on its own. A few cases may continue into adulthood, though. Just keep the affected area clean by applying a warm, wet compress. Sponging with water once or twice a day will help the area heal.

ACNE

SYMPTOMS
Blackheads and pimples; red or swollen skin; irritation or pain on the chin, lips, or muzzle

HOME CARE
Apply damp heat to chin daily; cleanse twice daily with plain water, or use cleansers like benzoyl peroxide–type solutions

VET CARE
When infected, clip fur; professionally clean with oral or topical antibiotic

PREVENTION
Most dogs outgrow the condition; use stainless steel bowls instead of plastic

When crusty sores persist, medicated ointments and shampoos or antibiotics available from your veterinarian may help. Use peroxide diluted half-and-half in water, or an antibacterial soap like pHisoHex twice a day to cleanse the area, then apply an antibacterial ointment recommended by your veterinarian. Products containing benzoyl peroxide have a flushing action that helps keep the follicles clean, and are quite effective. Check with your veterinarian for a safe recommendation.

Addison's Disease

Technically referred to as *hypoadrenocorticism*, Addison's disease is a malfunction of part of the endocrine system. The condition is named for the nineteenth-century English doctor who first described it in humans.

Endocrine glands include the pituitary gland, thyroid, pancreas, and adrenal glands as well as others located throughout the body. Each gland secretes specific hormones directly into the bloodstream that help regulate various body functions.

Addison's disease results when the adrenal glands, located adjacent to the kidneys, fail to produce enough of the hormones cortisone and aldosterone. These hormones help regulate the blood concentrations of the electrolytes sodium, chloride, calcium, and potassium, and without regulation, the dog becomes very sick.

The cause of the disease is not known, but it is suspected that most cases result from a malfunction of the IMMUNE SYSTEM. There is no one breed more prone than another, but most cases of Addison's disease affect young female dogs four to five years old or younger.

Initially, signs of illness are subtle, and they may become apparent only when the dog suffers some stressful event, such as boarding. Intermittent loss of appetite, weakness, VOMITING, and increased thirst and urination are early symptoms.

As the adrenal glands become more and more damaged, the dog suffers severe illness even without a stressful event. Vomiting worsens, and DIARRHEA and DEHYDRATION develop, with dogs typically suffering a severe weight loss. In some cases, the dog's skin may become dark. Without prompt treatment, the dog will go into SHOCK, then coma, and ultimately will die.

The diagnosis is made by testing the blood for telltale signs of electrolyte abnormalities and hormone imbalance. Dogs in crises require fluid therapy and replacement of the hormones.

Because the cause isn't known, there is no way to predict which dogs may be affected or to prevent the disease from developing. A properly treated dog

a

ADDISON'S DISEASE (HYPOADRENOCORTICISM)

SYMPTOMS
Loss of appetite; weakness; vomiting; slow heart rate; diarrhea leading to dehydration; eventually shock, coma, and death

HOME CARE
None

VET CARE
Address shock with fluid therapy; replace hormones

PREVENTION
None; once diagnosed, monthly injections or daily oral hormone replacement; reduce dog's stress levels; daily prednisone helpful during stressful times

can lead a happy, relatively normal life, but maintenance therapy is required for the remainder of the dog's life. Monthly injections or daily oral medications supply your dog with the necessary hormones depleted by this disease.

Administer Medication

All dog owners will eventually need to medicate their dogs. The task may be simple or problematic, depending on the size and temperament of your individual pet.

But almost all treatments, from topically applied ointments and salves to oral medications like pills or liquids, and even injections, can be given at home, once you learn how. And in many instances, treating your dog at home may be easier on him—and you—than the stress of a ride to the veterinarian's office.

Whether your dog is big, small, or in between, it's beneficial to enlist an extra pair of hands for medicating. That way, one person can RESTRAIN and comfort the dog, while the other performs the treatment. Wrapping a small to medium-size dog in a blanket or towel may help restrict his movements enough for you to treat without a second person's help. For those confident owners who have established a trusting relationship with their dogs, restraints may not be necessary.

Topical Treatments: Dogs usually accept *skin medications* without restraints, unless the area is very sore. When the area being treated is within licking

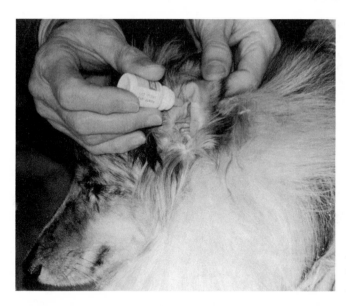

Medicating the ear *(Photo credit: Amy D. Shojai)*

range, though, care must be taken that the dog does not clean off the medication. Some medicines may taste bad and keep your dog from licking, but don't
count on that deterring a determined canine. After applying the lotion or
cream, engage your dog in a favorite game or keep him quiet for fifteen minutes or so until the medication is dry or absorbed. Other times, it may be necessary to apply a restraint to keep your dog from bothering the wound (see
ELIZABETHAN COLLAR).

EAR *medicating* also usually requires minimal restraint, unless the ears are
very tender. Have your dog lie down on his side so the opening of the affected
ear is directed at the ceiling. Then grasp the external ear flap with one hand
and drip in the medication. Avoid sticking anything inside the sore ear;
gravity will ensure the treatment gets deep inside the ear. Gently massaging
the outside of the ear base may help evenly spread the medication (see also
EAR MITES). Then ask your dog to turn over, and repeat the procedure on the
other ear, if necessary.

When *medicating* EYES, take care you do not touch the dog's eye with the
applicator. A second pair of hands may be necessary to steady your dog's
head so that his movement doesn't inadvertently injure him. Liquids can be
easily dripped into the affected eye by first placing one hand beneath the
dog's chin and tipping his face toward the ceiling. Ointments are squeezed
into the cupped tissue of the lower eyelid, or into the corner of the dog's eye.
Once applied, gently close the eyelid to spread the medicine over the surface
of the eye.

a

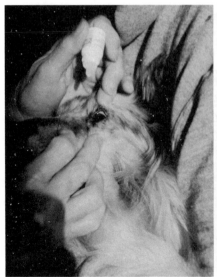

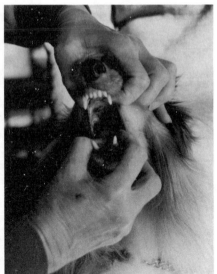

Medicating the eye *(Photo credit: Amy D. Shojai)*

Opening a dog's mouth *(Photo credit: Amy D. Shojai)*

Oral Treatments: Swallowed, or oral, medications may be in liquid, paste, or pill forms. Liquids and pastes come in squeeze bottles or are applied with eyedroppers or syringes that make medicating the dog quite simple. Generally, they are flavored, as well, so that your dog willingly accepts them. Tip back your dog's head, insert the applicator in the outside corner of his mouth, and squirt the medication into his cheek. Then hold his mouth closed, keeping his head tipped up, and stroke his throat until you see he swallows.

Pilling a dog involves opening his mouth, placing the capsule or tablet on the back of the tongue, closing his mouth, and inducing him to swallow. Generally, dogs are easy to pill, particularly large dogs that have handle-shaped muzzles. If you have the least doubt about your ability to pill your dog, enlist an extra pair of hands to open his mouth while you place the pill inside. Blanket-wrap a small dog, or kneel on the floor with the dog between your legs facing out, so he can't squirm away.

Most dogs have incredible jaw strength that makes it difficult to lever the mouth open against their will. Rather, your job is to induce the dog to open wide on his own. Place the palm of one hand over the dog's muzzle so that the thumb on one side and middle finger on the other fit behind the upper canine (long) tooth on each side. Tilt the dog's head back so he's looking at the ceiling. Gently press the dog's lips against his TEETH to encourage him to open his mouth. Or simply slip one finger inside your dog's mouth and press on the roof of his mouth, and he'll open wide. Then use your other hand to push the pill

a

to the back of his tongue, quickly close his mouth, and stroke his throat until he swallows.

A pill syringe available at most pet-supply stores works well for some owners who don't want to risk putting their fingers in the dog's mouth. Your veterinarian can demonstrate its safe use so you won't hurt the back of your dog's throat.

Hiding medication in treats works very well with dogs, who tend to gulp food whole. Check with your veterinarian first, though, because some drugs should not be mixed with certain foods. Use a hunk of cheese, a dab of peanut butter, or anything you're sure the dog will eat in one swallow. Mixing medicine in the whole bowl of food isn't recommended, because the dog may not be properly medicated if he doesn't eat it all at once.

Unless the medication is a time-release treatment that's supposed to dissolve slowly, the pill can be crushed and mixed into a strong-tasting treat. Use the bowl of a spoon to powder the pill and combine with a mouthful of canned food. If you're hiding medication in treats, be sure to offer them before meals to ensure every bit is eaten.

Following any treatment, reward your dog with positive attention. Give him lots of praise and play his favorite game so that he associates the activity with good things for him. That should help make the next session run even more smoothly.

Adoption, of Dog by Human

Adoption refers to the act of actively accepting another being into your life. By adopting your dog, you acknowledge responsibility for the life, health, and welfare of that dog.

Finding a dog to adopt is easy. Newspaper advertisements are glutted with giveaway animals, and worthy candidates abound at animal welfare organizations. Often, a friend or acquaintance has available an adoptable dog, or you may be taken in by the adorable STRAY that appears in your yard. Many people prefer a specific canine size, type, or personality to better fit their lifestyle, and more than four hundred distinct canine BREEDS are available. Professional breeding kennels produce puppies according to standards defined by various dog associations (see Appendix A, "Dog Associations and Breeds"); however, purebred registered animals, particularly those that are relatively uncommon, are typically more costly because of the expense involved in producing healthy animals of a particular type.

All dogs require routine health care, nutritious food, and a secure, safe place to rest, exercise, and relieve themselves. Successful adoptions match a

a

dog that has the look, care demands, and personality that fulfill an owner's expectations. For instance, dogs with abundant coats require more GROOMING than short-coated dogs; puppies need TRAINING and greater supervision than a staid adult dog who may already be trained; big dogs need more room and time to exercise than miniature varieties; unaltered male or female dogs can display behaviors that are obnoxious (see NEUTERING and SPAYING); and the pets you already have need consideration (see INTRODUCTIONS).

A number of difficulties can be avoided by adopting a dog that is healthy. The healthy dog's fur is clean and shiny, without bald patches or red, scaly skin. Eyes, nose, and ears are free of discharge, and the dog's bottom is clean without sign of DIARRHEA. A veterinary exam is always advisable to rule out hidden problems. Reputable shelters or kennels may provide preliminary health care prior to adoption, such as basic first VACCINATIONS or discount spaying or neutering. Some offer limited guarantees on the health of the animal.

Adoption should not be a whim; it is not a temporary arrangement, but is

Friends for life (*Photo credit: Ralston Purina Company*)

a

for the lifteime of the dog. We do not give back the human children we adopt when the "cute" stage passes or when they become inconvenient to have around; neither should a dog be a disposable commodity. At its best, adoption is a joyful yet serious act undertaken only after careful consideration.

Adoption, of Puppies (or Others) by Dog

Some dogs exhibit nurturing behavior toward other animals and seem to "adopt" puppies or others that are not their own. The behavior most often occurs when a female dog is still nursing and is hormonally ready to nurse and care for another animal's offspring. In kennel situations, if a litter for some reason is not accepted by the mother, the breeder may induce a "foster-mom dog" to take on the challenge, by making the strange puppies smell like the foster-mom's babies. Other times, dogs take on the responsibility without persuasion. Dogs have been known to nurse and raise kittens, puppies, and even rabbits or other species.

Dogs that have given birth often retain mothering urges even after being SPAYED, and some dogs that have never given birth—even male dogs—enjoy interaction with youngsters so much they take fostering responsibility very seriously.

In most instances, dogs that adopt other puppies or animals enjoy positive interspecies experiences during their impressionable weeks of life (see PUPPY, Socialization).

Affection

Dogs have well-known reputations as loyal, loving companions—the quintessential "man's best friend," and deservedly so. Dogs are naturally social creatures that thrive on interaction.

Dogs COMMUNICATE their moods, emotions, and desires in a variety of ways, from obvious to subtle. Although affection should be reciprocal, our dogs are unique in that many offer us blind adoration, whether we deserve it or not. It is the rare dog who is indifferent to people, although mistreatment

a

and/or poor breeding can warp the canine personality into a dysfunctional animal. Dogs are also individuals, with a wide range of personalities.

Dogs show their affection toward other dogs—and even cats or other pets—by sleeping together and by licking or nuzzling each other. Simply sharing space can be a subtle sign of affection between dogs. Affectionate dogs may share toys or food and enjoy PLAYING together.

Dogs often show affection to humans in the same ways. They beg for attention by crawling into your lap, sleeping next to you, and licking your face and hands. Dogs exuberantly invite owners to play, and want you to share your food. They want contact with you and may sleep across your feet or lean against your leg. Some dogs actually learn to "grin" to show their happiness.

Often, animal "experts" are reluctant to say any creature experiences the same emotions as people. Obviously, we can't know for certain what our dogs are feeling. But from every indication, dogs are every bit as devoted to us as we are to them.

Aggression

Aggression is the forceful reaction of a dog that feels threatened. Aggression can be normal behavior under certain circumstances. Dogs are naturally protective and will often defend their territory (including owners) from any perceived threat. It doesn't matter if your dog is the retiring, shy type, or a confident, macho canine; any dog may become aggressive given the right circumstances. Growls, snarls, barks, and bites are your dog's way to control the situation. But when aggression becomes unreasonable or uncontrollable, the aggressive dog is a danger to everyone, including himself.

Dogs that are in PAIN or ill often become short-tempered and exhibit aggressive behavior when the owner unknowingly touches a sore place. If your usually easygoing dog suddenly growls, snaps, or bites for no apparent reason, have him examined by a veterinarian.

Heredity plays a large role in how aggressive your dog may be. Certain breeds tolerate close contact with other dogs or strange people better than others do. Also, owners may consciously—or unconsciously—encourage aggressive behavior during their pet's puppyhood because they want a "guard dog."

Aggression can be categorized by the cause, or trigger, that prompts the behavior. Poor behavior can result from FEAR or anxiety, overly enthusiastic PLAY, misplaced predatory behavior, excessive DOMINANCE, or a combination

a

of these or others. Physical punishment won't work and will likely make the aggressive behavior even worse. Once aggression is a problem, the trigger must be identified so that a treatment specific to that cause can be initiated.

Territorial aggression is a natural phenomenon in dogs; after all, he's barking and snarling to protect his home and family from that scary stranger. Problem territorial aggression generally involves aggressive behavior toward strangers (human or other pets) who trespass on the dog's perceived turf, which can include the house, yard, car, or even the sidewalk down the block.

But *fear* is the operative word here; the dog often isn't so much aggressive as scared spitless. And when he snarls and snaps, the mailman goes away, rewarding the action, which actually trains your dog that snarling and snapping at strangers is the proper way to behave.

Treat these dogs by ensuring they receive enough exercise; boredom can increase STRESS level and push some dogs to the trigger point. Training is one of the best ways to increase your dog's confidence, and a confident dog no longer needs to rely on fear-bluffing. Desensitize your dog to the triggers by gradually exposing him to the situations that cause problems (see INTRODUCTIONS).

Dominance-related aggression (see DOMINANCE) refers to the dog that sees himself as king of the roost and wants to call the shots. These dogs primarily exhibit aggressive behavior—growling, snapping, or biting—toward human or other pet family members when something doesn't go their way: during grooming; when competing for food, attention, or toys; or when getting disciplined. Increasing the dog's exercise can help. All dogs benefit from a twenty- to thirty-minute romp every day. Also, avoid rough play (tug-of-war games are a no-no!) and brush up on obedience training. Learn to anticipate situations that may prompt poor behavior, and try to avoid or defuse them ahead of time. For instance, if your dogs compete over food, feed them in separate rooms.

Dogs may also exhibit aggressive behavior when overstimulated by a game. This is more typical of youngsters who have not yet learned to inhibit their bite and may attack your ankles as you walk by. Don't allow your hands or feet to be targets—*ever*. Playing rough games of wrestling or tug-of-war with your puppy encourages him to be aggressive as an adult.

Also, many of the terrier breeds have a highly developed predatory instinct similar to cats. They enjoy games of chase and pounce, and this can be dangerous for smaller pets in the household. Households with terriers should avoid keeping other pets like rabbits, ferrets, and smaller cats or dogs that tend to be prime targets for such breeds. Again, brush up on obedience training with your dog, and make it unpleasant for him by squirting him with water or using a noisemaker to distract him if he becomes aggressive. Offer your dog

a

plenty of "legal" opportunities to indulge his love of the chase. Games of fetch-the-ball or Frisbee are excellent.

In many cases, aggression can be greatly reduced by NEUTERING before the dog reaches sexual maturity. In addition, proper socialization during puppyhood prepares your pet for dealing with life without resorting to aggression (see PUPPY, Socialization).

Another type of aggression, commonly referred to as *rage syndrome*, is a pathological disorder. An abnormality of the brain causes seizurelike episodes of inexplicable rage in which the dog may attack anything—living or not—within sight with little or no provocation. The rage disappears as suddenly as it appears. Certain breeds are associated with this condition, in particular Springer Spaniels. Bull Terriers and Cocker Spaniels also are implicated. The dog's history along with a neurological examination are required to diagnose the problem. Behavior modification techniques that work with other aggression problems are ineffective in rage syndrome, but some types of seizure medications, like phenobarbital, help some dogs. One hundred percent cures are impossible, and sadly, in cases where the dog presents a danger, euthanasia is the only option.

For your safety and that of others, familiarize yourself with the signs of aggression (see COMMUNICATION) so that you can avoid provoking an aggressive dog to attack. Above all, do not hesitate to seek professional help. In many cases, an aggressive dog is an accident waiting to happen; if your dog's actions make you fear for your own safety or others', his aggression is best diagnosed and treated by a professional animal behaviorist or therapist. Some dogs also benefit from psychoactive drug therapy (see Appendix C, "Veterinary Resources").

Allergy

Allergy is an overreaction of the IMMUNE SYSTEM. Antibodies are specialized cells of the immune system that protect the body from foreign invaders, such as viruses and bacteria; specific white blood cells, such as eosinophils, also play a role. Sometimes these protective cells misrecognize harmless substances like dust, mold, or pollen as dangerous, and attack. The heightened response to these substances, called *allergens*, results in the allergy symptoms your dog suffers.

Dogs theoretically can develop allergies to anything, just like their human owners can. To develop an allergy, the dog must have been exposed to it in the past; this primes, or sensitizes, the body's immune system to overreact. In other words, a dog that has never been exposed to fleas will not suffer a reaction on first contact, but may develop an allergic response with subsequent exposure. A tendency to develop some allergies is inherited and so are more common in certain breeds.

Although people typically suffer from "hay fever" that makes them sneeze, their eyes itch, and their nose run, allergic dogs usually develop itchy skin diseases. Effective treatment requires eliminating the allergen that causes the reaction.

FLEA *bite hypersensitivity* is the most common allergy affecting dogs, with some surveys estimating 40 percent of the dog population affected. Allergic dogs develop skin disease when they react to a protein in flea saliva, and it may take only one bite to provoke all-over itching. Signs are seasonal, which typically are the warm summer months of flea season but can be year-round in some parts of the country. The most common sign is extreme itchiness on the rear half of the dog, particularly the area on the back immediately above the tail. Flea control is essential for dogs suffering from flea allergic dermatitis. There are many products available to safely eliminate fleas on your dog and in his environment.

Another 10 to 15 percent of the dog population is allergic to something they breathe from the environment, making *inhalant allergy*, or *atopy*, the

ALLERGY

FLEA ALLERGY	INHALANT ALLERGY	FOOD ALLERGY
SYMPTOMS		
Seasonal itchiness, especially of rear back and tail area; hair loss; scabby skin; visible fleas, or pepperlike debris on skin	Front-half itching, with face rubbing, foot licking, armpit scratching, and neck and chest itchiness	Intense all-over itching all year long: rarely, vomiting or diarrhea
HOME CARE		
Treat the dog and home or outside environment for fleas	Keep dog's coat and environment clean	Feed appropriate diet
VET CARE		
Sometimes steroids to reduce inflammation or itchiness; veterinary-prescribed flea treatments	Skin testing; allergy shots; sometimes dietary supplements of EFAs	Elimination diet to diagnose; sometimes prescription diet
PREVENTION		
Avoid fleas	Avoid dust, pollens, or whatever causes the problem	Avoid problem foods once identified

a

second most common allergy in dogs. Atopy can develop in any dog, but does have a genetic component. Breeds most commonly affected include the small terriers, especially the West Highland White Terrier, as well as Boxers, Dalmatians, Golden Retrievers, English and Irish Setters, Lhasa Apsos, Miniature Schnauzers, and Chinese Shar-Peis. Most signs first develop when the dog is between one to three years old.

Some surveys indicate that nearly half of all flea-allergic dogs also suffer from atopy. This allergy is the equivalent to human "hay fever," with dogs reacting to the same things owners do. Pollen, mold, fungi, and even the house dust mite make people cough, wheeze, and have difficulty breathing, but atopic dogs more typically suffer itchiness on the front half of their body. This includes recurrent ear infection, face rubbing, foot licking, armpit scratching, and neck and chest scratching. Atopy, like flea allergy, may also be seasonal.

To get rid of the allergen, you must first know what's causing the problem, and that can be hard to determine. Although blood tests are available, they aren't considered reliable by most veterinarians and researchers. Instead, intradermal skin testing helps diagnose atopy. Suspect allergens are injected into the shaved skin of the sedated dog. In five to fifteen minutes, positive reactions become swollen, red, and elevated, while negative reactions fade away.

Dogs may react to a single or multiple allergens, but even when you know your dog reacts to house dust, it's nearly impossible to eliminate exposure. The dog's fur is a magnet that attracts and captures environmental allergens. Rinsing away dust, pollen, and other debris on the fur helps reduce the atopic dog's symptoms, so regular bathing is helpful.

Totally eliminating exposure to environmental allergens is impossible with dogs, which typically are indoor/outdoor pets. After all, an owner can't vacuum the yard or filter the air. But reducing indoor exposure can be helpful, and cleanliness is key. Reservoirs that attract and capture allergenic substances should be reduced or eliminated; trade rough surfaces like carpeting and upholstery for linoleum or wooden floors and smooth fabrics that are easier to keep clean. Water filters on a vacuum help scrub particles from the air; avoid brooming, which tends to float allergens rather than capture them. High-Efficiency Particulate Air (HEPA) filter systems can be helpful, too.

Other treatments may help relieve your dog's symptoms, even if eliminating exposure is impossible. Veterinary-prescribed antihistamines relieve the symptoms in some dogs, and cortisone-containing drugs can help reduce itching. Some dogs benefit from dietary supplements of the essential fatty acids (EFAs) that help promote healthy skin and fur. The proper combination of these compounds appears to reduce the inflammatory skin response that results from atopy. Your veterinarian can recommend appropriate products.

Hyposensitization, or immunotherapy, may also help certain dogs. The treatment is a gradual process in which the dog's resistance to allergens is enhanced by exposing him to gradually increasing amounts of the substances. After skin tests determine the culprits, the dog is "vaccinated" with minute amounts of the allergens in the hopes that resistance to them will build and reduce the dog's sensitivity and resulting symptoms. Because improvement from immunotherapy is slow, injections are usually continued for at least a year. Maintenance injections may be required for life.

Depending on whom you speak with, *canine food allergies* are considered both common and rare. The incidence is estimated to be 1 to 10 percent of the total dog population. However, diagnosis is difficult and may be complicated by other allergies. Those dogs that are food allergic react to one or more ingredients in a diet. Usually the culprit is a protein—like beef, milk, corn, wheat, or eggs—that is common in commercial pet foods.

The typical food-allergic dog is two years old or older and suffers intense all-over itchiness that occurs year-round. Canine food allergy less often results in VOMITING and DIARRHEA. There may be an increased risk in West Highland White Terriers, Miniature Schnauzers, Golden Retrievers, and Chinese Shar-Peis. However, any dog can develop the condition at any age, even as early as six months old.

As in other allergies, avoiding the allergen—the food ingredient(s)— relieves the symptoms. A ten- to twelve-week-long veterinarian-supervised elimination diet diagnoses food allergy and identifies the culprits.

The dog is fed a special diet that contains unique protein sources that he's never before eaten and so should not be allergic to. Commonly, this limited antigen diet contains only one unique protein and carbohydrate, such as rabbit and potato, or venison and rice. Once the dog stops itching, the ingredients from his original diet are added to the diet one at a time to see which cause symptoms to return. When the culprits are identified, you simply feed your dog a diet without the offending ingredient.

The term *hypoallergenic diet* means it minimizes allergic reactions, and since every dog is different, there is no such thing as a one-fits-all canine hypoallergenic diet. The Food and Drug Administration (FDA) says diets labeled to control allergies can be prescribed and distributed only by veterinarians, and there are several on the market.

But understandably, some owners are reluctant to put their pet through the tedious diagnosis process of an elimination diet that still may not pinpoint the problem. Prescription diets from your veterinarian are typically higher cost, and this may also be a factor. Some food-allergic dogs do well when fed lamb- and rice-based commercial diets, as long as they haven't previously eaten these ingredients. Just remember that lamb- and rice-based diets often contain other ingredients, which may still cause your dog to react. And over time, dogs may become allergic to any unique ingredient.

Contact allergy is relatively uncommon to dogs, probably because of their

a

protective fur covering. When it occurs, the reaction is similar to what people experience when exposed to poison ivy. The reaction may happen hours after contact, or it may take weeks of repeated exposure before symptoms develop. Signs include itchy bumps, reddened skin, weepy sores and/or crust, blisters or pustules at the place of contact, and thinning coat or hair loss. Signs of contact allergy may be mistaken for atopy, RINGWORM, or SEBORRHEA.

Typical sites of contact-allergy skin disease are the sparsely furred areas of the body, like the feet, abdomen, muzzle and chin, groin, testicles, and the hocks and stifles (which are the areas of the legs that contact the ground when your dog reclines). Left untreated, the area of first contact may spread and involve more of the body, because the dog will scratch and further damage the skin. Potentially, any substance could result in a contact allergy, but the most common culprits are household products, like detergents and soaps; insecticides, like flea powders or collars; plastic or rubber dishes or toys; and the dyes typically found in indoor/outdoor carpets. Diagnosis is based primarily on incriminating signs, and identifying and removing the allergen will resolve the problem. Cortisone-type medications prescribed by your veterinarian help control the itching and keep your dog from further damaging himself until the lesions heal.

Allergies cannot be cured, and avoiding the allergy source is the only way to control the symptoms. To complicate matters, multiple allergies make identification of the culprit(s) nearly impossible.

Dogs are often sensitive to more than one thing, and allergies tend to be cumulative. For instance, if your dog is allergic to both fleas and pollen, they individually may not cause him problems, but the combination of the two pushes him over his *allergy threshold* so that he itches. Every allergic dog has an individual "itch" threshold, which is the amount of allergen necessary to provoke signs of disease.

This is actually good news, for although eliminating all allergens may be impossible, simply *reducing* the amount of exposure may substantially relieve your dog's symptoms. In other words, get rid of the fleas, and your dog may be able to handle exposure to house dust without scratching.

There can be many causes for itchy skin, and only a veterinarian can diagnose canine allergy. Identifying the allergen(s) and treating the signs should be a joint venture between you and your veterinarian, to best serve the health of your dog.

Amputation

Amputation is the surgical removal of part of the body, most usually an extremity like a leg or the tail. Amputation may be required when there is nerve damage from a traumatic injury, like FROSTBITE or FRACTURE, which renders the tail or limb useless. Some dog breeds are "tail-beaters," so happy that they wag their tails against objects and repeatedly injure themselves. Slow-healing invasive infections can destroy muscle tissue and threaten the integrity of the rest of the body. And sites damaged by CANCER may be impossible to cure. When the body becomes irreversibly damaged, amputation removes the injured or diseased portion and allows the rest of the body to remain healthy.

Once healed, otherwise healthy dogs are rarely slowed down by the loss of a leg or tail, and typically the cosmetic effect bothers owners more than it bothers their dog. Further, dogs that have suffered discomfort from the injury often rebound quickly once the PAIN—along with the limb—has been removed. Three-legged dogs navigate surprisingly well, often able to run and even jump. (See also DOCKING and CROPPING.)

Anal Gland

All dogs have two anal glands, or sacs, located beneath the skin at about eight and four o'clock on either side of the rectum. The pea-size glands are similar to a skunk's scent organs, but in the dog's case are used primarily for identification rather than protection. They give the dog's feces an individual scent. Dogs sniff each other's tail regions when they meet as a way of "reading" each other's scent-name.

The glands secrete a liquid—sometimes a creamy brown to yellow substance—and are usually expressed whenever the dog passes a stool. They may also be expressed when the dog suddenly contracts the anal sphincter, the circular muscle that controls the rectum. The contraction may occur when your dog is frightened or stressed, and can result in a strong odor.

Most dogs don't require help with anal gland maintenance. But others have overactive sacs that can cause an odor problem, and these dogs need help keeping the glands expressed. Smaller breeds most typically develop impacted anal glands if the sacs fail to empty normally. This can be due to overactive glands, to smaller-than-normal gland openings, or to soft stools that don't supply enough pressure to empty the sacs. The secretions become pasty and thick when not regularly expressed, and simply plug the normal exit.

a

ANAL GLAND PROBLEMS

SYMPTOMS
Excessive licking of anal area; scooting; strong odor; bloody or puslike discharge; soft, red to purple swelling beside the rectum

HOME CARE
Wet warm cloths applied for fifteen minutes several times daily

VET CARE
Express contents of glands; apply antibiotic ointment into gland opening; sometimes oral antibiotics or surgical lancing or removal of infected gland

PREVENTION
None; if this is a chronic problem, routine emptying of glands by owner or groomer

Signs of a problem include your dog licking herself excessively and/or giving off an offensive odor.

Left untreated, impacted anal glands can become painfully infected. The area on one or both sides of the rectum will swell. Your dog may lick herself to relieve the discomfort, or scoot on her bottom—sit down and pull herself forward while dragging her anal region against the floor—to try to clear the blockage. When infected, the secretions from the glands will contain blood or pus. In severe cases, an ABSCESS may develop at the site, characterized by a soft, red to purple, hairless swelling on one or both sides of the rectum.

The treatment in all instances is manual expression of the anal glands. Your veterinarian or groomer can perform this service for your dog, especially if the dog is very tender. Improper manipulations of the glands can force the matter deeper into the tissue, causing further problems, so it's best to ask your veterinarian or groomer for a demonstration if you'd like to care for your dog in the future.

Here's how it's done. Wear gloves for the procedure, then lift your dog's tail and find the sacs on each side of the anus. (They'll feel a bit like small marbles beneath the skin.) With your thumb and forefinger on the skin at each side of the gland, gently push in and upward, and squeeze as you would to express a pimple. Use a damp cloth to wipe away the smelly discharge as the sac empties.

When the glands are infected, they'll need to be expressed every week and an antibiotic infused directly into the sac itself. Ointments like Panalog work well; the tip of the tube is inserted into the sac opening, and the gland filled with the medicine. Usually it's best if your veterinarian applies the medication into the anal gland. An oral antibiotic administered at home may also be prescribed. Warm, wet compresses applied to the infected area for fifteen minutes two or three times daily will help the infection resolve more quickly.

Abscesses require surgical lancing so that the infection inside can be flushed out and drained away. The incision is left open so that the wound will heal from the inside out. The opening should be rinsed daily with a fifty-fifty solution of hydrogen peroxide and water, and the dog typically is also given an oral antibiotic.

In most cases, the abscess heals without complications. Dogs that suffer recurrences of impaction or infection require that the owner, veterinarian, or groomer empty the anal glands on a regular basis, at least once a week. In some instances, surgical removal of the problem glands may be necessary.

Anaphylaxis

An anaphylactic response is an extremely rare but potentially lethal ALLERGIC reaction. It can result from any substance, but most commonly is associated with reactions to medicine such as penicillin or a VACCINATION, or to INSECT STINGS and bites.

The immune system overreacts to the offending substances and responds by flooding the body with immune components like histamine that are supposed to neutralize the offender. Instead, the histamine causes intense inflammation both locally and throughout the body, with itchiness appearing on the head and face (sometimes in hives) and constriction of the respiratory system. Quite simply, the affected dog can't breathe. Severe anaphylactic reactions can kill a dog within minutes.

ANAPHYLAXIS

SYMPTOMS
Salivation; drooling; difficulty breathing; uncontrolled urination; incoordination; vomiting; collapse

HOME CARE
EMERGENCY! SEE VET IMMEDIATELY!

VET CARE
Intravenous administration of epinephrine (adrenaline), and oxygen therapy

PREVENTION
Avoid medicating dog without veterinary advice; prevent insect bites or stings

a

Signs of reaction include excessive salivation and drooling, difficulty breathing, uncontrollable urination, incoordination, VOMITING, and collapse. *This is an emergency situation that needs immediate veterinary attention.* The treatment of choice is administration of intravenous epinephrine (adrenaline), glucocortocoids, and fluid therapy along with oxygen therapy. (See also INSECT STINGS.)

Anemia

Anemia is a disorder of the BLOOD in which there is a lower-than-normal number of red blood cells. Anemia is the most common blood disorder in dogs and can affect any dog of any age or breed. However, because puppies have less blood volume to begin with, anemia in these youngsters can become serious much more quickly. There are a number of underlying causes, but in general, the signs are the same.

Dogs suffering from anemia usually act depressed, lose their appetite, sleep a great deal, show an overall weakness, and may lose weight. Severe anemia may cause PULSE and RESPIRATION rate to increase, and dogs may suffer a heart murmur (see ARRHYTHMIA). Excessive exercise can cause the anemic dog to faint. Such dogs appear pale, which is most easily seen in the normally pink mucous membranes like the gums.

Red cells in the dog live only about 110 to 120 days. They are constantly being replaced by the bone marrow as the old ones die, so the number of red cells remains relatively fixed. *Regenerative anemia* results when the bone mar-

ANEMIA
SYMPTOMS
Depression; increased sleep; anorexia; weakness; weight loss; rapid pulse or breathing; pale gums or tongue; fainting spells during exercise
HOME CARE
Nutritional support; needs veterinary care
VET CARE
Blood transfusion; treatment for underlying cause; other medication as needed
PREVENTION
Flea and tick treatment; regular fecal exams and deworming as needed

row still creates new red cells, but can't keep up with their loss or destruction. The most common cause of this is trauma that results in excessive BLEEDING. More subtle causes include parasites like FLEAS, TICKS, or HOOKWORMS, which can remove red cells from circulation. These result in a chronic loss that is insidious, and signs worsen over time.

Autoimmune hemolytic anemia (AIHA) can occur if your dog's immune system misrecognizes red cells as foreign. When this happens, the body attacks and destroys its own red blood cells, a process referred to as *hemolysis*. The cause usually cannot be determined, but many cases are thought to be associated with exposure to certain drugs or viruses, diseases like CANCER and LUPUS ERYTHEMATOSUS, or blood parasite diseases like BABESIOSIS and EHRLICHIOSIS. Some dogs may inherit an enzyme defect that shortens the life span of red cells. Feeding a dog onions also can result in AIHA. And in certain instances, newborn puppies may suffer a hemolytic reaction when their mother's protective immunity, which is passed to them through her milk, attacks the puppies' red cells (see BLOOD, Neonatal Isoerythrolysis; IMMUNE SYSTEM; and VACCINATIONS).

Dogs may also suffer anemia from bleeding disorders resulting from clotting defects in the blood. Clotting problems are most often associated with POISONS like rat bait, but may also result from diseases like HEMOPHILIA and VON WILLEBRAND'S DISEASE.

When the bone marrow stops making red cells, *nonregenerative anemia* results. This kind of anemia can be caused by chronic diseases, tumors, and infections that suppress the bone marrow function. Toxins, poisons, and drugs may also cause suppression of the bone marrow, as can KIDNEY DISEASE. When the kidneys malfunction, they're unable to produce enough of the hormone erythropoietin, which prompts the bone marrow to produce red cells.

The best way to prevent anemia is to protect your dog from blood-sucking parasites like fleas, ticks, and hookworms. Keeping your dog confined in a fenced yard or under leash control will help prevent traumatic injuries and bleeding from encounters with cars.

Anesthetic

Drugs used to block the sensation of TOUCH, pressure, and/or PAIN are referred to as *anesthetics*, or *anesthesia*. These drugs may or may not cause a loss of consciousness. They are used to prevent pain or stress during surgical or traumatic procedures. As we can't explain to our dogs what is happening or ask them to hold still, anesthesia is an important veterinary tool we can use to immobilize a dog during treatment.

a

Anesthetic drug doses are determined by your dog's weight. However, some dog breeds, like Afghan Hounds, Whippets, and others, seem to have a low tolerance for these drugs and may require less anesthetic than other breeds of the same size. And even dogs of the same breed and size may react differently to anesthetics. For that reason, such drugs should be given only under veterinary supervision. Often, they are given in repeated small doses until the desired effect is attained.

When treatment is isolated to the skin surface, a local anesthetic, like Xylocaine, may be used. A local anesthetic blocks feeling on only a small area and allows the dog to remain conscious. Locals can be applied to the skin as an ointment, spray, or cream or may be injected into surrounding tissue. Sedatives and tranquilizers affect the whole dog, acting to calm him down but not put him to sleep, and may be used to make your dog easier to handle. Local anesthetics are appropriate for such problems as removing PORCUPINE QUILLS, but aren't suitable for major procedures like NEUTERING.

For major surgeries, a general anesthetic is used to render the dog unconscious and prevent pain. Certain drugs have amnesiac properties so your dog won't remember any unpleasantness. A wide array of general anesthetic agents is available, and they often are used in combination to reduce potential side effects. Both injectable drugs, like Telazol, and inhaled anesthetic gases, like halothane and isoflurane, are common. Inhalant anesthetic is usually delivered to the lungs through an endotracheal tube that carries the gas into the dog's lungs; sometimes a mask, which fits over the dog's face, is used instead.

Anesthetics are eliminated from the body by the lungs, kidneys, and/or liver, and if any of these organs are compromised by disease, your dog may suffer complications from the drugs. Anesthetics also affect the way the heart works, and dogs with heart disease require special anesthetic consideration.

Overall, modern veterinary anesthetics are very safe and quite effective. Even dogs with preexisting problems can be anesthetized safely as long as the risk is known ahead of time and the proper precautions are taken. Screening tests prior to surgery determine what anesthetics are best for your particular dog, especially if he is very young, old, or ill.

Anorexia

Anorexia refers to a dog losing her appetite. The onset of the condition may be abrupt, where your dog suddenly refuses to eat, or gradual, where she eats less over the long term. Anorexia is the most common sign of illness in dogs and often occurs in conjunction with fever. Your dog may also show signs of weight loss, depression, and sometimes VOMITING.

Some finicky dogs develop preferences for certain foods and refuse to eat anything else. When you give in and feed the desired ration, you've trained the dog how to get her own way (see FOOD).

Most often, though, dogs that refuse food are suffering from a physical or emotional problem. STRESS can suppress your dog's appetite; being left at the kennel or enduring the loss of a beloved family member (human or another pet) can quell the dog's appetite. And refusing to eat can be an early sign of nearly any disease, including DIABETES MELLITUS, LIVER DISEASE, CANINE DIS-TEMPER, and CANINE PARVOVIRUS. Other times, PERIODONTAL DISEASE may make the dog's mouth so sore, she refuses to eat. Even a respiratory infection that stops up the dog's NOSE can spoil her dinner by ruining her sense of smell and taste. Anorexia can make healthy dogs ill, and sick dogs even sicker. Good NUTRITION is necessary to fight disease and keep well dogs healthy, and there are only a few instances where withholding or reducing food intake is recommended. (OBESITY, or chronic DIARRHEA or VOMITING may be examples.)

In most instances, if your dog refuses to eat or her appetite is markedly reduced for longer than three or four days, consult with your veterinarian. The underlying cause for the anorexia must be identified, and the condition treated to resolve the problem.

At home, you can stimulate your dog to eat by making her food more palatable. Try adding warm water to dry foods. While adding supplements to a balanced diet shouldn't be done on a routine basis, spiking a regular ration with pureed chicken or beef baby food, yogurt, or cottage cheese may tempt your dog's palate. A canned product with high-meat and high-fat content is also a good alternative. Also, some dogs will eat if the owner hand-feeds.

In severe cases, the veterinarian may recommend drugs to help stimulate your dog's appetite. Other times, force-feeding may be recommended. Typically the diet is made into a paste that's syringe-fed to the dog (see ADMINIS-TER MEDICATION, Oral Treatments). In rare cases, the veterinarian may resort to placing a feeding tube directly into the stomach to force-feed the dog.

Antifreeze

Antifreeze is one of the most frustrating poisons for dog owners, because pets willingly drink the sweet-tasting substance. Composed of ethylene glycol, the odorless, colorless fluid is used to protect cars from freezing temperatures. It's also used to remove rust and is found in some color-film-processing solutions used in home darkrooms.

Antifreeze is deadly; it takes very little to make the dog mortally sick—

a

about one-half teaspoon per pound of dog is lethal. That means a ten-pound dog could ingest as little as five teaspoons and be affected, while an average-size dog weighing forty-five pounds would need to drink less than half a cup. It's estimated that approximately ten thousand dogs each year are poisoned by antifreeze, and nearly 88 percent of pets that drink antifreeze die. All dogs are at risk, but those younger than three years old are affected most often, probably because of the curious nature of youth. Most poisonings take place during the fall, winter, and early spring when antifreeze is routinely used.

Your dog's survival depends on quick treatment, because the poison is rapidly absorbed into the system. Peak blood concentrations occur in dogs within one to three hours after ingestion, with initial signs appearing approximately one hour after poisoning. Dogs may die from kidney failure in as little as four to eight hours.

From the blood, the poison enters the brain and spinal fluid, causing neurologic signs, with the dog staggering as though he's drunk. Other signs include weakness, depression, loss of appetite, PANTING, and rapid heart rate. Convulsions, though rare, can also be a sign of poisoning. Although the substance is not particularly irritating to the gastrointestinal tract, sometimes the dog will suffer VOMITING. One of the earliest signs of antifreeze ingestion is an increased thirst; as a result, urine output of approximately six times the norm has been observed in dogs within three hours of ingestion.

The more antifreeze that is passed in the urine early on, the better, because the substance is at first relatively harmless. But quite soon the ethylene glycol is processed by the body into oxalic acid, an extremely toxic substance used as a

ANTIFREEZE POISONING

SYMPTOMS
Drunken behavior; excessive thirst; increased urination; diarrhea; vomiting; convulsions; loss of appetite; panting

HOME CARE
EMERGENCY! SEE VET IMMEDIATELY! If help is not available, induce vomiting, and/or administer activated charcoal within two hours of ingestion, then get dog to the vet

VET CARE
Induce vomiting; pump stomach; treat with intravenous fluids and 100-proof alcohol, or with 4MP; provide supportive care

PREVENTION
Store out of dog's reach; use pet-safe products

bleaching and cleaning agent that literally corrodes the urinary tract. It's not the antifreeze itself, but the oxalic acid that poisons the pet. Oxalic acid often also combines with calcium and forms crystals that block the flow of urine.

Your dog may seem to return to normal in about twelve to eighteen hours, but then the depression will return, although the intoxication goes away. Damage continues, sometimes over a week's time, with the kidney damage finally resulting in the dog ceasing to urinate. Coma and death are the end result of renal failure (see KIDNEY DISEASE).

If your dog is to survive, treatment must begin as soon as possible; treatment begun after twenty-four hours following poisoning offers only a slim chance of recovery. *If you suspect your dog has swallowed antifreeze, see your veterinarian immediately.*

If help is more than two hours away, though, and you've seen your dog drink antifreeze, making him vomit the poison can improve his chance of survival. Beyond this two-hour window, the poisoning will already be in his system and vomiting won't help. *Note:* Don't induce vomiting if your dog is acting depressed, is not fully conscious, or is acting drunk.

Induce vomiting using one of the following: one to two teaspoons of fifty-fifty water and hydrogen peroxide (3 percent solution); one to two teaspoons of dry mustard; or one tablespoon of dry mustard mixed in one cup of water (see ADMINISTERING MEDICATION, Oral Treatment).

Administering activated charcoal (available from your drugstore) will also help improve your dog's chance of survival. After you've induced vomiting— or if you're unable to get him to vomit—give him the crushed tablets (approximately 20 to 120 milligrams per kilogram of the dog's weight) mixed with water. Charcoal binds the poison to prevent its absorption in the intestinal tract. Any home remedy should be followed by a veterinarian's evaluation as soon as possible.

Your veterinarian's treatment is designed to prevent further absorption or metabolism of the poison and to increase excretion—urination—to get rid of it. Up to three hours following ingestion, the veterinarian will flush the dog's stomach with a saline-charcoal solution. Intravenous fluid therapy helps head off DEHYDRATION and also encourages your dog to urinate as much antifreeze as possible before it's changed into its more lethal form.

In the past, dogs were treated for antifreeze intoxication by administering 100-proof ethanol alcohol intravenously on a continuous basis for several days. By raising the dog's blood/alcohol content, the liver is forced to address the alcohol instead of changing the antifreeze to oxalic acid. Consequently, this gives the body time to pass the unchanged antifreeze through urination.

However, a new antidote for antifreeze poisoning in dogs became commercially available in January 1997. Distributed by Orphan Medical, Antizol-

a

Vet (fomepizole) is given in only three intravenous doses to the dog at twelve-hour intervals. Also known as 4-methylpyrazole or 4MP, the substance prevents the liver from metabolizing the poison so that the dog's body eliminates the antifreeze naturally through urination. However, early treatment is still required. This antidote is effective only when injected into the dog's bloodstream prior to complete metabolism of ethylene glycol.

When enough of the poison has already been changed, the kidneys will be damaged. People suffering from kidney failure benefit from dialysis machines, but this luxury is rarely available for our pets. However, peritoneal dialysis is effective; it consists of fluid being pumped into the abdominal cavity where it absorbs waste the damaged kidneys can't process, and then is drawn back out. It's hoped the procedure will offer the body time to heal the kidneys, so that normal function can return.

When damage to the kidneys is severe, it may be permanent; lesser damage may be reversible, and the kidneys may return to normal or near-normal function in three to four weeks. Aggressive supportive therapy (even ongoing veterinary hospitalization) may be necessary.

Prevent the possibility of antifreeze intoxication by keeping antifreeze out of your dog's reach. Garages and storage areas where antifreeze may be found should be off-limits to your pets. Dispose of drained radiator fluid in a sealed container and be sure to clean spills immediately. Alternative antifreeze products that use less-toxic chemicals such as propylene glycol are also available. Ask your veterinarian for a recommendation. (See also POISON.)

Arrhythmia

The term *arrhythmia* refers to a heartbeat that is abnormal. The natural rhythm of the dog's heart is stimulated by electrical impulses. Changes in the impulse may result in increased heart rate (tachycardia), decreased rhythm (bradycardia), or irregularity. Turbulence in the blood flow through the heart results in a distinctive sound, referred to as a *heart murmur*.

Drugs, toxins, and electrolyte or a body acid/base imbalance resulting from severe VOMITING or DIARRHEA, kidney stones, bladder stones, urinary blockage, and HEART DISEASE all are potential causes of arrhythmias. Drugs are available that help control and regulate the beat of the heart. The underlying cause, however, must be addressed if the problem is to be resolved.

Arthritis

The term *arthritis* covers a vast array of joint disorders that are generally divided into two groups: inflammatory and noninflammatory. Inflammatory joint disease is characterized by pain and swelling in one or more joints, while noninflammatory joint diseases are usually caused by degeneration of the joints and characterized by PAIN and stiffness.

The joints of the body are the "hinges" between two or more bones that allow movement by providing a smooth, lubricated surface composed of cartilage. The cartilage is coated with a lubricated fluid similar to plasma and encased in a joint capsule. This firm yet somewhat spongy surface offers ten times less friction than any man-made ball bearing system. The fluid feeds the joint, and motion of the joint pumps fluid to the cartilage to maintain joint health and nutrition.

Joint disease occurs when the cartilage is injured through trauma; the function of the joint is compromised from bone, muscle, or ligament injury; or disease attacks the joint components. The resulting pain restricts movement, which in turn interferes with joint nutrition when the fluid distribution is curtailed. Consequently, a vicious cycle is born.

Joint disease is quite common in dogs and results in painful movement. It's often associated with a lifetime of wear and tear on the joints, and large or heavy dogs tend to be affected most often because of the additional stress placed on their joints. It can develop in young dogs, but usually doesn't become apparent until the dog reaches ten years old or older.

ARTHRITIS

SYMPTOMS
Stiff joints; difficulty rising; lameness, especially in the morning; limping or holding up a leg; reluctance to move, particularly in cold weather

HOME CARE
Gently massage joints; apply heat to painful areas; moderate exercise, especially swimming; veterinary-prescribed buffered aspirin or other drugs

VET CARE
Sometimes steroids to reduce pain; buffered aspirin or other analgesic drug; occasionally orthopedic surgery

PREVENTION
Prompt veterinary treatment of joint or bone injury; keep dogs slim

a

There are several kinds of arthritis. *Rheumatoid arthritis* affects the connective tissue throughout the body and is considered rare in dogs. Most often it affects small or toy breeds. The cause isn't known, but it's thought that the IMMUNE SYSTEM may be involved.

Signs of rheumatoid arthritis in dogs include morning stiffness, lameness that may move from leg to leg, and swollen joints, especially the small ones of the legs. The dog may also exhibit swollen glands, with fever and depressed appetite. The condition is diagnosed with X RAYS, analysis of joint fluid, and blood tests.

Autoimmune arthritis is a relatively rare group of diseases in which the immune system erroneously attacks the joints and causes the problem. The most common of these is idiopathic nonerosive arthritis; again, the cause isn't known, but it usually affects large-breed young adult dogs, especially Doberman Pinschers and German Shepherd dogs. Signs include loss of appetite, joint swelling and stiffness in one or more legs, and intermittent fever. Typically, treatment includes immune-suppressing drugs and anti-inflammatory medications like corticosteroids. (See also LUPUS ERYTHEMATOSUS COMPLEX.)

Dogs may also suffer from *septic arthritis* when bacteria infects the joint space. This can occur when a penetrating wound gives access to the area, or bacteria spreads from nearby bone infections or through the bloodstream. ROCKY MOUNTAIN SPOTTED FEVER and EHRLICHIOSIS—both infectious rickettsial diseases spread by TICKS—may also cause septic arthritis, and LYME DISEASE (also carried by ticks) may result in septic arthritis due to the spirochete. Several weeks of oral or intravenous antibiotic therapy is the treatment of choice.

The most common type of canine arthritis is *osteoarthritis* or *degenerative arthritis*. It's a chronic disease that occurs when simple wear and tear slowly destroys the thin layer of cartilage protecting the joint surface. Usually, it's the weight-bearing joints—hip, stifle, shoulder, and elbow—that are affected. Most cases affect older dogs, but the condition can develop at any age from injury to the bone, cartilage, or ligaments, especially in large-breed or heavy dogs. Dogs suffering HIP DYSPLASIA often suffer from arthritis. As the cartilage wears away, the area becomes inflamed and painful, which in turn causes even more cartilage damage. A vicious cycle of joint degeneration is born; once started, arthritis is a progressive disease that doesn't stop.

Dogs with osteoarthritis will suffer varying degrees of lameness or stiffness that is typically worse in the morning. The affected dog may limp, hold up the affected leg, or simply refuse to move. Wet or cold weather aggravates the pain. Dogs may be reluctant to move, particularly after they've been resting. Moderate exercise is beneficial and keeps the joints loose and the muscles warmed up so that the pain lessens.

Diagnosis of osteoarthritis is based on X RAYS that show characteristic changes in the bone. The space between the joints may narrow, new but abnormal bone may form in and around the joint, and destruction of the bone surface may be apparent. Also, the veterinarian can manipulate the joint by flexing the affected limb and may detect a "grating" sensation. Usually the affected joint is warm to the touch and sometimes swollen, which the veterinarian can detect by feeling, or palpating, the area.

Treatment of osteoarthritis is aimed at relieving the dog's pain, maintaining muscle tone, and preventing stiffness. Moderate exercise helps keep the joint limber and promotes sound muscle, which helps to support the joint. It also keeps the dog fit and prevents weight gain, which can further stress diseased joints. Swimming is a particularly good exercise for arthritic dogs; however, be sure to warm and dry your dog thoroughly after swimming. Moderate exercise promotes the natural lubrication and nutrition of the joints.

To help ease your dog's arthritic condition, intersperse daily exercise with frequent rest periods and cut back on play if your dog becomes noticeably lame. Some dogs must be physically restrained from overdoing, since they'd rather put up with the pain than not join you for your jog or hunt. Overweight arthritic dogs should be put on a reducing diet (see OBESITY).

Veterinarians typically prescribe pain-relieving medications with anti-inflammatory properties like ASPIRIN. Buffered aspirin is the best and safest choice, but be sure to consult your veterinarian for the proper dosage; too much can cause gastrointestinal bleeding, and some aspirinlike products can also cause kidney toxicity and cartilage destruction.

Do not give your own arthritis medication to your dog. The canine body uses drugs differently than a human's does, and you may inadvertently poison your pet. Steroid-type medications that relieve inflammation may be prescribed by the veterinarian as injections, pills, or even skin patches to help relieve discomfort. A new drug called Rimadyl (Pfizer Animal Health) offers promising results in relieving the discomfort of arthritic dogs, with studies suggesting that nearly 80 percent of dogs showed up to an 80 percent improvement in their signs of pain. Ask your veterinarian if Rimadyl is appropriate for your dog.

In severe cases, surgery that fuses the joint may relieve pain and restore partial movement of the affected limb. Joint-replacement surgery or removal of the femoral head ("ball" of the bone) may be an option, particularly in dogs suffering from hip disease.

Massaging your dog can help relieve his aching joints and loosen tight muscles. Use gentle circular rubbing motions all over his body, from head to tail, and flex his joints to keep them limber. Try using hot-water bottles, heating pads, or circulating-water blankets (buffered with layers of towels) on sore joints.

a

Age-related arthritis can't be prevented, but treating the signs early can keep your dog more comfortable. Should your dog suffer a joint, bone, or ligament injury, prompt treatment will minimize the chance of developing arthritis down the road. Keeping your dog slim will reduce the stress and strain on his joints and may slow down the effects of arthritis.

Artificial Insemination (AI)

AI is the procedure of breeding by collecting semen from a male and introducing it into the vagina of a female. Most commonly, AI is chosen when the dogs are unable to breed naturally. Reasons may include a great size difference between the pair, anatomical problems like a too-narrow vagina or muscle weakness that interferes with the male mounting, inexperience or even antagonism between the pair, or the breeding pair being separated by great geographic distance. The procedure is usually performed by a veterinarian or an experienced professional breeder. Often, the owner's help is enlisted to hold and calm the dogs during the procedure.

Semen is collected from the stud dog using an artificial vagina and a clear plastic tube. The presence of a female dog in heat may be necessary to give the male the proper signals. Once the semen is collected, the male dog is removed from the room. The semen is drawn from the tube into a sterile syringe, and then a catheter is attached to the syringe. AI must take place within ten to fifteen minutes for the semen to remain viable. Cooling the semen (fresh-cooled) or freezing the sample extends its viability; samples may be shipped to the BITCH across the country.

The catheter is fed into the bitch's vagina, and the semen delivered through the catheter into the dog. It's recommended that the bitch's posterior be elevated for ten to fifteen minutes following the procedure.

AI used to produce smaller litters than natural breeding, but has become a preferred method by some professional breeders. It is a viable option in circumstances where normal breeding is not possible (see also REPRODUCTION).

Artificial Respiration a

Artificial respiration is the procedure of supplying air to a dog that has stopped breathing.

Respiratory distress in dogs is characterized by gasping, panting, or slowed breathing. When your dog isn't receiving adequate oxygen, the gums in his mouth, the rims of his eyes, and/or the inside of his ears become pale or slightly blue. Sometimes, the dog will lose consciousness. Your dog may stop breathing due to the trauma of being hit by a car, or as a result of ELECTRICAL SHOCK or DROWNING. A strong blow or penetrating chest wound can damage the lungs or tear the diaphragm (a muscle separating the abdomen from the chest cavity that normally works to expand the lungs). A SWALLOWED OBJECT that becomes stuck and blocks the airways also may interfere with breathing.

If you can see an obstructing toy, bone, or other object, you can attempt to re-move it with tweezers, pliers, or your fingers. However, leave string-type ob-jects for your veterinarian to address; the other end may have something sharp, like a fishhook, attached.

When unable to remove the object, lay your dog on his side, place the heel of your hand directly behind the last rib, and gently thrust upward three or four times in quick succession. In many cases, this modified Heimlich

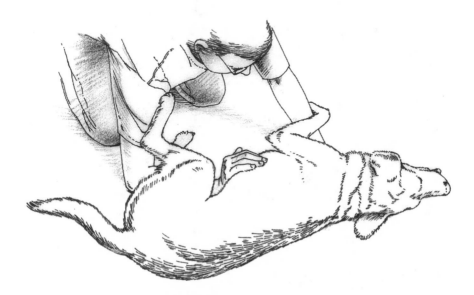

Modified Heimlich Maneuver

a

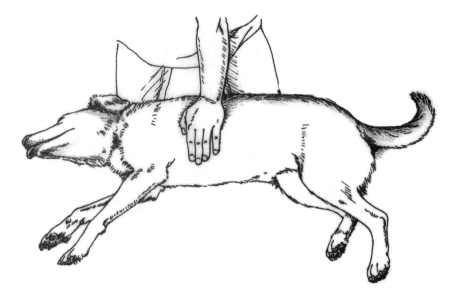

Press dog's ribs

Blow air into dog's lungs

maneuver will dislodge the obstruction; if it doesn't, get your dog immediate veterinary assistance.

When respiratory distress isn't due to obstruction, you must breathe for your dog until you can get him to a veterinarian. First, remove his collar. Then place your dog on his right side on a flat, firm surface; a table or kitchen counter works well for small dogs, while medium to larger dogs can be positioned on the floor. Pull the dog's tongue forward to keep it from blocking the airway, then gently close the mouth with his tongue extended outside. Extend your dog's neck forward from the body, keeping the chin slightly raised. Then place the flat of your hand on your dog's ribs and press down sharply to express the old air from his system, then quickly release. When the diaphragm is intact, the lungs will fill with air naturally when you release the pressure.

If this recoil mechanism doesn't work, you must breathe air into your dog's lungs. The mouth-to-nose method is the most effective. Keep his tongue forward, then place both hands about your dog's muzzle to seal his lips so the air will not escape. Then place your lips over your dog's nose and blow gently into the nostrils. A successful breath will cause his chest to expand; each time this happens, stop blowing to let air back out. When the chest doesn't expand, try blowing harder, or adjust the positioning of your dog's neck. Breathe for your dog once every four to five seconds, or twelve to fifteen respirations a minute. Continue to ventilate your dog as long as his heart beats, until he starts to breathe on his own, or until you arrive at the veterinarian's office. (See also CARDIOPULMONARY RESUSCITATION).

Aspirin

Aspirin (acetylsalicylic acid) is a common pain reliever used by people, and sometimes used in veterinary medicine for dogs. Aspirin is commonly prescribed to relieve the discomfort of canine ARTHRITIS. However, your dog's body metabolizes, or breaks down, aspirin at a different rate than a human's body does. That means the dosage for dogs is going to vary from that for people, so always consult your veterinarian to be safe before giving her aspirin. Also, use only buffered or enteric coated aspirin products, or you risk stomach upset or worse.

Giving your dog too much aspirin, particularly the nonbuffered or uncoated type, may result in an ulcer, or bleeding of the stomach (see ULCER).

a

ASPIRIN POISONING

SYMPTOMS
Vomiting blood that looks like old coffee grounds; weight loss; anemia; abdominal pain

HOME CARE
Stop giving the aspirin

VET CARE
Supportive care; sometimes ulcer-type medication

PREVENTION
Give medication only with your veterinarian's direction

Asthma

Asthma is a sudden narrowing of the airways that results in breathing distress. It's thought to be caused by inhalant ALLERGY, which triggers the bronchials—muscles and glandular structures surrounding the lower airways in the lungs—to constrict.

Asthma is considered to be very rare in dogs. Signs include audible wheezing, straining to breathe, coughing, and sometimes collapse from lack of oxygen. Treatment seeks to open the breathing passages and reduce accompanying inflammation so the dog can breathe. Antihistamines are effective and help dilate the airways and calm the inflammation. Their sedative effect acts to reduce

ASTHMA

SYMPTOMS
Gasping; panting; wheezing; straining to breathe; loss of consciousness; blue gums

HOME CARE
EMERGENCY! SEE VET IMMEDIATELY!

VET CARE
Antihistamines; steroids; oxygen therapy; bronchodilating drugs

PREVENTION
Reduce triggers like dust or stress; use humidifier

the dog's excitability. In some instances, steroids may be helpful as well to re-duce inflammation and the allergic reaction. Your veterinarian will prescribe the most appropriate medication for your dog's situation. Reducing house dust or other possible allergy triggers may help improve your dog's condition.

a

Babesiosis

Babesiosis is a disease caused by a blood parasite, a protozoa belonging to the genus *Babesia* that's transmitted by TICKS. There are more than seventy kinds of *Babesia* parasites that affect domestic and wild animals; most are both tick and host specific, which means they preferentially target certain ticks and animals. Dogs are affected by *Babesia canis* and *Babesia gibsoni*. All dogs are susceptible, but more cases occur in the southern United States and South Africa where the tick vectors *Dermacentor marginatus* and *Rhipicephalus sanguineus* are found. Puppies are more susceptible to *B. canis* disease than are adult dogs, but disease caused by *B. gibsoni* may kill dogs of any age.

The parasite is passed to the host through tick saliva when the tick takes a blood meal. There, the protozoa infects and destroys the red blood cells. The dog's own body also destroys red cells when the IMMUNE SYSTEM attacks the parasite. Dogs suffering from the disease may show sudden severe (acute) signs; a gradual onset of ongoing symptoms (chronic); or no signs at all. Ticks become infected by feeding on dogs already infected with the parasite.

The disease results in severe ANEMIA that ultimately can impact the liver, kidneys, and spleen. The first sign is fever that may reach as high as 107 degrees. The dog suffers from lethargy and/or loss of appetite. When severe anemia is present, the urine will turn dark due to leakage of hemoglobin (red-blood-cell pigment) into the urine; this is sometimes referred to as *red water*. When the liver is involved, JAUNDICE is apparent (yellow tinge to light areas of skin), and when the central nervous system (CNS) is affected, the dog will exhibit incoordination, teeth grinding, and mania, followed by coma. Four to eight days following the first symptoms, the dog may die.

Diagnosis is made by finding the parasite in the blood during microscopic

BABESIOSIS

SYMPTOMS
Anemia; high fever; lethargy; loss of appetite; dark urine; jaundice; incoordination; teeth grinding; coma

HOME CARE
None

VET CARE
Antiprotozoal drugs; fluid therapy; blood transfusions

PREVENTION
Prevent ticks by using appropriate insecticides and/or promptly remove attached ticks

b

examination, or sometimes by testing the blood for antibodies against the parasite. There are a variety of antiprotozoal treatments that, when given early, offer good results; however, currently many aren't approved for use in the United States.

The specific drug, dosage, and treatment depends on the goal of the treatment, which may range from alleviating signs, to eliminating or even preventing infection. Some of these drugs are so effective that one treatment will kill the parasite. When treated before severe anemia or CNS signs become apparent, dogs usually recover without further supportive therapy. But fluid therapy, blood transfusions, or other measures may be required, particularly in late-stage disease.

Babesiosis can be prevented by protecting your dog against ticks. In most cases, the tick must be attached to your dog for twelve to twenty-four hours before the parasite will be passed, so prompt removal of ticks will prevent transmission of the disease. Even better, modern acaricidal preparations work to prevent ticks from ever attaching to your dog at all.

Bad Breath

Also referred to as *halitosis*, offensive mouth odor is not normal for your pet. "Doggy breath" may result from strong-smelling canned foods for a short time following meals, but a persistent bad breath odor commonly indicates a health problem.

Dogs are susceptible to the same dental problems that people suffer, and

b

BAD BREATH	
SYMPTOMS	
Mouth odor	
HOME CARE	
Feed dry, crunchy foods; clean teeth	
VET CARE	
Anesthesia and dentistry; sometimes antibiotics	
PREVENTION	
Routinely brush dog's teeth; regular veterinary dental care	

are at even higher risk because they aren't able to care for their own teeth through brushing. The earliest sign of gum and tooth infections is bad breath.

Mouth odor can signal disease or even POISONING. Arsenic poisoning causes a strong garlic breath, and a symptom of late-stage DIABETES is acetone breath, which smells something like nail polish remover. Signs of KIDNEY DISEASE include mouth ulcers and ammonia-like mouth odor.

Your dog's pungent breath isn't something to disregard, and it cannot—should not—be masked with a mint. To resolve the issue, the cause must be diagnosed by your veterinarian. Usually, bad breath resulting from PERIODONTAL DISEASE can be prevented with routine dental care.

Balanoposthitis

Balanoposthitis is the inflammation and sometimes infection of the penis and/or its fleshy covering (prepuce). Mild cases are common in male dogs. Normally, there is either no discharge or only an occasional small amount of yellow-white secretion from the prepuce. An abnormal condition should be suspected anytime there is a discharge of pus from the opening.

Balanoposthitis may result from injury or from the intrusion of a foreign body that prompts overgrowth of the normal microorganisms. Dogs suffering severe cases can suffer sudden swelling and inflammation of penis and prepuce, lots of discharge, and PAIN. Typically, the dog will engage in a great deal of licking of the area. Without treatment, an ABSCESS can develop.

Treatment involves thoroughly cleaning the area with sterile saline solutions, along with administering antibiotic therapy. Medicated ointments are typically infused into the prepuce cavity over a two- to four-week period.

BALANOPOSTHITIS

SYMPTOMS
Abnormal discharge from penis or prepuce; swelling; redness; pain with or without licking

HOME CARE
Clean with sterile saline solutions; apply veterinary-prescribed medications

VET CARE
Same; also infusion of medicated ointments into prepuce and/or oral antibiotics prescriptions

PREVENTION
None; when problem is chronic, keep area clean

Sometimes oral medication is also prescribed. Dogs that have suffered a bout of balanoposthitis often have recurrences of the problem, and owners should remain vigilant to catch future problems early on.

Bitch

A bitch is a female dog, specifically those of reproductive age. The term is considered derogatory when applied to anything other than dogs, but is both accurate and highly appropriate when used in its proper context. The word differentiates between male and female canines, particularly in professional circles, where the male is the *dog* and the female is the *bitch*.

Bladder Stones

Also referred to as *urolithiasis*, the development of microscopic to egg-size mineral deposits, or stones, in the urinary tract is considered relatively common in dogs. When people suffer this problem, the stones typically develop in the kidneys, but for dogs the more common location is in the bladder.

It's estimated that nearly 3 percent of dogs suffer from urolithiasis, with most cases occurring in two- to ten-year-old animals; however, some dog breeds are predisposed to the condition. The Miniature Schnauzer, Dachshund, Dalmatian, Pug, Bulldog, Welsh Corgi, Basset Hound, Beagle, and terrier breeds are at highest risk.

BLADDER STONES

SYMPTOMS
Break in house-training; dribbling urine; "posing" without production; bloody or strong-smelling urine; whining during urination; excessive licking of genitals; splay-legged posture during urination; splatter or weak urine stream

HOME CARE
None

VET CARE
Usually surgical removal; occasionally prescription diets to dissolve stone; antibiotics

PREVENTION
Low-dose antibiotics to reduce recurrence; encourage drinking of water, and moderate exercise; Dalmatians benefit from special diets and the drug allopurinol

The stones are actually crystalline substances composed of a combination of minerals and organic substances found in the dog's urine. For stones to form, one or more of these minerals must be present in the urine in the right concentration. Also, the urine must remain a sufficient time in the urinary tract for crystals to precipitate. Finally, the urine must be a favorable pH for crystallization.

These three factors—and thus, stone formation—are influenced not only by genetics, but also by infection, diet, digestion, volume of urine, and frequency of urination. The causes of some types of stones are known, while others remain a mystery. For instance, urate stones are caused by metabolic problems, while struvite stones usually are associated with urinary-tract infections.

Stone types are classified according to composition, and some breeds more typically suffer one type of stone over another. High-risk dog breeds most commonly suffer from struvite, while in non-high-risk breeds, the most common composition is cystine and, to a lesser extent, struvite. Other common compositions are oxalate stones, urate stones (most common in Dalmatians), and silicate stones (most common in German Shepherd Dogs), with a variety of other minerals occurring less frequently. However, any dog can develop any type of stone.

Knowing the stone composition is important, because the chemical composition of the stone often points to the cause, which when treated may help prevent recurrence of the problem. Treatment may differ depending on the type of stone. Some mineral compositions can be dissolved by feeding a special diet, although most large stones require surgical removal.

Stones irritate the lining of the urinary tract; can cause CYSTITIS; and in the most serious cases, may block the passage of urine. Signs of bladder stones range from none to severe and also may vary between male and female dogs because of anatomical distinctions. Signs are any one or combination of the following: a break in house-training; dribbling urine; spending lots of time "posing" in the yard with little result; bloody urine, or urine with a strong ammonia smell; whining during urination; excessive licking of the genitals. Dogs of either sex may assume a strange splay-legged position when urination is painful. Partial obstruction may result in a weak, splattery stream of urine even when your pet shows no other signs of distress.

If crystals or stones cut off the passage of urine, life-threatening blockage occurs and is an emergency. Blockage is more frequently suffered by males, because of the narrower urethral passage. This is an excruciating situation for your pet, because with no place to go, the urine simply fills the bladder like a balloon and eventually backs up into the kidneys. Blockage may develop suddenly or over days or weeks. Even partial blockage causes severe damage that can result in renal failure (see KIDNEY DISEASE). *Complete blockage can kill your dog within seventy-two hours and requires immediate veterinary assistance.*

The bladder must be emptied before it bursts; rupture causes PERITONITIS, which dogs rarely survive. It's sometimes possible to pass a catheter through the dog's urethra past the blockage, or to flush the urolith back into the bladder; this is usually done with the dog anesthetized. Other times, a needle is inserted through the abdominal wall and into the bladder to drain the urine, a process called *cystocentesis*. The blockage may require surgical intervention.

Dogs often require supportive care, such as fluid therapy, particularly when dehydrated or depressed. Dogs require close monitoring for at least a week following relief of obstruction, to ensure it does not recur. Owners must remain vigilant for several weeks even after the dog is sent home.

Diagnosis of bladder stones is usually based on signs, X RAYS, and/or palpating, or "feeling," the bladder through the abdominal wall. The type of stone is usually indicated by the dog's breed, sex, diet, and the presence (or absence) of urinary-tract infection and its cause. However, specific determination of the stone conformation can be determined only by special laboratory analysis. Knowing stone composition is necessary for the veterinarian to manage and prevent recurrence of stones.

Often, surgical removal of the stones is required, along with flushing the urinary tract of any remaining crystals. There are commercially available (by veterinary prescription) calculolytic diets that dissolve struvite and ammonium urate stones within two to twenty weeks, which may be appropriate in certain cases. Great care must be taken in using these diets, though, as oftentimes the stones are of mixed composition and not all of the stone will be dissolved—or the stone may shrink to a size that allows it to pass into and block the urethra.

Depending on the type of stone, a mineral- and protein-restricted diet may help prevent recurrence. Also, the urine is analyzed and when infection is present, an appropriate therapy such as penicillin is instituted. A low-dose antibiotic medication may be prescribed thereafter as a preventative, because keeping the urinary tract free of bacteria will prevent further development of such "infection stones."

Dalmatians are the only breed that inconsistently metabolizes uric acid, which results in urate stones. Diet greatly influences the concentration of uric acid, as does the medication allopurinol. The combination of using a modified prescription diet and the drug allopurinol is instrumental in controlling the formation of such stones in the Dalmatian.

If your dog is of a breed that is considered at high risk for bladder stones, remain vigilant to catch the earliest sign of distress. Encourage your dog to drink by keeping plenty of fresh water available, and promote moderate exercise. Dietary and antibiotic therapy are not recommended as a preventative for dogs that have never before suffered an episode of urinary-tract stones.

Bleeding

Bleeding occurs whenever the integrity of the body's tissue is breached and cuts a blood vessel, and the bleeding itself helps to cleanse a wound. Bleeding results from cuts, abrasions, and lacerations, and clotting factors in the blood help protect injuries during healing by forming a scab over the wound. A veterinarian should address any deep or gaping injury, whether accompanied by excessive bleeding or not.

Capillary bleeding from abrasions or scratches typically produces oozing wounds with negligible bleeding. *Arterial bleeding* results in a spurting flow of bright red blood that surges with each beat of the dog's heart. *When a vein is cut*, the blood is dark red and flows evenly.

Generally bleeding can be stopped by applying even, direct pressure to the wound. Cover the area with a clean cloth or gauze pad and press firmly for five to seven minutes, then check if the bleeding has stopped by carefully lifting the cloth. Continue the pressure until the bleeding subsides. Be careful when moving the pad, as it may stick to the wound as the new scab forms. If this happens, simply place a fresh pad or cloth over the first.

b

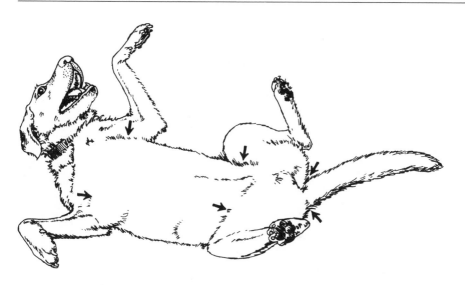

Pressure Points

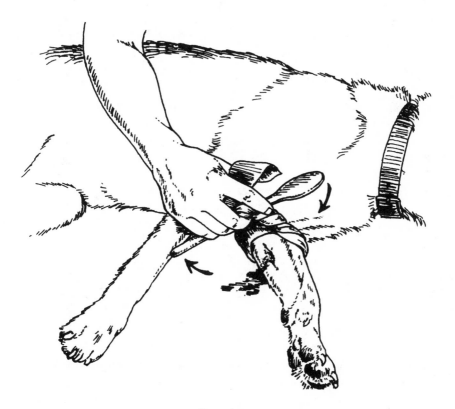

Tourniquet

b

When bleeding continues despite direct pressure, raising the injury above the heart level helps slow the bleeding by using gravity to reduce the blood pressure to the wound. It also may help to apply indirect pressure to the arteries between your dog's heart and the injury. Find the pressure points inside each leg at the "armpit" on front legs and the crotch where the hind legs connect to the torso. The underside of the tail base is another pressure point. With a cut vein, applying pressure *below* the injury stops bleeding.

When excessive bleeding continues despite your efforts, and if the injury is to a leg or tail, you may use a tourniquet when the life of the dog is at stake. Tourniquets are considered tools of last resort, however, because their improper use may damage the limb or tissue to the point that AMPUTATION becomes necessary.

Use a strip of cloth, gauze, or even one leg from a pair of panty hose to fashion your tourniquet. Be sure the material is at least one inch wide to reduce the risk of cutting your pet's skin. Circle the limb twice with the fabric, positioning the material about two inches from the wound. Tie the ends once, then securely knot a pencil or comparable object like a kitchen knife or wooden spoon above the first tie. Slowly turn the pencil to twist and tighten the material; stop as soon as bleeding slows to a trickle, and fasten the pencil in place. The pressure must be released every five to ten minutes for a brief period to allow circulation into the affected limb. Your dog should be seen by a veterinarian immediately.

Internal bleeding is more difficult to detect because bruises and swellings are often hidden beneath the fur (see HEMATOMA). Bleeding from the anus or mouth, blood in the urine, stool, or vomit, or loss of consciousness may all be signs of internal bleeding. Bloody urine or feces, or bleeding from the mouth, EARS, NOSE, or EYES can also point to POISONING or advanced LIVER DISEASE. Bloody urine may indicate CYSTITIS or BLADDER STONES.

Unless the injury is limited to a scratch or simple abrasion, any dog that is bleeding should see a veterinarian immediately.

Bloat (Gastric Dilatation-Volvulus)

Known more commonly as bloat, gastric dilatation-volvulus (GDV) is a poorly understood syndrome affecting up to sixty thousand dogs each year. Gastric dilatation is the painful swelling of the stomach with gas and/or frothy material; volvulus is the rotation, or twisting, of the stomach. Bloat refers to one or both scenarios, and either can result in death.

When bloat occurs, the stomach contents cannot be expelled by either VOMITING, burping, or passing into the intestines. The stomach distention causes pressure on other internal organs, which results in SHOCK. If the stomach twists, circulation is cut off and the stomach and spleen can die; the rotation also compresses a vein that returns blood to the heart, resulting in severe depression of normal blood circulation. Slowed circulation increases the chance that bacteria may leak from the intestines into the bloodstream and cause infection. When both distention and twisting are present, multiple organ failure and death typically occur within hours as a result of the shock.

All dogs can be affected, but purebred dogs are three times more likely to suffer bloat than mixed-breed dogs are. Breeds that have a narrow but deep chest have the greatest incidence of the condition, with surveys indicating the high-risk breeds include Chow Chow, German Shepherd Dog, Great Dane, Labrador Retriever, Weimaraner, Saint Bernard, Gordon Setter, Irish Setter, Standard Poodle, Irish Wolfhound, Borzoi, Bloodhound, Mastiff, Akita, and Bullmastiff. It's not known whether the dog's sex influences incidence. Age is considered a factor, though, with dogs seven years or older considered at twice the risk compared to dogs aged two to four years old. Stress is a risk factor in bloat, with very nervous dogs considered twelve times more likely to be at risk than calm dogs. One study indicated that incidence of the syndrome was lowest during morning hours and increased throughout the day, peaking during late evening.

The definitive cause has not been determined. The gas appears to arise simply from swallowing large amounts of air. Fearfulness, nervousness, pain,

BLOAT (GASTRIC DILATATION-VOLVULUS)

SYMPTOMS
Restless behavior; unproductive attempts to vomit or defecate; swollen, painful stomach; pale gums; irregular breathing; collapse

HOME CARE
EMERGENCY! SEE VET IMMEDIATELY!

VET CARE
Passage of stomach tube to vent gas; emergency surgery

PREVENTION
Gastropexy surgery to fix stomach in place; avoid sudden diet changes; feed meals in small amounts several times daily rather than once; enforce rest for at least one hour prior to and two hours following a meal

and excitement have all been shown to increase air swallowing in people, and the same seems to be true for dogs.

Dogs suffering from bloat typically eat a great deal, gulp lots of water after eating, and then strenuously exercise within two to three hours after meals.

Signs of bloat develop within only a few hours after eating. The first sign is sudden discomfort exhibited by restless behavior: your dog may whine, lie down then get up, and pace in an effort to get comfortable. The dog may attempt to vomit or defecate without success. The stomach becomes visibly swollen and is painful to the touch. Signs of SHOCK—pale gums, irregular or shallow breathing, rapid heartbeat—soon develop, leading to collapse. *Bloat is a life-threatening emergency that requires immediate veterinary intervention if your dog is to survive*.

The symptoms presented in a high-risk dog breed are usually suggestive of the condition, but X RAYS may be required to confirm the diagnosis. Treatment is aimed at relieving the pressure in the stomach by venting the gas and removing the solid contents. Approximately 30 to 60 percent of dogs suffering severe bloat will die.

When possible, the veterinarian passes a stomach tube down the throat and into the stomach. However, if the stomach is so twisted a tube won't pass, then emergency surgery is required to realign the stomach and remove its contents and any damaged tissue in the gastrointestinal tract.

Even when decompression is accomplished with the stomach tube, gastropexy surgery is recommended. This procedure fixes the stomach to the body wall and prevents a recurrence of the condition in more than 90 percent of cases.

Although bloat can't be completely prevented, predisposing factors can be reduced and should be taken into account, particularly if your dog is a high-risk breed. Avoid sudden changes in food, which can prompt gorging behavior. When a diet change is necessary, introduce it gradually over a seven- to ten-day period. Feed your dog small quantities of food several times a day, rather than feeding meals all at once. And if there's food competition between your dogs, feed them in separate rooms to help slow down gulpers and calm their anxiety over stolen food. Try mixing dry food with water to reduce your dog's urge to gulp water; this also increases the food volume, which may help slow fast eaters.

Some veterinarians recommend using gastropexy surgery in high-risk dogs as a preventative; the procedure is considered relatively uncomplicated on an otherwise healthy dog and can be done at the same time the dog is spayed or neutered.

Also, prevent exuberant exercise and excitement for at least one hour before and two hours after each meal.

Blood b

This liquid is composed of a number of specialized cells and serves as the body's transportation system. Plasma—the yellow, liquid portion of the blood—ferries clotting agents, nutrients, immune components, and waste products to their various destinations throughout the body. Plasma also transports the solid components of blood: the red cells, white cells, and platelets.

Red cells (erythrocytes) carry oxygen throughout the body. Hemoglobin is the oxygen-carrying pigment that gives these cells their red color. Platelets and specialized proteins make clotting possible and serve to control and stop bleeding. Five kinds of white cells—neutrophils, monocytes, lymphocytes, eosinophils, and basophils—are variously involved with the body's IMMUNE SYSTEM. Along with antibodies, the white cells help identify and protect against viral or bacterial infection.

Blood components are the same in all dogs, but concentrations of the individual components may vary between breeds. For example, racing Greyhounds have a much higher red cell volume than other breeds (60 in Greyhounds compared to 40 in all other dogs), probably because of the greater need for oxygen demanded by racing.

But just like people, there are important differences between individual dogs. Blood groups and types vary from dog to dog, and the differences are inherited.

Antigens on the surface of the blood cells define a blood type. Antigens are proteins, toxins, or other substances to which the body responds by producing antibodies. Eight different canine blood groups have been identified, with possibly more to be named in the future. Previously, canine blood groups were identified with letters similar to human blood types, but currently they're designated *DEA* (dog erythrocyte antigen) with a number that identifies each. The canine blood groups most commonly recognized are DEA-1.1, DEA-1.2, DEA-3, DEA-4, DEA-5, DEA-6, DEA-7, and DEA-8. When a dog has those specific antigens on its red cells, it's said to be positive for that particular group; if the red cells do not have a given antigen, then the dog is negative for that blood group.

This is important, because when a dog is injured or ill, a transfusion with whole blood or blood components may be necessary to save the dog's life. But giving the wrong type of blood can have dire consequences.

People (and cats) have very strong antibodies against the wrong type of blood. Our immune system recognizes noncompatible blood as foreign and attacks and destroys the blood as if it were a virus or bacteria. When a person receives a blood transfusion and the wrong blood is given, this transfusion reaction can quickly kill the individual.

b

Dogs rarely have naturally occurring antibodies the way people and cats do, however. The dog's immune system doesn't seem to immediately recognize incompatible blood, but must be first exposed to incompatible blood before building antibodies against it. For that reason, most dogs can receive a transfusion from any other blood group the first time. After that, though, the immune system is "primed" to recognize the foreign blood, and if it's given again, a life-threatening transfusion reaction can happen.

Blood incompatibility can cause problems in breeding situations (although this is considered much more rare in dogs than in cats). Called *neonatal isoerythrolysis (NI)*, the condition results when the dam's blood is incompatible with that of her puppies. This can happen if she has preformed antibodies (considered rare), or if she's been sensitized by a previous transfusion. In either case, these antibodies will be in the mother dog's milk when she gives birth. By breeding a male dog with DEA-1.1-positive blood to a female dog with DEA-1.1-negative blood, resulting puppies that have their father's blood type are at risk; when they drink the mother dog's first milk (colostrum), antibodies it contains attack and destroy the puppy's red cells. Suffering from FADING PUPPY SYNDROME, such puppies start out healthy, but become weaker and weaker and usually die within the first week of life. NI in dogs is considered by some to be extremely rare, while other researchers argue it's much more common than many believe. A thorough investigation of how blood types contribute to fading puppy syndrome has not been done, but blood compatibility can be a matter of life and death for all dogs.

A *hemolytic transfusion reaction* happens when the red cells are attacked by the immune system and broken down. In an acute reaction, the affected dog can show nearly immediate signs of distress: heartbeat and RESPIRATION slow, there's a loss of blood pressure, and the dog may uncontrollably vomit, defecate, and/or urinate and finally collapse. More commonly, the reaction is milder and develops over a period of hours as the transfusion is given. A delayed reaction is also possible, in which the dog tolerates the transfusion at first, then develops signs down the road when the body destroys the blood faster than it normally would.

Some blood types cause more dangerous transfusion reactions than other blood types do, with DEA-1.1-positive being the worst offender; an incompatible transfusion can result in both clumping and destruction of the red cells. Reactions to DEA-1.2 aren't quite as severe, while DEA-7 may produce delayed transfusion reactions.

Many times, a dog's first transfusion takes place under emergency circumstances to save the dog's life. If he's never before been transfused, it's likely he'll have no adverse reaction to the blood, even if it is incompatible. But it's advisable whenever possible—and *always* after your dog has been previously transfused—to identify the dog's blood type so that sensitization of your dog's blood and/or a possible life-threatening reaction can be avoided.

Specialized tests are necessary to identify canine blood types, and only a few places in the United States, such as veterinary schools and certain commercial labs and animal blood banks, have the capability. There are new in-house test kits available for your veterinarian to screen for the most problematic blood types in their office; however, in-house testing for all known canine blood types is not yet available.

Cross-matching can be done in your veterinarian's office. It won't determine the type, but will tell if the donor's blood is compatible with the recipient's—in other words, whether a transfusion reaction will occur or not. Cross-matching won't be helpful if the dog has never before been transfused, but is highly recommended in cases where the dog has received blood before. A drop of serum or plasma from the recipient dog is mixed with a drop of blood from the prospective donor dog; clumping indicates the blood is incompatible.

Certain blood types are more desirable for transfusion than others. Those that are the least antigenic—least likely to cause a reaction—are best. DEA-1.1 is often the donor blood type of choice, because it will not sensitize or cause a reaction in a DEA-1.1-negative dog; a large percentage of the dog population is this type and won't have a reaction. DEA-4-positive is also a good choice, because it causes little problem when there is a reaction, and about 98 percent of all dogs are positive for this blood type and would have no reaction.

Many veterinarians keep a dog on call that serves as a blood donor. Teaching hospitals at veterinary schools often operate their own animal blood banks, and commercial animal blood banks also make a variety of products available (see Appendix C, "Pet Services"; see also BLEEDING).

Botulism

Botulism is not an infection, but is an intoxication resulting in a usually fatal paralysis caused by ingestion of the toxin produced by the bacteria *Clostridium botulinum*. Thankfully, botulism intoxication is a rare condition.

The organism grows in decomposing animal tissue and sometimes plant material and is probably found in the highest frequency in domesticated chickens and wild waterfowl, like ducks. Dogs may contract the toxin by eating improperly canned food, raw meat, or rotting carcasses, or by wound contamination that results in the toxin being produced in the dog's damaged tissue. Dogs are comparatively resistant to ingested botulism.

BOTULISM

SYMPTOMS
Vomiting or regurgitation; abdominal pain (hunching posture); dry mouth; weakness; progressive paralysis; difficulty chewing and swallowing

HOME CARE
None

VET CARE
Antitoxin early in the disease; supportive therapy to relieve symptoms

PREVENTION
Keep dog from scavenging garbage or dead animals; attend to any wounds promptly

The neurotoxin targets the nerve endings that control the muscles. Signs of botulism intoxication include VOMITING or regurgitation, abdominal pain characterized by a "hunching" or arched-back posture, dry mouth, and progressive weakness beginning in the hind legs that produces an odd hopping gait. Paralysis eventually spreads to include the whole body, and the dog typically has trouble seeing and difficulty chewing and swallowing. Death usually results from respiratory and/or cardiac paralysis.

Diagnosis is difficult, because it's hard to find the toxin in the dog's blood, tissues, vomit, or feces, or even in the suspect food. Most commonly, diagnosis is determined by suspect signs and eliminating other causes for the paralysis. Unlike some other paralytic diseases that have similar signs, botulism intoxication also affects muscles in the head.

An antitoxin is available for treatment when botulism is suspected, but is not terribly helpful unless administered very early in the disease. Antibiotic therapy offers little help, either. Treatment is almost exclusively supportive, aimed at relieving the dog's symptoms and keeping him alive until his own body can clear the toxin. It may take a week or longer before supportive care results in any visible improvement in the dog's symptoms, and even then the chance of recovery is poor.

Botulism intoxication is best prevented by keeping your dog from raiding the garbage or from scavenging the remains of wildlife. Any wound should be promptly seen and attended by a veterinarian.

Breed b

Breed refers to a distinct type of dog having predictable physical and/or temperament characteristics that are consistently reproduced in that dog's offspring.

A dog of a particular breed has a known, traceable ancestry referred to as the *pedigree*. A purebred dog is one produced by mating a male and female dog of the same breed. Registering the litter produced from such a breeding authenticates breed status of those puppies by placing them on record in a dog registry association. There are over four hundred distinct dog breeds recognized around the world; more than one hundred are described in this book (see Appendix A, "Dog Associations" and "Dog Breeds").

Dogs have been associated with humans for at least fifteen thousand years, with recent genetic research pointing to as early as one hundred thousand years ago. Consequently, the form and function of dogs have been altered throughout history, and the domestication process has literally molded dogs into new forms.

Natural dog types, like the Alaskan Malamute and Saluki, appeared in nature. They have probably changed very little over the centuries; selective breeding by dog fanciers only refined these breeds.

Spontaneous mutations are inexplicable deviations of nature that dog fanciers promoted and developed into new breeds. Mutations range from body shape and size, ear placement, and tail carriage, to scenting and sighting ability, or even hair coat and color. Size mutation examples include the giantism (acromegaly) of mastiff-type breeds, like the Great Dane and Saint Bernard, or midgetism of toy breeds, like the Toy Poodle, which are simply miniature versions of larger breeds. Dwarfism (achondroplasia) results in shortened, somewhat curved leg bones of breeds like Dachshunds and Basset Hounds.

Hybrids are created by combining existing breeds to form new ones; however, most existing dog breeds are so ancient, that although it's likely many are hybrids, their origin is obscure. Many of the variety of breeds we know today have been around for three thousand years or longer.

Despite the great variety in size and shape, all dogs are easily recognizable as canines. Dog breeds range in size from two- to three-pound teacup sizes, to pony-size two-hundred-pound-plus canines. Mastiff-type breeds are larger and tend to be more heavily muscled and cobby (compact, short-bodied), while sight-hound breeds, like Greyhounds and Whippets, are no less muscled but appear more lithe—and there are a wide range between the two extremes.

Some of the earliest mutations had to do with the dog's coat, which today is found in a wide range of lengths, textures, and colors. Coat color offers a

b

rainbow of hues: Westie white, Kerry Blue blue, Weimaraner silver, Scottie black, and a range of browns from light tan to Golden Retriever gold, Irish Setter red, and Labrador chocolate. Dogs in solid colors are referred to as *self-colored*.

Pattern is equally diverse. *Ticked* refers to small, isolated areas of black or colored hairs over a white ground color. *Sable* is produced by black-tipped hairs on a background of silver, gold, gray, fawn, or brown. *Brindle* is a pattern of black tigerlike stripes on a lighter background (usually tan). *Parti-color* (also *pied* or *piebald*) refers to patches of two or more colors on the coat. *Harlequin* is patches of color (usually black or gray) on a white background. *Tricolor* is a coat with three distinct colors, usually white, black, and tan. *Merle* color pattern has dark blotches against a lighter background of the same color, while *mottled* pattern is characterized by round blotches of color on a lighter background. *Points* are the same color on the face, ears, legs, and tail and are usually white, black, or tan. *Grizzle* (also called *roan*) is a mixture of black or red hairs with white and is often a bluish gray to iron gray color, or may be orange or lemon.

Mixed-breed dogs come in a variety of colors, shapes, and sizes that rival any purebred. Also referred to as *random-bred* or *mutt* dogs, they are the result of unplanned breedings of various purebred or other mixed-breed dogs. They have no pedigree, are not often registered, but may superficially resemble a purebred; however, it is impossible to predict what their offspring will be like. They make wonderful pets, though, and are the dog type of choice for many households throughout the world.

BREEDS AT A GLANCE

Every dog is an individual, and generalities may not apply to every dog of a given breed: dogs may be biters or good with kids due to training or circumstances apart from breed tendencies. And dogs may never experience the listed health concerns or may develop others not mentioned.

BREEDS	SIZE breed standards for weight and shoulder height	COAT TYPE	COAT CARE	ATTITUDE	COMMON HEALTH CONCERNS
Affenpinscher	6–8 lbs 9–11.5"	medium	medium	likes older kids; smart but resistant to training; likes to dig; usually quiet	periodontal disease, slipped kneecap, kidney problems, heart murmurs, hypothyroidism, hip problems

b

BREEDS	SIZE breed standards for weight and shoulder height	COAT TYPE	COAT CARE	ATTITUDE	COMMON HEALTH CONCERNS
Afghan Hound	50–70 lbs 25–27″	long	high	not good with kids; high activity; quiet; aggressive toward small animals; needs lots of exercise; likes privacy	hip dysplasia, allergies, cataracts, demodicosis, ear infection, hypo-thyroidism, PRA
Airedale Terrier	45–52 lbs 23″	short	low	not good with kids; protective; inde-pendent; aggressive; moderate exercise	hip dysplasia, gastritis, skin disease, hypo-thyroidism, PRA
Akita	80–110 lbs 24–28″	short to medium	low	not good with kids; dog-aggressive; one-person dog	bloat, PRA, cataracts
Alaskan Malamute	75–85 lbs 23–25″	medium	medium	loyal but indepen-dent freethinker; needs lots of exercise; likes to howl and bark; dog-aggressive	hypothyroidism, zinc-responsive dermatosis, PRA, bronchitis, hemolytic anemia, cataracts
American Eskimo Dog	25–35 lbs 15–18″	long	high	likes older kids; playful; likes to bark; high-energy dog needs lots of exercise	none mentioned
American Foxhound	55–75 lbs 21–25″	short	low	good watchdog; high energy; needs to hunt; older kids okay	none mentioned
American Staffordshire Terrier	55–70 lbs 12–19″	short	low	needs early training; dominant personality; not for homes with kids	demodicosis, PRA
American Water Spaniel	25–45 lbs 15–18″	medium	medium	not good with kids; lots of exercise; suspicious of strangers; possessive of toys; needs firm hand	none mentioned
Australian Cattle Dog	35–45 lbs 17–20″	short	low	not good with kids; suspicious of strangers; great watch-dog; high-energy dog; needs work	PRA
Australian Shepherd	45–60 lbs 18–23″	medium to long	high	enjoys older kids; suspicious of strangers; highly intelligent and trainable; needs lots of exercise	deafness, PRA, cataracts, Collie eye
Australian Terrier	10–18 lbs 10–11″	medium	medium	likes older children; not good with small pets	PRA, upper-airway disease

b

BREEDS	SIZE *breed standards for weight and shoulder height*	COAT TYPE	COAT CARE	ATTITUDE	COMMON HEALTH CONCERNS
Basenji	21–25 lbs 16–17″	short	low	good with kids; energetic; barkless but noisy yodeler; hard to train; moderate exercise	hernias, gastritis, anemia, inflammatory bowel disease, hemolytic anemia, kidney disease, cataracts
Basset Hound	30–55 lbs 14″ or less	short	low	moderate exercise; good with older kids; calm; loyal; good- natured; easily distracted; tends to be noisy	bladder stones, disk disease, lymphoma, otitis, ectropion or entropion, glau- coma, conjunc- tivitis, obesity, skin disease, cherry eye, Von Willebrand's disease, PRA, spine problems
Beagle (two sizes)	18–35 lbs 13″ or less or 13–15″	short	low	good with kids; likes to run and bark; extremely friendly; a gentle, happy, and curious dog; good family pet	bladder stones, bronchitis, Cushing's disease, diabetes, obesity, glaucoma, hyper- thyroidism,ectro- pion, cherry eye, cataracts, heart disease, epilepsy, allergy, disk disease, periodontal disease, hemolytic anemia, demodicosis, PRA
Bearded Collie	45–55 lbs 20–22″	long	high	good with kids; needs lots of exercise; will chase cars and kids; smart but stubborn	PRA, possibly ivermectin sensitivity
Bedlington Terrier	17–23 lbs 15.5–16.5″	short to medium	low to medium	not good with small kids; moderate exercise; stubborn; may be aggressive to other pets (especially small animals); likes to bark and dig	PRA, cataracts, copper poisoning, kidney disease
Belgian Malinois	55–80 lbs 22–26″	short	low	protective and affectionate; highly trainable; likes to chase cars, bikes, and joggers	none mentioned

b

BREEDS	SIZE breed standards for weight and shoulder height	COAT TYPE	COAT CARE	ATTITUDE	COMMON HEALTH CONCERNS
Belgian Sheepdog	55–80 lbs 22–26″	long	high	protective and affectionate; highly trainable; likes to chase cars, bikes, and joggers	none mentioned
Belgian Tervuren	55–80 lbs 22–26″	long	high	protective and affectionate; highly trainable; likes to chase cars, bikes, and joggers	epilepsy
Bernese Mountain Dog	70–100 lbs 23–27.5″	medium	medium	not good with kids; stubborn; aloof with strangers; needs lots of exercise	entropion, PRA
Bichon Frise	7–12 lbs 9–12″	medium to long	high	good with kids; needs light exercise; an active, playful, and curious dog; sometimes shy; great family pet	runny eyes, cataracts, otitis, skin disease, obesity, tremors, entropion
Black and Tan Coonhound	70–90 lbs 23–27″	short	low	not good with kids; needs to run and hunt; best in hunting home	PRA
Bloodhound	80–110 lbs 24–26″	short	low	not good with kids; needs to work; best in hunting home	bloat, cherry eye, entropion
Border Collie	38–52 lbs 17–21″	medium	medium to high	good with older kids; highly intelligent and trainable; suspicious of strangers; likes to chase cars, etc.; needs a job to do	PRA, Collie eye, ivermectin sensitivity
Border Terrier	11.5–15.5 lbs 9–11″	short	low	affectionate; enjoys kids; likes to dig; a good family dog	none mentioned
Borzoi	55–105 lbs 26–28″	long	high	not good with kids; needs lots of exercise; docile; aloof; loves to run; needs privacy	allergy, bloat, leg fractures, gastritis
Boston Terrier	15–25 lbs 11–14″	short	low	likes older kids; needs light exercise; playful; intelligent; sensitive but sometimes independent;	cataracts, PRA, cherry eye, Cushing's disease, demodicosis,

b

BREEDS	SIZE *breed standards for weight and shoulder height*	COAT TYPE	COAT CARE	ATTITUDE	COMMON HEALTH CONCERNS
Boston Terrier (cont'd)				may be aggressive toward smaller pets; likes to bark and dig; good apart- ment pet	respiratory problems, heat- stroke, kneecap slipping, mast cell tumor, whelping difficulty; perio- dontal disease, corneal ulcers, epilepsy, hydrocephalus
Bouvier des Flandres	65–95 lbs 23.5–27.5″	long	high	easygoing; learns slowly; likes known kids; loves to chase cars	laryngeal paralysis, bloat, glaucoma
Boxer	55–70 lbs 21–25″	short	low	likes kids; protective; courageous; intelligent; needs moderate exercise	acne, allergy, cancer, cherry eye, Cushing's disease, demodicosis, hyperthyroidism, hypothyroidism, inflammatory bowel disease, periodontal disease, respiratory problems, heat- stroke, heart disease, hip dysplasia, spine problems, mast cell tumors, hemangiosarcoma
Briard	55–90 lbs 22–27″	long	high	reserved with strangers; likes older kids; easily trained; needs lots of exercise; likes to chase cars, etc.	none mentioned
Brittany	30–40 lbs 17.5–20.5″	medium	medium	likes kids; needs lots of exercise; friendly; intelligent; wants to please; good with other dogs; good family dog	hypothyroidism, PRA
Brussels Griffon (rough- and smooth- coated)	8–12 lbs 9–10″	short to medium	low to medium	affectionate; intelli- gent but stubborn; reserved with strang- ers; slow learner; likes to dig and bark	PRA, slipped kneecap
Bulldog	40–50 lbs 13–15″	short	low	likes kids; needs moderate exercise; gentle; calm;	bladder stones, demodicosis, hypothyroidism,

BREEDS	SIZE breed standards for weight and shoulder height	COAT TYPE	COAT CARE	ATTITUDE	COMMON HEALTH CONCERNS
Bulldog (cont'd)				friendly; great family dog; noisy breather (snores, etc.)	obesity, respiratory problems, heat-stroke, heart disease, cherry eye, entropion, whelping problems, acne, spine problems, disk disease, corneal ulcers
Bullmastiff	100–130 lbs 24–27"	short	low	docile dog; affectionate protector to family; unpredictable with strangers; snores and drools	bloat, spine problems
Bull Terrier and Miniature Bull Terrier	40–55 lbs 15–22" or 10–20 lbs 10–14"	short	low	likes older kids; playful; gentle; aggressive toward other pets or small kids; stubborn; tends to be slow learner	deafness, allergy, obesity, heart problems, hernia, rage syndrome, zinc-responsive dermatosis, kidney disease, demodicosis, eye problems, laryngeal paralysis
Cairn Terrier	13–14 lbs 9.5–10"	medium	medium	not good with kids; moderate exercise; loyal but jealous; dangerous toward smaller pets; likes to bark and dig	allergy, diabetes, obesity, PRA, kidney disease, glaucoma
Canaan Dog	35–55 lbs 19–24"	short	low	territorial dog; reserved with strangers; good watchdog; may be dog-aggressive	none mentioned
Cavalier King Charles Spaniel	12–18 lbs 11–12"	long	high	loves kids (and everyone!); sweet, gentle dog; exceptional family/ apartment pet	heart disease, cataracts, eye problems, slipped kneecap, hip dysplasia, deafness, epilepsy, thyroid disease, allergies
Chesapeake Bay Retriever	55–80 lbs 21–26"	short	low	not good with kids or other dogs; needs lots of exercise; dominant; stubborn; territorial; needs firm hand; barks a lot; best for hunter	bloat, hip dysplasia, entropion, PRA, cataracts, obesity

b

BREEDS	SIZE breed standards for weight and shoulder height	COAT TYPE	COAT CARE	ATTITUDE	COMMON HEALTH CONCERNS
Chihuahua (smooth- or long-coated)	6 lbs or less 6–9"	short or long	low to medium	not good with kids or other pets; light exercise; loyal but jealous; needs lots of attention; tends to yap	demodicosis, fractures, periodontal disease, heart disease, slipped kneecap, epilepsy, hydrocephalus
Chinese Crested	6–10 lbs 11–13"	none to short	low	older kids okay; playful and devoted dog; slow to learn; good house dog	hairless variety often missing teeth or nails
Chinese Shar-Pei	40–55 lbs 18–20"	short	low	aggressive toward other dogs, pets, and kids; one-person dog; unpredictable with strangers; very dominant; can be dangerous	allergy, cherry eye, demodicosis, entropion, inflammatory bowel disease, kidney disease, skin problems, hypothyroidism, megaesophagus
Chow Chow	44–70 lbs 17–20"	long	high	not good with kids; moderate exercise; loyal to one or two people; dog-aggressive; stubborn; independent; can be dangerous	hot spots, hip dysplasia, heatstroke, entropion, demodicosis, PRA, kidney disease, glaucoma
Clumber Spaniel	55–85 lbs 17–20"	medium	medium	not good with kids; moderate exercise; suspicious of strangers; possessive; easily scent-distracted	obesity, otitis, disk disease, joint problems, entropion
Cocker Spaniel	26–34 lbs 14–15"	long	high	not good with kids; needs moderate exercise; gentle, playful, happy dog; bright but stubborn; hard to housebreak; can be aggressive and tends to bite; needs a firm hand	hernia, slipped kneecap, otitis, allergy, obesity, entropion, ectropion, cataracts, cherry eye, glaucoma, rage syndrome, hypothyroidism, heart disease, allergy, skin disease, periodontal disease, hemolytic anemia, PRA, kidney disease

BREEDS	SIZE breed standards for weight and shoulder height	COAT TYPE	COAT CARE	ATTITUDE	COMMON HEALTH CONCERNS
Collie (rough and smooth)	50–75 lbs 22–26″	short or long	low or high	likes kids; needs lots of exercise; can be high-strung and stubborn, intelligent; affectionate; eager to please	Collie eye anomaly, demodicosis, deafness, lupus erythematosus complex, PRA, cataracts, ivermectin sensitivity
Curly-Coated Retriever	55–75 lbs 22–25″	medium	high	tolerates kids; needs lots of exercise; independent; stubborn; loves water; best in hunting home	PRA
Dachshund (standard and miniature, long-haired, smooth, or wirehaired)	16–32 lbs 9″ or 16 lbs or less 5–6″	short to medium	low to medium	good with kids; moderate exercise; lively; clever; wants to be center of attention; tends to stubbornness	bladder stones, alopecia, demodicosis, Cushing's disease, disk disease, diabetes, heart disease, hypothyroidism, obesity, PRA, portosystemic shunt
Dalmatian	45–59 lbs 19–23″	short	low	likes older kids; needs lots of exercise; courageous; loyal; needs firm hand; difficult to train; may tend to snap	allergy, demodicosis, diabetes, laryngeal paralysis, hip dysplasia, deafness, allergy, bladder stones, urethral obstruction, spine problems
Dandie Dinmont Terrier	18–24 lbs 8–11″	medium	medium to high	likes kids; stubborn; slow to learn; aggressive toward smaller pets; good house dog	none mentioned
Doberman Pinscher	55–90 lbs 24–28″	short	low	older kids okay; needs lots of exercise; bold and loyal; good watchdog; aggressive and independent; very trainable but needs a firm hand; can be dangerous	acne, arthritis, demodicosis, hypothyroidism, liver disease, copper poisoning, wobbler's syndrome, Von Willebrand's disease, skin problems, gastritis, immune problems, hemophilia, heart disease, joint disease,

BREEDS	SIZE breed standards for weight and shoulder height	COAT TYPE	COAT CARE	ATTITUDE	COMMON HEALTH CONCERNS
Doberman Pinscher (cont'd)					obesity, diabetes, PRA, bloat, bone cancer, cataracts, kidney disease
English Cocker Spaniel	26–34 lbs 15–17"	medium to long	high	likes kids; needs moderate exercise; friendly; affectionate; sometimes stubborn; good family dog	PRA, glaucoma, cataracts
English Foxhound	50–65 lbs 23"	short	low	good watchdog; high energy; needs to hunt; older kids okay	none mentioned
English Setter	50–70 lbs 24–25"	medium	high	likes kids; needs lots of exercise; stubborn; easily distracted; likes to bark; very active; great family dog	allergy, PRA
English Springer Spaniel	49–55 lbs 19–20"	medium	medium	not good with kids; needs lots of exercise and attention; intelligent; easily bored; may snap and bite when surprised	eye disorders, hip dysplasia, skin disease, otitis, PRA, rage syndrome, hemolytic anemia, progressive neurological disorder (weakness)
English Toy Spaniel	8–14 lbs 9–10"	long	high	good with kids; affectionate; easily trained; great house pet	slipped kneecap, cataracts, inguinal hernia, heart murmurs, sensitive to anesthesia
Field Spaniel	35–55 lbs 17–18"	medium	high	likes older kids; needs moderate exercise; smart; easily scent-distracted; timid with strangers	otitis, eye infections, PRA
Finnish Spitz	25–35 lbs 15.5.–20"	medium	medium	likes older kids; cautious of strangers; good watchdog; likes to bark; hard to train; can be dog-aggressive	none mentioned
Flat-Coated Retriever	60–80 lbs 22–24.5"	medium	high	likes kids; needs lots of exercise; has a Golden personality; easily scent-distracted; great family dog	cataracts

b

BREEDS	SIZE breed standards for weight and shoulder height	COAT TYPE	COAT CARE	ATTITUDE	COMMON HEALTH CONCERNS
Fox Terrier (smooth and wire)	16–18 lbs 15.5″	short	low	independent; smart and friendly; okay with older kids; dangerous for small pets and kids; hard to train; loves to dig and bark	cataracts; smooth: progressive neurological disorder (weakness); wire: megaesophagus
French Bulldog	28 lbs or less 10–12″	short	low	loves everybody; happy, quiet dog; needs light exercise; ideal apartment dog	breathing problems
German Shepherd Dog	60–85 lbs 22–26″	medium	medium	likes kids; needs lots of exercise; highly trainable but firm handling required; intelligent; loyal; affectionate; likes to chase cars, etc.; aloof with strangers; may be dog-aggressive	hip dysplasia, gastritis, skin disease, diabetes, megaesophagus, Von Willebrand's disease, inflammatory bowel disease, malabsorption syndrome, arthritis, hyperthyroidism, hemangiosarcoma, demodicosis, epilepsy, hyperparathyroidism, pannus, lupus, bloat, bone cancer, PRA, heart disease, spine problems, cataracts, anal gland problems
German Shorthaired Pointer	45–70 lbs 21–25″	short	low	tolerates kids and other dogs; needs lots of exercise; intelligent; excitable; stubborn; needs to hunt	hip dysplasia, spine problems
German Wirehaired Pointer	50–70 lbs 22–26″	medium	medium	not good with kids; stubborn; suspicious of strangers; needs firm hand; ignores everything for a scent; needs to hunt	none mentioned
Giant Schnauzer	65–95 lbs 23.5–27.5″	medium	medium to high	not good with kids; stubborn; dog-aggressive; highly trainable; loyal and courageous; good watchdog	bloat, PRA

b

BREEDS	SIZE breed standards for weight and shoulder height	COAT TYPE	COAT CARE	ATTITUDE	COMMON HEALTH CONCERNS
Golden Retriever	55–75 lbs 21.5–24″	medium	high	likes kids; needs lots of exercise; intelligent; eager to please; loyal; gentle; may be pushy for affection	allergy, epilepsy, hyperthyroidism, hypothyroidism, obesity, hip dysplasia, PRA, cataracts, entropion, heart problems, diabetes, bloat, bone cancer, portosystemic shunt, Von Willebrand's disease, hot spots, otitis
Gordon Setter	45–80 lbs 23–27″	medium	high	likes kids; wary of strangers; needs lots of exercise; stubborn; easily bored	bloat, PRA
Great Dane	100–165 lbs 28–32″	short	low	likes kids; needs lots of exercise (and room!); gentle; calm; affectionate; can be dog-aggressive; can be dangerous	acne, bloat, bone cancer, demodicosis, hypothyroidism, megaesophagus, entropion, hip dysplasia, wobbler's syndrome, tumors
Great Pyrenees	85–100 lbs 25–32″	long	high	confident and gentle with family; protective; suspicious of strangers; hard to train; dog-aggressive; needs to work	bloat, bone cancer
Greater Swiss Mountain Dog	125–130 lbs 25–28″	short	low	not good with kids; stubborn; aloof with strangers; needs lots of exercise; can be dangerous	bloat
Greyhound	60–90 lbs 26–28″	short	low	not good with small kids; needs lots of exercise; gentle; sensitive; can be shy; may be aggressive to small pets	allergy, periodontal disease, PRA, pannus
Harrier	40–55 lbs 19–21″	short	low	outgoing; likes other dogs; a hunting dog (not a pet)	none mentioned

BREEDS	SIZE breed standards for weight and shoulder height	COAT TYPE	COAT CARE	ATTITUDE	COMMON HEALTH CONCERNS
Ibizan Hound	45–50 lbs 22.5–27.5"	short	low	quiet, reserved dog; friendly but needs privacy; aggressive to smaller pets and kids; likes to run; slow learner	none mentioned
Irish Setter	60–70 lbs 25–27"	long	high	likes kids; needs lot of exercise; energetic; excitable; sometimes clownish; needs firm hand; loyal; pushes for affection; easily distracted	allergy, bloat, hypothyroidism, skin disease, hip dysplasia, otitis, PRA, entropion, heart disease, epilepsy, megaesophagus, digestive problems, bone cancer
Irish Terrier	25–27 lbs 17–18"	medium	low to medium	likes kids; good watchdog; likes to bark and dig; stubborn	none mentioned
Irish Water Spaniel	45–65 lbs 21–24"	medium	medium	likes kids; needs lots of exercise; clownish personality; curious; stubborn; suspicious of strangers; dog-aggressive; needs firm hand; needs to work	none mentioned
Irish Wolfhound	105–120 lbs 30–32"	medium	medium	needs to run; suspicious of strangers; dog-aggressive; quiet, gentle, affectionate dog to those he knows	bloat, hypo-thyroidism, porto-systemic shunt
Italian Greyhound	7–13 lbs 13–15"	short	low	not good with kids; needs light exercise; calm; sometimes timid; likes privacy	fractures, PRA, epilepsy, periodontal disease, hypo-thyroidism, slipped kneecap
Jack Russell Terrier (smooth and wire)	10–16 lbs 12–15"	short	low	high-energy, clever dog; likes to bark and dig; very affectionate but stubborn; hard to train	progressive neurological disorder (weakness)
Japanese Chin	4–7 lbs 8–9"	long	high	not good with kids; needs light exercise; playful and bright; resists training; easily spoiled	respiratory problems, heatstroke, eye problems, spine problems, heart

b

BREEDS	SIZE breed standards for weight and shoulder height	COAT TYPE	COAT CARE	ATTITUDE	COMMON HEALTH CONCERNS
Japanese Chin (cont'd)					disease, periodontal disease
Keeshond	35–42 lbs 17–18"	long	high	likes kids and strangers; intelligent and highly trainable; likes to bark	epilepsy, hyperpara- thyroidism, kidney disease, diabetes
Kerry Blue Terrier	33–40 lbs 17.5–19.5"	medium	medium	not good with kids; dog-aggressive; stubborn; hard to train; intelligent, lovable dog	none mentioned
Komondor	80–120 lbs 23.5" or more	long	medium to high	wary of strangers; good watchdog; highly territorial; best as a working dog, not a family pet	bloat
Kuvasz	70–115 lbs 26–30"	medium	medium	not good with kids; aggressive toward strangers and other dogs; protective guard dog; best as a working dog, not a pet	bloat
Labrador Retriever	55–75 lbs 21.5–24.5"	short	low	likes kids; needs lots of exercise; gentle; intelligent; loyal; gregarious; demands attention; great family dog	hip dysplasia, cataracts, PRA, entropion, obesity, epilepsy, oral cancer, hemo- philia, otitis, portosystemic shunt, mega- esophagus, spine problems, bloat, diabetes
Lakeland Terrier	17 lbs 13–15"	medium	medium	likes older kids; quiet, slow-to-learn dog; aggressive toward smaller pets; likes to dig	none mentioned
Lhasa Apso	13–15 lbs 10–11"	long	high	not good with kids; needs moderate exercise; one- or two- person dog; playful; easily spoiled; slow to train	allergy, eye problems, kidney problems, periodontal disease, epilepsy
Maltese	4–7 lbs 7–8"	long	high	older kids okay; quiet, smart, easily trained dog; affectionate;	spine problems, periodontal disease, slipped kneecaps,

b

BREEDS	SIZE breed standards for weight and shoulder height	COAT TYPE	COAT CARE	ATTITUDE	COMMON HEALTH CONCERNS
Maltese (cont'd)				good house dog	heart disease, tremors
Manchester Terrier (and Toy)	12–22 lbs 15–17" or 12 lbs or less 8–13"	short	low	devoted but bossy pet; likes older kids; aggressive toward smaller pets; likes to dig	slipped kneecaps, periodontal disease, Von Willebrand's disease, hypothyroidism, epilepsy, hip problems
Mastiff	170–200 lbs 27.5" or more	short	low	likes kids; needs moderate exercise; independent; can be aggressive; loyal; gentle and good-natured with firm handling; can be dangerous	bloat, hip dysplasia, bone cancer
Miniature Pinscher	8–10 lbs 10–12.5"	short	low	not good with kids; needs light exercise; independent; bold; big dog in small package (but not a lap dog!); tends to be dog-aggressive	kidney stones, obesity, periodontal disease, hip problems, pannus
Miniature Schnauzer	13–15 lbs 12–14"	medium	medium	good with older kids; moderate exercise; loyal and playful; sensible; likes to bark and dig	allergy, obesity, bladder stones, hypothyroidism, cataracts, liver disease, heart disease, diabetes, acne, pancreatitis, PRA, kidney disease, Von Willebrand's disease
Newfoundland	100–150 lbs 26–28"	long	high	outstanding kid's pet; needs lots of exercise; loyal, smart, easily trained dog; great family dog	bloat, bone cancer, hypothyroidism
Norfolk Terrier	11–12 lbs 9–12"	medium	low	not good with young kids; needs moderate exercise; likes to dig, bark, and chase; affectionate and loyal	allergy
Norwegian Elkhound	48–55 lbs 19.5–20.5"	medium	medium	likes older kids; intelligent and trainable dog; high-energy pet	hyperparathyroidism, PRA, kidney disease, glaucoma

b

BREEDS	SIZE breed standards for weight and shoulder height	COAT TYPE	COAT CARE	ATTITUDE	COMMON HEALTH CONCERNS
Norwegian Elkhound (cont'd)				not happy confined indoors	
Norwich Terrier	12 lbs 10″ or less	medium	low	not good with kids; needs moderate exercise; similar to Norfolk Terrier	allergy
Old English Sheepdog	60–90 lbs 21″ or more	long	high	likes kids; needs lots of exercise; lovable; loyal; easygoing; adopts kids as "part of flock"; likes to chase	allergy, cataracts, deafness, demodicosis, diabetes, spine problems
Otter Hound	65–115 lbs 23–27″	medium	medium	boisterous dog; needs lots of exercise; best when given work to do	none mentioned
Papillon	8–10 lbs 8–11″	long	high	not good with kids; needs light exercise; energetic and playful; highly trainable; protective of owner; likes to bark	fractures, periodontal disease, portosystemic shunt, cataracts, PRA, collapsing trachea, sensitive to penicillin and some drugs
Pekingese	14 lbs or less 8–9″	long	high	not good with kids; needs light exercise; stubborn, likes to bark; hard to train; best as pet of single person	entropion, eye problems, respiratory problems, disk disease, slipped kneecap, hernia, difficult whelping, epilepsy, hydrocephalus
Petit Basset Griffon Vendeen	35–45 lbs 13–15″	medium	medium	happy dog; likes kids; easily scent-distracted; hard to train; can be stubborn; good family pet	none mentioned
Pharaoh Hound	45–60 lbs 21–25″	short	low	affectionate, playful dog; loves to run; older kids okay; needs privacy and her own space	none mentioned
Pointer	45–75 lbs 23–28″	short	low	tolerant of kids; needs lots of exercise; lives for scent; high-energy; friendly; good with other pets	none mentioned

b

BREEDS	SIZE breed standards for weight and shoulder height	COAT TYPE	COAT CARE	ATTITUDE	COMMON HEALTH CONCERNS
Pomeranian	3–7 lbs 5–7"	long	high	intelligent, affectionate dog; loves kids; good watchdog; excellent house pet; easily spoiled	hypothyroidism, slipped kneecap, periodontal disease, epilepsy, hydrocephalus
Poodle (Miniature)	15–35 lbs 10–15"	medium to long	high	likes kids; needs moderate exercise; intelligent and highly trainable; good family dog	bronchitis, diabetes, cataract, Cushing's disease, epilepsy, hypothyroidism, hemolytic anemia, glaucoma, PRA, respiratory problems, portosystemic shunt
Poodle (Standard)	50–65 lbs 15" or more	medium to long	high	loves kids; needs lots of exercise; intelligent and highly trainable; excellent family dog	bloat, cataract, epilepsy, Addison's disease, disk disease, kidney disease, Von Willebrand's disease
Poodle (Toy)	7–12 lbs 10" or less	medium to long	high	not good with young kids; needs moderate exercise; playful; sometimes high-strung; intelligent; easily spoiled and sometimes stubborn; can be yappy	bronchitis, glaucoma, cataracts, dry eye, otitis, allergy, heart disease, epilepsy, slipped kneecap, PRA, collapsed trachea, Cushing's disease, epilepsy, hypothyroidism, whelping problems
Portuguese Water Dog	35–60 lbs 17–23"	medium to long	high	high-spirited, dominant dog; needs firm direction; not good with kids; a working dog	none mentioned
Pug	14–18 lbs 9–11"	short	low	good with older kids; needs light exercise; sturdy; clever; affectionate; often a one-person dog; slow to learn; good apartment dog	bladder stones, demodicosis, periodontal disease, whelping problems, proptosis of eyeball, respiratory problems, gastritis, encephalitis, eye problems, heart disease, cherry eye, heatstroke, slipped kneecaps

b

BREEDS	SIZE breed standards for weight and shoulder height	COAT TYPE	COAT CARE	ATTITUDE	COMMON HEALTH CONCERNS
Puli	28–35 lbs 16–17"	long	high	not good with kids; excellent watchdog; bonds with one person; dog-aggressive; likes to bark and chase	none mentioned
Rhodesian Ridgeback	65–75 lbs 24–27"	short	low	likes older kids; great protector and guard dog; smart dog that needs firm training	bloat, spine problems
Rottweiler	85–115 lbs 22–27"	short	low	not good with kids; needs lots of exercise; needs firm handling; intelligent; strong; alert; can be dangerous	hip dysplasia, obesity, entropion, joint problems, inflammatory bowel disease, bloat, spinal cord problems
Saint Bernard (long- and (short-coated)	120–170 lbs 25" or more	short or long	low to high	likes kids; needs lots of exercise; easygoing; cheerful; loyal and patient; good family dog; snores and drools	bloat, bone cancer, epilepsy, hip dysplasia, joint problems, entropion, ectropion, spine problems
Saluki	40–60 lbs 23–28"	short	low	affectionate but needs her space; loves to run; slow learner; prefers quiet home without kids or other pets	none mentioned
Samoyed	35–55 lbs 19–23.5"	long	high	likes kids; needs moderate exercise; independent; intelligent; needs firm hand or can get into trouble	hip dysplasia, PRA, glaucoma, skin problems, zinc-responsive dermatosis, cataracts, spine problems, kidney disease, portosystemic shunts
Schipperke	12–18 lbs 10–13"	medium	medium	devoted to owners; reserved with strangers; likes to bark	none mentioned
Scottish Deerhound	75–110 lbs 28–32"	medium	medium	not good with kids; requires lots of running room; a loyal, devoted companion; aggressive toward other pets	bloat, bone cancer

b

BREEDS	SIZE breed standards for weight and shoulder height	COAT TYPE	COAT CARE	ATTITUDE	COMMON HEALTH CONCERNS
Scottish Terrier	18–22 lbs 10″	long	medium	not good with kids; needs moderate exercise; independent; loyal to one person; curmudgeon	allergy, deafness, lymphoma, oral tumors, periodontal disease, obesity
Sealyham Terrier	20–24 lbs 10–11″	medium	high	good watchdog; friendly to family; stubborn	none mentioned
Shetland Sheepdog	14–18 lbs 13–16″	long	high	older kids okay; needs moderate exercise; intelligent; eager to please; loyal; may be shy; likes to bark and chase	PRA, Collie eye, heart disease, epilepsy, deafness, obesity, hypothyroidism, lupus, pancreatitis, Von Willebrand's disease, possible ivermectin sensitivity
Shiba Inu	17–23 lbs 13.5–16.5″	short	low	independent and affectionate to family; aggressive with strange people or pets; stubborn to train; good apartment dog	none mentioned
Shih Tzu	9–17 lbs 9–10.5″	long	high	not good with kids; needs light exercise; affectionate; playful; can be stubborn; needs lots of attention; easily spoiled	obesity, respiratory problems, periodontal disease, otitis, kidney disease, eye problems, Von Willebrand's disease
Siberian Husky	35–60 lbs 20–23.5″	medium	medium	friendly; affectionate; needs lots of exercise; very vocal; stubborn and slow to train	cataract, laryngeal paralysis, lupus, Rocky Mountain spotted fever, zinc-responsive dermatosis, glaucoma, bronchitis
Silky Terrier	1–10 lbs 9–10″	long	high	likes older kids; curious and affectionate; aggressive toward smaller pets; likes to bark and dig	slipped kneecaps, diabetes, epilepsy, collapsed trachea, hip problems
Skye Terrier	20–25 lbs. 9.5–10″	long	high	not good with kids; affectionate; cautious with strangers; slow to learn	copper poisoning

BREEDS	SIZE breed standards for weight and shoulder height	COAT TYPE	COAT CARE	ATTITUDE	COMMON HEALTH CONCERNS
Soft-Coated Wheaten Terrier	30–40 lbs 17–19″	long	high	sensitive, affectionate dog; needs moderate exercise; intelligent; needs slow training	kidney disease
Staffordshire Bull Terrier	24–38 lbs 14–16″	short	low	affectionate to those he knows; aggressive toward other animals; dominant dog; can be dangerous	demodicosis, cataracts
Standard Schnauzer	30–45 lbs 17.5–19.5″	medium	medium to high	likes older kids; great watchdog; good family pet	none mentioned
Sussex Spaniel	35–45 lbs 13–15″	medium	high	not good with kids; needs moderate exercise; reserved with strangers; scent-distracted; stubborn; can be noisy (baying); hard to housebreak; needs job to do	otitis, eye problems
Tibetan Spaniel	9–15 lbs 10″	medium	medium	not good with small kids; affectionate and sweet, but suspicious of strangers; stubborn; good watchdog	PRA
Tibetan Terrier	18–30 lbs 14–17″	long	high	loves kids and other pets; happy, friendly dog; great family dog	none mentioned
Vizsla	45–60 lbs 21–24″	short	low	likes kids; needs lots of exercise; playful; happy; sensitive yet stubborn; easily scent-distracted; timid around strangers; needs to hunt	none mentioned
Weimaraner	45–70 lbs 23–27″	short	low	not good with kids; needs lots of exercise; stubborn; independent; best as hunter	hip dysplasia, allergy, tumors, bloat, spine problems
Welsh Corgi (Cardigan)	25–38 lbs 10.5–12.5″	short	low	not good with kids; needs moderate exercise; intelligent; obedient; playful and friendly; big dog in small package	PRA, bladder stones, glaucoma, disc disease, hip dysplasia, obesity

BREEDS	SIZE breed standards for weight and shoulder height	COAT TYPE	COAT CARE	ATTITUDE	COMMON HEALTH CONCERNS
Welsh Corgi (Pembroke)	25–30 lbs 10–12″	short	low	not good with kids; needs moderate exercise; intelligent; obedient; playful and friendly, big dog in small package	PRA, bladder stones, glaucoma, disc disease, hip dysplasia, obesity, kidney disease, Von Willebrand's disease
Welsh Springer Spaniel	35–45 lbs 17–19″	medium	medium	good with older kids; needs moderate exercise; timid of strangers; easily bored; needs a job	cataracts
Welsh Terrier	20 lbs 15–15.5″	medium	medium	not good with kids; friendly; dog-aggressive; likes to dig and bark	none mentioned
West Highland White Terrier	15–22 lbs 10–11″	medium	medium	not good with kids; needs moderate exercise; affectionate; loyal to owner	allergy, copper poisoning, liver disease, hernia, glaucoma, heart disease, tremors, cataracts
Whippet	18–30 lbs 18–22″	short	low	likes kids; needs moderate exercise; bright; affectionate; gentle; likes to run	gastritis
Wirehaired Pointing Griffon	50–65 lbs 20–24″	medium	medium	not good with kids; needs lots of exercise; good watchdog; needs firm training; not a house dog; needs a job to do	none mentioned
Yorkshire Terrier	7 lbs or less 7–9″	long	high	not good with kids; needs light exercise; intelligent; courageous; affectionate; can be stubborn; likes to bark	eye problems, periodontal disease, slipped kneecap, liver disease, PRA, heart disease, spine problems, pancreatitis, porto-systemic shunts, hip problems

b | Bronchitis

Characterized by bursts of dry, harsh, honking coughs, bronchitis is the inflammation of the large breathing tubes (bronchials) of the lungs. Chronic bronchitis is a common problem in older dogs and is seen a great deal in small-breed dogs, like terriers, Poodles, and Beagles.

Some cases of bronchitis are caused by ALLERGY. Dogs suffering from allergic bronchitis frequently cough all year long. The cough may be prompted simply by massaging the dog's throat or induced by excitement, exercise, tugging against the leash, or even drinking. As with most inhalant allergies, only rarely can the cause be identified.

The condition causes an increase in the production and accumulation of mucus in the airways. The thick, sticky substance is very irritating and difficult to move. Dogs cough from the resulting inflammation and also in an attempt to clear their lungs. Dogs aren't able to spit, so they often gag or retch at the end of a coughing spell.

In most cases, the cause of chronic bronchitis isn't known, and the dog is otherwise quite healthy. There currently is no evidence that viral or bacterial infections play any role in the condition.

Chronic bronchitis is diagnosed by the presence of an ongoing cough and by ruling out other causes such as KENNEL COUGH, HEARTWORM DISEASE, or CANCER. An examination of the airways and/or x RAYS may confirm the diagnosis. When the culprit is an allergy, an analysis of a tracheal wash usually reveals no bacteria, but many eosinophils (white cells important to allergic response).

BRONCHITIS
SYMPTOMS
Bursts of dry, harsh, honking coughs prompted by pressure against throat, drinking, or excitement and exercise
HOME CARE
If due to allergy that can be identified, avoiding the allergen is beneficial
VET CARE
None, unless severe; then sometimes long-term low doses of corticosteroids, expectorants, and/or bronchodilator drugs
PREVENTION
None; if allergy is diagnosed, avoiding the allergen helps reduce signs

Even when chronic bronchitis is diagnosed, unless the coughing is severe, treatment may not be required. In fact, cough suppressant medications may actually exacerbate the problem by interfering with the mechanism that clears the mucus.

When the condition is considered severe, your veterinarian may prescribe long-term low doses of corticosteroid drugs to help control the inflammation. Expectorant medications are also helpful, which help break up mucus and other secretions and aid in coughing them up. Bronchodilator drugs that open the airways and help breathing seem to benefit some dogs.

There's no way to prevent chronic bronchitis from occurring. However, if the cause is due to allergy and the culprit can be identified, avoiding that allergen will help relieve the dog's symptoms (see ALLERGY, Atopy).

Brucellosis

This canine venereal disease is caused by the bacterium *Brucella canis* (*B. canis*) and causes a number of problems, including abortions. *B. canis* was first recognized in the mid-1960s and is found in dogs all over the world. It's estimated that about 1 percent of pet dogs and 5 percent of strays are infected, but the incidence of disease varies depending on the geographic region.

Most cases of canine brucellosis are associated with dogs in breeding kennels. Female dogs harbor the organism in the greatest concentration in the placenta and vaginal secretions, while male dogs pass the infection through their semen. Brucellosis is transmitted through sexual contact or through

BRUCELLOSIS

SYMPTOMS
Sometimes lymph node enlargement; weight loss; fatigue; loss of libido; females suffer late-term abortion, stillbirth, fading puppies; males suffer swollen testicles or wasting testicles, back pain

HOME CARE
None

VET CARE
Antibiotic therapy

PREVENTION
Test dogs and remove positive animals from kennel/breeding situations; kennel dogs in separate runs

h

ingestion of the bacteria from contact with contaminated surfaces. Infected BITCHES can infect kennel runs with their uterine discharges or aborted fetuses, which may potentially spread disease to other dogs.

Once the bacteria has been introduced either orally or sexually, the organism multiplies in the nearest lymph nodes—either the neck and head or the groin region. The nodes may become slightly enlarged, but rarely are fever or other signs of illness seen. Occasionally, the dog may lose weight, appear fatigued, or seem to lose interest in mating. The organism then spills into the dog's bloodstream and can maintain a presence for two years or longer. During this period, the bacteria infects the prostate and testicles of male dogs and the pregnant female dog's placenta.

As the infection progresses, a dog typically develops immunity to the bacteria and eventually clears the organism from his body. After ten to twenty-four months, most dogs have self-cured and appear to become immune to reinfection. But during infection, dogs continue to spread the disease. Infection in the pregnant female results in late-term abortion (forty-five to fifty-five days into gestation); stillbirth at or near term; or weak puppies that die within days of birth. Rarely will puppies survive, but when they do, they become carriers of the bacterium. Infected bitches usually abort puppies only during the pregnancy that initially follows infection; sometimes, though, the disease also kills puppies in the second or even third pregnancy following infection.

In male dogs, permanent damage can occur. Brucellosis results in infertility caused by inflammation and atrophy of the testicles. The testicles may swell and then shrink and waste away as the sperm-producing tissue is destroyed. Low sperm count, production of abnormal sperm, and/or sterility results. Some dogs develop back problems caused by inflammation of the disks in the lower back.

Dogs are diagnosed by testing a sample of their blood for the bacteria. There are several types of tests available, and the most accurate (blood culture) is also the most expensive, especially when a group of dogs must be screened. Another test screens the blood and measures the level of antibodies specific for the disease, which indicates the dog has been exposed to brucellosis. Therefore, a negative test is quite accurate—no antibodies means no exposure and no disease—but a positive means only that exposure has occurred, not necessarily that infection is present. A positive antibody test for brucellosis should be confirmed with a more specific test.

There is no vaccine available to prevent the disease. Several antibiotics will clear the bacteria from the dog's bloodstream. However, the organism "hides out" in the lymph nodes and other tissues of the body and can reinfect the bloodstream once therapy is stopped.

Brucellosis is controlled by testing all dogs before introducing them into a kennel situation and by removing any dogs that carry the bacteria. Particularly in breeding situations, prior screening of both the male and female is essential to protect both dogs and any subsequent puppies that may be born. Kennels that keep dogs caged individually typically have a lower incidence of the disease.

There have been rare cases of humans contracting brucellosis, usually through contact with aborted puppies or laboratory exposure. It's not currently considered a common hazard to people, but when it does occur, people typically experience flulike symptoms. Intermittent headache, fever, swollen lymph nodes, chills, muscle pain, and sore throat are some signs. Unlike the canine disease, antibiotics are very effective in eliminating *B. canis* infection in people (see also ZOONOSIS).

Burns

A burn is an injury resulting from exposure to fire, heat, caustic substances, electricity, or radiation. Dogs can suffer burns from kitchen accidents involving spills of hot cooking oil or boiling water; from walking through fresh tar on the road; from chemical burns (see POISON), from chewing electric cords (see ELECTRICAL SHOCK); from overexposure to the sun (see SUNBURN); and (rarely) from direct contact with fire. FROSTBITE also resembles a burn injury.

BURNS

SYMPTOMS
Red skin; blistering, swelling, tender to painful area; severe burns are sometimes charred, with fur easily pulled out

HOME CARE
Soak cloth in cool water, apply to injury, then see vet as soon as possible

VET CARE
Depending on severity, cold compresses, salves, or ointments; surgical removal of dead tissue; sometimes fluid therapy or pain medication

PREVENTION
Confine dog in safe place when access to hazards are unavoidable; tape down electrical cords or paint with dog repellent; keep caustic solutions out of reach

The extent of damage depends on the intensity and length of exposure. A minor burn will cause the skin to turn red and sometimes blister or swell, and the area will be tender. Deeper burns char or turn the tissue white. Fur in the affected areas will become loose and is easily pulled out.

Severe burns cause excruciating PAIN. They are usually accompanied by excessive loss of fluid and SHOCK. When 30 to 40 percent or more of the body surface is burned, the outlook is grim.

First aid involves relieving the pain and stopping further damage. Soak a towel in cool water and apply to the injured area to alleviate the pain. For superficial burns, clip away the surrounding fur, rinse gently with cool water, and blot dry with a clean, soft cloth. A topical antibiotic, like Neosporin, will help prevent infection and keep the area moist while it heals. You may need to employ an ELIZABETHAN COLLAR to prevent the dog from licking the wound.

Moderate to severe burns should be addressed by your veterinarian. Even a superficial injury can be more serious than you think, because damage may be hidden by the hair coat.

To avoid burns, make the kitchen off-limits to your dog when you're cooking. When open flame is accessible, such as candles or fireplace, either confine the dog to a safe place or increase your vigilance to prevent accidents. Dogproof your house by making electrical cords inaccessible or unattractive. Tape electrical cords out of the way and/or apply a bad-tasting solution, like Bitter Apple, to deter persistent CHEWING. Supervise your dog's outdoor excursions to prevent his blundering into a sticky situation and getting into hot water—or tar.

Callus

A callus is a hard, thickened area of gray, hairless skin that forms as a protective barrier, usually on a pressure point above bone. Calluses can form anywhere on the body but typically develop on the elbow, usually as a result of the ongoing pressure of contact when the dog lies down. Small calluses aren't usually a concern, but they can develop into problems, particularly in dogs housed in kennels with cement floors.

Callus sores occur most frequently in large-breed or heavy dogs. In addition to developing on the elbows, they may develop on the underside of the forelegs or the outside of the rear legs, thighs, and buttocks. Draining pressure sores can develop at these sites if the irritation is not relieved. Infected sores are treated like an ABSCESS.

Prevent problem calluses by padding your dog's sleeping areas, particularly concrete runs, with blankets, rugs, or foam rubber pads. This helps distribute the dog's weight more evenly and alleviates the pressure on the callus.

Cancer

The term *cancer* refers to an abnormal growth of cells that interfere with normal body functions. All body cells have a finite life span. When they die, cells are replaced through a process called *mitosis* in which a single cell splits into two cells identical to the parent cell. For reasons we don't fully understand, normal cells sometimes mutate during mitosis, producing fast-growing abnormal cells that act like parasites, invading and replacing healthy tissues.

Under ideal circumstances, the body's IMMUNE SYSTEM recognizes these cells as foreign and eliminates them before they can cause problems. But all too often, the body can't fight off the attack. Growths of abnormal cells, called *tumors* or *neoplasms*, are the result. Those that remain localized and relatively harmless are termed *benign*, while potentially deadly tumors are called *malignant*.

Malignant tumors can be confined to one area, but often they spread, or *metastasize*, throughout the body. The seriousness of a specific kind of cancer is determined by how malignant it is. The most treatable are considered low-grade cancers because although they reach a great size, they tend not to metastasize until relatively late in the disease. The most dangerous cancers are already spreading at the earliest stages, when the point of origination is still very small or even nearly undetectable. A malignant tumor becomes deadly when it interferes with normal body processes.

Cancer is considered a disease of older dogs, and the incidence of tumors in dogs increases with age. The prevalence of canine cancer is difficult to determine, but the Veterinary Cancer Society believes cancer accounts for nearly half of the deaths of pets over ten years of age. About 25 percent of all pet dogs will develop cancer.

The exact cause of cancer remains a mystery, but we do know that cancer-causing agents, referred to as *carcinogens*, may increase the risk of developing certain kinds of disease. Cumulative exposure over a dog's lifetime may be why older dogs develop cancer more often.

Exposure to ultraviolet rays (sunlight) increases the risk of skin cancer. Certain components in foods may increase a dog's risk of cancer, or they may protect against it; the role diet plays in cancer is not yet fully understood. However, the relation between sexual hormones and some types of cancers

---

THE VETERINARY CANCER SOCIETY'S TOP TEN SIGNS OF CANCER IN ANIMALS

1. Abnormal swelling that persists or continues to grow
2. Sores that do not heal
3. Weight loss
4. Loss of appetite
5. Bleeding or discharge from any body opening
6. Offensive odor
7. Difficulty eating or swallowing
8. Hesitation to exercise or loss of stamina
9. Persistent lameness or stiffness
10. Difficulty in breathing, urinating, or defecating

CANCER

SYMPTOMS	
See Top Ten Signs of Cancer in Animals	
HOME CARE	
Maintain good nutrition; nursing care	
VET CARE	
Surgery; chemotherapy; radiation	
PREVENTION	
Spay females before first heat cycle, neuter males before puberty; avoid sun exposure in light-colored dogs; remain alert to lumps and bumps	

has been well documented. The risk of mammary cancer in female dogs and prostate and testicular cancer in male dogs can be reduced or even eliminated by neutering or spaying the dog. There also can be inherited tendencies, with certain breeds—or families or lines of dogs within a certain breed—being more prone to some cancers.

Early detection greatly improves your dog's prognosis and chance for successful treatment. Any lump or bump you find on your dog should be evaluated immediately by your veterinarian. However, symptoms of cancer are often similar to other illnesses or conditions. Most canine cancers are external, but a dog's fur can make lumps or sores difficult to detect. And when a cancer is internal, you may not notice anything is wrong until your dog becomes sick. Be vigilant for any physical and/or behavioral changes in your dog and alert your veterinarian immediately.

Dogs can suffer from more kinds of cancer than any other domestic animal, including the same variety of cancers that people do. It's impossible to catalog them all here. But the cancers people commonly suffer—cancer of the lungs, cervix, prostate, colon, and pancreas—are relatively uncommon in dogs.

Skin cancer is the most common canine cancer. Several types affect dogs, and some studies estimate that up to 30 percent of canine cancers arise from the skin. The most common are sebaceous adenomas; thankfully, about 75 percent are benign. These tumors develop from the oil-producing sebaceous glands and are seen most commonly in Cocker Spaniels. They resemble a cauliflower and are usually less than an inch in size; sometimes the skin surface ulcerates.

Mast cell tumors account for 12 to 21 percent of all canine skin cancers and are common in Boxers and Boston Terriers. These tumors are usually less than an inch in size with a bumpy surface and are found most often on the lower abdomen, hind legs, and prepuce. About 30 percent of mast cell tumors are malignant and metastasize to other organs.

Squamous cell carcinoma is associated with overexposure to sunlight. This skin cancer most frequently affects the belly of white dogs, like Dalmatians and American Staffordshire Terriers, and the faces of white-faced dogs, but can also appear on the feet and legs. It looks like a cauliflower, or like a grayish, hard, flat, nonhealing ulcer. Although squamous cell carcinoma rarely spreads throughout the body, it is locally invasive and can be very damaging to the surrounding areas.

Mammary gland cancer is considered the second leading cancer in dogs, accounting for 25 to 42 percent of tumors in BITCHES. Up to 50 percent of canine mammary gland tumors are malignant and occur most frequently in intact (nonspayed) females. There also appears to be an increased risk in the sporting breeds of dogs. Usually, a painless lump or enlargement appears in the breasts closest to the rear legs. Malignant and benign mammary tumors look alike, and physical examination alone can't determine which is which. Most females affected with mammary gland cancer are older than six years old, with the average being ten years of age. The breast cancer usually spreads to the lungs. Spaying female dogs before the onset of their first heat cycle nearly eliminates their risk of developing mammary cancer. Risk is also reduced in bitches spayed before they are two years of age, but there appears to be no cancer-protective benefit if spay surgery is delayed beyond this age.

Lymph gland cancers are devastating because they commonly spread throughout the body. Several breeds, including the Boxer, Basset Hound, Saint Bernard, and Scottish Terrier, have an increased risk for developing lymphomas. The lymphatic system also includes the blood cell–forming organs—bone marrow and spleen. Splenic hemangiosarcoma (cancer of the spleen) seems to affect middle-aged to older German Shepherd Dogs most frequently. Affected dogs commonly are diagnosed on an emergency basis as their tumors rupture and cause PAIN, collapse, severe BLEEDING, SHOCK, and eventually death if not treated. Unfortunately these tumors usually metastasize early, and the expected life span after diagnosis is three to twelve months even with surgical treatment and chemotherapy.

Oral tumors account for about 8 percent of all malignancies seen in dogs, and most growths in the middle-aged or older canine's mouth are malignant. Squamous cell carcinomas, melanomas, and fibrosarcomas (cancers of connective tissue) affect the mouth, and all tend to spread throughout the body. Malignant melanomas tend to occur most frequently in dark-pigmented dogs. Scottish Terriers, black Labrador Retrievers, black Poodles, and other dark dogs are most susceptible. Epulides are benign growths of the tissue surrounding the teeth, which may need to be surgically removed for comfort. So watch for a mass on the gums, bleeding, mouth odor, or difficulty eating.

Bone cancer is another common canine cancer, rated by some in the top five. Osteosarcomas arising from the bone-forming cells are the most common type and are almost always malignant. They have a high probability of spreading, often to the lungs. Typically they affect the long bones of the legs, or the skull, and are most common in large- and giant-breed dogs like Saint Bernards, Great Danes, and Newfoundlands; rarely does bone cancer occur in small dogs. The disease is excruciatingly painful. Affected dogs typically limp on the affected limb, which may have swelling.

Testicular cancer is considered relatively common in dogs; the testicle typically enlarges, or a mass grows on the scrotum. In cases where one or both testicles fail to descend from the abdomen into the scrotal sac (see CRYP-TORCHID), there is a thirteen-times-greater incidence of tumors in the retained testicle. Fortunately, most testicular cancers tend not to spread, and neutering the dog usually cures the problem. Intact male dogs also tend to get perianal tumors—growths beneath the tail adjacent to the anus—that often are benign, but can be malignant.

The appearance of a tumor along with the dog's other symptoms (see chart) can point to cancer. Lumps that grow fast, change size or shape over weeks or months, ooze or break open, are firm and tightly fixed to body tissue, or are abnormally colored are most likely to be malignant. However, only microscopic examination and identification of the tumor cells will render a definitive diagnosis. Your veterinarian may be able to collect a sample by inserting a needle directly into the tumor and withdrawing tumor cells into the syringe. Other times, cancer cells may be identified in the circulating blood, or even in a urine specimen. However, often cancers require a biopsy (removal of a piece of tissue) for specialized laboratory analysis.

Biopsy not only identifies the kind of cancer, but also evaluates its current state of progression. These two parameters define which treatment will be most effective (various cancers respond differently to available treatments) and help predict your dog's chance of survival and/or recovery.

Prognosis depends on the type of the cancer, how advanced it is, and whether it has—or will—spread. It also depends on how healthy your dog is in other respects, because an elderly or ill dog may not handle the stress of cancer therapy as well as a robust dog might. In the best circumstances when the cancer is detected early and treated aggressively, cures are possible.

There is no one magic bullet for treating cancer, either in human or veterinary medicine. The three major cancer therapies applied to people are also used to treat canine malignancies, either singly or, more often, in combination. Cancer treatment is aimed at neutralizing as many abnormal cells as possible by attacking the cancer from multiple angles, while doing as little damage as possible to healthy tissue.

The cancer treatment of choice in veterinary medicine is *surgical removal of the tumor*, which is particularly effective when the cancer is localized and has not spread. For instance, bone cancer is usually treated by AMPUTATION of the affected limb. Cost varies greatly depending on the cancer and the individual dog.

Unfortunately, surgical cure is rare because it's difficult to remove every cancerous cell. Leaving behind a single cell allows the cancer to recur and/or spread. In fact, the disturbance caused by surgery is sometimes thought to increase the chance that cancer cells will be disseminated; instead of conventional scalpels, lasers may be used to excise tumors to decrease this potential. Surgery alone may give your dog another six to twelve months. Other forms of treatment often follow surgery in an effort to rid the body of any malignant cells that may have been missed.

Some cancers that encroach upon vital organs, nerves, or muscles can be difficult to surgically remove without damaging normal tissues. In those instances, *radiation* may be used. Brachytherapy is one form of radiation treatment in which radioactive elements are surgically planted into the tumor and left there for several days. However, this treatment is not widely available because it's more expensive and fewer places are equipped to do it. Conventional beam therapy is most commonly used; it consists of a beam of very intense X RAY being shot directly into the cancer to kill the cells. Radiation therapy is most successful when used in combination with other treatments. We don't understand exactly how radiation kills cells, but cancers and tissues of rapidly dividing cells (like bone marrow and the skin) are most sensitive to radiation therapy. However, cancer cells aren't more sensitive than normal cells, and normal tissue can be damaged during treatment. Radiation works best on cancers confined to one area that are difficult to treat surgically, such as a skin cancer around the dog's eye. The treatment regime varies, but often may be performed three times a week for a month.

In order to irradiate only the target area, the dog must be anesthetized for each treatment. Anesthetic risk may be a concern when the dog is old or ill, as well as increasing the cost of an already expensive treatment. Because of regulatory burdens associated with the machines, and the cost of the machines themselves, only veterinary cancer centers, universities, or research facilities can make this treatment available. Still, radiation therapy is often effective in curing up to 80 percent of some kinds of cancer.

Chemotherapy is the third cancer treatment commonly used with dogs, and it is most useful in treating cancer that's spread throughout the body. A wide variety of *cytotoxic* (cell-poisoning) drugs is available and may be used singly or in combinations as pills or intravenous injections. The specific drug(s) used depend on the kind of cancer; many of the same human medications are effective against cancer in dogs. Often, initially intense therapy is followed by lower doses as the treatment progresses.

The drugs are used to destroy as many cancer cells as possible—or at a minimum, to slow the growth rate of the tumor. But the drugs affect healthy tissue as well as cancerous growths, which is what causes unpleasant side effects in people. These symptoms vary depending on the drug and the dose; however, most dogs undergoing chemotherapy have few to no side effects compared to people. They may lose their appetite for a short time or act lethargic during the most intense part of the treatment. But most dogs don't lose their hair or suffer bouts of vomiting.

Lymph gland cancers are considered one of the most rewarding canine cancers to treat using chemotherapy. Tumors shrink often within days of initial treatment, and up to 85 percent of treated dogs go into remission for nine to eighteen months. A small percentage of these dogs are cured or remain in remission for several years.

Chemotherapy is also a boon in treating bone cancer. Traditional treatment involves amputation, or sometimes replacement of the diseased bone with donor bone transplanted to "spare" the limb. A newer, limb-sparing treatment called *bone transport* actually grows new bone in the gap left after the bone tumor is removed. A special device is used that induces the body to believe there's a fracture so that new bone is generated to heal the gap. However, when only surgery is performed on osteosarcoma cases, 80 percent of the time the cancer spreads to the dog's lungs and kills the dog in three to five months. Chemotherapy using the drugs cisplatin and doxorubicin, in addition to surgery, prevents lung metastasis for more than a year in most cases, with up to 30 percent of these dogs living beyond two years. The University of Illinois College of Veterinary Medicine is currently investigating use of a biodegradable polymer sponge that dissolves over time when implanted in the dog's body, providing a slow-release chemotherapy. It's believed this new technique will be less toxic than IV chemotherapy, require fewer doses, and help control recurrence or spread of the tumor. Since canine cancer sufferers typically are middle-aged or older when first diagnosed, this can mean the dog remains cancer-free for the remainder of his natural life.

Because the drugs are prescribed according to the dog's body weight, cost of chemotherapy varies depending on the drug(s) and the individual dog. The cost for small animals tends to be relatively low, but can mount when your dog is quite heavy or is affected by other medical problems that increase the cost of treatment.

Experimental therapies also show promise and are being used particularly in veterinary teaching institutions. *Immunotherapy* is mostly investigational at this time. It employs special agents, including drugs, that help stimulate the body's immune system to prevent cancers from developing or to help destroy existing tumor tissue.

Cryosurgery uses selective freezing to damage and destroy cancerous tissue. A substance that produces intense cold—usually, liquid nitrogen—is carefully applied directly to the tumor itself, leaving surrounding healthy tissue intact. Cryosurgery works best on localized tumors that don't invade too deeply into the body, such as oral tumors or perianal tumors.

Hyperthermia, or heat therapy, is the opposite of cryosurgery: it heats the cancer cells to kill them. The proper temperature destroys the tumor without damaging normal tissue. Hyperthermia enhances the effect of other cancer treatments.

Lasers, in addition to being used as a cutting and cauterizing instrument, can also be used in a kind of light therapy against cancer. Called *photodynamic therapy* (*PDT*), a special drug is injected into the tumor. Within a day or two, the drug sensitizes the tumors to the effects of light. When the tumor is then exposed to light, the drug is activated and completely destroys any cancer cells around it.

Diet therapy is also being investigated. Preliminary studies suggest that cancer—specifically, lymphoma—changes the way a dog uses nutrients. Recent research suggests that dogs fed a specially developed diet in conjunction with conventional chemotherapy improved the dogs' quality of life and extended longevity by nine months to three years (see Appendix C, "Canine Research Foundations").

With few exceptions, cancer cannot be prevented. You and your dog are best served by remaining vigilant to early warning signs and seeking veterinary intervention as early as possible.

The maintenance of quality of life is the underlying goal of all cancer therapies, because a cure rarely is possible. Your veterinarian can help you recognize when a longer life isn't necessarily a *better* life. When the time comes, love will tell you the best decision to make for your dog (see also EUTHANASIA).

Canine Coronavirus (CCV)

Canine coronavirus is a highly contagious gastrointestinal disease first identified in 1971 in a group of military dogs in Germany. The virus has since been found in Europe, North America, and Australia, but likely occurs throughout the world.

The canine coronavirus is related to the feline forms that cause feline infectious peritonitis and feline enteric disease; however, CCV causes disease only in coyotes, foxes, and dogs. All dogs are susceptible, but the signs are most severe in puppies and may develop suddenly. Studies have shown that more than 25 percent of pet dogs have been exposed to CCV.

Dogs usually are infected through contact with sick dogs or their droppings. Once the virus is swallowed, infection develops within one to three days. Many dogs will show no signs, while others rapidly become sick and die. Most cases are seen in kennel situations.

CANINE CORONAVIRUS (CCV)

SYMPTOMS
Loss of appetite; fever; vomiting; depression; liquid, yellow-orange diarrhea that may contain blood or mucus; dehydration

HOME CARE
Nursing care

VET CARE
Fluid therapy; antibiotics; sometimes medication to control vomiting and diarrhea

PREVENTION
Prevent contact with strange dogs; practice good sanitation by picking up yard; high-risk dogs may benefit from vaccination

Early signs include loss of appetite (see ANOREXIA), sometimes fever, VOMITING, and depression. This is followed by loose to liquid DIARRHEA, which may contain blood or mucus and has a characteristic yellow-orange color and foul odor. Life-threatening DEHYDRATION can develop quickly.

CCV infects a specific part of the lining of the small intestine. The small intestine is lined with hill-shaped structures called *villi* that are covered with tiny hairlike projections (microvilli) that absorb nutrients. CCV infects the "hilltops" of the villi, compromising the body's ability to process food. However, the "valley" portion contains microvilli-producing crypt cells that can completely replace the tips about every three or four days. For that reason, the virus tends to produce only a mild to moderate, usually self-limiting disease; in most cases, dogs will recover within seven or ten days. However, some dogs may relapse three or four weeks following apparent recovery.

Diagnosis is made on the basis of symptoms and sometimes identification of the coronavirus by electron microscope examination of a stool sample. There is no specific treatment for CCV, but supportive care helps speed recovery. It's mostly aimed at counteracting fluid loss and vomiting. Fluid therapy helps combat dehydration that often results from the vomiting and diarrhea, and antibiotics reduce the number of bacteria in the bowel so they do not infect the bloodstream through the compromised bowel lining. Medication is often prescribed to control the diarrhea and vomiting.

The disease by itself is rarely fatal; however, when the dog is already compromised by intestinal parasites or other illness, CCV can kill. In particular, dogs infected with CANINE PARVOVIRUS along with CCV can have up to a 90 percent mortality rate.

Prevention of the disease is best managed by avoiding contact with infected animals and their droppings. Sanitary procedures, such as picking up the yard and kennel area, help a great deal. Preventative VACCINATIONS are available and may be recommended for high-risk dogs, such as those exposed through kenneling or dog shows.

Canine Distemper Virus (CDV)

Canine distemper, first recognized in Europe in the eighteenth century, is still considered the most important viral disease of dogs. CDV is similar to the human measles virus, and in dogs it is the most commonly known infectious disease of the nervous system. This highly contagious, often fatal virus is excreted in the saliva, respiratory secretions, urine, and feces and is transmitted through the air (sneezing and coughing) and by contaminated objects (in the same way a cold virus spreads in people). Contact with infected secretions spreads the disease. Rarely, unborn puppies are infected by their mother, which may result in stillbirths, abortions, FADING PUPPY SYNDROME, and central nervous system signs in four- to six-week-old puppies.

CDV can infect and be carried by many species besides the dog, including the wolf, coyote, raccoon, ferret, mink, skunk, otter, and weasel. These wild populations probably help maintain the infection, despite good preventative vaccination practiced by responsible pet-dog owners. Unfortunately, even the

---

CANINE DISTEMPER VIRUS (CDV)

SYMPTOMS
Loss of appetite; yellowish diarrhea; difficulty breathing; seizures; behavior changes; weakness; incoordination; thick discharge from the eyes and nose; sometimes thickened, cracked footpads

HOME CARE
Nursing care; VETERINARY CARE ESSENTIAL IF THE DOG IS TO SURVIVE

VET CARE
Supportive care; fluid therapy; antibiotics; drugs to control vomiting and diarrhea; sometimes anticonvulsive medication to control seizures

PREVENTION
Vaccinate your dog as recommended by your veterinarian; prevent contact with other unvaccinated dogs

highly effective commercial vaccines are not 100 percent effective, and even vaccinated dogs can become infected by and clinically ill from the disease. Puppies are more susceptible than adult dogs, but during their lifetime, most dogs will be exposed to distemper. In particular, dogs that are kenneled or regularly boarded, and those that routinely hunt or are shown, have a higher risk because of increased exposure to other dogs. Dogs obtained from the less-than-ideal conditions of some animal shelters or pet stores, particularly at nine to twelve weeks of age, are often affected. They may appear healthy but be incubating the disease when adopted (even if they've been vaccinated), then become sick once in their new home.

There are several strains of the virus, and some are more virulent than others. In general, about 85 percent of puppies exposed to the virus when they are less than a week old develop distemper within two to five weeks and die, while older puppies and adult dogs develop fatal disease only about 30 percent of the time. Older puppies and adult dogs have more mature immune protection and so are better able to fight off the infection if they are exposed.

The virus attacks various body tissues, especially the epithelial cells that line the surfaces of the body, like the skin, the conjunctiva of the eyes, the respiratory and urinary tracts, and the mucous membranes lining the gastrointestinal tract. It also infects lymph nodes, kidneys, liver, spleen, and the brain and spinal cord. Whether or not the infected dog survives depends on the effectiveness of her individual IMMUNE SYSTEM.

Within two days following infection, the virus spreads to the bronchial lymph nodes and tonsils, and then throughout the body's lymphatic system (bone marrow, spleen, and other lymph nodes). Within five days, virus infects and begins destroying the white blood cells, which results in leukopenia (low white blood cells), and a fever develops for a day or two.

By nine to fourteen days following infection, 75 percent of dogs that have competent immune systems will kill the virus and won't become sick. Dogs that aren't able to mount an early immune response develop sudden devastating signs of disease, including ANOREXIA, yellowish DIARRHEA, trouble breathing, and central nervous system signs, such as seizures, behavior changes, weakness, and incoordination. A characteristic thick, white to yellow discharge from the eyes and nose is often seen as well. This looks similar to signs of a cold, but as dogs don't catch colds like humans do, this is a serious warning of illness.

Other symptoms vary, depending on what organs are affected by the virus. Infection of the respiratory system may prompt the dog to cough and develop PNEUMONIA. Gastrointestinal infection can cause bloody or mucoid diarrhea, the eyes to ulcerate or even become blind, and the skin (particularly the footpads) to thicken, crack, and bleed. Dogs that survive infection during

C

puppyhood may suffer enamel hypoplasia—poorly developed tooth enamel that's pitted and discolored—as adults. Even dogs that recover from infection may suffer permanent damage to the central nervous system that results in recurrent seizures or palsy for the rest of the dog's life. Diagnosis of CDV is usually based on the signs of disease.

Because of an impaired immune system, dogs suffering from distemper may also develop bacterial, fungal, or parasitic infections that can make the dog even sicker and increase the risk of death. Without veterinary intervention, dogs experiencing severe symptoms usually die within three weeks.

There is no cure for distemper, only supportive treatment that addresses individual symptoms to make the dog more comfortable until—and if—her own body is able to overcome the infection. Hospitalization is usually necessary if the dog is to survive. Stricken dogs are treated with antibiotics to combat infections that often result from immunosuppression, along with fluid therapy and medications to control diarrhea and vomiting to counteract DEHYDRATION. Anticonvulsant medication may be necessary to control seizures. No one treatment is specific or always effective, and it may take ongoing therapy for up to six weeks to conquer the disease.

Dogs sick with CDV also shed the virus for up to ninety days and are sources of infection for other healthy dogs. Sick dogs must be QUARANTINED away from healthy animals. Plus the virus can live in a frozen state for many years, thaw out, and still infect your dog. However, it is relatively unstable in hot or dry conditions, and it can be killed by most disinfectants, such as household bleach, a solution of 0.5 percent formalin in water, or a quaternary ammonium (0.3 percent) disinfectant.

The decision to attempt to save the dog is based on her overall health, the seriousness of the disease, and the potential for permanent health problems. Each dog responds differently to treatment. For some, symptoms get better, then worsen before recovery. Other dogs show no improvement despite aggressive treatment. Often, after consulting with their veterinarian, owners make the difficult decision to EUTHANIZE the sick dog.

VACCINATIONS work with the immune system to help protect the majority of dogs from contracting this disease. However, an unknown number of dogs do not develop an immune response (i.e., antibodies in the bloodstream) to vaccines, and these dogs may be susceptible to infection when exposed, even though they've received adequate vaccination. STRESS and debilitation from other illness not only predispose dogs to contracting CDV, they also interfere with the effectiveness of vaccines. Occasionally, puppies that are born with a deficient immune system may actually become sick with CDV as a result of vaccination. This is considered extremely rare, though, and the risk of disease from withholding vaccination is much greater.

The best way to protect your dogs from CDV infection is to vaccinate as recommended by your veterinarian and prevent contact with other unvaccinated dogs.

C

Canine Herpesvirus (CHV)

Canine herpesvirus is one of a wide variety of herpesviruses affecting many species and is the most common cause of FADING PUPPY SYNDROME. A TEMPERATURE of about 98 degrees is ideal for virus growth, which is why CHV attacks youngsters (while body temperature averages 96 to 100 degrees) rather than adult dogs (whose body temperature normally ranges 100.5 to 102.5 degrees). The virus can be found in the lower temperature areas of the genital and respiratory tracts of healthy adult dogs, where it remains dormant and doesn't cause deadly disease in the host, but may be shed intermittently.

The virus is transmitted through contact with infected oral, nasal, or vaginal secretions. Puppies may be infected during whelping—that is, as they pass through their mother's vaginal canal during birth. Carrier adult dogs, though not sick themselves, may spread infection to susceptible puppies. The virus can also spread to puppies by an owner who has handled an infected dog. Less commonly, puppies are infected by their mother before they're born.

At birth, puppies typically appear normal in every way and nurse and even thrive. The virus attacks puppies five to twenty-one days after birth.

CANINE HERPESVIRUS (CHV)

SYMPTOMS
Adults rarely sicken; puppies at birth appear normal, then stop nursing; their stomachs swell; they lose coordination, excrete a soft, odorless, yellow-green feces, may have nasal discharge or tummy rash; death may occur within twenty-four to forty-eight hours

HOME CARE
None

VET CARE
Hyperimmune serum may reduce mortality

PREVENTION
Keep puppies warm and isolated from other adult dogs

C

CHV first infects the tonsils and nasal cavity, then is carried in the bloodstream to a variety of organs throughout the body. Within days of initial infection, many major organs, including the kidneys, lungs, liver, gastrointestinal tract, lymph nodes, spleen, and brain, are attacked by the virus. CHV kills the organs' cells and causes bleeding. The first sign of disease is a sudden cessation of nursing. Then puppies' body temperatures drop, their tummies distend, they lose coordination, and then cry out during ongoing, excruciating abdominal muscle spasms. Typically, they excrete soft, odorless, yellow-green feces. They also may have a nasal discharge or a rash on the tummy. Late-stage disease results in central nervous system signs, such as blindness. Nothing is able to relieve their pain, and the puppies die within twenty-four hours. Those few babies that do survive the initial infection are likely to suffer permanent neurological and organ damage, are chronic carriers of the virus, and often succumb within six months.

Diagnosis of the disease is usually based on the signs. Mother dogs that lose a litter to CHV typically develop immunity to the virus; they then pass on the immunity to subsequent litters that will not be affected. Unfortunately, there are no recommended preventative measures available, nor is there a recommended treatment for this devastating illness.

Canine Parvovirus (CPV)

This highly contagious and often lethal virus was first identified in 1978 and is found throughout the world. It is believed that CPV arose as a mutation of a parvovirus of wildlife, or perhaps from the feline parvovirus (feline panleukopenia virus). In addition to affecting pet dogs, CPV also affects coyotes and some other wild canids.

CPV affects dogs of any age. However, puppies are the most susceptible, with up to a 20 percent mortality rate even in pups that receive treatment. Those pups that are already stressed from parasites or from surgical procedures like tail DOCKING or ear CROPPING are at highest risk for severe disease. Rottweilers and Doberman Pinschers seem to be more severely affected by parvovirus than other breeds are. The highest incidence of CPV occurs in kennels, pet stores, shelters, and poor-quality breeding facilities (see PUPPY MILLS).

The virus is shed in the droppings of infected dogs for about two weeks, and the disease is spread by direct contact with this infected material. Dogs are usually infected when they swallow the virus after licking contaminated material.

CPV is one of the most hardy viruses and can live in the environment for at least five months and sometimes for years. Direct dog-to-dog contact isn't necessary to spread the disease. The virus can be picked up simply by walking

CANINE PARVOVIRUS (CPV)

SYMPTOMS
Some puppies suffer sudden death, or succumb with retching, convulsions, or foaming at the mouth; more typically, puppies and adults suffer anorexia, bloody diarrhea, and vomiting with fever

HOME CARE
Nursing care; veterinary hospitalization usually required if dog is to survive

VET CARE
Fluid therapy; antibiotics; medications to control vomiting and diarrhea; bland food

PREVENTION
Vaccinate your dog as recommended by your veterinarian

through a yard contaminated with infected feces or by contact with kennels or other objects that have been contaminated by an infected pet. Your pet could be exposed to the virus from your *shoes* after you've walked through an infective area! The virus is resistant to most common disinfectants and household detergents, but thorough cleaning with household bleach will kill the virus; a dilution of one part bleach to thirty parts water is recommended.

Following exposure, symptoms usually occur in five to eleven days. The parvovirus causes two forms of disease. *Myocarditis* was much more common when the disease first appeared. It affects the heart muscles in young puppies four to eight weeks old. Affected puppies are infected before birth, or shortly thereafter, and typically stop nursing, gasp for breath, and may cry in distress. Retching, convulsions, and foaming at the nostrils or mouth may occur. Other times, the disease causes a sudden-death syndrome that may occur within hours or a few days of onset. Those pups that survive initial infection may develop congestive heart failure and die weeks to months later. Today, this form is rare because puppies are usually protected by maternal antibodies (see IMMUNE SYSTEM and VACCINATIONS).

The incidence of the *enteric* form of parvovirus has been reduced with proper vaccination, but is still prevalent. The tonsils are infected first, and from there the virus travels to the lymphatic system, which routes it to the bloodstream. Then the virus travels throughout the body, ultimately infecting the crypt cells of the intestinal lining.

The small intestine is lined with hill-shaped villi containing tiny hairlike projections called *microvilli*. It's here that the majority of digestive absorption takes place. Crypt cells down in the "valleys" replace the microvilli every three to four days, and these new microvilli migrate toward the "hilltops" of the villi. Parvovirus kills the crypt cells that make the nutrient-absorbing microvilli. It takes three to four days for crypt cells to heal and begin to repopulate the villi. During that time, the dog's body is unable to effectively process food and water.

Dogs die from DEHYDRATION, electrolyte imbalance, SHOCK, or secondary infections. Puppies often collapse and die in as little as twelve hours following the onset of symptoms. *Immediate veterinary help is critical.*

Signs of illness are similar to CANINE CORONAVIRUS. Infections with both CCV and CPV occur about 20 percent of the time and result in the most severe signs; symptoms include depression, usually a fever of 104 to 106 degrees, refusal to eat or drink, and severe VOMITING along with DIARRHEA. Vomiting is often the first sign, with diarrhea usually appearing within twenty-four to forty-eight hours. Vomitus may be clear, yellow, or blood-tinged; diarrhea is often bloody, smells rotten, and may have mucus present. The acute form of the disease, however, may result in sudden severe stomach pain and depression, followed by shock and sudden death before any other symptom becomes apparent. A long illness is rare; dogs typically either recover quickly, or they die.

In most cases, parvovirus is suspected in any young dog with vomiting, bloody diarrhea, and a fever, especially unvaccinated dogs under twelve months of age. But because these signs are not restricted to CPV, diagnosis is confirmed only by finding the virus in the feces. There is no cure or specific treatment for parvovirus, but early detection and treatment increase the chance for survival. Therapy is centered upon good nursing and supportive care. Essentially, a sick dog must be kept alive long enough for his own immune system to suppress and clear the virus from his body. Dogs that survive for three to four days following the onset of vomiting and diarrhea generally recover rapidly and will become immune to the enteric form of the disease.

Food and water are usually withheld for two to four days to give the digestive system a chance to rest. Fluid therapy helps counter the devastating dehydration and returns electrolyte balance to normal. Antibiotics may be administered to fight secondary infection, along with medications to control vomiting and diarrhea. Septi-serum may be used when septic shock is present. Once vomiting and diarrhea have subsided, water and a bland food, like cottage cheese and rice, or a veterinary-prescribed diet are offered in small amounts several times daily. The normal diet is then reintroduced gradually as the dog recovers over the next several days.

Strict isolation helps control the spread of disease. Sick dogs should remain isolated for thirty days after recovery and bathed thoroughly before being brought into contact with other dogs. Everything that comes in contact with the infected animal—including your own skin—must be disinfected with the bleach solution. The best way to prevent CPV is to protect your dog with a preventative vaccination.

Canine Scabies

Canine scabies, in the past often referred to as sarcoptic MANGE, is a disease caused by *Sarcoptes scabei* var. *canis*, a circular, short-legged, microscopic mite that burrows in the skin.

Canine scabies can affect any dog regardless of age, breed, or coat type. It's rare for only one dog in a multipet home to exhibit clinical signs; the disease is so contagious that usually if one is affected, all animals are infected.

The female mite burrows into the skin, forms a tunnel, and lays three to five eggs daily. Larvae emerge within another three to eight days, and after hatching, those that migrate across the surface of the skin often will die. But most larva stay in the tunnel or its extensions (called *molting pockets*), where they develop into nymphs.

Some nymphs stay in the original tunnels and molting pockets, while others burrow and form new tunnels. A few wander on the skin surface, where the potential for transmission to yet another host becomes possible. The next molt produces adult male and female mites. The cycle from egg to adult takes seventeen to twenty-one days. Adult females live about four to five weeks, while the males die shortly after mating.

The mite is usually transmitted by direct dog-to-dog contact. The mite lives out its entire life cycle on the dog, but mites can survive up to forty-eight hours off a host. This means your dog could pick up the mites simply by sleeping on a blanket used by an infested dog.

It takes as little as a week for signs of disease to develop following exposure. The mite prefers sparsely furred areas of the body, like the hock, elbow,

CANINE SCABIES (SARCOPTIC MANGE)

SYMPTOMS
Intense itching; skin inflammation; red papules; sores; crusting; hair loss; thickened, wrinkled skin

HOME CARE
Once diagnosed by vet, clip dog's fur; bathe with antiseborrheic shampoo, as recommended by vet

VET CARE
Same as home care; sometimes ivermectin injections

PREVENTION
Prevent contact with strange dogs

area surrounding the eyes and muzzle, stomach, ear flap, and root of the tail. The dog's back is rarely involved.

Burrowing mites produce intense itching, which prompts the infested dog to chew, scratch, and rub the affected areas. The scratch reflex in affected dogs can be easily stimulated; by merely manipulating the pinnae of the ear, the dog will often kick a hind leg in reaction. Excessive scratching results in skin inflammation, and red papules and sores and secondary infections often develop. Crusts form on the surface of affected skin, and as the disease intensifies, the skin thickens. Untreated dogs will have dry, deeply wrinkled, and thick skin. Damaged skin causes loosened hair to fall out, and the sparseness of hair in turn provides the mite with an even better environment in which to proliferate.

Left untreated, the disease may continue for months to years. Victims with advanced mite infestation become irritable and are restless and subsequently begin to lose weight. Diagnosis is based on signs of disease and on finding the mite in microscopic examination of skin scrapings. Scabies can be difficult to diagnose because the mites can be hard to find; in only about 30 percent of canine scabies cases can a mite actually be located in skin scrapings. For this reason, the condition may be confused with SEBORRHEA, flea ALLERGY, or other skin conditions. When scabies is highly suspected but skin scrapings aren't able to confirm the diagnosis, a flotation technique may work: skin-scraping debris is mixed with special solutions, heated, and centrifuged to better isolate the mite.

Treatment is often the best diagnosis. Dogs that respond favorably to therapy are deemed to have scabies. Treatment consists of clipping the dog's fur, bathing with an antiseborrheic shampoo, and treating with a miticide like lime sulfur dip. Because the condition is so contagious, all dogs and cats in contact with the affected animal should be treated. Some dogs may be carriers of the mite, without ever showing clinical signs themselves.

Several effective scabicides are currently on the market and are available from your veterinarian. Multiple treatments over several weeks—typically an application every five days for six treatments—are generally needed for satisfactory results. Ivermectin, which is the active ingredient in some HEARTWORM preventatives, is also effective against sarcoptic mange.

Secondary infections generally respond to the medicated shampoos and miticidal therapy, so antibiotics are not usually necessary. However, in severe cases of sarcoptic infection, use of concurrent therapy may be warranted. A high-quality, well-balanced diet is important as well.

Canine scabies almost exclusively affects dogs, but can also cause skin disease in cats or in people. It most commonly affects owners who allow the dog to sleep in their bed or who hold the dog a great deal. In people, the mite causes itching and inflammation, and prolonged exposure may produce sores.

However, the mite does not reproduce on people, and curing the dog typically also cures the owner within seven to twenty-eight days following treatment of the affected dog.

Once cured, dogs are not immune to reinfection. Part of the treatment should include disinfection of the dog's bedding, grooming tools, collar, and carriers to prevent reinfestation. Reduced exposure to other dogs and vigorous treatment at the earliest warning will keep your pet free of this debilitating, potentially deadly disease.

Carbon Monoxide Poisoning

Carbon monoxide is an odorless, colorless, tasteless gas that is deadly to people and their pets. This natural by-product of fuel combustion is present in car exhaust and improperly vented gas furnaces or space heaters.

The gas causes the same problems in dogs as in people. However, carbon monoxide is lighter than air, so dogs that live at human knee level may not show symptoms as quickly as their owners. If you notice any change in your dog's behavior or your own symptoms that coincides with cold weather or the furnace coming on, consult your veterinarian and doctor.

Carbon monoxide passes into the lungs, and then binds with hemoglobin, the oxygen-transporting component of BLOOD. This effectively prevents the hemoglobin from utilizing or transporting oxygen to the body. The gas creates a kind of chemical suffocation.

The most common symptoms of human carbon monoxide poisoning are headache, confusion, disorientation, and flulike symptoms with vomiting. Ultimately, the poison victim falls into a coma and dies. We don't know if poisoned dogs suffer headaches, but they do act confused, lethargic, and drunk like human victims. A distinctive sign common to both people and pets are bright cherry-red gums in the mouth. When the victim is asleep during exposure to the poison, the dog—or the person—may never wake up.

The body can get rid of the poison bound to the hemoglobin only by breathing it out or by replacing the poisoned hemoglobin with new. The liver and spleen replace hemoglobin about every ten to fifteen days. When only a small amount of the blood is affected, the victim recovers without treatment as long as no more poison is inhaled.

But high levels of blood saturation will kill the person or pet unless emergency treatment is given. A 25 percent saturation level is considered dangerous for people. Usually, though, both people and pets should be treated when the carbon monoxide saturation level is 10 percent or higher.

CARBON MONOXIDE POISONING

SYMPTOMS
Confusion, disorientation, and difficulty walking; vomiting; lethargy; extreme sleepiness; cherry-red color to gums

HOME CARE
Provide fresh air. EMERGENCY! SEE VET IMMEDIATELY!

VET CARE
Oxygen therapy

PREVENTION
Have heating units safety-checked each fall before using them

Administering high concentrations of oxygen is the treatment of choice, because it increases the amount of gas that is breathed out. Many hours of oxygen therapy may be required. In some cases, ventilation may be necessary. To protect yourself and your pets from carbon monoxide poisoning, have heating units inspected each fall before you start using them.

Cardiopulmonary Resuscitation (CPR)

CPR is the means of providing mechanical heart action and ARTIFICIAL RESPIRATION for dogs whose breathing and heartbeat have stopped. Heartbeat and respiration may stop due to POISONING, ELECTRIC SHOCK, or injury, like being hit by a car. CPR is a short-term method of keeping your pet alive, while stimulating her heart and breathing to resume working on their own.

Use CPR *only* when both the heart and breathing have stopped and the dog is unconscious; you risk injury to the dog if CPR is administered when the heartbeat or respiration are normal. Monitor the motion of the dog's chest to check for breathing. To find the heartbeat, place your flat palm on the dog's left side just above and behind the elbow of the front leg. *When the heart is beating, but the dog isn't breathing, refer to the section on* ARTIFICIAL RESPIRATION.

CPR requires two people to apply artificial heart contractions and artificial breathing, one after the other, in an ongoing rhythm. A third person can drive you to the veterinary clinic while CPR is administered. Experts agree

CPR – small dog/puppy

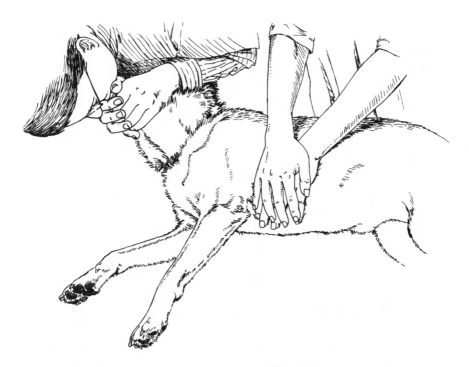

CPR compressions and breathing

that it is difficult and nearly impossible to restart a heartbeat without special-ized veterinary equipment. Although rare, an arrested heart may resume beat-ing when stimulated by external compressions.

Refer to the entry on artificial respiration (page 35) for instructions in that technique. The degree of heart compression depends on the size of the dog; about a 50 percent compression of the chest wall is required.

For small dogs and puppies, external heart massage is accomplished by placing the palm of your left hand beneath the dog's chest, so that your thumb rests on her left side at the point of her elbow, and the other fingers are flat on the right side for compression. Squeeze firmly but gently three times, about twice every second, then follow with one breath of artificial respiration.

Medium to large dogs should be placed on a rigid flat surface with their right side down. Place the heel of your palm on the dog's chest immediately behind the elbow and over the heart, and press down sharply and firmly three times about twice a second. Follow with a breath of artificial respiration.

Repeat the six compressions/breath sequence until the dog begins breathing on her own, or until no heartbeat is felt for five to ten minutes, after which revival is unlikely.

Carnivore

A carnivore is an animal that eats other animals. The name comes from specialized molars, TEETH in the side of the jaw that evolved with early meat-eating mammals. These carnassial teeth offer a scissor-action that slices flesh and makes it easier to eat.

Although dogs prefer meat in their diets, they have evolved to be omnivores like people. This opportunistic ability—being able to survive on nearly anything at hand—means dogs are able to eat and thrive on both plant and animal source foods. Dogs may do well on largely plant-source-based diets, when formulated correctly (see FOOD and NUTRITION).

Car Sickness

Young dogs often become sick to their stomachs during car rides. The motion of the car stimulates the area of the brain that stimulates VOMITING. Stress and excitement also impact how well a dog tolerates car rides.

Acclimate young dogs slowly to car rides by making the experiences very short and pleasant. While he's still young, drive with him around the block, and end the ride with a special treat or favorite game so he associates the car with good things. If he shows signs of vomiting (salivation, excessive swallowing), stop the car and let him walk on a leash for a moment or two to allow his stomach to settle.

CAR SICKNESS		
SYMPTOMS		
Agitation; whining; shivering; vomiting; excessive salivation or drooling		
HOME CARE		
Position dog/carrier so he has a view, or block his view with a towel		
VET CARE		
Prescription sedative or Dramamine-type car-sickness medication		
PREVENTION		
Withhold food for six to eight hours prior to trip; acclimate dog to car in short trips; use favorite toys/games or other rewards to make experience more pleasant		

Some dogs experience fewer problems when allowed to watch the view, while others do better traveling blind; in that instance, place a towel or blanket over the dog carrier or crate. Your veterinarian also may prescribe a mild sedative to calm your pet's nerves, or a drug like Dramamine to soothe an upset tummy.

Dogs travel best on an empty stomach. Withhold food for at least six to eight hours prior to a long car ride and give any veterinary-prescribed medication one hour before you leave. Never give your dog anything for car sickness without first consulting with your veterinarian. Most young dogs outgrow the problem.

Cataract

A cataract is the opacity of the lens inside the EYE. The lens is located directly behind the pupil and normally is transparent.

A cataract interferes with normal vision. It's often classified by age of onset—congenital, juvenile, or senile—along with the cause and the degree of cloudiness. The opacity can vary from a little spot of white to a totally opaque structure that affects the entire lens. If the lens becomes completely masked, the result is blindness. Depending on the degree of opacity, you may notice cloudiness within the pupil space that looks like a white marble inside the eye.

Dogs suffer from cataracts more commonly than any other species. Cataracts can develop at any age, but most cases are found in dogs over five years of age.

Several things can result in lens changes. Trauma and/or resulting

CATARACT

SYMPTOMS
Cloudiness to lens (inside) of eye; loss of sight; bumping into walls

HOME CARE
None

VET CARE
Address underlying cause; sometimes surgery

PREVENTION
None

inflammation may cause a cataract, but usually to only one eye. Some puppies are born with the cataracts. Cataracts resulting from poor nutrition are possible, but rare because of modern advances in canine diets. And in some cases, the cataract is idiopathic, which means the cause cannot be identified.

Dogs most often suffer from senile, or "old age," cataracts; almost all dogs older than eight years suffer some degree of cloudiness to the lens of the eye. Cataracts in dogs also may result from DIABETES MELLITUS when the lens protein is injured by metabolic changes.

But most canine cataracts are inherited, especially in certain breeds. Poodles, Cocker Spaniels, Boston Terriers, Wirehaired Fox Terriers, Siberian Huskies, Golden Retreivers, Old English Sheepdogs, and Labrador Retreivers are reported to be affected most often.

A cataract may affect only a portion of the lens, and consequently some dogs show few signs at all. Even the cataract that covers the entire lens may still allow some vision. Treatment may not be necessary until a high degree of vision is lost and cataracts become problematic for the dog. Often, even blind dogs continue to do well in familiar surroundings by relying on their other acute senses. The underlying cause is treated when possible.

Puppies born with congenital cataracts can improve as they mature. The lens grows along with the dog, while the area of cloudiness on the lens remains the same size and, at maturity, is relatively small. By adulthood, many dogs born with cataracts are able to compensate and see "around" the cloudiness.

In dogs that have trouble navigating due to vision loss, sight can be restored to near normal by surgery. This procedure is not indicated when the cataract is caused by inflammation, however.

The same surgical techniques used on people for cataracts are applied to dogs and cats. Most veterinary ophthalmologists in private practice or at a university can do the surgery. This long procedure done under general anesthetic removes most but not all of the affected lens. The lens itself is contained in a kind of capsule, like an eggshell. Most commonly, surgery removes the front part of the shell and the contents inside, while leaving the back half of the capsule/shell intact. In some cases, the whole lens is removed and a new lens is transplanted to replace the damaged lens. A procedure called *phacoemulsification* produces high-frequency sound waves—ultrasound—to break up the lens, which is then removed by suction or aspiration. Dogs that have the surgery do quite well. (See also EYES.)

C

Cesarean

This procedure is a surgical delivery performed by the veterinarian when a natural birth is not possible. A difficult birth may occur even in the healthy BITCH, and those in poor health often need assistance.

Sometimes, the bitch's uterus is too weak to propel puppies through the birth canal. In these instances, medications may be administered to stimulate uterine contraction, but this isn't always successful.

A difficult birth results when puppies are too large, which can occur in a single-pup litter (since all nutrients went to one pup instead of several). A single baby is common in miniature and small breeds, like the Chihuahua, whose tiny frame also may impede normal delivery of a jumbo-size baby.

A small pelvis also can interfere with normal delivery. Trauma such as broken bones, nutritional deficiency, or heredity may result in a pelvic size and shape that make natural birth difficult. In particular, brachycephalic (flat-faced) dog breeds, like Boston Terriers, Bulldogs, and Pugs designed to have large heads with wide shoulders and narrow hips, commonly suffer difficulty whelping naturally.

A cesarean is performed by the veterinarian, and the dog is under general anesthetic, with risk to the bitch usually nominal. Owners of breeds known to be prone to difficult births should consult with their veterinarian and plan for the possibility when the dog is bred. This reduces the risk of prolonged unproductive labor, dead puppies, uterine rupture, or toxicity, which increase the risks for the bitch.

Within a few hours of the surgery, the mother is usually awake and able to nurse her puppies. She may or may not require a cesarean with future pregnancies, depending on the circumstances for the first. (See also REPRODUCTION.)

Chasing Animals/Vehicles

Dogs evolved as endurance specialists that use speed to run down prey. The urge to pursue moving objects is hot-wired into the canine brain; this natural HUNTING BEHAVIOR is demonstrated whenever your dog chases a ball, Frisbee, or squirrel. However, chasing inappropriate objects, like bicycles or cars, or animals, like the neighbor's cat or livestock, can become a problem that may have unfortunate or even deadly consequences.

All dogs enjoy the chase, but particular breeds developed for specific kinds of work are typically more obsessive than others. For instance, sight hounds, like Greyhounds and Whippets, and most terriers are attracted to pursuing and even attacking small animals and can pose a danger to cats, smaller dogs, or farm animals, like chickens or rabbits. Shepherd breeds are more likely to chase larger livestock, as well as cars, bicycles, and jogging people, in a misguided effort to herd them.

The owner of a dog that chases inappropriately is liable, should any property be damaged or person injured. The chasing dog is also at risk from being injured or killed by the vehicle, or by the other animal or person defending themselves. In some areas, property owners are within their rights to shoot dogs that harass livestock.

To teach what *not* to chase, your dog must first be trained to the leash and the "sit" and "stay" commands (see TRAINING). Then expose your dog to staged situations that prompt chasing behavior, such as livestock or cars. Place your dog on a long six-foot leash (as a safety precaution, should he bolt) and give him the sit/stay command. Next, have a friend ride the bicycle or drive the car slowly by the dog, while you continue to enforce your dog's sit/stay position. It may help to have the decoy person armed with a long-distance squirt gun, so that your dog learns inappropriate behavior prompts being sprayed. Distract your dog with a food reward, praising him for not chasing. Gradually increase the speed of the vehicle, and continue to intermittently reward your dog for sitting still with the treat. That way, he can't predict when he'll get a tidbit, and will more consistently perform in the hopes that *this* time he'll get that treat!

It's impossible to eliminate chasing behavior, but it can be redirected. Prevent inappropriate chasing habits from the beginning; remember, what's cute in a ten-pound puppy is dangerous in a fifty-plus-pound adult. Reduce opportunities for mistakes by enforcing boundaries; a fenced yard, or leash confinement when off your property, teaches him the rules and prevents him from chasing livestock on your neighbor's property. Obedience training is necessary if you are to control your dog's bad habits.

Offer your dog safe outlets to satisfy this normal urge. Interactive games, such as fetch, not only satisfy your dog, but provide a bonding experience for the two of you. There are also organized dog sports, such as herding trials for shepherd breeds, lure coursing for sight-hound breeds, and go-to-ground trials for terriers, that reward these innate behaviors in controlled settings (see also HUNTING and TRIALS).

Cherry Eye

This condition occurs when the pinkish red tear gland at the inner corner of the eye protrudes, or prolapses. The smooth mass swells to the size of a small cherry. There may be a purulent discharge if infection is present. The cause of the condition has not been determined.

Cherry eye is common in young dogs and can occur in one or both eyes of any breed dog. However, it is most common in Beagles, Bloodhounds, Boston Terriers, Boxers, Bulldogs, Cocker Spaniels, Lhasa Apsos, Mastiffs, and Chinese Shar-Peis. Prolonged exposure of the gland can cause irritation to the eye. Sometimes, anti-inflammatory topical medications may resolve the problem. More commonly, surgery is necessary to correct the condition.

CHERRY EYE

SYMPTOMS
Red, swollen tissue at inside corner of the dog's eye, sometimes with a discharge

HOME CARE
None

VET CARE
Anti-inflammatory ointments; more often, surgery

PREVENTION
None

Chewing

C

Just like human babies, puppies put things in their mouths as a way to explore their world. Particularly when teething, young dogs chew objects to relieve the discomfort. But unlike people, dogs don't outgrow the habit of mouthing and gnawing.

Your dog doesn't have hands and instead uses her mouth. Canines are mouth-oriented creatures with an incredible ability to control the intensity of

Dogs love to chew
(Photo credit: Amy D. Shojai)

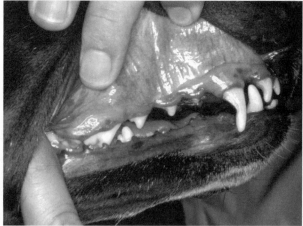

Chewing can wear or break teeth
(Photo credit: Ralston Purina Company)

Chewing sticks can cause problems *(Photo credit: Betsy Stowe)*

their bite. Modern pet dogs use their powerful teeth and jaws to pick up and carry things, to eat, for defense, and for recreational chewing. Gnawing objects simply feels good to dogs.

This oral fixation tends to get dogs into trouble, however, because they aren't always particular about the objects they target. Canine chewing not only can damage your property, but can injure the dog when teeth are broken or an object is swallowed (see SWALLOWED OBJECTS and PERIODONTAL DISEASE).

Items that carry their beloved owner's scent—like leather shoes—are often targeted, but nothing is sacred. Dogs who are bored and have nothing else to do tend to be problem chewers.

Chewing is normal, natural behavior for dogs and cannot—should not—be eliminated. It is up to owners to provide their pets with appropriate and safe chewing outlets to satisfy these doggy cravings.

Avoid offering objects that may confuse your dog. If she's not to chew your new shoes, don't offer the old ones; dogs may not be able to tell the difference. Choose instead a dog toy sold in grocery or pet stores. The key to solving problems is to reduce your dog's opportunities to make mistakes. Don't leave tempting items scattered about the house, and confine your dog to a "safe" zone when you aren't there to supervise her activity. When you catch her chewing a forbidden object, tell her "no" and take it away (or remove her from the table leg), and provide her with an allowed alternative. A product like Bitter Apple applied to dangerous objects, like electrical cords, will help train your dog to leave forbidden items alone.

Never offer your dog bones to chew on. Raw bones are unsanitary, and both raw and cooked bones can splinter under the dog's assault. Swallowed fragments could cause lethal internal trauma by puncturing or blocking the gastrointestinal tract.

A number of commercial chew objects are available, including a variety of flavored rawhide toys. Rawhide is fine in moderation, but large dogs tend not only to chew, but to eat the things. In excess, rawhide can interfere with sound nutrition when your dog eats these treats instead of her food. They can also cause CONSTIPATION and sometimes blockage if large enough pieces are swallowed.

Commercial hard rubber chew objects are available in sizes and even chicken and liver flavors to suit nearly every dog. The Nylabone and Gumabone products are excellent, offering a nearly indestructible source of chewing delight.

Cheyletiellosis

Also called *Cheyletiella* dermatitis, this condition in dogs is usually caused by a mite called *Cheyletiella yasguri*. The mite lives on the surface of the dog's skin and causes a contagious disorder that tends to be limited to scaling and crusting of the skin. Typically, the dog's fur looks filled with dandruff. The skin may be itchy or not, and occasionally the lymph nodes will also swell. Some dogs may harbor the mite without showing any signs, yet spread the disease. Any

CHEYLETIELLOSIS

SYMPTOMS
Scaly, crusty skin; the fur is filled with dandrufflike flakes; sometimes the skin is itchy, and the lymph nodes swell

HOME CARE
Flea treatment

VET CARE
Same as home care

PREVENTION
Routine flea prevention

dog is susceptible, but the bug most commonly affects puppies and young dogs. It is contagious to other pets and to people.

This mite is quite large, and an infestation looks like white specks on the dog's skin or fur; it can be seen with (sometimes without) the aid of a magnifying glass. The entire life cycle—egg, larva, nymph, adult—is completed on the host. However, adult female mites can survive for an extended period off the host, increasing the risk of contagion to other victims.

Diagnosis is based on the signs and by finding the mite during microscopic examination of skin debris. *Cheyletiella* mites are easily killed with flea treatments as recommended by your veterinarian. In fact, the condition is rarely a problem in areas where routine flea prevention is practiced. Treatment should be applied to other pets (including cats) that are in contact with a diagnosed animal, and environmental treatment is also recommended.

Chocolate Toxicity

Many dogs have a sweet tooth and relish the taste of chocolate, but the candy is toxic to both dogs and cats. The incidence of chocolate toxicity increases around the holidays, when owners have more candy available.

Chocolate is made from the roasted seeds of cocoa plants and contains a substance called *theobromine*, along with small amounts of caffeine; both are toxic to pets. Milk chocolate found in candy bars contains about forty-two milligrams of theobromine per ounce. Typically, a toxic dose of milk chocolate

CHOCOLATE POISONING
SYMPTOMS
Drooling; vomiting and/or diarrhea; excessive urination and thirst; hyperactivity; irregular heartbeat; muscle tremors; seizures; coma; sometimes sudden death without signs
HOME CARE
EMERGENCY! SEE VET IMMEDIATELY! If ingested in last two hours, induce vomiting
VET CARE
Induce vomiting; give activated charcoal; flush stomach; supportive care, like fluid therapy and sedatives
PREVENTION
Keep chocolate out of dog's reach

is five ounces per pound of body weight, so while a bite of chocolate generally isn't a concern, a ten-pound dog may get very sick from eating as little as eight ounces of milk chocolate.

Unsweetened baking chocolate is much more dangerous because it contains nearly ten times as much theobromine as milk chocolate does, about 450 milligrams of theobromine per ounce. Baking chocolate is used to make brownies, chocolate cake, and other desserts. A lethal dose of theobromine is 0.67 to 1.3 ounces of baking chocolate per 2.2 pounds of dog. That means your ten-pound dog can become sick simply by licking off the chocolate frosting on a large cake!

Signs of chocolate poisoning are often delayed for up to eight hours following ingestion, with death occurring twelve to twenty-four hours postpoisoning. Some dogs show few signs, then suddenly die of heart failure. If you suspect your dog has eaten chocolate, don't wait for symptoms; get help immediately!

The theobromine and caffeine are stimulants that affect the dog's nervous system, causing hyperactive behavior along with other signs. Dogs may pass large amounts of urine due to the diuretic effect of the drug, which also relaxes bladder control. Dogs often drool, act thirsty, and may suffer VOMITING and/or have bouts of DIARRHEA. The drug may either increase the dog's heart rate or cause irregular heartbeat. The signs of poisoning may eventually include muscle spasms or tremors, seizures, coma, and ultimately death.

There is no antidote for chocolate poisoning. Affected dogs are offered supportive treatment to prevent further absorption of the poison and hasten elimination, along with symptomatic treatment.

When you know your dog has eaten chocolate, it's generally recommended that the owner make the dog throw up as soon as possible. Chocolate isn't absorbed very quickly, so emetics may be helpful for six to eight hours after ingestion.

Refer to the section on ADMINISTERING MEDICATION. An effective emetic is one tablespoon of a 3 percent solution of household hydrogen peroxide for every ten pounds of pet. Repeat the dose in ten minutes if the first dose doesn't do the trick. Whether successful in inducing vomiting or not, bring your dog to the veterinary hospital so further help can be offered.

Activated charcoal may be administered to help prevent additional absorption of the theobromine into the dog's system. Signs of SHOCK are addressed with fluid therapy, and seizures, heart irregularities, vomiting, and diarrhea are each specifically treated with appropriate medications. The treatment is often prolonged, because the half-life of theobromine—the time it takes the body to eliminate it—is seventy-two hours in dogs.

The best way to deal with chocolate toxicity is to prevent the problem from ever happening. If your dog has a sweet tooth, keep chocolate out of reach (see also POISON).

Coccidiosis

Coccidiosis is an intestinal disease caused by coccidia, a common protozoal parasite that affects both domestic and wild animals. Twenty-two species of coccidia infect the intestinal tract of dogs, with four species of *Cystoisospora* (formerly called *Isopora*) being most common.

Coccidiosis is relatively common in dogs. The parasite colonizes the lining of the intestine, and adult dogs often have coccidia in their system without getting sick. Puppies less than a month old are affected most often with intestinal disease.

Dogs are infected by swallowing the immature parasite. Five to seven days later, the eggs, called *oocysts*, develop in the dog's intestine and are passed in the stool. These microscopic oocysts require several days in the soil to become infective. Dogs contract coccidia by swallowing this infective stage, either from licking themselves or contaminated objects, or by eating raw meat or other infected animals. Puppies stressed by other illness, an unsanitary environment, and/or the crowded conditions of pet stores and shelters are at highest risk for coccidiosis.

The earliest sign typically is a mild DIARRHEA that becomes more severe until it contains mucus and sometimes blood. ANOREXIA, weight loss, and DEHYDRATION follow. This acute phase lasts up to ten days, and severely affected puppies may die. Diagnosis is made by finding oocysts during a microscopic examination of a stool sample.

Puppies are usually treated with a sulfa-type drug for five days to two to three weeks to eliminate the parasite. Typically, resolution of the symptoms is

COCCIDIOSIS
SYMPTOMS
Mild diarrhea with mucus and blood; loss of appetite; weight loss; dehydration
HOME CARE
None
VET CARE
Sulfa-type drugs; sometimes fluid therapy or blood transfusion in severe cases
PREVENTION
Prompt cleaning of feces from yard; treat runs and kennels with ammonium hydroxide or boiling water to disinfect; prevent dogs from eating wild animals; preventative prescription medication may help

C

slow once signs develop, and it may require a week of therapy before improvement is seen. Severe cases may demand hospitalization to counter dehydration with fluid therapy.

Sanitation is the single most important prevention of coccidiosis, particularly in kennels or other environments where large numbers of dogs are housed. Environmental control is key: remove feces promptly from the yard or kennel to prevent infection or reinfection. Coccidia are resistant to common disinfectants, but a strong ammonium hydroxide solution or heat treatment using boiling water, steam, or a flame gun (on cement or gravel runs) is effective. Also, disinfect runs, cages, and food bowls every day to destroy infective organisms.

In high-risk environments, puppies may benefit from use of the preventative drug amprolium. However, it's only effective against one stage of the protozoan's life cycle, so it must be administered for about seven days until all parasites reach this stage and are destroyed. Also, amprolium can cause a thiamine deficiency in puppies if used beyond ten days, and should be used only under your veterinarian's supervision.

Colitis

Colitis is an inflammation of the lining of the large bowel or colon, which is at the end of the gastrointestinal tract. Colitis accounts for about half of DIARRHEA problems in dogs.

The colon acts as a dehydration organ, pulling water from the solid waste that's passed. Inflammation inhibits water removal and interferes with organ contraction and movement of the fecal material.

COLITIS

SYMPTOMS
Straining to defecate; frequent liquid stools containing mucus and bright red blood

HOME CARE
None

VET CARE
Address the specific cause; oral medications and high-fiber diets

PREVENTION
Prevent intestinal parasites; avoid abrupt diet changes

Signs of colitis include urgent straining and painful defecation. Affected dogs commonly produce very frequent (several in an hour) liquid stools that have a great deal of mucus and bright red blood.

Colitis may be caused by a variety of conditions, including intestinal parasites like WHIPWORMS, HOOKWORMS, or GIARDIA. When the causative parasites are eliminated through proper treatment, the colitis usually goes away. Rarely, the inflammation is due to a food ALLERGY, and avoiding the food ingredient will relieve the situation.

Sometimes, a specific cause for the colitis can't be determined. Cases of idiopathic colitis may benefit from high-fiber, low-fat diets fed in small, frequent meals (three to six times a day). The diet content and feeding schedule may slow the transit time of the material in the dog's colon, allowing the organ to better function. Your veterinarian may also prescribe oral medications (see also INFLAMMATORY BOWEL DISEASE).

Collapsed Trachea

This syndrome occurs when the normally rigid structure of the trachea—the breathing tube leading down the throat to the lungs—weakens. The trachea is then easily collapsed from such things as the dog tugging against his collar, or heavy panting during exercise. The cause of tracheal collapse is unknown, but it is most common in toy and miniature breeds, like Terriers and Poodles, and frequently in obese dogs. Although the syndrome can occur alone, dogs can also have other concurrent respiratory or HEART DISEASE.

Signs are a chronic honking cough along with difficulty inhaling or exhaling.

COLLAPSED TRACHEA
SYMPTOMS
Honking cough; difficulty inhaling or exhaling, particularly during exercise or excitement; coughing fits with gagging, retching, or vomiting
HOME CARE
Restrict dog's activity; avoid stress; use vet-prescribed cough suppressants
VET CARE
Antibiotics; bronchodilator drugs; sometimes surgery
PREVENTION
Keep dog trim; prevent excess stress and activity; do not let dog overheat

C

In mild cases, the dog may show signs only during heavy exercise or excitement. In more extreme cases, dogs at rest or only mildly excited suffer coughing fits that end with gagging, retching, or even VOMITING; occasionally, the dog passes out.

Tracheal collapse is suspected whenever an otherwise healthy small-breed dog suffers a chronic cough. Diagnosis is confirmed by X RAYS or endoscopic examination.

Dogs suffering from this syndrome can often lead relatively normal lives. Most mild cases can be controlled by restricting the dog's activity, reducing opportunities for excitement and stress, and treating the dog with cough suppressants. When the dog is obese, weight reduction is important (see OBESITY).

When other medical conditions, such as ASTHMA, are present, they must be treated as well. Antibiotics and bronchodilator drugs may be helpful. Severe cases that threaten the dog's life may be helped surgically by removing and replacing the portion of trachea that is affected or by implanting a prosthesis to hold the airway open.

Collie Eye Anomaly (CEA)

This inherited condition of Collies and Shetland Sheepdogs is an interruption in the development of the EYE, which impairs vision.

Lesions form on the retina at the back of the eye and on the optic disk, which is the contact point at the back of the eye for the optic nerve leading to the brain. In some cases, the retina is detached. Puppies are born with CEA in both eyes, and when the retina remains intact, the condition is static and does not worsen over time.

The degree of vision impairment varies from dog to dog. Mild cases can result in "blind spots" that don't bother the dog and may be hard for your veterinarian to detect. CEA characterized by retinal detachment will ultimately result in complete blindness.

There is no treatment for CEA. Reputable breeders are working with researchers to discover how the problem is inherited. It is hoped that eventually the incidence can be reduced or even eliminated from these breeds.

Communication

Communication is a process by which information is transmitted from one individual to another using a system of common signals. Understanding each other becomes particularly important when individuals must frequently interact.

Social groups are individuals that come together for a common purpose. The ancestors of dogs survived by forming packs that hunted together, communally protected young, and defended territory from outsiders. But as numbers of any group increase, so does the potential for conflict. Understanding each other, as well as having a system to resolve conflict, is essential if the group is to survive.

Therefore, your dog's social system is based on rules of behavior, a kind of canine etiquette that all dogs understand and obey. Very simply, canine culture is structured as a hierarchy of dominant and submissive individuals, with the dog at the top serving as leader of the pack and the others following in a stair-step pecking order below. Most dogs don't particularly care whether they are the leader or not, as long as they belong to a family.

Canine communication is a complex system of sign language, vocalization, and even scent cues (see MARKING) that serve to reinforce the dog's social position within the group. Dogs are quite flexible regarding members of their group, particularly when the dog has been properly socialized (see PUPPY). In other words, your dog considers you—and other people and pets in the household—to be a part of his family group, and acts accordingly.

If your relationship is to reach its full potential, it is important that you, and not your dog, be the leader of the "pack." For this to happen, you must understand each other's language.

Human hearing and scenting limitations make it impossible to understand subtle signals of canine language. But an attentive owner can learn to interpret the more obvious canine signals and pave the way for smoother interspecies communication. Many dogs meet us halfway by learning a large human vocabulary, particularly when words are used with consistency (see TRAINING).

Dogs are more highly attuned to body language, however, and this silent communication is given greater weight. Your dog's dedicated observation can make him appear psychic—for example, he always hides when a bath is imminent—when in fact he's simply reacting to nonverbal cues you may be unaware you're broadcasting. That's why when you smile during a verbal reprimand, your dog reads amusement rather than reproach, and acts accordingly.

Each type of canine communication has advantages and disadvantages. Sound carries over long distances, but a bark may alert adversaries as well as pack members. A body posture can be held nearly forever, while a growl can be sustained only one breath at a time. And scent signals can be left behind for others to read the way people leave messages on the answering machine.

Dogs use combinations of each technique to communicate meaning. Very

C

basically, canine communication is used to *decrease* the distance between individuals with signals that solicit attention, or to *increase* distance between individuals with warning signals. Most often, vocalizations punctuate what the body movements are saying (in the same way people use inflection to impart emotion and meaning). And because dogs realize people rely on verbal communication, our pets have become much more vocal than their ancestors.

For instance, barking is rare in wolves, but is the most common vocal signal in dogs. It's used during play, defense, and as a greeting, and it's considered a sign of DOMINANCE but not always of AGGRESSION. Barking is a canine fire alarm, a call to action that alerts the family group to the unusual. This may be anything from the arrival of friend or foe, to an unexpected sound like thunder, or the strange sight of you wearing a hat. Some dogs bark to relieve boredom, particularly when left alone for hours at a time. Dogs also bark together as a joyful expression of happiness; that's why yelling at a dog to stop barking rarely works—he thinks you're joining in a communal bark-fest, and barks even louder.

Dogs use howls to express emotion and to announce their location to missing pack members. Usually, a howl is a dog's cry of loneliness that implores others to come join him; dogs left home alone or sequestered by themselves in a room may howl. Howls seem to be contagious, with a single lone call often answered by any other dog within hearing. Dogs may interpret a siren or even human singing as an invitation to sing along.

Whining, whimpering, and yelping are used to communicate submission, pain, or fear. They may also be used as solicitations to a dominant individual (usually the owner) for attention, food, or to go in or out.

Growls and snarls are distance-increasing signals that are warnings to stay away. Snarls display the teeth and aren't always accompanied by sound; they signify slight fear. Growls indicate deeper concern and can be made with the mouth open or closed. A dog's growl is used in defense and as a threat. Dogs that aren't sure how they feel may bark, snarl, and growl all at the same time—which usually means they're more scared than aggressive.

Silent canine communication makes use of the dog's body from nose to tail. The position and movement of his tail, his facial expression, and even his posture is telling.

EYES communicate volumes. Droopy eyelids indicate pleasure, and your dog may squint and moan with delight when his ears are rubbed. Alert dogs keep their eyes open wide. An unblinking stare is a challenge and shows dominance, while averting the eyes shows canine submission. The pupils of a dog's eyes indicate aggression and imminent attack when they suddenly dilate wide. Avoid locking eyes with a strange dog, for such a challenge may incite him to aggression.

The dog's mouth is also quite expressive. In general, when the lips lift

Alert   Fearful

Aggressive   Submissive

Soliciting play/attention

C

Alert

Fearful

vertically to show the long dagger-shaped canines, the dog is showing aggression or fear. Lips pull back horizontally to show more teeth in a canine grin of submission, which is often used as an appeasement gesture toward a dominant individual. A flicking tongue signals intent to lick, which when aimed at the face or hands is also an appeasement gesture. The relaxed, happy dog may sit with his mouth half-open and tongue lolling out as he pants.

The EARS are barometers of mood. The shape of the dog's ears—whether erect or pendulous—also influence how easy ear language is to understand. For the sake of this discussion, the ear conformation of the German Shepherd Dog will be used. When the ears are erect and facing forward, the dog is interested and possibly aggressive. The ears flatten against the head by degrees depending on how fearful or submissive the dog feels.

Tail talk is perhaps the dog's most obvious signal to people. Again, the conformation of the dog's tail—from long to docked, corkscrew or curled— will determine the extent of your dog's tail semaphore.

Aggressive

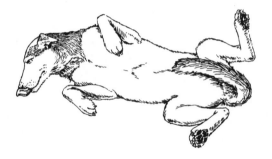

Submissive

Soliciting play

In most cases, a wagging tail is a distance-reducing signal that declares the dog to be friendly. However, what the tail says depends to a great degree on what the rest of the body is doing.

A relaxed pet's tail curves down and back up in a gentle U. As interest grows, the higher the tail will be held. Dominant and confident dogs hold their tails high and wag rapidly in tight, sharp arcs. Aggressive dogs also hold their tails high, often tightly arched over their back with just the end jerking very quickly back and forth. This indicates imminent attack and usually includes relevant vocalizations and facial expressions.

Holding the tail in a low position indicates submission. A dog shows his subordinance by wagging in loose, wide, low arcs that often include hip wags as well. Tucking the tail between the legs signals submission and fear. A tucked tail is the canine equivalent of hiding the face. Tucking the tail between the legs covers the genitals and interferes with the sniffing behavior that identifies him to other dogs.

Your dog's carriage and even his fur position show how he feels. Dogs bump, push, or lean against people or other animals as a sign of dominance. Erect posture is a sign of confidence typical of dominant dogs, who seem to stand nearly on tiptoe when in the presence of another dog they want to impress. The aggressive dog leans forward, toward whomever he wants to cow, while the fearful dog leans backward. Piloerection—fluffing the fur along the ridge of his back (the hackles)—makes the dog look bigger and more impressive, and may be used to bluff. Both fearful and aggressive dogs raise their hackles.

The opposite is true when a dog shows submission: he tries to look smaller

A dog in a submissive pose
(*Photo credit:*
Betsy Stowe)

than he is. Dogs cry "uncle" by flattening their ears, tucking their tail, crouching as low as possible, and perhaps offering a paw in a placating gesture in prelude to rolling over. Exposing the tummy, perhaps even urinating in this position or when crouched before the aggressor, is the dog's ultimate sign of deference.

All these signals must be read together to place your dog's meaning in proper context. Often, mixed signals may be sent, with the snarling front half of the dog indicating aggression while the back half wags submissively. Dogs may "pretend" to be submissive to invite PLAY, and they indicate it's a game by using exaggerated signals.

Canine language serves to smooth relationships, offering a way for dogs to get along with each other and the people who make up their families. Communicating submission to a dominant individual reinforces each of the dog's position within the family group. For the most part, place is determined simply by posturing alone, and fights are rarely necessary. Dominant dogs practice chivalry and let lower-ranking dogs off the hook when they cry "uncle."

Constipation

Constipation refers to the difficult, less-frequent-than-normal passage of dry, hard feces. If defecation is delayed and feces remain in the colon for two or three days, too much moisture is removed by the organ, which makes elimination painful. A constipated dog may squat and strain unproductively for long periods of time. Ongoing constipation may result in a loss of appetite and the

CONSTIPATION

SYMPTOMS
Straining without passing stool, or hard, dry stools accompanied by dark brown liquid

HOME CARE
Add milk to dog's regular diet, or nonflavored Metamucil, bran cereal, canned pumpkin, or squash; offer fresh celery as a snack; increase the dog's exercise

VET CARE
Suppositories, enemas, or laxatives; sometimes mechanical removal of blockage; fluid therapy if dehydrated

PREVENTION
High-fiber diets; groom to remove mats; keep dog from ingesting nonfood items; limit rawhide-type treats; don't feed bones

dog losing weight. When the condition becomes chronic, the bowel lining may become inflamed, which stimulates a release of dark fluid that accompanies the hard, dry fecal matter.

Dogs may become constipated for a variety of reasons, including SWALLOWED OBJECTS. Besides the danger of puncture, swallowed bone fragments turn feces into cementlike masses that block the colon. Dogs are notorious for chewing and swallowing nondigestible objects like paper, sticks, grass, and cloth, which tend to turn into wads that cause impaction. Rawhide chews, if eaten in excess, promote constipation.

High-meat diets with little fiber produce stools that are small and sticky and difficult to pass. STRESS can also influence the condition; dogs boarded or in strange surroundings may voluntarily delay defecation and become constipated. Elderly dogs commonly suffer bouts of constipation, which may be due to a combination of weak abdominal muscles, reduced exercise, or improper diet (see GERIATRIC DOG). Poor GROOMING, especially of long-haired dogs, may also promote constipation when fur beneath the tail mats with feces and causes anal inflammation that results in painful defecation; mats may even cause external blockage that interferes with normal defecation. Keep the anal region of long-haired dogs clipped to prevent mats from developing.

Another common cause of constipation is prostatitis. In unneutered male dogs, the prostate swells and blocks the colon in the pelvic region. Rectal exams should be part of the annual exam for intact males over five years of age. Tumors of the prostate or rectum or perianal region also can cause constipation. Constipation can also be a sign of kidney disease or diabetes; with either condition, there is excessive urine production, which prompts the colon to conserve water—and that causes a dry stool that can lead to constipation.

Laxatives may be helpful, but human medications can be dangerous and should be given only with veterinary approval. Your veterinarian may prescribe enemas or suppositories; ask for a demonstration before attempting to administer these treatments yourself or you risk injuring the dog. Many times, evacuating the colon requires a veterinarian's help, and often the dog must be sedated.

Treating constipation must address the specific cause to be effective, but in general, treatment for canine constipation is the same as for people. A diet containing 7 to 13 percent fiber (look on the label), drinking lots of water, and a regular exercise regimen (a daily twenty-minute walk) are beneficial, as is increasing the dog's exercise. Old dogs may benefit from a higher water content in their diet; feed canned food, or soak the kibble with equal parts water for twenty minutes before feeding.

Veterinary-approved stimulant laxatives are available, but shouldn't be overused or they may interfere with normal colon function. Mild cases of constipation may benefit from temporarily adding milk to the diet, which has a laxative effect in some dogs. Give your small dog one-eighth cup twice a day, and a large dog one-half cup twice a day until he is regular again.

Another choice is laxatives, like Metamucil, that contain cellulose ingredients, which attract water and add bulk to the stool. Mix nonflavored Metamucil with your dog's food; one teaspoon twice a day for small dogs, and two to three teaspoons twice a day for large dogs, is helpful. Bran cereals and canned pumpkin and squash are natural sources of fiber that also work well, and dogs seem to like the flavor. To promote regularity, add one-half teaspoon to your small dog's food, or about two tablespoons to the big dog's diet. For dogs that relish vegetable snacks, offer a stick or two of celery; the fiber and liquid help reduce constipation, and celery also gives your dog an outlet for CHEWING urges. Don't give your dog bones, and offer rawhide treats only if he chews but doesn't swallow them.

Contraception

Contraception is the means of preventing pregnancy. In dogs, the most common and effective contraceptive procedure is SPAYING. Spay surgery is a permanent, irreversible procedure that offers health and behavior benefits, and it is recommended for female dogs not in a professional breeding program or show career.

When a BITCH is left intact, the onset of heat (see REPRODUCTION) may interfere with participation or performance in certain dog sports. The owners of field TRIAL, hunting, racing, and show dogs may choose to delay the onset of estrus by using drugs that don't prevent future pregnancy. However, these drugs should be used only with the recommendation of a veterinarian, as they may have severe side effects when misused.

Ovaban (megastrol acetate) is a synthetic progesterone given as a daily pill that prevents or postpones heat depending on when and how long it is given. It should not be used in dogs with existing uterine disease, breast tumors, or DIABETES MELLITUS, and it may cause uterine damage when used to prevent or delay more than two consecutive heat periods. The drug can adversely affect unborn puppies and delay whelping; it should never be given to a pregnant—or suspected pregnant—dog.

Cheque (mibolerone) is a synthetic male hormone given as a liquid that's added to the dog's food. It is not recommended for dogs that will be bred. It can inhibit bone growth in immature dogs, and it is not recommended for dogs with existing LIVER or KIDNEY DISEASE; when used longer than six months, the dog's liver and kidney function should be regularly screened. Use of mibolerone seems to promote some male-dog-type behaviors, such as aggressiveness and mounting.

New methods of canine contraception, such as a "vaccination" that immunizes the bitch against pregnancy, are being investigated. The vaccination tricks the dog's IMMUNE SYSTEM into attacking and sterilizing the dog's eggs. Safety and effectiveness studies are still under way. Until the protocol is approved by the regulating bodies, the best choice for canine contraception will remain spay surgery.

Copper Poisoning

Copper naturally occurs in certain foods, such as organ meats like liver and kidneys. Copper is an essential nutrient affecting the formation of bone. It is normally metabolized in and the excess removed by the liver.

However, some dogs, particularly Bedlington Terriers and West Highland White Terriers, have an inherited tendency to an increased sensitivity and aren't able to get rid of excess copper. Doberman Pinschers are also prone to copper toxicity secondary to LIVER DISEASE. The inherited tendency is similar to Wilson's disease in people, in which copper cannot be metabolized but collects in various organs and causes damage.

In dogs, the copper typically accumulates in and damages the liver. Although excess copper can be demonstrated in the liver by six months of age, signs of disease usually aren't evident for several years. Symptoms are the same as for liver disease, and damage to the organ is irreversible once signs develop. Without treatment, the dog will die.

Up to 50 percent of Bedlington Terriers develop the disease, and West Highland White Terriers are also at high risk. It is recommended that dogs of these breeds be fed a low-copper diet from puppyhood on as a preventative measure; such a diet is indicated in any dog diagnosed with the condition. Ask

COPPER POISONING

SYMPTOMS	
Loss of appetite; vomiting; diarrhea; weight loss; lethargy; jaundice; swollen abdomen; bloody urine and/or feces	
HOME CARE	
None	
VET CARE	
Drugs that help the body excrete copper in the urine; zinc supplements	
PREVENTION	
High-risk breeds should be fed low-copper diet and be given zinc supplements	

C

your veterinarian for a recommendation. In addition, zinc supplements may prove beneficial as a preventative and treatment in such dogs, since it inhibits copper absorption and may even help eliminate copper stored in the liver. Some drugs also increase the excretion of copper in the urine and may be helpful for dogs with this condition.

Coprophagia

This is a fancy term for the practice of a dog eating feces—his own or another animal's. In fact, this is a common behavior of dogs. Mother dogs ingest their puppies' stool as a means of keeping the nest clean. Outside of this context, though, the behavior becomes objectionable to most owners.

Usually the behavior is first noticed in puppies aged four to nine months old, with the frequency increasing after one year of age. Some dogs outgrow the nasty habit, but it can persist throughout the dog's life. In some dogs, the behavior may indicate a nutritional or gastrointestinal disorder in which food isn't being completely digested. PANCREATITIS, parasites, or starvation may prompt the dog to eat his own waste in an effort to utilize the nutrients that it contains.

But in most instances, nutritional deficiency has nothing to do with the behavior. Dogs are historically scavengers, and this is a scavenger behavior that causes some dogs to relish cow piles or to eat from the cat's litter box.

In most instances, though, the behavior is simply an attention-seeking behavior, or a bad habit prompted by anxiety or boredom. Increase playtime with your dog; most need about forty-five minutes of aerobic exercise each day to stay healthy. And increase the number of toys in the house to keep him busy when you're away.

Retraining is also key, and preventing the dog's access to feces is the obvious answer. Walk the dog on a leash and pick up droppings promptly. A muzzle may be beneficial to prevent the dog from eating anything when he can't be supervised. Put a cover on the cat's litter box and/or use a baby gate to limit the dog's access to the cat's toilet area.

The behavior resolves itself in some dogs who are fed a high-protein, low-carbohydrate ration twice a day. Adding a tablespoon of vegetable oil to the food every day seems to help in some cases.

When all else fails, a commercial product called ForBid can be added to your dog's diet. When eaten with his food, the powder makes the dog's feces taste bad. Feeding the dog MSG, garlic, or pumpkin is also thought to give feces a bad taste and make it less attractive to the dog. ForBid and other commercial products are available at many veterinary offices or pet supply stores.

Cropping

Otoplasty, commonly called *cropping*, refers to the practice of surgically altering the shape of the dog's external EAR. The procedure may be done to correct congenital defects or damage from injury or disease. More commonly, the procedure is not required for the dog's health, but is done purely for cosmetic reasons, to change a folded or hanging conformation to an erect or "pricked" ear.

In the United States, ear cropping is historically performed to conform to the specific look of each breed standard. The surgery is typically performed on eight- to ten-week-old puppies (Bostons, more typically at four to six months of age) and requires general anesthesia and the expertise of a veterinary surgeon. Splinting and other specialized ear-bandaging techniques help form the puppy's ears following the surgery and will need to be monitored and changed as the ears heal. Medication to relieve postoperative PAIN is recommended.

In recent years, the ethics of cosmetic ear cropping has been called into question both in the United States and abroad. The American Kennel Club standards for these breeds generally include descriptions of both the ideal cropped, as well as the natural ear conformation. Show dogs in some other countries may be disqualified if the ears are cropped.

This standard Manchester Terrier is cropped (*Photo credit: Amy D. Shojai*)

The practice of surgically altering the conformation of a dog's ears is expensive, painful, tedious, and not always successful. Please consult with your veterinarian—and consider your own motives—before putting your pet through this elective procedure.

C

Cryptorchid

The testicles of puppies are generally descended into the scrotal sac by ten days after birth. Male puppies that fail to have their testicles descend into the scrotal sac by eight weeks of age are said to be cryptorchid; occasionally, the organs will descend by six months of age. When they don't, the testicles are retained within the abdomen. When only one is retained, it's called *monorchid*.

Cryptorchid dogs are sterile, although monorchid dogs may be able to father puppies. This isn't considered a good idea, though, because the tendency to retain a testicle is thought to be inherited. It is also more common in purebred dogs. Dogs with a retained testicle cannot be shown in conformation, and surgically moving the organ into the scrotum is considered unethical.

The testicles generate male hormones even when they are retained in the abdomen, which means cryptorchid dogs exhibit the same behavior as any intact male (see REPRODUCTION). These dogs are also at higher risk for testicular CANCER. For all these reasons, cryptorchid dogs should be NEUTERED. The veterinarian then must surgically go into the abdomen to find and remove the organs.

Cushing's Disease

More correctly referred to as *hyperadrenocorticism*, Cushing's disease was named for the doctor who first described this syndrome in people. It is a common metabolic disorder of dogs, in which the adrenal gland produces too many steroid hormones, especially cortisol.

This particular hormone affects the metabolism of carbohydrates, proteins, and fats. It also suppresses the body's inflammatory and immunological responses. Consequently, excess amounts reduce the body's resistance to bacteria and viruses and promote infection.

About 15 percent of cases are caused by a tumor of the adrenal gland, which can be benign or malignant. Most, though, result from an often microscopic and otherwise benign tumor that affects the pituitary gland in the brain, which in turn overstimulates the adrenal gland. It also can result when cortisone-type medications (often used to control itchy skin conditions) are overused.

C

CUSHING'S DISEASE (HYPERADRENOCORTICISM)

SYMPTOMS
Increased appetite and thirst; excessive urination; lethargy; sometimes pacing, circling, drunken behavior, or seizures; symmetrical hair loss on the body; potbellied appearance with thin, wasted legs; skin disease

HOME CARE
None

VET CARE
Surgery to remove tumor when possible; drug therapy to control symptoms; sometimes radiation therapy

PREVENTION
Avoid the overuse of steroid drugs

The condition can affect any dog, but most typically is seen in dogs that are six years old or older. Beagles, Boston Terriers, Boxers, Dachshunds, and Toy and Miniature Poodles appear to have an increased risk for the condition. The disease is a progressive one that is slow and insidious.

Signs of Cushing's disease are increased appetite and thirst, excessive urination, and lethargy. When caused by a tumor in the brain, neurologic signs may include pacing, circling, a drunken walk, head pressing, or seizures. Dogs also typically suffer a symmetrical hair loss on their body and often develop a progressive potbellied appearance, with wasting and weakening of the leg muscles. Color changes in the fur and/or the skin are typical, along with skin disease that includes thinning and loss of elasticity, flaky scales, bumpy irregularities, blackhead pimples (particularly surrounding the nipples and genitals), and bleeding.

Only a veterinarian can diagnose Cushing's disease; diagnosis requires a battery of laboratory tests. Blood tests evaluate the adrenal gland function by measuring the amounts of circulating hormones when the dog is at rest, and in response to adrenal-gland-stimulating and -suppressing drugs. Treatment depends on where the tumor is located.

Tumors of the adrenal gland can be surgically removed. Dogs that undergo a removal of benign tumors, or of malignant tumors that haven't yet metastasized, usually recover. When the malignancy has spread to other sites, the prognosis is poor, even with surgery; such dogs usually die within a year.

Tumors on the pituitary gland are treated with the drug mitotane, which helps control the symptoms. Mitotane destroys controlled amounts of the cortisol-secreting cells, and usually quickly reverses many of the symptoms. The medication must be continued for the rest of the dog's life. Water and food consumption, as well as urination, return to normal within days, physical activity and muscle strength return in weeks, and substantial hair regrowth occurs within the first three months of treatment. If the tumor has progressed to causing neurologic signs, radiation therapy may help. A new drug, Anipryl, may also control symptoms but won't cure the disease. Ask your veterinarian about the best treatment options for your pet.

Dogs typically are middle-aged or older at the time of diagnosis. Successful treatment will generally keep the dog comfortable and prolong his life for an additional two years beyond diagnosis. Dogs diagnosed at an earlier age and successfully treated often live for another five to ten years.

Cuterebra

Cuterebra is the larval stage of the botfly, a parasite that afflicts rabbits and mice and can infect pets that hunt these creatures. Cats are at highest risk, but dogs are not immune. Cuterebra infection is seen most often during the summer months.

Botflies lay up to two thousand eggs in their lifetime, infecting the soil or vegetation surrounding mouse and rabbit runs. Eggs are triggered to hatch when sensors pick up the body heat of a nearby host. The larvae enter the body through the nose or mouth when the dog sniffs or lick-explores an infected environment. Once inside, the parasite migrates and forms a CYST beneath the dog's skin, usually in the chest or neck region. This area swells as the parasite matures.

Initially the swelling is firm, then softens as it fills with fluid, which escapes from a central vent hole through which the parasite breathes. The larva continues to grow and molt, and the spine-covered brownish cuterebra may reach over an inch in length and a half inch in diameter. After about a month

CUTEREBRA INFESTATION

SYMPTOMS	
Soft swelling beneath skin, usually of the neck or chest region	
HOME CARE	
None	
VET CARE	
Surgical removal	
PREVENTION	
Prevent dogs from hunting and roaming	

spent in the host, the parasite exits the skin and drops to the ground, where it spends the winter in a pupal stage. Pupae hatch into adult botflies in the spring.

Dogs aren't generally bothered by cuterebra infection, but the cysts may become infected. In very rare instances, the cuterebra may migrate into the nostrils, spinal column, or scrotum, or even into the brain, which can have life-threatening consequences.

Do not attempt to remove the parasite yourself, and *never squeeze the swelling to express the cuterebra from the skin*: crushing the parasite may cause a life-threatening ANAPHYLACTIC reaction in your dog. Cuterebra parasites should be carefully removed through the vent hole by surgically enlarging the opening. The empty cyst is then cleaned and treated to prevent infection.

Prevent your dog from unsupervised roaming and hunting to reduce cuterebra exposure and risk of infection.

Cyst

A cyst is a saclike cavity filled with foreign matter that is contained by a thickened capsule of tissue. Cutaneous cysts (those found in the skin) are quite common in dogs and can appear anywhere on the body. Some breeds, including Kerry Blue Terriers, Schnauzers, and Spaniels, tend to be affected most often.

Cutaneous cysts are usually filled with fluid or a semisolid cheeselike substance. They are firm to soft, well-defined round areas that move freely beneath the skin. The most common type in dogs are follicular (epidermoid) cysts that arise from the hair follicles; they are commonly—and erroneously—referred to as *sebaceous cysts*.

Cysts often grow to an inch or more in diameter and may rupture and drain from a central opening. Manual expression of a cyst can cause severe inflammation and is discouraged. Surgical removal is the recommended therapy.

Fluid-filled ovarian cysts may develop in intact female dogs and can grow quite large, producing hormones that interfere with the dog's fertility. Surgical removal of the cysts may correct the problem and allow conception to occur. SPAYING removes the reproductive organs, including the affected ovaries. And spaying your dog before her first heat cycle prevents the problem from ever occurring.

Cystitis

Cystitis is an inflammation of the membrane lining the urinary bladder and is usually caused by bacterial, viral, or fungal infection. Bacterial urinary-tract

CYSTITIS

SYMPTOMS
A housebroken dog dribbling urine or urinating in unusual locations; frequent voiding of small amounts of urine; sometimes bloody urine

HOME CARE
None

VET CARE
Antibiotics; sometimes therapeutic diets

PREVENTION
Offer access to lots of fresh water; offer plentiful bathroom breaks; encourage exercise

infections are common in dogs, estimated to affect more than 10 percent of all dogs. Cystitis typically affects females more often than it affects males. The condition can occur at any age and may be present prior to or in conjunction with the development of BLADDER STONES.

People suffering from this condition may feel the need to urinate more frequently and may suffer pain during urination. Such signs in dogs, though, may not be noticed unless a housebroken dog has an accident in the house. Occasionally, the dog's urine will contain blood.

Left untreated, the infection and inflammation can spread up into the kidneys and cause scarring or even kidney failure. The condition may lead to PROSTATE INFECTION or invade the testicles of male dogs; in both male and female dogs, untreated urinary-tract infections may result in infertility.

Diagnosis is made by examination of the dog's urine. Both a urinalysis and a urine culture may be performed to identify the cause of the infection, so that an appropriate medication can be prescribed.

Cystitis is typically treated with an antibiotic for two to three weeks. To help prevent future bouts, provide your dog with access to plenty of clean, fresh water, offer ample opportunities for appropriate elimination, and encourage your dog to exercise regularly.

Dam

The term *dam* is used by canine professionals in reference to a dog's mother.

Dehydration

Dehydration is a water deficit of the body. Dogs lose water every day during elimination, the exhalation of each breath, and through the evaporation of saliva during PANTING. About 75 percent of water loss is due to urination, and another 20 percent occurs through the respiratory tract, mouth, and skin. These fluids are replaced when the dog eats and drinks. Anything that increases the fluid loss, or interferes with the body's recouping moisture, may result in dehydration.

Dehydration can occur as a result of any illness that causes DIARRHEA or VOMITING, or an excessive fever, which may result from HYPERTHERMIA. Excessive urination that occurs in DIABETES MELLITUS and KIDNEY DISEASE; BLEEDING; or any condition that causes a reluctance to eat or drink can result in dehydration.

A normal adult dog's total body water is approximately 60 percent of his body weight. Signs of dehydration become apparent with losses of as little as 5 percent of normal body water. A 12 to 15 percent loss of total body water results in SHOCK and imminent death.

The earliest noticeable sign of dehydration is dry mucous membranes in which the dog's gums and tongue are sticky instead of wet. The saliva may become sticky or even stringy.

DEHYDRATION

SYMPTOMS

Loss of skin elasticity; dry mouth; stringy saliva; delayed capillary refill time; sunken eyeballs; muscle twitches; cold paw pads

HOME CARE

Give lots of water and/or solutions like Pedialyte as directed by the veterinarian

VET CARE

Fluid therapy; supportive care; sometimes blood transfusion

PREVENTION

Provide lots of fresh water at all times; offer shelter from the heat

A more obvious sign is loss of skin elasticity. A dog's skin normally fits like a comfortable coat, with some room to move, particularly in the shoulders. Grasp the skin over your dog's neck and shoulders and gently lift; when normally hydrated, the skin quickly springs back into place upon release. The skin retracts slowly when the dog is 7 to 8 percent dehydrated; a dehydration of 10 percent or more is serious, and the skin will remain in a ridge when retracted, and not spring back into place.

Capillary refill time is an accurate measure of hydration. This is the time it takes for blood to return to tissue after pressure is applied; it can be demonstrated by gently pressing a finger against your dog's gums. This briefly blocks blood flow so the tissue turns white when the pressure is quickly released. When your dog's hydration is normal, it takes less than two seconds for the white to return to normal pigment. A dehydration of 7 to 8 percent will delay capillary refill time for two to three seconds. Longer than four or five seconds indicates severe dehydration—an extremely dangerous situation. These dogs also exhibit sunken eyeballs, involuntary muscle twitches, and cold extremities. Dogs suffering from moderate to severe dehydration require immediate veterinary attention if they are to survive. Intravenous fluid therapy will be required to rehydrate the dog and return his electrolyte (mineral) balance to normal.

In mild cases in which vomiting is not a problem, simply getting the dog to drink water will be helpful (see ADMINISTER MEDICATION); under normal circumstances, a thirsty dog willing to drink is able to recoup a 6 percent water deficit in about an hour. Your veterinarian also may prescribe products like children's Pedialyte, which provides lost minerals.

The underlying cause of the dehydration will need to be treated. Specific medication to control diarrhea and vomiting may be required to prevent further fluid loss.

Demodicosis

Demodicosis is a skin disease caused by *Demodex canis*, a cigar-shaped micro-scopic mite that is a normal inhabitant of canine skin and found on most healthy dogs. The mite infests hair follicles and occasionally the sebaceous glands of the skin. When present in excess numbers, the mite causes demodi-cosis, also called demodectic or red MANGE.

Demodicosis is not contagious. Puppies are infected the first two or three days after birth through close contact with an infected mother. In normal dogs, a few of these mites may be found in the hair follicles of the face. It ap-pears that a normal IMMUNE SYSTEM keeps the mite population in check, so that no disease results.

Typically, it is the immune-compromised individual unable to stop mite proliferation that develops disease. The life cycle of the mite is spent entirely on the host animal and takes about twenty to thirty-five days to complete. Spindle-shaped eggs hatch into small, six-legged larvae, which molt into eight-legged nymphs, and then into eight-legged adults.

Demodicosis typically affects puppies three to twelve months old. Adult-onset disease is considered rare and, when it does occur, usually is a result of compromised immunity associated with other systemic disease like CUSHING'S DISEASE or CANCER.

Two forms of disease occur. The condition always begins as the *localized* form, which is limited to a spot or two on the face and legs. Localized de-

---

DEMODICOSIS (DEMODECTIC MANGE)

SYMPTOMS
Small, circular areas of hair loss on face or forelegs with or without itching; or massive patchy hair loss over entire body with red, crusty skin, swollen paws, and "mousy" body odor

HOME CARE
Once diagnosed by vet, provide Canex or Goodwinol Ointment on localized lesions; benzoyl peroxide shampoos and/or dips as prescribed by vet for generalized disease

VET CARE
Amitraz dips; sometimes antibiotics

PREVENTION
None

modicosis is quite common in puppies and typically is a mild disease that resolves by itself. It typically consists of one to five small, circular, red, and scaly areas of hair loss around the eyes and lips, or on the forelegs. The lesions may or may not be itchy. Most cases resolve by puberty and rarely recur. But when the localized form spreads, involving large areas of the body with severe disease, it is termed *generalized* demodicosis. Generalized demodicosis is considered uncommon.

But again, it is youngsters that are most commonly affected with generalized demodicosis, usually prior to age eighteen months. Such dogs may have a genetic defect in their immune system. Any dog may develop the disease, but an inherited predisposition appears to increase the incidence of the disease in the Afghan Hound, American Staffordshire Terrier, Boston Terrier, Boxer, Chihuahua, Chinese Shar-Pei, Collie, Dalmatian, Doberman Pinscher, English Bulldog, German Shepherd Dog, Great Dane, Old English Sheepdog, Staffordshire Bull Terrier, and Pug.

Generalized demodicosis is a severe disease characterized by massive patchy or generalized hair loss and skin inflammation, often complicated by bacterial infection that may cause the feet to swell. Mites (all stages) may also be found in lymph nodes, intestinal wall, blood, spleen, liver, kidney, bladder, lung, urine, and feces. The canine's skin is red, crusty, and warm and has many pustules. It bleeds easily, becomes very tender, and has a strong "mousy" odor due to bacterial infection on skin. The condition can ultimately kill the dog.

Diagnosis is based on signs of the disease and finding the parasite in skin scrapings or biopsies. Occasionally treatment is not necessary for localized demodicosis, which may clear up by itself. When desired, a miticide such as Canex or Goodwinol Ointment may be applied to the affected areas only.

Generalized demodicosis requires aggressive therapy, however. Typically, the dog is shaved to offer better access to the skin, and is given weekly or every-other-week whole-body dips with a miticidal preparation. Mitaban (amitraz) is quite effective against the mite, but has some contraindications. Chihuahuas are particularly sensitive to the chemical, and occasionally dogs suffer side effects such as drowsiness, VOMITING, lethargy, and drunken behavior. So use this product only with veterinary supervision.

Antibiotic therapy is required to fight secondary infections. Exfoliating shampoos, such as those containing benzoyl peroxide, are helpful. Unfortunately, dogs suffering from generalized demodicosis have a guarded prognosis and may never achieve a cure. EUTHANASIA is sometimes the kindest choice. Because of the potential heritable components involved in this disease, dogs that have suffered generalized demodicosis should not be bred.

Dermatitis

d

Dermatitis refers to skin disease and is an inflammation that can involve the entire body or be isolated to specific areas. Canine dermatitis is most often associated with ALLERGY or skin parasites that cause MANGE. It can also result from metabolic disorders, like CUSHING'S DISEASE, or from SUNBURN, and very rarely is a psychological disorder related to STRESS. Signs and treatment vary depending on the cause.

Diabetes Mellitus

Diabetes mellitus is a common endocrine disorder of dogs, in which an insulin deficiency prevents the normal metabolism of carbohydrates. In other words, the body of a diabetic dog is unable to use the food that she eats.

The pancreas, a gland located near the stomach and liver, produces the hormone insulin, which stimulates the movement of glucose (sugar) from the blood into the cells of the body where it is used. Diabetes mellitus in dogs results from conditions that either suppress the action of existing insulin (*Type II, noninsulin dependent*) or interfere with the production of insulin (*Type I, insulin dependent*).

Insulin resistance is often seen in dogs suffering from hyperadrenocorticism (see CUSHING'S DISEASE) and can result from overuse of glucocorticoid (steroid) drugs. A large percentage of body fat also tends to suppress insulin function, which means OBESITY can result in diabetes mellitus.

DIABETES MELLITUS

SYMPTOMS
Increased eating with weight loss; increased drinking and urination; possible breaks in house-training

HOME CARE
Administer insulin injections as instructed by veterinarian

VET CARE
Stabilize dog with fluids and other medications; regulate diet and monitor urine and blood; determine proper insulin dosage

PREVENTION
Prevent obesity; trim down pudgy pooches

However, the disease usually arises from damage to the pancreas that interferes with insulin production. Damage can be caused by a variety of conditions, but most often, canine diabetes mellitus is a result of PANCREATITIS.

About one in two hundred pet dogs is estimated to develop the condition. Most dogs are middle-aged or older, and females are affected twice as often as males. Although any dog can develop the disease, there appears to be an increased incidence in Beagles, Cairn Terriers, Dachshunds, Miniature Poodles, Miniature Schnauzers, Keeshonds, Golden Retrievers, Labrador Retrievers, and Doberman Pinschers.

The onset of diabetes is insidious and is often undiagnosed until relatively advanced. Signs are increased consumption of water and food, increased urination, and weight loss. Diabetic dogs also can suffer sudden blindness as a result of CATARACTS.

The food eaten by a diabetic dog is turned into glucose by digestion, but without insulin, it cannot be further used. Glucose levels in the blood continue to rise as the dog eats more and more to satisfy her hunger. Eventually, the glucose in the blood is excreted in ever-increasing volumes in the urine, and the sugar in the urine causes an osmotic diuresis that pulls even more liquid out of the dog's body. The resulting increase of urination makes the dog thirsty, so she drinks more water, which increases urine volume, and so on. The increased need to urinate may cause a break in house-training, which may be one of the earliest signs an owner may notice. Left untreated, the diabetic dog will eventually begin to rapidly lose weight.

Diagnosis is based on the signs of the disease, along with evaluation of the blood and urine. Sugar and sometimes acetone in the urine, along with a high blood sugar, indicate diabetes mellitus. Pet owners may notice the dog has sticky urine.

Left untreated, dogs develop a life-threatening ketoacidosis. When the body is unable to metabolize glucose for energy, it instead switches to catabolism, a destructive process in which fat and muscle tissue are broken down for energy. Ketone bodies are a normal by-product of fat metabolism, but an excess of ketone bodies in the blood and urine results in a diabetic coma and death. A characteristic sign is a sweet-smelling breath similar to the odor of nail polish. Treatment for ketoacidosis should include fluid and electrolyte replacement and insulin therapy, and bicarbonate may be needed to correct acid-base balance.

Diabetes mellitus cannot be cured, but in most dogs it can be controlled. Treatment addresses any complications of the disease and replaces the insulin the dog's body cannot provide. Management is accomplished more easily in some patients, however, than in others.

Many dogs suffering from Type II (noninsulin dependent) diabetes mellitus improve when fed high-fiber diets. These diets appear to reduce insulin requirements and also help overweight dogs lose weight. High-fiber diets help relieve the surge of glucose that increases insulin requirements shortly after eating certain foods and are helpful in any dog that suffers from diabetes mellitus. Most dogs with the condition, though, also require insulin injections.

The trick is to find the right type and amounts of insulin, balanced with proper diet and exercise. Commercial insulin is derived from a variety of sources, most notably beef, pork, and synthetic human insulin, or combinations thereof; all are effective in dogs. These products are categorized by promptness, duration, and intensity of action. The mixture most appropriate for your dog's condition must be determined by your veterinarian. Typically, the dog's blood and urine glucose levels are monitored for several days, and hospitalization is often required to obtain these baseline readings. Even then, adjustments to the dose may be necessary, and the dog should be reevaluated by your veterinarian two or three times a year.

Dog owners usually become quite adept at giving their dogs insulin injections once the dosage has been determined by a veterinarian. Most dogs require twice-daily beneath-the-skin (subcutaneous) injections. In addition to insulin, how often and how much the dog is fed and exercised influence treatment success. Too much or not enough of either may cause problems. Therefore, the diabetic dog's diet and exercise must remain constant, with regularly scheduled feedings, and no unauthorized snacks or romps.

Diabetic coma may result if not enough or too much insulin is given, if the dog doesn't eat on schedule or exercises too much, or if the insulin has expired and isn't effective. The dog loses consciousness and can't be roused. *This is an emergency that your veterinarian must address.*

Too much insulin can cause insulin reaction, referred to as *hypoglycemia*. Symptoms include disorientation, salivation, weakness and hunger, lethargy, shaking, or head tilt. Without treatment, the dog will suffer convulsions, coma, then death. *Giving the dog a glucose source, such as Karo syrup or honey, should reverse signs within five to fifteen minutes. Then get your dog to the veterinarian immediately.*

Diarrhea

The frequent passage of soft or fluid stools is referred to as *diarrhea*. Diarrhea is not a disease, it is a sign of illness, and it is typical of a variety of health conditions. Any change of bowel habits that continues for more than twenty-four hours should be addressed by the veterinarian.

Dogs frequently suffer gastrointestinal upsets, and diarrhea is the most common sign. The condition may be of acute (sudden) onset, or chronic, which is an ongoing condition. Food normally spends about eight hours in the dog's small intestine, where most of the bulk, and nearly 80 percent of the moisture, is absorbed. As the remainder moves through the colon, the waste is concentrated, as much of the remaining water is removed. Diarrhea results when food passes too quickly through the intestine and is incompletely digested. Rather than solid, well-formed feces, the waste is soft or liquid.

Diarrhea usually is caused by an irritation of the bowel lining that causes the rapid transit of food. Common causes include intestinal parasites, like HOOKWORMS, or viruses, like CANINE DISTEMPER and CANINE PARVOVIRUS. Dogs are notorious gorgers, and overeating or an abrupt change in diet may bring on diarrhea. Unhealthy FOOD SUPPLEMENTS, like table scraps, can cause upset digestion. MILK causes problems for many dogs because they may lack the dietary enzyme that allows them to digest it properly. Indiscriminate eating habits, such as snacking from the garbage, eating varmints, or ingesting toxic substances (see POISON), also may result in diarrhea. Some dogs develop ALLERGIES to their food. And swallowing foreign material may also result in diarrhea (see SWALLOWED OBJECTS).

Treatment must address the underlying cause whenever possible. If the problem is caused by a parasite, deworming medicine is given. Diarrhea resulting from viral diseases may require treatment to counteract such consequences as DEHYDRATION. Only in the mildest cases would an antidiarrheal medication

DIARRHEA

SYMPTOMS
More frequent than normal bowel movements that are soft or fluid

HOME CARE
Withhold food for twenty-four hours, offering water or ice cubes to lick; offer bland first meal—either therapeutic diet recommended by your vet, or one part broiled lean hamburger, boiled egg, or cottage cheese, with two parts rice or boiled macaroni—in several small servings, then mix with regular diet, (equal-size portions of each); gradually increase ratio of normal diet over four-day period; alternatively, try adding one tablespoon natural wheat bran or Metamucil to food

VET CARE
If intestinal parasites diagnosed, specific medications prescribed; antidiarrheal medication; sometimes fluid therapy, or other medications depending on diagnosis

PREVENTION
Vaccinate dog against viral illnesses; pick up yard to reduce parasite risk; keep outside dogs confined to yard to prohibit them from eating vermin; avoid sudden diet changes, table scraps, garbage, and milk treats

be the sole treatment, because if the underlying cause isn't removed, the condition will return.

Acute diarrhea is usually treated by withholding food for at least twenty-four hours to rest the gastrointestinal tract. As long as there is no vomiting along with the diarrhea, offer small amounts of water or ice cubes during this time. The first meal should be bland and offered in four to six servings throughout the day rather than one big meal. A therapeutic diet prescribed by your vet may be helpful, or you can feed a mixture of one part broiled lean hamburger and two parts cooked rice, or try one part cottage cheese or boiled egg mixed with two parts rice or cooked macaroni. Feed this diet for three days, even if the dog's diarrhea has stopped. On the fourth day, mix this special diet half-and-half with your dog's regular diet. Reduce the mixture until, by the end of the week, your dog is again eating only his normal ration. Sometimes mixing in a tablespoon of a fiber supplement helps firm the stool; try natural wheat bran or unflavored Metamucil.

Only your veterinarian should prescribe an antidiarrheal medication for your dog. *It's dangerous to give your dog over-the-counter medication without your veterinarian's direction.*

When diarrhea becomes a chronic problem, symptomatic treatment usually doesn't work. Whenever you suspect your dog has swallowed something dangerous, or if the stool contains blood, see a veterinarian immediately. A black, tarry stool indicates upper-digestive-tract bleeding, while bright red blood or clots arise from the colon.

If diarrhea doesn't resolve with the above steps, is accompanied by other signs like refusal to eat or VOMITING, or if it persists for more than twenty-four hours, see your veterinarian. A further diagnosis is necessary to understand what's causing the problem before it can be appropriately treated. (See also COLITIS, ENTERITIS, INFLAMMATORY BOWEL DISEASE, and MALABSORPTION SYNDROME.)

Digging

Dogs excavate for a variety of reasons. Digging is a natural canine behavior that evolved as a means of survival. The dog's footpads are very thick and callused and are the toughest area of her body. Dogs use their claws and paws to shovel dirt when pursuing burrowing varmints, to bury food or toys for safekeeping, and to create nests in the snow or dirt that protect them from the cold of winter or the heat of summer. Dogs also dig to escape, by tunneling beneath fences meant to confine them.

All dogs dig, but terrier breeds live for the joy of kicking up dirt. The word *terrier* means *of the earth*; terriers were developed specifically to dig in pursuit of belowground prey.

Digging becomes a problem when your dog is given no opportunity to indulge the urge; left to her own devices, she'll often choose an inappropriate outlet. Dogs dig holes in the yard, unplant your flower bed or potted plants, empty the cat's litter box, or even attempt to tunnel through carpeting, upholstery, and hardwood floors. When confined, dogs often scratch at doors or the floor in an effort to get out.

Digging becomes particularly problematic in dogs that are bored; to dampen your dog's digging enthusiasm, give her something better to do. First, be sure you provide your dog with at least twenty minutes (forty is even better!) of aerobic exercise every day. Burn off her energy by playing games of fetch or taking her on a brisk walk. If you have a terrier and space allows, provide her with a "legal" area, like a sandbox in the yard, where she can dig to her heart's content.

If your dog is caching toys or food, then allow her to have these items for fifteen or twenty minutes at a time; this will just about exhaust her attention span. Take them away when she begins to lose interest, and offer them again at a later time. Some dogs bury objects of importance to them to prevent another dog from stealing them. Give your dog privacy away from the competition if this is the case, so that she won't be inclined to hide her toy.

Some dogs love to dig (*Photo credit: Betsy Stowe*)

d

Digging holes to stay cool can be cured by providing your dog with a shaded area out of the sun, such as access to the covered porch or patio. A dog run with a concrete floor and shaded roof will provide a secure, comfortable outdoor area that can't be pockmarked by digging.

Dogs that dig to escape confinement may be discouraged when their holes are filled with bricks, for eventually, the dog should become convinced he'll run into bricks wherever he digs. Dogs also dislike digging up feces, so you may discourage a hard-case digger by "planting" his own feces in the holes and covering them up as a sort of booby trap.

Indoor digging may require more specialized corrections. Provide some distraction, like Nylabone chews or a favorite toy, to give the bored dog something to do. Put a cover on the cat's litter box or move it out of reach. Cover the surface of large potted plants with gravel or larger rocks to make the contents unattractive to canine diggers.

Obedience training is the single most important step dog owners can take to prevent and correct problem behaviors like inappropriate digging. See TRAINING for further instructions on using effective and humane canine corrections.

Disk Disease

Just like their owners, dogs may suffer debilitating spinal injury and back problems. Disk disease is most common in small breeds, and particularly in those with long backs and short legs, like Dachshunds and Basset Hounds.

DISK DISEASE

SYMPTOMS
Weak, wobbly gait in rear legs; hunched, painful posture; refusal to move; paralysis

HOME CARE
Confinement; restrict activity, especially running or jumping; pain medication only if prescribed by vet

VET CARE
Same as home care; sometimes pain medication; commonly anti-inflammatory drugs; occasionally, back surgery

PREVENTION
Prevent obesity; restrict jumping, particularly in small dogs or high-risk breeds; remain vigilant for problems; enforce rest when necessary

The spine is a chain of bones held together by ligaments, with intervertebral disks in between each vertebra that act as cushions. These disks provide the spine's flexibility. The spinal cord is strung through a bony canal inside each vertebra and is the neurological highway that speeds nerve impulses from the brain throughout the body.

The disks act as shock absorbers for the back and are filled with fluid, collagen, and other substances. Disk disease typically begins as early as seven months of age, when the disk suffers a loss of this fluid and begins to calcify and loses its resiliency. Eventually, the degenerated disk may rupture, which compresses the spinal cord. That causes the dog severe pain in the neck or back and may compromise function and feeling in the legs.

Signs depend on the site of the damage. Ruptured disks located in the lower back cause a weak, wobbly gait in the rear legs. Ruptured disks located in the neck cause the dog to tilt his head down in a hunched, painful posture and may cause front-leg weakness; the dog may even refuse to move. The most severe signs are complete paralysis due to compression and/or damage to the spinal cord.

Diagnosis is based on signs, and sometimes x rays confirm the condition and pinpoint the location of the problem. Treatment depends on the severity

Dachsunds are prone to disk pain (*Photo credit: Amy D. Shojai*)

of the signs, and prompt veterinary help improves your dog's chance for a complete recovery. Initially, confinement and enforced rest for four to six weeks may return the dog to mobility.

The discomfort that arises from the degenerated disk helps restrict the dog's activities; otherwise, the dog may move too much and cause further damage. For that reason, PAIN medication and anti-inflammatory drugs, like steroids, are prescribed with caution. Most dogs improve from mild symptoms after three or four days of crate rest.

With more severe symptoms or those that don't improve with rest, more aggressive therapy such as surgery may help. Surgical decompression of the spinal cord creates a "window" in the vertebrae to remove the encroaching disk material from the spinal canal. Prognosis can vary depending on the severity of the signs and how long the dog has suffered the problem. Some veterinary researchers report significant improvement in some dogs suffering disk disease by combining conventional therapies with veterinary acupuncture treatments. Complete recovery may take as long as six months and typically requires physical therapy.

However, dogs may suffer permanent nerve damage so that full recovery isn't possible. A veterinarian can best evaluate each individual situation (see also WOBBLER'S SYNDROME).

Docking

Docking refers to the amputation of all or a portion of the dog's tail. Docking may be done for medical reasons, such as damage resulting from FROSTBITE or FRACTURE. Some dogs are "tail beaters" in a constant state of bloody injury from flailing their tails against objects. However, most cases of tail docking are performed purely for cosmetic reasons, so that the dog will look a certain way.

Historically, tails were docked (or "curtailed") to prevent injury to them during work, or to differentiate a commoner's "cur" from a purebred dog owned by the aristocracy. Today, the practice is more a tradition than a health consideration; the American Kennel Club standards specify docked tails in more than forty breeds.

The length of the docked tail varies depending on the specific breed. Typically, the surgery is performed on three- to five-day-old puppies. It should be done under sterile conditions by a veterinarian familiar with breed standards.

d

Viszla tails are docked long
(Photo credit: Amy D. Shojai)

Dominance

Dominance is behavior used to achieve command over another individual. Most dogs are happy to simply belong to a family and know their ranking within that social group. However, some dogs that have forceful personalities aren't satisfied unless they are in charge.

The canine social system defines how your dog behaves. It is based on a hierarchy of dominant and submissive individuals that rank in a stair-step order, with most dominant at the top and more submissive individuals below. Submissive dogs yield to those in power, be that another dog or pet, or the owner. But a dominant dog wants to call the shots and may challenge an owner's authority. However, dominance is not necessarily expressed as AG-GRESSION; even the tiniest and seemingly most compliant pet may assert his dominance by wrapping the unsuspecting owner around his furry paw.

Dominant behavior may be expressed in a variety of ways. Dogs that beg constantly for food, attention, or to go inside or out are asserting their dominance. Such dogs may growl or snap at another pet or the owner when displeased or challenged, demand the choicest resting areas, like the sofa or the bed, hog all the toys, and eat from other pets' bowls. A dominant dog isn't necessarily large, either; tiny dogs, like a Chihuahua or Toy Poodle, often buffalo their owners into pampering them.

It is vital that you, as the owner, be the leader in your dog's social group. Dogs communicate dominance with attitudes expressed through posture, vocalization, and body position (see COMMUNICATION). Use your dog's language to establish yourself as leader: speak with a commanding voice, stand tall, make eye contact, and enforce your authority with appropriate TRAINING. Do not allow a dominant dog to sleep with you on the bed; sleeping on the same level as the leader confers status and is a signal to the dog that he is your equal.

Don't allow yourself to be trained by the dog. If he whines and pushes against you for attention, then pet him only when he's quiet and ignore him when he's noisy. If he begs to be fed, feed him before he turns up the noise, and don't give in to pleas at any other time. Consistency is key; owners reinforce the dog's identity as king by giving in just one time. Dogs know that if it worked once, it will likely work in the future. Have the dog earn your attention. The person in the family group who controls access to food, toys, and attention is the leader. Rule judiciously.

Dogs are particularly sensitive to territorial issues. Dogs consider their house, the yard, and their owner to be owned by them, and defend this "property" against threat. Dominance becomes most problematic in multipet households where property must be shared. If your dog feels his territory is threatened—the mailman or a strange animal crosses the yard, a new baby is taking your time, the cat sits on his favorite chair—the dominant dog may react with aggressive behavior or some other action to reestablish his dominance.

It is very important in multipet homes that owners do not interfere with or try to influence a pet's social status among his furry peers. Dangerous aggression cannot be permitted, but in all else, allow the pets to work out their own ranking. There is often posturing and skirmishes before one is established as top dog, and your interference prolongs this sorting-out process and can make life miserable for the lower-ranking pet. Treating a low-ranking animal the same as his superior puts the dominant dog's nose out of joint, and he feels compelled to reinforce his position by harassing his subordinate. The best way to handle the situation is to side with the dominant pet; dog society is not democratic, and you must recognize this.

Feed the dominant dog first. If he routinely steals from the other pets, feed them in separate rooms. And when the dominant dog chases your other pet off the sofa, don't try to correct the situation; simply allow the lower-ranking dog quality time with you when the dominant dog is otherwise engaged.

Most dogs sort out their own social order with few squabbles. The dominant dog typically is a confident, secure individual that has nothing to prove; after all, the other pets know he's king and reinforce his status by displaying submissive behaviors, so King Dog can afford to be tolerant. (See also INTRO-DUCTIONS and SUBMISSION.)

Dreaming

Animals with highly developed brains dream, and it's no surprise that dogs indulge in these canine fantasies. At birth, the area of the puppy brain that keeps her awake and alert is poorly developed; consequently, puppies spend the first two weeks of their life sleeping 70 percent of the time (the remainder is spent eating). This early sleep is characteristic of the dream state in older animals and people and is punctuated with muscle twitches and vocalizations. As the puppy's brain matures, another type of nondreaming, quiet sleep develops; however, like people, dogs continue to dream throughout their lives.

Why people and animals dream isn't known, but like their owners, dogs appear to relive the activities of everyday life in their dreams. The dog's muscles relax, her eyes move rapidly beneath her eyelids (REM, or rapid-eye-movement phase) during dream sleep, and she is difficult to wake up. A trusted owner whose scent and touch are familiar may even be able to move the dog without awakening her. A dreaming dog's paws, legs, or tail may move during sleep, and she may whine, whimper, or growl as she fetches the ball of her dreams.

Drooling

Saliva that escapes from the mouth is referred to as *drooling*. Saliva is the alkaline fluid produced by four pairs of salivary glands, which help lubricate the mouth and food and aid in digestion. The evaporation of moisture from the mouth during PANTING helps control the dog's body temperature. An excess production of saliva results in drooling.

Dog breeds that have loose, pendulous lips and jowls tend to drool more than others. In particular, Bloodhounds, Great Pyrenees, Newfoundlands, and Saint Bernards produce an excess of thick, mucoid saliva that tends to hang from the corners of their mouths.

The secretion of saliva may be stimulated by a variety of things. A dog's mouth may water in the presence of enticing food. Conversely, dogs drool as a prelude to VOMITING. Illnesses as innocuous as CAR SICKNESS, to deadly ones like RABIES and CANINE DISTEMPER, may be associated with drooling. STRESS may cause dogs to drool when they are fearful or nervous. Injury or foreign

d

Otter Hounds may drool (*Photo credit: Amy D. Shojai)*

objects in the mouth, throat, or esophagus often cause drooling (see SWAL-LOWED OBJECT, and PERIODONTAL DISEASE); a sore throat may prompt a reluctance to swallow, resulting in drooling (see KENNEL COUGH). Also, POISON like arsenic causes excessive drooling.

When drooling is a problem, treatment depends on discovering the underlying cause and addressing it. Owners of dog breeds that have a tendency to drool may benefit from frequently wiping the dog's face and shielding furniture and carpets with towels. Sedatives, tranquilizers, or anti-motion-sickness medications are available that may help relieve stress-caused drooling. Your veterinarian may prescribe a drug to help reduce the amount of saliva produced.

Drowning

Drowning is suffocation resulting from inhaling water. Water in the lungs impairs or even stops normal respiration and may also stop the heart.

Dogs are natural swimmers, and certain breeds (especially retrievers) are drawn to water. Other dogs may prefer dry land, particularly if a heavy coat tends to become waterlogged and uncomfortable. Puppies and small dogs are at highest risk for drowning; their inexperience, curiosity, and fearlessness may prompt them to explore, yet they may be unable to climb out when they fall into even small bodies of water. However, all dogs are at risk for drowning. Hazards like ponds, rivers, and streams are often involved and are especially dangerous during winter months, when dogs venture out on thin ice and break through. Swimming pools and hot tubs pose a year-round risk.

Treatment requires removing water from the lungs and getting the dog to resume breathing. For a large dog, one person should grasp him about the abdomen just in front of his hind legs and turn him upside down with his head pointing to the ground, while the second person thumps both sides of the dog's chest with the flat of each palm so water runs out of his throat and windpipe. With small to medium-size dogs, one person can grasp the dog with both hands about the lower abdomen and swing the dog's head down for twenty to thirty seconds. This should remove most of the water, and in some cases, the dog will begin breathing again.

DROWNING

SYMPTOMS
Loss of consciousness; no breathing apparent; dog found in or near water

HOME CARE
Grasp small dog's lower abdomen and swing downward to express water; grasp bigger dogs about chest with their head to the ground while a second person thumps dog's chest; begin resuscitation; once dog is breathing, keep warm and get to a veterinarian

VET CARE
Oxygen therapy; possible rewarming therapy; precautions against pneumonia

PREVENTION
Bar the dog from exploring dangerous waterways; supervise young puppies and dogs around toilet bowls, whirlpools, bathtubs, etc.

If he's still not breathing, begin ARTIFICIAL RESPIRATION to get air into the dog. If the water was cold, the dog's body will need to be warmed as quickly as possible. *Seek veterinary attention immediately.* Such pets are frequently at risk for PNEUMONIA. (See also CARDIOPULMONARY RESUSCITATION and HYPOTHERMIA.)

Dry Eye (Keratoconjunctivitis Sicca)

This condition is exactly what it sounds like: an insufficient lubrication of the EYE. Normally, tears are secreted by specialized glands that keep the eye wet. Dry eye results from a malfunction of these glands, resulting in inadequate tear production.

Injury or disease can damage the nerves of the tear glands or the tear glands themselves, so that tear production is reduced or stopped. Normal age changes in the elderly pet may result in problems, or chronic eye infections may block the tear ducts. The syndrome can also occur as a result of corrective surgery for CHERRY EYE, which may remove one of the tear glands. In most cases, the condition affects older dogs.

Signs are dullness to the surface of the eye, along with a thick, stringy discharge that's difficult to clean away. Without enough lubrication, blinking begins to cause the dog pain and the eye will become infected and inflamed and develop ULCERS. Dogs suffering from dry eye typically squint the affected eye and are reluctant to blink. In some cases, the nostril on the same side of the face is also affected, and the dog will repeatedly lick his nose to keep it moist.

DRY EYE (KERATOCONJUNCTIVITIS SICCA)
SYMPTOMS
Dull-looking eye; thick, stringy discharge; redness or ulcer; squinting; sometimes excessive licking of nose
HOME CARE
Artificial tears administered at two-hour intervals throughout the day; meds as prescribed by vet
VET CARE
Prescription drugs (ointments or drops) to stimulate tear flow; sometimes surgery
PREVENTION
None

When the cause is reversible, most cases recover within sixty days with appropriate treatment. Treatment consists of reestablishing the flow of tears, controlling infection with antibiotics, and reducing inflammation in the eyes with appropriate medications. Your veterinarian may prescribe drugs that stimulate the production of tears.

When dry eye is the result of nerve damage or age changes, the condition may be permanent. Artificial tears provide some relief for the dog, but usually must be administered throughout the day at two- to four-hour intervals to be effective. Some ointment-based medications are available (see ADMINISTER MEDICATION). The immune-suppressant drug cyclosporine is helpful for some dogs that don't respond to treatment; ask your veterinarian if these eyedrops are appropriate for your dog. In severe cases, surgery is an option. One of the salivary glands can be transplanted to the eye to provide moisture from saliva.

Early diagnosis and treatment is essential for best recovery results and to preserve vision in your pet's eyes.

Ear

The dog's ears are sensory organs of hearing and also provide a sense of equilibrium, or balance. Canine hearing is remarkably acute; it's used in hunting, protection, and play, and is an important tool that keeps dogs in touch with their world.

The structure and function are categorized as the external, middle, and inner ear. The visible portion, called the *pinna*, is a triangular cartilage flap covered on both sides by skin and fur. The size and shape varies among breeds. Some are erect (prick ears), like the German Shepherd Dog; folded to some degree (drop ear), as in the Collie; or pendulous, as in Cocker Spaniels. The pinna of some dogs is surgically altered to conform to a breed standard (see CROPPING).

The pinna is extremely mobile, with more than twenty separate muscles that provide 180 degrees of movement. This mobility helps collect, capture, and direct sound further into the organ. It also aids in canine COMMUNICATION by offering a host of expressive ear positions.

The pinna funnels sound down the L-shaped auditory canal. This configuration, a vertical passageway ending in a right-angle turn inward (the foot of the L), helps protect interior structures. However, it also makes dogs prone to ear infections when debris or moisture collects in the foot of the L. Hair that grows in the ears of a number of dog breeds may compound the problem (see OTITIS).

Sound waves pass through the auditory canal and strike the tympanic membrane, or eardrum. The resulting vibration is passed to a chain of three tiny ossicles (bones called the *hammer*, *anvil*, and *stirrup*) of the middle ear. The eustachian tube, which helps equalize pressure within the ear, is also located in the middle ear and connects this area to the back of the throat.

Vibrations are transmitted by ossicles to the inner ear, a bony chamber containing four fluid-filled organs responsible for hearing and balance. Chalk-like particles float in the fluid inside the semicircular canals, utricle, and sac-cule, and as the dog moves his head, they brush against tiny hairs that line these organs. That signals directional information to the brain and gives the dog his sense of equilibrium.

Sound vibration is read by the fluid-filled cochlea, a snail-shell-like coil of tubing lined with a membrane called the *cochlear duct* that spirals its length. The organ of Corti, a specialized area of this lining, is where hearing actually takes place. Vibration-sensitive hairs that cover the organ of Corti pass infor-mation through the auditory nerve to the brain, where the vibration is inter-preted as sound.

These intricate organs enable your dog to hear sounds you cannot detect, particularly at high frequencies and at soft volumes. People are able to hear low-pitched tones about as well as dogs do, but while we typically hear sound waves up to twenty thousand cycles per second, dogs may hear frequencies as high as one hundred thousand cycles per second. The size of the dog doesn't matter, with Chihuahuas able to hear just as well as Great

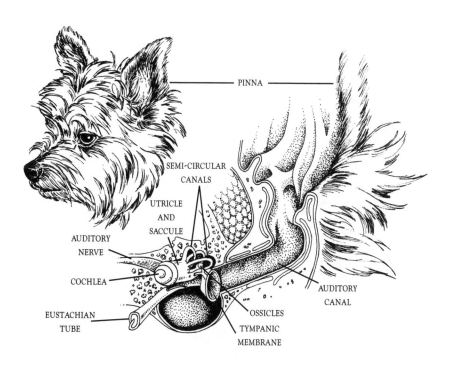

PINNA

SEMI-CIRCULAR
CANALS

UTRICLE
AND
SACCULE

AUDITORY
NERVE

COCHLEA

EUSTACHIAN
TUBE

OSSICLES

TYMPANIC
MEMBRANE

AUDITORY
CANAL

Ear

Danes. However, age tends to temper the dog's hearing, and young dogs hear better than old dogs.

Varying degrees of deafness develop with age, resulting from nerve degeneration of the cochlea and a lessening of ossicle mobility. But a dog may suffer hearing loss at any age from ear infection (see EAR MITES, HEMATOMA, and OTITIS). Dogs may be born deaf when the nerves of the ear fail to properly form. Congenital deafness is often associated with merle or piebald coat patterns (see BREED). Commonly affected breeds include the Dalmatian, Australian Shepherd, Old English Sheepdog, Collie, Shetland Sheepdog, and Bull Terrier. Ethical breeders are aware of potential problems and are working to eliminate deafness in these dogs through stringent breeding practices.

You may not immediately be aware your puppy is deaf. Specialized electrodiagnostic tests available at some veterinary universities can determine the extent of hearing loss. Most owners realize there's a problem during TRAINING when voice commands are ignored or other noise fails to draw the dog's attention. Deaf dogs may bark less than other dogs, and their voice may sound odd. They frequently develop behavior problems because of their inability to understand human communication, and because they may be easily startled or frightened by the unexpected. Some deaf dogs may be able to hear the frequencies of special whistles or feel the vibration of a stomped foot and may compensate enough for day-to-day living.

Dogs with a gradual hearing loss tend to do well as long as they remain in familiar, safe surroundings. Routine ear cleaning is important to stay ahead of possible health problems (see GROOMING). Dogs with hearing loss are a challenge for many owners, but patient owners can train them to understand hand signals rather than voice commands.

Ear Mites

These aggravating parasites commonly afflict dogs and often lead to secondary ear problems. Ear mites (*Otodectes cynotis*) are a type of arthropod that resembles ticks. They colonize the ear, where they feed on cellular debris and suck lymph from the skin. Only three or four adult mites in the ear can wreak considerable discomfort.

The life cycle takes three weeks, from the time eggs are laid and cemented in place within the ear canal. Eggs incubate four days, then hatch into six-legged larvae, which feed for another three to ten days. The larvae develop into eight-legged protonymphs, which molt into the deutonymph stage. At this point, the immature deutonymph attaches itself to a mature male ear mite

EAR MITES

SYMPTOMS
Black to brown tarry or crumbly debris in ears; itchy ears; scratching or rubbing of ears; shaking head; holding ear toward ground

HOME CARE
After diagnosis by vet, clean ears with prescribed medication

VET CARE
Sometimes sedation of dog to flush ears clean; sometimes medication to reduce inflammation or itching; mite-killing medication

PREVENTION
Monitor ears; prevent contact with other possibly infected animals

using suckers on its rear legs. If the deutonymph becomes a female adult, fertilization occurs and the female bears eggs.

Ear mites are one of the most common causes of OTITIS, and signs of infestation include brown, crumbly debris in the ear canal, and/or crust formation. Mites crawling about inside the ear cause intense itching, and dogs

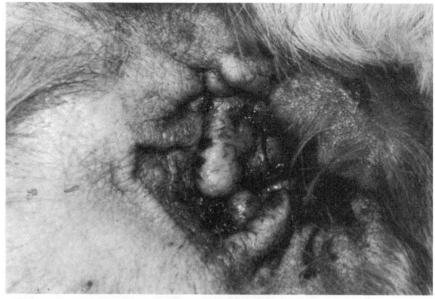

An infected ear *(Photo credit: Ralston Purina Company)*

typically shake their heads, dig at their ears, or rub their heads against the floor or furniture.

Trauma to the ear often results when the dog's efforts to relieve the itch bruise the pinna, the external ear flap. Scratching and head shaking, especially in pendulous-eared dogs like Beagles, often results in a kind of blood blister called an aural HEMATOMA.

Ear mites are extremely contagious and also affect cats, rabbits, ferrets, and other pets. Puppies often acquire ear mites from their mother. If one pet has ear mites, all animals in contact with that pet must be treated to prevent reinfestation. When left untreated, ear mites can lead to infections of the middle and inner ear, which can damage hearing or affect balance.

Characteristic dark ear debris and behavior signs generally point to ear mites. The veterinarian confirms the diagnosis by finding the mite in a sample of ear debris that's examined under the microscope. The parasite is tiny, white, and nearly impossible to see with the naked eye. Never treat your dog for ear mites until the diagnosis has been confirmed, or you risk masking other ear problems, or complicating the canine's proper diagnosis and treatment.

The ears are treated by flushing away the debris and mites using an insecticide such as a carbaryl or pyrethrin that kills the bug (see GROOMING and EAR). The medication is often suspended in a bland medium, like mineral oil, which when squirted into the ear helps float debris out of the ear canal as the ear base is gently massaged. A number of commercial products are available for treating ear mites; ask your veterinarian for a recommendation. Depending on the medication prescribed by your vet, it may be necessary to treat the ears as often as twice a day or as little as once a week for two to three weeks to get rid of the problem, because eggs will continue to hatch for at least that time

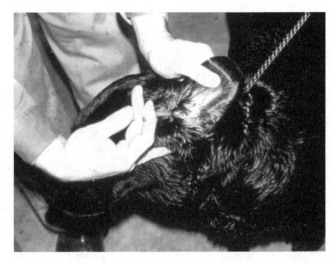

Medicating the infected ear (Photo credit: Ralston Purina Company)

and can quickly reinfest the ears. Steroid medications may be necessary to soothe inflammation, or antibiotic ointment may be required to treat bacterial infections.

Ear mites sometimes travel outside of the ear to other parts of the dog's body. Resulting sores may resemble an ALLERGY to fleas; this condition is called otodectic MANGE. So when your dog is diagnosed with ear mites, don't neglect the rest of his body. FLEA products also kill ear mites, so choose an appropriate product and do whole-body treatments along with ear treatments. (*Note: Flea products should never be used in your dog's ears.*)

Ear mites may infest the environment for several months, and premise control is helpful, particularly in homes with many pets. To get rid of ear mites in the environment, follow the same procedures and use the same products as you would for premise control of fleas. Treat your house and yard for at least four weeks; experts suggest treating the environment two weeks beyond the pet's apparent cure.

Often, the dog's ears are so sore that sedation is necessary for the initial ear treatment. Some dogs are too difficult for owners to continue treating at home, and in certain instances, an injectable medication may be recommended. One or two beneath-the-skin injections of the insecticide ivermectin has been reported to cure the problem, with preliminary tests suggesting the treatment is very safe and effective. However, because this protocol has not yet been approved in the United States, veterinarians may use the drug "off label" with the informed consent of their clients. *Note: Ivermectin is highly toxic in Collies, Collie-cross dogs, and Australian Shepherds and should not be used in these dogs.*

Eating

Dogs are passionate about food. In fact, many dogs will eat anything that doesn't move faster than they do, and so it's up to owners to ensure that the canine diet is appropriate for their pet.

The canine style of eating is rooted in evolution. Dog ancestors hunted in packs and required large animal prey to sustain the group. The mouse or rabbit an individual might catch was eaten outright, but larger animals posed a problem. What wasn't immediately eaten drew scavengers ready and willing to steal leftovers out of canine mouths; that's why most modern dogs are gorgers.

Like their ancestors, dogs can eat huge quantities of food at one time. Such a meal would last wild canines several days, which meant they didn't need to hunt or eat as often. Modern hunting breeds—Labrador Retrievers and Beagles especially—tend to be gorgers that gulp mouthfuls of food without chewing until they reach the bottom of the bowl.

Dogs love food
(Photo credit: Ralston Purina Company)

Dog ancestors also developed the ability to benefit from vegetables, which is why modern canines share the human enthusiasm for sweet foods. Sweetness is the signal that a plant has reached ultimate ripeness and its highest nutrient value. This diet flexibility gave dogs an edge in survival by allowing them to eat whatever was at hand.

A dog's TEETH are designed for an omnivorous diet, one composed of both animals and vegetables. Dagger-shaped canine teeth are designed to hold and slash prey, while the small incisors across the front of the jaw gnaw flesh from bone. Molars are used to crush bone, shear meat, and grind vegetable matter. Drinking is accomplished by curling the tongue into a spoon to scoop liquid. In this way your dog throws water up into his mouth and swallows every two to three laps.

Dogs are happy to eat anytime—or all the time—but it's healthier and easier for you to manage their feeding on a routine basis. Feed your dog in the same place and at the same time every day. Most dogs consider eating a social event and enjoy company while dining. However, if you have more than one pet, competition may be a problem. Dogs tend to eat more when another pet is present because of their gorger mentality: "If I don't eat it, he will." Make sure each pet has his own bowl, and feed them at separate ends of the kitchen, or even in separate rooms, if necessary. Plenty of clean water should be available at all times.

A number of bowl designs are available, from trendy fashion statements personalized with your dog's name, to disposable paper trays. The best are utilitarian, easy-to-clean dishes that stay in place.

Lightweight plastic bowls are difficult to keep clean and may skid about the room when under an eager canine's assault. Ceramic dishes are a better choice because of their solid weight and ease in cleaning. Buy American, though, as the glazes of some products manufactured in foreign countries may contain lead. Heavy glass bowls are also good choices, but be careful of using breakable dishes. Stainless steel bowls are the veterinarian's choice because they are easily sterilized and won't break. But empty pans—even metal pans—may turn into dog toys or chew objects, so keep this in mind when you choose.

Specialty bowls come in designs to keep long ears from falling into food, or with platforms so that tall or arthritic dogs won't have to bend to eat. There are also bowls that keep water from freezing in winter, or keep food and water cool in warm weather. A variety of automatic bin feeders and waterers are also available.

Puppies should be weaned by the age of six to seven weeks and eating an appropriate commercial puppy ration at that time. PUPPY tummies are too small for the dog to eat adequate amounts at one feeding, so for puppies up to six months old, offer puppy food three times a day. Stick to the same schedule every day, which will also aid in HOUSE-TRAINING. For puppies under nine weeks of age, it may be necessary to moisten dry foods to make the kibble easier to eat; mix three parts dry food to one part water (not MILK) to soften the food. Offer each meal for about twenty to thirty minutes at a time and allow the puppy to eat his fill. Always throw out the uneaten portion, because wet food spoils if left out too long. Dogs over six months of age should be fed twice a day.

Soft diets may be fed for your dog's lifetime, but can be quite expensive (especially for large dogs) and also tend to contribute to dental plaque or tartar. Puppies are able to eat plain dry food with appropriately sized kibble by about three months of age. Gradually decrease the amount of water over a week's time until the food is completely dry. Feed your puppy a commercial puppy ration as long as he is growing, at least for a year; as some breeds continue to grow beyond this point, ask your veterinarian or a knowledgeable breeder for a recommendation. Once-a-day feedings may lead to overeating and obesity or may prompt begging or even a garbage raid should the dog become hungry, so twice-daily feedings are highly recommended for all adult dogs.

When they've stopped growing, most pet dogs thrive on a commercial adult-maintenance ration. Change to a new diet gradually to avoid causing upset stomachs that can result in DIARRHEA. Introduce new food over a week's period by mixing it with the familiar food. Gradually increase the proportion of new food while reducing the amount of old ration until the dog is eating only the new diet.

The quantity of food required depends on the dog and the individual food. Big dogs need more than small dogs, and working dogs, like hunters or herders, require more than couch-potato lap pets. Dogs need to eat less of nutrient-dense superpremium foods than other category diets. But dogs that weigh less than twenty pounds need about 30 percent more calories per pound of body weight than dogs weighing twenty to seventy-five pounds. And dogs weighing over seventy-five pounds require about 15 percent fewer calories, pound for pound, than dogs in the twenty- to seventy-five-pound group. Commercial dog foods publish feeding guidelines on their packages, and your veterinarian can offer recommendations. However, the best indication is your dog. If he begins to gain weight, reduce the amount he is fed or choose a lower-calorie diet; conversely, if he is losing weight, increase the amount or choose a more nutrient-dense product.

Your dog's appetite may vary some from day to day, but a loss of appetite for several days may indicate illness, so see a veterinarian.

Most dogs do best being meal-fed—that is, having food offered only for a limited period of time for each meal. This also helps alert owners when he may be feeling ill, aids in scheduling bathroom breaks, and limits the amount of food a gorger otherwise would eat. Canned rations will spoil if left out all day.

Some dogs that don't tend to overeat do well on free feeding of a dry food. The kibble can be left in the bowl all day without spoiling, so the dog can nibble at his leisure. This is convenient for both the dog and the owner. (See also FOOD and NUTRITION.)

Eclampsia

Eclampsia is a condition caused by a low calcium level in the blood. Also called *milk fever*, eclampsia is associated with a large litter of PUPPIES, which depletes the BITCH's calcium stores. Most commonly, the condition arises in the first weeks following the birth during the heaviest nursing, but may also develop prior to whelping or, more rarely, into the sixth or seventh week of nursing. Eclampsia usually affects toy breeds and small dogs that have large litters.

The mother dog initially acts restless and anxious. She leaves her babies and paces, breathes rapidly, and sometimes exhibits a stiff-legged, uncoordinated gait. Her TEMPERATURE may soar as high as 106 degrees. The condition causes tetany—a constriction of the muscles—and the affected dog's face may tighten to expose her teeth in a strange grin. She may have muscle twitching of her shoulder or thigh regions. Her gums and lips will appear pale. Finally she collapses, suffers muscle spasms with all four legs kicking wildly, and drools. Left untreated, eclampsia results in respiratory failure, brain damage,

ECLAMPSIA (MILK FEVER)

SYMPTOMS
Restlessness; pacing; ignoring puppies; stiff-legged gait; drunkenness; rapid breathing; high fever; grimacing expression; pale lips and gums; drooling; collapse with muscle spasms

HOME CARE
EMERGENCY! SEE VET IMMEDIATELY!

VET CARE
Intravenous calcium treatment; therapy to counter high fever

PREVENTION
None; avoid oversupplementing with oral calcium, which may encourage eclampsia

and HYPERTHERMIA; the combination can be fatal within a few hours. *This is an emergency that must be immediately addressed by a veterinarian.*

Diagnosis is based on characteristic signs in a nursing bitch. Immediate administration of an intravenous organic calcium solution, such as calcium gluconate, is the treatment of choice. Given in time, treatment results in a rapid, dramatic improvement within fifteen minutes of administration. When the dog's temperature exceeds 104 degrees, she may require treatment for heatstroke as well.

Puppies should be removed from nursing and bottle-fed with an appropriate milk replacer (see MILK, AS FOOD) for at least twenty-four hours. Depending on the mother's condition and the age of her puppies, you may need to take over feeding for Mom permanently, or perhaps wean the puppies. Puppies may be weaned at three weeks in these instances.

Be aware that a bitch that has previously suffered an episode of eclampsia is at higher risk for a recurrence during subsequent pregnancies. However, adding calcium to the bitch's diet prior to whelping will *not* prevent eclampsia and, in fact, may promote the condition. Feed only a complete and balanced ration that contains the recommended calcium-to-phosphorus ratio. (Calcium and phosphorus must be in the proper balance, and increasing the calcium without adjusting the phosphorus also causes health problems, like bone malformation.)

Ectropion/Entropion

These terms refer to the abnormal conformation of a dog's eyelids. Entropion is the rolling inward of the lid, while ectropion is the reverse, in which the lower eyelid turns outward.

In either instance, the eye may become damaged. Inward-turning lids place eyelid hairs and lashes against the sensitive cornea and interfere with the tear coating that keeps the eye healthy. An eversion of the eyelid increases the chance of irritation or injury by exposing the eye; it is mostly seen in dogs with loose facial skin, like hounds and spaniels.

Ectropion and entropion eyelids are usually congenital and often inherited. The highest incidence of entropion occurs in Basset Hounds, Bernese Mountain Dogs, Bloodhounds, Bulldogs, Chesapeake Bay Retrievers, Chinese Shar-Peis, Chow Chows, Cocker Spaniels, and Rottweilers. Ethical breeders are aware of the inheritance factors predisposing certain dogs to such conditions and are seeking to reduce the incidence of these problems. Surgery is often required to correct the defect.

ECTROPION/ENTROPION

SYMPTOMS

Rolling inward or outward of eyelid margins; red, watery eyes; reluctance to blink; mattery discharge

HOME CARE

Keep eyes clean by wiping away discharge; vet care required

VET CARE

Surgical correction

PREVENTION

None

Ehrlichiosis

e

This disease goes by many names, including tropical canine pancytopenia, canine typhus, canine hemorrhagic fever, Nairobi bleeding disease, and tracker dog disease. Canine ehrlichiosis is caused by *Ehrlichia canis (E. canis)*, a kind of specialized bacteria that requires an intermediate host, or vector, to infect its victim. The brown dog TICK *(Rhipicephalus sanguineus)* is the primary vector.

The disease has been reported worldwide wherever the brown dog tick is found. Most cases in the United States are reported to occur in dogs living in the Texas Gulf Coast regions and other southern states but can occur anywhere the brown dog tick is found. All dogs are susceptible, but those with greater exposure to ticks—outdoor dogs, working dogs, and hunting dogs—are at highest risk. Ehrlichiosis is diagnosed most often during the warm months of tick season.

The tick becomes infected when it bites an exposed dog and ingests infected blood. The tick may transmit the disease for up to five months after engorgement with infected blood. Once infected, transmission of the disease to dogs can occur in any stage (by larva, nymph, or adult tick). It is even possible for ticks to survive winter months and infect susceptible dogs in the spring.

The organism is passed to dogs in the tick saliva when the infected parasite takes a blood meal. BLOOD transfusion from an infected donor dog also has the potential to transmit the disease. *E. canis* initially invades and damages the white blood cells of the host dog. From there, the rickettsiae spread via the blood to lymphatic tissue including the liver, lymph nodes, and spleen.

Signs of the disease can vary greatly from case to case, making canine

EHRLICHIOSIS

SYMPTOMS
Presence of ticks; fever; eye and nasal discharge; anorexia; depression; swollen legs; lameness; muscle twitches; weight loss; nosebleeds; bloody urine; bruising

HOME CARE
Remove ticks; vet care required

VET CARE
Remove ticks; antibiotic therapy

PREVENTION
Use appropriate insecticides to keep ticks off your dog; promptly remove ticks that do attach to the dog

ehrlichiosis an extremely frustrating disease to diagnose. Dogs suffering stress are also more susceptible.

There are both acute and chronic stages of the disease. Dogs suffering from the acute phase exhibit sudden severe symptoms or show few or no signs at all. Signs may include a weeklong fever, eye and nasal discharge, ocular lesions, loss of appetite, depression, swollen legs, stiffness and reluctance to walk, and weight loss. Some dogs show neurologic symptoms, such as muscle twitches, and x rays may reveal signs of pneumonia. The acute stage lasts two to four weeks; dogs either recover or proceed to the chronic phase of disease.

The chronic stage of the disease can last for several months and appears to affect dogs with suppressed IMMUNE SYSTEMS. The bone marrow is compromised, resulting in a reduction in the production of blood cells. Often, the dog will develop KIDNEY DISEASE. Low platelet counts may cause bleeding tendencies, and long-nosed breeds, like shepherds, may suffer nosebleeds. Fatigue, bloody urine, and discoloration and bruising of the skin occur in all breeds.

Diagnosis is based on signs of disease along with history of tick exposure; laboratory tests of the blood that find the organism will confirm the diagnosis. The antibiotics tetracycline and doxycycline are effective against E. canis when administered early in the course of the disease. Dogs may require six weeks or more of treatment before being cured, and some may benefit from fluid therapy or blood transfusions.

Recovered dogs tend to be immune to subsequent infection or develop only mild disease. However, dogs with chronic disease in which bone marrow is irreparably damaged may require months of therapy before any improvement is apparent; their prognosis is not good, and often the dog dies despite treatment.

There is no VACCINATION available to prevent canine ehrlichiosis. The best way to protect your dog is to reduce or prevent his exposure to ticks. In high-risk environments (i.e., kennel situations where the disease has been diagnosed), a daily low dose of tetracycline may be used as a preventative.

Electrical Shock

Dogs are often injured or killed from encounters with electricity. Lightning, fallen electrical cables, or faulty circuits offer opportunities for disaster, but most accidents result from the puppy or dog CHEWING through an electric cord. Electrical current may cause muscle contractions that make your dog bite down even harder and prevent her from releasing the cord.

If you find your dog in such a situation, shut off the current and disconnect the plug before attempting to touch her or you risk being shocked, too. Then, if the dog has stopped breathing, begin ARTIFICIAL RESPIRATION.

Keep electrical cords out of reach (*Photo credit: Fran Pennock Shaw*)

Injury varies depending on the degree of the voltage and the pathway taken through the body by the current. Usually, electrocution causes burns at the point of contact, which is most often the mouth area in dogs. The lungs often fill with water within twelve hours after the incident, due to the electricity rupturing tiny capillaries in the lungs. The fluid leaks into the lungs and makes it difficult for the dog to breathe.

Current passing through the heart may prompt an irregular beat and circulatory collapse, while a central nervous system injury may affect breathing and other bodily functions. Unless treated promptly, the dog may fall into a coma, suffer convulsions, and die. Pets who survive can suffer permanent nerve damage. The trauma typically causes SHOCK and should be treated accordingly.

Surgery may be necessary to remove the damaged tissue caused by BURNS from electrical shock. Antibiotics are used to fight possible infections, and when mouth burns are severe, a feeding tube may need to be passed through the nose to bypass the damaged oral cavity. Drugs are often needed to stabilize an irregular heartbeat, and fluid therapy combats circulation problems and shock. Diuretic drugs, like furosemide, help eliminate water in the lungs, and bronchodilating drugs and oxygen therapy help the dog breathe. Some dogs may need mechanical help breathing until their lungs can compensate. Electric-shock victims must be seen by a veterinarian as soon as possible.

It's easier to prevent electrical shock than deal with the consequences. Puppies that are teething are at particularly high risk, but all dogs investigate their

e

ELECTRICAL SHOCK

SYMPTOMS
Mouth burns; difficulty breathing; convulsions; loss of consciousness; shock

HOME CARE
Shut off current first, then administer resuscitation if dog isn't breathing. EMERGENCY! SEE VET IMMEDIATELY! Nutritional support during convalescence

VET CARE
Oxygen therapy; drugs to rid fluid from lungs; surgical removal of burned tissue; antibiotics; possible placement of feeding tube and prescription nutrition

PREVENTION
Supervise dogs and puppies around electrical cords

---

world with their mouths. Unplug appliances that aren't in use, and tape down cords to make them less tempting. Use a dog repellent like Bitter Apple on dangerous items to keep them out of your dog's mouth. *Watch* your dog to prevent her from dangerous contact with electrical cords. When you can't watch her, crate the dog (especially puppies) to prevent exposure to electric cords.

Elizabethan Collar

An Elizabethan collar is a cone of stiff material placed about the dog's neck to prevent him from bothering, licking, or biting at healing wounds. The contraption is named after the elaborate ruffled stiff collars of the Elizabethan period. In veterinary medicine, the collar is typically made of plastic or cardboard and extends outward in a cone to just beyond the end of the dog's nose. Pet-supply stores and veterinarians offer the collars in various sizes.

You can make a serviceable Elizabethan collar by cutting the bottom from a plastic pail or wastebasket or by using stiff cardboard. The actual size should depend on your dog's dimensions. Cut out a twelve- to thirty-two-inch circle and, at the center, cut a neck-sized opening (plus an inch or so). Measure the dog's collar for the right size; the depth should reach from point of neck contact to the tip of the dog's nose.

Remove a pie-shaped wedge from the circle (about one-fourth of the diameter) and tape the edges to form the cone. Buffer the inside opening with

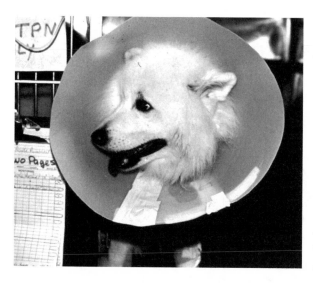

An Elizabethan collar
(Photo credit: Ralston Purina Company)

e

tape to cushion the dog's neck, and punch three to six holes to accept string, to bind the contraption to the dog's collar.

When fitted properly, some dogs may be able to eat or drink while wearing the collar, but for dogs that have difficulty or refuse to eat, remove the collar for dining—and supervise to keep them from nibbling themselves. The collar impairs peripheral vision, and dogs shouldn't be allowed outdoors unattended while wearing the collar.

Enteritis

An inflammation of the small intestines and/or stomach is called *enteritis* and can result from several diseases. Dogs suffering enteritis may lose their appetite and commonly exhibit watery DIARRHEA along with periodic VOMITING.

Most cases of enteritis in dogs arise from their less-than-discriminatory eating habits. Raiding the garbage, EATING table scraps, food ALLERGY, SWALLOWED OBJECTS, or simple gluttony often result in gastrointestinal upset. Any sudden change in diet, even from one commercial food to another, potentially may cause enteritis.

When acute signs are due to dietary indiscretion, vomiting and diarrhea usually resolve simply by resting the gastrointestinal tract and treating the symptoms. Withholding food for twelve to twenty-four hours is often all that's required, but in some instances, your veterinarian will prescribe medication to control the vomiting and/or diarrhea.

e

ENTERITIS (UPSET STOMACH)

SYMPTOMS
Loss of appetite; vomiting; watery diarrhea

HOME CARE
Withhold food and offer only ice cubes to lick for twelve to twenty-four hours to rest the system; if symptoms continue longer, see a veterinarian

VET CARE
Fluid therapy; diagnostic tests; treatment specific to cause

PREVENTION
Feed canine gluttons smaller portions to slow down eating; cut out table scraps or other inappropriate supplements; when diet change is necessary, do so gradually

When signs don't respond to symptomatic therapy, a diagnosis of the underlying problem is necessary if the condition is to be reversed. A number of viral diseases cause similar signs and can be life-threatening, and intestinal parasites are also a common cause. In some instances, fluid therapy may be required to counteract dehydration resulting from diarrhea and vomiting. (See also ALLERGIES, CANINE CORONAVIRUS, CANINE PARVOVIRUS, COCCIDIOSIS, GIARDIASIS, HOOKWORMS, LEPTOSPIROSIS, ROUNDWORMS, SWALLOWED OBJECTS, and WHIPWORMS.)

Epilepsy

This generic term describes a brain disorder characterized by seizures, also called *convulsions* or *fits*. A seizure is a loss of motor and/or emotional control that results from abnormal nerve impulses arising in the brain.

The brain employs neurons as messengers, which function by sending tiny electrical charges through the nervous system. The nervous system is structured like a web of highways, a neural network that provides pathways to every area of the body so that instructions from the brain can be delivered to prompt body functions.

Epilepsy happens when neurons misfire. A kind of biological power surge blows out the breakers of the brain and temporarily shuts down normal function. The result is a seizure.

Seizures can be acquired and develop as a result of head trauma, POISON, or metabolic disease. Toxicities resulting from ANTIFREEZE or inappropriate use of FLEA preparations often result in seizures. A blow to the head from being hit

EPILEPSY

SYMPTOMS

Seizures usually characterized by falling down with involuntary jerky or paddling motions of legs, grinding of teeth, loss of bladder and bowel control

HOME CARE

None; see veterinarian for diagnosis; do not interfere with seizuring dog; seizures lasting longer than five minutes are a MEDICAL EMERGENCY! SEE VET IMMEDIATELY!

VET CARE

Diagnostic tests; medications to control seizure episodes

PREVENTION

Once diagnosed, medication may reduce the frequency; there is no prevention

by a car often injures the brain; seizures may not begin until several days or even weeks following the accident. Severe KIDNEY or LIVER DISEASE, tumors, or organic or infectious disease, like CANINE DISTEMPER or DIABETES MELLITUS, may cause seizures. ECLAMPSIA, HYPERTHERMIA, intestinal parasites, and tick-borne diseases may induce seizures.

When the cause is identified and successfully treated, seizures are usually eliminated. Seizures may occur only once in the dog's life, or continually recur. Seizure disorders in dogs may also be inherited. Beagles, Belgian Tervurens, German Shepherd Dogs, Golden Retrievers, Irish Setters, Keeshonds, Labrador Retrievers, Poodles, and Saint Bernards are predisposed to inherited epilepsy.

When the first seizure occurs in a dog older than six, it's commonly due to a tumor. Acquired disease may appear at any age, but usually occurs for the first time in older dogs. The majority of epileptic dogs are between one and five years of age and act normally between episodes; this form is typically termed IDIOPATHIC EPILEPSY, which means the cause cannot be determined. Seizures in dogs less than a year of age are likely caused by inherited problems, infections, or toxins. Idiopathic and inherited epilepsy may appear in the first year, but more commonly are noticed during the dog's second year.

Dogs usually suffer major motor seizures, also called *grand mal* or *tonic/clonic episodes*, which affect the entire body. Partial motor seizures strike only specific groups of muscles; for instance, an ear may flick or the dog's lip may spasm.

Psychomotor seizures affect behavior; the dog suddenly hallucinates, becomes aggressive or fearful, or exhibits obsessive-compulsive behavior. During

e

an episode, the dog may chase his tail, a ball, or a stick. Some dogs inexplicably attack objects, owners, or invisible items without warning, or may even maim themselves. English Springer Spaniels, Cocker Spaniels, and Bull Terriers appear to be prone to obsessive-compulsive disorders and rage syndrome (see AGGRESSION), which some experts believe may be caused by psychomotor seizures. Cavalier King Charles Spaniels may exhibit "fly-catching" behavior, snapping at the air when nothing is there.

Seizures rarely last longer than a few minutes and are characterized by three phases. The first is an altered period of behavior immediately prior to the seizure, called the *aura*. Dogs stare, seem "out of it," or act disoriented, apprehensive, or restless. They may sniff the air or snap as though seeing or smelling a hallucination. Your dog may seek you out during this period and whine.

In the next stage, *seizure*, the convulsion begins. The dog loses consciousness and falls over with legs rigid and outstretched, and breathing is irregular or stops. This rigid period lasts ten to thirty seconds. It's followed by an agitated period in which dogs paddle or jerk their legs, chew and grind their teeth, blink their eyes, drool, and foam at the mouth. Often they urinate or defecate at this time. Their eyes dilate, and their fur stands on end. The first two phases typically last one to three minutes.

During the *postseizure* phase, the convulsion stops but the dog acts exhausted or confused. Complete recovery varies between individuals; some are back to normal within minutes, while others act disturbed for hours. The dog may immediately suffer another seizure, particularly if stimulated by loud noises, bright lights, or excitement.

Leave your dog alone during a seizure. *And don't try to put anything in your dog's mouth.* He isn't aware of his actions, and the involuntary muscle contractions may result in your being severely bitten. Move a seizuring dog only if he might fall and further injure himself; cover him with a towel or blanket to reduce outside stimuli. When the convulsion stops, call your vet for advice on what to do next.

Most convulsions in dogs are more frightening than dangerous. However, seizures that continue for longer than five minutes are an emergency and need immediate veterinary attention. Rapidly recurring seizures without recovery in between, or ongoing prolonged convulsions, are referred to as *status epilepticus*. These uncontrolled seizures can cause permanent brain injury, severe metabolic problems, and death. The seizure itself burns so many calories that body temperature rises and blood sugar levels drop—and both conditions stimulate seizures to continue. Intravenous administration of valium is the treatment of choice to stop status epilepticus.

Seizures are usually controlled with oral anticonvulsant medication the owner gives the dog at home. Maintenance therapy is warranted only when dogs suffer recurrent seizures that interfere with a quality life. One seizure rarely prompts medication, and dogs who suffer only occasional episodes may not require medication at all.

The condition is not curable; in certain instances, where metabolic disease damage can be reversed, epilepsy may be transient. Treatment for ongoing epilepsy, however, attempts to reduce the frequency, shorten the duration, and/or reduce the severity of seizures, with a minimum of side effects. Limiting recurrence to one or two seizures per month is considered a success.

Some of the same human medications for controlling seizures are also used in veterinary medicine. Phenobarbital and primidone are most often used in dogs; Dilantin, which works well in people, is metabolized too rapidly in dogs to be particularly helpful to them. An experimental drug that is effective in some dogs is potassium bromide, which may reduce the amount of other anticonvulsants necessary to control the seizures. Some dogs suffering from psychomotor seizures have been helped with medications that control obsessive-compulsive disorders, such as Prozac and similar drugs. Ask your veterinarian for the best program for your dog.

Dosage varies from dog to dog, and it's important to work closely with your veterinarian to find the ideal maintenance dose. Side effects such as sedation or increased thirst, appetite, or urine output are seen in some patients. Once anticonvulsant therapy has begun, missing a dose can actually cause a seizure, so owner attention and compliance is important if the dog is to do well. Most dogs are helped by therapy, but about 20 to 30 percent require intensive medical attention and may be helped by a veterinary specialist. Most dogs with idiopathic epilepsy can, with treatment, enjoy a quality life.

Euthanasia

Euthanasia is the act of causing merciful death. When your dog suffers an injury or illness with no reasonable hope of recovery, euthanasia may be the kindest choice. Deciding to put your dog "to sleep" isn't easy and should be made with the understanding and guidance of a compassionate veterinarian.

All of us who love and care for dogs understand that we will outlive our pet and ultimately have to say good-bye. But knowing that doesn't make the reality any easier. Quality care can prolong the lives of our pets only for so long.

It is incumbent upon caring owners to make the wisest, most compassionate—and certainly, the most difficult—decisions for our dogs. The time will come when a longer life isn't necessarily a better life. When the joy of living is gone, when pain replaces pleasure, and when your dog is ready to leap forward into the next adventure beyond your side, you can grant her the greatest gift of all: a merciful death.

An anesthetic agent is administered by your veterinarian so that your dog will fall immediately asleep. Her heart will stop, and she will feel no more pain. Most veterinarians allow you to be with your pet as she passes from this life to the next. A beloved pet's final moments are often difficult for your veterinarian and staff, too. Many practitioners offer counseling and emotional support (see Appendix C, "Pet Services").

Eyes

The dog's eyes are sensory organs that translate images carried by light into meaning. Besides providing vision, dog eyes are also important in canine COMMUNICATION.

Structurally, the canine eye is similar to our own. It is designed to function well in both high- and low-light situations. Eyes situated toward the front of the face provide binocular vision and an acute depth perception important for a successful predator. But eye placement—and so, visual acuity and field of vision—varies from breed to breed, with the eyes of flat-faced dogs, like the Pug, being more forward-facing, and the eyes of narrow-headed breeds, like the Collie, being placed further toward the sides.

Each eyeball is cradled in fat and positioned inside a bony socket in the dog's skull. Eyelids support the front of the eye and glide across the eyeball on a coating of tears. Dogs have a third eyelid that begins at the inside corner of the eye. Called the *nictitating membrane* or *haw*, this membrane lubricates and protects the eye. It is more prominent in some breeds than in others, but is usually not particularly noticeable when the other eyelids are open. It functions by sliding across and wiping the surface clean.

A thin layer of clear cells, called the *cornea*, cover the front surface of the dog's eyeball. The "white" of the eye, or sclera, isn't nearly as obvious in dog eyes as in our own. The conjunctiva is a thin, protective layer of tissue that covers the inside of the eyelids, sides of the nictitating membrane, and sclera. Tear glands located in the eyelids produce lubricants that also contain bacteria-fighting substances that help protect the eyes from infection.

Behind the cornea, the front portion of the eye is filled with watery fluid that holds the structures of this anterior chamber in place. The center black area is the pupil, an opening directly behind the cornea through which light passes into the eye. Surrounding the pupil is the colored portion of the eye, called the *iris*. It is actually a special muscle that controls the opening and closing of the pupil to regulate the amount of light allowed into the eye. In

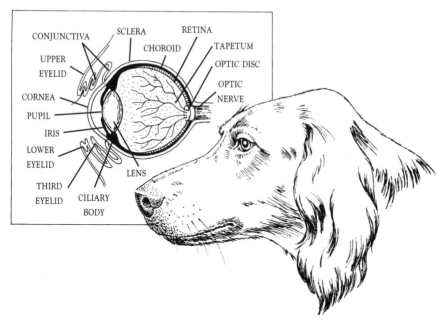

CONJUNCTIVA
SCLERA
RETINA
CHOROID
TAPETUM
UPPER EYELID
OPTIC DISC
OPTIC NERVE
CORNEA
PUPIL
IRIS
LOWER EYELID
LENS
THIRD EYELID
CILIARY BODY

Eye

very bright light, the iris closes the pupil to a pinpoint, while in low light, it dilates the pupil into a wide circle to capture as much light as possible.

The posterior chamber of the eye is situated behind the pupil and iris and contains a gel-like material that helps give the eye its shape. Called *vitreous*, this substance keeps the inner structures like the lens in place. The lens focuses light that enters through the pupil onto the retina at the back of the eye.

The retina is covered with highly specialized light-receptor cells, called *rods* and *cones*, which react to the light in various ways. Cones provide color sense, while rods allow the dog to see shades of white, black, and gray. The optic nerve is connected to the retina and carries these signals to the brain's visual center, where the impulses are translated into meaningful images.

The dog's cones allow him to see a dichromatic, or two-color, system (blue and green, and their combinations) rather than the three (red/yellow/blue and combinations) that people see. Dogs can be readily trained to distinguish between certain colors, but probably don't see them the same way that we do. Under normal light, dogs likely see blue and green as much brighter than red, because they have few to no red-sensitive cones.

This lack of color perception is balanced by dogs having many more rods than people do. The retinal illumination of the dog is about three times more efficient than ours, which means dogs see much better in low-light conditions than people do. A layer of reflective cells behind the retina, called the *tapetum lucidum*, enhances the light-gathering efficiency of canine eyes by nearly 40 percent by reflecting back any light that enters the eye. This gives the dog's eyes a second chance to use existing light, and it also accounts for the eerie glow of canine eyes at night as light escapes.

Eyes that face forward allow the dog's field of vision to overlap, providing three-dimensional or binocular sight. The degree of binocular vision varies from breed to breed, with flat-faced dogs having more, and narrow-headed dogs less. Cocker Spaniels and Greyhounds have about 80 degrees of binocular vision, compared to our own 120, which means they can see less in-depth than we can.

Dogs tend to see better at middle to far distances and have trouble focusing on objects closer than about ten inches. Rather than focus, dogs tend to rely more on motion. That's why dogs may be unable to see the last piece of food in the bowl, but will respond to strong hand signals at a distance of up to a mile away. And they may not recognize an owner who wears a hat until scent or sound of voice offers identification.

Eyes are prone to conditions that can be extremely painful to the dog and require immediate veterinary attention. Signs of a painful eye include squinting, tearing, avoiding light, and tenderness to touch. A visible nictitating membrane is often a sign of pain. Flat-faced breeds that have more prominent eyes, like the Pekingese, may require routine cleaning of their eyes (see GROOMING). Signs of injury and/or disease may include any kind of eye discharge, redness, crusting, cloudiness to the eye, or a hard or soft eye. Problems of the eye should be evaluated as soon as possible by your veterinarian to prevent loss of vision or even the loss of the eye. (See also CATARACT, DRY EYE, ECTROPION/ENTROPION, GLAUCOMA, and UVEITIS.)

Fading Puppy Syndrome

This term refers to puppies that appear healthy at birth, then inexplicably "fade away" and die. Such puppies fail to gain weight, stop eating, and become weak. It is likely that a variety of conditions result in the syndrome, either singly or in combination. Factors such as the immune competence of the DAM, environmental stress, congenital defects, viruses, or even inherited blood defects such as neonatal isoerythrolysis (see BLOOD) may contribute. If the cause is treatable and can be identified in time, the condition may be reversible. (See also CANINE HERPESVIRUS.)

FADING PUPPY SYNDROME
SYMPTOMS
Puppies that appear healthy at birth, then fail to thrive, stop eating, become weak, and die
HOME CARE
Nursing care; supplemental feeding; keep warm
VET CARE
Supportive care; treatment depending on cause
PREVENTION
Ensure the mother dog is healthy and has been wormed and vaccinated prior to pregnancy

False Pregnancy

Also called *pseudopregnancy*, this condition is exactly what it sounds like. The dog exhibits physical and behavioral signs of pregnancy following estrus when, in fact, no PUPPIES have been conceived. The condition may occur whether the dog has been mated or not and is an exaggeration of a clinically normal condition.

False pregnancy is a relatively common occurrence in intact female dogs. Behaviorists believe the condition in wolf ancestors served a survival function. Female wolves that did not become pregnant were nevertheless biologically prepared to nurse and mother the offspring of other pack members.

False pregnancy results when ovulation occurs but fertilization does not take place. It is not caused by an excess of progesterone, though. The level of this hormone, which prepares the dog's body for pregnancy, remains normal, but the body is somehow fooled into behaving as though it has become pregnant.

Signs develop about six to ten weeks following estrus and vary from dog to dog. Some canines exhibit only subtle changes in appetite, with perhaps a slight swelling of the abdomen. Other dogs "adopt" and mother inanimate objects, like a stuffed animal or a shoe, or other puppy substitutes. Dogs suffering a false pregnancy often produce milk and may even go through labor.

Treatment is rarely necessary for this condition, which will resolve itself within one to three weeks following the onset of signs. However, producing milk without nursing puppies to relieve the pressure can prove uncomfortable for the dog and is a potential cause of infection (see MASTITIS). Dogs suffering from false pregnancy actually stimulate the ongoing production of milk by mothering objects or licking their own breasts; even the presence of another dog's puppies may prompt milk production. An owner's efforts to relieve the dog's distress can make the condition worse; cold or warm packs applied to the swollen mammary glands also stimulate milk production.

If the condition doesn't resolve within three weeks, try removing the "adopted" objects and apply an ELIZABETHAN COLLAR to prevent the dog's continued self-stimulation. In some instances, more aggressive intervention by a veterinarian may be required.

Dogs that suffer from false pregnancy once will likely do so again. When puppies are not desired, SPAYING prevents future occurrences. (See also REPRODUCTION.)

Fear

Fear is a strong emotional response to a perceived threat. Dogs typically exhibit fear when confronted with unfamiliar people, animals, or situations. This normal emotion is a protective mechanism that prompts the dog to either fight or flee the danger.

There are limitless circumstances that may prompt fearful or anxious behavior in the dog. Anything outside the dog's experience is typically perceived as a potential threat, particularly by submissive dogs. Strange noises, being left alone, or a stranger's approach are common triggers of fear. Dogs may react fearfully to unfamiliar animals, children, or babies; people in uniforms or wearing hats are common fear inducers.

The dog's response to fear depends on the circumstances and how dominant or submissive the dog may be. When the opportunity is available, dogs may run away or try to hide from the threat. Dogs fearful of being left alone (separation anxiety) may try to escape by clawing windows or doors, crying or howling for company, or even CHEWING or eliminating inappropriately. When escape isn't possible, and when the dog feels cornered or is defending his property (the yard or an owner), the result may be a fear-induced AGGRESSION.

Your dog COMMUNICATES his fear and tries to drive the threat away using growls and snarls, barks, raised hackles, and/or flattened ears. If these distance-producing signals don't work, the dog may attack. But a submissive dog crouches in a low position, rolls on his back, and urinates submissively (see SUBMISSION) in an attempt to appease the perceived threat.

Many young dogs tend toward shyness during adolescence, at about four to five months of age. However, most of these fear-related behaviors fade as the dog matures, gains confidence, and becomes used to the triggering situation. Exceptions can develop into problem behaviors, though. In particular, some of the northern breeds, like Siberian Huskies, as well as larger-breed dogs, like German Shepherd Dogs and Labrador Retrievers, tend to be more likely to develop phobias about loud noises, like thunderstorms or fireworks. And a dog that is frightened by something specific during the socialization period (see PUPPY) may thereafter react in a fearful manner.

Punishing the dog for fearful behavior *does not work* and in some instances will escalate the behavior. The best way to prevent fear in dogs is to build confidence at an early age by exposing them to a variety of positive new experiences.

When the dog is older, a program of desensitization is required. In effect, the dog is trained to recognize a benefit to conquering his fearful behavior. He is exposed to the fear-inducing situation time after time—a man in a hat, tape-recorded thunder, the departure of a loved one—initially for extremely short periods followed by progressively longer sessions. He is rewarded (praised, given a treat, etc.) only when he behaves appropriately. Eventually it is hoped that the dog will learn to relate the formerly fearful encounter with good things for himself.

Separation anxiety is a common problem in dogs who are left alone during the day by owners who work. Typically, the dog follows the owner about the house, can't bear to have the owner out of his sight, and becomes increasingly distraught as the owner prepares to leave. To make up for this, owners may tend to overdo good-byes. But in fact, this can accentuate your dog's feeling of abandonment once you leave the house. Instead, ignore the dog for ten minutes or so immediately prior to departure. And get him used to your leaving; stage your absences, first for only a minute or two, then five minutes, ten, and so on. Offer your dog a flavored chew, like a Nylabone, before you go to keep him pleasantly distracted while you're gone.

Some dogs urinate submissively in an effort to defuse a threat. Raising your voice or offering a physical correction will not work, but instead escalates the problem; the dog urinates even more to try to block the growing threat of your displeasure. Instead, simply walk away when the dog begins to urinate submissively. Do this consistently, and clean up any mess in a moment or two after the situation has defused. The dog will soon learn that urinating results in an absence of attention and that controlling himself prompts positive owner attention.

Dogs that are particularly submissive may benefit from obedience TRAIN- ING and interactive play sessions. Nothing builds canine confidence like being praised for doing something well. Tug-of-war with a towel is a great confidence boost for dogs; let your pet win. *Caution: Use tug-of-war games only for this purpose*, as they tend to escalate aggression in dominant dogs.

An extremely fearful dog, especially one who reacts with aggressiveness, may need more help than you can offer. Consult a professional animal behaviorist for advice. Some dogs may benefit from antianxiety medications (see Appendix C, "Veterinary Resources").

Feral

As it applies to our pets, *feral* refers to a domesticated dog that has reverted to the wild state. Feral dogs are usually lost or abandoned dogs forced to live on their own (see also STRAY). Some may crave human attention, but most learn to fear people and avoid close contact.

Feral dogs are found in both cities and farm settings. They typically survive as scavengers, eating from Dumpsters or overturning garbage cans, or from the handouts of sympathetic humans; sometimes they steal cat or dog food left out for other pets. Rarely are they effective hunters, although they may catch the occasional rabbit or feed on dead livestock or roadkill. Occasionally, a dog or a group of feral dogs learns to kill young calves or sheep, pet cats, or small dogs.

Groups of feral dogs rarely are larger than three individuals, with these small groups sometimes interacting loosely with other small packs. Larger groups may hang out together for only short periods of time. Although the group may collectively help guard puppies that are born and protect territory from trespass, the interactive group-rearing that is typical of wolves has not been observed in feral dogs. In fact, because of high levels of disease, poor nutrition, and the threat of injury from automobiles or other predators, puppies born to feral dogs rarely survive to adulthood.

Well-meaning individuals who feed these dogs without addressing other issues may perpetuate the problem. Feral dogs are a nuisance and pose a health risk to pets and people. Particularly in the southwest United States, populations of feral dogs provide a reservoir for the spread of RABIES. Local health departments may resort to trap-and-kill programs to control the problem.

Some feral dogs can become pets again, or at least learn to tolerate human contact. However, this often requires great patience and dedication on the prospective caretaker's part and should not be undertaken lightly. Animal welfare organizations and concerned citizens groups may be able to offer educational support for people who are interested in helping feral dogs in their area (see Appendix C, "Animal Welfare and Information Sources").

Flatulence

Also referred to as *passing gas*, this condition is both offensive and embarrassing to a dog owner. Gas is produced naturally in the intestines during digestion, and some dogs produce more than others. Usually, the obnoxious condition isn't dangerous, but flatulence can be the sign of a health problem.

What and how the dog eats influences how much gas will be produced and ultimately passed. Inappropriate FOOD SUPPLEMENTS, snacking from the garbage, or any sudden change in diet can make the problem worse. Diets that include highly fermentable substances or large quantities of milk, or simply gulping air when eating or drinking, are common causes.

Gorging allows food to stay in the stomach for extended periods and tends to make dogs more prone to gas. So feed your dogs separately to cut down on fast eating because of competition. Slow the gulper by placing a large, non-swallowable ball in the food bowl so she must eat around it.

Try offering your dog a more digestible diet. Check the ingredient list on the package (see READING FOOD LABELS) and ask your veterinarian to recommend an appropriate choice. Always change diets gradually over a week's period, by initially mixing two-thirds of the old diet with one-third new. Progress to half-and-half, then one-third to two-thirds, and finally the new diet entirely.

Another helpful option is garnishing the dog's regular diet with a tablespoonful of plain yogurt, which contains bacteria that helps digestion and re-

FLATULENCE
SYMPTOMS
Passing gas; offensive odor
HOME CARE
Provide a more digestible diet; cut out table scraps; feed activated charcoal as directed by vet, or add yogurt to the diet
VET CARE
Prescription for gas control like Flatulex or CurTail; sometimes antibiotics for bacterial overgrowth
PREVENTION
Slow down gulping of food (and air) by feeding free choice, or in smaller quantities several times a day, or away from other pet competition; limit rawhide treats

duces flatulence. Many dogs love the flavor. As a last resort, your veterinarian may prescribe a human medication that contains simethicone and activated charcoal to control the gas. There is also an antigas veterinary product called CurTail that contains an enzyme that aids food digestion and reduces flatulence.

Fleas

This external bloodsucking parasite is the most common complaint of dog lovers. There are more than 250 kinds of fleas in the United States, but the cat flea *Ctenocephalides felis* afflicts pets most often. With the exception of pets living in mountainous regions exceeding elevations of five thousand feet or in dry areas like deserts that are inhospitable to fleas, every dog is at risk for flea infestation. Fleas thrive in warm summer weather, but because most dogs spend time both outside and indoors, fleas carried into homes often set up housekeeping and afflict dogs all year long.

Fleabites can cause a variety of problems, and while some dogs don't seem bothered at all, others suffer skin irritation, itchiness, or even severe ALLERGIC reaction. Blood loss from fleas can cause ANEMIA or even death, especially in very young or ill dogs. Fleas should never be taken lightly, because they are also potential carriers of other diseases and parasites, such as PLAGUE and TAPEWORMS.

Fleas belong to a group of insects designated *Siphonaptera*, meaning *wingless siphon*, which refers to piercing-sucking mouthparts. The flea cuts into the dog's skin and inserts a suction tube to feed upon blood. They are also equipped with a specialized protein, called *resilin*, that functions like elastic to propel the flea great distances. The resilin is compressed by leg and thorax muscles, then quickly released, and the recoil action flings the flea as much as eight inches vertically and sixteen inches horizontally. Six hooked legs are used to cling to any host within reach.

The flea's flat body is armored with cuticle plates that make it nearly crushproof, and the narrow profile promotes easy movement through fur. An adult flea can live from a few weeks to more than a year, but more typically lives about thirty days. Fleas set up permanent housekeeping on the pet and stay there unless involuntarily evicted.

However, adults represent only about 5 percent of the total flea population. The remaining 95 percent of the bug count is composed of immature life stages: eggs, larvae, and cocoons.

After mating, female fleas store sperm to use as needed; a blood meal stim-

FLEA INFESTATION

SYMPTOMS
Presence of fleas; black pepperlike residue on skin; itchiness, particularly of the back above the tail; tapeworm segments; extreme cases show lethargy with pale lips and gums from anemia

HOME CARE
Treat dog and environment with appropriate insecticides

VET CARE
For anemia cases, fluid therapy and/or blood transfusions, then appropriate flea treatment; sometimes steroid therapy to relieve itching

PREVENTION
Routine flea control; confine dog to finite outdoor area

ulates her to lay eggs. She can produce over two thousand eggs in thirty days and up to fifty each day. Eggs typically fall from the host and may remain dormant in the environment—the carpet or yard—for as long as six months. But normally, eggs hatch into tiny, maggotlike larvae within one to two weeks. They are virtually invisible to the naked eye and subsist on the waste passed by adult fleas (sometimes referred to as *flea dirt*) and other organic material.

Larvae spin cocoons in about three weeks, where they mature into adults. From inside the cocoon, the flea's antennae and bristles are able to detect body heat and odor, changes in light, touch, and moisture, and even traces of carbon dioxide exhalation of a nearby host. This prompts the flea to emerge from the cocoon and immediately snag a canine victim. The cycle from egg to adult takes about thirty days.

Flea infestation is diagnosed by actually seeing the bugs on the dog, but fleas move so quickly they may be hard to find. Other incriminating evidence, like dark brown specks of digested blood excreted by the flea, also diagnoses the condition. The parasite tends to like the dog's flanks and lower back above the tail. Flea dirt can be found on the skin in these areas by parting the fur. Try standing your dog on a light-colored towel or sheet and comb his rear quarters, and the evidence will pepper the fabric below. When the specks are placed on a damp cloth, they dissolve and turn red. Evidence of tapeworms also points to flea infestation. Look for dried ricelike grains in the dog's bedding or in the fur below the dog's tail.

A range of products is available for addressing the problem, but flea control is complicated by both flea biology and pet sensitivity. Simply put, there is no quick fix.

Fleas cause dogs to itch and scratch *(Photo credit: Fran Pennock Shaw)*

Because the lion's share of the flea population isn't even on the dog, it's crucial to treat the environment as well as your pet. Treating only your dog may kill the adult fleas, but leaves the remaining life stages to mature and begin the cycle all over again. Dogs that come indoors for even brief periods will seed flea eggs in your house, which, given time to mature, quickly turn your house into a flea hotel. And if your dog spends any amount of time outdoors, he is exposed to fleas and is potentially reinfested. The weapons you choose to battle fleas depend on your particular circumstances.

Historically, flea control relied on various classes of chemical insecticides applied to the dog or environment as sprays, bug "bombs," powders, shampoos, and dips. Inappropriate or careless application of chemical insecticides are potentially toxic to the pet. *Always read, understand, and follow product directions for use.*

The effects of a class of chemicals called *cholinesterase inhibitors* can be cumulative. What may be safe when used by itself can become toxic, or even deadly, when combined with another product. For instance, dipping your dog with one product, then spraying the house with another, can result in toxic levels that poison the dog. This group of chemicals includes organophosphates such as chlorpyrifos (Dursban), malathion, Diazinon, cythioate, and fenthion, and carbamates like carbaryl and propoxur. Products containing chlorinated hydrocarbons (DDT, lindane, methoxychlor) are highly toxic and must be used with extreme caution.

Botanicals are chemical compounds derived from plant sources and typically are less dangerous to the dog. Pyrethrins, made from a relative of the chrysanthemum flower, are one of the safest insecticides for pets available. They kill fleas quickly on initial contact, but have little residual effect; because they degrade when exposed to ultraviolet light, pyrethrin-based products aren't particularly effective for environmental protection. Synthetic pyrethrins called *pyrethroids* include permethrin and provide a broader and longer flea-killing action than natural pyrethrins.

Some products are combined with synergists, compounds like piperonyl butoxide (PBO) that increase the effectiveness of insecticides and allow lower, safer concentrations of the chemical to be used. Microencapsulation is a technique used to reduce toxicity to the pet while enhancing the product's long-term effect; the chemical is encased in permeable microcapsules that release small amounts of insecticide over a longer period of time.

Insect growth regulators (IGRs) are a relatively new class of flea control that is extremely safe for pets because they affect insects, not mammals. Methoprene and fenoxycarb are two of these hormonelike compounds. IGRs work by changing the insect's metabolic process to prevent maturation of the flea, or reproduction. In either case, the life cycle is broken. Some IGR products are used in the environment, while others address the dog. The IGR lufenuron (Program) is given to the dog as a once-monthly pill; fleas that bite a dog treated with lufenuron won't produce eggs able to hatch. However, fleas that bite still cause itchy skin, so this isn't the best choice for flea-allergic dogs. Lufenuron is available only through veterinarians.

New chemical products are also available for flea control that are safer for the dog and the environment, while providing better and longer-lasting flea control. Two new products affect only the insect's nervous system, not the dog's. Imidacloprid (Advantage) kills adult fleas, and fipronil (Frontline Top Spot) kills both adult fleas and TICKS. Both products are applied once a month as drops to the skin of the dog's shoulder blades. Imidacloprid spreads through the skin, while fipronil spreads to the hair follicles, where it coats each hair as it grows. These products kill fleas before they bite, which prevents the allergic reactions sensitive dogs suffer. These products are currently available only through veterinarians.

How the product is applied influences ease of use and effectiveness. Flea collars, shampoos, dips, powders, and sprays are the more traditional delivery systems. The "one-time application" of flea collars appeals to dog owners for its easy use, but historically hasn't been particularly effective; after all, the collar is on the dog's neck, while the fleas are on his rump. Newer collar products that spread the flea treatment over the entire pet are more effective.

Shampoo products kill fleas only while on the dog; rinsing off the suds eliminates the action (see GROOMING, Bathing). Powders and dust last longer, but are messy and can dry the skin. Sprays for small dogs may be a good choice, because they offer a good initial flea kill, and some repel fleas or offer residual protection; these can be costly for big dogs, though. Dips are applied wet and allowed to dry, and offer good residual protection because they penetrate the hair—but typically must be applied three times a month for complete protection. Again, these can be messy to apply, particularly if your big dog objects to bathing. Some dogs are sensitive to these strong dips.

"Natural" products are touted as an alternative to chemical flea control; however, please be aware that some of these work better than others, and the claim "natural" does not necessarily mean it is safe for your dog. Rotenone and d-limonene are effective when used properly; they are made from roots and citrus fruit extracts and are considered botanicals. Desiccants are drying agents that cause fleas to dehydrate and die; derivatives of borax used by some commercial pest-control companies on carpet do kill flea larvae, which helps break the life cycle. Desiccant diatomaceous earth (DE or Diatom Dust) also has a drying effect against a certain percentage of fleas and larvae, but is messy to apply. Certain kinds of nematodes (worms) that eat immature fleas are sold in pet stores and garden shops in powder form, to be mixed with water and sprayed in the yard. Herbal preparations in the environment, like peppermint, shoo away fleas because of the strong odor, but don't kill fleas—and the smell may be offensive to your pet as well as to the flea and can sometimes be toxic to pets.

A bath or dip helps get rid of fleas
(Photo credit: Ralston Purina Company)

Compounds claiming to have activity against parasites are required to pass Environmental Protection Agency (EPA) guidelines for safety and effectiveness claims and will have an EPA registration number on the label. Some products avoid these expensive tests by calling themselves "natural." A product without the EPA registration may work and be safe—or it may be dangerous and ineffective. There's no way to predict.

For the most effective and safest flea treatment protocols for your individual needs, consult with your veterinarian. In many cases, (such as flea-allergic dogs) the best options are to use an IGR-containing product that breaks the flea life cycle, along with an appropriate adulticide product to kill adult fleas on the dog.

Outside treatments are effective only if your dog is confined in a limited area; it's impossible to treat the whole of the great outdoors. The ideal flea habitat is moist and cool; fleas tend to avoid the hot, drying sun, so focus treatment in shaded areas of the yard. Trim grass short and pick up the brush to let the sun chase the bugs away. Check with your local county extension agent to learn what environmental insecticides are approved for use in your area. Some products containing IGRs can control fleas for up to twelve months, but be aware that some IGRs may also affect beneficial insects, like bees or butterflies, so choose your weapons wisely.

Indoors, vacuum carpets several times to lift the flea eggs and larvae to the surface so flea products can reach them. Change the vacuum bag frequently to keep surviving bugs from reinfecting the house. Follow product directions to treat the house and yard, and don't allow pets or people access until these areas are completely dry.

Flukes

This is a kind of trematode, a flatworm parasite that varies from one-sixteenth inch to two inches in length. There are many kinds of flatworms, but they are uncommon parasites of dogs. When they do infest dogs, they are found in the intestines or lungs.

Typically, the fluke is covered with hard cuticle scales or spines and has a pair of suckers on its underside. Most flukes have both male and female reproductive organs and are capable of independent reproduction. There are five life stages from egg to adult, and each stage may depend on a specific host for development. Dogs contract the parasite when they eat one of these host animals.

Lung flukes cause a chronic cough as a result of cysts that form in the dog's lungs. Dogs may contract lung flukes by eating infected crayfish or snails, or the frogs, birds, snakes, or rodents that eat these snails or crayfish. The highest incidence occurs in dogs that live near the Great Lakes, and in the Midwest and southern states.

Intestinal flukes are most common in dogs of the Pacific Northwest and are contracted by eating raw fish. Most commonly, they cause an ENTERITIS with DIARRHEA. However, this parasite is particularly dangerous because it carries a rickettsial disease that can be deadly (see SALMON POISONING).

Diagnosis is based on signs of disease and on finding the eggs during fecal examination. Occasionally, lung cysts will be seen on an X RAY. A medication like praziquantel effectively kills the parasite.

Prevent your dog from contracting flukes by keeping him from hunting along waterways where infective snails, crayfish, or frogs are found. Do not allow your dog to scavenge dead fish.

FLUKES	
SYMPTOMS	
Coughing; diarrhea	
HOME CARE	
None	
VET CARE	
Medication to kill the parasite	
PREVENTION	
Keep dog from eating varmints	

Food

Food is organic material consumed by an organism to nourish and sustain life. Food promotes body growth, repairs tissue, maintains vital bodily processes, and provides the energy necessary for work and play. Like their hunter-scavenger ancestors, our dogs enjoy chasing the occasional bunny or raiding the garbage. But left to his own devices, your dog's gustatorial adventures can get him into all kinds of nutritional trouble. It's up to responsible owners to provide balanced and complete foods for their dogs.

An appropriate diet must consider the individual dog. The right recipe for your dog is influenced by his age, lifestyle, activity level, health status, and sometimes breed. Growing PUPPIES need more calories than adults do, and dogs with special health conditions, as well as GERIATRIC DOGS, often require specific diets. Formulating dog foods is extremely difficult—even for professional canine nutritionists. Only in special cases are homemade diets appropriate for your dog, and then only under a veterinarian's supervision.

You will find the best food choices for your dog in a wide array of commercial products, which are designed to provide appropriate nutrition for every dog and condition imaginable. Reputable pet-food companies invest years in ongoing research to ensure the diets they produce fulfill the various needs of pet dogs.

Commercial dog-food companies design their products to please owners, as well as the pet. Dog food must be attractive to human consumers because unless you buy the product, your dog will never eat it. Certain elements, like the color of the food, are designed to prompt owners to open their wallets. Dogs actually don't care what food looks like; just think of some of the things your dog puts in his mouth. So try not to be swayed by packaging, but choose a food that best addresses your dog's nutritional requirements.

Commercial pet-food products typically fall into one of three broad categories: superpremium products, premium products, and low-cost products. The category that is best depends on the age, body condition, and activity level of the individual pet.

Superpremium foods tend to be highest in nutrient density and digestibility and use high-quality ingredients; consequently, this category is the most expensive. Higher fat content makes the foods very tasty so dogs tend to eagerly accept these diets. Nutrient density means the dog doesn't need to eat as much volume as in other categories, while high digestibility allows his body to use a high percentage of nutrients; the end result is less waste, and a smaller volume of stool to clean up from the yard. Superpremium foods are marketed primarily through specialty pet stores or veterinary clinics.

Feed dogs a good quality diet (*Photo credit: Ralston Purina Company*)

Grocery stores typically stock premium name-brand products, which may also be found at large pet stores and some department stores. These diets are more economical than superpremium dog foods, and the average dog will thrive on the nationally distributed brands. However, because premium name-brand products aren't as nutrient dense as superpremium diets, dogs must eat more to obtain equivalent calories. Select products made by reputable manufacturers that have been tested through feeding trials to ensure the diet is of a consistent quality and provides complete and balanced nutrition.

Low-cost products are known for being the least expensive pet foods and typically are sold in the grocery store or discount chain stores sometimes as the "store brand." These foods often are not as readily accepted by the dog because they may not be particularly tasty, a result of using the least-expensive ingredients to keep cost down. This also results in lower digestibility, which means a great deal of the diet isn't usable and instead ends up out on the lawn. House-brand products claim nutritional value equal to that in national name-brand products, but at a lower cost. Some dogs may do fine on these foods; however, dogs may have trouble eating enough of these diets to obtain adequate nutrition. It's very difficult to predict the quality of these low-cost products, which can vary from batch to batch. And if a product costs less per pound of food, but your dog must eat more volume to meet his needs, the food is no longer "cheap." Avoid generic dog foods, and choose quality over cost to ensure your dog receives the best possible nutrition. Ask your veterinarian whether a superpremium, premium, or other product is most appropriate for your dog's circumstances.

Before making your final choice, also consider the form of the food. Dog foods come in three basic forms: soft-moist, canned, and dry. They vary in the moisture content, cost, palatability, convenience to the owner, and the amount of nutrition delivered per pound of food.

Soft-moist foods appeal to consumers primarily for their convenience; they can be stored without refrigeration and typically come in single-serving packages that are particularly helpful when traveling with the dog. Ingredients like corn syrup that keep the food moist and prevent it from drying out tend to make the dog thirsty. High-quality soft-moist foods are more palatable than dry foods are (but less than canned forms); these foods also tend to be more expensive than dry foods are. Semimoist foods contain about 16 to 25 percent protein, 5 to 10 percent fat, 25 to 35 percent carbohydrate, and 30 to 50 percent water.

Canned dog food and human canned food products are processed in the same way. Once nutritionists design the formulation (recipe), the ingredients are ground together and placed in cans at high-speed filling lines run by computers. The food mixture in the cans is cooked and sterilized in giant pressure cookers, sealed, then labeled and shipped. This process preserves food without adding chemicals. Until it's opened, a canned product stays fresh nearly indefinitely. Canned dog foods contain about 8 to 15 percent protein, 2 to 15 percent fat, and 72 to 78 percent water.

Dry-food ingredients are mixed into a dough or batter, cooked under extreme pressure for a short time, then pushed through a die plate to give the food its characteristic shape. Called *extrusion*, this process dries the kibble and gelatinizes the starches in the grain ingredients to make them more digestible. Dry dog foods generally contain 18 to 27 percent protein, 7 to 15 percent fat, less than 12 percent water, and about 35 to 50 percent carbohydrate.

The quality of the diet—whether name-brand, premium, or super-premium—depends more on the ingredients, formulation, and processing rather than the form of the food. Complete and balanced nutrition may be obtained from any of the forms, but some food types may have certain advantages or disadvantages for an individual dog.

Canned diets tend to have a higher protein and fat content and lower carbohydrate content than dry foods have. Carbohydrates don't can well, so only small amounts are used in canned foods. There is a perception that canned dog foods contain primarily meat and fat; in fact, some do, and only add necessary vitamins and minerals to balance the diet. Meat meal is more typically used in dry foods, while canned products often contain fresh meats cited on the label as beef, chicken, and meat by-products. However, some canned products contain an extruded soy product that is less expensive but looks like meat. The label identifies such ingredients as textured vegetable protein, soy protein, or soy protein isolate. As long as they're formulated correctly, soy-ingredient diets are fine for the dog.

The lower carbohydrate and fiber content of canned diets may result in the dog producing softer stools, since fiber helps form feces. Carbohydrates are useful in formulating low-calorie rations, and again, canned "lite" diets are difficult to produce. And because carbohydrates help food retain its form, canned foods must instead rely on gum arabic, xanthan gums, and vegetable gums as viscosity enhancers to help the food set up. These ingredients create the "gravy" in canned products. Color enhancers, like iron oxide and caramel, may be added to make the food look more like something the owner would want to eat. Some products are designed to look like human beef stew, complete with veggies.

Canned foods are extremely palatable because water releases odor and flavor, both appealing to canine taste buds. The canning process requires liquid—raw meat is approximately 83 percent water—which is why canned foods are high in moisture. Some foods add palatability enhancers, like garlic powder, caramel, and onion powder.

Canned foods are also easier to chew. Small dogs with very small mouths, or older dogs with no teeth, prefer to eat them. However, canned and soft-moist foods tend to stick to teeth and may impact the dog's dental status (see PERIODONTAL DISEASE).

Canned foods also appeal to dog owners who fear their dog will become bored with one food. Dry products are available in larger quantities, while canned foods are packaged in single servings. This makes offering the dog on a canned-food diet a buffet of choices easier for his owner—even though the dog does not require variety in the diet.

A drawback of canned diets is they spoil quickly once opened, cannot be fed free choice, and require refrigeration for any leftovers. Canned dog foods, compared to dry forms, cost much more, because dogs may need to eat three times as much canned food as dry to compensate for the bulk added by water. This may make feeding canned diets cost-prohibitive for certain breeds; for example, it may take a great many cans to satisfy the appetite of a 120-pound dog.

Dry dog foods offer two advantages to the owner: cost and convenience. Dry diets can be purchased in large quantities. The bags are easily stored and do not require refrigeration after being opened. Owners can feed dry diets free choice, filling the dog's bowl with food and allowing him to eat at his convenience. Most experts believe feeding two to three small measured meals is healthier for the dog, particularly for breeds prone to BLOAT. Dry diets tend to be more energy-dense than canned or soft-moist forms are, which means your dog can eat less volume of the food, while getting the same amount of energy.

Palatability of a given food is influenced by "mouth feel" as well as flavor and smell. Some dogs prefer crunchy food, which offers the dog an opportunity to indulge his love of chewing.

While the food form does influence dental disease, feeding your dog a dry diet will not prevent tooth problems. Still, kibble won't stick to teeth the way canned foods do, and eating dry foods may slow down the development of tartar or even help reduce dental plaque. But veterinary dentists estimate the detergent action of eating a dry diet helps, at best, by about 10 percent. Only proper veterinary dental care, including regularly brushing your dog's teeth, will control tartar.

Fat makes food taste good so the dog will eat it. However, if fat isn't protected with preservatives, it deteriorates (oxidizes) within hours of a dry food's manufacture. To slow down this process and prevent fats from turning rancid, preservatives keep dry food fresh for up to a year after manufacture so that optimum nutrition is delivered when the food is eaten. Antioxidants like BHA, BHT, ethoxyquin, vitamin E, and vitamin C are often used to help maintain freshness. (See also FOOD ADDITIVES, NUTRITION, and READING FOOD LABELS.)

Food Additives

These are ingredients included in diet formulations that enhance the food in some way. Food additives may be nutritional or nonnutritional.

Nutritional additives are the vitamins, minerals, and fats that are incorporated to make the diet nutritionally complete and balanced. Flavorings, texture enhancers, colors, and preservatives are nonnutritional supplements added to enhance the taste or appearance of the food. Laws that regulate pet food require that any additive in pet foods be proven harmless to pets. Many currently used in dog foods are also approved for use in people foods.

Organic food dyes, such as caramel or carotene, and artificial colorings, like iron oxide, provide a consistent appearance or distinguish between various particles in multiparticle foods. Sugar-type additives, like guar gum, gum arabic, xanthan gum, carrageenan, and cellulose flower, are used to give foods a characteristic texture. These ingredients create the aspic or jellylike consistency of certain canned foods, as well as the gravylike sauces. They prompt owners to buy these foods by making dog food look more like something people would want to eat themselves. Texturizers also are designed to make food "feel good" in the dog's mouth.

Some pet foods add flavor enhancers to increase palatability. Palatability is incredibly important, because a food has no benefit unless the dog accepts and eats it. Dogs love the flavor of animal digest, which is enzymatically degraded (predigested) meat or animal organs; animal digest is often sprayed on dry foods to make them taste good to the dog. Canned foods typically are already highly palatable, but some add flavorings, like garlic powder, caramel, or onion powder.

Food additives also include preservatives, which are designed to guard the nutritional quality of foods by slowing or preventing food from degrading (spoiling). Canned diets rarely contain preservatives, because the canning process itself offers the necessary protection. However, dry and semimoist forms of food require preservatives to prevent the breakdown (oxidation) of the nutrients. Oxidation is the reaction of oxygen with other compounds, especially fats, and has been described as a kind of biological rust. Preservatives, also called *antioxidants*, help food taste fresh, protect fat from becoming rancid, and keep essential fatty acids and fat-soluble vitamins at optimal nutrient value.

A variety of natural and synthetic antioxidants is used in commercial pet foods. Chemical preservatives, such as sorbic acid or potassium sorbate, are humectins that hold water and help keep soft-moist products moist and also protect these foods from mold and bacterial growth. The synthetic antioxidants most commonly used in dry pet foods include ethoxyquin, BHT (butylated hydroxytoluene), and BHA (butylated hydroxyanisole).

Ethoxyquin has been used in pet foods since the mid-1950s when five-year efficacy and safety studies were done. Ethoxyquin is considered by many pet-food nutritionists to be the most effective preservative on the market, with BHA and BHT rating fairly close behind. However, recent questions regarding the safety of ethoxyquin have been raised, prompting new studies.

The most recent report concluded that ethoxyquin levels above the current tolerance in dog foods produced *no* adverse effects; however, there remains a concern that safety margins might not be adequate for puppies or nursing bitches. That's because lactating females in the study showed some liver changes, which is thought to be due to their eating two to three times more of these foods than nonnursing dogs eat. Consequently, the FDA's Center for Veterinary Medicine released an August 1997 recommendation that commercial pet-food companies voluntarily lower ethoxyquin levels to half the previous recommendations in complete dog foods. Many pet-food companies had already suspended use of ethoxyquin pending these studies, and further analysis of the preservative is anticipated.

Natural antioxidants are preservatives found in nature and include ascorbic acid (vitamin C) and tocopherols. Tocopherols are chemical compounds collectively referred to as vitamin E. Natural antioxidants are typically used in combinations and potentially provide good preservation but don't tend to last as long as synthetic forms. Foods preserved with mixed tocopherols should usually be used within three to six months of manufacture, or by the product's expiration date.

Food Supplements

A food supplement is anything fed to the dog above and beyond an otherwise complete and balanced diet. Dogs fed homemade diets that may not be adequate in terms of the vitamin and mineral balance, and dogs suffering from certain medical conditions, may benefit from dietary supplementation. Food supplements may be necessary to stimulate a dog's food intake, particularly in hardworking dogs or in bitches nursing a litter, who require higher levels of energy. But always consult a veterinarian before supplementing your dog's diet.

Food supplements range from nutritional components, like vitamins and mineral tablets, to table scraps and commercial treats. When a dog is already eating a complete and balanced diet, food supplements throw the nutrition out of balance. Choose a complete and balanced diet for your dog by learning to READ PET-FOOD LABELS.

Nutrients work together and are needed in the right combinations and amounts; too much can sometimes be as bad as too little. High-quality commercial dog foods are formulated with a safety margin for all the essential nutrients, to compensate for any normal loss through processing or storage and for variations in the needs of individual dogs. Further, offering your dog vitamins or other treats beyond what's required can potentially cause nutritional imbalances and can be dangerous.

For instance, too much dietary calcium can cause bone and cartilage deformities and interferes with absorption of phosphorus, iron, zinc, and copper, which may cause deficiencies of these minerals. Such deficiencies can result in skin disease, reproductive problems, nervous system dysfunction, and impaired immunity.

Feeding excessive amounts of raw liver can cause a calcium deficiency and possibly vitamin A toxicity, resulting in crippling bone disease, weight loss, anorexia, even death. And a deficiency of vitamin D (which is involved in the absorption of calcium) may result in rickets. Vitamins D and E are found in wheat germ, liver, and fish oils, and dogs may relish these treats. Yet too much can cause toxicities that can result in skeletal deformity, reproductive problems, and even calcification of soft tissues. Eating onions or garlic in excess (equal to or greater than 0.5 percent of the dog's body weight) can cause hemolytic ANEMIA that can kill the dog.

Adding raw egg white to the diet can cause a vitamin deficiency. The protein avidin is found in raw egg whites; avidin destroys biotin, one of the B vitamins, and can result in poor growth and hair loss in the biotin-deficient dog. Raw foods are particularly dangerous because they carry parasites and bacteria like SALMONELLA and TOXOPLASMOSIS.

Because dogs are omnivores willing to eat anything, they often beg for and relish scraps from the table. Besides unbalancing the dog's diet, such treats increase your dog's risk for OBESITY, gastrointestinal problems that result in upset tummies with signs like VOMITING or DIARRHEA, or even metabolic problems such as PANCREATITIS. Table scraps should make up no more than 5 to 10 percent of the total amount of food your dog eats and even then should be healthy scraps—that is, vegetables, grains, and fruits along with the occasional meat tidbit—never exclusively fat trimmings. But many veterinarians recommend no table scraps at all.

Cooked bones are never a good choice, as they tend to splinter and can lodge in the dog's mouth or intestinal tract and cause life-threatening blockage (see SWALLOWED OBJECTS). Raw bones splinter less often, but are unsanitary and may break the dog's teeth. And although your dog may relish sweet treats as much as you do, candy of any kind is a no-no and can drastically increase dental problems or even be deadly (see CHOCOLATE TOXICITY and PERIODONTAL DISEASE).

Highly palatable treats like gravy or fat not only compromise the dog's health but can create behavior problems. Unlike people, who require many different foods to achieve nutrient balance, dogs are happy to eat the same commercial diet day in and day out—unless you train them to expect variety. Offering tasty treats or switching back and forth to different highly palatable foods tends to create finicky eaters. Find a complete and balanced diet your dog accepts, and stick to it.

Beware of diet supplements marketed as "natural"; there are few regulations that apply to such products, so approach them with caution. In fact, manufacturers can avoid certain expensive efficacy and safety tests by saying their product is natural. Many times this term is used as a marketing buzzword, because *natural* is often equated with *healthier*. Unfortunately, natural is not necessarily healthy, or even safe; some of the most dangerous poisons are natural. Ask questions of the manufacturer, and if you don't like the answers—or can't get any answers—avoid the product to protect your dog. Rely on the reputation of well-known pet-food companies that have been around for a while and have the nutritional research to back up their claims. And always ask your veterinarian's advice, as some "natural" products may have health benefits for your dog when used under an expert's supervision.

Treating your dog with an occasional healthy snack probably won't cause any problems. Dogs and owners seem to benefit most from the bonding experience of doing something "special" for the dog. A wide variety of commercial dog treats is available, and some are formulated to be complete and balanced so they don't cause nutritional difficulties (other than added calories).

If your dog isn't eating enough, a veterinary exam can rule out possible health problems. Adding one teaspoon of vegetable oil for every eight-ounce cup of dry food may tempt his appetite and also help improve his coat condition. A strong-smelling or flavored top dressing, like warm chicken broth, often prompts dogs to eat up to 10 percent more of the food. However, a better choice for dogs with small appetites and big energy needs is a more energy-dense ration, like a complete and balanced superpremium food. Such diets provide more calories even if the dog eats less volume.

A good way to treat the dog without unbalancing his diet is to reserve a portion of his regular ration. Offer this reserve as special tidbit feedings throughout the day. (See also NUTRITION and FOOD.)

Fracture

A fracture is an injury that results in partial or complete breakage of bone. The skeleton is a collection of bones that form the scaffoldlike structure that gives each dog her shape. Selective breeding has varied the size and shape of the canine skeleton, making the tiny, dome-headed Chihuahua distinctive from the giant, narrow-headed Wolfhound. Despite these differences, all dogs—no matter the breed—remain surprisingly similar beneath the fur, with about 319 separate bones making up the average canine skeleton.

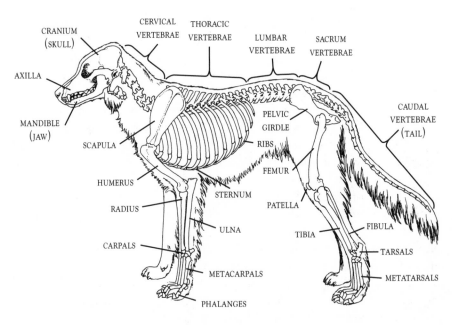

Skeleton

FRACTURES
SYMPTOMS
Floppy, "unhinged" legs or tail; limping; swelling; exposed bones; reluctance or inability to move
HOME CARE
Immobilize with temporary splint if possible, then get dog to the vet
VET CARE
Diagnosis with X ray; application of casts, surgical plating, wire, or pinning; sometimes antibiotic therapy; occasionally amputation
PREVENTION
Keep dogs away from car accidents by confining to yard or leash; remain vigilant to slamming doors, falls, or dog jumping from your arms, etc.

Fractures most typically are caused by trauma. Bones can withstand only small amounts of stress without fracturing. Other times, disease may weaken the bone until only minor stress results in damage.

Fractures are commonly categorized as fatigue fractures, pathologic fractures, or traumatic fractures. Fatigue fractures result from ongoing stress to a bone; they are not common in dogs, but may occur in dogs that do repetitive strenuous work. Illnesses like CANCER or HYPERPARATHYROIDISM may weaken individual bones or the entire skeleton and result in pathologic fractures. The disease as well as the fracture must be treated in these instances. The growing bones of puppies tend to crack or split rather than break; these fractures are called *greenstick fractures*. Elderly dogs may develop brittle bones that break more easily than healthy adult dogs' bones.

Dogs most commonly suffer traumatic fractures, which usually result from being hit by cars. But a broken bone is often only one part of a litany of other injuries. A fracture is painful, but conditions like BLEEDING and SHOCK may be life-threatening and must take precedence before anything else. In these instances your dog should see a veterinarian as soon as possible.

A complete break in the bone is classified by whether or not the skin is breached. It's called a *closed fracture* when the skin is not broken; when bone protrudes from the skin, it's termed a *compound*, or *open, fracture*. Such injuries increase the risk for tissue or bone infections, which are painful and can result in limb loss or even death.

Although any bone may be broken, some are more susceptible to fracture than others. The dog's pelvis is broken the most often. The femur (thigh bone) is the next most common fracture site. The lower bones of the hind legs (tibia/fibula) and the forelegs (radius/ulna/humerus) also commonly suffer fractures—especially when dogs jump from high surfaces.

Dogs can also suffer fractures of the skull, which could cause brain injury or concussion. A broken palate (roof of the mouth) or jaw (mandible) are common injuries. Severe damage including paralysis may result from spinal fractures, and broken ribs may puncture internal organs and threaten the dog's life. Crushing injuries may occur when a tail is caught beneath a chair or shut in a door.

There may be blood present with compound fractures, which also have the bone exposed. Closed fractures may be more difficult to detect. Dogs suffering from a fracture often hold the affected limb off the ground at an odd angle or may limp. The leg or tail may move or hang disjointedly. The injured area may be swollen. Dogs with pelvic fractures often have trouble standing or supporting their weight and may walk with a wobbly gait in their hind limbs. Some dogs will simply refuse to move.

If you suspect your dog has suffered a broken bone, limit his movement as much as possible. Avoid touching or manipulating the affected area. Broken bone is sharp, and fooling with the injury may punch bone through skin or damage veins, arteries, internal tissues, organs, or nerves. Handle your dog carefully to prevent further injuries to him, or to yourself (see RESTRAINT).

For pelvic injuries—and especially suspected back fractures—limit the dog's movement as much as possible. Ideally, the dog should be placed on a rigid surface for transport to the veterinarian. For small dogs, a cookie sheet, TV tray, or even the flat blade of a snow shovel may work; a large board or something like an ironing board may be better for a larger dog. If rigid material of an appropriate size isn't available, use a sheet or blanket. Place the conveyance on the ground next to the dog and carefully slide—don't lift—her onto it. For large dogs, you'll need a person at the head end and one at the tail end (and possibly, a person in the middle) to lift the dog all in one motion. With fabric carriers, try to keep the blanket taut and as level as possible during transport. Once the dog is in the car, get her to the emergency room as soon as possible and let your veterinarian get the dog out of your car. He'll have the appropriate dog-size stretcher.

When the dog has an open fracture, protect the wound by loosely covering it with sterile gauze or a clean towel. Temporary splints are helpful for immobilizing fractures of the leg below the elbow or knee. The splint must extend beyond the joints both above and below the injury to be effective. With fractures above the elbow or of the thigh, use a towel or sheet to wrap and hold the limb snugly against the body.

A temporary splint may be fashioned from almost any long, rigid material. A rolled length of newspaper, the cardboard cylinder from paper towels, even a pair of wooden cooking spoons may work. Split cardboard tubes so the injured limb can be laid inside. Use a wooden spoon (or a tightly rolled newspaper) on the inside and one on the outside of the leg, and wrap with gauze, a towel, or even panty hose or a necktie. A simple hand towel by itself wrapped about the limb may be sufficient, or use tape over the gauze, towel, or cardboard to hold it in place. Once the limb is immobilized, get your dog veterinary attention as soon as possible.

Fractures may be obvious, but more often require specific diagnostic procedures to determine the best procedure for repair. Veterinarians palpate (feel) the injury and use X RAYS. Sedation or anesthesia may be required to take the X rays and treat your dog. Treatment consists of setting the fracture (called *reduction*). A range of procedures is available to position bone appropriately so that healing will take place. The type of fixation depends on the kind of fracture, its location, the individual dog, and owner compliance.

Greenstick fractures and breaks in the midportion of the legs may be sufficiently treated with a simple splint or cast. This method has the greatest success when bone fragments fit back together easily. However, fractures near a joint, or bones with multiple fractures, are more difficult to fix.

Complicated fractures may require intramedullary pinning, which is the insertion of a stainless-steel rod that strings the pieces back together like threading a needle. Small external metal pins may be inserted through the skin and muscle and into the bone, with the visible portions outside fixed to a single connecting bar that holds everything in place. Metal plates and wire may be required to surgically fix bone fragments back into place, so that healing can begin. The hardware may become a permanent part of the dog or may be removed after the fracture heals.

Canine bones heal relatively quickly and easily, especially those of growing puppies. Pelvic fractures may heal by themselves even when multiple fractures are present, although sometimes surgery must repair the damage when the pelvis is too unstable. In either case, the dog's mobility must be restricted, though, so that new bone called *callus* forms across the fracture site and helps stabilize it. Hard bone formation follows shortly, with an eventual return to normal function.

Dogs that fracture the ball-and-socket formation of the hip may regain partial to full limb function within three to five weeks simply by resting the affected leg. In some instances, the damaged femoral head and/or neck are surgically removed, and the body creates a new false joint out of tissue that functions like the original.

Sometimes a fracture refuses to heal; this often occurs with broken tails or toes, and AMPUTATION may be necessary. Dogs rarely seem to miss toes or tails, and many do quite well when they have lost a leg.

Unsupervised outdoor dogs are at highest risk for fractures from car accidents. But indoor injuries can also result in fractures when the dog or puppy falls from an owner's arms or lands wrong after jumping on or off furniture. Most tail and paw injuries can be prevented by remaining aware of rocking chairs and slamming doors that can crush legs or tails.

Frostbite

This term refers to partial or complete freezing of the extremities of the body. Dogs most typically suffer frostbite on their ears, toes, scrotum, and tail.

Like our own, a dog's body is composed of more than 90 percent water. Freezing causes great damage because water expands when frozen, rupturing the integrity of the living cells and destroying tissue. Frostbite causes severe tissue damage, infection, and even loss of body parts.

Cases of frostbite are categorized from mild to severe. Mild frostbite turns the affected area white and pale; then, as the area rewarms and blood circulation returns, the injury reddens and may swell. Severe frostbite looks very similar to BURNS. The affected area first blisters, then peels, and dead skin eventually sloughs off.

Treatment consists of rewarming the frozen area. First aid at home is extremely important to minimize damage. Do not massage or rub the area, and don't apply snow or ice; that will further damage the tissues and make recovery more difficult. To thaw frozen tissue safely, soak in warm 104- to 108-degree water for fifteen to twenty minutes until the skin becomes pink. Typically, the area will begin to weep serum, and as feeling returns, the dog will feel PAIN. Apply a triple-antibiotic ointment, like Neosporin, to the affected area. Restrain the dog from licking or biting the area (see ELIZABETHAN COLLAR).

FROSTBITE	
SYMPTOMS	
Initially very pale to white flesh on affected areas, commonly the ear tips, nose, testicles, tail, and toes; areas then swell, turn red, and may blister; finally, tissue peels and may fall off	
HOME CARE	
Soak affected white areas in 104-degree water for fifteen to twenty minutes until tissue is flushed, then apply antiseptic ointment like Neomycin; veterinarian must evaluate damage	
VET CARE	
Antibiotics; pain medication; possible amputation of affected tissue	
PREVENTION	
Confine dogs indoors during cold weather; provide outdoor shelter from wind, wet, and cold	

It may be difficult to evaluate the extent of the injury until a few days have passed. Often, an area that appears only mildly affected on initial examination later exhibits severe damage. *Frostbite should always be evaluated and monitored by a veterinarian.* Prescription antibiotics and pain medication may be necessary, and severe cases may require surgery to remove damaged or dead tissue. Healing may take several weeks. Dogs that have suffered frostbite in the past are prone to recurrence.

Prevent frostbite by confining your dog indoors during cold weather. Outdoor dogs require protection from the weather; a warm, dry shelter away from the wind is best. (See also HYPOTHERMIA.)

Fungus

A fungus is a kind of primitive plant that lacks energy-producing chlorophyll and instead subsists as a parasite. The term *fungus* refers to molds, mushrooms, and yeast; all function to promote decay and decomposition of organic matter.

A variety of fungi are able to produce mild to serious disease in dogs. The most common types affect the skin or mucous membranes and tend to be self-limiting problems that are relatively easy to treat. RINGWORM is the most common example.

Candidiasis is a relatively uncommon yeast infection of the mucous membranes in the mouth, genitals, and respiratory tract. Signs of localized infection are ULCERS, moist DERMATITIS, or a purulent white discharge from the genital tract. Candidiasis is diagnosed by culturing the organism or by finding the organism during microscopic examination of a skin scraping or tissue sample. Localized infections are typically treated with topical antifungal medications.

Occasionally, the infection spreads throughout the body, resulting in a variety of signs from fever and generalized pain, to abscesses and lymph node enlargement. Whole-body or systemic disease caused by fungus is quite rare in dogs and most commonly affects dogs with IMMUNE SYSTEM defects. These organisms may be resistant to treatment and can be life-threatening to the host. Prognosis for this form of fungal infection isn't good.

Blastomycosis, coccidioidomycosis, cryptococcosis, and histoplasmosis are four other kinds of systemic fungal diseases that can affect dogs. Each is found in specific geographic regions (detailed below). In each, the organism is inhaled by the dog, and in most cases, this prompts a strong immune response that keeps the dog healthy and protected from infection. In rare instances, the dog succumbs to infection, and the organism spreads from the lungs throughout the body, infecting the organs and tissues. Diagnosis is made by microscopic examination of affected tissues that identifies the organism.

FUNGUS

	BLASTOMYCOSIS	COCCIDIOIDOMYCOSIS	CRYPTOCOCCOSIS	HISTOPLASMOSIS	CANDIDIASIS
SYMPTOMS	Coughing; labored breathing; pneumonia; weight loss; refusal to eat	Mild flulike signs; sometimes progression to cough and fever; refusal to eat; lethargy; weight loss; lameness; draining sores; neurological signs	Neurologic signs including head tilt, rapid eye movement, circling, paralysis, seizures	Mild to severe coughing, sometimes with blood; lethargy; fever; watery to bloody diarrhea; anemia	Ulcers; moist, sore skin; white discharge from genitals
HOME CARE	None	None	None	None	None
VET CARE	Systemic antifungal medication	Systemic antifungal medication	Systemic antifungal medication	Systemic antifungal medication	Topical antifungal medication
PREVENTION	Prevent dog's access to bird droppings; remain vigilant for signs; seek prompt treatment	Prevent dog's access to bird droppings; remain vigilant for signs; seek prompt treatment	Prevent dog's access to bird droppings; remain vigilant for signs; seek prompt treatment	Prevent dog's access to bird droppings; remain vigilant for signs; seek prompt treatment	None

Systemic illness can be difficult to treat and isn't always successful, and dogs diagnosed with systemic fungal disease may ultimately be euthanized. When treated, prolonged systemic antifungal therapy is required, which also can cause side effects in the dog. The medication can have adverse affects on the kidneys and liver, with side effects that include DIARRHEA, VOMITING, kidney failure, and ANEMIA.

Blastomyces dermatitidis causes blastomycosis and is found in moist, shaded soil rich in rotting organic matter like bird droppings. The organism is most prevalent along the Ohio/Mississippi river valley, north-central states, and mid-Atlantic seaboard. Young male dogs, often hunting breeds, are most often affected. Infection causes skin, eye (see UVEITIS), and respiratory disease and may result in neurological signs. The most common signs are coughing, labored breathing, PENUMONIA, weight loss, and ANOREXIA. Prognosis is guarded, and treatment takes weeks to months of aggressive therapy.

Coccidioides immitis is the organism that causes coccidioidomycosis, also called *valley fever*. It is found in the same regions where the creosote bush thrives: in the dry soil of the southwest, from California to Texas. Most cases cause only mild flulike signs, but at other times, infection spreads beyond the lungs into the bones and joints, eyes, kidneys, liver, and even the spinal cord and brain. Signs include chronic harsh cough and fever, anorexia, lethargy, weight loss, lameness, joint enlargement, draining tracts over infected bones, and neurological signs. Treatment takes six to twelve months and can be successful, but lifetime therapy may be required.

Cryptococcus neoformans causes cryptococcosis, a yeastlike fungus that prefers tissues of the central nervous system. It is most commonly found in pigeon droppings. Cryptococcosis is uncommon in dogs, but when it occurs, lower respiratory signs are most common. Other signs may include neurologic involvement such as head tilt, rapid eye movement, circling, varying degrees of paralysis, disorientation, incoordination, and seizures. Dogs may exhibit dilated pupils and blindness. Diagnosis can be made from examination of nasal discharge, skin scrapings, or biopsy. Treatment is difficult, but can be effective.

The soil fungus *Histoplasma capsulatum* causes histoplasmosis and is found most commonly in the Ohio, Mississippi, and Missouri river valleys. The organism likes to grow in bird, chicken, and bat droppings. Signs of infection are usually mild coughing, lethargy, and fever, with watery to bloody diarrhea, and mucus in the stool; more severe disease may include anemia, chronic cough, and coughing up of blood. A minimum of four to six months of systemic antifungal therapy is required.

Keeping a dog in optimum health is the best prevention. Additionally, prevent dogs from access to bird droppings.

Geriatric Dog

Geriatric refers to the condition of aging, which is a gradual decline in the effective functioning of the body. Dogs age at different rates, and this is dependent to a large degree upon an individual animal's genetics. Big dogs tend to age more quickly than small dogs. Breeds like Great Danes are elderly at age seven; German Shepherd Dogs, at nine to ten years of age; medium-sized dogs, at ten to twelve years; and smaller breeds, like Toy Poodles and Yorkshire Terriers, at fourteen to sixteen years old. But just like their owners, signs of aging are extremely variable. The better care a dog receives throughout his life, the longer he can be expected to live.

STRAY and FERAL dogs that don't have these benefits rarely live to experience geriatrics; they die early and young, usually from a combination of disease, malnutrition, and trauma. But pet dogs are living longer, healthier lives than ever before, due in great part to advances in canine nutrition and medicine.

However, canine longevity means owners are faced with more geriatric issues than ever before. Many parallel the health issues that people can expect as they age. Elderly dogs are less active, sleep more, and may become forgetful. They aren't able to withstand extremes of temperature as well as youthful dogs can. They lose muscle and may become unsteady on their feet or unable to sustain the activities of their youth. Typically, the thighs and forelimbs become thinner, while the neck and body thicken, and the abdomen sags; exertion may result in tremors of fatigue. Joint pain from ARTHRITIS is a common complaint and often slows the dog down or results in a short temper. Like a set-in-his-ways human, the oldster canine gets cranky and less tolerant of changes in routine.

AGE COMPARISON

Each dog ages differently. The rate at which a dog ages depends on his lifestyle, health status, the care he receives early on and throughout his life, and even his genetics. Small dogs live longer than large dogs. A dog's maturity at one year old is roughly equivalent to a young human adolescent. Emotional and physical maturity quickly follow.

AGE OF SMALL DOG	AGE OF MEDIUM DOG	AGE OF LARGE DOG	AGE OF GIANT DOG	HUMAN AGE
1	1	1	1	15
2				18
3	2	2	2	24
4				29
5	3	3	3	34
6	4			38
7	5	4	4	42
8	6	5		46
9	7	6	5	50
10	8	7		54
11	9		6	58
12		8		62
13	10			66
14		9	7	70
15	11			74
16				78
17	12	10	8	82

g

The dog's senses tend to dull with age, which can be upsetting to your pet when he can't see, smell, or hear the way he used to. Most old dogs suffer some degree of dental problems, which can be painful (see PERIODONTAL DISEASE). Senior dogs tend to eat less and may lose weight due to PAIN when eating or due to other problems; this is a sign that something is wrong, and your pet should be checked by the veterinarian. But geriatric dogs usually suffer from OBESITY from eating more than they need and exercising less, and in fact, obesity tends to shorten the life span.

Old dogs may have problems with irregularity (see CONSTIPATION), may suffer from senility, and often their house-training becomes less reliable. The skin loses elasticity and tends toward dryness when oil-producing glands slow down. When activity declines, so does the normal wear of TOENAILS, which may seem to grow faster. Special attention to your aging dog's grooming helps him look and feel healthier.

The geriatric dog's health becomes more fragile because the immune system's competence also fades with age. Old dogs get sicker quicker and recover more slowly than healthy young dogs. It is vital to provide prompt veterinary attention to keep old dogs healthy.

Recognize that dogs age more rapidly than humans; after age three, each canine year is roughly equivalent to four human years. More frequent veterinary evaluations are therefore particularly important for the aging dog; twice a year after age eight is a good goal. Canine geriatric medicine attempts to reduce physical discomfort and emotional stress, as well as slow the signs of aging as much as possible. Often, special NUTRITIONAL concerns must be addressed.

A number of diseases and conditions typically affect geriatric canines. Renal failure is probably the most common cause of death in aged dogs (see KIDNEY DISEASE). Kidneys just seem to wear out more quickly than other organs. HEART DISEASE is another consequence of canine aging, because the muscle tends to weaken after a lifetime of use. CYSTITIS and urinary-tract infections also occur frequently in aging dogs. The risk of CANCER increases as the dog ages. CATARACTS are very common in old dogs, and GLAUCOMA or DRY EYE may also develop with age. Intact male dogs may develop PROSTATE INFECTION. And because of a compromised immune system, geriatric dogs may suffer a wide range of opportunistic infections. Elderly dogs may not tolerate hospitalization that separates them from their owners very well, though, and in these cases your veterinarian may show you how to treat your dog at home.

Proper nutrition is vital to the old dog's health. "Mature" or "senior" formulations of commercial diets are available for the special needs of older dogs. In most animals, energy requirements decrease with age, and since this is thought to be true in dogs, most commercial canine geriatric rations are reduced in calories. Often, elderly dogs do best on food that's easily digested and/or chewed.

Most dogs can live comfortably and happily into old age, but some environmental modifications may help. If stair steps are a problem, provide a ramp to make familiar haunts more accessible. Move sleeping quarters to a warm, cozy spot. Keep your dog warm when he accompanies you on outings by perhaps providing him with a sweater. Daily grooming keeps your dog looking and feeling good and also provides an opportunity to find problems early. Give your old dog lots of attention and understanding; he's given you the best times of your life, and you can now be his comfort and friend during his golden years. Encouraging moderate exercise will keep him fit and limber longer and make the last years of his life more comfortable and enjoyable for you both.

Giardiasis

This is an illness caused by a protozoan of the *Giardia* species, a single-cell organism that parasitizes the small intestine. Canine infection is becoming more common and typically affects pups.

The organism compromises the dog's ability to properly process food. Signs of infection are DIARRHEA sometimes mixed with mucus and blood. Other times the stool may simply be soft and light colored, or even normal-appearing, but the dog often develops a poor hair coat and the tummy swells from gas. Infected dogs may have trouble gaining or maintaining weight.

The infective cyst stage of the organism lives in the environment, most usually in standing water. Dogs tend to contract the parasite by drinking from mud puddles or other contaminated water sources. The disease is also spread through contact with infected feces.

Diagnosis is made by finding the protozoan during microscopic examination of stool samples. However, infected dogs pass the organism only intermittently, and a fresh stool sample may be negative even when giardia are present. Repeated tests are often necessary before the tiny parasite is detected. Some dogs may not show signs of illness themselves, yet are infected and spread the parasite.

Giardia can be treated with the prescription drug Flagyl (metronidazole) to kill the parasite. This drug can injure unborn puppies, however, so medication such as albendazole may be a safer option for treating pregnant dogs. Keeping the yard picked up and restricting your dog's access to unsanitary water helps prevent the chance of infection.

GIARDIASIS

SYMPTOMS
Soft stools; poor hair coat; swollen abdomen; trouble gaining or maintaining weight

HOME CARE
None

VET CARE
Treatment with drug to kill parasite

PREVENTION
Keep yard clean; restrict access to mud puddles or other unsanitary water sources; vaccinate as recommended

Waterborne diarrheal disease in humans is also commonly caused by *Giardia* (see ZOONOSIS); however, it's not known if the same kind of organism affecting dogs causes the disease in people. Reasonable hygiene practices—washing hands after cleaning up after puppies—prevents the possibility of contracting the infection from a pet. Researchers at the University of Calgary (Alberta, Canada) have developed a new protective vaccination against *Giardia* infection in puppies. Ask your vet if the vaccine is right for your pet.

Gingivitis

This refers to an inflammation of the gums. The tissue that surrounds the dog's teeth becomes red and may be tender or bleed when hard food is chewed. Gingivitis is an early sign of dental disease (see PERIODONTAL DISEASE).

Glaucoma

Increased pressure inside the eyeball is referred to as *glaucoma*. It causes damage to the retina and optic nerve (see EYES), which results in blindness if not treated in time.

Any dog may be stricken with glaucoma, but it's more common in some dogs than in others. Glaucoma is categorized as either primary or secondary. Primary glaucoma arises spontaneously due to congenital or inherited conditions. It's an inherited defect in Beagles and also commonly affects Cocker Spaniels and Basset Hounds.

Secondary glaucoma results from an injury or disease. Most often, the condition develops due to trauma that causes bleeding inside the eye or that displaces the lens. Conditions like UVEITIS or tumors that cause intraocular inflammation also may result in glaucoma.

Directly behind the cornea, the front portion of the eye is filled with aqueous humor, which is manufactured by a membrane called the *ciliary epithelium*. This specialized liquid holds the internal structures in place, and the fluid level is constant, but not static. It drains out, but at the same time is replaced with fresh by the membrane. The excess fluid drains through the iridocorneal angle where the cornea and iris meet. Anything that interferes with the drainage creates a rise in pressure due to the increased liquid inside the eyeball; this can result in glaucoma.

In glaucoma, the sphere of the eye keeps filling, and it swells when the drain is plugged and the fluid can't escape. The condition is excruciating for

GLAUCOMA

SYMPTOMS
Painful eye with squinting; pawing at the eye; tearing; bloodshot or cloudy-looking eye; swelling of the eyeball; dilated nonresponsive pupil

HOME CARE
None

VET CARE
Medications to control pressure; pain medications; possibly surgery; sometimes removal of affected eye

PREVENTION
None

g

the dog. The increasing pressure destroys his vision by pushing the internal structures out of position.

Signs of glaucoma may occur suddenly, or they may appear gradually and be quite subtle. Often, signs aren't noticed until they become severe, at which time it may be too late to save the dog's vision. High intraocular pressure can permanently damage the eye within only a few days, and suspected glaucoma should be considered an *emergency*, with veterinary evaluation sought immediately. The painful eye produces excess tears, is cloudy or bloodshot, and the dog squints or paws at the eyeball, which eventually swells. Finally, the dilated pupil no longer responds to light.

Diagnosis is made using a Schiotz tonometer, an instrument that measures pressure inside the eye. Eyedrops are administered so that the dog feels no discomfort, and then the veterinarian gently balances the instrument on the cornea. A mercury level on the tonometer measures the pressure within the eye.

In secondary glaucoma, the condition may be reversible if inflammation is caught early. Eyedrops help relieve pain and contract the pupil, steroids relieve inflammation, and intravenous and oral medications promote water transfer and decrease the production of fluid within the eye. However, medications aren't effective for long-term control; when glaucoma is primary in origin, surgery may remove the membrane that produces the fluid.

When damage is severe or the cause cannot be successfully treated, glaucoma will result in blindness. In some instances, medication doesn't relieve the dog's pain, and removing the eye (enucleation) is necessary. Usually, the eyelid is sewn closed over the empty socket. Sometimes a prosthetic eye replaces the real one for cosmetic reasons. Yet dogs tend to compensate admirably with only one eye; because dogs tend to rely more on hearing and scent for orientation, blind dogs do very well in familiar surroundings. And when the source of their pain is removed, dogs feel and act better almost immediately.

Grass, Eating

Dogs are omnivores, which means they can eat nearly anything, including vegetables or fruits. Wild canids like coyotes typically eat vegetable matter found in the stomach and intestines of prey animals, but may also eat roots, grasses, and even fruit. Our dogs often beg for and enjoy snacks of raw vegetables, like lettuce, green beans, and carrots.

Most pet dogs occasionally eat grass, which may be used as a natural emetic to stimulate VOMITING when the dog feels unwell. However, grass eating does not always result in vomiting; some dogs may simply relish the flavor or texture. Some speculation exists that grass grazing may provide trace elements of vitamins.

Indoor dogs may indulge their urge to graze by nibbling houseplants which, depending on the plant, may be dangerous (see POISON). Occasional grass eating isn't a cause for concern. However, if grazing becomes a habit, and especially if grass eating prompts vomiting more than two days in a row, your dog should be examined by a veterinarian to rule out a health problem.

Grooming

Grooming refers to the proper cleaning and conditioning of the body. Grooming keeps your dog looking and feeling good; it requires attention to the HAIR coat, EARS, EYES, TOENAILS, ANAL GLANDS, and TEETH. Grooming not only addresses the dog's physical needs, but promotes bonding between the owner and pet because the contact and attention simply feel good (see TOUCH).

Grooming promotes healthy SKIN. The sebaceous glands at the base of each hair root secrete an oily substance, called *sebum*, which is spread over the fur during grooming. Sebum helps waterproof the fur and gives the hair coat its healthy sheen. Grooming also removes loose hair that can tangle the fur and produce painful mats.

A healthy coat is not only attractive, it's the dog's first line of defense against injury. Fur lies in loose protective layers that shield skin from damage and provide insulation from temperature extremes. A properly groomed coat is weather-resistant and sheds rain, and it keeps the dog warm in the winter and cool in the summer. A dog's SWEAT GLANDS are not particularly effective for cooling—he primarily uses PANTING to cool off—and the coat must remain free of mats to allow air to pass between the hairs when it's hot. Healthy fur traps warm air next to the skin when it's cold.

Dogs attend to some grooming themselves. They scratch with rear toenails; use their teeth to nibble burrs, dirt, or parasites from their fur (see FLEAS, TICKS, and LICE); and clean their genitals by licking. Some breeds are more fastidious than others. For instance, the Basenji licks himself all over like a cat to keep clean. Dogs may also become overly enthusiastic in licking or nibbling and develop HOT SPOTS, lick granulomas, or HAIR LOSS. For the most part, dogs must rely on the owner for proper grooming care.

Grooming Your Dog: The length and type of coat varies from breed to breed. Dogs with smooth, short hair require less coat care than longer-furred breeds, but every dog benefits from regular grooming attention. Besides making your dog look and feel good, grooming provides an excellent opportunity to examine your dog for health problems.

Begin grooming your dog during puppyhood, so he'll learn to anticipate and enjoy the attention. Even reluctant dogs accept grooming when the sessions are kept brief. There's no rule that says you must groom the whole dog at one time, so break off the session if it becomes a struggle, and finish later. Make grooming as enjoyable for you both as possible by being prepared. Have all your supplies and equipment close at hand, stop before your dog becomes antsy, and then reward his patience with a treat or game.

Big dogs can be groomed on the ground as you kneel beside them; medium to small dogs should be placed on a table at waist level, which helps confine their movements. Your dog may accept grooming better if lightly restrained by a second pair of hands while you handle the comb and/or brush. Many dogs, though, love the sensation of being brushed and will beg you to go on and on.

A wide variety of tools is available, especially for show grooming. A professional groomer or breed expert can best guide you regarding the extravagant show trims of curly or woolly-coated dog breeds, like Poodles. But even if your dog isn't a show contestant, you should learn how to keep the fur clean and prevent painful mats.

Teflon-coated combs are best, because they don't break or pull the fur and they reduce static-electricity shocks that turn many dogs off to grooming. Combs are designed with fine, medium, and coarse teeth, which is the amount of space between the tines. The widest-toothed comb is best for long, thick fur, while fine-tooth combs work well on dogs with short fur.

Brushes also come in many styles. Dogs with short fur can get by with a rubber curry brush that smoothes the coat and pulls off dead hair. A slicker brush has bent wire bristles set close together in a rubber pad, and is designed

g

Show dogs need special grooming *(Photo credit: Amy D. Shojai)*

to remove mats and shed fur; they come in small, medium, and large for different size dogs. The pin brush, with long, rounded, stainless steel or chrome-plated pins, works well on long, thick coats. A pin palm brush has round-tipped pins set in an oval rubber pad and is designed for brushing the face and leg fringes of terriers. The bristle brush has natural and/or nylon bristles for smoothing the coat of short, medium, or long coats. There are also electric clippers, stripping knives, and other specialized grooming equipment for specific coat situations.

There are five basic coat types, and care is slightly different with each. *Long fur with undercoat* includes breeds like Collies and German Shepherd Dogs and requires combing two or three times weekly, followed by brushing. *Nonshedding curly coat* includes the Poodles and Bedlington Terriers; their fur grows continuously and must be trimmed with electric clippers about every two months and combed weekly in between. *Silky coat* breeds include the Afghan Hound, Lhasa Apso, Maltese, Pekingese, setters, and spaniels. They may require daily combing and brushing to prevent matting. *Smooth coat* dogs include the Boxer, Rottweiler, and Greyhound. Their fur can be maintained with a comb and/or bristle brush, and very short coats may need only a curry brush or chamois cloth. Slip an old pair of panty hose over your hand and stroke the dog with that; it works as well as expensive grooming equipment to polish the fur. *Wiry coat* dog breeds include most terriers and the Schnauzer. These breeds need weekly combing. They may also require plucking about four times a year, which removes the dead hairs from tight, wiry coats; a professional groomer can show you how.

For routine care, always begin by allowing your dog to sniff and investigate the grooming tools, especially if the experience is new to him. Start with petting, or finger-combing, your dog, to familiarize yourself with the contours of his body and discover any problem areas, like mats, ahead of time. Initially comb or brush with short, light strokes in the direction the fur grows. Thick, long fur needs to be combed before brushing; comb through the surface first, then work your way deeper until you're combing clear to the skin. Always be careful not to press too hard, though, or you risk hurting tender skin.

Create a grooming ritual that's always the same, so your dog knows what to expect. Groom him in the same time and place and always finish with something pleasant like a game or treat, so he'll equate the experience as positive.

Begin by grooming each side of his face, progress to his throat and neck, then move to the sides of his body. The backbone and nipples are tender areas, so use a light stroke in these areas. Don't forget the tail, especially the underside. Dogs generally let you know what they like by moaning with enjoyment; they particularly like having their chest and tummy brushed. Pay attention to the flanks inside and out.

When old, dead fur falls out and is caught in long outer hairs, painful knots develop. These mats often form during spring and fall SHEDDING, but can be a problem year-round in silky-coated dogs. Problem areas are the

Comb long hair to detangle
(Photo credit: Amy D. Shojai)

Brush to smooth the coat
(Photo credit: Amy D. Shojai)

"armpit" regions of all four legs, behind the ears, and beneath the tail. Regular grooming can prevent mats from developing. Minor mats may be teased out with a coarse-toothed comb, starting at the very tips and slowly working deeper. Don't use scissors; inevitably, you'll also cut the skin. A badly matted coat may require electric clippers and is best addressed by a professional.

Clipping Your Dog's Nails: Most active dogs allowed to run outside wear the nails to a manageable length naturally and may not need frequent trimming. However, dogs that spend most of their time inside often require monthly nail attention. The toenails of some dog breeds, like the Chihuahua, seem to grow quickly and may need more frequent trims.

Overgrown nails tend to curl, can become caught in bedding and carpets, and may split or tear. Keeping the toenails trimmed is healthier for the pet and helps reduce inappropriate digging some dogs are prone to indulge in. Dew-claws on the inside of the lower leg need particular attention since they never contact the ground.

A variety of commercial nail trimmers are available from your veterinar-

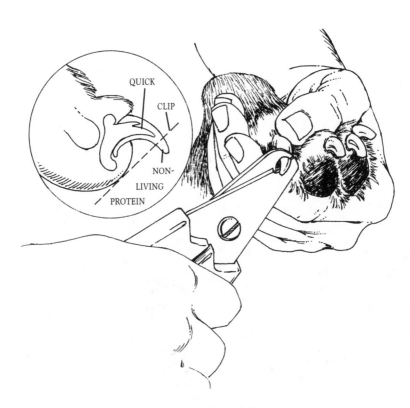

Clipping dog's nails

ian, pet-supply store, or mail-order catalog. They are typically either scissor-action or guillotine-type clippers designed to cut the dog's toenails at the proper angle without splitting or crushing the nail. The clippers you choose must be sharp, and you must be comfortable using them. Dog nails may also need to be filed after trimming. Use a human emery board or a nail file available from a pet-supply store to smooth the edges and keep them from getting caught in the carpet.

It's helpful to regularly handle your puppy's paws and trim just the tip of his nails, even if he doesn't need it. This gets him used to the idea. What he learns to accept as a puppy is more easily endured as an adult. This is particularly helpful with large-breed dogs that can be handled more easily while puppy size.

All four feet don't have to be done in the same session. If you're having difficulty getting the job done, finish the other toes later. It's helpful to have two pairs of hands during nail trimming; ask someone else to restrain and steady the dog while you wield the clippers (see RESTRAINT). A wiggling dog makes it more likely you'll "quick" the nails, or cut into the living vessels that feed the nail bed, causing them to bleed. Also take care not to catch the fur in the clippers. This is uncomfortable for your dog, distressing for you, and will make you both reluctant to try again in the future.

Nails at their longest should just clear the ground when the dog is standing. If you hear him clicking over the linoleum like a tap dancer, he needs a trim. Overgrown nails cause the foot to spread or splay, and can even curl and grow back into the dog's flesh.

When the nails are white or clear, the pink quick is visible and makes it easy to avoid the danger zone. Clip just outside the pink line showing in white nails. However, dog toenails are often dark or opaque, and the quick can't be seen. Rather than trimming blind and taking too much, clip off only the tips—the hooklike portion that turns down. This is especially important if the nail has been allowed to overgrow, because the quick will grow further down, too. Tipping the nails will then prompt the quick to draw back up, so you can trim a little more each week until reaching the proper length. Don't forget the dewclaws, the extra "toe" that some dogs have high on the inside of their legs. Dewclaws are often removed by the veterinarian soon after a puppy is born (except in the Briard and Great Pyrenees breeds, which call for this in the standard). If you do happen to quick a nail, use a styptic pencil or cornstarch, and apply direct pressure to stop the bleeding. You can also rake the claw through a bar of soap.

Always reward your dog for enduring a nail trim. Tell him what a good dog he is, and engage him in a game to show how pleased you are. Dogs like to please us, and consistent positive reinforcement helps make future sessions less traumatic.

Bathing Your Dog: Dogs tend to be bathed more often than is necessary. Excessive baths can strip natural oils from the coat and dry the skin. Unless they get quite grubby or are show animals, most dogs that are regularly groomed shouldn't need a bath more than one to four times a year, depending on coat type.

Puppies shouldn't be bathed until they are at least four weeks old. Old or sick dogs can be stressed by bathing. Puppies and GERIATRIC DOGS have trouble regulating body temperature and can become chilled and easily develop PNEU-MONIA. If your dog is in one of these categories, consult with your veterinarian before bathing your animal.

Poodle-type coats require the most bath time and should be washed with each trim—about every two months. Silky and wiry coats do well with four baths a year. German Shepherd Dogs and similarly coated dogs need a bath a couple of times a year; spring and fall is good, following their normal shed. Smooth-coated pets, like Rottweilers, may need a bath only once a year, and then only if they get smelly or dingy-looking.

Assemble all the supplies you need beforehand. Be sure there are no mats by thoroughly combing and brushing your dog; water turns mats into solid masses impossible to remove without electric clippers. Bathe large to medium dogs in the bathtub, or if the day is warm, the garden hose in the backyard or patio may be appropriate. A waist-high sink works well for small dogs and is easier on your knees.

Use only shampoos approved for pets. People products—even human baby shampoo—are much too harsh and will dry the dog's skin and possibly cause allergic reactions. *Do not use dishwashing soap, laundry detergent, turpentine, gasoline, kerosene, or other household cleaners or chemicals; they can be toxic to your dog.* Should your dog get paint, tar, or tree sap in his coat, it's best trimmed out with electric clippers. If you don't want to do this, try soaking the area in vegetable or mineral oil for twenty-four hours, then wash out with dog shampoo. Some sticky substances, like chewing gum, may be removed by rubbing peanut butter into the mass, and then washing it out. Strong odors or toxins may need specific attention (see POISON and SKUNK ENCOUNTERS).

Dogs object to baths when they're frightened, so prepare ahead of time out of his sight. You'll need dog shampoo, mineral oil, cotton balls, a washcloth, and towels. The bigger the dog, the more towels you'll need. Place everything near your sink, tub, or patio within easy reach. When bathing indoors, the area should be warm and draft-free. Be sure to push shower curtains and any breakables that could spook your dog out of the way. If you're container-bathing, fill the tub or sink with dog-temperature water (about 102 degrees) before you bring in the victim—er, your pet. He won't enjoy having to watch the preparations beforehand.

It's easier to bathe your dog when two hands are free. Bath tethers are

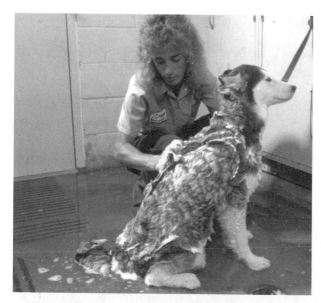

Use a pet-safe shampoo to clean, and then rinse out all the soap *(Photo credit: Ralston Purina Company)*

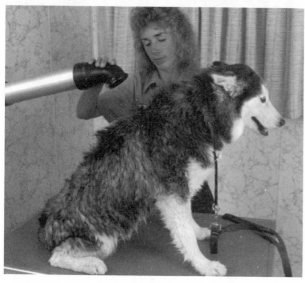

Dry your dog thoroughly *(Photo credit: Ralston Purina Company)*

available that have a suction cup that secures one end to the tub or sink while the other clips to the dog's collar. When bathing outdoors, tether the dog with a short lead to a fixed object.

Before beginning, place cotton in the pet's ears to keep out the water. A drop of mineral oil or artificial tears in each eye helps to protect them from er-rant suds. Place the dog in the standing water. It doesn't need to cover him;

level with his knees is fine and lets him feel he can stand above it without risk of drowning.

Use a plastic cup or ladle to dip water over the pet, or use a handheld sprayer. Many dogs are frightened by sprayed water, so use only a low force and keep it against the coat to soak the fur. Don't spray or dunk the dog's face; that is very scary and upsetting to the animal. Instead, use a washcloth to clean and rinse the face. Once the fur is wet, apply a thin stream of pet shampoo along the back—or lather the shampoo in your own hands and then apply—and suds your dog thoroughly, then rinse. If you're using a FLEA product, suds the dog's neck first to create a flea barrier the bugs won't cross. Most shampoos, especially flea products, work best if left on the dog for ten to fifteen minutes.

The most critical part of bathing your dog is the rinse cycle; leaving soap in the coat can cause an allergic reaction, can attract dirt, and makes the fur look dull and dingy. After you've thoroughly rinsed the dog, do it once more before calling it quits. Then allow your dog to do what he's been yearning for the whole time: a good shake. If his shaking doesn't fling out the cotton from his ears, then you should remove it. Leaving the cotton in can cause ear infection. After bathing, always dry your dog's ears with a commercial drying solution and/or a cotton ball and cotton swabs to prevent ear infections.

Smooth-coated dogs air-dry very quickly. Dogs with more fur require lots of towels. As much as dogs may dislike the bath, they often relish the toweling-off afterward. Some dogs will tolerate a blow-dryer on a low setting, which will help fluff up the fur. Be sure the dog is dry to the skin before allowing him outside if it's a cold day.

Caring for Your Dog's Eyes: Just like people, dogs may develop "sleepy crust" in the corners of their eyes when tears spill out and dry. Some dog breeds, like Poodles and Maltese, have large, prominent eyes that tend to water.

Others that have many nasal folds, like the Pekingese, Pug, and Bulldog, may have hairs that grow too near the eye and cause irritation. Tears can stain the fur, particularly in white or light-colored pets, and can crust the fur, irritate the skin, and lead to infection. A groomer can show you how to use electric clippers to keep these areas trimmed and prevent eye irritation. Wipe out the skin folds regularly with a warm, wet cloth to help prevent skin irritation or infection.

Clean around the dog's eyes each day to prevent problems from developing. A cotton ball or soft cloth moistened with warm water or contact lens saline solution works well to soften the secretion and wipe it away. Stained fur is usually at the inside corners and below the dog's eyes; commercial products available from pet stores can help remove the stain from fur.

Caring for Your Dog's Ears: Different dogs require various amounts of ear care. Healthy ears are pink, and a small amount of amber wax is normal and helps protect the ear canal. A discharge, bad smell, and/or dark or crumbly

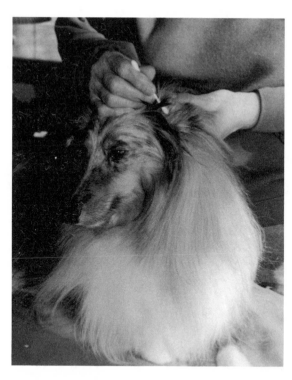

Use swabs only on visible portions of the ear (*Photo credit: Amy D. Shojai*)

material may indicate an infection or EAR MITES. Check your dog's ears at least once a week and clean at least monthly, unless your veterinarian recommends that you do so more often.

Commercial ear-cleaning solutions are available from veterinarians and pet stores, but a fifty-fifty vinegar-and-water solution is fine for general cleaning. Place a small amount of solution on a cotton ball, soft cloth, or cotton swab, and gently wipe out only the visible portions of the ear. Never drip cleaner or put any instrument down into the ear canal unless instructed to do so by your veterinarian. You may inadvertently damage your dog's ear.

The pendulous ears of breeds like Cocker Spaniels tend to trap moisture, and the poor air circulation provides a perfect environment for ear infections. If your dog has this type of ear, he'll benefit from a weekly cleaning with a drying agent (epiotic solution), or an "airing out": Draw the ears up over his head or behind his neck and tape them in place for a few hours. It looks funny, but can prevent ear problems down the road.

In Poodles, Cocker Spaniels, Schnauzers, Lhasa Apsos, Bouviers des Flandres, Old English Sheepdogs, and some other breeds, hair actually grows inside the ear canal. This tends to block air circulation, holds moisture, and makes these dogs prone to ear infections. Every one to three months, use electric clippers to trim the hair around the ears, and pluck out the fur growing inside the ear.

Serum that oozes from the hair pores after plucking is an ideal medium for bacterial growth. Follow ear plucking with an antibiotic ointment as recommended by your veterinarian to prevent infection (see OTITIS). You may be able to perform plucking service for your dog once a veterinarian or professional groomer shows you how.

Caring for Your Dog's Teeth: See PERIODONTAL DISEASE.

g

Hair

Hair is the colored threadlike structure made of keratin that grows outward from the skin. Individual hairs combine to make up your dog's distinctive coat.

Fur is a protective barrier shielding the dog's skin from the elements and regulating body temperature. Hair also acts like a "wick" that routes scent-producing chemicals related to identification and sexual status from the skin into the air.

All healthy dogs have fur, but the amount and type of hair coat varies in individuals and from breed to breed. Even the hairless variety of the Chinese Crested dog breed has hair on the face, feet, and tail.

Hairs are composed of the hair shaft, which is the visible portion of the hair, and a root that's generated by a hair follicle within the skin. Dogs have compound follicles, which means multiple hairs are produced (as many as twenty!) from a single pore; people have simple follicles, which produce only one hair for each pore (see SKIN).

In general, dogs have three kinds of hairs, which are characterized by length and diameter. Guard, or primary, hairs are the longest, coarsest hairs of the outer coat. Secondary hairs of various lengths make up the undercoat, which is composed of medium-length awn hairs of the intermediate coat; and soft, short, cottonlike fur that's curly or crimped. All three types may sprout from a single compound follicle. Sinus hairs, also called WHISKERS or VIBRIS-SAE, are found on the face and offer specialized sensory input.

The length of the hair shaft and the ratio of guard to undercoat hairs varies from breed to breed. When the hair follicle that produces the hair is slightly twisted, the hair that grows is curly. These differences, as well as a variety of colors and patterns, produce each dog's distinctive coat.

h

The Chinese Crested is bald in places
(Photo credit: Amy D. Shojai)

The Lhasa Apso has lots of hair
(Photo credit: Amy D. Shojai)

**The Komondor has a
corded coat** *(Photo credit:
Amy D. Shojai)*

The Irish Water Spaniel is curly *(Photo credit: Amy D. Shojai)*

h

Hair grows from the root outward in a cycle of rapid growth (called *anagen*); shrinkage (called *catagen*, in which the root detaches from the follicle); and a resting period (called *telogen*). Old, loose hairs in the telogen phase are pushed out by new hairs as the anagen cycle begins (see SHEDDING). Shed fur is composed of telogen hairs.

A single human hair may grow for up to six years before being shed and replaced by a new one. However, the growing cycle of canine hair is much shorter and more synchronized, which accounts for the massive shed. It varies from breed to breed, but the growth cycle averages about 130 days. The exception is the so-called nonshedding breeds, like the Poodle and some terriers, whose coats actually grow for several years before being replaced.

A healthy coat is possible only with proper NUTRITION, because hair is 95 percent protein. Your dog's coat retains its healthy glow from the proper balance of fats and other nutrients. Poor nutrition is first reflected in the skin and hair coat by dry, lifeless fur or abnormal HAIR LOSS. GROOMING is beneficial for all dogs and particularly important for dogs with thick, long coats.

Hair Loss

Also referred to as *alopecia*, hair loss is normal for dogs as new growth replaces old, dead fur (see SHEDDING). Dogs with long, thick coats, like the Chow Chow, typically lose heavy undercoats in clumps, which may give them a shocking, moth-eaten appearance. But normally, every time a hair is lost, it is replaced like clockwork.

Isolated areas of hair loss not due to normal shedding can arise from parasite infestation or skin disease, such as ALLERGIES, FLEAS, or MANGE. A veterinary diagnosis is necessary before the proper treatment can begin.

Pattern baldness is a common syndrome found in Boston Terriers, Dachshunds, Manchester Terriers, Miniature Pinschers, Whippets, Italian Greyhounds, and Chihuahuas, and there is currently no treatment. Typically, dogs show a slow, progressive thinning of the coat, particularly of the ears, but also of the neck, chest, thighs, abdomen, and around the anus.

Hair loss may occur when the normal hair-growth cycle gets out of synch, and the telogen phase is prolonged (see HAIR). In almost all instances, this is due to an underlying metabolic disease, such as CUSHING'S DISEASE. Stress from metabolic insult, a high fever, or serious illness may also cause a sudden loss of coat, which usually regrows two to three months later.

Destruction of the hair follicles from bacterial or fungal infection (see RINGWORM) may also cause permanent hair loss. It may also develop from constant traction placed on the hair from rubber bands or barrettes used to decorate toy breeds, like Poodles, Yorkshire Terriers, or Maltese.

Occasionally, dogs suffering psychological STRESS lose hair by obsessively licking, biting, and pulling at their fur. This can become a habit if the stressful conditions are not addressed. Sometimes, these dogs may be helped with anti-anxiety drugs.

Heart Disease

A number of conditions can adversely affect the function of the heart. Heart failure results when the damaged muscle is no longer able to move blood throughout the body. Without treatment, the dog will die.

Signs of heart disease vary from type to type, but many times the affected dog suffers exercise intolerance (becomes exhausted quickly), may act weak, or have a bluish tinge to the skin from lack of oxygen. In most cases of chronic (long-standing) heart failure, the dog's body retains fluid (edema). This is due to the body trying to compensate for reduced heart efficiency; the result is a retention of sodium and fluid, increased blood volume and constriction of the blood vessels, and increased blood pressure. Heart disease has a cascading effect on the whole body and can lead to damage of other organs, like the kidneys, liver, and lungs.

When the left side of the heart fails, fluid collects in the lungs (pulmonary edema) and results in a cough, labored breathing, and PANTING. OBESITY complicates heart disease and makes it more difficult to treat, but some dogs suffer weight loss and seem to waste away. Dogs sit with elbows spread and neck extended while straining to breathe, and may even try to sleep in this position to ease respiration.

When the right side of the heart fails, fluid collects and swells the abdomen (ascites), accumulates beneath the skin (edema—the legs may swell), and/or fills the chest cavity (pleural effusion). This fluid accumulation results in congestive heart failure. Often, dogs suffering from heart failure will have a heart murmur (see ARRHYTHMIA). Many times, right heart failure develops as a result of the strain from existing left heart failure.

Congenital heart diseases may or may not be inherited and are quite rare. *Patent ductus arteriosus* (PDA) is the most common, with highest incidence in Miniature Poodles and German Shepherd Dogs. The ductus arteriosus allows blood to bypass the fetal puppy's lungs. The duct normally closes after birth, and if it doesn't, blood leaks back into the heart and leads to left heart failure. Surgery is the treatment of choice and usually cures PDA.

Small-breed dogs may be affected by *congenital pulmonic stenosis*. It's a

HEART DISEASE
SYMPTOMS
Tires easily; weakness; blue tinge to skin; swollen abdomen or legs; coughing, especially at night; labored breathing; sitting with "elbows" out to aid breathing
HOME CARE
Nutritional support, such as a therapeutic diet recommended by your vet, and any prescribed medications
VET CARE
Drug therapy to get rid of excess fluid, aid breathing, and control heart action; oxygen therapy as needed; sometimes surgery
PREVENTION
Heartworm preventative; routine dental care; prevent obesity; encourage moderate exercise

narrowing of the connection between the right ventricle and pulmonary artery that leads to the lungs, which makes it harder for the heart to push blood through the narrow opening. Often, the heart muscle compensates by growing stronger. When the narrowing is severe, the dog may be treated with balloon valvuloplasty, which widens the narrowed opening, or with corrective surgery.

Large-breed dogs, like Golden Retrievers, are prone to *aortic stenosis*, a narrowing of the connection between the left ventricle and the aorta. Again, the heart tends to compensate for this condition by enlarging so blood can be pumped with more force. Although many dogs show no signs of problems, a few may collapse after exercise or die suddenly without warning. Surgery is the treatment of choice, but is risky, expensive, and available only at veterinary schools that have access to cardiopulmonary bypass machines.

Unlike congenital forms, *acquired heart diseases* develop over time and commonly are due to other conditions, like CANCER, parasites (see HEART-WORM DISEASE), or infectious diseases (see PERIODONTAL DISEASE). *Acquired valvular heart disease* is the most common cause of heart disease in the dog. Valvular heart disease is considered a disease of old age, with about one-third of all dogs over the age of twelve affected. It's most common in smaller breeds.

The heart valves simply begin to wear out, and leak blood backward instead of pumping it all forward. This puts extra strain on the heart muscle. In some instances, the valves are damaged by infection when bacteria enters the bloodstream and attacks the heart. Bacterial endocarditis also causes the dog to develop a fever, and may prompt the formation of blood clots that can cause lameness when they block blood flow to a leg. Along with therapies aimed at relieving the heart failure, bacterial endocarditis is also treated with antibiotics.

Dilated cardiomyopathy may also cause heart valve problems. Cardiomyopathy is a disease of the heart muscle rather than the valves, and the dilated form results in systolic dysfunction: the heart muscle loses the ability to adequately contract and pump blood out of the heart. The heart itself enlarges, but becomes flaccid, and the muscle walls become thin. It is not a disease of old age, but typically develops between the ages of two and five, although signs may not become apparent right away. The disease is thought to have a genetic factor, because more than 90 percent of canine cases occur in Boxers, Cocker Spaniels, Doberman Pinschers, German Shepherd Dogs, and Golden Retrievers. Most times the cause remains unknown, but Boxers, Dobermans, Saint Bernards, and Cocker Spaniels that develop the condition may respond to nutritional supplementation with the amino acids taurine and/or carnitine (see NUTRITION). But most dogs with dilated cardiomyopathy die within six months of diagnosis. Treatment is designed to prolong life and make them more comfortable during this period.

Diagnosis of heart disease is made using X RAYS, ULTRASOUND, and electrocardiograms that pick up irregular heart rhythms. Dogs with congenital heart disease, endomycardial cardiomyopathy, and heart disease due to heartworms can be cured if diagnosed and treated early.

Dogs with acquired valvular heart disease can often be helped with drugs that improve the heart's performance and reduce fluid accumulation. A diuretic drug like Lasix (furosemide) forces the kidneys to eliminate excess salt and water, and special prescription diets can compensate for the potassium, chloride, and magnesium lost due to increased fluid excretion. Vasodilator drugs like enalapril and captopril help open the lungs and control congestion. Digoxin, digitoxin, or hydralazine may help improve heart muscle performance in certain types of heart disease; other kinds of heart disease may respond to the calcium channel blockers diltiazem and verapamil, or beta-blockers like propranolol.

Appropriate treatment can potentially increase the life expectancy of a dog with some kinds of heart disease, or at least can make the dog more comfortable during the time he has left. Proper nutrition is very important.

h

Heartworm Disease

Heartworm disease was first described in 1922. It is caused by a type of round-worm called *Dirofilaria immitis* that belongs to a group of parasites termed *filarids*. Adult worms live in the pulmonary arteries and heart chambers and can damage the heart muscle and interfere with its function. An intermediate host, the mosquito, is necessary to transmit the disease to dogs. The life cycle takes about six to seven months.

HEARTWORM DISEASE
SYMPTOMS   Difficulty breathing; shortness of breath; reluctance to exercise; weight loss; sudden collapse; coughing, sometimes of blood; swollen abdomen or legs
HOME CARE   Supportive care; reduce stress; limit activity; requires vet treatment
VET CARE   Medication to kill both adult and immature heartworms
PREVENTION   Routine heartworm blood testing; heartworm preventative medication

All dogs can get the disease, but those exposed more often to mosquitoes—i.e., outdoor dogs living in close proximity to mosquito breeding grounds like swamps or standing water—are at highest risk.

An infected dog's blood contains circulating microfilariae, the immature stage of the heartworm. Mosquitoes become infected by ingesting baby heartworms when taking a blood meal from an already infected dog. The immature parasites spend about three weeks developing inside the mosquito, then the larvae migrate to the mouthparts of the insect. When the mosquito again takes a blood meal, larvae are deposited upon the skin and gain entrance to the new host's body through the bite wound left by the mosquito.

The heartworm undergoes many more molts and development stages during the next several months, during which time it migrates inside the animal's body, ultimately arriving at the heart and pulmonary arteries where it matures. Adult worms can reach four to twelve inches in length. Adults mate and females shed as many as five thousand microfilariae each day into the dog's bloodstream. These microfilariae must be ingested by a mosquito to continue their development, but can remain alive and infective in the dog's bloodstream for up to three years.

It's not uncommon for infected dogs to carry dozens of worms; more than 250 have been found in a single dog. Heartworm disease is a chronic condition in which worms live in the dog for up to five years. Initially, the dog may not show any ill effects, but symptoms develop and grow worse over time. Common signs are coughing, shortness of breath, and reluctance to exercise; dogs may faint after exertion. Eventually the dog becomes weak, listless, loses weight, and may cough up blood. Severe signs of late-stage disease are congestive heart failure, including labored breathing and edema. The condition may result in sudden collapse and death.

Heartworm disease is diagnosed based on signs of disease and blood screening techniques. Traditional tests look for microfilariae in the blood. However, a dog can be infected without microfilariae being present. This may result from single-sex infections—worms present in the heart are the same sex—in which reproduction can't happen. Other times, the dog's immune system clears away the microfilaria, but leaves the adults in the heart. Newer, more accurate tests detect the antigen that worms release into the bloodstream, or screen for antibodies made by the dog's IMMUNE SYSTEM in defense against the worms. Tests may be used in combination, or occasionally, X RAYS or echocardiograms may help diagnose the disease.

Once diagnosed, dogs are evaluated for liver and kidney competency—and treated for problems, if necessary—before being treated. Very rarely are the worms removed surgically. Sometimes they are treated with injections of the drug thiacetarsamide (Caparsolate), which is a derivative of arsenic. It's administered intravenously in two doses each day for two days, and hospitalization is required to monitor the dog for any adverse reactions to the drug. The medication is also toxic to the liver and may cause loss of appetite, VOMITING, or jaundice (yellow tinge to skin) from liver involvement. Treatment is stopped if the dog suffers these side effects; when begun again a month later; such side effects rarely recur. The medication kills about 70 percent of the worms, so some dogs require a repeated treatment to address the remaining worms.

The newest and safest treatment is with a drug called Immiticide. One injection is given in the muscle daily for two days. This drug eliminates virtually all side effects and is much more effective in producing a complete cure.

The treated dog can go home, but must undergo an enforced rest for

h

A dog taking a heartworm preventative (*Photo credit: Merial Limited*)

several weeks until the dead worms are absorbed by the body. This prevents the sudden movement of dead-worm debris that might result from sudden exertion and that could cause a life-threatening blockage, or embolism, when the parts of the worm lodge in the bloodstream. Embolism can cause lung damage and/or heart failure. In severe cases, treating the dog with buffered aspirin before and after treatment appears to reduce this risk by helping make the blood less "sticky." Your vet should prescribe the proper dosage.

In three to six weeks following thiacetarsamide injections, the dog is treated with an oral medicine like levamisole, Interceptor, or ivermectin to kill the microfilariae that still circulate in the bloodstream. Any one of these drugs may cause side effects, such as vomiting and listlessness or DIARRHEA. Ivermectin, however, can cause life-threatening reactions in Collies and Collie-crosses and should not be used in these dogs.

It is much easier to prevent heartworm disease than to diagnose, treat, and cure it once infection is present. Preventing mosquito bites will eliminate the risk of disease; however, this is nearly impossible. Keeping dogs indoors during mosquito feeding times, like late afternoons and evenings, will help. Preventative medications are a more effective option and are quite safe.

Several preventatives have been available for dogs for many years; these are generally given as daily or monthly pills. Some also prevent certain intestinal parasites, and a new product also contains lufenuron to control FLEAS. Always have your dog tested to ensure she is not already infected with heartworms before giving her a preventative medication; some medications can cause dangerous reactions if given when microfilariae are present in the dog's body.

Hematoma

This term refers to a blood blister, a swelling beneath the skin that contains blood. Hematomas typically result from a bruise or blow and usually resolve by themselves. However, surgical drainage may be required when the hematoma is large.

Dogs most commonly suffer aural hematomas in the skin of the EAR flap (pinna). This is often a result of trauma from scratching or rubbing the ear, due to parasites or ear infection. The ear cartilage is separated from the skin when the area between suddenly swells with blood and fluid. The soft swelling is usually on the inside but can be on the outside surface of the pinna. Aural hematomas most commonly affect dogs with floppy, pendulous ears that easily

HEMATOMA

SYMPTOMS
Soft swelling of (usually) the inside or sometimes the outside of the ear flap

HOME CARE
None

VET CARE
Surgical drainage and repair; medication to treat underlying cause

PREVENTION
Routine ear cleaning to prevent self-trauma from scratching at parasites (like ear mites) or infection

h

bruise when the head is shaken to relieve itchy ears. The underlying cause must be treated as well as the hematoma (see OTITIS and EAR MITES).

The trapped blood must be drained to prevent the ear cartilage from scarring. When the hematoma is small, removing the fluid with a syringe, followed by firm bandaging for seven to ten days, may be sufficient. More commonly, the hematoma recurs in a day or two as new blood and serum fill the cavity.

Shaking ears can lead to hematomas *(Photo credit: Betsy Stowe)*

Surgery offers the best results. The dog is ANESTHETIZED, and a small incision opens the inside surface of the pinna. The opening is drained and cleaned, and the separated flaps of cartilage and skin stitched back together. A narrow opening is left at the incision line so that fluid will drain as the incision heals rather than reinflating the wound. Often, a soft padded bandage is used to help the ear retain normal shape as it heals; the bandage may anchor the ear against the head or collar to prevent a recurrence of ear-flapping injury. Typically, dogs that undergo this surgery are fitted with an ELIZABETHAN COLLAR to prevent their scratching at the wound.

h | Hemophilia

Hemophilia is an inherited bleeding disorder, and it has been found in nearly all of the popular dog breeds. Affected dogs lack an essential clotting component of blood. The body is unable to stop bleeding from even minor injuries.

Signs of the condition include recurrent bruising or blood pockets beneath the skin (see HEMATOMA), bleeding into the joints and resultant lameness, and internal hemorrhage that often results in severe ANEMIA and death. Dogs diagnosed with hemophilia should not be bred, as the condition can be passed on to offspring. (See also VON WILLEBRAND'S DISEASE.)

HEMOPHILIA

SYMPTOMS
Recurrent bruising; blood pockets beneath skin; lameness; failure of bleeding injuries to scab or clot; anemia

HOME CARE
None

VET CARE
Blood transfusions; supportive care

PREVENTION
None; once diagnosed, avoid trauma and elective surgeries and remain vigilant for signs; seek prompt treatment should bleeding occur

Hernia

A hernia is the abnormal protrusion of abdominal contents through a natural or unnatural opening in the body wall. Hernias are characterized as either reducible or nonreducible (incarcerated). The reducible type is characterized by a soft, painless, and compressible swelling that's easily manipulated back into place and may vary in size from time to time. A nonreducible hernia is hard and painful and cannot be moved. A nonreducible hernia should be treated as an emergency, because the protruding tissues may die as a result of strangulation if blood supply is pinched off.

There is no way to prevent congenital hernias. When a dog is born with a hernia, inguinal (groin) or umbilical (naval) hernias are the most common. Typically, congenital hernias are corrected during spay or neuter surgery.

Occasionally, adult dogs suffer from perineal herniation, which is the protrusion of the rectum through the pelvic muscles. Affected dogs are typically six- to eight-year-old unneutered animals, and incidence seems highest in Boston Terriers, Boxers, Collies, Corgies, and Pekingese. You'll see a bulge alongside the anus, which may grow larger as the dog strains. The feces caught in this area can become impacted and block normal defecation. Surgery corrects the defect.

Herniation can also be the result of trauma. The severe blow a dog suffers when hit by a car often causes a diaphragmatic hernia. The diaphragm is the muscle and tissue structure that divides the abdominal cavity from the chest. The tear allows abdominal organs to intrude into the thorax, which interferes

h

HERNIA

SYMPTOMS
Soft, compressible, but painless swelling, or hard and painful swelling adjacent to the navel or genitals; or labored breathing following trauma, such as being hit by car

HOME CARE
None; hard, painful swelling that can't be moved, or respiratory distress following trauma are EMERGENCIES! SEE VET IMMEDIATELY!

VET CARE
Surgery

PREVENTION
None; remain vigilant for signs; seek prompt treatment

with the dog's ability to expand his lungs. Affected dogs typically exhibit labored breathing while sitting with the neck extended or head hanging in an effort to ease respiration. Diagnosis is based on signs, a history of trauma, and x rays. Surgical correction is the only treatment.

Sometimes a dog suffers an abdominal or thoracic hernia during an attack by a larger dog. The sharp canine teeth can penetrate the muscles of the abdomen or thorax and tear the body wall—sometimes without even causing a noticeable skin injury. These hernias also require surgical repair, and the entire contents of the abdomen or thorax should be evaluated since trauma can also occur to structures like the intestines, kidney, spleen, bladder, or lungs. Prognosis is guarded when repairing a traumatic diaphragmatic hernia.

There is no way to prevent congenital hernias. Risk of traumatic herniation can be reduced by supervising your dog's outdoor adventures, confining him to the yard, and keeping him safe from cars and other dogs.

Hip Dysplasia

Hip dysplasia is a progressive, degenerative disease that causes joint instability due to an abnormality of the hips and/or head of the femur (thigh bone). It is the most common cause of rear-end lameness in dogs and is most often seen in large breeds, like German Shepherd Dogs, Saint Bernards, and Greater Swiss Mountain Dogs. However, any size dog may be affected. Male and female dogs are affected with equal frequency.

The cause of canine hip dysplasia isn't known. The condition is thought to have a genetic link, and dogs suffering from hip dysplasia should not be bred; their puppies will be two times more likely to develop the disease than puppies born to parents with normal hips. However, even dogs with normal parents can develop hip dysplasia.

Dogs typically are born normal, but as the puppy matures, the hip joint alignment becomes progressively worse. Normally, the pelvis has a kind of a cup or socket (acetabulum) into which the rounded head of the femur fits. This ball-and-socket arrangement forms the joint, and muscles and tendons hold the joint together and allow the leg movement. Dogs suffering from dysplasia typically have a very shallow socket and/or loose muscles and tendons. This allows the joint to work loose, which places abnormal stress and wear on the bones when they rub together and causes further joint degeneration. Bones respond to stress by growing thicker, which makes the fit even worse.

Severe hip dysplasia may become noticeable as early as four months of age, but more typically is seen in the nine- to twelve-month-old dog. The painful condition causes limping and favoring of limbs, and difficulty in rising, running, or jumping. Dysplastic dogs may exhibit an odd, wavery gait when walking, and a "bunny hop" when running (which helps minimize joint stress). Stairs can prove a challenge to these dogs, and sore hips may prompt the dog to snap or flinch when touched.

However, hip dysplasia is not a finite condition; there are degrees of severity, and some dogs may show minimal to no signs at all. Mild cases may go undiagnosed until the dog reaches middle age or older. How quickly or to what extent degeneration occurs is in part determined by the dog's activity level. While healthy, normal hips probably won't be adversely affected by hard work, the dog with mild to moderate hip dysplasia develops more severe signs more quickly when excessive stress is placed on these joints.

As the hip joint becomes damaged, inflammation of surrounding tissues weakens the joint further. The ligaments become swollen and stretched and ultimately rupture. The cartilage that covers and cushions the bones is worn down. Thigh muscles and muscles of the hip joint atrophy. Dogs with hip dysplasia often develop ARTHRITIS.

Diagnosis is made using X RAYS of the pelvis and hips once the dog is placed under general ANESTHESIA. Characteristic changes in the joint may not be evident until the dog is two years old.

There is no cure for hip dysplasia. Treatment is aimed at relieving PAIN and improving joint function. How well treatment works depends on the severity of the problem.

Often, mild to moderate cases of hip dysplasia can be managed with moderate exercise, a healthy diet, and oral pain relievers, like buffered aspirin or Rimadyl as prescribed by the veterinarian. Moderate exercise helps maintain and improve the dog's muscle tone, which alleviates painful wear and tear on

HIP DYSPLASIA
SYMPTOMS
Lameness; limping; favoring of rear legs; difficulty rising, running, or jumping; wavery gait, or bunny hops when running
HOME CARE
Encourage moderate exercise; provide good nutrition; offer pain relievers as recommended by vet
VET CARE
Pain medications; sometimes surgery
PREVENTION
None; provide good nutrition and keep dogs lean to delay progression of disease

the joint. Encourage your dysplastic dog to take short walks with you; swimming is ideal, but jumping and prolonged running should be discouraged. Keep him lean; OBESITY increases joint strain and exacerbates the condition.

Severe cases of hip dysplasia may benefit from surgery that rebuilds or removes bone, or alters the muscles and tendons to reduce pain. Such procedures may not fully restore joint function, but can give the dog improved movement.

Pectineus myotomy or tendonectomy surgically divides muscles or tendons connected to the hip to afford relief from pain; however, this procedure does not alter the progression of bone degeneration. A femoral head osteotomy, which removes the femoral head, prompts the dog's body to create a new "false" joint from fibrous scar tissue. Total hip replacement is often quite successful, in which the entire ball-and-socket joint is replaced by a stainless steel apparatus similar to what's used in human medicine. However, the cost for this procedure often makes it prohibitive. A newer procedure, called a triple pelvic osteotomy, creates a new socket in the pelvis; when done correctly, this procedure seems to slow the progression of joint disease and restores normal function. In this procedure, the pelvic bone is cut in three places and the acetabulum is rotated into a better position over the femoral head to provide a normal fit.

There is no way to prevent hip dysplasia in dogs, although acquiring your puppy from parents certified to have normal hips will reduce his chances of having the condition. Reputable breeders should be able to tell you about their dogs' history. The Orthopedic Foundation for Animals (OFA) provides a consulting service for purebred dog owners and breeders (see Appendix C, "Canine Research Foundations"). OFA reviews hip X rays provided by an owner to evaluate the dog's conformation and, when normal, certifies that fact.

Development of the condition is delayed and the severity is lessened when the growth rate of puppies (during the first four months) is restricted; conversely, the condition in prone puppies can be brought on more quickly when the growth rate is accelerated. Feeding a high-quality puppy ration that provides a moderate and healthy growth rate is important, particularly in high-risk large breeds. Manage the dog's diet appropriately and encourage regular exercise to keep the dog fit and lean. Most dogs with hip dysplasia can lead happy, otherwise healthy lives when owners remain vigilant regarding their special needs.

Hookworms

Hookworms are a common intestinal parasite of dogs. They grow to less than half an inch long. Depending on the species, they suck blood and/or take bites out of the wall of the dog's small intestine, which can result in severe hemorrhage. All dogs are susceptible, but puppies are at highest risk because they may not have the immunity to the worms that adult dogs usually develop (see IMMUNE SYSTEM). Dogs typically become immune to the worms after several bouts of infection; such immunity doesn't necessarily clear all the parasites, but it does help diminish their effects.

Several kinds of hookworms affect dogs. *Ancylostoma caninum* is the most important and, along with *Ancylostoma braziliense*, is found in warm climates. *Uncinaria stenocephala* also occasionally affects dogs and is found in cool climates. The highest incidence of disease is found in southern states, where higher humidity and temperature conditions provide an ideal environment for the parasite.

The adult hookworms mate inside the dog's intestine, and females lay eggs, which are passed with the stool. The eggs hatch in about a week, then develop further in the environment into infective larvae. In warm and wet conditions, larvae may live for two months. They prefer sandy soil, but may crawl onto grass seeking a host.

Dogs can be infected in several ways. Oral ingestion after investigatory sniffing or licking is a common route of infection when the dog picks up larvae

h

HOOKWORMS
SYMPTOMS
Anemia; bloody to black tarlike diarrhea; weight loss; low energy; sometimes vomiting; painful, swollen, cracked feet
HOME CARE
None
VET CARE
Hookworm medication; supportive care, such as fluid therapy or blood transfusion; treatment to relieve enteritis
PREVENTION
Pick up feces promptly and keep yard clean; disinfect kennels with rock salt, borax, or 1 percent bleach solution, certain heartworm preventatives also deworm the dog

from soil or feces. Larvae are also able to penetrate the skin directly, usually the dog's footpads.

(*Note:* Infective hookworm larvae are capable of penetrating human skin, causing cutaneous larval migrans in which migrating larvae in the skin cause small, red, itchy trails [see ZOONOSIS].)

Puppies often contract hookworms through transmammary infection—by drinking infested mother's milk—or less often, before birth while in the uterus. Dogs also may be infected by eating an infected mouse or cockroach.

After being swallowed or penetrating the skin, the immature worms take about two weeks to migrate into the bloodstream, through the lungs, and into the intestine where they mature. When the dog is older and has an established immunity to the parasite, the larvae may never reach the lungs, and instead remain in arrested development in various tissues throughout the body. When a dog becomes pregnant, the worms migrate to the mammary glands, or less commonly, the uterus, and subsequently infect puppies before or shortly after birth. In males and nonpregnant females, tissue-infesting larvae may "leak" back into circulation, mature, and become reproducing adults. The larvae migrate from the tissue into the bloodstream, to the lungs, and on to the intestines.

The most common clinical sign of infection is blood loss resulting in ANEMIA. When young puppies are exposed to hookworms for the first time, they have no natural defense and can quickly become overwhelmed by a massive infestation. Acute hookworm disease arises suddenly, and in addition to signs of profound anemia, these pups may have a bloody to black tarlike DIARRHEA. A severe infestation can cause sudden collapse and death.

Adult dogs more typically develop chronic, or ongoing, disease. Dogs that are stressed, malnourished, or in an endemic region are at highest risk, and chronic infection typically is characterized by mild diarrhea or VOMITING. But if the dog's immunity fully breaks down, chronic hookworm disease can turn deadly even in adults; signs are similar to the acute infection. *This is an emergency situation, which may require hospitalization, a blood transfusion, and supportive care.*

Hookworms are diagnosed by finding eggs during microscopic examination of the stool. However, young puppies may suffer acute disease without any eggs being present if the worms are too young to reproduce. A liquid oral worm medication, like pyrantel pamoate, or febantel and praziquantel may be given, usually in two doses two weeks apart. This kills the adult worms in the intestinal tract, but may not clear larvae in arrested development in other tissues.

Sometimes older dogs with ongoing exposure to the parasite develop a hookworm DERMATITIS at the site of skin penetration. This most commonly affects the footpads and is referred to as *pododermatitis*. The dog's feet become painful, swell, feel hot, and become soft and spongy. Without treatment, the footpads may separate, nails become deformed, and the pads turn dry, thick, and cracked. Treatment is the same as for intestinal infestation, but in addition, a medicated paste is applied to affected skin to kill the larvae.

Preventing hookworm infection can be done simply by giving a monthly heartworm preventative that also prevents hookworms. Otherwise, female dogs that are to be bred should receive worm medication prior to the birth to help kill the larvae that may infect her puppies. The best prevention is to practice good hygiene; clean up stools promptly from the yard (it takes six days for larvae to leave the stool). Outdoor exposure has the greatest risk in damp, shaded areas. Keep kennel areas dry and clean. Direct sunlight will help curb the worm population in the environment. Gravel or sandy runs may benefit from applications of rock salt or borax, which will kill the larvae; however, these substances also kill grass. Concrete runs should be washed down with a 1 percent solution of bleach.

Hot Spots

Also referred to as *acute moist* DERMATITIS, a hot spot is a localized area of self-induced trauma that becomes infected. Dogs suffering from atopy are at highest risk (see ALLERGY), but all dogs can develop these sores. Dog breeds with heavy double coats, like Chow Chows and German Shepherd Dogs, seem most prone to developing hot spots immediately prior to shedding, when dead hair may be trapped next to the skin. For unknown reasons, Golden Retrievers tend to develop deeply infected hot spots.

Hot spots can appear anywhere on the dog's body, but the rump, tail, back, and flanks are common sites. Usually, the hot spot appears suddenly as an initially small circular area of hair loss, but it can spread rapidly. Sores can grow to several inches in diameter within a few hours. The infection often smells bad and secretes pus, and hot spots typically are moist due to licking and/or the weeping of the wound, and hot because of infection and inflammation.

No one is certain what causes a hot spot to form, but it's thought to be prompted by some minor irritation, like a fleabite. Itchiness and discomfort prompts licking and nibbling, and when the dog can't leave the wound alone, a hot spot erupts.

Treatment consists of getting air to the infection so it will heal and dry, and preventing further self-mutilation. An ELIZABETHAN COLLAR keeps a dog from licking or nibbling the sore.

Hot spots are both itchy and painful, and they often require a veterinarian

HOT SPOTS

SYMPTOMS
Small but quickly growing round circle of itchy hair loss with moist, painful, inflamed skin

HOME CARE
Clip fur surrounding area; cleanse with diluted hydrogen peroxide or benzoyl peroxide cleanser; apply medication like Burrow's solution to dry lesion

VET CARE
Same as home care; often sedation is necessary; prescription ointments or injections that soothe the itch; sometimes antibiotics and corticosteroids; address underlying cause

PREVENTION
Groom dogs to prevent mats; provide proper flea and tick control; treat wounds promptly

h

to sedate the dog before treatment can begin. The fur surrounding the area is clipped away, and the skin cleansed with an antibacterial preparation, like diluted hydrogen peroxide, Nolvasan, Betadine, OxyDex, or pHisoHex. Pet formulations of benzoyl peroxide–containing cleansers help reduce the itchiness, dry the lesion, and flush out hair follicles, as well as kill certain bacteria.

Once cleansed, a medication like Burrow's solution, available at most drugstores or pet stores, may be applied and seems to work quite well to dry the sore. The veterinarian may prescribe ointments, like Panolog or Neocort, or short-acting corticosteroids, like prednisone, that reduce the irritation. Occasionally, antibiotics are required to clear up deep infection. The underlying problem—fleas, allergy, or whatever—must also be addressed.

Since dogs aren't able to adequately groom themselves, owners must take great responsibility for seeing that coat care is provided. GROOMING during shedding season is particularly important and can help prevent problems like hot spots from developing.

House-Training

House-training refers to teaching dogs proper bathroom etiquette. Dogs that share house privileges with you must learn where appropriate facilities are located and how to alert you to their need.

"Accidents" that occur in the house can indicate a health or behavior

Affenpinscher
PHOTO CREDIT: AMY D. SHOJAI

Afghan Hound
PHOTO CREDIT: AMY D. SHOJAI

Airedale Terrier
PHOTO CREDIT: AMY D. SHOJAI

Akita
PHOTO CREDIT: AMY D. SHOJAI

Alaskan Malamute
PHOTO CREDIT: AMY D. SHOJAI

American Eskimo, standard
PHOTO CREDIT: ANDREW HEISTER

American Staffordshire Terrier
PHOTO CREDIT: AMY D. SHOJAI

American Water Spaniel
PHOTO CREDIT: JOHAN
ADLERCREUTZ

Australian Cattle Dog
PHOTO CREDIT: AMY D. SHOJAI

Australian Shepherd
PHOTO CREDIT: AMY D. SHOJAI

Australian Terrier
PHOTO CREDIT: AMY D. SHOJAI

Basenji
PHOTO CREDIT: AMY D. SHOJAI

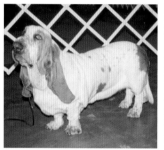

Basset Hound
PHOTO CREDIT: AMY D. SHOJAI

Beagle
PHOTO CREDIT: AMY D. SHOJAI

Bearded Collie
PHOTO CREDIT: AMY D. SHOJAI

Bedlington Terrier
PHOTO CREDIT: AMY D. SHOJAI

Belgian Malinois
PHOTO CREDIT: AMY D. SHOJAI

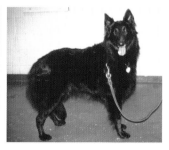

Belgian Sheepdog
PHOTO CREDIT: AMY D. SHOJAI

Belgian Tervuren
PHOTO CREDIT: AMY D. SHOJAI

Bernese Mountain Dog
PHOTO CREDIT: BERND GÜNTER

Bichon Frise
PHOTO CREDIT: AMY D. SHOJAI

Black and Tan Coonhound
PHOTO CREDIT: WILLIAM SEDLAK

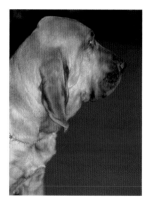

Bloodhound
PHOTO CREDIT: AMY D. SHOJAI

Border Collie
PHOTO CREDIT: AMY D. SHOJAI

Border Terrier
PHOTO CREDIT: AMY D. SHOJAI

Borzoi
PHOTO CREDIT: DONNA MAHARAN

Boston Terrier
PHOTO CREDIT: AMY D. SHOJAI

Bouvier des Flandres
PHOTO CREDIT: AMY D. SHOJAI

Boxer
PHOTO CREDIT: DONNA MAHARAN

Briard
PHOTO CREDIT: AMY D. SHOJAI

Brittany
PHOTO CREDIT: AMY D. SHOJAI

Brussels Griffon
PHOTO CREDIT: AMY D. SHOJAI

Bulldog
PHOTO CREDIT: AMY D. SHOJAI

Bullmastiff
PHOTO CREDIT: AMY D. SHOJAI

Bull Terrier
PHOTO CREDIT: AMY D. SHOJAI

Cairn Terrier
PHOTO CREDIT: AMY D. SHOJAI

Canaan Dog
PHOTO CREDIT: BOOTH
PHOTOGRAPHY

Cavalier King Charles Spaniel
PHOTO CREDIT: AMY D. SHOJAI

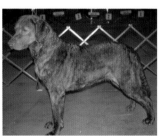

Chesapeake Bay Retriever
PHOTO CREDIT: AMY D. SHOJAI

Chihuahua, long coat
PHOTO CREDIT: AMY D. SHOJAI

Chihuahua, smooth coat
PHOTO CREDIT: AMY D. SHOJAI

Chinese Crested, powderpuff
PHOTO CREDIT: AMY D. SHOJAI

Chinese Crested, hairless
PHOTO CREDIT: AMY D. SHOJAI

Chinese Shar-Pei
PHOTO CREDIT: AMY D. SHOJAI

Chow Chow
PHOTO CREDIT: AMY D. SHOJAI

Clumber Spaniel
PHOTO CREDIT: AMY D. SHOJAI

Cocker Spaniel
PHOTO CREDIT: AMY D. SHOJAI

Cocker Spaniel, English
PHOTO CREDIT: AMY D. SHOJAI

Collie, rough
PHOTO CREDIT: AMY D. SHOJAI

Collie, smooth
PHOTO CREDIT: AMY D. SHOJAI

Curly-Coated Retriever
PHOTO CREDIT: MARILYN SMITH

Dachshund, smooth
PHOTO CREDIT: AMY D. SHOJAI

Dachshund, wirehaired
PHOTO CREDIT: AMY D. SHOJAI

Dachshund, longhaired
PHOTO CREDIT: AMY D. SHOJAI

Dalmatian
PHOTO CREDIT: AMY D. SHOJAI

Dandie Dinmont Terrier
PHOTO CREDIT: AMY D. SHOJAI

Doberman Pinscher
PHOTO CREDIT: AMY D. SHOJAI

English Setter
PHOTO CREDIT: AMY D. SHOJAI

English Springer Spaniel
PHOTO CREDIT: AMY D. SHOJAI

English Toy Spaniel
PHOTO CREDIT: AMY D. SHOJAI

Field Spaniel
PHOTO CREDIT: AMY D. SHOJAI

Finnish Spitz
PHOTO CREDIT: AMY D. SHOJAI

Flat-Coated Retriever
PHOTO CREDIT: PETER ELEY AND
KELLICK FLAT-COATED RETRIEVERS

Foxhound, English
PHOTO CREDIT: AMY D. SHOJAI

Fox Terrier, wire
PHOTO CREDIT: AMY D. SHOJAI

Fox Terrier, smooth
PHOTO CREDIT: AMY D. SHOJAI

French Bulldog (puppy)
PHOTO CREDIT: AMY D. SHOJAI

German Shepherd Dog
PHOTO CREDIT: AMY D. SHOJAI

German Shorthaired Pointer
PHOTO CREDIT: AMY D. SHOJAI

German Wirehaired Pointer
PHOTO CREDIT: AMY D. SHOJAI

Giant Schnauzer
PHOTO CREDIT: AMY D. SHOJAI

Golden Retriever
PHOTO CREDIT: AMY D. SHOJAI

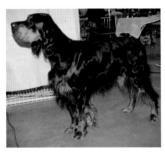

Gordon Setter
PHOTO CREDIT: AMY D. SHOJAI

Great Dane
PHOTO CREDIT: AMY D. SHOJAI

Great Pyrenees
PHOTO CREDIT: AMY D. SHOJAI

Greater Swiss Mountain Dog
PHOTO CREDIT: AMY D. SHOJAI

Greyhound
PHOTO CREDIT: AMY D. SHOJAI

Harrier
PHOTO CREDIT: AMY D. SHOJAI

Ibizan Hound
PHOTO CREDIT: AMY D. SHOJAI

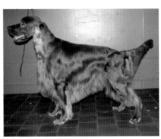

Irish Setter
PHOTO CREDIT: AMY D. SHOJAI

Irish Terrier
PHOTO CREDIT: AMY D. SHOJAI

Irish Water Spaniel
PHOTO CREDIT: AMY D. SHOJAI

Irish Wolfhound
PHOTO CREDIT: STEVE MCCROSSAN

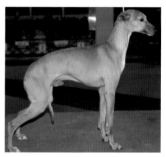

Italian Greyhound
PHOTO CREDIT: AMY D. SHOJAI

Jack Russell Terrier
PHOTO CREDIT: MICHELLE WARD

Japanese Chin
PHOTO CREDIT: AMY D. SHOJAI

Keeshond
PHOTO CREDIT: AMY D. SHOJAI

Kerry Blue Terrier
PHOTO CREDIT: AMY D. SHOJAI

Komondor
PHOTO CREDIT: AMY D. SHOJAI

Kuvasz
PHOTO CREDIT: AMY D. SHOJAI

Labrador Retriever
PHOTO CREDIT: AMY D. SHOJAI

Lakeland Terrier
PHOTO CREDIT: AMY D. SHOJAI

Lhasa Apso
PHOTO CREDIT: AMY D. SHOJAI

Maltese
PHOTO CREDIT: AMY D. SHOJAI

Manchester Terrier, standard
PHOTO CREDIT: AMY D. SHOJAI

Mastiff
PHOTO CREDIT: AMY D. SHOJAI

Miniature Pinscher
PHOTO CREDIT: AMY D. SHOJAI

Miniature Schnauzer
PHOTO CREDIT: AMY D. SHOJAI

Newfoundland
PHOTO CREDIT: AMY D. SHOJAI

Norwegian Elkhound
PHOTO CREDIT: AMY D. SHOJAI

Norwich Terrier
PHOTO CREDIT: DONNA MAHARAN

Old English Sheepdog
PHOTO CREDIT: AMY D. SHOJAI

Otterhound
PHOTO CREDIT: AMY D. SHOJAI

Papillon
PHOTO CREDIT: AMY D. SHOJAI

Pekingese
PHOTO CREDIT: AMY D. SHOJAI

Petit Basset Griffon Vendeen
PHOTO CREDIT: AMY D. SHOJAI

Pharaoh Hound
PHOTO CREDIT: AMY D. SHOJAI

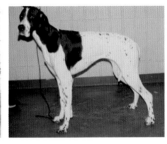

Pointer
PHOTO CREDIT: AMY D. SHOJAI

Pomeranian
PHOTO CREDIT: AMY D. SHOJAI

Poodle, miniature
PHOTO CREDIT: AMY D. SHOJAI

Portugese Water Dog
PHOTO CREDIT: AMY D. SHOJAI

Pug
PHOTO CREDIT: AMY D. SHOJAI

Puli
PHOTO CREDIT: AMY D. SHOJAI

Rhodesian Ridgeback
PHOTO CREDIT: DONNA MAHARAN

Rottweiler
PHOTO CREDIT: AMY D. SHOJAI

St. Bernard
PHOTO CREDIT: AMY D. SHOJAI

Saluki
PHOTO CREDIT: AMY D. SHOJAI

Samoyed
PHOTO CREDIT: AMY D. SHOJAI

Schipperke
PHOTO CREDIT: AMY D. SHOJAI

Scottish Deerhound
PHOTO CREDIT: DONNA MAHARAN

Scottish Terrier
PHOTO CREDIT: AMY D. SHOJAI

Sealyham Terrier
PHOTO CREDIT: BACKSTAGE

Shetland Sheepdog
PHOTO CREDIT: AMY D. SHOJAI

Shiba Inu
PHOTO CREDIT: AMY D. SHOJAI

Shih Tzu
PHOTO CREDIT: AMY D. SHOJAI

Siberian Husky
PHOTO CREDIT: AMY D. SHOJAI

Silky Terrier
PHOTO CREDIT: AMY D. SHOJAI

Skye Terrier
PHOTO CREDIT: J. K. KERNAN

Soft Coated Wheaten Terrier
PHOTO CREDIT: AMY D. SHOJAI

Staffordshire Bull Terrier
PHOTO CREDIT: AMY D. SHOJAI

Standard Schnauzer
PHOTO CREDIT: AMY D. SHOJAI

Sussex Spaniel
PHOTO CREDIT: AMY D. SHOJAI

Tibetan Spaniel
PHOTO CREDIT: AMY D. SHOJAI

Tibetan Terrier
PHOTO CREDIT: AMY D. SHOJAI

Viszla
PHOTO CREDIT: AMY D. SHOJAI

Weimaraner
PHOTO CREDIT: AMY D. SHOJAI

Welsh Corgi (Cardigan)
PHOTO CREDIT: AMY D. SHOJAI

Welsh Corgi (Pembroke)
PHOTO CREDIT: AMY D. SHOJAI

Welsh Springer Spaniel
PHOTO CREDIT: CHRISTOPHER FORD

Welsh Terrier
PHOTO CREDIT: AMY D. SHOJAI

West Highland White Terrier
PHOTO CREDIT: AMY D. SHOJAI

Whippet
PHOTO CREDIT: AMY D. SHOJAI

Wirehaired Pointing Griffon
PHOTO CREDIT: ROBERT GERITY

Yorkshire Terrier
PHOTO CREDIT: AMY D. SHOJAI

problem. Leg-lifting in the house is a DOMINANCE display and a part of MARK-ING behavior, and defecating on an owner's property, such as the bed or shoes, can be an expression of STRESS. Many times, however, inappropriate elimination habits are due to deficient house-training. Puppies require specific instruction, and adult dogs often need refresher courses to enforce good habits.

For effective house-training, four things are required: patience, consistency, timing, and confinement. A plain cardboard box or dog crate is the ideal teaching tool.

Given a choice, both adult dogs and puppies will eliminate far away from where they eat and sleep. The most effective house-training methods use the dog's natural inclination toward cleanliness to prompt proper elimination. Puppies aren't physically able to control elimination until they reach about five weeks of age, and complete bladder control develops later. However, it's important to institute the rules of the house as soon as you bring your puppy home.

During house-training, whenever the dog or puppy is not under your direct supervision (i.e., your eyes on her at all times!), she should be confined in a small space large enough for only bedding and a bowl of water. Use a crate or cardboard box, which the dog will readily identify as her "den." She'll do her best to wait until released from confinement, so she won't have to live with her own waste. *A small area like the powder room or laundry room won't work*, because your dog will simply use one corner as a toilet and sleep in the other

A crate helps house train *(Photo credit: Ralston Purina Company)*

"den" end. The idea is that she must live with the consequences of her mistake should she produce a puddle or pile.

During the confinement, offer your dog plenty of opportunities to eliminate in the *right* location. This is where timing is important. Puppies have a limited capacity to control their bowels and bladder, and need frequent potty breaks. A good rule of thumb is after each nap, meal, and play session, and the first thing every morning and last thing at night. Adult dogs can hold out for longer at a time, but offer more opportunities for good behavior rather than less.

Consistency is extremely important in training. Feed your dog at the same times each day, so her body establishes an internal clock that you can anticipate. Designate the dog's toilet area from the beginning, and always take her to the same place so that she'll associate the sight and scent with what's expected. There's no need to first "paper-train" your dog if she's to use the yard as an adult; that simply adds an extra step, and she'll have to unlearn using the house and switch her bathroom allegiance to outdoors. From the beginning, physically take her to a specific corner of the yard and wait for her to "do her duty," then praise the dickens out of her so she knows she's been a good girl. Wait until she's consistent and knows what's expected before simply letting her out the back door into your fenced yard.

High-rise apartments or other housing that offers no yard privileges require you to designate an area of your home as the dog's bathroom. Older dogs may eventually develop the control to be able to "hold it" until they can reach the neighborhood park or nearest fire hydrant; in most cases, you'll need to address any pooper-scooper requirements. House-training is identical; timing, consistency, and confinement are still required, but instead of taking your puppy outside you take her to your indoor facility.

Traditionally, paper-training has involved layering newspaper on an area of easily cleaned floor, such as the linoleum of a bathroom. However, some hardheaded dogs have trouble distinguishing between the newspapers in the potty area, and the ones you've left beside your chair after reading them. A better and probably more hygienic alternative is to use jumbo-size absorbable pads available from pet-supply stores—or use disposable diapers. Some small dogs will accept using a cat litter box.

To avoid accidents on the way from confinement to the doggy toilet, either carry the dog if she's small enough, or put her on a leash so she's under your command. Dogs are less likely to eliminate when they're "working." Confine her until she's reliable; that means, whenever you're talking on the phone, eating dinner, watching television, or otherwise do not have your eyes glued to the fuzzy puddle-maker, she should be in the box or crate. This ensures that if a mistake *is* made, you catch her in the act and can correct her appropriately.

Dogs have a short-term memory regarding inappropriate behavior. Unless a correction is made during or *immediately* following the infraction (within thirty to sixty seconds), your dog won't understand why she's being reprimanded and the correction won't have any effect. If you discover a puddle or pile under the dining room table after you left her unsupervised to answer the door, all you can do is clean it up and resolve to watch her closer next time. Incidentally, rubbing your dog's nose in her mess—even when caught in the act—is not helpful, and is even counterproductive. It confuses the dog and can make her think you object to any elimination when in fact it's the location that's the problem. Some dogs may simply think you've lost your mind.

A more effective method is to say no when she begins to pose, and immediately remove her to the designated area. Offer extravagant praise when she's productive in the right place. Link a command to the action by saying, "Hurry up, hurry up" as she squats, then praise her when she's done. Soon, she'll understand what's expected when she hears the "hurry up" command.

Eliminate opportunities for mistakes by confining her when she cannot be watched. Dogs respond more readily to positive reinforcement (praise) than negative (chastisement), so give her every chance to be a good dog. She'll soon learn to let someone know when she needs to go out, in order to avoid messing her bed.

Dogs and puppies typically are eager to please, and most learn the concept within the first several days. Even hard-case adult dogs can be house-trained within two or three weeks with consistent confinement. Puppies may understand the concept, but may be physically incapable of reliable control until they're about six months old. However, confinement needn't continue the whole time, as she should learn to notify you of her needs whether in confinement or not. Once your dog has proved able to keep the box or crate clean, expand her territory by degrees (every two weeks) until she considers the entire house a den and treats it appropriately (see also TRAINING).

Hunting Behavior

This refers to behaviors that allow the dog to detect and capture prey. Dogs evolved as hunters in order to survive, and all modern dogs are born with innate predatory skills specific to hunting prey. This applies whether the dog is a free-living feral animal who relies on these behaviors to eat, or a pampered house dog that never wants for food. Many PLAY behaviors use the same techniques as those used for hunting.

But instinct alone does not make every dog a successful hunter. Not all dogs have the same abilities to hunt, and technique is learned only through practice. Each PUPPY hones technical skill through play and sometimes an adult's example. Dogs never exposed to prey as puppies can learn by trial and error in concert with instinct to become successful hunters as adults.

Dogs do not necessarily hunt to eat. Hunger does not trigger the behavior; for most dogs, scent drives hunting behavior, and is used to both identify and locate prey (see NOSE). Sight and sound also play a role. Even a pampered lap dog reacts to a leaping squirrel, the rustle of leaves, or the scent of a bunny hiding in the shrubs. The urge to track and chase prey is ingrained in the canine psyche, and a number of refined behaviors used singly or together compose the dog's hunting repertoire.

Typically, the dog's smell sense alerts him to the presence of prey, and he tracks game by following the scent trail. This may be done with head held high and reading scent cues from the air, or with a nose-to-ground posture. As he nears the target, he slows his gait and lowers his head in the classic stalking pose. His eyes remain glued to the prey, and he may pause and freeze in position with his body pointed at the target. Once within striking range, the dog flushes the bird or bunny from hiding. The prey's attempt to escape prompts

Hunting dogs like this Flat-Coated Retriever love the water *(Photo credit: Susan D. Cooper)*

the hunter's chase impulse. He drives the animal mercilessly, using his stamina to run it to exhaustion. When working with a pack, individual canines may run large prey in relays until it gives up, or may herd it into the waiting jaws of compatriots.

Dogs use powerful jaws and sharp canine TEETH for a slashing attack. But the neck and shoulder muscles usually provide the lethal blow when the dog grasps the animal and shakes it furiously to break its neck. Larger prey requires a different technique, but are rarely hunted by domestic dogs. The dog's wolf cousins may first cripple very large prey, like caribou, by slashing their legs and then the torso; the animal simply weakens from blood loss and is easily brought down. Canines eat prey on the spot, but may carry small animals home when they have puppies to be fed.

Not all hunting behaviors are seen in all dogs, though. One or more of the tracking, stalking, pointing, herding/driving, attacking, killing, and retrieving behaviors have been selectively augmented or even eliminated in certain dog breeds through the domestication process. These changes better fit specific breeds to their roles in the service of humans. In most breeds, the attack-and-kill-sequence behaviors have been inhibited, while others have been enhanced.

For instance, the Bloodhound has been selectively bred to be an expert tracker, and lives for scent—he cares about little else. Sight hounds, like the Afghan Hound and Greyhound, and many of the terriers, trigger more to movement than scent and rely on sight to track prey. The former are racers that love the chase, while the latter react similarly to cats in their stalk-and-pounce techniques.

Sheepdogs, like Border Collies, employ the stalk, stare, and chase to herd their woolly charges, but the final attack-kill sequence has been bred out. The behaviors of "hunting" breeds have been refined to those that only locate prey for the human hunter (pointers and setters), and those that bring it back once killed (retrievers and spaniels). Some dogs have been bred with an exceptionally inhibited bite that promotes a "soft mouth" to keep the dog from damaging the game as it is retrieved. Conversely, some hunters, like the Foxhound, even today remain adept at attacking and killing prey.

Eating wild game exposes dogs to the risk of parasites like TAPEWORMS or HOOKWORMS. In farming communities, the indiscriminate hunter can become a menace to livestock and poultry. The only way to prevent unacceptable hunting is by keeping the dog under your direct supervision. Confine him to a fenced yard or keep him on a leash when outside. It's best to offer dogs the opportunity to use their skills by actually hunting, herding, or tracking with their owner, or participating in mock exercises like field trials, lure coursing, herding exhibitions, or other outlets (see TRIALS). Some pets may be satisfied with alternative outlets for hunting behavior (see PLAY).

Hyperparathyroidism

This condition refers to the excessive production of parathyroid hormone (PTH or parathormone). PTH is produced by a pair of parathyroid glands located adjacent to each lobe of the thyroid gland in the dog's neck. PTH normally acts to pull calcium out of the bones and into the blood, which lowers blood phosphorus levels. It also increases intestinal calcium absorption and kidney calcium retention. (See also HYPOPARATHYROIDISM.)

When too much PTH is produced, it causes an abnormal increase in blood calcium levels and decrease in blood phosphorus levels. Bone formation in young dogs is impaired due to increased losses of calcium. Adult dogs with this condition suffer a softening and weakening of the bone, which makes them highly prone to FRACTURE. The most common cause of hyperparathyroidism is a noncancerous tumor involving one or more of the parathyroid glands. Another cause is long-standing KIDNEY DISEASE, which results in retention of phosphorus in the blood that, in turn, stimulates excessive production of PTH to counter the resulting low calcium serum level. A third cause is a dietary deficiency of calcium or vitamin D, or an excess of phosphorus (see NUTRITION and FOOD SUPPLEMENTS).

Most affected dogs are ten years or older. It appears most commonly in Keeshonds, German Shepherd Dogs, and Norwegian Elkhounds, which indicates there may be a genetic predisposition.

Mild forms of the disease may not cause obvious signs, but usually the dog exhibits increased thirst and urination, loss of appetite, lethargy and weakness, and VOMITING. Unless treated, the dog will ultimately suffer kidney failure.

HYPERPARATHYROIDISM
SYMPTOMS
Increased thirst and urination; loss of appetite; lethargy and weakness; vomiting
HOME CARE
Nutritional support
VET CARE
Surgery; sometimes vitamin supplementation
PREVENTION
Feed complete and balanced dog food

Diagnosis is based on signs and on laboratory analysis of the blood levels of calcium, phosphorus, and PTH. Surgical removal of the abnormal parathyroid tissue is the treatment of choice. When the condition is a result of nutritional inadequacy, feed a complete and balanced diet with appropriate calcium or vitamin D supplementation as advised by your veterinarian. In most cases, the chance of recovery is good. However, when the condition involves kidney failure, the prognosis is guarded and treatment must address renal disease.

Hyperthermia
h

Also referred to as *heatstroke*, hyperthermia is body TEMPERATURE above normal that cannot be reduced through natural means. The condition occurs when the body's cooling system is unable to lose heat as fast as it is gained.

The most common causes of hyperthermia are fever, excessive exertion, and confinement in a hot and/or humid area. Poor ventilation and direct sunlight are predisposing factors, and dogs are most often afflicted during the warm summer months. Dogs usually are able to lose excessive body temperature by elevating, or "fluffing," their fur to allow ventilation next to the skin, and by PANTING. When the outside temperature is close to or exceeds the dog's normal temperature (about 102 degrees), this cooling mechanism becomes much less effective.

HYPERTHERMIA (HEATSTROKE)
SYMPTOMS
Panting; drooling; vomiting; muscle tremors; temperature to 106 degrees; rapid pulse; staring; diarrhea; bright red gums; bloody nose; severe weakness; coma
HOME CARE
EMERGENCY! Wrap dog in cool, wet towel, or immerse in cool water until temperature drops to 103; SEE VET IMMEDIATELY!
VET CARE
Cool-water enemas; oxygen therapy; fluid therapy to fight dehydration; medications to treat bleeding tendency; possibly blood transfusion
PREVENTION
Keep cool water and shade available at all times; provide good ventilation; never shut dog in closed car; keep fur well groomed; restrict exercise during hottest times of the day

Most cases of canine heatstroke result when the dog is left in a poorly ventilated car parked in the hot sun. Other times, dogs don't know when to call it quits, and they overexercise during hot, humid weather. Being confined on a concrete shadeless run can also raise body temperature. Hot apartments, rooms, or dog crates that have poor circulation can also be dangerous. And dogs being groomed that are muzzled while exposed to a hot-air dryer can also suffer problems. Dogs with preexisting respiratory problems, like ASTHMA, short-nose dogs, like Pugs and Bulldogs, and OBESE dogs are highly susceptible to the condition.

Heat exhaustion is the beginning stage of hyperthermia. Dogs suffering heat exhaustion may simply collapse, exhibit VOMITING, muscle tremors, rapid heart rate, and/or pant very rapidly. Sometimes they'll faint, but more commonly the dog remains alert and has only a slightly elevated temperature. In heat exhaustion, the dog's body still works and tries to cool her.

In the more serious heatstroke, the body's temperature-regulating mechanism shuts off. All the signs are similar, except the body gets hotter faster. A rectal temperature over 106 degrees is diagnostic for heatstroke. In severe cases, the dog's gums become bright red, and she may develop a bloody nose. At temperatures over 108 degrees, the cells begin to die as they are literally cooked from the inside out. Among other things, the kidneys and liver stop working, the heart fails, and the brain is irreparably damaged. Without prompt treatment, the dog becomes comatose and will die.

Heatstroke is a medical emergency that must be treated immediately. Treatment consists of cooling the dog as quickly as possible. When the dog's rectal temperature is 104 to 108 degrees, simply soak the dog's fur in cool (not ice) water and turn on a fan to aid evaporative cooling. If the dog's temperature exceeds 108 degrees, immerse her in ice water. A cold-water enema may be required to cool her from the inside out. Check her temperature every ten minutes, and continue cooling until the temperature drops to at least 103 degrees. If she loses consciousness—and even if she doesn't—get your dog veterinary attention as soon as possible. Some cases may require hospitalization to counter damage.

Cases of severe hyperthermia will also require treatment for SHOCK, including fluid therapy to combat DEHYDRATION. Oxygen therapy helps prevent brain damage. Sometimes heatstroke may cause the dog's throat to swell, further compromising the situation and requiring a cortisone injection to counter the inflammation.

Prevent heatstroke by restricting your dog's activity during the hottest times of day, particularly in humid summer weather. A matted coat keeps heat from escaping; keep your full-coated dogs properly GROOMED and mat-free, or clip the coat short during summer months. Pay particular attention if your dog already suffers respiratory problems, or is a high-risk flat-faced breed (i.e.,

Boston Terrier, Bulldog, Pug, etc.). Always provide access to plenty of fresh drinking water, and when she must be confined, be sure she has proper ventilation and adequate shade. *Never leave your pet in a parked car*, not even with the window cracked. Even shaded cars reach 120 degrees in less than ten minutes.

Hyperthyroidism

The term *hyperthyroidism* refers to overactivity of the thyroid gland. The condition is considered rare in dogs and most commonly affects dogs older than ten years old. Any dog can be affected, but Beagles, Boxers, Golden Retrievers, and German Shepherd Dogs appear to have the highest risk.

The thyroid gland has two lobes and is located at the base of the dog's neck. It secretes the hormones thyroxine and triiodothyronine, which help regulate metabolism, the rate at which food and oxygen are turned into energy by the body. Canine hyperthyroidism occurs when a tumor forms on the thyroid gland and secretes excess hormones into the blood, speeding up the dog's metabolism.

The tumor may be benign, but more commonly is a large, malignant mass that encroaches into the dog's esophagus and trachea and surrounding tissues. These tumors frequently spread to the lungs or lymph nodes throughout the body.

Signs of hyperthyroidism include a ravenous appetite, increased thirst and urination, weight loss, hyperactivity, and increased AGGRESSION. Diagnosis is based on clinical signs, on tests that measure levels of thyroid hormones (T3

h

HYPERTHYROIDISM

SYMPTOMS
Ravenous appetite; increased thirst and urination; weight loss; hyperactivity; increased aggression

HOME CARE
None

VET CARE
Surgery; sometimes radiation or chemotherapy, or radioactive iodine therapy

PREVENTION
None; remain vigilant for signs; seek prompt treatment

and T4) in the circulating blood, and on the evaluation of a sample of tumor tissue. Treatment depends on the individual dog's age, ANESTHETIC risk, and health status.

Removal of the tumor has a good chance of curing the dog. Benign tumors and small cancerous tumors that have not yet spread are treated surgically. If all of the thyroid gland must be removed, a daily thyroid supplement provides the necessary hormone.

Tumors that are large and invasive and/or have spread can be treated with therapies that may combine radiation therapy, surgery, and chemotherapy (see CANCER). Radioactive iodine, which selectively destroys thyroid tissue, may also be used. However, dogs suffering from such tumors have a very poor prognosis.

Hypoparathyroidism

This condition refers to the deficiency of parathyroid hormone (PTH or parathormone). PTH is produced by a pair of parathyroid glands located adjacent to each lobe of the thyroid gland in the dog's neck. Normally, PTH maintains the blood calcium and phosphorus levels. (See also HYPERPARATHYROIDISM.)

A lack of PTH results in a deficiency of blood calcium levels, with a corresponding excess of blood phosphorus levels. The cause of the condition isn't known, but is commonly thought to result from an abnormal immune reaction that destroys parathyroid tissue.

Most affected dogs are females less than six years old, but there is no ap-

HYPOPARATHYROIDISM	
SYMPTOMS	
Signs appear during stress or exercise and include seizures, muscle twitching or spasms, nervousness, weakness, drunken behavior, loss of appetite, excessive panting, face rubbing	
HOME CARE	
None	
VET CARE	
Calcium and vitamin D supplements	
PREVENTION	
None; remain vigilant for signs; seek prompt treatment	

parent breed prevalence. Signs are severe and are due to lack of calcium (hypocalcemia). They tend to appear without warning, often during periods of exercise or stress. Signs include seizures (see EPILEPSY), muscle twitching or spasms, nervousness, weakness, and uncoordinated drunken gait. Dogs tend to lose their appetite, have no energy, pant excessively, and may exhibit intense facial rubbing.

Diagnosis is based on signs, along with laboratory analysis of calcium and PTH in the blood. Normal blood levels can usually be maintained by calcium and vitamin D FOOD SUPPLEMENTS as prescribed by the veterinarian. A maintenance dose of vitamin D supplements may be required for the rest of the dog's life, but in most cases, a full recovery can be expected.

Hypothermia

Hypothermia is the opposite of hyperthermia and results when body TEMPERATURE falls below normal. Dogs have many protective mechanisms for regulating body heat. Their fur insulates by trapping air next to the skin, which is warmed by the body. Dogs conserve heat by curling up in protected areas sheltered from wind and wet, and their own bodies heat the area and help keep them warm.

When they feel cold, dogs burn more calories at the cellular level, a kind of furnace that increases body temperature and helps keep them warm. Shivering is a spontaneous action of the body designed to generate heat. Cold weather also prompts the body to divert blood circulation from the ears, toes, and tail and pour more into the trunk to protect and keep warm the important internal organs. Failure of any one or several of these protective mechanisms can predispose to loss of heat and may result in hypothermia. In fact, the very action that protects organs from the cold actually promotes damage to the extremities (see FROSTBITE).

Outdoor dogs are at highest risk for hypothermia. It's seen most often in toy breeds and dogs with short fur. Very young PUPPIES are unable to regulate their own body temperature and are at high risk for hypothermia. Body heat is produced by burning muscle and fat, which are less available in very young and very old dogs (see GERIATRIC DOG). However, any dog that is exposed to extreme or long-term cold, a long anesthetic procedure, or that becomes wet or that suffers SHOCK risks hypothermia.

The severity of the hypothermia is designated *mild*, *moderate*, or *severe*, depending on the dog's body temperature. Mild hypothermia results in lethargy, excessive shivering, and sometimes muscle tremors, and the dog will feel cold to your touch. Rectal temperatures down to about 96 degrees are categorized

HYPOTHERMIA

SYMPTOMS
Lethargy; shivering; loss of shivering impulse; body temperature less than 98 degrees; loss of consciousness; slowed body function; dog appears dead

HOME CARE
If still shivering, wrap in blanket or give warm bath when already wet; when dog stops shivering and/or has subnormal temperature, it's an
EMERGENCY! SEE VET IMMEDIATELY!

VET CARE
Aggressive rewarming with heating pads, water bottles, warm-water enemas, heated oxygen, and/or heated intravenous fluids

PREVENTION
Confine dogs indoors during cold weather, and provide outdoor shelter from wind, wet, and cold; feed outdoor dogs more, or a higher-calorie food during cold weather

h

as mild and can be treated using passive rewarming techniques. If your dog is dry, simply cover him loosely with a blanket and allow his own body to rewarm itself. When the dog is wet, a warm bath will help rewarm him. Dry him thoroughly with towels. Warm a blanket or towel in the dryer, and keep him covered until he's no longer wet.

Dogs are moderately hypothermic when their rectal temperature falls between 96 and 82 degrees. At this point, the dog's shivering response will stop, and natural metabolic warming is no longer possible. Severe hypothermia occurs at body temperatures below 82 degrees; typically, the dog loses consciousness, and the heart and respiration become so slow he may be mistaken for dead. Veterinarians have special thermometers able to record these low body temperatures, but standard rectal thermometers measure only as low as 93 degrees. *If your dog feels cold to the touch but has stopped shivering, and/or loses consciousness, veterinary attention is necessary if he is to survive.*

Moderate to severe hypothermia requires aggressive rewarming techniques to reduce further heat loss, prevent organ damage, and keep vital organs working. Moderate hypothermia calls for rewarming with hot-water bottles, electric blankets, recirculating water blankets, heating pads, heat lamps, or other heat sources. Extreme care must be taken, though, because too-rapid surface warming can cause a drop in blood pressure, when the outside returns to normal more quickly than the depressed heart can handle. Heating sources are applied only to the *trunk* of the body; this keeps the extremities cool, to prevent shock that may kill the dog. Even then, the heat sources must be buffered and not in direct contact with the skin; hypothermia prevents the body from conducting excessive heat away, so the dog can be easily burned. A heat lamp should ideally be placed about thirty inches away for optimum impact without burning the dog.

Core warming is reserved for cases of severe hypothermia, and in these cases the dog is literally reheated from the inside out. A veterinarian's help is usually required. Treatment can involve warm-water enemas, warm intravenous fluid therapy, airway rewarming with oxygen, and even heart-lung bypass machines to warm the blood. Fluids may be repeatedly flushed into the abdomen to warm the organs and tissues, then drawn back out, until body temperature returns to normal. Sadly, the chance for full recovery from severe hypothermia is small, because often the organs and tissues are severely damaged.

If you suspect your dog is suffering from moderate to severe hypothermia but are unable to reach veterinary help, treat the dog by using the external warming techniques described above. Fill hot-water bottles with warm (not burning!) water that's about 100 degrees, and wrap them in a towel. Place the buffered water bottle, heating pad, or other rewarming device on the dog's chest and abdomen, and in the armpit areas beneath his legs. Monitor the dog's temperature—don't try to rewarm too quickly; a degree or two each hour is about right—until it reaches 100 degrees. If the dog begins to stir and move, when he's conscious offer him one to two tablespoons of honey or Karo syrup. Get your dog a veterinary evaluation as soon as possible.

Prevent hypothermia by protecting your dog from inclement weather. Most cases occur during cold winter months, but a brisk wind and damp weather raise the risk of hypothermia. Wet fur compounds the effects of cold, and wind strips away the protective warm-air layer caught in the dog's fur.

Provide outdoor dogs with shelter from the wet, wind, and cold. Bedding such as a blanket or loose straw makes a fine nest that holds pockets of warmer air. Heat lamps, warming pads, or simply standard light bulbs are helpful; however, they should be situated so the dog can escape direct warmth to avoid burns.

Outdoor dogs require a higher-calorie and energy-dense ration during cold weather, because the body burns more energy to generate heat. Increase both the amount and frequency of feedings. Your veterinarian can recommend a good product; a high-quality adult ration or a high-calorie puppy food is appropriate. The best way to prevent hypothermia in dogs is to keep the dog inside.

Hypothyroidism

This disease condition results from an inadequate production of the hormones thyroxine (T4) and triiodothyronine (T3) from the thyroid gland. Hypothyroidism is the most common hormonal disease condition of dogs, and it is caused by destruction of thyroid tissue due to immune-mediated disease, inexplicable atrophy, and rarely, CANCER.

All dogs are susceptible, but certain breeds appear to have an increased risk. Mid- to large-size breeds are most commonly affected, and the condition is rare in toy and miniature breeds. Some researchers report that the Afghan Hound, Airedale, Alaskan Malamute, Beagle, Boxer, Brittany Spaniel, Chow Chow, Cocker Spaniel, Dachshund, Doberman Pinscher, Bulldog, Golden Retriever, Great Dane, Irish Setter, Irish Wolfhound, Miniature Schnauzer, Newfoundland, Pomeranian, Poodle, and Shetland Sheepdog are most likely to develop hypothyroidism. Spayed females are also at higher risk.

Hormones excreted by the thyroid gland, located in the base of the dog's neck, regulate the body's metabolism. When not enough hormones are produced, energy levels fall and body processes (even at the cellular level) slow down.

Clinical signs of disease begin to appear between two to six years of age and can be mild to severe. The onset of symptoms can be very gradual, and mild disease may not be noted for some time. Typically, the dog becomes lethargic, reluctant to exercise, and loses mental focus and acts dull. Some dogs gain weight and may become obese, even though appetite and food intake remain the same. The dog suffering from hypothyroidism has trouble regu-

HYPOTHYROIDISM
SYMPTOMS
Lethargy; reluctance to exercise; dullness; weight gain and obesity; seeks warm places; thick and rough skin with symmetrically thinning fur; sometimes puffy face
HOME CARE
None
VET CARE
Blood tests to diagnose and monitor; hormone replacement therapy
PREVENTION
None; remain vigilant for signs; seek prompt treatment

lating body temperature and is more prone to HYPOTHERMIA; such dogs are heat seekers and will search out warm places to rest. Hormone deficiency also causes changes in the skin and hair coat, but the dog does not act as if he itches. Skin thickens, becomes rough and dark, sometimes is oily and scaly, and is prone to bacterial infections. The hair becomes brittle and is easily pulled out, and the affected dog exhibits excessive SHEDDING. Symmetrically thinning fur is particularly apparent on the dog's trunk and tail. In moderate to severe cases, dogs develop puffiness to the skin, which is particularly apparent in the face, with thickened, droopy eyelids and skin folds on the forehead.

Intact dogs, both male and female, will also experience fertility problems. Female difficulties include irregularity of or failure to cycle, abortion, poor litter survival, and infertility, while males may suffer testicular atrophy, low sperm count, lack of libido, and infertility.

Diagnosis is based on signs and on laboratory tests including blood analysis that measures levels of circulating hormone. The dog is conclusively diagnosed with hypothyroidism if she responds to therapy; with appropriate treatment, clinical signs usually can be reversed. Improvement in the skin and hair-coat condition may be seen after one to two months of therapy.

Treatment consists of replacing the missing hormone with a daily oral synthetic thyroid hormone called Thyroxine. Dogs will require this replacement therapy thereafter. Most recover and can lead an otherwise normal life.

h

Ibuprofen

Ibuprofen (propionic acid) is a common human pain reliever found in products like Motrin and Advil. It is one of a group of nonsteroidal anti-inflammatory drugs (NSAIDs) that includes naproxen (Aleve). Dogs benefit from pain-relieving medication when they suffer from such conditions as ARTHRITIS. However, a dog's body metabolizes, or breaks down, NSAIDs at a different rate than a human's body does.

For example, naproxen takes about fourteen hours to be eliminated from the human body, but requires up to ninety-two hours in dogs. Consequently, the equivalent of a human dose of naproxen can kill a dog. *Ibuprofen and other NSAIDs should never be given to your dog without a veterinarian's specific direction.*

Use of these pain relievers can cause ulcers, gastrointestinal bleeding, kidney damage, or stomach perforation. VOMITING is the most frequent sign, with the digested blood making the vomitus look like old coffee grounds; occasionally, bright red, fresh BLOOD is seen. Ongoing bleeding will cause weight loss over time, and ANEMIA can result.

Diagnosis is based on history of the drug used, X RAY evaluation, and/or by gastroscopy (visual examination of the gastrointestinal tract using a special instrument called an *endoscope* that's fed down the dog's throat). Treatment includes stopping use of the NSAID and prescribing ulcer medication similar to what is used in humans. Veterinary supervision is necessary.

If you suspect that your pet has ingested ibuprofen, induce vomiting (see ADMINISTER MEDICATIONS) using 3 percent hydrogen peroxide, one tablespoon per ten pounds of pet, and immediately contact your veterinarian.

NSAIDS POISONING (TYLENOL, ASPIRIN, IBUPROFEN)

SYMPTOMS
Vomiting bloody or coffee-ground-like material; weight loss; anemia

HOME CARE
EMERGENCY! SEE VET IMMEDIATELY; stop administering the NSAID medication immediately.

VET CARE
Stop administration of NSAID drug; ulcer medication; sometimes fluid therapy or other support

PREVENTION
Don't give your dog medication without a vet's advice

i

Identification

All dogs should wear identification. This protects them from being stolen and ensures their safe return should they become lost (see STRAY). Seventy percent of pets that arrive at shelters have no identification and so cannot be reunited with owners. Most of these animals are EUTHANIZED.

Although every dog is unique, it's hard for an outsider to tell the difference between like-colored dogs of the same breed; to the uninitiated, one Golden Retriever may be indistinguishable from other Goldens. For that reason, it's a good idea to record your dog's appearance with photographs. Shoot a close-up of the face and make full-body shots from both sides and the back. Also, document any distinguishing marks; perhaps your Dachshund has a thumb-size birthmark on her tummy, or your Dalmatian has three dark spots on his left hip that look like Mickey Mouse. Your description also should include the pet's color, breed, sex, age, weight, height at shoulder, length of tail, ear set, and any other distinctive markings.

Should the worst happen and the dog become lost, have photos and a description ready so that you can make posters and advertise the loss. Leave copies at area shelters to alert them; sometimes people will call shelters after finding a dog, but be hesitant to turn him in. Remember that it may not be particularly helpful to describe your hybrid dog as a Labrador/Poodle or "whatever" cross when the combination can be so varied; rather, describe exactly what the dog looks like—curly chocolate fur, forty-five-pound neutered male, drop ears, docked tail—and attach pictures.

Other identification is even more important, and several systems are available. The most common and easiest to use is a plastic or metal tag that attaches to the dog's collar. Tag identification may contain a variety of information, such as the owner's contact information, dog license number, RABIES vaccination verification, or contact information for the dog's veterinarian. The dog must wear a collar to benefit from this form of identification, though, and some pets are notorious for slipping out of collars. Be sure your dog's collar fits correctly, not too tight or not too loose; you should be able to easily slip two fingers beneath a snug-fitting collar.

Tattoos are a more permanent means of identifying your pet. Often, the owner's Social Security number or the dog's registration number is tattooed onto the skin inside of the thigh or the ear. The tattoo number can then be registered in a local or national database able to access owner contact information should the dog become lost. However, over time a tattoo may fade or be obscured by fur. Whoever finds your lost dog must know to look for the tattoo, and also know what to do with that information to reunite you with your pet.

Microchip identification is one of the newest forms of pet identification. A tiny silicon chip no larger than a grain of rice is encoded with an identification number, encased in surgical glass, and implanted beneath the loose skin of the dog's shoulders. A specialized scanner (similar to equipment used by grocery stores to read prices) retrieves the microchip information. Owner

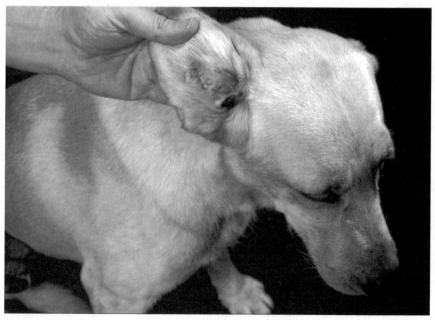

Tattoos can identify dogs (*Photo credit: Ralston Purina Company*)

and pet information is kept current by a database service, which can then match the identifying microchip code on the found animals to the owner so that the lost dog can be returned (providing that whoever finds the pet is aware of the existence of this kind of technology). Many veterinary clinics and shelters are now equipped with microchip technology (see Appendix C, "Pet Services").

Immune System

This refers to the body's complex defense system that protects your dog from microscopic organic invaders that cause injury or disease. The immune system patrols the body seeking foreign substances (antigens), then tries to either neutralize or destroy them. Antigens include viruses, bacteria, toxins, and abnormal cells like CANCER.

The immune system is composed of both primary and secondary lines of defense. The bone marrow and thymus gland are part of the primary immune system. They produce protective disease-fighting cells and molecules that patrol the blood and lymphatic system for anything that doesn't belong. The secondary immune system includes the lymph nodes and spleen, which are a part of an intricate bodywide filter that removes antigens from circulation.

There are also two types of immune responses. A *humoral immune response* refers to the custom creation of a kind of protein called an *antibody*. Antibodies are created in response to a specific antigen and are designed to attach themselves to that single kind of antigen. This marks the antigen as dangerous, so that other specialized cells can destroy it. The second type of immune response is *cell-mediated immunity*. Specialized cells like macrophages and lymphocytes attack and destroy virus-infected cells or tumor cells without the aid of antibodies.

The dog's body also has a kind of immunity memory, referred to as *active immunity*. Once an antigen is marked by antibodies and then destroyed, the remaining antibodies still programmed to recognize the disease continue to circulate. They can react immediately to the antigen should it ever return. In this way, active immunity prompts an early immune response before damage can be done. How long active immunity lasts depends on the particular antigen involved. It can be artificially created by stimulating the dog's immune system with VACCINATIONS to protect him from various diseases.

Puppies receive a transient passive immunity from their mother when they nurse her antibody-rich first milk, called *colostrum*. However, a puppy's passive immunity lasts only about four months.

Infectious Canine Hepatitis (ICH)

Also referred to as *Rubarth's disease*, ICH is a contagious viral disease of dogs caused by the canine adenovirus-1 (CAV-1). It was first described in the 1920s in foxes, and it also affects wolves, coyotes, skunks, and bears. However, it is not contagious to people. The virus is related to CAV-2, one of the causative agents of KENNEL COUGH, but the disease primarily affects the dog's liver.

Any dog can be affected, but young dogs and particularly puppies are at highest risk. The disease varies from mild fever to fatal illness, and signs may be confused with CANINE DISTEMPER.

The virus is spread via direct dog-to-dog contact by ingesting infected urine, feces, or saliva. Incubation—the time it takes for signs to appear—is four to nine days following exposure. The virus first infects the tonsils, spreads to the lymph nodes, and then the blood. The bloodstream carries the virus everywhere, but CAV-1 particularly likes and targets the liver, eyes, kidneys, and cell lining of the blood vessels.

The first symptom is fever up to 106 degrees, which may come and go and lasts one to six days. Shortly after the initial fever appears, dogs develop *leukopenia*—a low white-blood-cell count. This is important because white cells act as part of the immune system's defense team. The degree of leukopenia directly correlates with the seriousness of the illness. When the fever lasts only one day, leukopenia may be the only sign that develops. But if the fever continues longer than that, severe illness develops.

INFECTIOUS CANINE HEPATITIS (ICH)

SYMPTOMS

High fever to 106 degrees; bloody diarrhea; anorexia; thirst; lethargy; eye inflammation; eye and nasal congestion; "hunching" from painful abdomen; swelling of body, head, and neck; bleeding from mouth, nose, urinary tract, or rectum; sometimes corneal opacity

HOME CARE

EMERGENCY, SEE VET IMMEDIATELY!

VET CARE

Supportive therapy; blood transfusions; fluid therapy; antibiotics

PREVENTION

Vaccinate your dog as recommended by your vet

The most severe cases affect puppies less than four months old, and especially those aged two to six weeks. In the fatal fulminating form of the disease, the dog suddenly develops bloody DIARRHEA, collapses, and dies in a single day; other puppies die without any warning at all. To the owner, it may appear the puppy has succumbed to POISON.

The acute form most commonly affects puppies aged six to ten weeks, but can afflict dogs of any age. Signs include ANOREXIA, thirst, lethargy, conjunctivitis (inflammation of mucous membranes of eyes), and mucoid congestion of the nose and eyes. Sometimes, the dog will exhibit a "hunching" posture indicating abdominal pain resulting from a swollen liver, and may suffer bouts of bloody VOMITING and diarrhea. Edema—swelling of tissues with fluid—can develop in the neck, head, and body. Dogs with healthy immune systems are able to produce an antibody response in about a week and tend to recover. Other dogs develop bleeding disorders between the second and fifth day of infection. Hemorrhage is caused by infection of the blood vessels and results in bleeding gums, HEMATOMAS, and sometimes bleeding from the mouth, nose, urinary tract, or rectum (see also BLEEDING). Bleeding is particularly dangerous because clotting ability is also compromised by this disease.

Diagnosis is based on the abrupt onset of signs, especially the prolonged bleeding. Virus isolation techniques and other laboratory tests including analysis of a tissue sample from the liver (biopsy) may be necessary to distinguish ICH from distemper.

There is no cure for ICH. Rather, treatment is aimed at stabilizing the dog's condition and offering support until hopefully his immune system takes over and eliminates the virus. Treatment may require BLOOD transfusion in severely ill dogs, along with intravenous fluid therapy to combat SHOCK, ANEMIA, and DEHYDRATION. Subcutaneous administration of fluids (beneath the skin) can prove dangerous to dogs, because of the potential for excessive bleeding. Antibiotics are also administered; tetracycline is effective for adults, but can cause tooth discoloration in puppies and shouldn't be used unless the dog already has permanent TEETH.

Seven to ten days following the disappearance of signs, about a quarter of infected dogs develop a transient opacity of the cornea (see EYES), referred to as *blue eye*. In mild cases of ICH, this may be the only indication of disease. Treatment for the opacity is rarely required; it usually resolves on its own. Recovering dogs continue to shed virus in their urine for up to six months and should be QUARANTINED during this period. CAV-1 in the environment can be killed using iodine, sodium hydroxide, or a mixture of one part bleach and thirty-two parts water.

Highly effective preventative VACCINATIONS are available to protect your dog against ICH.

Inflammatory Bowel Disease

This syndrome refers to a group of disorders characterized by chronic inflammation of the intestine. Nobody knows what causes the disease, but several theories have been proposed. Symptoms may result from any one or a combination of an inappropriate response of the IMMUNE SYSTEM, food ALLERGY, infection, parasites, or even drug reactions. Whatever the cause, the result is inflammation that clogs the microscopic filaments lining the intestinal tract that transfer nutrients into the bloodstream.

Affected dogs suffer ongoing bouts of COLITIS. Chronic DIARRHEA is the most common sign, with frequent straining but minimal passage of stool, which may be streaked with blood. Episodes may be sporadic and occur during times of STRESS, or can be continuous.

Any dog may be affected at any age, but the condition most frequently occurs in middle-aged dogs. The Basenji, Boxer, Chinese Shar-Pei, German Shepherd Dog, and Rottweiler breeds appear to be more prone to inflammatory bowel diseases than other breeds are.

Diagnosis usually is made only after ruling out other causes for diarrhea, such as WHIPWORMS or a SWALLOWED OBJECT. Conclusive evidence requires a biopsy of the intestine, in which a sample of tissue is removed surgically from the ANESTHETIZED dog for microscopic evaluation. Sometimes a special instrument called a *colonoscope* is inserted into the dog's rectum to view the tissue. Visualization and biopsy help determine the specific type of disease by the kind of inflammation and location in the intestinal tract that's affected.

INFLAMMATORY BOWEL DISEASE
SYMPTOMS
Chronic diarrhea, sometimes streaked with blood; straining to defecate with minimal results
HOME CARE
Vet diagnosis and treatment required, then feed and medicate as recommended
VET CARE
Treat underlying cause, if it can be determined; sometimes antibiotics or immune-suppressing drugs, or limited-antigen diet or high-fiber diet
PREVENTION
None

Affected dogs cannot be cured, but their symptoms may be relieved through treatment. Because signs of disease most likely are prompted by some type of allergic response, treatment is aimed at identifying and eliminating the offending substance (if possible) and attempting to block or suppress the hypersensitive reaction.

If it's determined that a food allergy is causing problems, then a limited-antigen diet may prove helpful. Immune-suppressing drugs and medications to calm inflammation, such as corticosteroids, are often prescribed. Drugs to treat bacterial overgrowth or GIARDIA infection may be necessary. Occasionally, feeding a diet higher in fiber is recommended.

Insect Stings

Dogs are afflicted by the same bugs that pester people. Stings and bites potentially spread disease and often result in ALLERGIC reactions that make the dog itch. More often, a single sting from a bee, wasp, spider, or fly causes local irritation, but multiple stings—and sometimes even a single bite or sting—potentially may result in life-threatening reactions.

Dogs don't routinely hunt bugs the way cats do. However, puppies enjoy chasing insects, and some—especially terriers—may carry the urge into adulthood. Common insects like crickets and butterflies are harmless, but catching a bee, spider, or other biting or stinging insect can have severe consequences.

The dog's body is usually protected by fur. Most insect bites and stings are located on the less-protected lips or inside the mouth when your dog tries to catch the bug. A puppy also may suffer massive bites on the tummy and inner flanks if she walks into a fire ant mound.

Insect bites and stings typically cause painful localized swelling and/or itching. When the mouth is the target, the dog may drool and be reluctant to eat. If a stinger can be seen (bees leave them behind), remove it with tweezers or scrape it free with a credit card.

A paste of baking soda and water is an effective home remedy that eases the sting, and calamine lotion relieves itching; however, both are messy when applied to fur and would be appropriate only on the sparsely furred areas like the belly. Ice packs reduce swelling, and a dab of ammonia directly on the bites (use a cotton ball or swab) helps soothe the pain and itch.

Injuries inside the mouth are more difficult to address. When the dog is amenable, flush the area with a teaspoon of baking soda mixed in a pint of water. A turkey baster or squirt gun works well to aim the fluid onto the area, but take care the dog doesn't inhale the liquid.

A sting is often painful and only occasionally dangerous. However, dogs

BUG BITES AND STINGS
SYMPTOMS
Local irritation; swelling or itching at site; drooling or difficulty eating when stung in the mouth; anaphylactic shock happens nearly immediately and is an EMERGENCY—signs of this are drooling, difficulty breathing, swelling of face, drunken behavior, collapse
HOME CARE
Apply ice packs or dab ammonia on spots to relieve the sting; apply baking soda paste or flush with baking soda and water to soothe; anytime dog has trouble breathing, SEE VET IMMEDIATELY!
VET CARE
An injection of epinephrine (adrenaline) counteracts life-threatening reactions; more commonly, antihistamines and/or steroids are given
PREVENTION
Avoid contact with dangerous insects by supervising outdoor activities

can have a life-threatening reaction to a single bite or sting, and multiple stings tend to cause the worst reactions. The mouth, nose, or throat can swell until it's difficult for the dog to breathe. An allergic reaction called ANAPHY-LACTIC shock results in the airways closing down. The affected dog struggles to breathe, drools, become uncoordinated, and finally collapses. These signs appear almost immediately following the bite or sting. *Anaphylactic shock is an emergency that must be immediately addressed by a veterinarian if your pet's life is to be saved.* Your vet will give the dog an injection of the drug epinephrine (adrenaline) to counter the life-threatening signs.

Some spiders, like black widows, Missouri brown spiders, and tarantulas, inject a venom with their bite that causes pain at the site, followed by chills, fever, labored breathing, and SHOCK. Centipede and scorpion stings can also cause severe illness and slow-healing wounds. The bite of TICKS can cause a variety of life-threatening diseases (see BABESIOSIS, EHRLICHIOSIS, LYME DIS-EASE, ROCKY MOUNTAIN SPOTTED FEVER, and TICK PARALYSIS).

Introductions

Dogs are inherently social creatures who develop strong emotional family ties. To your dog, his family group includes human owners, as well as other pets. However, dogs are also territorial by nature, and a new family member upsets the status quo. For that reason, introduction of a new pet or person into the household should be done gradually, with attention to the resident dog's feelings.

Many dogs enjoy meeting new pets and people. Dogs tend to get bored, and a new playmate—human or otherwise—can be a welcome diversion. Other dogs, though, may be shy of new experiences, and FEAR can result in either withdrawal or hostility. Excessively DOMINANT dogs may be possessive of space or an owner's attention. How well your dog accepts another pet (cat or dog) or new family members (spouse or baby) depends the most on the dog's own personality and sense of self.

The degree to which your dog has been socialized (see PUPPY) has a great deal to do with how well he accepts new family members. Obedience TRAINING also impacts the situation. Confident dogs are more readily accepting than shy dogs. The dog that has been trained to obey your directives is more confident, less stressed, and more willing to accept new situations.

The finesse of initial introductions can tip the scales. Unless care is taken, a dominant dog may become AGGRESSIVE to the interloper, while fearful, insecure dogs can become depressed.

Dogs typically are more accepting of kittens or puppies that don't threaten an adult's status. Introducing an adult resident dog (R.D.) to a new adult cat or dog can be done successfully, too; however, the pair must themselves sort out who is to be leader of the pack—and it may not be the resident dog.

Before anything else, consider these key factors. When there is a large size difference between the two, care must be taken that the bigger pet doesn't injure (accidentally or otherwise) the smaller. After all, the gentlest Saint Bernard can cause damage simply by sitting on a Chihuahua or kitten.

Also consider the breeds, because predatory nature can to a degree be predicted by this (see HUNTING). A highly predatory dog may have difficulty stemming his impulse to chase and injure the new dog or cat. Be particularly careful when introducing a resident terrier dog to a prey-size newcomer pet, or a resident prey-size dog to a newcomer terrier or jumbo-size cat.

When possible, let R.D. learn about the newcomer ahead of time by introducing the new pet's scent on a sock or handkerchief. Simply stroke the new animal with the cloth item, then leave the scented item in your house for R.D. to find, sniff, and investigate.

One room of the house should be made temporarily off-limits to R.D. and function as the new pet's home base. That way, your dog doesn't feel all of his territory has been invaded by the new pet, only a portion. Further, the newbie has a private place to become used to the new situation.

There are a few differences to be considered when introducing a cat or a dog to your R.D. When introducing two dogs, it's helpful to make first meetings on neutral territory—in the park, a friend's house, or your neighbor's

i

**Dogs and cats can be
great friends** *(Photo
credit: Betsy Stowe)*

Take care during introductions *(Photo credit: Fran Pennock Shaw)*

yard. That way, R.D. doesn't feel defensive about his property and can let his natural curiosity prompt more amenable introductions. Both dogs should be under leash control. A new puppy typically will lick R.D.'s face and roll on her back in deference to the dominant adult. Adult dogs may posture a bit (see COMMUNICATION); allow sniffing and playing, but excessive growling or escalating aggression are your cue to take a break.

When introductions are to be made at home (which is necessary when introducing a kitten or cat), R.D. and the new pet should first get to know each other by sniffing under the door. Some cats will posture, hiss, and growl; others will ignore the entire venture until they think you're not watching. Either behavior is normal. Be encouraged if the pair begin poking and playing with each other's paws under the door.

Make every effort to make the introductions seem like a part of normal life. Don't pay too much attention to the new pet, or you risk putting R.D.'s nose out of joint. If anything, give your old friend more attention, so he'll associate the new pet with good things for him. If he's a shy, retiring dog, he may feel threatened and begin to withdraw if he feels he's losing your attention.

With dog-to-cat introductions, keep the pair separated by the private room for two or three days, allowing interaction only beneath the door. Then have them switch places for half an hour or so. This gives the pair an opportunity to investigate each other's smells and to become comfortable with the rest of the house.

When the new pet is a puppy, kitten, or a cat, R.D. should be on a leash for the first nose-to-nose meeting. When the newcomer is small, it can be placed in a pet carrier and initial sniffs can occur through the grille.

When both parties appear friendly and eager, simply open the door to the room—or the carrier—and allow the pets to meet at their own pace. R.D. should still be on a leash. New puppies typically race to meet adult dogs, but kittens and cats may be more circumspect. Don't force things; you're there to keep R.D. from becoming too excited and losing control.

When introducing two adult dogs, both should be on a leash. Get your spouse, an older child, or a friend to hold R.D.'s leash while you handle the newbie; that sends an unmistakable message to R.D. that this newcomer is welcome by the pack leader (you) and that he should follow your example. Every case is different. Initial introductions can prompt love at first sight—or the opposite.

Typically, female dogs concentrate on sniffing the newcomer's neck and face, while a male dog's interest is the genital region. Both male and female dogs try to prevent themselves being sniffed in the anal region, and they may turn circles trying to sniff each other while blocking themselves from being investigated.

Usually, it's the resident dog that takes charge, but that's not always the case. There may be some hissing or growling, but unless the situation escalates to imminent attack, let the pets sort things out (see AGGRESSION). Interrupting too soon may actually delay the determination of who's to be top dog, and force a replay of the display at a later date.

Remember, it's not always the smaller pet that's at a disadvantage. A big but shy dog may be buffaloed by an intimidating puppy or kitten, particularly if he's never before experienced another pet. Always provide an escape route for both R.D. and the newbie so they can have some privacy when they've had enough. A crate works well for dogs, while cats typically can get out of reach on a tabletop. Until the pair have accepted each other, keep them separated when you are not there to supervise.

A baby gate is a great tool for introductions. It keeps pets separated while allowing them limited interaction through the grillework. Once you are satisfied R.D. understands Newbie is a part of his family (and vice versa), you can take down the gate. In some instances, the baby gate will allow the smaller pet to regulate interaction by coming and going through the grill, while keeping out the larger pet. Use the leash until you're satisfied no fur will fly.

The same principles apply when introducing new human family members to your resident dog. When he's still a puppy, introducing him to a variety of people of all ages will prepare him for such changes as an adult and make both of your lives easier. An adult dog who has had you to himself can become difficult if you later decide to marry. And a new baby can turn the most benevolent dog into an excitable yapper.

Use a scented sock to familiarize R.D. with the new family member ahead of time, just the same as with a new pet. Tape your fiancé's voice and play it while you pet your dog, or have the fiancé bring special treats or new toys. Your dog should associate a new family member's presence with only good things.

When your family is expecting an infant, record baby sounds for the dog to hear. Don't shut out the dog—your old baby—when the new one arrives; let him be a part of your happy event. If you don't want him in the nursery, set up a baby gate so he can at least observe as you paint, change wallpaper, set up the crib, and get things ready. Wear baby powder so he associates baby smells with good things—you. Excluding the dog from this important event makes him feel left out, confused, and even scared he's losing you.

Dogs have a built-in inhibition to injuring infants—including human babies. That's why the typical dog puts up with puppy and baby antics that would prompt mayhem if they came from an adult. In fact, many dogs are delighted by babies, as long as they're made to feel a part of things. You want R.D. to recognize your baby as a part of his family, to be cherished and protected by him.

When you bring home your new baby, act like it's no big deal, even though it is. You want your dog to believe this is an expected part of dog life. Introductions shouldn't be forced; most dogs will be interested and will approach by themselves. If R.D. is calm, let him sniff the baby's foot or hand. He should know what smells so different and sounds so interesting, so he knows it's nothing to fear.

Praise your dog when he acts well. Most dogs follow your lead; be sure to continue giving your dog plenty of quality time, so his nose won't get out of joint. Play a special game with your dog that's associated only when the baby is present; that way, R.D. will welcome the baby rather than resent the baby as an interloper. If you like, your dog can be allowed in the nursery when you are there to supervise. Be aware, though, that some dogs become solicitous and protective quite early; this can be good, but can be taken to extremes. You want yourself, not the dog, to be the parent, so make it clear who is responsible for cleaning up the baby's messy face (and other areas) or you may have competition.

As the child grows, be sure she understands R.D. is not a toy. Dogs often have great patience with young children, but it's the dog's home, too. And the dog could lose self-control if hurt by the child, and cause injury.

Prevent tragedies from happening by teaching your children to respect pets from an early age. Teach your baby how to pet and hold the dog, and how to care for R.D. Love of dogs begins during childhood and can be based only on mutual respect. Such love can last a pet's lifetime, and beyond.

Jacobson's Organ

Dogs have a secondary scenting mechanism, called the *vomeronasal*, or *Jacobson's organ*. The organ is situated in the roof of the dog's mouth, between the hard palate and nasal septum. It's connected to a nasopalatine canal, or incisive duct, which opens behind the upper incisor TEETH in the mouth and allows communication with the nasal cavity.

Theoretically, the scent particle is captured on the tongue, then transferred to the incisive duct in the mouth. Fluid in the organ sacs is pumped into the ducts, then drawn back up once it captures the chemical scent, and the scented fluid is read by the organ.

Although all dogs have these specialized scent organs, experts disagree whether or not they actually use them. Cats exhibit a distinctive facial grimace, called *flehmen*, when using the organ to detect sexually specific scents, called *pheromones*. Dogs do not display this behavior (although coyotes do). Some studies conclude the organ has become nonfunctional in domestic dogs, based on the fact that no chemical receptors can be found in the sacs.

Jaundice

Jaundice refers to the abnormal yellow discoloration of bodily tissues and fluids. In dogs, jaundice is most easily seen in thinly furred or light-colored areas of the body, such as the insides of the ears or whites of the eyes. It is a sign of abnormal liver function and results from the abnormal deposition of bile pigments throughout the body (see LIVER DISEASE).

Jumping Up

Dogs tend to jump up toward people to compensate for their size. It is normal greeting behavior for dogs to nuzzle and lick each other's faces; a SUBMISSIVE dog aims attention at a DOMINANT individual's eyes and mouth. Therefore, licking the owner's face is a canine "howdy!"—a way to solicit attention.

Since most dogs cannot reach us any other way, they jump up to aim their attention at our faces, particularly during greetings. Perhaps this doesn't bother you. Many people consider jumping up cute when the dog's a puppy, but the attraction tends to fade as the dog matures. Jumping up then becomes obnoxious or even dangerous, depending on the size of the dog and the attitude of his target. There are some people in the world who dislike or are even frightened by dogs, and they will not appreciate your dog jumping up on them.

As in all problem behaviors, your dog can be trained to an acceptable alternative. Obedience TRAINING is the best way to teach appropriate canine manners. It promotes canine confidence—because, after all, she is rewarded and praised for doing well—and more important, establishes you as the boss.

Canine jumping up is a way for your dog to adore you with an appropriate greeting. Once she realizes her behavior offends you, she'll strive to find another way to say hello. Wanting to please the leader—you—is simply part of being a dog. The difficult part for the owner is explaining to the dog what you want in terms she understands.

Your goal is to give your dog every opportunity for good behavior; don't wait for her to do something wrong and then shame her. Instead, anticipate problems and structure the situation to avoid the problem.

Does your dog always jump up when you arrive home? when the doorbell rings to announce guests? when the neighbors' kid walks by? Then anticipate her behavior, and be ready with an alternative.

As your dog becomes poised to jump, say, "Sit" in a firm, commanding tone, then praise her when she does. She should wear a buckle collar during such training sessions, so that you can grasp the collar and enforce the sit if necessary.

Don't step on her toes and don't knee her in the chest. Either action can be painful, which tends to prompt avoidance behavior or even AGGRESSION. Instead of teaching your dog to greet you appropriately, such actions tell her to avoid greeting you altogether—and that's no fun for anybody.

Enlist the aid of family and friends. Drill with your dog, until sitting during greeting prompts more attention for her than jumping up ever did. It may be difficult to get strangers to conspire with you, for dog lovers may protest that they really don't mind the attention.

If a wet slurp across the mouth doesn't offend you, then you kneel down on your dog's level to put yourself in range of her kiss so she doesn't have to leap. And remember, there's nothing to stop you from training your extremely well-behaved dog to jump up—but only on your command.

Kennel Cough

Canine infectious tracheobronchitis, generically referred to as *kennel cough*, is a highly contagious and common condition affecting dogs. The disease causes an inflammation of the dog's larynx, trachea, and bronchi (tubes leading to the lungs).

All dogs are susceptible, but the disease is most common in dogs exposed to crowded conditions, such as kennels (hence, the name), shows, or other stressful conditions. Most cases cause only mild disease with signs that tend to be more aggravating to owners than dangerous to the dog. But kennel cough in puppies can cause stunted lung development and/or develop into life-threatening PNEUMONIA.

The disease can be caused by any one or a combination of several different infectious agents. The most common culprits are bacteria called *Bordetella bronchiseptica*, the canine parainfluenza virus, and the canine adenovirus-2 (CAV-2). These agents attach themselves to the delicate hairlike cilia in the dog's trachea or actually cause the removal of the cilia. Cilia normally protect the tracheobronchial tract by clearing away irritants like bacteria and other microorganisms with wavelike motions similar to wind moving a grassy field. When they are destroyed—or the agent can't be dislodged from remaining cilia—the protective mechanism breaks down, resulting in further irritation to the dog's respiratory tract.

The typical sign of kennel cough is, in fact, a chronic, high-pitched, honking cough. It can easily be prompted by excitement, drinking, or gentle pressure applied to the base of the dog's neck; the dog tugging at his leash may result in a paroxysm. Rarely there is also a nasal or eye discharge, and dogs

KENNEL COUGH

SYMPTOMS
Chronic, high-pitched, honking cough prompted by excitement, drinking, or pressure against throat; occasionally, eye or nasal discharge, slight fever, or loss of appetite

HOME CARE
None

VET CARE
Cough suppressants; antibiotics; sometimes anti-inflammatory drugs or bronchodilators to help dog breathe

PREVENTION
Reduce exposure to other dogs; vaccinate when dog will be kenneled

k

may suffer a slight fever or loss of appetite. The signs can last from a few days to several weeks.

Infection is spread through the saliva and nasal secretions and may occur by direct nose-to-nose contact. However, coughing also transmits the agents through the air from one dog to another. Signs develop four to six days following exposure.

Diagnosis is based on the dog's recent history and clinical signs. Because the disease results in a vicious cycle of irritation causing the cough, and the cough causing further irritation, cough suppressants to relieve persistent coughing are very important.

Antibiotics may be required when bacterial infections are involved. Anti-inflammatory drugs and bronchodilators that open breathing passages may also be prescribed.

Preventative vaccinations are available. However, protecting a dog from kennel cough is complicated by the fact that many different infectious agents may be involved. Some vaccinations are given by injection, while others are given as drops in the nose to stimulate a local immunity in the nasal passages (see IMMUNE SYSTEM). However, local immunity is relatively short-lived and may protect the dog for only six months or so.

Dogs at high risk may benefit from annual or more frequent vaccinations. These vaccinations may be given alone or in combination and are often recommended when you anticipate your dog will be placed at risk for exposure, such as boarding at a kennel over the holidays.

Keratitis

Keratitis is the inflammation of the cornea (see EYE). The inflammation may include an ULCER, or hole, in the cornea, or it may affect the surface only. Keratitis can be caused by an injury to the eye surface, such as a scratch or other trauma. It can also occur as a result of disease caused by bacteria or virus.

Any dog may develop keratitis, but breeds with prominent eyes, like Pekingese and Boston Terriers, are particularly prone to injury. Dogs suffering from ECTROPION or ENTROPION or from DRY EYE may also develop keratitis. The cause of German Shepherd Pannus, a noninfectious, nonulcerative, progressive keratitis, remains unknown. It can affect other breeds, as well, and result in blindness if not aggressively treated. Radiation therapy and sometimes surgery is required.

Signs are squinting from PAIN, and a loss of the transparency of the cornea. It will at first look dull, then hazy or cloudy, and finally completely opaque.

Left untreated, keratitis may result in perforation of the cornea with damage to or complete loss of sight. Deep ulcers may heal and form vision-impairing scars. Treatment depends on the underlying cause, which must also be addressed. Topical antibiotics, anti-inflammatory solutions, and pain-relieving medications are often necessary, and surgery may be required.

Most cases of keratitis can be prevented by routine eye care (see GROOMING, Eyes). Anytime you suspect injury to your dog's eye, prompt veterinary attention is important to prevent superficial injury from becoming serious, and serious injury from causing blindness.

k

KERATITIS

SYMPTOMS
Squinting; dull, hazy, or cloudy cornea; sores on eye surface

HOME CARE
Keep eye clean

VET CARE
Treat underlying cause; topical antibiotics; anti-inflammatory medications; pain-relieving drugs; possibly surgery

PREVENTION
Routine eye care, keeping eyes clean and hair clipped away from eyes

Kidney Disease

Kidney disease refers to any condition that damages or impairs the function of the kidney organs. Kidneys screen organic waste and toxins or infectious agents from BLOOD and excrete them in urine that's voided from the body. These living filters also govern the fluid composition of the dog's body, as well as the nutrient content of the blood. Kidneys also manufacture hormones that control red-blood-cell production and blood pressure.

Kidney disease is characterized as *acute* (of recent origination) or *chronic* (of long duration). Acute kidney disease affects dogs at any age and is caused by trauma, disease, or *poison* that damages the kidney. Common causes of acute kidney disease include chemical toxins, like ANTIFREEZE or certain prescription drugs; infectious agents, like LEPTOSPIROSIS; or periods of inadequate blood flow to the kidneys. If the blood pressure falls below a certain level, which may be due to DEHYDRATION, blood loss, SHOCK, or HEART DISEASE, the kidneys aren't able to function adequately.

Dogs suffering from acute kidney failure often benefit from IV fluids, which may bring the dog back to normal. Other times, dogs suffering acute kidney failure require dialysis on a temporary basis, in the hope that once the underlying condition is treated, the kidneys will begin working again. However, the machines used to clean the blood in human medicine are rarely available, or are prohibitively expensive, for veterinary applications. Peritoneal dialysis is a more commonly used option. It is a procedure whereby fluid is pumped into the dog's abdominal cavity, where it absorbs waste products, then is drawn back out.

KIDNEY DISEASE	
SYMPTOMS	
Increased thirst and urination; loss of appetite; weight loss; depression and weakness; hunching posture from pain; break in house-training; dehydration; brown-colored tongue; sores in the mouth; ammonia breath	
HOME CARE	
Supportive care; good nutrition	
VET CARE	
Supportive care; peritoneal dialysis; drugs to normalize blood; prescription diets	
PREVENTION	
Avoid toxins like antifreeze and NSAID; provide regular dental care	

Chronic kidney disease is considered a common condition of GERIATRIC DOGS. It is estimated that 10 percent of all dogs over the age of fifteen suffer from chronic renal failure, but the cause is rarely diagnosed. It's speculated that as the dog ages, the kidneys simply wear out from a lifetime of work and become less efficient.

Signs of kidney disease appear abruptly in the acute form, but develop slowly over time when the condition is chronic. The organs are able to compensate and continue to work even when severely damaged; dogs rarely show signs of illness until up to 70 percent of kidney function is gone. An owner may not notice signs of chronic kidney disease until the condition is quite advanced. Without treatment, kidneys will fail; the dog ultimately dies, either suddenly or after first falling into a coma.

Signs of kidney disease vary depending on the cause. The earliest signs include increased thirst and urination due to the inability of the kidneys to concentrate urine. Your dog drinks more water to counteract the water loss from increased urination, and the increased water intake also increases urine volume so he must urinate more often; a vicious cycle is born.

A dog suffering kidney failure tends to drink his bowl dry and may slake his thirst by drinking from toilet bowls, fish tanks, or other unusual locations. He may suffer "accidents" in the house when he can't contain himself to reach the yard in time.

As the disease progresses, other signs develop, including ANOREXIA and weight loss, weakness and depression, VOMITING, DIARRHEA, and CONSTIPATION. Infections may cause PAIN, with the dog exhibiting a hunched posture. Sores appear on the tongue and in the mouth, along with a brownish discoloration on the tongue, and breath that is foul and may smell like ammonia.

The diagnosis is based on signs, along with blood and urine tests. Special examination of the kidneys with X RAYS or ULTRASOUND may be necessary. The prognosis depends on how much damage has been done. Dogs may be able to live with mild to moderate kidney disease for months—or even years—following diagnosis and treatment.

Chronic renal disease is irreversible; it cannot be cured. Treatment, however, is aimed at stopping or delaying the progression of the disease and alleviating the symptoms to keep the dog comfortable as long as possible.

Because of the damage, the dog isn't able to effectively filter from blood all waste products that result from normal metabolism of protein. Dogs suffering kidney failure also have trouble excreting phosphorus, and the excess can result in secondary problems.

Reducing the stress on the kidneys will help slow the progression of the disease. This is accomplished by feeding a high-quality therapeutic diet that reduces or adjusts the levels of waste products produced. Reduced phosphorus helps lessen the strain on the kidneys, and restriction of salt helps manage arterial hypertension associated with canine kidney disease. Reduced protein is also important in dogs suffering *uremia*—that is, excessive levels of waste products, such as urea, in the blood. Protein restriction in these dogs helps minimize signs such as mouth sores and foul breath. Drugs like sodium bicarbonate help normalize the blood if it becomes too acidic, and potassium supplementation can help even out the blood potassium level. Lots of fresh water should be available at all times.

Although kidney transplant is now a reality in the treatment of feline kidney failure, the procedure is more complicated and rarely successful when applied to dogs. The organ is usually rejected by recipient dogs and works only if it's from a compatible sibling.

Early detection by using blood and urine tests is the best prevention. Laboratory screening techniques can identify kidney problems before they become severe. All middle-aged and older dogs should undergo periodic examinations. Routine checks—whether he's showing signs or not—can keep your dog healthy as he enters his golden years.

k

Kneecap, Slipping

Technically termed *patellar luxation*, this condition refers to the patella (kneecap) becoming dislocated due to trauma or inherited conditions. The condition is considered common in toy-breed dogs, but can affect any size or breed of dog.

In a normal position, the small bone sits on top of and protects the stifle joint of the hind leg, where the femur and tibia (thigh bones) meet. The patella is held in place by ligaments and slides over the head of the femur in grooves.

SLIPPING KNEECAP (PATELLAR LUXATION)
SYMPTOMS
Intermittent lameness; limping on affected limb or loss of its use
HOME CARE
None
VET CARE
Surgery
PREVENTION
None

A shallow groove, weak or lax ligaments, or poor muscle tone and alignment predispose the dog to a slipped kneecap. Any one or a combination of these conditions may occur due to injury, or the dog may simply be born with the condition. Rather than staying in place, the patella slips to the inside or outside of the knee. When this happens, the dog isn't able to fully straighten the knee.

Dogs may show no signs at all or may suffer intermittent lameness and limping as the kneecap slips in and out of place. Some dogs may lose all use of the limb. Keeping your dog slim and preventing excessive jumping can reduce the risk of repeat injury.

Your veterinarian diagnoses the condition by palpating, or feeling, the joint and being able to manipulate the patella in and out of place. When the condition is painful and/or causes loss of leg use, surgery to deepen the groove or realign the tendons is recommended.

k

Laryngeal Paralysis

This common condition is the abnormal movement of the vocal folds, the structures that shape the dog's voice. Movement of the vocal folds is normally tied to respiration: timed to open during inhalation and partially close with exhalation. When the timing is out of sync, or the folds don't move at all, the airway may become blocked.

Laryngeal paralysis is a rare congenital defect in the Bouvier des Flandres, Dalmatian, and Siberian Husky, but can affect any breed or age dog. It is most common in elderly hunting dogs, but is also a problem in large and giant breeds, like the Labrador Retriever and Great Dane.

LARYNGEAL PARALYSIS

SYMPTOMS
Dry cough; change in voice; noisy inhalation; excessive panting; difficulty breathing; sensitivity to heat and exercise, which may prompt blue gums and collapse

HOME CARE
Restrict exercise; reduce stress

VET CARE
Tranquilizers; corticosteroids; sometimes surgery

PREVENTION
None; once diagnosed, avoid excess stress and heat, and prevent obesity

The cause of the syndrome remains uncertain. In the past, it was considered due to HYPOTHYROIDISM, but recent studies indicate the condition is likely due to muscular and/or neurological inflammation.

Signs include a dry cough, change in voice sounds (i.e., the bark sounds different), and noisy breathing especially during inhalation. Dogs tend to pant excessively, may be sensitive to heat, and often suffer labored breathing or collapse prompted by exercise or stress. Diagnosis is based on the signs and confirmed by examination of the larynx using a laryngoscope while the dog is sedated.

Treatment depends on the severity of the signs and is aimed at relieving airway obstruction. Mild cases respond to tranquilizers and anti-inflammatory drugs like corticosteroids. Severe obstruction may require surgical correction to enlarge the opening.

Laryngitis

This is the inflammation of the larynx, which is the upper portion of the trachea that contains the sound-producing vocal cords. *Laryngitis* more commonly refers to the condition of losing one's voice, which often results from such inflammation. But the condition can become dangerous if inflammation and localized swelling interfere with breathing.

In dogs, laryngitis typically results from irritation. This may occur secondarily to an upper-respiratory-tract infection, such as KENNEL COUGH or CANINE DISTEMPER. Inhalation of an irritant like smoke or dust or the presence of a foreign body may also cause the dog to temporarily lose his voice. Trauma can also be a cause and may result from surgery that requires the placement of an endotracheal tube to administer oxygen or gas. Dogs may also suffer laryngitis as a result of simply barking too much.

The most common signs are a harsh, dry cough, gagging, and/or changes in the sound of the dog's voice; some dogs may be unable to produce any sound at all. Diagnosis is based on clinical signs and sometimes on visual examination of the tissues using a laryngoscope while the dog is sedated.

Most cases of canine laryngitis are self-limiting. That means no treatment is necessary because the dog will get better on his own simply by resting his voice. Try to avoid exposing your dog to situations that prompt excessive barking.

However, sometimes the condition can turn more serious if the inflammation proceeds to swelling. Then the dog may exhibit noisy breathing, particularly on inhalation, as breathing becomes more difficult. The dog may stand with his mouth open and his head hanging between his braced front legs. As

---

LARYNGITIS

SYMPTOMS

Harsh, dry cough; gagging; voice changes or loss of voice; sometimes noisy inhalation and difficulty breathing; head-hanging posture to ease respiration; blue gums

HOME CARE

Reduce barking opportunities; humidify air; feed soft foods; breathing difficulties (blue gums, labored breathing) are an EMERGENCY! SEE VET IMMEDIATELY!

VET CARE

Treat underlying cause; often resolves without treatment; sometimes antibiotics and cough suppressants

PREVENTION

Reduce excessive barking

---

the larynx swells, oxygen is blocked, and the dog's gums and tongue may turn blue, while TEMPERATURE and PULSE rate increase. *Obstruction of the airways—labored breathing, blue gums—is an emergency that must be seen by a veterinarian immediately;* it may require surgical tracheotomy to open a passage in the dog's throat so he can breathe.

When laryngitis is not due to excessive barking or the placement of a breathing tube for surgery, treatment depends on the underlying cause. Infections are treated with appropriate antibacterial medications. Cough suppressants, inhalation of humidified air, and feeding soft foods help speed the dog's recovery.

Lead Poisoning

Lead poisoning, though less common than in the past, is still a frequently diagnosed poisoning in veterinary medicine. It affects dogs most often because of their less-than-discriminatory eating habits and high susceptibility to the POISON.

Dogs like to mouth, bite, and chew nonfood objects. They may be exposed from swallowing the lead weight from a curtain, or a shotgun slug; when the metal remains in the stomach, ongoing exposure builds over time. Dogs may also suffer ongoing exposure by eating peeling paint, crumbling plaster, or linoleum.

LEAD POISONING

SYMPTOMS

Loss of appetite; vomiting; hunching posture from stomach pain; diarrhea or constipation; depression, or hyperactivity with excessive barking, teeth grinding, and seizures

HOME CARE

EMERGENCY! SEE VET IMMEDIATELY!

VET CARE

Stomach lavage; treat with chelating agents, like edetate calcium disodium or d-penicillamine; supportive care

PREVENTION

Monitor dog's activities; prevent her swallowing or chewing dangerous items

Any dog is susceptible, but puppies are more severely affected because of their smaller size. Most signs stem from gastrointestinal and/or neurologic systems. Initial signs in dogs are ANOREXIA, VOMITING, hunching posture from stomach PAIN, and DIARRHEA or CONSTIPATION. Neurological signs may be either depression or, more commonly, sudden hyperactivity with hysterical barking, teeth grinding, seizures, and muscle spasms. *Without treatment, the dog will die.*

Diagnosis is based on signs of illness, and lead poisoning should be suspected anytime a dog exhibits acute neurological signs but has no previous history of neurological problems. Blood tests or analysis of tissue samples from the kidneys or liver confirm the diagnosis.

Prognosis depends on the extent of injury to the nervous system, which is irreversible. In severe cases, treatment will not help and euthanasia is the kindest choice. However, in some instances, flushing the dog's gastrointestinal tract will help clear out any remaining lead.

Mild to moderate toxicities may respond favorably to treatment. Edetate calcium disodium (CaEDTA) mixed with saline or dextrose solution can be administered to the poisoned dog in several doses given every other day for three days. CaEDTA helps move lead out of the tissues and enhances its excretion through the urine. A repeat of the treatment may be necessary, after giving the dog a week of rest. Dogs may also benefit from the oral chelating agent d-penicillamine, given daily for a two-week period. Close veterinary supervision during treatment is required.

It's much easier to prevent lead intoxication than to treat its devastating effects. Monitor your dog's investigatory behavior and prevent him from chewing or swallowing dangerous items. *Note:* Whenever lead poisoning is diagnosed in a dog, any young children in the home should also be examined by a pediatrician, as they likely have also been exposed to the risk.

Leptospirosis

This disease is caused by a *spirochete*, a type of spiral-shaped bacteria that is common in many wild and domestic animals, including dogs. There is a wide variety of bacteria that can cause leptospirosis, but the canine disease most often results from *Leptospira canicola (L.canicola)*. Dogs are the natural reservoir for this bacterium, but infection usually causes mild to no signs of illness at all. Dogs may also be infected with the leptospires commonly found in the urine of livestock or rodents.

Dogs can develop life-threatening disease from any one of these agents. This is particularly important because *leptospirosis is extremely contagious and can be transmitted from infected dogs to people* (see ZOONOSIS). Fortunately, canine leptospirosis is relatively uncommon.

The bacteria infects the dog by entering through a break in the skin or when the dog swallows contaminated water or food. Drinking from standing water in cattle pens is a common route of infection in farm dogs. All dogs are susceptible, but those with outdoor exposure are at highest risk.

LEPTOSPIROSIS

SYMPTOMS
Low-grade fever; listlessness; loss of appetite; increased thirst and urination; hunched posture due to kidney pain; diarrhea; vomiting; reluctance to eat due to mouth pain; bloodshot eyes; reddened gums; brown coating on tongue; jaundice; sometimes bleeding

HOME CARE
Supportive nursing care; soft food; usually, dog must be hospitalized and treated under quarantine

VET CARE
Antibiotics; diuretic drugs to promote urination; fluid therapy; medication to control vomiting and diarrhea; sometimes blood transfusion

PREVENTION
Vaccinate your dog to reduce severity of disease; provide ample fresh water and supervise outdoor activities to prevent exposure to contaminated water

Owners probably won't notice signs of mild disease. When obvious illness develops, infection typically causes an acute inflammation of the kidneys with reversible kidney damage.

Common symptoms include low-grade fever with mild to moderate listlessness, loss of appetite, and increased thirst and increased urination. PAIN in the kidneys causes the dog to walk in a hunched posture. In severe disease, DIARRHEA and VOMITING develop, and mouth ULCERS can make eating painful. The dog may exhibit bloodshot eyes or reddened gums. A brownish coating on the tongue may be seen. Occasionally, the liver becomes affected, resulting in JAUNDICE. In rare cases, leptospirosis causes a generalized bleeding disorder that also affects the kidneys and liver.

Diagnosis can usually be made by the signs themselves, and the disease is confirmed by finding the bacteria in the dog's urine or blood. When diagnosed early and treated aggressively, most dogs recover.

The bacteria are killed and further organ damage arrested using a combination of antibiotic therapies, such as penicillin and dihydrostreptomycin. Antibiotics may be required for several weeks to ensure all the bacteria are eliminated.

Diuretic drugs that promote urination help with the kidney failure. Supportive care such as fluid therapy to control dehydration, along with medication to help minimize vomiting and diarrhea, are often required. If hemorrhage is present, the dog may need blood transfusion. Most cases require the dog be hospitalized and treated under quarantine; this not only allows the illness to be adequately treated, but also prevents transmission of the disease to people. Some dogs shed bacteria in their urine for up to a year following infection.

To reduce the chance for human infection when the dog is recovering at home, owners should wash their hands thoroughly with soapy, warm water after handling the dog. Confine the dog away from where you prepare and eat your meals. If you suspect you may have been exposed, consult your physician.

Vaccinations are available, but they *do not* prevent infection. Rather, vaccination reduces the chance of infection, and if the dog becomes infected, vaccination helps lessen the severity of disease. The best way to prevent leptospirosis in your dog is to provide him with annual vaccinations but also prevent his opportunity for infection. Don't allow him to roam unsupervised, and provide fresh drinking water so he's less tempted to drink from contaminated puddles.

Lice

Lice are wingless, flat insects that parasitize the skin using either biting or sucking mouthparts to feed. There are countless varieties, but each species prefers a specific host and tends to remain on one animal for its entire life. Dogs in North America may be afflicted with the sucking louse *Linognathus setosus*, which feeds on blood, or the biting varieties *Trichodectes canis* and *Heterodoxus spiniger*, which feed on skin debris.

Louse infestation, called *pediculosis*, is rare in dogs. This may be because flea treatment also kills lice. When it does occur, dogs contract the bugs from direct contact with an infected animal. Typically, they infest skin beneath areas of matted fur, around the head and neck, and near the anal area. Itching and poor hair coat and/or loss of fur are common signs. Severe infestations can result in life-threatening ANEMIA, particularly in small dogs or puppies.

Diagnosis is based on signs; usually owners will see the parasite or the eggs (nits) glued to the individual hairs. Nits look like white sand and are hard to brush off. Sucking lice move quite slowly, while biting lice are quicker. Both kinds are pale and small (about two or three millimeters long).

Pediculosis is treated using an appropriate insecticide; most flea preparations also kill adult lice. However, the immature nits are very resistant, and so ongoing treatment is necessary to kill these babies as they hatch. Weekly topical treatment of a dog-safe flea product is necessary for up to

LICE	
SYMPTOMS	
Scaling or scabby skin; itchiness; poor hair coat (often matted); hair loss; visible bugs or eggs stuck to hairs; sometimes anemia	
HOME CARE	
Treat weekly with a topical flea product; destroy infected bedding; thoroughly vacuum premises; provide high-quality nutrition	
VET CARE	
Rarely necessary	
PREVENTION	
Keep dog well groomed; avoid contact with other dogs; provide good nutrition	

five weeks. Anemic dogs may require fluid replacement therapy or blood transfusions.

The bugs can't survive for long when off the host. Destroy the dog's bedding and thoroughly vacuum carpets to help eliminate the parasite from the environment. Most affected dogs are run-down, poorly kept, and undernourished. Prevent lice infestation by regularly GROOMING your dog, keeping her skin and fur coat healthy and clean, and providing optimum NUTRITION.

Lick Sores

More correctly termed *acral lick dermatitis*, this is a common condition usually born of canine boredom. The affected dog incessantly licks a selected area, usually on a lower leg, which creates a raised, hairless ulcerative plaque—almost a CALLUS that surrounds the never-healing sore. The constant licking makes the area itch and can cause secondary bacterial infection. This prompts further licking to relieve the itch, and a vicious cycle is created.

Any dog can be affected, but the condition most commonly affects males older than three years. The syndrome is often seen in large, active-breed dogs that demand a lot of owner interaction, such as Golden Retrievers, Labrador Retrievers, Doberman Pinschers, Great Danes, and German Shepherd Dogs.

Diagnosis is based on the clinical signs, history, and microscopic exami-

LICK SORES
SYMPTOMS
Raised, hairless ulcer; calluslike plaque, usually on lower leg; incessant licking of sore
HOME CARE
Apply Elizabethan collar
VET CARE
Treat underlying cause, if it can be determined; sometimes antibiotics or immune-suppressing drugs; occasionally, tranquilizers or antidepressant medication may be helpful
PREVENTION
Reduce dog's boredom and alone time by playing; perhaps adopt second pet

nation of the lesion (biopsy). Treatment is difficult, and some dogs may never be completely cured. Infections may respond to antibiotics, and steroid injections may temporarily soothe itchiness. The best treatment is to alleviate the dog's boredom and give him something better to do with his time.

An owner's interaction—spending more one-on-one time with the dog playing games, walking, or training—is beneficial. Dogs that are confined alone for long periods of time tend to have more problems with boredom, and so avoiding extended confinement can help. Some dogs respond favorably when another pet is adopted into the home (see INTRODUCTIONS).

The habit may be interrupted in some dogs through the use of veterinary-prescribed tranquilizers. Antidepressant drugs such as Prozac (fluoxetine) and Anafranil (clomipramine) used in treating obsessive-compulsive disorders may be effective in certain instances.

Liver Disease

This refers to any disease or condition that interferes with any of the liver's normal functions. The liver is an organic filter that removes waste and detoxifies drugs and POISONS, and acts as a factory that manufactures and processes nutrients and enzymes.

Food in the intestine is absorbed into the BLOOD, which then ferries specific components to the liver. There, sugars and fats are processed, amino acids are produced, and certain vitamins and minerals are stored. The liver also manufactures hormones, important blood-clotting enzymes, and a substance called *bile* that allows fats to be absorbed. These products are delivered by the blood as needed by the body.

Other substances, such as drugs, that are carried by the blood are metabolized, or altered, by the liver into other forms. Foreign matter, including viruses and bacteria or poisons, are filtered out in an effort to protect the rest of the body from damage. For that reason, the dog's liver is exposed to disease and injury more than any other part of the body. Other conditions affecting liver function include birth defects, parasites, and CANCER. *Liver disease is serious and often life-threatening to the dog.*

The signs of liver diseases are remarkably similar, whatever their cause. Commonly, liver dysfunction results in ANOREXIA, VOMITING, DIARRHEA, weight loss, and lethargy. When bile backs up in the circulation, it can turn light-colored areas of the dog's body pale yellow or tea-colored. This is called JAUNDICE and is most easily seen in the whites of the eyes, gums, or inner sur-

LIVER DISEASE

SYMPTOMS
Refusal to eat; vomiting; diarrhea; weight loss; lethargy; sometimes jaundice to inside of ears or whites of the eyes or gums; swollen abdomen; bloody urine or stool

HOME CARE
EMERGENCY! SEE VET IMMEDIATELY! Once diagnosed, supportive nutrition

VET CARE
Treat the specific cause; supportive care; steroid-type drugs; prescription diet; sometimes drugs to kill parasites; congenital defects are surgically corrected

PREVENTION
Keep poisons out of reach of the dog

faces of the ear flap. Increased pressure of the veins that drain into the liver may result in *ascites*, which is an accumulation of fluid in the abdomen. The dog's abdomen will appear swollen or bloated. Hemorrhage is another sign of advanced canine liver disease, with BLEEDING into the stomach, intestines, and urinary tract; blood in the stool or urine is the sign.

Unfortunately, a wide variety of other illnesses may also involve the liver. Early signs can be vague, so that the dog owner may not realize there's trouble until the disease is quite advanced.

Treatment depends on the specific cause of the disease. Diagnostic blood tests look for changes in liver enzymes, and an ULTRASOUND is also helpful. A definitive diagnosis requires a microscopic examination or culture of the liver tissue, but the dog should be screened for any bleeding disorders before undergoing biopsy, which may require surgery. Other times, cells may be collected for examination using a fine needle inserted into the liver through the abdominal wall. This procedure—an ultrasound-guided fine-needle aspirate—requires ultrasound so that the needle can be accurately placed.

Chronic hepatitis, or inflammation of the liver, is the most common liver disease of dogs. All dogs are at risk, but mature dogs six to eight years old (especially Doberman Pinschers) are at highest risk. Most cases are idiopathic, which means no cause can be determined; a virus, drug toxicity, or abnormal immune response is thought to be at fault. When a cause can be determined, it's often due to another generalized disease such as CANCER,

KIDNEY DISEASE, or infection. Treatment consists primarily of supportive care and removal of the cause, if known. Prognosis depends on the cause, but usually isn't too good. About 30 percent of dogs suffering from hepatitis will die within one week of diagnosis, despite treatment. The remaining dogs, when treated with immune-suppressing drugs like corticosteroids and fed a veterinarian-prescribed therapeutic diet, tend to live longer. When diagnosed and treated very early, liver damage in some instances may be reversible.

Degenerative changes in the liver may occur due to anorexia, DIABETES MELLITUS, PANCREATITIS, gastrointestinal disease, or cancer. When the cause can be controlled, it's expected the liver can return to normal function.

A congenital defect may result in a *portasystemic shunt*, an abnormal connection of a vein into the liver that should normally close off shortly after the puppy is born. When the vein remains open, blood is shunted through this opening instead of passing through the liver. Small dog breeds, like Yorkshire Terriers and Miniature Schnauzers, are most commonly affected, although all dogs are at risk. Any dog with this defect will usually show signs of liver disease before reaching a year old; occasionally, dogs will not show any signs until they are older. Diagnosis can be confirmed by a combination of blood tests, ultrasound, special X RAYS, and/or exploratory surgery. Surgical correction is the treatment of choice for some types of shunts, and a reduced-protein diet in the interim relieves the clinical signs of the condition.

A diet with a nonmeat protein source places less strain on the liver and gives it a chance to heal. Some experts recommend a soy, tofu, or cottage cheese diet combined with a bland carbohydrate source like boiled white rice, and supplemented with an appropriate vitamin and mineral mix. However, it's best to follow your veterinarian's advice since he or she is most familiar with your dog's diagnosis, clinical condition, and dietary needs. Also, protecting your dog from poisons helps prevent toxicity-induced liver damage. (See also COPPER POISONING, FLUKES, and INFECTIOUS CANINE HEPATITIS.)

Lungworms

Lungworms are slender, hairlike worms that parasitize the branches of the respiratory tract. Two kinds of lungworms affect dogs: *Filaroides osleri* are contracted when the dog swallows the eggs or larvae found in infected feces or saliva; *Capillaria aerophila* are contracted by a dog eating infected earthworms.

Adult worms live in the lung tissue, where they lay eggs. The hatched larvae are coughed up and usually swallowed by the dog. Puppies may be infected by contact with their mother when she licks them. Finding larvae or eggs in a stool sample during microscopic examination is diagnostic; sometimes a sample is taken directly from the trachea and bronchials using needle aspiration.

The two types of lungworms cause different kinds of disease. *Capillaria aerophila* live in the nasal cavities and upper airways and rarely cause symptoms. It takes about thirty days from the time the dog swallows the infective earthworm for adult lungworms to emerge. At most, dogs may suffer a chronic cough and harsh sneezing. The eggs found in the stool sample closely resemble those of WHIPWORMS, and misdiagnosis is common.

Infestation of *Filaroides osleri* are more dangerous and are largely a problem in kennels, where they can affect entire litters of puppies, which contract the parasite from infected feces or saliva. It takes about ten weeks for worms to develop in the dog. The parasites are isolated in encapsulated, grayish, wartlike growths up to three-quarters of an inch in diameter within the trachea. These nodules can result in BRONCHITIS, causing harsh, dry coughing spells. ANOREXIA and weight loss may result, and in severe cases, up to 75 percent of affected puppies in a litter may die.

Bronchitis may be treated with antibiotics and requires a veterinarian's care. Worm medications such as fenbendazole and levamisole are effective against *Capillaria aerophila*, but currently there is no effective medication to kill *Filaroides osleri*. Routinely picking up feces and practicing good hygiene in the kennel, as well as preventing dogs from eating earthworms, will help prevent infection.

LUNGWORMS
SYMPTOMS
Harsh, dry cough; labored breathing; refusal to eat; weight loss
HOME CARE
None
VET CARE
Antibiotics; medication to kill the parasite
PREVENTION
Prevent the dog from eating earthworms; limit contact with other dogs

Lupus Erythematosus Complex

This refers to an autoimmune disease that may affect only the skin (usually of the face) or, in rare cases, the entire body. Essentially, instead of acting in a normal fashion to protect the body from outside invaders, the dog's IMMUNE SYSTEM goes haywire and attacks itself.

The first type, *discoid lupus erythematosus*, is considered quite common. It can affect any dog at any age, but is most common in Collies, Shetland Sheepdogs, German Shepherd Dogs (white German Shepherds are at particularly high risk), and Siberian Huskies.

Because of the high incidence of the condition in Collies, and the possible influence of sunlight, the condition has in the past been referred to as *Collie nose*, or *nasal solar dermatitis*. Whether or not there is a direct causal relationship between exposure to ultraviolet radiation and development of discoid lupus erythematosus isn't known, but sun exposure does aggravate an existing condition. Lesions are more severe during the summer months and in high-exposure geographic regions such as high altitudes.

The first signs are loss of skin color and reddened, scaly skin particularly on the bridge of the nose. The dog loses hair in the affected regions, which develop crusting sores. The leather of the nose (the tip) is also affected and

LUPUS ERYTHEMATOSUS COMPLEX

SYMPTOMS
Loss of skin color and reddened, scaly skin on bridge of nose; eroding nose tip; ulcers and crusting sores around mouth and eyes; sometimes footpad ulcers and joint disease

HOME CARE
Protect dog from direct exposure to sunlight; use sunscreens on high-risk areas

VET CARE
Same as home care; also, anti-inflammatory creams or ointments, or sometimes pills or injections; treat systemic illness with supportive care, along with immune-suppressing drugs

PREVENTION
Protect dogs from sunburn, particularly white-faced and sparsely furred dogs; keep dogs inside during high sun-exposure hours, and/or protect with sunblock

seems to erode. Sores and ulcerations grow progressively worse and may also involve the muzzle, lips, around the eyes, and ear margins.

Diagnosis is based on clinical signs and on skin biopsy in which a sample of the affected tissue is examined for characteristic changes. Treatment is similar to that for SUNBURN. Affected dogs should be kept away from direct sunlight, and owners should apply sunscreen to the dog's nose, ears, or other high-risk areas. The veterinarian may prescribe anti-inflammatory creams or ointments for affected tissues; anti-inflammatory pills or injections are only rarely used.

Systemic lupus erythematosus (SLE) is considered quite rare in dogs, and it appears to be similar to the condition in people. Skin sores similar to the discoid lupus condition also appear in this disease, and dogs may also develop footpad ulcers; however, SLE affects the whole body, attacking blood, joints, kidneys, heart, and other organs, often at the cellular level.

Signs of disease depend upon the organ affected and the severity of disease. Diagnosis is similar to that of discoid lupus erythematosus, in that skin biopsy and clinical signs are evaluated. In addition, a blood test can detect the antibodies that attack DNA; their presence provides definitive diagnosis in both dogs and people. Immune-suppressing drugs such as corticosteroids offer the best treatment hope for dogs suffering SLE. Such dogs should also be protected from exposure to the sun. Their prognosis is guarded.

Lyme Disease

Lyme disease was first identified in 1975 when a cluster of childhood arthritis cases were reported in Lyme, Connecticut. It's caused by a spirochete, a type of bacteria named *Borrelia burgdorferi*, that occurs naturally in white-footed mice and deer. The organism is transmitted to people and dogs by TICKS.

A number of tick species are able to carry *B. burgdorferi*, but the deer tick, *Ixodes scapularis* (formerly called *Ixodes dammini*) is the most effective transmitter of the Lyme bacterium. It's found most commonly in the northeastern, north central, and Pacific Coast states.

Deer ticks mature in a two-year cycle, progressing from egg to larvae, nymph, and then adult. Adult ticks prefer to feed on deer, but immature stages feed on white-footed mice and sometimes other warm-blooded animals. The Lyme bacterium makes its home in deer and mice, which don't become sick, but spread the disease to ticks at any stage when they feed on infected blood. Both the nymph and adult tick are able to transmit the disease to people and dogs and will make do with such victims when a preferred host isn't available.

LYME DISEASE

SYMPTOMS
Sudden lameness with limping; painful, swollen joints; sometimes fever; history of tick infestation

HOME CARE
Remove ticks; requires vet treatment

VET CARE
Antibiotics; sometimes supportive care

PREVENTION
Put tick repellents and insecticides on dog and environment; prompt mechanical removal of ticks; vaccination when recommended by vet

Human symptoms include a red rash around the tick bite in a kind of "bull's-eye" pattern. Other early signs involve flulike symptoms, including fever, headache, stiff joints, and swollen lymph nodes. The disease can ultimately cause ARTHRITIS, lethargy, heart disorders, and damage to the nervous system.

The most common sign of Lyme disease in dogs is a sudden lameness (limping) from painful, swollen joints; dogs may also run a fever. Diagnosis is based on the presence of these signs, a history of being in an endemic region, and blood tests. However, blood tests that measure antibodies to the bacteria do not confirm the disease and indicate only that exposure has taken place. In endemic regions, up to 50 percent of tested dogs will show they have been exposed to the bacterium, yet may show no signs of disease.

A positive reaction to antibiotic therapy is a better confirmation of diagnosis. Dogs may refuse to walk, yet within twenty-four hours of antibiotic treatment (usually tetracycline) appear to be fully recovered. Antibiotics are most effective when given soon after onset of the symptoms.

There is a preventative vaccine available for dogs; ask your veterinarian if it is appropriate for your situation. Deer ticks are found in high grass and weeds between the lawn and the woods, and pets and people that roam these areas are more likely to pick up ticks. Use veterinarian-approved tick repellents or insecticides like fipronil (Frontline Top Spot), which kills both FLEAS and ticks.

Prevention also includes removing ticks promptly. The tick must feed twelve to twenty-four hours before the organisms will be transmitted into the host; when your dog comes inside, immediately inspect him for ticks and remove them with tweezers to avoid exposing yourself. People don't become infected from their pets, but you can become sick by touching infected ticks, so wear gloves.

Application of insecticide directly to the tick-infested environment is another method of control. However, since the tick's life cycle is two years, one application isn't enough.

People living in endemic areas should wear light-colored clothing, tape socks over pants cuffs, and use insect repellents on clothing and exposed skin when in tick-infested areas. For further information, call the Lyme Disease National Hot Line at (800) 886-LYME.

Malabsorption Syndrome

This uncommon condition refers to the inability of the dog's body to digest and/or to absorb food that is eaten. Any dog may be affected, but German Shepherd Dogs appear to have the highest incidence.

Dogs with this condition may have a healthy appetite, but appear malnourished and thin and have a poor hair coat despite eating well. The dog produces a large volume of stool that typically contains a great deal of fat, giving it a characteristic rancid odor. The fur surrounding the anus is often greasy or oily.

The most common cause of malabsorption syndrome is pancreatic insufficiency, when the pancreas fails to produce the necessary digestive enzymes (see also PANCREATITIS). This syndrome is most common in dogs two to three years old.

LIVER DISEASE is another cause, which results in a lack of bile, the substance that allows fats to be absorbed. Parasites or viral or bacterial infections that cause intestinal damage may also result in malabsorption. A more recently identified cause of the syndrome is bacterial overgrowth of the small intestine, in which normal bacteria proliferate to excess levels.

Treatment depends on the cause of the condition, and a variety of specialized laboratory tests may be required for diagnosis. Analysis of the stool reveals the presence of undigested dietary fats, starches, and/or muscle fibers. A blood test may confirm pancreatic insufficiency. A biopsy of the intestinal tissue may be necessary.

Depending on the cause, treatment may include replacing the missing components necessary for digestion of the dog's diet. For instance, the missing pancreatic enzymes may be added as a powder to the food. When bacterial

MALABSORPTION SYNDROME

SYMPTOMS
Malnourished appearance despite healthy appetite; poor hair coat; large stool volume; fatty, rancid-smelling stool; oily fur surrounding anus

HOME CARE
Feed a highly digestible diet, as directed by vet

VET CARE
Treat underlying cause; supplement diet with pancreatic enzymes; sometimes antibiotic therapy; prescription diet, such as cottage cheese or tofu with boiled rice

PREVENTION
None

---

overgrowth is the cause, antibiotic therapy is the treatment of choice. Other times, feeding a diet that is more easily digested may be required for the rest of the dog's life; a combination of cottage cheese or tofu with boiled rice along with a balanced vitamin and mineral supplement may be recommended. Always consult with your veterinarian to ensure your dog receives the best treatment and diet for his situation. (See also INFLAMMATORY BOWEL DISEASE.)

Mammary Glands

Also called *breasts*, mammary glands are modified sebaceous glands of adult mammals that provide nourishment to offspring by secreting milk through nipples. Both male and female dogs typically have eight breasts located in four pairs along the abdomen, but most male dogs do not produce milk.

When not producing milk, mammary glands remain nearly flush with the abdomen and are apparent only by slightly elevated, light pink nipples. Milk production causes swelling of the breast tissue and darkening of the nipples, and the fur surrounding the nipples may thin. The breasts nearest the flanks tend to produce the most milk and so are often favored by puppies.

A lump, bump, or swelling of the breast not associated with milk production requires immediate veterinary evaluation to rule out CANCER. If a mother dog suffers a high fever during nursing, this may indicate trouble; stop the pups from nursing and take the DAM to see a veterinarian (see ECLAMPSIA and MASTITIS).

Mammary glands give milk to pups *(Photo credit: Ralston Purina Company)*

m

Mange

Mange is a generic term that describes a skin condition caused by microscopic parasites, called *mites*, that live on or in the skin. Mites are similar to insects, but are actually more closely related to spiders.

Mange is caused by a wide variety of mites, but only three kinds typically cause problems in dogs (see CHEYLETIELLOSIS, DEMODICOSIS, and CANINE SCABIES). Depending on the mite involved, skin disease can be mild to severe.

Marking

Marking is a behavior used by dogs to identify territory. Dogs primarily use urine, and possibly scratching, to leave visual and scent cues. These signals not only indicate ownership, but also act as a canine bulletin board to tell other dogs who have been there before them, how long ago the mark was left, the sexual status of that dog, and other important information. However, because the scent of urine tends to fade as soon as it contacts the air, markings must be constantly freshened with new markings on top of or nearby the original.

Marking is different from elimination behavior. When the purpose is to simply void a full bladder, female dogs usually urinate downward in a crouched position over a flat surface like the ground; males may also squat to urinate. In contrast, marking is done from a standing position by cocking a rear leg and aiming the urine stream at a (usually) vertical object. This places the scent at a convenient sniffing level, just as people would place a Post-it note at eye level to attract the most attention.

Both male and female dogs urine mark, but typically it is the male that is most enthusiastic. And it is the intact dog able to produce puppies that exhibits the most prominent behavior. Females also may leg-cock to announce their breeding availability to male dogs.

It takes very little urine to send the intended message. During walks with your dog, he may stop you every five yards or so to leg-cock against a tuft of grass, telephone pole, or other obvious landmark. By the end of the walk, he may run out of urine but continue to leg-cock, in effect simply going through the motions. This is thought to be a visual signal to any watching dogs.

Urine marking is a sign of DOMINANCE that has great social and sexual significance to dogs. However, sometimes they get carried away and mark inappropriate targets. Extremely dominant dogs may even urinate against a

m

Dogs scent-mark with urine *(Photo credit: Betsy Stowe)*

person's leg, and intact indoor dogs often feel compelled to scent their household top to bottom. NEUTERING greatly reduces leg-cocking behavior, thereby curtailing the baptism of bedroom walls, tires, and furniture.

Altered dogs of either sex that excessively mark with urine usually are experiencing STRESS. When feeling insecure, a dog attempts to assert control over his or her environment by aggressively marking territory with the comforting familiarity of personal scent. SOILING may also be due to medical problems.

Another behavior thought to be a part of canine marking repertoire is the ground-scratching or dirt-kicking common to many male dogs and, less often, females. These dogs typically scratch the ground after urinating or defecating. The behavior isn't completely understood.

One theory says that perhaps scratching or kicking the ground following elimination helps spread the scent; however, dogs may move after splashing urine on the side of a building and kick up grass some distance away. Others believe there may be scent left during the scratching or kicking behavior from glands in the dog's feet, similar to what cats use when scratching objects. The scarred ground could also be a visual sign of territorial marking.

m Mastitis

Mastitis is an inflammation of the milk glands in the breast. Infection most commonly develops in one of two ways: Either bacteria is introduced by a scratch or puncture wound from the puppies' claws during nursing, or not enough milk is evacuated from the breasts and they become blocked or caked (galactostasis).

Caked breasts are more uncomfortable than dangerous, but can lead to infection if not addressed. It's usually the two hindmost breasts that are affected. The condition may result when too much milk is produced; puppies don't suckle adequate amounts to relieve the pressure; or a deformed nipple prevents milk from being expressed. Sometimes dogs suffering from FALSE PREGNANCY produce milk, then develop caked breasts when there are no puppies to suckle.

Breasts that are caked will be swollen, hard, warm to the touch, and very sensitive and painful. When the condition progresses to infection, the mother dog also loses her appetite and refuses to eat, is listless and/or restless, and develops a high fever.

Both the tissue and the MILK produced are affected. The milk may appear normal, but often is tinged with blood or has a yellowish cast, or is thick or stringy. Normal bitches' milk has a pH between 6.0 to 6.5, and you can test

MASTITIS

SYMPTOMS

Swollen, hard, hot, and painful breasts; high fever; anorexia; yellow or blood-streaked milk, or milk that's stringy or thick

HOME CARE

EMERGENCY! Remove puppies and hand-feed, and SEE VET IMMEDIATELY! Once diagnosed, massage affected breast several times daily, apply cold, wet compresses, and medicate as directed

VET CARE

Culture milk to diagnose; administer appropriate antibiotics; sometimes surgical drainage is required

PREVENTION

Clip puppies' claws; spay dog to prevent future pregnancies

the acidity of the milk using litmus paper. Milk from caked breasts should be evaluated by your vet or tested with litmus paper before letting puppies nurse. If the litmus paper tests the milk at a pH of 7.0 or higher, the milk is infected and dangerous for the babies.

Puppies that ingest toxic milk become ill and can die. Signs of toxic-milk syndrome in puppies may include depression and lethargy, DIARRHEA, fever, and bloating. Puppies should be prevented from nursing from infected breasts. It is possible to tape over the nipples of the infected breasts to prevent puppies from suckling; however, it's safer to bottle-feed the babies using a canned commercial canine milk replacer available from your veterinarian (see MILK, AS FOOD).

In the meantime, get the BITCH to a veterinarian immediately. Infected milk must be cultured to discover the type of bacteria involved, so the appropriate antibiotic may be administered. If an abscess develops, surgical drainage of infected glands may be necessary.

Caked breasts may be resolved using gentle massage of the affected gland twice a day. Application of cold packs helps relieve the pain and also reduces milk production. If nursing is no longer necessary, your veterinarian may administer the drug bromocriptine (Parlodel), which helps dry up the milk and stop lactation.

Megaesophagus

This condition refers to an enlargement of the esophagus, the tube that moves food down the throat and into the stomach. Megaesophagus results in a partial or complete paralysis of the esophagus. The nerves that tell the tube to move food simply don't work, and the food when swallowed must fall downward to get to the stomach. Unfortunately, food comes back up even more easily.

In some instances, adult dogs can develop the condition. However, most cases are congenital; puppies are born with the defect. Congenital megaesophagus appears to primarily affect larger-breed dogs, such as German Shepherd Dogs and Great Danes.

Affected dogs typically have a voracious appetite, but are underweight because of difficulty holding food down. Often, the puppy or dog suffers chronic regurgitation in which food comes back up immediately after eating, or hours thereafter. Rather than immediately passing into the stomach, the food may sit in the esophageal passage, ballooning and enlarging the tube even more.

Diagnosis is based on clinical signs. X RAYS using swallowed barium as a contrast medium are required to confirm the diagnosis and to evaluate structure and function of the esophagus.

Unfortunately, there is no effective treatment for congenital megaesophagus. Feeding the affected dog in an elevated position—having him stand on his hind legs while he eats from a table, chair, or elevated box—may help keep food down. Semiliquid diets may pass more easily into the stomach than solid foods do. However, the condition makes puppies and dogs prone to pneumo-

MEGAESOPHAGUS
SYMPTOMS
Dog is always hungry but underweight; suffers chronic regurgitation
HOME CARE
Feed dog from a table so she stands on her hind legs; offer semiliquid food
VET CARE
Treat underlying cause when possible
PREVENTION
Be vigilant to swallowed objects or poisons

nia if vomitus is inhaled on the way up. Prognosis is poor in cases of mega-esophagus, and often the puppy is humanely euthanized.

Cases of acquired megaesophagus may be reversible when adult-onset magaesophagus is due to SWALLOWED OBJECTS, CANCER, nerve disorders, or toxins like LEAD POISONING. Supervise your dog's recreational chewing to prevent his swallowing inappropriate objects that might lead to this condition.

Metritis

Metritis is the inflammation and/or infection of the uterus; it typically occurs shortly after giving birth. Some cases are caused when not all the placenta and birth materials are expelled from the uterus. Others result from contamination of the birth canal when unsterile fingers or instruments are used to help during whelping.

The most common sign is fever, and BITCHES should be examined by a veterinarian immediately after they have whelped. An injection of oxytocin may be administered to induce the uterus to expel the placenta. Antibiotics are usually prescribed to treat metritis. The condition can be prevented by SPAYING the dog and preventing pregnancy.

m

METRITIS

SYMPTOMS
Fever following the birth of puppies

HOME CARE
None

VET CARE
Antibiotics

PREVENTION
Veterinary injection of oxytocin after whelping to clean out uterus; spay the dog to prevent future pregnancy

Milk, as Food

As soon as they're born, puppies begin suckling and thrive on their mother's milk. If a PUPPY is orphaned or the mother can't feed the baby, milk is the obvious substitute.

However, the composition of BITCH's milk and cow's milk is quite different; cow's milk provides only half the necessary nutrients for a growing puppy. Also, the lactose content of cow's milk is three times higher than bitch's milk. Lactose is a kind of sugar in the milk, and many puppies and adult dogs have inadequate amounts of the enzyme lactase in their intestinal tract that's necessary to break it down. Feeding cow's milk to puppies or adult dogs often results in DIARRHEA. Lactose-free milk may work better for giving adult dogs a treat.

But on a calorie basis, cow's milk has 15 percent less protein than bitch's milk, which makes it inappropriate as a substitute for puppies. Human baby formula is similar in composition to cow's milk, and so isn't a good substitute. An interim option (emergency only) is using canned evaporated milk; dilute three parts milk with one part water.

The best choice for long-term supplemental or replacement feeding of puppies is commercial puppy milk replacers. These are formulated to closely resemble the nutrient composition of bitch's milk. Esbilac (PetAg) and other brands are available from your veterinarian and pet store.

Many adult dogs may like the taste of milk, but treat your dog with caution until you determine whether or not an upset tummy will result. There are a few commercial lactose-free milk drinks made for pets for owners who want to treat the dog without risking diarrhea.

Mismating

Mismating is the application of medications designed to terminate an unwanted canine pregnancy. BITCHES that are in heat are notoriously difficult to protect from the attentions of amorous males (see REPRODUCTION). A couple of options are available, depending on the specific circumstances.

One option is veterinary administration of the estrogen (hormone) compound estradiol cypionate (ECP), which usually has no adverse affect on the dog's future fertility. The drug prevents normal implantation of the fertilized eggs into the wall of the uterus. However, the FDA has not approved this method because use of estrogen is associated with side effects, including severe—even fatal—suppression of bone marrow function. Dogs may also suffer dangerous infections of the uterus (see PYOMETRA) or prolonged heat cycles. If you choose this method, the dog *must* receive the drug within seven days of the mating.

Yet another choice is clinical abortion, which can be induced for up to forty days into gestation. Injections of prostaglandin are used, which stop the normal production of the hormone progesterone. The lack of progesterone prompts the uterus to contract, resulting in an abortion of the developing puppies. Hospitalization is required to monitor side effects. These can include PANTING, DROOLING, VOMITING, and DIARRHEA, but are typically not life-threatening.

When the bitch is not to be used in a professional breeding program, the best choice is SPAYING. It is an economical, permanent solution that can be safely performed during early pregnancy with almost no risk to the dog. Later-stage surgery is also possible, but is more involved and does pose some risk.

Muzzle

m

The muzzle is the front part of a dog's face that includes the nose, mouth, and jaw. The term also refers to confining or enclosing this part of the dog's anatomy, to prevent him from using his teeth and/or mouth and to protect handlers from injury.

Commercial muzzles are available from veterinarians or pet-supply stores. Most are designed to fit over the dog's face and are secured behind his ears. Homemade muzzles are also effective. (See also RESTRAINT.)

Navigation

Navigation refers to the dog's ability to find his way home. Canines allowed to roam may cover territory of several square miles. The homing mechanism for FERAL or free-roaming dogs is a survival tool that guides them to familiar territory after distant exploration.

Dogs "map" their territory using MARKING behavior that leaves scented signposts along the way. The scent-oriented breeds are particularly adept at simply backtracking by sniffing their own paw-steps. Also, dogs may note visual landmarks or familiar sounds, such as a stream or a noisy highway. By reading these signals, most dogs can easily retrace the route home.

The roaming canine is equally familiar with the smells of other dogs in adjacent or overlapping territories, which tell him how far and in which direction from home he may be. Should he become separated from his owner—say, he leaps the fence chasing a squirrel from Grandma's yard during your out-of-town visit—some dogs are able to use this knowledge to return home. Behaviorists believe dogs travel in a kind of ever-increasing spiral until they run across a familiar scent—like a neighboring dog's scented signpost. This gives them their bearings, so they can from that point head directly home.

What of the tales of amazing journeys in which dogs traveled hundreds of miles to be reunited with loved ones? Again, when returning to familiar territory, it's believed that displaced dogs may be stimulated to travel in a certain direction to make the relationship between the sun's position and his own internal clock "feel" normal again. Dogs may be able to use the position of the sun or setting stars to point them in the right direction, just as migrating birds use a kind of internal compass.

In fact, microscopic deposits of iron have been found in the front part of the brains of cats and some other animals, like homing pigeons, and it's possible that dogs may have this as well. Scientists believe the substance acts like a neurological compass that responds with geomagnetic sensitivity to the earth's magnetic field.

Nobody knows whether a mysterious compass or inexplicable psychic ability accounts for the extraordinary homing ability of some dogs. However, there are many more dogs lost each year than ever find their way home. Few dogs are blessed with an infallible homing ability; some can become lost only a block away from home, while others may be fatally injured or killed during their ramblings.

The best way to ensure your dog's safety is to confine him in the house or an enclosed yard whenever not under your direct supervision. Your pet should also always carry some form of IDENTIFICATION so that should you become separated, you can be reunited.

Neutering

Neutering, also called *altering* or *sterilizing,* refers to the surgical removal of an animal's reproductive organs. In pets, *neutering* usually refers to males, while *spaying* refers to females. A male's testicles are removed in surgery called a *gonadectomy* or *castration.*

Neutering not only prevents the births of unwanted puppies, it reduces—and in some cases, eliminates—certain health and behavioral problems. Excessive roaming and AGGRESSION, which can result in ABSCESSES; excessive MARKING behavior; and embarrassing "mounting" behavior are all greatly reduced in neutered dogs, making them better pets. Castration also eliminates any chance of testicular cancer, which accounts for up to 7 percent of all canine tumors. Prostate problems are suffered by more than 60 percent of sexually intact male dogs over the age of five (see PROSTATE INFECTION); neutering drastically reduces the chance of your dog ever having these problems.

To reap the greatest benefits, avoid behavior problems, and prevent unplanned puppies, dogs ideally should be neutered before reaching sexual maturity. Timing varies from dog to dog and from breed to breed, but most male dogs are able to reproduce by five or six months of age. Healthy dogs may be castrated at any time, and the procedure can be done safely on puppies as early as eight weeks of age. The American Veterinary Medical Association currently endorses four months of age to be an ideal time for the surgery.

Neutering is performed while the dog is under a general ANESTHESIA. A

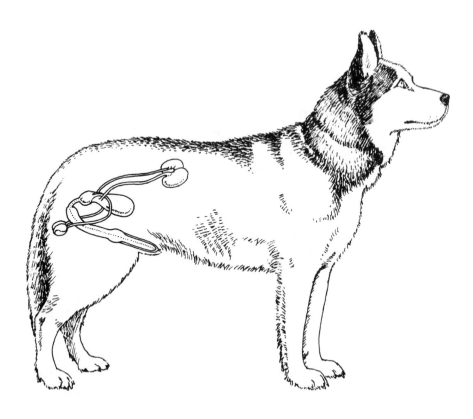

N

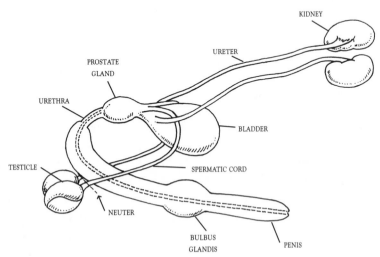

KIDNEY

URETER

PROSTATE
GLAND

URETHRA

BLADDER

TESTICLE

SPERMATIC CORD

NEUTER

BULBUS
GLANDIS

PENIS

Male Urogenital Tract

combination of injectable drugs and/or inhalant anesthetics may be used. Depending on the pet, preanesthetic blood work may determine which anesthetic is best for the animal.

Your dog's stomach should be empty during the procedure so that the danger of aspiration is reduced. Inhaling foreign material such as food or vomitus into the lungs can cause life-threatening complications, including PNEUMONIA. For this reason, it's usually recommended that food and water be withheld for a period of time prior to the surgery. Should your dog sneak an unauthorized snack, tell the veterinarian so that appropriate precautions can be made or the surgery can be delayed.

Once the dog is comfortably anesthetized, the surgical site is prepared. Sterile procedures include removing the hair from the site and disinfecting the area with solutions like Betadine and alcohol, or chlorhexidine and alcohol. The dog is placed on a towel or heating pad positioned on the surgery table to keep his TEMPERATURE constant. The surgeon wears sterile gloves and uses sterile surgical instruments, and the dog is draped with sterile cloth or towels to keep the site clean.

The two fur-covered spheres seen between the male dog's rear legs are the scrotum, skin sacs that contain the sperm-producing testicles. Each testicle is joined to a spermatic cord that contains an artery and the spermatic duct.

The surgical procedure to neuter your dog is typically done in one of two ways. When the dog is very small, as in tiny breeds or young puppies, each testicle is expressed through a separate incision made in each scrotal sac. With older or larger dogs, a single one- to two-inch incision is made in front of the scrotum at the base of the dog's penis, and then each testicle in turn is pushed out of the scrotum through that single incision.

The attached spermatic cords are tied with suture material to prevent bleeding, then the testicles are cut free. The stub of the spermatic cord recedes back into the surgical opening, leaving the scrotal sac empty. An antibiotic may be sprayed into the scrotal cavity, and scrotal incisions may be closed with internal stitches or glue. Male dogs that lick at the site may need a restraint like an ELIZABETHAN COLLAR that prevents them from bothering the incision until it heals. Other times, absorbable stitches close the incision from the underside and won't need to be removed. A routine castration takes ten to twenty-five minutes of actual surgical time.

In rare cases, there's a failure of one or both testicles to descend from the abdomen into the scrotal sac as the dog matures. This inherited condition is called CRYPTORCHID. Dogs with this condition have a thirteen-times-greater incidence of tumors in that retained testicle. Because both testicles must be removed to prevent unwanted sexual behaviors, a veterinarian must go into the abdomen to castrate a cryptorchid dog. Your veterinarian should check for this condition prior to performing a castration surgery.

Following the surgery, dogs may be held for only a few hours, or overnight, for monitoring by the veterinarian. Until the anesthesia wears off, they often act drunk or disoriented, but typically are fully awake and functional within an hour or so of the surgery.

The dog's activities should be restricted for two or three days following the surgery. Outdoor dogs should be kept inside for several days and prevented from lying in the dirt until the incision has healed. The neutered dog doesn't need to see the veterinarian again unless there's a problem.

Postneutering difficulties are rare, but monitor the incision site for inflammation or swelling. See the veterinarian if there is a discharge or puffiness at the surgery site. Most problems are minor and involve the dog licking the incision.

Nose

The nose contains the scent-detecting organs that provide the dog with olfaction, or sense of smell. More than looks or a name, it is scent that identifies each dog as an individual among other dogs. Smell distinguishes friend from foe, provides sexual information, and is important to communication and social interaction.

The shape and size of the external nose, which is part of the MUZZLE, varies greatly between dog breeds. The profile of flat-faced dogs, like the Pekingese, which have a "break" or indentation at the eyes, may be many inches shorter than that of Roman-nosed and long-muzzled breeds, like the Collie, and there are many breeds that fall in between the two extremes.

In fact, the short skulls of certain snub-nosed breeds can distort and narrow the nasal passages and airways. Dogs like Bulldogs and Boston Terriers may have abnormally small nasal openings and excessively long soft palates, which makes them work harder to breathe. When the condition results in breathing problems, it's referred to as *brachycephalic upper-airway syndrome*. Physical activity, excessive heat, or stress make breathing more difficult and can prompt wheezing and noisy breathing; affected dogs often snore. Surgery to increase the size of air passages may be necessary.

The hairless end of the nose is called the *leather* and is usually dark, but may be brown, pink, or spotted to match the coat color. The leather contains the nostrils (nares) through which airborne scent enters. The leather is typically cool and moist from mucous glands that lubricate the area.

Nostrils open into the nasal cavity, which is enclosed in bone and cartilage and runs the length of the muzzle. This cavity empties into the throat

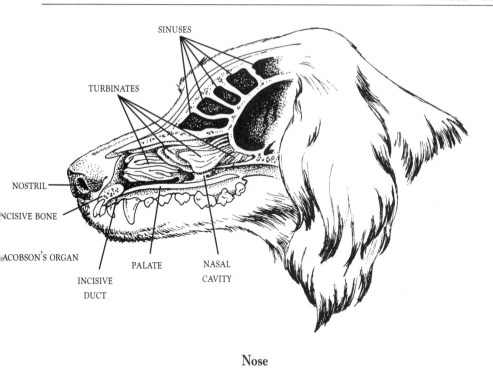

SINUSES

TURBINATES

NOSTRIL

INCISIVE BONE

JACOBSON'S ORGAN

PALATE

INCISIVE
DUCT

NASAL
CAVITY

Nose

behind the soft palate. Open spaces in the bone (sinuses) connecting to the nasal cavity help shape a dog's vocalizations.

The nasal septum is a midline partition made of bone and cartilage and lined by mucous membrane. It divides the nasal cavity into two halves, one for each nostril. Within the nasal cavity are a series of scrolled bony plates, called *turbinates*. Those situated nearest the nostrils clean, warm, and humidify air as it's inhaled. This protects the dog's delicate internal nasal structures by screening the air before passing it on to the sensitive scent-detecting portions.

Further inside, additional turbinates are covered by thick, spongy membrane, called the *olfactory mucosa*. It is this structure that contains the scent-detecting nerves and cells. Depending on the breed of the dog and size of the muzzle, dogs have from seven to sixty square inches of olfactory mucosa, compared to the human's one square inch.

A long muzzle accommodates more scent-detecting equipment, which is why longer-nosed breeds tend to be better sniffers and hunters than the flat-faced dogs. Humans have between 5 million and 20 million scent-analyzing cells, but canine scent sense varies between breeds. For instance, the Dachshund has about 125 million such cells, compared to the German Shepherd

Dog's 200 million. The best sniffer of them all—the Bloodhound—is said to have 300 million olfactory cells. The flat-faced breeds have far less, but no matter their conformation, all dogs have an extraordinary ability to detect scent.

Odor particles that are inhaled must first be dissolved in the moist layer of mucus that coats the inside of the nose. Millions of microscopic hairlike cilia sprout from the olfactory cells up into this thin layer of mucus. Odor-detecting receptors are found on the cilia. When the dissolved odor particle makes contact, it somehow excites the receptor, which in turn feeds the impulse down to the olfactory cell.

Every odor is thought to have a distinctive molecular "shape," which defines the amount of excitement stimulated in a given nerve cell. In turn, these nerves signal the olfactory bulbs, which send the information directly to the brain where the smell is interpreted as a rabbit, or whatever. A second scenting mechanism may play a role in interpreting sexually related odors (see JACOBSON'S ORGAN).

The internal structures of the canine nose are also protected by a layer of moisture produced by serous glands and mucous glands throughout the nasal cavity. The mucociliary blanket is composed of microscopic cells covered with hairlike cilia that move the moisture toward the nostrils and throat. This mucus coating protects the body against infection by trapping foreign material.

Because dogs tend to meet the world nose-first, they are often exposed to illnesses and infected through inhaling bacteria or virus. Dogs do not get "colds" the way people do. A nose dripping clear, watery fluid may be due to canine nervousness or excitement and usually goes away when the dog settles down. If it doesn't, or the discharge is anything other than clear, there

---

BLOCKED NASAL PASSAGES

SYMPTOMS
Head tilt or eye squint on affected side; sudden violent sneezing; pawing at nose; open-mouth breathing; thick discharge or bleeding

HOME CARE
None; see veterinarian if the signs don't resolve within twenty-four hours

VET CARE
Sedate or anesthetize dog, and remove the foreign body; sometimes surgery or antibiotics

PREVENTION
Supervise sniffing activities to prevent foreign-body inhalation

may be a problem. Nasal disorders such as thick discharge, sneezing, or BLEEDING from the nose can indicate a number of different conditions, such as CANINE DISTEMPER, RHINITIS, CANCER, POISONING, or a foreign object in the nose.

Dogs may tilt the head to one side or squint the eye on one side when a foreign body lodges in the nasal passages. Sudden symptoms include violent sneezing and pawing at one side of the nose. Dogs with blocked nasal passages may resort to open-mouth breathing—not PANTING, which is normal. Foreign matter like grass, an insect, or dust may work its way out by itself; other times, a veterinarian's help is advisable. *Don't try removing foreign bodies yourself.* The nasal structures are very sensitive and bleed easily, and you could injure the dog without meaning to.

Nutrition

Nutrition refers to the food your dog eats. Eating a complete and balanced diet is required to maintain optimal health. *Complete* means all essential nutrients are present in the diet, while *balanced* means these components are in the proper proportions as compared to each other.

Nutrients are the elements of food that provide nourishment. It's necessary they be present in the correct amounts and also in the proper balance, because they benefit the dog both individually and also by interacting together. Dogs require six different classes of nutrients for optimum health: water, protein, carbohydrates, fats, minerals, and vitamins.

Water is the most important nutrient. Sixty percent of a dog's body weight is water; the ratio is even higher in puppies. Water lubricates the tissue and helps electrolytes like salt to be distributed throughout the body. Moisture is used in digestion and elimination and helps regulate the body temperature. Even a 15 percent loss of body water, referred to as DEHYDRATION, results in death.

Protein builds and maintains bone, blood, tissue, and even the immune system. Proteins are composed of twenty-three different chemical compounds called *amino acids*. Ten of these amino acids cannot be produced by the body in sufficient amounts and are called *essential* because they must be supplied by the diet. Dogs require dietary arginine, isoleucine, lysine, phenylalanine, histidine, leucine, methionine, threonine, tryptophan, and valine.

Dogs require much lower levels of dietary protein than do cats, but more than people. A dog's life stage or lifestyle may influence his protein requirement. For example, GERIATRIC DOGS need higher levels of protein in their diet compared to young adult dogs.

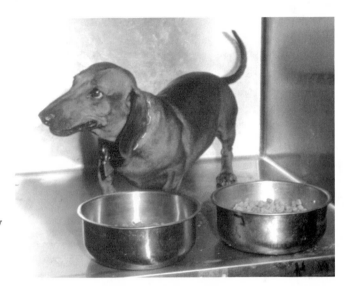

Proper nutrition keeps dogs healthy
(Photo credit: Ralston Purina Company)

Proteins are derived from both plant and animal (meat) sources; however, most single protein sources (except for eggs) don't contain an ideal balance of the essential amino acids. A single meat or single vegetable protein source won't provide balanced nutrition for the dog. When chosen properly, combinations of two or more protein sources will complement each other by providing the amino acids the others lack, and so together will provide adequate protein. It is possible to formulate a complete and balanced canine vegetarian diet, but an all-meat diet is not balanced. Signs of a protein deficiency may include loss of appetite, weight loss, poor hair coat, poor growth, and impaired reproductive performance.

Carbohydrates are starches, sugars, and dietary fiber; they provide ready energy when the body breaks it down into glucose. Carbohydrates are obtained primarily from cereal grains and sugars like lactose (milk sugar). Fiber gives minimal energy, but helps regulate the bowels, assists in normalizing the bacterial populations living in the gut, and may give a full feeling for obese dogs that are dieting. An excess of carbohydrates will be turned to fat. Not enough carbohydrates may cause problems in whelping and interfere with the development of healthy puppies.

Dogs use protein, carbohydrates, and fats as sources of calories, or energy. *Fats* provide 2¼ times the available energy per unit of weight than carbohydrates or proteins do, because up to 95 percent of dietary fats can be digested and used. Fats are particularly important for dogs with high energy requirements, like pregnant or nursing BITCHES and hardworking dogs that hunt or herd. However, excess intake of calories from fat or other sources can lead to OBESITY.

Fat also helps make food taste good to the dog. Fats are the only source for linoleic acid, an essential fatty acid that helps in the absorption of fat-soluble vitamins. Dogs are able to efficiently use both animal and vegetable-source fats. Fatty acids and fats promote healthy skin and fur, but too much can result in obesity. Fat deficiency is rare, but when it occurs, it produces greasy fur, dandruff, weight loss, and poor healing of wounds.

Minerals are needed in relatively tiny amounts but are essential for nerve conduction, muscle contraction, acid/base balance, fluid stability inside the cells, and many other things. Necessary minerals include calcium, phosphorus, magnesium, potassium, sodium, chloride, sulfur, and the trace minerals copper, iodine, iron, manganese, selenium, and zinc. Minerals work together, and the balance is as important as the amount. Too much can be as dangerous as too little. An imbalance can cause bone deformities, ANEMIA, muscle weakness, HEART or KIDNEY DISEASE, and countless other problems.

Vitamins are used in biochemical processes inside the cells, and very small amounts are sufficient. Vitamins are divided into two groups. The fat-soluble vitamins A, D, E, and K are stored in the body. The B-complex vitamins are water-soluble, are not stored in the body, and must be replaced every day in the diet. B vitamins include thiamin, riboflavin, pyridoxine, vitamin B_{12}, folic acid, niacin, pantothenic acid, biotin, choline, and inositol. Unlike people, dogs don't require vitamin C in their diet, because their bodies produce adequate amounts of this vitamin.

Vitamins must be in proper combinations and amounts, or severe problems may result. Oversupplementation can be toxic to the dog, while insufficiency can cause dangerous diseases. Too much or too little of certain vitamins may result in problems including bone deformities like rickets, ANEMIA, eye disease, ANOREXIA, BLEEDING, and even death.

Nutrient requirements for dogs vary depending on several factors, including the animal's age, health status, activity level, and living conditions. Every dog is different, but most are able to obtain optimum nutrition by eating commercial dog foods that have been properly formulated.

Staged feeding refers to your dog's life stage and generally has been divided into three broad categories: growth (puppies), reproduction and lactation (mother dogs bearing and nursing puppies), and maintenance (adults). Pregnant bitches, those nursing a litter, and growing puppies require much higher levels of energy than do most adult dogs. Among other things, puppies need more protein, fat, and calcium than mature dogs do. Conversely, adults may gain too much weight if fed a high-calorie puppy ration. Relatively recently, some pet-food companies have added a "geriatric" or "senior" life stage for older pets.

Always choose a food that is appropriate to your dog's life stage and lifestyle. High-quality commercial pet foods clearly label their products for growth and reproduction (pregnant or nursing mothers and puppies); maintenance (adult dogs); or all life stages (from puppyhood to motherhood and adult maintenance). Feed only products that have been tested in feeding trials and are proven to be complete and balanced.

Select a diet that contains a calorie or energy level appropriate to the activity level of your dog; higher fat levels usually indicate more calories. Very active dogs, such as working animals, require more calories than sedentary pets require. Choose appropriate diets by READING FOOD LABELS.

Specialty diets are also available that address a number of nutrition-related concerns. Those that help control health problems generally are available only through a veterinarian and should be used only as prescribed. Many are designed to relieve specific clinical signs of disease by manipulating nutrient profiles, and are not appropriate for routine maintenance in healthy dogs. (See also EATING; FOOD; FOOD ADDITIVES; FOOD SUPPLEMENTS; GRASS, EATING; and MILK, AS FOOD.)

n

Obesity

Obesity is an excess of body fat that impairs health or normal body function. The condition is considered the most common and important nutritional disorder of dogs and is estimated to affect about 25 percent of pet dogs seen by veterinarians.

The incidence of canine obesity has drastically increased compared to twenty years ago. Obesity is caused by eating more energy than is expended through exercise. In the past, most dogs lived most, if not all, of their lives outdoors, which offered them greater opportunity for exercise. Many modern pets are house dogs that are left confined during the day while owners work, and so lead a more sedentary lifestyle. These dogs may also eat more than in the past because modern foods are extremely tasty, and because often there's little else for the bored dog to do. And the higher the fat and calorie content of food, the greater is the dog's risk for obesity.

All dogs can potentially become overweight, but the incidence is greatest in middle-aged dogs between five to ten years of age. The dog's activity levels slow as she ages, and metabolic changes may also occur that promote obesity. The tendency to become overweight can also be inherited; certain breeds or lines of dogs seem to be more prone to obesity than others, suggesting there is a "fat gene" in dogs. Breeds that tend to suffer from obesity more commonly include Labrador Retrievers, Cairn Terriers, Shetland Sheepdogs, Basset Hounds, Beagles, Golden Retrievers, Cocker Spaniels, Dachshunds, and Miniature Schnauzers. Certain diseases, like HYPOTHYROIDISM, can cause obesity by changing the dog's metabolism.

Neutered and spayed dogs are more prone to obesity than intact ones are. Neutering alters the behavior of dogs, and the resulting decline in activity can

An obese dog
(*Photo credit:*
Ralston Purina
Company)

result in weight gain when the diet isn't adjusted. There is also some evidence that neutering may cause metabolic differences with reduced calorie requirements due to hormonal influences. Owners must adjust diets accordingly or risk weight gain. (See NEUTERING and SPAYING.)

In humans, excessive weight raises the risk for a number of conditions, including atherosclerosis. However, atherosclerosis is not a problem in dogs. Canine obesity does cause and/or significantly increase the risk for a number of other health problems, though.

Obesity can increase your dog's risk for DIABETES MELLITUS, CANCER, skin problems, and lameness due to ARTHRITIS or HIP DYSPLASIA. Severely overweight dogs are more likely to suffer surgical complications from BLEEDING or ANESTHESIA, heat or exercise intolerance, and complications from cardiovascular diseases.

Obesity is commonly defined as exceeding "ideal" body weight by 20 to 25 percent. But weight alone isn't a good measure of the ratio between body fat and muscle/bone mass. A better method is evaluating your dog's body condition by looking at her profile and feeling her body.

You should be able to feel your dog's ribs, but not see them. (Coursing breeds, like Greyhounds, that have thin coats and light fat cover are the exceptions to this rule; you'll see their ribs!) Also stand above your dog and look for an "hourglass" figure. There should be an indentation at the waist beginning at the back of the ribs to just before the hips. Again, the degree of the indentation depends on the breed; a Scottish Terrier will be more level, while a Whippet is quite extreme without being underweight. Finally, look at your dog's profile for a tummy tuck beginning just behind the last ribs and going up into the hind legs. Again, there are extremes like the Greyhound, and more moderate tuck-ups like the flatter tummy on a West Highland White Terrier. If you can't feel the dog's ribs, and/or she has a pendulous or bulging tummy, your dog is too pudgy. Overweight dogs often develop rolls of fat on the lower back above the tail. To evaluate your dog's condition, compare her appearance to the illustrations in the "Body Condition System" chart.

Before beginning a diet, have a veterinarian examine your dog to rule out hypothyroidism or diabetes mellitus. Controlling hypothyroidism will often help correct the weight problem as well. Then evaluate your current feeding protocol. Your veterinarian can help calculate how much weight your dog needs to lose, and advise you on the best way to proceed. Most diets target losing about 1 to 1.5 percent of the dog's starting weight per week.

For some dogs, simply eliminating the treats (see FOOD SUPPLEMENTS) and slightly reducing the amount of their regular ration is adequate. Because of the water content, canned food is less calorie dense than dry foods. Rather than free feeding dry food, success may be obtained by meal feeding with canned. However, dry food is absorbed more slowly, so may provide a greater feeling of fullness. Divide the food into four or even five small meals a day to help keep your dog from feeling deprived. Multiple small meals also tend to increase the body's metabolic rate, which can help the corpulent canine slim down.

In other cases, switching the dog to a lower-calorie, lower-fat diet is a better option. Special "lite" diets are designed to provide complete and balanced nutrition in a reduced-calorie, reduced-fat formulation that also satisfies the dog's need to feel full. These diets typically replace fat with indigestible fiber, dilute calories with water, or "puff up" the product with air. However, special reducing diets may not work when offered free choice, because dogs that are gorgers simply eat more of the reduced-calorie food. Measuring the amount of food given will help with weight loss and will help to keep it off.

The definition for reducing products historically has varied between pet-food companies, so that one company's "lite" product actually might have more calories than the next company's "regular" food. Pet-food regulators have recently defined the term to establish an industrywide standard. For example, the new standard requires dog foods labeled *lite* to contain not more than 3100 calories per kilogram (about 1400 calories per pound). These products can still vary in the calories per cup. Also, other terms like *lean* or *reduced* have different meanings.

BODY CONDITION SYSTEM

1 EMACIATED Ribs, lumbar vertebrae, pelvic bones and all bony prominences evident from a distance. No discernible body fat. Obvious loss of muscle mass.

2 VERY THIN Ribs, lumbar vertebrae and pelvic bones easily visible. No palpable fat. Some evidence of other bony prominence. Minimal loss of muscle mass.

3 THIN Ribs easily palpated and may be visible with no palpable fat. Tops of lumbar vertebrae visible. Pelvic bones becoming prominent. Obvious waist and abdominal tuck.

4 UNDERWEIGHT Ribs easily palpable, with minimal fat covering. Waist easily noted, viewed from above. Abdominal tuck evident.

5 IDEAL Ribs palpable without excess fat covering. Waist observed behind ribs when viewed from above. Abdomen tucked up when viewed from side.

6 OVERWEIGHT Ribs palpable with slight excess fat covering. Waist is discernable viewed from above but is not prominent. Abdominal tuck apparent.

7 HEAVY Ribs palpable with difficulty, heavy fat cover. Noticeable fat deposits over lumbar area and base of tail. Waist absent or barely visible. Abdominal tuck may be absent.

8 OBESE Ribs not palpable under very heavy fat cover, or palpable only with significant pressure. Heavy fat deposits over lumbar area and base of tail. Waist absent. No abdominal tuck. Obvious abdominal distention may be present.

9 GROSSLY OBESE Massive fat deposits over thorax, spine and base of tail. Waist and abdominal tuck absent. Fat deposits on neck and limbs. Obvious abdominal distention.

This Body Condition System was developed and tested at the Purina Pet Care Center and has been documented in the following publications: Laflamme DP. Body Condition Scoring and Weight Maintenance. Proc N Am Vet Conf, Jan 16-21, 1993, Orlando, FL, pp 290-291. Laflamme DP, Kealy RD, Schmidt DA. Estimation of Body Fat by Body Condition Score. J Vet Int Med 1994; 8:154. Laflamme DP, Kuhlman G, Lawler DF, Kealy RD, Schmidt DA. Obesity Management in Dogs. J Vet Clin Nutr 1994; 1:59-65.

Body Condition System (*Photo credit: Ralston Purina Company*)

In extremely obese dogs, veterinary-prescribed reducing diets in conjunction with a therapeutic weight-loss program supervised by the veterinarian is the safest option. Gradual weight loss is best; she didn't gain it all at once, so give her time to trim it off. If your dog needs to lose a quarter of her current weight, expect her to take at least three months to slim down. Increasing the dog's exercise is encouraged to help get—and keep—the weight off.

To keep your dog in condition, choose a quality complete and balanced diet. Think thin from the moment you get your dog; a fat puppy may be cute, but tends to become a fat adult. Monitor the dog's body condition and adjust the amount of food offered as needed. Don't feed table scraps and severely limit treats; reward your dog with attention rather than snacks. And PLAY interactive games with your dog, like fetch, and take her on walks to promote healthy exercise; start slow and work up to two or three fifteen-minute sessions a day. Once she's lost the weight, keep her on a regular exercise program. Nearly all dogs require forty-five minutes of aerobic exercise every day to stay healthy. (See also NUTRITION and FOOD.)

Otitis

Otitis means inflammation of the EAR and refers to a condition that may develop suddenly (acute) or be ongoing (chronic). The condition is categorized by the area of the ear affected.

Dogs with drop ears are more prone to developing otitis than breeds with erect ears. In fact, up to 80 percent of canine ear problems treated by veterinarians occur in drop-eared dogs. The infection is typically brought on by poor air circulation that promotes moisture in the ear canal conducive to the growth of bacteria, yeast, or fungus.

Anything that throws off the normal balance of the ear secretions can result in otitis. This can be caused by something as simple as getting water or soap in the ears during a bath (see GROOMING). Other common causes include a foreign body (like a grass seed), parasites like mites or TICKS, excess hair or mats in or around the ears, ALLERGIES, or excess wax production.

Most cases are confined to the external portion of the ear canal and/or the ear flap (pinna) and are termed *otitis externa*. Otitis externa occasionally advances into the middle ear (otitis media) and even more rarely into the inner ear (otitis interna).

Signs of otitis include painful and sometimes itchy ears that may be red, raw, or even bloody if the dog has scratched them. Dogs typically hold the painful ear down, tipping their head. Excessive shaking or scratching may result in a HEMATOMA. A bad odor from the ear indicates infection, as does any

OTITIS

SYMPTOMS
Itchy or painful ear that may be red or raw; head shaking, or scratching at ears; ear discharge and/or bad odor; sometimes a head tilt; eye squint, or circling

HOME CARE
After veterinary diagnosis, gently clean and treat ears with prescribed medication

VET CARE
Thorough cleaning may require sedation; antibiotics, steroids, antifungal creams, and/or ear mite preparations; sometimes surgical reconstruction of ear canal

PREVENTION
Proper ear maintenance; avoid water in ears from bathing or swimming

sort of discharge. Normal wax is light amber; an abnormal discharge is anything different.

Red, itchy ears without discharge are probably due to allergy, but may progress to infection due to scratching trauma. An acute bacterial infection is often due to the staphylococci organism, and the discharge will be light brown. Chronic bacterial infections may be caused by the proteus organism and will typically result in a yellow discharge; or they may be caused by the pseudomonas organism, characterized by a soupy, black discharge. When the infection is due to EAR MITES, a crumbly brown to black debris will be present. A buildup of oily, yellow wax may be a sign of *ceruminous otitis*, which is a sign of SEBORRHEA or HYPOTHYROIDISM. A thick, dark, or waxy discharge characterized by a distinctive musty odor is a sign of yeast or fungal infection.

Otitis media usually results from an ascending infection from the external ear canal, or penetration of the eardrum by a foreign object. From there, the problem can progress into otitis interna, which can cause severe signs and permanent damage.

Signs of nerve involvement, such as head tilt, droopy eyelids, or a facial palsy on the affected side, indicate middle to inner ear involvement. Inner ear infections can interfere with balance, and dogs will walk in circles and/or fall toward the affected side. Severe damage from otitis may result in deafness.

Treatment depends on identifying and addressing the cause of the inflammation. Sedation is often required, because the ears are typically very sore. An instrument called an *otoscope* that has a magnifying lens and light allows the veterinarian to examine the horizontal and vertical ear canal to see if the eardrum is intact.

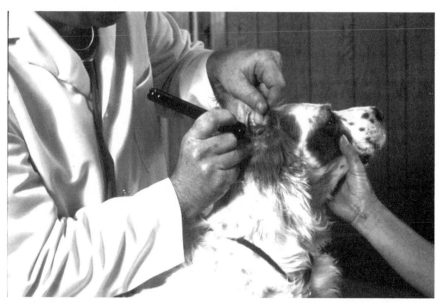

Vet checks dog's ear *(Photo credit: Ralston Purina Company)*

The status of swelling or scarring of the ear canal is evaluated during the exam, and it's determined if a foreign body is involved. The veterinarian also collects a sample of the discharge when present, and examines it under the microscope to identify the type of bacteria, yeast, fungus, or parasite that is involved.

Treatment must first begin with thorough cleaning and drying of the ears; general ANESTHESIA may be required. Your veterinarian will know which cleaning solutions are most appropriate. If the eardrum is ruptured, some solutions or medications can actually damage the middle ear and make a bad situation even worse. Wax-dissolving solutions are particularly helpful with dogs suffering from seborrhea.

After the initial cleaning and flushing of the affected ears, most cases can be treated by owners at home (see ADMINISTER MEDICATION). Topical antibiotic ointments and drops, sometimes with steroids to reduce itchiness and inflammation, are generally prescribed for bacterial infections. Medicine is usually administered twice a day for two weeks.

Fungus and yeast infections typically take longer to resolve and often recur. They require antifungal medications, such as nystatin. Medication generally is applied twice daily for two weeks, then once a day for another week. If the infection is caused by more than one thing, an antifungal-antibacterial cream may be prescribed to address all issues.

Treatment usually resolves acute otitis within two or three days, but chronic problems take much longer to cure and often recur. If the eardrum is punctured, six weeks or more of treatment may be required to prevent permanent damage to hearing or balance. Sometimes the veterinarian must lance the eardrum to relieve the pressure of infection that has built up if this happens; usually the eardrum heals quickly.

Chronic infections tend to leave the ear canal swollen. When this is the case, or when infections are deep inside the ear, drops and ointments may not reach the source, and surgery may be necessary to clean out these pockets of infection. Long-term oral antibiotics are given to fight the infection, along with steroids to address inflammation and protect nerve involvement.

Surgical restructuring of the ear canal may be required in cases of severe chronic infection. The vertical portion of the canal is removed, and a new opening created to allow better aeration and drainage. When there is severe damage to the middle or inner ear, neurologic signs, like head tilt or circle walking, may continue for the rest of the dog's life even after the infection is cured.

The best way to prevent otitis is to keep your dog's ears clean and dry. Avoid getting water into the ears during baths and inspect the dog's ears for grass awns or other debris, particularly after rambles through brush. Your veterinarian may dispense a drying agent or acidifying solution for use in your dog's ears, particularly water-loving dogs that are hard to keep out of the water.

O

Pain

Pain refers to extreme discomfort resulting from injury or illness. It is usually limited to one specific area of the body. Dogs feel pain similarly to their owners, and the unpleasant sensation can arise in the skin, bone, joint, or muscle, and even within internal organs.

Pain serves to protect the body from harm by stimulating a reaction that interrupts the action causing the pain, which in turn prevents further injury. For example, a burn prompts the dog to withdraw his nose from sniffing the flame, while the pain of a FRACTURE motivates resting the area to help speed the healing.

Before treatment can begin, the cause of the pain must be determined. Pain is caused by any number of things, including injury due to trauma or surgery, illnesses like CANINE PARVOVIRUS, or conditions such as ARTHRITIS, PERITONITIS, or PERIODONTAL DISEASE.

Pain medications, termed *analgesics*, are appropriate to relieve moderate to severe pain in the dog. However, painkillers must be used with discretion. Otherwise, removing the discomfort may allow the dog to overdo and further injure himself. *Analgesics should never be used without consulting a veterinarian*, nor should they take the place of identification and treatment of the cause.

Narcotic pain relievers, such as morphine, codeine, and Demerol, are available by prescription only and should be used only under veterinary supervision; dosage requirements and effects in dogs are quite variable. Your vet may dispense an anti-inflammatory drug if your dog suffers pain from joint or bone disorders.

ASPIRIN can be used for pain relief in dogs; however, dosage is quite different than for humans, and misuse can cause ULCERS and BLEEDING. IBUPROFEN

SIGNS OF PAIN

Dogs in pain don't act like themselves. Retiring dogs may become
demanding, while friendly dogs become irritable. It's hard to tell sometimes
what your dog is trying to say. Be alert for these signs, and have the dog
checked by your veterinarian if you suspect he is in pain.

1. Hides
2. Remains very still and quiet
3. Becomes vocal, whines, whimpers, or cries
4. Acts agitated, paces, can't get comfortable
5. Pants or drools
6. Refuses food
7. Flinches, yelps, or snaps when touched in tender place
8. Trembles
9. Limps or carries paw, begs for attention
10. Assumes hunched posture
11. Squints eyes or has watering eyes

isn't as effective and causes more side effects, and acetaminophen (i.e.,
Tylenol) can help reduce fever but is usually contraindicated unless the dog's
TEMPERATURE is extraordinarily high. *Misuse of human pain-relief medications
can POISON your dog.* If you suspect your pet is in pain, have the veterinarian
examine him to determine the underlying cause. Give medication for pain
only upon advice from your veterinarian.

P

Pancreatitis

Pancreatitis is the inflammation and/or infection of the pancreas, an organ situated near the liver that provides digestive enzymes and insulin. The condition is not uncommon in dogs and typically affects adult dogs aged two to
seven years old.

In about a third of pancreatitis cases, the cause is unknown, but probably a
number of factors are involved. OBESITY, sudden high levels of dietary fat (such
as meat and fat scraps from your dinner plate), trauma, and overuse of corticosteroid drugs are thought to contribute to the condition. Pancreatitis may be
related to kidney, liver, or gastrointestinal disease, or systemic infection.

The inflammation causes the pancreas to swell and release digestive enzymes into the bloodstream and surrounding abdominal cavity, instead of into

the small intestine. The misdirected enzymes digest fat and tissues in the abdomen, or even in the pancreas itself.

Signs of the disease may be mild and easily missed, or acute with sudden illness. Signs of canine pancreatitis include a high fever, hunching posture from abdominal PAIN, VOMITING, weight loss, DIARRHEA, listlessness, and ANOREXIA, or even death.

Diagnosis is based on signs of the disease and confirmed with blood tests that measure the level of the circulating pancreatic enzyme, lipase. An ULTRASOUND is also useful to confirm the diagnosis.

Treatment varies depending on how severe the disease is, and may include pain relievers and drugs to control vomiting. Fluid therapy is particularly important and helps restore normal pancreatic circulation and calms the inflammation. Antibiotics to fight the infection may be prescribed, and initially the dog may be fasted—food withheld—until the vomiting is under control. After recovery, typically the dog is placed on a special low-fat diet, such as boiled white chicken and rice, or a veterinarian-prescribed therapeutic diet. Some cases require dietary enzyme supplementation.

Dogs that recover from an acute attack may develop chronic disease and have occasional flare-ups the rest of their life. They are at increased risk for developing DIABETES MELLITUS or MALABSORPTION SYNDROME secondary to the disease.

Dogs with a history of pancreatitis may benefit from a low-fat diet and avoidance of sudden dietary changes. Your dog's risk of developing pancreatitis can be reduced by watching her weight, encouraging regular exercise, and feeding a healthy commercial ration while avoiding fatty table scraps.

P

PANCREATITIS

SYMPTOMS
High fever; hunching posture from abdominal pain; vomiting; weight loss; diarrhea; listlessness; anorexia

HOME CARE
Supportive care; special diet as recommended by vet

VET CARE
Drugs to control vomiting; sometimes pain medication; fluid therapy; antibiotics; fasting the dog; prescription diet

PREVENTION
Keep dog slim; avoid feeding fatty table scraps

Panting

Panting refers to the moderate to rapid open-mouthed respiration dogs use as a means to lower their body TEMPERATURE. This normal cooling mechanism is necessary because dogs do not have an effective system of SWEAT GLANDS like people do.

Instead, dogs cool their bodies using the evaporation of moisture from the mouth and tongue, and by exchanging the hot air of their lungs with cooler external air. The panting dog breathes with his mouth open and tongue somewhat protruding.

Panting should not be confused with labored breathing, which is strained and may be accompanied by sounds of distress or whistles due to blockage.

p

Panting cools hot dogs
(Photo credit: Ralston Purina Company)

Rapid or labored breathing can be a sign of heatstroke (see HYPERTHERMIA), which needs emergency attention.

Periodontal Disease

Periodontal disease refers to disorders that affect the TEETH, oral bones, and gums. Oral disease is the number one diagnosed health problem in dogs and cats, with 85 percent of dogs developing some degree of gum disease by age three. The condition tends to worsen as the dog ages.

Some dogs are more prone to dental problems than others are. Small dog breeds are more likely to develop periodontal disease than large dogs because the teeth of small dogs are often crowded and are too large for their mouths. For instance, although the teeth of the Yorkshire Terrier and Doberman Pinscher are very similar, the Yorkie has much less jawbone to support the teeth and is affected more severely by gum disease. Breeds like the Pug and Yorkie tend to develop periodontal disease quite early; however, all dogs are at risk.

Bacteria readily grows in food that sticks to the teeth. As the bacteria grows, a soft, sticky, colorless film called *plaque* forms on the tooth surface. Eventually, plaque turns to a chalklike material that mineralizes and forms hard deposits called *calculus* or *tartar*. This is the yellow to brown crusty debris you may see on your dog's teeth. These deposits increase bacterial activity in the mouth, resulting in BAD BREATH, which is the earliest warning sign of dental disease.

p

PERIODONTAL DISEASE

SYMPTOMS
Bad breath; yellow to brown debris on teeth; red, swollen gums that easily bleed; loose or broken teeth; receding gums; reluctance to eat; sometimes nasal involvement with discharge; pawing at face; constant nose licking or nosebleeds

HOME CARE
None

VET CARE
Anesthetize dog to clean and/or extract decayed teeth; sometimes antibiotics are required

PREVENTION
Clean dog's teeth regularly (weekly); avoid feeding exclusively soft diets

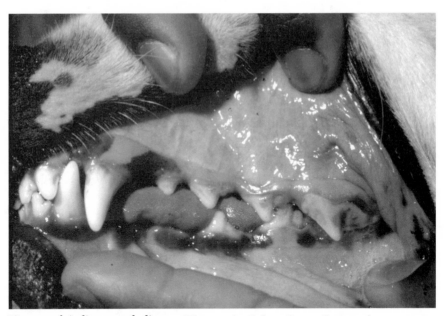

Nasty teeth indicate tooth disease *(Photo credit: Ralston Purina Company)*

The bacteria release enzymes that attack the surrounding tissue, causing gum inflammation (see GINGIVITIS), which is another early sign of periodontal disease. The gums at the tooth line become red, tender, and swollen and may easily bleed.

The IMMUNE SYSTEM attacks the bacteria, but this results in even more inflammation and tissue destruction. Chronic infection is characterized by deep pockets of plaque and pus between the gum and tooth root, which hold decaying food particles. The gums try to pull away from the resulting toxins, which causes even more gum recession and bone destruction; teeth become so loose they fall out.

When canine cavities occur, they develop at the gum line secondary to plaque accumulation. Yet dogs rarely develop cavities; this may be in part because their diets lack the high sugar content common in human foods. However, feeding a dog human foods (see FOOD SUPPLEMENTS) may increase the risk of cavities.

Because dogs typically use their mouths to explore their world, teeth often are broken, especially by overenthusiastic chewers. Hard objects, like cow hooves, are particularly hazardous. A dog with a broken tooth may chew only on the unaffected side, salivate at the food bowl, or refuse to eat at all. Tooth fractures or cracks in the crown that expose the internal pulp can become abscessed if not treated appropriately. An abscessed tooth typically causes sudden severe swelling of the face, and sometimes a puslike discharge from the face, chin, gums, or nose that produces sneezing and nasal discharge. A painful mouth is characterized by a reluctance to chew toys or hard food, pawing the face, sneezing, constant nose licking, or nosebleeds.

Mouth infections are not only painful, but also impact the dog's overall health. Chewing literally pumps the bacteria into the bloodstream and can spread infection throughout the body. Periodontal disease may cause lung, heart, liver, and/or kidney disease.

Dentistry is now a veterinary specialty that offers teeth cleaning, fillings, crowns, root canals, and even orthodontia work—just like a human dentist. Treating periodontal disease involves a thorough cleaning, which requires general anesthesia. Tartar is scaled from the teeth above and below the tender gum line using an ultrasonic cleaner. This is followed by polishing to smooth the enamel and eliminate irregularities on the tooth surface that collect plaque. Treatment concludes with a protective fluoride treatment.

Antibiotics are often necessary when infection is present. Usually, decayed or abscessed teeth are extracted, and extremely loose teeth may also be lost due to bone degeneration. Once the tartar is removed, there's often nothing left to hold teeth in place. Removing the painful teeth may offer such relief that the dog acts young again.

Canine periodontal disease is a preventable condition. The development of plaque and tartar depends on several things, particularly food. Textures and chemicals in food affect how the ration impacts dental health. Canned diets that stick to teeth stay in the oral cavity longer and offer more opportunity for bacterial growth than dry foods. Conversely, the chewing of kibbled chunks provides some detergent action that helps scrub tooth surfaces above the gum line, much the way crunching an apple helps human dental health. For that reason, dry foods are often promoted as being beneficial for your dog's teeth.

Be aware, though, that dry food alone does not prevent problems from occurring. Veterinary dentists estimate eating dry food helps at best about 10 percent. Dogs don't tend to chew, but rather gulp their food, so the detergent benefit is less helpful than in people. Also, canine dental problems tend to occur at or below the gum line, not on the crown of the tooth where the kibble makes contact.

Ongoing research is investigating pet diets that promote dental health. New dog foods with added fiber may augment the detergent action, and special chemicals and enzymes added to food may help prevent plaque and calculus from attaching to teeth. However, manual cleaning of the teeth remains an important part of good dental care.

Veterinary dentists recommend having your dog's teeth professionally cleaned as often as your own—about once a year—as a preventative measure. High-risk breeds, like toy dogs, probably benefit from more frequent attention. Feeding a dry ration rather than canned and cleaning your dog's teeth at home may reduce how often professional cleanings are needed. If you and your dog are lucky, he may need professional attention only two or three times in his lifetime.

Brush your dog's teeth as frequently as your own—after each meal. This isn't always possible, but aim for at least two to three times a week; once a week is better than nothing. Toothbrushes and pastes designed for dogs are available from veterinarians and specialty pet stores. Avoid human products; our toothbrushes generally are too stiff and too large for the dog's tender mouth. And as dogs can't spit, swallowing human toothpaste can upset their stomachs; it also contains high fluoride levels that may damage the dog's kidneys when ingested. They also find the foaming action distasteful.

Pet toothbrushes are typically smaller with softer bristles than those designed for people (although human baby toothbrushes may be appropriate for medium to large dog mouths). Also, finger toothbrushes with tiny rubber bristles that slip over the owner's finger are accepted more readily by some dogs. Canine toothpastes don't foam, and they come in beef or poultry flavors that most dogs savor.

Dogs should be introduced to home dental care gradually by making it a natural part of the human-canine interaction. Most dogs are quite mouth-oriented and often mouth an owner's hands and fingers without prompting. Capitalize on this; stroke your dog's lips and handle his mouth for short times, and reward his acquiescence with a play session or a healthy treat. Then try rubbing the teeth and gums with one finger. There's no need to force open the mouth, just slip your finger through the lips into the cheek. Try flavoring your finger with meat-flavored broth like bouillon or the canine toothpaste.

Progress to using a soft cloth wrapped around your finger. Spread the paste on the cloth, and massage your dog's teeth and gums as long as he allows. Be satisfied if you complete one side, and don't force the dog beyond his tolerance level; you can always finish the rest at the next session.

A toothbrush is the next step, but the cloth or finger brush work fine and often are better tolerated because they are an extension of you. Dental rinses with antibacterial properties that help prevent plaque buildup, promote healing, and control bad breath are also available.

Don't expect success the first time you attempt to clean your dog's teeth. Puppies often tolerate brushing well, but most adult dogs will need gentle persuasion. The trick is to convince the dog that the attention is pleasant and rewarding. Patient consistency goes a long way toward encouraging a dog to accept dental care. And it's worth the effort, for routine brushing will not only alleviate bad breath, but will extend your dog's life.

Peritonitis

Peritonitis refers to inflammation and/or infection of the abdominal cavity. The condition is caused by introduction of bacteria, usually as a result of a puncture wound to the stomach, intestines, or uterus. This can happen due to infections, like PYOMETRA, or from SWALLOWED OBJECTS that puncture or cut.

The dog suffers abdominal PAIN and may "hunch" her back and tuck up the abdomen to protect the stomach area. Dogs may assume a stiff-legged gait when walking, or may refuse to move at all. A high TEMPERATURE is characteristic, and typically the dog refuses to eat and acts depressed. Sometimes the abdomen swells.

Prognosis for dogs suffering peritonitis is very poor. When diagnosed in time, treatment includes supportive care and massive antimicrobial therapy to fight infection and try to stabilize the pet. Surgery is required to repair the damage and clean out the infection.

PERITONITIS

SYMPTOMS
Extreme abdominal pain; hunching posture; stiff-legged walk or refusal to move; anorexia; shock; depression; fever; swollen abdomen

HOME CARE
None; EMERGENCY! SEE VET IMMEDIATELY!

VET CARE
Emergency surgery to clean out infection and repair damage; antimicrobial therapy to fight infection; fluid therapy; possibly blood transfusion

PREVENTION
Keep inedible objects away from the dog

p

Plague

Plague is a deadly bacterial disease historically associated with humans and wild rodents. Although it can cause deadly illness in cats and in people, it rarely affects dogs.

The disease is caused by the bacterial organism *Yersinia pestis* and most commonly affects rodents and the FLEAS that live on them. In the United States, prairie dogs and ground squirrels are the primary reservoirs. According to the Centers for Disease Control, the states of New Mexico, Arizona, Colorado, and California account for about 90 percent of reported plague cases, with more than half occurring in New Mexico. Plague has also been reported in Texas, Montana, Wyoming, and Utah. On average, ten to fifteen cases of human plague are reported each year in the United States.

People typically become infected from bites of infected rodent fleas, which are different from the fleas that typically affect pets. Plague fleas prefer rat, squirrel, or prairie dog blood, but will readily feed on any available pet or human they encounter. Pets are exposed from the bites of infected fleas or by eating infected animals. Dogs that roam and hunt endemic regions are at highest risk; although they may not become sick themselves, a dog may carry the dangerous bugs home, where they can potentially infect people. Plague can occur anytime, but the incidence appears highest during flea season.

Dogs appear to be resistant to the disease, but when they become ill, signs are usually mild and characterized by a moderate fever and enlarged lymph

PLAGUE
SYMPTOMS
History of prairie dog or ground squirrel exposure in endemic regions; mild fever; lethargy; enlarged lymph nodes
HOME CARE
None; HIGHLY CONTAGIOUS TO PEOPLE! SEEK HELP IMMEDIATELY!
VET CARE
Tetracycline-type antibiotics
PREVENTION
Prevent dogs from hunting plague-carrying rodents; clean out rodent habitat; use flea control

nodes. (Conversely, cats run a high fever and usually develop a draining bubo beneath the chin that looks like an ABSCESS [see PLAGUE in *The Purina Encyclopedia of Cat Care*].) If you suspect your dog is suffering from plague, alert the veterinarian so appropriate precautions may be taken.

Because plague is a human health risk (see ZOONOSIS), suspect cases must be reported to public health officials. Diagnosis is confirmed by blood tests, and dogs are commonly treated with tetracycline or comparable medications and usually recover.

Protect your dogs and yourself by preventing exposure to infected rodents and fleas. Keep dogs confined in fenced yards or under your supervision when outdoors in endemic regions. Use appropriate flea control and destroy prime rodent habitat to evict plague-carrying varmints. Clean out brush and woodpiles, barns and sheds.

Play

Play refers to a group of canine behaviors that people interpret as recreational in nature, because the activities appear to have no clear function. In the past, it was assumed that PUPPY play was instinctive behavior designed to develop survival skills necessary for life in the wild. The thinking that followed was

Playing is serious puppy business
(Photo credit: Fran Pennock Shaw)

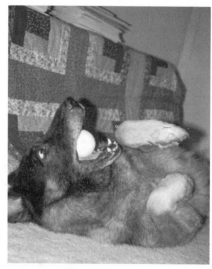

Adult dogs like to play, too
(Photo credit: Amy D. Shojai)

that adult pet dogs continue to play as a replacement for hunting or defense urges frustrated by the confines of a domestic lifestyle.

However, few studies have specifically examined the role of canine play and how it influences the dog's behavior. In fact, many wild animals continue to play as adults, and domestic dogs that practice these skills through hunting TRIALS continue to engage in play. Today, many researchers agree that one of the major benefits of play is that participants develop COMMUNICATION skills through these behaviors. In any event, it's obvious that play is great fun for dogs, whether puppy or adult—and that in itself should be enough.

Each dog is different, and all dogs play. But because behaviors and attitudes vary significantly across breed lines, some dogs tend to be more playful than others. For example, in one survey of fifty-six dog breeds, Airedale Terriers, English Springer Spaniels, and Irish Setters scored high in playfulness, while Bloodhounds, Bulldogs, and Chow Chows scored very low.

Play behavior can be categorized as social, locomotory, or object play. Social play is interactive; wrestling, biting, play fighting, and chase games characterize social play. Locomotory play in adults usually involves a pair or group of dogs, running, jumping, and rolling about, but puppies may indulge in such activities on their own. Object play describes interaction with some interesting object, such as chasing or tossing about a ball, rag, or stick.

During play, puppies realize what is and isn't acceptable behavior, learn to inhibit their bites, and discover the limitations of their bodies and the world around them. Puppies of both sexes may exhibit sexual behavior as early as four weeks of age, mounting each other during play games. Prey-killing behavior—like pouncing and object shaking—is also seen, and the language of DOMINANCE and SUBMISSION is learned. Although wolf pups may establish the dominant "top wolf" at eight weeks of age, most experts today agree that dominance status expressed in play by puppies at these early ages is *not* a good predictor of future status.

Puppies begin social play as early as three weeks of age, with play biting, pawing, and barking. The intensity escalates and becomes more complex as the dog matures. The first play-eliciting gesture seen in puppies is the raised paw. The play bow—butt end up, front down—is the classic invitation for a canine romp and is used by older pups and adults, along with barking, face pawing or licking, and leaping forward to nose-poke and then withdrawing. Exaggerated and highly ritualized gestures characterize canine play, in order to avoid misunderstandings that might result in fights.

It appears that dogs, being such social creatures, have an innate need to play. Most dogs continue to play in one form or another throughout their life. Self-directed play, such as tail chasing or pouncing on imaginary objects, is thought to be a replacement for social play when a play partner isn't available.

Puppies are curious and respond differently to new situations (*Photo credit: Ralston Purina Company*)

Play behavior is also an expression of emotion and seems to characterize an individual dog's personality; styles vary somewhat across breeds. Some dogs are more athletic and tend to enjoy games of chase, others like to fetch, and retrievers are fascinated by water.

Dog toys, like balls, the Kong, or Frisbees, that prompt the dog to chase, leap, and fetch are some of the best interactive dog games available. The Nylabone and Gumabone products are exceptional and offer CHEWING opportunities as well. Some toys even float for those water-loving canines. Dogs also enjoy soft stuffed or fuzzy toys, and most commercial products are available in a variety of colors or sizes to fit your dog's needs. Please be careful, however, of toys containing squeakers; they entice the dog, but if chewed out of the toy, they can be swallowed and cause serious problems (see SWALLOWED OBJECTS). A number of "tug" toys are also available; these are *not* appropriate for dominant or aggressive dogs, because tug-of-war games promote these behaviors. Toys don't need to be expensive to be successful; a tennis ball is popular, and even an old stuffed sock will provide hours of fetching fun.

Playing together serves to reinforce social bonds between group members. And because your dog considers you her leader and best friend, playing with your dog brings you closer together. In fact, play is often a particularly effective therapeutic tool for dogs with health or behavior problems. Interactive play encourages dogs to exercise and stimulates healthy weight loss in OBESE dogs. AGGRESSIVE dogs may benefit from play, which allows them to release their energy in a more productive way. And play can boost the confidence of a shy dog, distract the fearful dog, and help relieve STRESS.

Pneumonia

Pneumonia is an infection of the lungs caused by virus, bacteria, or parasites. It can also result from aspiration, the inhalation of something that should instead have been swallowed. Aspiration of vomit may occur with regurgitation during surgery when the dog is under ANESTHESIA, or when he suffers a seizure. Incorrect administration of liquid medications or foods (see MEGAESOPHAGUS) may also cause pneumonia. Inhalation of gaseous fumes from a fire or chemical spill may also cause pneumonia.

Usually, pneumonia affects very young or elderly dogs secondary to upper-respiratory infections, like KENNEL COUGH or CANINE DISTEMPER. EHRLICHIOSIS or ROCKY MOUNTAIN SPOTTED FEVER may also prompt the disease. Pneumonia resulting from fungal infection is rare in dogs and occurs most commonly in those that are already ill or that have suppressed IMMUNE SYSTEMS.

Signs usually include a high fever with rapid or strained breathing. Coughing helps clear the lungs, but dogs with pneumonia may have bubbly wheezing or rattling sounds when they breathe. Dogs that aren't able to get

p

PNEUMONIA

SYMPTOMS
High fever; rapid or strained or rattling breathing; wheezing; bubbly breathing sounds; blue-tinged gums; coughing; sitting with "elbows" out to aid breathing

HOME CARE
EMERGENCY! SEE VET IMMEDIATELY! Humidifier (or breathing in steamy bathroom) helps relieve breathing difficulty; offer plenty of water; fever-reducing meds as recommended by vet

VET CARE
Antibiotics; supportive care

PREVENTION
Vaccinate for distemper and kennel cough; prevent tickborne diseases with insecticides; feed dogs with megaesophagus from elevated bowl

enough oxygen may develop blue-colored gums. Typically, the breathing-impaired dog will sit with his front "elbows" turned out and head extended to aid breathing (rather than lying down, which may restrict expansion of the chest).

Diagnosis is based on examination of the lung secretions and chest X RAYS.

Humidifying the air may help ease your dog's breathing until you can get expert help. Try running a hot bath or shower so the dog can breathe the steamy air. *Pneumonia is often deadly, and requires prompt veterinary intervention, so get your dog to a hospital as soon as possible.* Treatment usually includes antibiotic therapy.

Poison

Poison refers to any substance that through chemical reaction impairs, injures, or kills your dog. *Poisoning is a life-threatening emergency that requires immediate veterinary help.* The sooner your dog's treated, the better her chance of survival.

Dogs are particularly prone to poisoning because of their less-than-discriminatory eating habits. Often, dogs are exposed when they mouth, chew, or even swallow nonedible items, like batteries or antifreeze. They may absorb toxins through their footpads when they wade or walk through toxic substances, like fresh tar, paint, or a salted icy sidewalk.

Anytime you suspect poisoning has occurred, immediately call your animal emergency center. Give them as much information as possible so they're prepared, then rush your dog to the hospital for expert treatment. The veterinarian needs to know the type of poison (check the label), how much was administered, time elapsed from exposure, and the symptoms your dog is showing. When available, take the poison package with you to help identify the poison, and if the dog has vomited, bring a sample.

Signs of poisoning vary depending on the chemical agent, the amount of exposure, and the individual animal. A certain antidote or treatment is often specific to the individual poison, which is why identification of the toxin is so important. The wrong treatment may cause more harm than good.

When your dog loses consciousness or seizures, first aid won't help; however, specific home treatments in certain situations will improve potential for survival, especially if immediate veterinary intervention isn't possible. (The home treatments follow shortly.) Therapy strives to eliminate or neutralize the toxin and often includes supportive care of the dog to combat SHOCK and systemic signs.

But never try to give oral medications unless the dog is completely awake and in complete control of her body. Putting liquids into an unconscious dog's mouth risks aspiration into the lungs that can cause PNEUMONIA or even suffocation.

Contact poisons usually are spilled onto the fur, or the dog walks through them; they affect the skin, and the longer they remain in contact, the more poison is absorbed into the body. Therefore, first aid consisting of flushing the affected area with plain water is extremely important. Wash or rinse the entire body (for whole-body poisoning) or the affected area for at least ten minutes. Dogs poisoned by natural gas, smoke, or carbon monoxide need fresh air as soon as possible.

When the toxin was ingested within the past two hours, VOMITING *may help eliminate a good portion of the poison.* (However, when caustic poisons, like drain cleaners, chlorine, lye, and dishwashing liquid, are involved, do not induce vomiting because the toxin can do as much damage coming back up as it did going down. If unsure, do not induce vomiting without checking with your veterinarian or local poison control hot line.)

Vomiting may be induced using one-quarter to one teaspoon of syrup of ipecac (smaller amounts for small dogs); however, *do not use syrup of ipecac in cats,* because it can be toxic. One to two tablespoons of 3 percent household hydrogen peroxide, mixed half-and-half with water, will foam when squirted to the back of the tongue, and may induce vomiting within about five minutes; the dosage can be repeated once, if the first attempt fails (see ADMINISTERING MEDICATION, Liquid). Your veterinarian has available even more effective emetic drugs, should your first-aid attempts prove fruitless.

For caustic poisons like drain cleaner or bleach, do not induce vomiting; not only will the poison burn on its way back up, but retching could cause the already damaged stomach to rupture. However, one to five teaspoons of lemon juice or vinegar helps neutralize the effects of caustic alkaline poisons such as drain cleaner. Acids like bleach or battery acid can be neutralized with milk of magnesia; give one teaspoon for every five pounds your dog weighs.

Encourage your dog to drink water or milk, which helps dilute ingested poisons. Milk also coats and soothes the injured stomach and can prevent certain poisons from being completely absorbed. Activated charcoal also helps absorb toxin. It's available at nutrition stores or drugstores; mix one capsule in ten teaspoons of water, and give one teaspoon of this liquid for every ten pounds your dog weighs.

Poisonous Flea Treatments: The most common poison affecting pets is the misapplication of FLEA products and other insecticides. Toxicities often result from the wrong combination of flea products (alone, they're fine, but combined, they become toxic), or misreading label applications and using too much of the substance.

A range of subtle to conspicuous behavior changes may result. Dogs poisoned by flea products may simply act lethargic and/or drool a lot with bouts of VOMITING and DIARRHEA. Shivering, incoordination, or even staggering gait may be seen.

Flea-product poisoning is usually a dermal exposure; the pet absorbs the toxin through the skin when the product is applied. For this reason, signs may not appear until several hours following exposure. Whenever you realize your dog has been poisoned, whether she's sick or not, rinse her thoroughly in plain lukewarm water to speed decontamination. Then see a veterinarian.

Home Medications: The second most common canine poisoning involves the misuse of medications, especially human pain relievers like acetaminophen (Tylenol), ASPIRIN, IBUPROFEN, and naproxen (Aleve). Dogs don't metabolize these drugs at the same speed or in the same ways as people do, which means smaller doses remain in the dog's system for much longer periods. Also, safe dosage varies dramatically between dogs, due to the differences in size. The most common effect of toxicity is gastrointestinal bleeding. Give these medications *only* when advised to do so by your veterinarian.

Dogs may also get into other medication and inadvertently overdose. Often, human pills are flavored to make them go down easier, and the scavenging dog may willingly eat a whole bottle of your medicine. The signs and treatments depend on the type of medication and how much was taken. Induce vomiting or give activated charcoal, then get your dog to the veterinarian. Take a sample of the drug with you.

Houseplants: A wide range of plants are poisonous to pets. The toxin may be only in the seed or leaves; other times, the entire plant is poisonous. In rare instances, simple contact with the plant causes a reaction the way poison ivy affects sensitive people. But the most dangerous plants require chewing and/or swallowing.

The symptoms of plant poisoning depend on the individual toxin and may be as innocuous as localized contact irritations and rashes, to systemic poisonings. DROOLING, vomiting, diarrhea, hallucinations, convulsions, and even death may result.

p

POISONOUS PLANTS

TOXIN	SIGNS/SYMPTOMS	TREATMENT
Apple seeds, Apricot pits, Cherry pits, Hydrangea, Peach pits	Difficulty breathing; muscle tremors; convulsion; death	SEE VET IMMEDIATELY! Induce vomiting if ingested recently. These contain cyanide, which acts to suffocate the dog. A chemical antidote administered by the veterinarian is usually required to save the dog's life.
Azalea	Salivation; vomiting and diarrhea; muscle weakness; seizures; coma; death	Administer lots of water to wash out the stomach, along with activated charcoal to absorb toxin, then see your veterinarian.

TOXIN	SIGNS/SYMPTOMS	TREATMENT
Belladonna, Datura, Henbane, Jessamine, Jimpson weed	Dry mucous membranes; excessive thirst; rapid heartbeat; dilated pupils; can lead to coma or convulsions, and death	SEE VET IMMEDIATELY! Supportive care along with chemical antidotes are required if the dog is to survive.
Bird of Paradise, Box, Crown of Thorns, Daphne, English Ivy, Honeysuckle, Iris, Snow-on-the-Mountain	Intestinal irritation with nausea and vomiting. (Dog exhibits stomach pain, suffers diarrhea immediately upon ingestion.)	Induce vomiting, administer lots of water to dilute toxin, or several tablespoons of milk to coat the stomach; giving activated charcoal helps absorb the poison. See a veterinarian as soon as possible.
Black Locust, Castor Bean, Rosary Pea	Signs can be delayed up to twenty-four hours after ingestion, then abdominal pain, bloody diarrhea, and vomiting. Dogs may suffer fever, act depressed; signs can progress to coma, seizures, and death.	HIGHLY POISONOUS: eating a single pea or bean can kill a dog. Induce vomiting, then SEE VET IMMEDIATELY!
Caladium, Dieffenbachia (Dumb cane), Jack-in-the-Pulpit, Philodendron (heart-leaf and split-leaf), Skunk Cabbage	Irritation of the mouth, tongue, and throat; increased salivation, with possible ulcers and swelling, which may interfere with breathing	DO NOT INDUCE VOMITING. Offer water or milk to cleanse the dog's oral cavity. Rarely fatal; should see veterinarian if breathing becomes difficult or severe oral irritation develops.
Chinaberry, Marijuana, Morning glory, Periwinkle	Bizarre or odd behavior; trembling; convulsions	Induce vomiting, and get to the veterinarian.
Creeping Fig, Chrysanthemum, Weeping Fig	Contact rash affecting skin surrounding and inside the mouth	Wash area with cool water to soothe rash. See veterinarian.
Daffodil, Tulip, Wisteria (especially the bulbs)	Gastric irritation; violent vomiting; possible depression; death in severe cases	Induce vomiting. Administer lots of water to dilute toxin, or several table-spoons of milk to coat the stomach; giving activated charcoal helps absorb the poison. SEE VET IMMEDIATELY!
English Holly, European Holly	Abdominal pain; vomiting and diarrhea when two or more berries are eaten; death reported rarely	SEE VET IMMEDIATELY! Supportive care is necessary to treat the digitalis-like toxin.
Foxglove, Larkspur, Lily of the Valley, Monkshood, Oleander	Slowed heartbeat (this plant contains digitalis), followed by severe abdominal pain and vomiting; finally, signs of agitation are exhibited, followed shortly by coma and death	SEE VET IMMEDIATELY! Induce vomiting if ingested recently. These plants' toxicity can stop your dog's heart.
Golden Chain, Indian Tobacco, Mescal Bean, Poison Hemlock, Tobacco	Salivation; incoordination; muscle twitches; rapid heartbeat; breathing becomes labored, and the dog can collapse in minutes to hours following ingestion	SEE VET IMMEDIATELY! These plants contain nicotine and requires a chemical antidote to save the dog.

TOXIN	SIGNS/SYMPTOMS	TREATMENT
Jerusalem Cherry, Potato (green parts and eyes)	Signs may not appear until eighteen to twenty-four hours following ingestion; then the dog exhibits a painful abdomen, bloody diarrhea, vomiting, and dry mouth; severe cases may proceed to tremors, paralysis, and cardiac arrest	DO NOT INDUCE VOMITING as this may further damage the gastrointestinal tract. SEE VET IMMEDIATELY!
Mother-in-law Plant	Vomiting; salivation; mouth irritation; diarrhea; occasionally staggering or collapse	DO NOT INDUCE VOMITING! Offer water or milk to cleanse the dog's oral cavity. Rarely fatal; should see veterinarian if dog loses coordination or collapses.
Poinsettia	Irritates mucous membranes of mouth; may cause excessive salivation or vomiting but not death	Offer water or milk to cleanse the dog's oral cavity. Consult your veterinarian.
Rhubarb (upper stem and leaves)	Vomiting; excessive salivation; abdominal pain; staggers, followed by convulsions	Induce vomiting, then get your dog to the veterinarian. Without treatment, the toxin causes extensive damage to the dog's kidneys.
Yew (American Yew, English Yew, Japanese Yew, etc.)	Irregular heartbeat; dilation of the pupils; shivering; nausea; abdominal pain; but death often occurs without warning signs	SEE VET IMMEDIATELY! Induce vomiting if possible.

Therapy is aimed at counteracting or preventing the effects of the poison. Depending on the individual plant, the toxin may be addressed either by flushing the area with water, inducing vomiting, or dilution or neutralization of the poison.

Household Products: Pets can be poisoned by almost any cleaning agent; bleach, drain cleaner, or phenol preparations like Lysol disinfectant or coal-tar products are common culprits. Most often, the dog is poisoned when the product is splashed on the dog, or she walks through a spill and/or licks the substance. Ice-melting chemicals and salt on sidewalks or roadways will severely burn your dog's footpads. Flush the area with lukewarm water to remove the toxin from the skin, and get your dog to a veterinarian. Other common household poisons that dogs relish are ANTIFREEZE and CHOCOLATE.

Pest Poisons: Dogs that catch or scavenge wild animals or bugs can be exposed by ingesting a poisoned pest like a rodent, roach, or snail. In addition, the same cereal grains often used in commercial dog foods are also used in rodent baits, so dogs may willingly seek out and eat the poison. There are three general groups of rodenticides: anticoagulants, cholecalciferol, and bromethalin. Anticoagulants like warfarin are the most common; they work by preventing blood from clotting, leading to uncontrolled and fatal bleeding from the rectum, nose, and even the skin. Cholecalciferol is a vitamin D analog that interferes with the body's ability to eliminate calcium, leading to toxicity and death. Bromethalin is a neurotoxin that causes irreversible damage to the nervous system. Strychnine can result in seizures, and arsenic can kill before signs develop (the dog's breath smells of garlic).

OTHER POISONS

TOXIN	SIGNS/SYMPTOMS	TREATMENT
Acid poisons (bleach)	When swallowed, drooling, pawing at mouth, painful abdomen; when spilled on skin, vocalizations, signs of distress, rolling, licking area	DO NOT INDUCE VOMITING! Flush the area of contact with plain water for at least ten minutes. If substance was swallowed, administer two teaspoons of milk of magnesia. SEE VET IMMEDIATELY!
Alkaline poisons (drain cleaner)	When swallowed, drooling, pawing at mouth, painful abdomen; when spilled, vocalizations, signs of distress, rolling, licking area	DO NOT INDUCE VOMITING! Flush the area of contact with plain water for at least ten minutes. If substance was swallowed, administer six tablespoons of half water and half lemon juice or vinegar to neutralize, then SEE VET IMMEDIATELY!
Antifreeze (ethylene glycol)	Drunken behavior; excessive thirst; increased urination; diarrhea; vomiting; convulsions; loss of appetite; panting	EMERGENCY! SEE VET IMMEDIATELY! If ingested in last two hours, induce vomiting and/or administer activated charcoal. Veterinary treatment administers 100 proof alcohol or 4MP.
Chocolate	Drooling; vomiting and/or diarrhea; excessive urination; hyperactivity; muscle tremors; seizures; coma	EMERGENCY! See vet ASAP. If ingested in last two hours, induce vomiting.
Coal-tar poisoning (phenol disinfectants like Lysol, treated wood, tar paper, heavy oil)	Depression; weakness; incoordination; coma; death	See vet ASAP. Lysol is absorbed through skin; wash dog immediately if exposed.
Flea products (organophosphates, carbamates, and chlorinated hydrocarbons)	Signs may be delayed due to skin absorption of toxin; a variety of signs possible, including apprehension, muscle twitches, shivering, seizures, drooling, diarrhea, hyperactivity, or depression	Wash dog as soon as you realize poisoning has occurred, even if several hours have passed and no signs are yet seen; then see vet ASAP.
Lead poisoning (insecticides, paint, linoleum, roofing shingles, plumbing materials, solder, batteries, golf balls)	Abdominal pain; vomiting; seizures; uncoordinated gait; excitation; continuous barking; hysteria; weakness; blindness; chewing fits	When ingestion is within past two hours, induce vomiting. See vet for specific treatment ASAP.

TOXIN	SIGNS/SYMPTOMS	TREATMENT
Medications, aspirin, ibuprofen, Tylenol, other NSAIDs	Blood in vomit that looks like coffee grounds	Stop administering the medication, then see your vet. If dog ingested more than one tablet in past two hours, induce vomiting, then see vet ASAP.
Medications, other	Various signs dependent upon toxic agent	Induce vomiting if ingested within last two hours. See vet ASAP.
Petroleum products (gasoline, kerosene, turpentine)	Vomiting; difficulty breathing; tremors; seizures; coma; respiratory failure and death	EMERGENCY! DO NOT INDUCE VOMITING! SEE VET IMMEDIATELY! If help is more than thirty minutes away, give the dog one to two ounces of mineral oil, olive oil, or vegetable oil by mouth; follow it in thirty minutes with Glauber's salt (sodium sulfate) to stimulate defecation. Be prepared to perform artificial respiration.
Pest baits, anticoagulant types (warfarin, pindone, d-Con Mouse Prufe II, Coumadin, Talon)	Bleeding in stool and/or urine, from nose, ears, and beneath the skin and gums; symptoms first appear several days after ingestion	EMERGENCY! Induce vomiting if ingested within past two hours, then see vet ASAP. Blood transfusions and treatment with intravenous vitamin K is a specific antidote.
Pest baits, arsenic (slug/snail bait, ant poisons, weed killers, insecticides)	Thirst; vomiting; staggers; drooling; abdominal pain and cramps; diarrhea; paralysis; strong garlic breath	EMERGENCY! Induce vomiting if poisoning occurred within last two hours, then SEE VET IMMEDIATELY! A specific antidote is available.
Pest baits, bromethalin (Assault and Vengeance rodenticides)	Muscle tremors; staggering gait; high fever; stupor; agitation; seizures	EMERGENCY! Induce vomiting if ingested within past two hours, then SEE VET IMMEDIATELY!
Pest baits, cholecalciferol (Rampage, vitamin D₃)	Vomiting; diarrhea; seizures; heart or kidney failure	EMERGENCY! Induce vomiting if ingested within past two hours, then SEE VET IMMEDIATELY!
Pest baits, metaldehyde (rat, snail, and slug bait)	Drooling; incoordination; excitability; muscle tremors; progressive weakness	EMERGENCY! Induce vomiting if ingested within past two hours, then SEE VET IMMEDIATELY!
Pest baits, phosphorus (rat and roach poisons, matches and matchboxes)	Vomiting; diarrhea; garlic breath; sometimes symptom-free period, then return of signs with painful abdomen, seizures, and coma	EMERGENCY! Induce vomiting if ingested within past two hours, then SEE VET IMMEDIATELY!
Pest baits, sodium fluoroacetate (rat poison)	Vomiting; agitation; straining to defecate or urinate; seizures (not triggered by external stimuli); staggering gait; collapse	EMERGENCY! Induce vomiting if ingested within past two hours, then SEE VET IMMEDIATELY! A specific antidote is available.
Pest baits, strychnine (rat, mouse, mole, coyote poison)	Agitation; apprehension; excitement; seizures prompted by noises like clapping hands; drooling; muscle spasms; chewing; collapse	EMERGENCY! SEE VET IMMEDIATELY! Cover dog with towel to prevent stimulation of further seizures. If poisoned within two hours and dog remains alert, induce vomiting.
Pest baits, zinc phosphide (rat poison)	Depression; difficulty breathing; weakness; seizures; vomiting (with blood); seizures; coma	EMERGENCY! Induce vomiting if ingested within past two hours, then SEE VET IMMEDIATELY!

TOXIN	SIGNS/SYMPTOMS	TREATMENT
Snakebite (copperhead, cottonmouth, rattlesnake, coral snake)	Restlessness; drooling; panting; weakness; diarrhea; collapse; sometimes seizures, paralysis, or coma	EMERGENCY! SEE VET IMMEDIATELY! If help is more than thirty minutes away, apply tight bandages between bite and dog's heart and loosen for five minutes once an hour. Keep dog quiet until help is available. *Don't wash bite, don't cut bite to suction out poison, and don't apply ice to bite:* all could increase venom absorption and/or damage tissue further.
Toad poisoning	Slobbering or drooling; pawing at mouth; seizures; coma; collapse	EMERGENCY! Flush dog's mouth with plain water for at least ten minutes; induce vomiting. Be prepared to perform artificial respiration. SEE VET IMMEDIATELY!

The common rodenticides take twenty-four to seventy-two hours to induce signs, but once the dog is showing distress, treatment may not be as effective and can be too late. Induce vomiting immediately if you see your dog swallow the poison, then get her to a vet; a specific antidote is available for each of these poisons.

If a veterinarian is unavailable, call the ASPCA National Animal Poison Control Center (NAPCC). They'll guide you step-by-step as to what home remedies are appropriate to your circumstance. Consultations can be charged to a credit card by calling (800) 548-2423 or to a phone bill at (900) 680-0000, or you can visit their Web site at http://www.napcc.aspca.org.

p

Porcupine Quills

Curious dogs, especially those living in rural areas, often encounter a porcupine with devastating results. The needlelike quills are up to four inches long and barbed to penetrate flesh and continue moving inward. The quills typically lodge in the dog's face or open mouth.

Porcupine quills are exceptionally painful. A dog typically loses self-control, rolls with PAIN, and may even reflexively strike out at concerned owners in his attempts to seek relief.

Visible quills should be removed as quickly as possible, and may be plucked out using needle-nose pliers; grasp the quill near the skin and pull straight out. Be aware, though, that the barbed ends can break off. Once beneath the skin, they travel inward and may result in deep infections. Also, a dog's fur may hide small quills that you may miss. Because a dog in pain is rarely able to hold still even for

PORCUPINE QUILLS	
SYMPTOMS	
Needlelike barbs protruding from body, particularly face or mouth; crying with pain; rolling; pawing at injured area	
HOME CARE	
If quill is accessible, grasp with needle-nose pliers close to skin, pull straight out, disinfect each wound; vet care usually required	
VET CARE	
Anesthetize dog, remove quills, swab each wound with disinfectant, like peroxide or Betadine; possibly oral antibiotics	
PREVENTION	
Supervise outdoor excursions	

a beloved owner's ministrations, a veterinarian is usually better equipped to do the plucking. Once anesthetized, a search and seizure of quills hidden by fur— and particularly inside his mouth—is more easily accomplished. The wounds are then treated with a disinfectant, like peroxide or Betadine.

The only way to prevent your dog from encountering an irate porcupine is to keep outdoor exploration confined to the yard by a fence, or supervise outside adventures from the end of a leash.

Progressive Retinal Atrophy (PRA)

PRA is an inherited EYE disorder characterized by degeneration of the retina, which ultimately results in blindness. Most dogs are first affected at age five to seven years.

There are two forms, referred to as *central* and *generalized*. The generalized form is most common, in which the light-detecting cells on the surface of the retina gradually stop working. This results in an overall loss of sight. It is recognized in many breeds, including the Irish Setter, Toy Poodle, Norwegian Elkhound, Yorkshire Terrier, Welsh Corgi, and others.

The central form is inherited in the Border Collie, Golden Retriever, English Springer Spaniel, Irish Setter, Labrador Retriever, and Shetland Sheepdog. It affects the deepest layer of the retina below the photoreceptor layer. Initially, it is the centermost portion of the retina that is destroyed, with peripheral vision the last to go.

Signs of both forms are similar and begin with the dog's loss of vision in

PROGRESSIVE RETINAL ATROPHY (PRA)

SYMPTOMS
Initial loss of night vision, progressing to total blindness

HOME CARE
None; maintain familiar surroundings to keep dog comfortable

VET CARE
None

PREVENTION
None

dim light, often characterized by night blindness. Dogs may try to compensate by staying near light sources at night. Others become increasingly dependent on the owner. Affected dogs may avoid stairs and jumping on furniture, and dislike unfamiliar environments.

Eventually, PRA progresses to total blindness. There is currently no effective treatment. Owners can make the vision-impaired or blind dog more comfortable by establishing a routine and not rearranging the dog's familiar surroundings.

Because this is an inherited condition, dogs suffering from PRA should not be bred. Conscientious breeders are aware of the potential for congenital eye disease, and high-risk dogs should be examined and certified free of the disorder before being bred. The Canine Eye Registration Foundation, Inc., issues certification and collects data, in conjunction with the Veterinary Medical Database at Purdue University (see Appendix C, "Canine Research Foundations").

Proptosis of Eyeball

A sharp blow to the head or a bite wound may cause the eyeball to prolapse, or "pop," from the socket. Sometimes tumors or infection may also cause the condition. This is not only disconcerting to the owner, but extremely painful for the dog and will result in permanent vision damage if not promptly addressed. *This is an emergency; see your veterinarian immediately.*

Dogs with large, prominent eyes, such as Boston Terriers, Pekingese, and Pugs, are most prone. Once the eye has left the socket, the eyelids may try to close behind the organ, blocking its return. Subsequent to the prolapse, tissue behind the eye will swell from the trauma, making the condition even more difficult to correct.

PROPTOSIS OF EYEBALL (EYE OUT OF SOCKET)

SYMPTOMS
Eye bulges out of socket

HOME CARE
EMERGENCY! Immediate vet care required to save dog's sight; place wet cloth over eyeball until you can get dog help

VET CARE
Mechanical replacement of eye; medications to reduce swelling and pain and prevent infection

PREVENTION
Remain vigilant to avoid trauma, such as bite wounds and sharp blows to head, especially in flat-faced breeds

To prevent the surface from drying, place a wet gauze sponge or wet cloth over the eye. Don't try to manipulate the eyeball back into place yourself; you could cause even more damage. Hold the covering in place either manually or with tape until you reach veterinary help.

The eyeball will need to be surgically replaced. Medications are prescribed to relieve the trauma and reduce and/or prevent further injury. It may take several weeks after the eyeball is replaced before the extent of the damage can be determined.

Prostate Infection

The prostate gland is located at the base of the bladder in male dogs and aids in REPRODUCTION. Bacterial infection of the prostate gland is quite common in dogs, and the agents involved are often similar to those causing urinary-tract infections.

Signs include lethargy, loss of appetite, bloody or puslike discharge from the penis, and a hunching posture indicative of abdominal PAIN. The condition is diagnosed based on these signs and on culture of the prostatic fluid, urine, or semen. The culture identifies the bacteria involved, so that a specific antibiotic is prescribed. Usually, at least three weeks of medication is required to ensure the infection has resolved.

Prostate infection, referred to as *prostatitis*, can become chronic if the infection cannot be resolved. This may prompt ongoing urinary-tract infections or even sterility in an otherwise healthy dog. In chronic cases, antibiotics are

PROSTATITIS

SYMPTOMS
Lethargy; loss of appetite; bloody or puslike discharge from penis; hunching posture from pain; constipation

HOME CARE
None

VET CARE
Antibiotic therapy; sometimes neutering

PREVENTION
Neuter the dog

indicated for at least three months, and sometimes for the life of the dog to control the infection. When there is no response to treatment, your veterinarian may recommend NEUTERING.

Prostatic hyperplasia is an enlargement of the prostate gland and is the most common prostate problem of intact older dogs. The condition is thought to be due to a lifetime exposure to male sex hormones. Often there are no symptoms, although constipation may be a problem. Neutering is the treatment of choice; typically, the dog's enlarged prostate will reduce in size within a couple of weeks following neuter surgery. For stud dogs, treatment with Ovaban (progesterone) often reverses the enlargement and returns the dog to potency.

p

Pulse

Pulse refers to the rhythmic movement of blood by the heart. The pulse rates of individual dogs vary depending on their age and size. The average-size adult dog's resting pulse rate ranges from 60 to 150 beats per minute; a large dog's pulse rate falls in the slower end, while a small dog's pulse rate is up to 180, and a puppy's may be 220 beats per minute. And just like athletic people, the working dog's pulse rate may be slower than the pulse rate of a couch-potato dog of the same size.

Your dog's pulse should be strong and steady. A rapid pulse rate indicates anything from excitement or exertion, to ANEMIA, infection, or HEART DISEASE; a slow pulse can indicate illness.

You can calculate your dog's pulse rate by counting the number of beats in a minute. The drumbeat can be felt by placing the flat of your fingers against the femoral artery in the groin, at the juncture of thigh and body. Or place your palm over the ribs on your dog's left side directly behind his front elbow.

Puppy

A puppy is an immature dog. Dogs are considered puppies from birth until fully grown (usually at about one year of age). However, each dog develops differently, with smaller dogs tending to mature earlier and some large breeds not physically mature before they are two years old.

Newborn puppies vary in size depending on the breed; tiny dogs, like the Chihuahua, produce puppies about four inches long, while giant-breed newborns, like Great Dane puppies, may be twice that size. Rate of puppy development also varies from breed to breed. For instance, Cocker Spaniel puppies open their eyes sooner than Fox Terrier puppies, and Basenji puppies develop teeth earlier than Shetland Sheepdog puppies. However, no matter the breed, all puppies are born totally dependent on the BITCH.

At birth, puppies are blind, deaf, and toothless, unable to regulate body temperature, or even urinate or defecate on their own. Puppies depend on their mother and littermates for warmth, huddling in cozy piles to conserve body temperature. A puppy separated from this warm, furry nest can quickly die, and cold, lonely puppies cry loudly to alert Mom to their predicament.

Puppies first experience the sensation of being petted when washed by their mother's stroking tongue. The bitch licks her babies all over to keep them and the nest clean, and also to stimulate them to defecate and urinate.

From birth, puppies are able to use their sense of smell and touch, which helps them root about the nest to find their mother's scent-marked breasts. The first milk the mother produces, called *colostrum*, is rich in antibodies that provide passive immunity and help protect the babies from disease during these early weeks of life (see IMMUNE SYSTEM and VACCINATIONS).

For the first two weeks of life, puppies sleep nearly 90 percent of the time, spending their awake time nursing. All their energy is funneled into growing, and birth weight doubles the first week. Newborns aren't able to support their weight, and crawl about with paddling motions of their front legs. The limited locomotion provides the exercise that develops muscles and coordination, and soon the puppies are crawling over and around each other and their mother.

The second week of life brings great changes for the puppy. Ears and eyes sealed since birth begin to open during this period (ears at about two weeks; eyelids, between ten and sixteen days). This gives the furry babies a new sense of their world. They learn what their mother and other dogs look and sound

p

Newborns pile together for warmth *(Photo credit: Ralston Purina Company)*

like, and begin to expand their own vocabulary from grunts and mews to yelps, whines, and barks. Puppies generally stand by day fifteen and take their first wobbly walk by day twenty-one.

By age three weeks, puppy development advances from the neonatal period to the transitional period. This is a time of rapid physical and sensory development, during which the puppies go from total dependence on Mom to a bit of independence. They begin to PLAY with their littermates, learn about their environment and canine society, and begin sampling food from Mom's bowl. Puppy TEETH erupt, until all the baby teeth are in by about five to six weeks of age. Puppies can control their need to use the bathroom by this age and begin moving away from their sleeping quarters to eliminate.

Following the transitional phase, puppies enter the socialization period at the end of the third week of life; it lasts until about week ten. It is during this socialization period that interaction with others increases, and puppies form attachments they will remember the rest of their lives. The most critical period—age six to eight weeks—is when puppies most easily learn to accept others as a part of their family.

The puppies learn to identify friend and foe during this time. Those exposed to friendly people, like babies, children, and strange adults, and other animals, like cats and dogs, during this impressionable period will more readily recognize

Puppies form attachments early *(Photo credit: Ralston Purina Company)*

Puppies learn social skills with their littermates *(Photo credit: Ralston Purina Company)*

them as safe and accept them as family members later in life. Puppies that miss out on these vital introductions will be fearful of strangers and have a more difficult time adjusting. Studies show that puppies handled daily by friendly people during this period learn more quickly and are more easily trained.

Beginning at four weeks of age, the bitch's milk production begins to slow down just as the puppies' energy needs increase. As the mother dog slowly weans her babies from nursing, they begin sampling solid food in earnest. Weaning typically is complete by week eight.

Nearly every waking moment is spent in play, which is not only great fun for the babies, but is great practice for canine life. Puppies learn how to do important dog activities like chasing, running, pawing, biting, and fighting. Social skills and canine etiquette are learned by interaction with littermates and Mom. Puppies learn to inhibit their bite when they are bitten by each other, and learn canine language (see COMMUNICATION). Through play, they practice dominant and submissive postures and prepare for life in the world (see DOMINANCE and SUBMISSION).

The juvenile puppy period generally begins at age ten weeks and lasts until puberty and the onset of sexual maturity (see REPRODUCTION). It is during this period that puppies begin to learn the consequences of behavior and determine what is most appropriate to certain circumstances. Puppies at this age have boundless curiosity, exasperating stubbornness, and enthusiastic AFFECTION. Expect your puppy to get into everything, and you won't be disappointed. This is an ideal time to begin TRAINING.

Puppies may be placed in new homes once they are eating well on their own; however, they will be better adjusted and make better pets by staying and interacting with littermates and the bitch until they are twelve weeks old. Puppies tend to make transitions from one environment to another more easily at this age.

A healthy puppy has bright, clear eyes and clean, soft fur. Her ears, eyes, nose, and anus should have no discharge. Well-socialized puppies are curious and friendly, will readily come to you with wagging tail, and are easily engaged in a game. Proper health care includes preventative vaccinations, screening for intestinal parasites, and a nutritionally complete and balanced puppy diet.

Puppy Mills

This derogatory term refers to the factorylike production of puppies by unscrupulous "backyard breeders" who care nothing for the health of the animals. Dogs of questionable parentage are constantly bred to produce supposedly "purebred" puppies, which are then sold for profit (typically in pet stores). To make more money, backyard breeders often don't provide proper care and housing. The result is sickly, emotionally bankrupt puppies that, if they live, make poor pets for the gullible, softhearted souls tricked into buying them for exorbitant prices.

In recent years, the horrors of puppy mills have been exposed by the national media, leading to a better awareness by the pet-loving public. Sadly, there are undoubtedly still some unscrupulous breeders making a buck at the expense of the innocent.

Most reputable pet stores no longer traffic in puppies and kittens, and often instead promote adoptions from animal welfare organizations. If you are interested in a pup of a particular breed, ask the registering organization for a reference in your area. Then, insist on viewing the breeder's accommodations for the dogs, and ask questions. A reputable breeder is more interested in finding an appropriate home for the puppies than making money and will be happy to satisfy your curiosity; in fact, you may need to convince the breeder that you've got what it takes to provide the best home!

Pyometra

Pyometra is a bacterial infection of the uterus that can spill into the bloodstream. *This is a life-threatening condition, and requires a veterinarian's immediate attention.*

The condition is most common in bitches over seven years of age and is thought to be due to hormone exposure. High levels of the hormones progesterone or estrogen can result in pyometra. Over a lifetime, the intact female dog cycling in and out of heat is exposed to these hormones, and with age, her risk of developing pyometra increases. Younger dogs may develop pyometra from exposure to estrogen used to interrupt pregnancy (see MISMATING). Ovaban, which is still used as a birth control in dogs, may result in pyometra if used for long periods.

P

PYOMETRA
SYMPTOMS
Loss of appetite; lethargy; increased thirst and urination; swollen abdomen; sometimes a creamy to greenish smelly discharge from vagina; low to subnormal temperature
HOME CARE
EMERGENCY! SEE VET IMMEDIATELY!
VET CARE
Spay surgery removes infected uterus; antibiotic therapy
PREVENTION
Spay dogs that aren't in a professional breeding program or show career

Signs typically develop four to eight weeks after the dog goes out of heat. Symptoms include loss of appetite, lethargy, and increased thirst and urination. When pus collects in the uterus, a painful swelling in the lower abdomen develops. Other times, the infection is termed *open* and will drain from the cervix; the discharge smells and looks like pus. The dog may have a low-grade fever or even a subnormal temperature, but sometimes the temperature remains normal.

Diagnosis is based on the signs and may be confirmed with an X RAY or ULTRASOUND. The treatment of choice is SPAYING the dog to remove the infected reproductive organs and prevent the condition from recurring (see also METRITIS).

p

Quarantine

Quarantine is the isolation of a dog for a period of time to prevent the potential spread of disease or pests to other pets or people. New dogs and puppies should undergo a veterinary examination and be given appropriate treatment before or shortly following ADOPTION. But it's prudent to isolate even healthy-appearing newcomers when they are to be introduced into a home that already has pets.

Any animal showing signs of illness should be isolated from healthy animals. However, it's possible for a new pet to expose resident animals to illness before they become sick themselves. That's because the incubation period—the amount of time between exposure to disease and the development of symptoms of illness—varies depending on the causative agent. For instance, the incubation period for CANINE PARVOVIRUS is five to eleven days, while RABIES can be months or even years. It is for this reason that some countries like the United Kingdom and states like Hawaii impose a quarantine of up to six months on pets imported into these areas.

In most cases, dogs incubating a highly contagious disease become sick within two to three weeks of exposure. If unsure of your new dog's recent health, quarantine him for at least two weeks (a month is better) to reduce risk of exposure for your other pets. If the newcomer remains healthy during the quarantine period, he can then be safely introduced to your home and other pets.

Segregate an area like the laundry room or enclosed porch, and furnish it with necessary canine paraphernalia—food and water dishes, toys, and bed. The new dog and your resident pets should have no direct contact, not even

Isolate dogs to quarantine them *(Photo credit: Ralston Purina Company)*

sniffing through the screen or beneath the door, as even this risks disease transmission.

Use a disinfectant to keep the quarantine area and canine necessities clean. A good all-purpose disinfectant is Clorox at a dilution of one cup of bleach to two gallons of water. Remember to also disinfect yourself following interaction with the new dog, particularly after cleaning up any accidental puddles or piles. Thoroughly clean your hands and even wipe down your shoes to prevent carrying something nasty out of the room that could infect your other pets.

Rabies

Rabies is caused by a bullet-shaped virus that belongs to the family *Rhabdoviridae*. It causes a devastating neurological disease that affects the brain, causing symptoms that are similar to meningitis. Once symptoms develop, the disease is always fatal.

Rabies is an ancient scourge that has been around for centuries and continues to appear throughout the world. The disease affects all mammals, most commonly wild animal populations, but also afflicts dogs, cats, and people. However, since 1884 when Louis Pasteur developed the first vaccine, rabies has been preventable. Some areas such as Hawaii and Great Britain eliminated the disease using strict QUARANTINE protocols.

Rabies still appears today in pets or people as a result of disease "spillover" from wild animals and parallels the incidence of rabies in these feral reservoirs. Animals most often associated with the disease include raccoons in the northeastern United States (New York, Connecticut, New Jersey, Maryland, and spreading); coyotes and gray foxes in Texas and the southwest; foxes in Alaska; and skunks in Kansas. Bats are also often associated with rabies. Pets allowed to roam in the regions cited are at highest risk for encountering a rabid animal and getting sick. Consequently, such high-risk pets place their owners in danger as well.

Infection requires direct contact with an infected animal. The usual transmission is through a bite that introduces infective saliva into the wound. There, the virus proliferates until it reaches the nerves, which carry the infection to the spinal cord. Ultimately the virus reaches the brain, whereupon symptoms develop.

Rabies has three recognized states of clinical disease: (1) incubation,

RABIES	
SYMPTOMS	Refusal to eat or drink; hiding; depression; drooling; throat paralysis and inability to swallow. Or vicious, violent behavior; excessive vocalizing; chewing or eating wood, rocks, or other inedible objects
HOME CARE	None; BUT EXTREMELY CONTAGIOUS TO PEOPLE (THROUGH BITES OR CONTACT WITH SALIVA)
VET CARE	None; euthanasia; test brain tissue to confirm diagnosis
PREVENTION	Vaccinate dog; prevent contact with wild animals

(2) clinical signs, and (3) paralysis terminating in death. The incubation period—the time from exposure (bite) to development of symptoms—takes fourteen days to twenty-four months to incubate, with an average of three to eight weeks for most species. From the brain, the virus spreads to other tissues, like the salivary glands.

Clinical signs are mild to severe behavior changes. The first symptom is refusal to eat or drink, and the stricken dog typically seeks solitude. The disease then progresses to one of two forms: *paralytic*, or *dumb, rabies* and *furious rabies*.

In the dumb form dogs act depressed, become insensitive to PAIN, and develop paralysis of the throat and jaw muscles. They salivate and drool, and because they can't swallow, it may appear something is stuck in their throat. Pets with dumb rabies usually fall into a coma and die within three to ten days of initial signs.

Furious rabies is the classic presentation of "mad dog" symptoms. Dogs become extremely vicious and violent, and any noise prompts attack. Such dogs snap and bite at real or imaginary objects and may roam for miles attacking anything in their path. They lose all fear of natural enemies and commonly chew or swallow inedible objects like stones or wood. Death occurs four to seven days after onset of clinical signs as a result of progressive paralysis.

The signs and course of rabies in people are similar to those in animals, and incubation ranges from two weeks to twelve months. There is no cure for rabies. Once signs appear, the mortality rate for the animal or person is virtually 100 percent.

For that reason, all pets should be protected with a rabies vaccination.

Even dogs confined to kennels should be vaccinated, to protect them should they inadvertently escape. Besides, you never know when a bat might wing through a window, or a raccoon shimmy down the chimney and invade your house dog's territory. Because of the human health risk (see ZOONOSIS), rabies vaccination of dogs is required by law.

Diagnosis of rabies can be accomplished only by microscopic examination of brain tissue from the suspect animal; this cannot be done while the animal is alive. Wild animals that act suspiciously or attack humans or pets should be euthanized immediately, and the brain examined for evidence of rabies. Dogs bitten by an animal that cannot be tested for the disease should be considered exposed to rabies.

Each state has established its own rules regarding rabies exposure in pets. Animals are thought to be infectious only shortly before and during the time they show symptoms. Therefore, a biting animal capable of transmitting disease at the time of the bite will typically develop signs within a ten-day period. For that reason, ten days is the recommended period of quarantine in such cases.

The human risk is so high when handling suspect animals that it's safest that unvaccinated pets exposed to rabies be euthanized, and then tested for the disease. However, some local or state laws may allow an exposed pet to live under stringent quarantine for six months and, if no signs develop, be vaccinated prior to release. Recommendations for pets whose rabies vaccinations are current but who are exposed to the disease include immediate revaccination and strict owner control and observation for not less than forty-five days.

Prevent exposure and protect your dog and yourself by restricting roaming and keeping his rabies vaccination current. Any contact with wild animals acting in an abnormal behavior, including STRAY or FERAL cats or dogs, increases your risk.

A number of states in endemic regions have implemented programs to immunize populations of wild animals in an effort to slow or prevent the spread of the disease. Vaccine-laced edible baits dropped from planes are seeded in rabies-prone areas.

The rabies virus is sensitive to many household detergents and soaps. Should you or your pet suffer a bite, thoroughly wash the wounds with soap and hot water to kill as much virus as possible, then consult a doctor or veterinarian immediately. The postexposure vaccine available for people is virtually 100 percent effective when administered in the right period of time.

Reading Food Labels

Pet-food labels are governed by regulations established and enforced by feed control officials in each state; however, most states based their regulations on those developed by the American Association of Feed Control Officials (AAFCO). Among other things, the AAFCO Model Regulations detail what and how information is presented on the label. Virtually all pet-food manufacturers with interstate distribution follow AAFCO label guidelines. Label information on pet foods must also follow rules and regulations established by the Food and Drug Administration (FDA), the U.S. Department of Agriculture (USDA), and the Federal Trade Commission (FTC). These national, state, and local rules regulate how pet food is distributed, what goes into the food, how it's sold, and even the way it's labeled. By reading and understanding food labels, dog owners are able to choose the best products for their pets.

All pet foods involved in interstate commerce must, by law, disclose on their labels a guaranteed analysis, a list of ingredients, and a statement and validation of adequacy. Canine nutritional needs continue to be studied and better defined as time goes on.

In 1991, a panel of canine nutrition experts from the FDA, academia, and industry developed nutrient profiles for dog foods intended for growth and reproduction or for adult maintenance. AAFCO has adopted these profiles as the industry standard, and pet foods formulated to meet these standards may claim to provide complete and balanced nutrition. Alternatively, pet-food manufacturers may use their own standards, which may be more stringent than the AAFCO standards. In either instance, nutritional adequacy of the products must be demonstrated through animal feeding trials, as discussed later.

The label includes the principal display panel, which identifies the product by brand and/or product name. Many times, a picture identifying the species (dog) is on the display panel along with the words *dog food* or a similar designation. The principal display panel must also disclose the total amount of food in the package and can also include a nutritional claim.

Even the name of the food is regulated by certain rules. A flavor may be used in the food name—*Beef Flavor Dog Food*—only if the product contains enough of that flavor to be recognized by the dog. Ingredients from animals, poultry, or fish must make up at least 25 percent of a product before that ingredient may be included as part of the product name, but a modifier, like beef "cakes" or liver "dinner," must also be used. For instance, a food called *Moochie Poochie's Beef Dinner* indicates that beef makes up at least 25 percent of the product. When the name includes an animal, fish, or poultry product *without* the modifier, the food must contain at least 95 percent of the named ingredient. *Moochie Poochie's Chicken* indicates that chicken comprises at least 95 percent of the product. *All* or *100 percent* means the product contains the named ingredient, with only water, preservatives, flavorings, vitamins, and minerals added.

The information panel contains a guaranteed-analysis statement listing minimum levels of crude protein and fat and maximum levels of crude fiber and moisture. *Crude* refers to the amount measurable by laboratory equipment, not the amount that can be used by the dog.

If the nutritional claim isn't on the display panel, it's on the information panel. Dog-food manufacturers may label the food *nutritionally complete and balanced* only if they meet AAFCO standards. These standards can be validated in one of two ways:

1. By laboratory chemical analysis or calculation of nutritional values. Products tested this way say, "[Name of product] is formulated to meet the nutritional levels established by the AAFCO Dog Food Nutrient Profile for [life stage]."

    However, calculation methods *don't* include feeding the food to dogs to ensure it's usable by their bodies. So this method costs less because long-term nutritional-adequacy tests (i.e., digestibility and other trials) are not conducted.

2. Feeding trials that determine whether dogs benefit from food. Products tested in this way will be labeled "Animal feeding tests using AAFCO procedures substantiate that [name of product] provides complete and balanced nutrition for [life stage]."

Feeding trials are expensive and time-consuming, but are the only way to ensure the nutrition is adequate for the dog's needs. *The best foods for your dog are complete and balanced products validated through feeding trials that determine whether the nutrients are truly usable by the dog's body.*

If the food doesn't say it's complete and balanced, choose a product that does. Some foods are formulated as gourmet treats designed as supplements to a complete and balanced diet. When research hasn't proven nutritional adequacy, the label must state that the product is "Not Intended for Sole Feeding Purposes."

Reputable pet-food manufacturers determine nutritional adequacy using long-term feeding trials that test for support of growth, adult maintenance, or reproduction. Reproduction trials must maintain the DAM through gestation and lactation, and the puppies through six weeks of age. Growth tests determine if a diet will support the normal growth of puppies; they begin at weaning and run approximately ten weeks. Adult maintenance trials run for about six months with dogs at least one year old. An "all life stages" claim is validated by testing the same animals through all stages of reproduction and growth.

Dog-food manufacturers also conduct short-term tests to determine digestibility and palatability of diets. *Palatability* refers to how tasty the dog considers a diet; it is determined by offering test dogs more than one choice in foods and measuring the quantity and how fast the food is eaten. *Digestibility* describes how well the dog's body is able to utilize the food; it is measured by comparing the difference between what's eaten and what comes out in the feces.

Some labels will include a statement of caloric content in the food. A calorie is a measure of energy produced by eating a specific food. A single calorie is such a small unit of measure that often a unit of 1000 calories, termed a *kilocalorie* (or interchangeably as a *Calorie*) is a more useful measure. Disclosure of Calories is not required on the label—except in diets making "lite" claims—but when it appears, it must be stated as "kilocalories per kg of food." For convenience' sake, it's also often labeled as "Calories per cup" or "per unit" of food.

Dry rations generally contain 1400 to 2000 metabolizable kilocalories per pound of diet (3080 to 4400 kcal/kg); semimoist have 1200 to 1350 metabolized kilocalories per pound of diet (2640 to 2970 kcal/kg); and canned rations provide only 375 to 950 metabolized kilocalories per pound of diet (825 to 2090 kcal/kg). That's why dogs must eat more canned foods than dry diets to obtain the same energy intake.

The amount of calories a dog requires varies widely from dog to dog; the animal's size, metabolism, age, and energy expended determine each dog's need. On average, large dog breeds need less food per pound of body weight than do small-breed dogs. For purposes of this discussion, small-breed dogs are those whose adult body weight is less than twenty pounds; they require about 50 kilocalories per pound of body weight each day. Medium-breed adult dogs are those weighing twenty to fifty pounds, which need approximately 30 to 40 kilocalories per pound of body weight each day. Large-breed dogs weigh fifty to one hundred pounds, while the giant breeds exceed one hundred pounds as adults; they need 20 to 30 kilocalories per pound of body weight each day, or less. Individual dogs can vary greatly from these averages due to differences in activity, lifestyle, or metabolism.

Growing puppies and reproducing female dogs require as much as two to four times more energy per pound of body weight than an adult dog. Working dogs like hunting or herding animals, those under STRESS, and outdoor dogs exposed to cold weather have much higher energy requirements. Inactive couch-potato dogs, and outdoor dogs exposed to hot weather, require much less.

Feeding guidelines are on the label only as a starting point for the amount to feed your dog. Be sure to decrease or increase the amount fed to keep your dog in ideal body condition.

The dog-food label must also list ingredients in the food in decreasing order of the amount present by weight. Therefore, ingredients listed first are present in the greatest amounts, while smallest amounts are listed last. Although the quality of individual ingredients may vary from very poor to excellent, pet-food manufacturers aren't allowed to cite the quality of their ingredients.

In general, the dog-food ingredient list should have:

1. *One or more protein sources*, which should be one of the first two ingredients in canned dog food, and one of the first three in dry dog food;
2. *Carbohydrate source*, such as cereals;
3. *Fat source*; and
4. *Large numbers of trace minerals and vitamin supplements*, which will be toward the bottom of the list.

Water content varies depending on the form of food: dry foods contain 6 to 12 percent moisture, soft-moist foods contain 23 to 40 percent moisture, and canned foods contain 68 to 82 percent moisture.

Any questions concerning a dog-food product should be directed to the manufacturer. Reputable manufacturers include an address or toll-free telephone number on the label.

Dog-food labels will not tell you everything about the food. There's no easy way to judge the overall quality of a dog food, but usually better foods cost a bit more because feeding trials and high-quality ingredients are more expensive than lower-quality generic food brands. It's also important to judge food quality by the manufacturer's reputation, including its history in nutritional research.

And although you may choose the finest ration available, it's worthless if your dog refuses to eat it. Smell, texture, and taste define whether your dog will like a food or not. Ultimately, it's the dog's sense of taste, not the label, that decides palatability. (See also FOOD, FOOD ADDITIVES, FOOD SUPPLEMENTS, and NUTRITION.)

Reproduction

Reproduction is the biological mechanism that allows dogs to create puppies. Dogs become sexually mature and able to breed at various ages, depending on the individual animal's health and breed. By four months of age, male dogs show interest in a sexually receptive female, but males typically aren't able to successfully breed until nine to ten months of age. Female dogs typically

Large dogs have large litters (*Photo credit: Ralston Purina Company*)

experience their first breeding cycle at about six months of age. Onset of sexual maturity varies between individuals as well as breeds, however. Large breeds of both sexes tend to mature more slowly and may take eighteen to twenty-four months to become sexually mature.

Ideally, females should not be bred until their second heat cycle, to allow them to fully mature first. A healthy BITCH will continue to cycle and be able to produce puppies all her life, but beyond the age of about eight, reproduction problems are more likely to develop. Males are able to sire puppies throughout their life. Size of the litter depends on the mother, with tiny dog breeds usually producing one to four babies and large-breed dogs giving birth to litters of eight, ten, and even more puppies. Females generally are able to produce one or two litters a year.

The estrus cycle is the period during which a female becomes sexually receptive to the male and breeding takes place. Nearly all dog breeds experience estrus about every seven months; some cycle more often, while a few (like the Basenji) cycle only once a year.

Canine estrus, also called *heat*, is categorized by distinct periods of time. Proestrus is the onset, lasts about nine days, and is distinguished by swelling of the vulva and a dark, bloody discharge. Ovulation, the release of the eggs, occurs during the next "standing heat" phase, which is technically termed *estrus* and which lasts another seven to nine days. Once the eggs are released, they must mature in the female for seventy-two hours before they can be fertilized by sperm. The vaginal discharge lightens to a faint pink color during this receptive period, during which the bitch will allow breeding to take place. Diestrus is the next stage; it begins at the end of standing heat and lasts about fifty-eight days. Hormone levels increase in response to the body's anticipation of developing puppies and birth. Anestrus is the final stage and lasts about four and a half months, beginning with whelping of the puppies, and ending with the beginning of a new cycle when proestrus returns. It may be difficult to tell exactly when one stage ends and the next begins in dogs that don't become pregnant.

The breeding period is also announced with subtle behavioral signals. The female may become more active or nervous during estrus. Her body gives off scented cues that males readily detect, and canine suitors are attracted from miles away. They MARK territory by leaving urine advertising their status as breeding males, and defend that territory from other dogs with raucous and often violent fights.

Canine breeding is a science that requires a comprehensive knowledge of canine health, anatomy, and genetics. It's also an expensive proposition, and only professional breeders—or those under the direct supervision of a professional—should attempt canine matchmaking. All too often, puppies are produced with little to no thought, which ultimately results in their deaths because, frankly, there simply aren't enough good homes to go around. Unless your dog is in a professional breeding program or is being shown in competition that precludes this option, surgically sterilize your dogs. NEUTERING males and SPAYING females prevents accidental breeding.

Before breeding, both the male and female dogs should be in optimal health. Males should be tested for BRUCELLOSIS, and females should receive any necessary medication, worming, and VACCINATIONS prior to pregnancy. This not only protects the health of the bitch, but also helps protect her puppies during development and for a period after birth.

The preliminaries to mating include a great deal of exploratory sniffing of the anal regions. Once she's ready and interested, the bitch presents her rear quarters to the male and flags her tail to one side in invitation. However, she may flag up to five days before she's actually fertile. The male mounts, clasping her with his forelegs while thrusting forward. Insertion of the penis takes place prior to erection. Following penetration, he treads with his rear legs as erection begins.

His penis swells inside the bitch's vagina. Muscles in her vagina constrict, tying the pair together. The first ejaculate (within the first minute of intromission) is sperm-free prostatic fluid, followed by a sperm-rich ejaculation within the next five minutes. Usually, the male lifts one rear leg over his penis after dismounting, and turns around so the breeding pair stand tail to tail. The genital tie lasts five to sixty minutes, during which prostatic fluid will continue to be produced. This tie is thought to have evolved to better ensure fertilization. Sperm survives in the female for up to seven days.

The female may immediately initiate another breeding, or subsequent encounters may be delayed for several hours or even a day or more. It's also possible for a single litter to be fathered by more than one male.

The dog's uterus is a Y-shaped organ; puppies develop within each arm of the Y. Gestation, the length of time between conception and birth, varies somewhat. The average is sixty-three to sixty-five days; however, it's not unusual for puppies to be born between day fifty-six and seventy-two.

The first signs of pregnancy are the dog's nipples swelling and darkening from light to rosy pink at about forty days into gestation; some dogs may suffer morning sickness between the third and fourth week. By day twenty-seven a veterinarian can detect individual babies by palpating, or feeling, the pregnant dog's abdomen (which won't noticeably swell until about the fifth or sixth week of pregnancy. Large dogs that carry babies high beneath their rib cage may not show at all).

The health of the bitch and her unborn puppies requires high-quality NU-TRITION. Most pregnant dogs eat more during this time, but overfeeding and excessive weight gain should be avoided. Offer her an appropriate commercial reproduction ration like an energy-dense puppy food as recommended by your veterinarian. FOOD SUPPLEMENTS are rarely required.

Within a few days prior to birth, the mother's breasts swell and further develop. Long fur should be clipped away from the breasts and genitals before the puppies are born. Nesting behavior becomes apparent twelve to twenty-four hours before whelping, or giving birth. Typically, canine mothers-to-be seek hidden, cozy spots, dig in the laundry, or rearrange the bedspread. A whelping box for dogs should be provided to dissuade Mom from giving birth on your cashmere sweater.

The dog's rectal TEMPERATURE drops from the normal range of 100.5 to 102.5 degrees to 98 or 99 degrees eight to twelve hours prior to onset of labor. The first stage of labor lasts six to twelve and sometimes twenty-four hours. During this time the bitch appears restless, may pant and shiver, vomit or pace, and scratch at the floor. She either seeks seclusion or looks for an appropriate nest. Give her some privacy so she can get ready.

Dogs with more than one puppy will alternate between the second and third stages of labor. Stage two consists of the birth of the baby, and stage three is the expulsion of the placenta; combined, they usually last only ten to thirty minutes, and rarely longer than ninety minutes. Placentas usually pass within five to fifteen minutes of each puppy birth.

Vaginal discharge signals imminent birth. Involuntary contractions begin until the bitch is fully involved and bearing down to deliver. *If the first puppy isn't born within an hour following these strong contractions, take Mom to a veterinarian.* Normally, a dark green-gray bubble, which is the placental sac containing the puppy, will emerge from the vagina and should be fully passed within thirty minutes. Normal presentation can be either tail or face first. Puppies are expelled from alternating arms of the Y-shaped uterus.

After each baby is born, the bitch cleans herself, may consume the placenta that follows, and bites through the umbilical cord. She licks her baby to clean away fetal membranes so it can breathe. Often, the mother dog may give birth to several puppies and then rest for several hours before resuming labor and delivering the rest of the litter. *Seek a veterinarian's help if labor does not resume within four hours, if Mom acts restless or feverish, ignores her puppies, or there's a white or foul-smelling discharge from the vulva.* An odorless green, dark red, or brown fluid discharge is usually normal.

The distinctive configuration of some dog breeds may interfere with a normal birth, or make it more difficult. Those that are tiny or that have a proportionally large head and a narrow pelvis may require help. The Bulldog, Boston Terrier, Pekingese, Toy Poodle, and Chihuahua are prone to whelping problems and may require a CESAREAN to deliver healthy puppies.

The mother dog remains with her newborns for the first day or so following the birth, leaving only to relieve herself or grab a quick bite to eat. Attention is focused on cleaning and feeding the babies. Mom's first milk, called *colostrum*, provides puppies with important nutrients and protective antibodies (see IMMUNE SYSTEM). Licking their anal region stimulates puppies to eliminate, and the bitch consumes the feces and urine to keep the nest clean.

A healthy puppy actively squirms and cries aggressively if moved away from his mother. Puppies that feel cold to the touch, move sluggishly, or make only weak sounds may be stimulated by massaging them with a dry, warm towel. Very cold puppies may be warmed by dipping them up to their neck in 100-degree water until they squirm. Then dry them off and give them back to Mom.

If Mom fails to remove fetal membranes from the face within a minute or two of birth, do it for her so the puppy can breathe. *Babies that fail to breathe need immediate help* and may need their airways cleared. Wrap the puppy in a dry, warm cloth, cup him in both hands, keeping his head secure, and swing him in a downward motion to help clear fluid from his lungs. When the baby begins breathing, give him back to the mother.

Nursing continues for up to eight weeks, and during this time the bitch also protects and teaches her babies how to be dogs. If Mom isn't able to feed her puppies, supplemental feeding may be necessary. Newborn puppies require feeding four or more times a day with an appropriate bitch's-milk replacer (see MILK, AS FOOD).

Respiration

Respiration is the act of breathing. Dogs on average breathe at a rate of about twelve to thirty respirations each minute when at rest; smaller dogs tend to breathe more quickly than larger breeds. The respiratory system includes the nasal passages of the NOSE, the throat, voice box, windpipe, bronchial tubes, and lungs.

The bronchial tubes repeatedly branch in a series of progressively smaller passageways, like a tree. They terminate in tiny air sacs deep inside the lung; it's here that the blood-oxygen exchange takes place. Muscles of the chest, including the diaphragm, pump air in and out of the lungs.

Breathing is normally rhythmic and even. Changes in the sound or rate of respiration may indicate a wide variety of illnesses and should be addressed by a veterinarian. Excitement, FEAR, PAIN, or fever may prompt heavy breathing in the dog. Typically, the dog suffering breathing problems is reluctant to lie down, and may sit with his front "elbows" held away from his body to make respiration easier.

Upper-respiratory infections such as CANINE DISTEMPER or KENNEL COUGH can cause obstruction of air and result in noisy breathing. Slowed respiration may indicate POISON. Increased respiration, or PANTING, is normal during exertion or hot weather and is a way for the dog to cool off. But prolonged, labored panting can be a sign of heatstroke (see HYPERTHERMIA).

r

RESPIRATORY DISTRESS

SYMPTOMS
Gasping; coughing; excessive panting; slowed or shallow breathing; whistling or strained breathing sounds; pale or blue color to lips, gums, or tongue; standing with front legs braced and head hanging, or sitting with "elbows" outward to aid breathing; loss of consciousness

HOME CARE
Remove blockage from mouth (if present) and/or give artificial respiration; EMERGENCY! SEE VET IMMEDIATELY!

VET CARE
Address the underlying cause; possibly oxygen therapy

PREVENTION
Prevent poisoning, electrical shock, or other traumas that can cause breathing problems; avoid overheating and obesity

When air must be forced through narrowed, constricted airways, the dog makes a whistling, wheezing sound during respiration. This sound is typical of dogs suffering from ASTHMA, but may also indicate LARYNGITIS, COLLAPSED TRACHEA, or even growths in the airways.

Painful breathing due to rib FRACTURE or other painful conditions causes the dog to breathe in shallow, quick breaths to keep from moving too much. A punctured lung or ruptured diaphragm also compromises normal respiration. Fluid in the chest, called *pleural effusion*, also results in shallow breathing.

Coughing may be the dog's attempt to clear a SWALLOWED OBJECT, like a piece of bone, from his throat. It can also be an indication of BRONCHITIS, congestive heart failure (see HEART DISEASE), or HEARTWORM DISEASE.

Restraint

This refers to restriction of the dog's movement so she can be safely and efficiently medicated or transported, while preventing injury to the person handling the dog. A dog suffering PAIN or FEAR may often become frantic or even violent and may injure herself or the person who comes to her aid.

The degree of restraint required depends on the individual circumstances, the competence of the handler, and the personality of the dog. A good rule is to restrict your dog only as much and as long as required to accomplish what needs to be done. Slow, gentle, and confident movements are best. Dogs that have obedience TRAINING are more easily handled and may require less restraint than others.

Avoid sudden movements, which can be frightening to a pet. When possible, gather your equipment and medication ahead of time so that you're prepared and don't feel rushed. The aim is to avoid the dog's TEETH, while keeping her from escaping. A two-person team is most effective; one restrains while the other attends the dog. A couple of restraint techniques are appropriate.

For small dogs, use one hand to firmly grasp the loose skin at the back of her neck (the scruff) while your other hand captures both of the hind legs above the hock. Simply stretch the dog gently on her side. A similar approach is to again lay the dog on her side, capturing the hind legs with one hand as before. But rather than grasping the scruff with your other hand, lay your forearm across the dog's shoulders and press her down to hold her in place; that hand captures the forelegs.

For medium and large dogs, the hugging technique works well. Place the dog in a sitting, standing, or reclining position—whichever is best for your treatment. Then, one arm goes under her neck and chin and snugs her head to your

r

Lay a dog on its side to restrain him *(Photo credit: Amy D. Shojai)*

Restrain a medium or large dog with the hugging technique *(Photo credit: Amy D. Shojai)*

chest, while the other arm goes across her back and around her tummy and hugs her body close. Whoever is restraining the dog should be well known and hopefully liked or at least respected by the dog; talk soothingly to the dog during the restraint, then reward her afterward with praise and petting or a game.

But it may become necessary to restrain and medicate your dog all by yourself. For some dogs, simply grasping the scruff and gently pressing her down with one hand while you medicate with the other may be sufficient. Other times, a MUZZLE may be helpful; it negates the dog's teeth, so you can

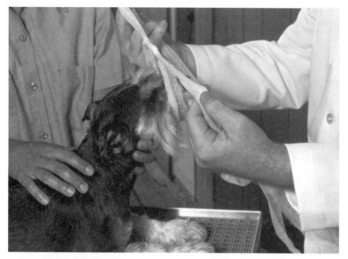

Use gauze or scarf to muzzle, looping around dog's jaw as shown (*Photo credit: Ralston Purina Company*)

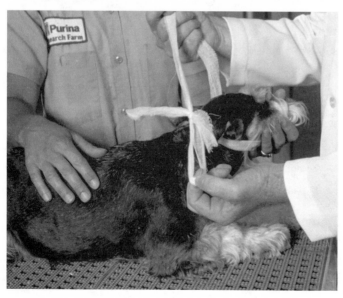

Then tie gauze behind head (*Photo credit: Ralston Purina Company*)

maneuver better with both hands. Placing the dog on a leash and tethering her to a table leg may also give you the necessary advantage.

Another highly effective method is to wrap your dog in a blanket or large towel while leaving the treatment area on her body uncovered. Drop the fabric over the dog (get her head end with all the teeth!), then wrap her up to immobilize her legs so she can't escape. Be sure to give her adequate breathing room, though. Often, the blanket trick helps calm the excited dog long enough for treatment to take place.

Rhinitis

Rhinitis is the inflammation of the nasal passages. It is a common condition of allergic humans who suffer symptoms of hay fever when allergens like pollens or molds are inhaled. However, allergic rhinitis is considered rare in dogs.

When it does occur, the dog may sneeze and snort, and suffer a clear, watery nasal discharge during typical ALLERGY season. Diagnosis is based on these signs and on microscopic examination of the nasal discharge.

Treatment is aimed at identifying and eliminating the problem allergen. However, even when the culprit is identified, it's rarely possible to eliminate such things as pollen from the dog's environment. When signs are severe, the veterinarian may prescribe low doses of corticosteroids to relieve the symptoms during peak allergy season.

r

RHINITIS

SYMPTOMS
Sneezing; snorting; clear, watery nasal discharge

HOME CARE
None

VET CARE
Treat underlying cause, if it can be determined; sometimes low doses of steroid-type drugs

PREVENTION
Avoid allergen when possible

Rickets

Rickets refers to a skeletal deformity characterized by weak, bent leg bones. The condition is caused by a nutritional deficiency or imbalance of calcium, potassium, or vitamin D. (See also NUTRITION.)

Ringworm

Ringworm isn't a worm, it's a fungal parasite (dermatophyte) that feeds on the outer dead surface of growing hair, skin, and toenails. There are many types of dermatophytes, but most cases of canine ringworm are caused by *Microsporum canis*. Ringworm also commonly affects cats and people (see ZOONOSIS).

Ringworm is named for the ringlike lesions typical of human disease. In fact, ringworm is comparable to a contact allergy. Skin inflammation results from a by-product produced by the fungus. The dermatophyte dislikes inflammation and continually moves beyond its point of origination in ever-widening rings, leaving the center to heal.

The sores in dogs grow outward in expanding areas of hair loss. Typically there is scaling and crusting at the margins of bald patches, with broken or stubbled hair in these areas along with variable itchiness. The inner hairless regions appear clear as they start to heal. The face, head, and forelimbs are the first areas affected, but the fungus potentially can spread and affect the dog's whole body.

r

RINGWORM

SYMPTOMS

Hair loss; skin inflammation in patchy areas and/or ever-increasing circles

HOME CARE

After veterinary diagnosis, miconazole preparations or lime sulfur dips; environmental treatment by thoroughly vacuuming and cleaning surfaces daily with bleach and water solutions (CONTAGIOUS TO PEOPLE)

VET CARE

Culture hairs to diagnose; prescribe antifungal medication (griseofulvin)

PREVENTION

Avoid contact with contagious pets; bring dog only to reputable groomers

The condition is transmitted by direct animal-to-animal contact, usually from infected hair or skin debris. However, ringworm is also transmissible from contaminated grooming equipment and can even be picked up from dermatophytes in the environment.

All dogs are at risk for ringworm, but the condition is most common in puppies and dogs less than a year old and in older dogs with compromised immune systems. Some pets are asymptomatic carriers; that is, they carry the fungus without showing signs themselves, while spreading it to other pets or people. If one pet in the house is diagnosed, all should be treated whether showing signs or not. Infected pets should be QUARANTINED from those not showing signs.

Canine ringworm is diagnosed by identification of the fungus. The veterinarian may use a Wood's lamp to screen suspect cases; about half of M. *canis* cases will "glow" when exposed to its ultraviolet light. Other times, a skin scraping collects debris from the lesions, which is then examined microscopically. Many cases are identified using a culture test that grows the ringworm fungus. A sample from the lesion is placed in a special medium designed to grow ringworm. But it may take up to three weeks before the test indicates a positive result.

In most cases, otherwise healthy dogs self-cure in sixty to one hundred days without any treatment at all. However, in severe cases and when the infected pet may expose humans to infection, specific topical or oral antifungal treatment may be recommended. People who are immune compromised, very young, or very old are at highest risk.

Ringworm fungus is difficult to eradicate. Human products like athlete's-foot preparations aren't effective; neither are captan or ketoconazole shampoos. Topical miconazole preparations do work, and lime sulfur dip is extremely effective for treating canine ringworm (but smells like rotten eggs). However, medicating sores with anything prior to a veterinary examination may interfere with an accurate diagnosis. So treat only after your veterinarian diagnoses the condition, and follow his or her recommendation.

The drug griseofulvin (Fulvicin) is also very effective in treating ringworm. Once swallowed, it is incorporated into the growing hair, where it slows the growth of the fungus. Pills are usually given for four to eight weeks and should be continued two weeks beyond the time symptoms have disappeared. Griseofulvin may be given as a preventative in pets that have been exposed but who have not yet developed signs. However, the drug is contraindicated in pregnant dogs, because griseofulvin may cause birth defects.

Contaminated hairs and skin debris shed into the environment remain infective for over a year and act as a reservoir for reinfection. Treating the environment helps reduce the numbers of fungal spores and helps prevent reinfection. But disinfectants used in the past for this purpose—such as chlorhexidine and water—have recently been proven to be ineffective against ringworm spores. Although concentrated bleach and a 1 percent formaldehyde solution are effective, they aren't very practical in a home environment.

Currently, experts recommend environmental control by daily cleaning of all surfaces using a diluted bleach solution (one part bleach to ten parts water), along with thorough vacuuming. Seal the vacuum bag in a plastic garbage sack and remove it from the house.

Rocky Mountain Spotted Fever

Rocky Mountain spotted fever is a rickettsial disease caused by the organism *Rickettsia rickettsii*. Rickettsiae are tiny bacteria-sized parasites that live inside cells, and most spend a portion of their life cycle in an insect vector, which then transmits them to an animal host, or reservoir. People and dogs are not the natural host for most of these agents, but can become ill when infected. Rocky Mountain spotted fever can be transmitted by several different kinds of TICKS, particularly the wood tick and the American dog tick. The illness affects both people and dogs.

The disease is seasonal, with most cases occurring from spring to early fall. It has been reported in nearly every state, but is most prevalent in the central states from Colorado west to the coast. Most infected dogs may not show any

ROCKY MOUNTAIN SPOTTED FEVER
SYMPTOMS
Fever; loss of appetite; lameness; coughing or labored breathing; hunching from abdominal pain; vomiting; diarrhea; swelling of face and legs; thick discharge from eyes and nose; poor balance; rigid neck; altered mental state; nosebleeds; bloody urine or feces; shock
HOME CARE
None
VET CARE
Treat with doxycycline or tetracycline; supportive care, including fluid therapy
PREVENTION
Use tick control, including insecticides and/or mechanical removal of ticks from your dog

signs at all, but others can suffer severe illness and rapid death. For unknown reasons, Siberian Huskies appear to be most severely affected.

The agent is transmitted to the dog from the bite of an infected tick, and the rickettsiae travel from the tissues to the lymphatic system. They proliferate in the cells found in the walls of small blood vessels throughout the body. This prompts an inflammatory response that results in blood-clotting and bleeding disorders and organ damage.

Signs begin with fever of up to 105 degrees, loss of appetite, signs of ARTHRITIS, coughing or labored breathing, abdominal pain, VOMITING and DIARRHEA, and swelling of the face or extremities. A thick mucoid discharge may be seen from the eyes and nose. Neurologic signs are also common and may include altered mental states, poor balance, and a rigid neck. Many of these acute signs are similar to CANINE DISTEMPER.

A week or two following initial signs, the dog develops bleeding disorders similar to EHRLICHIOSIS. Nosebleeds and bleeding beneath the skin or in the urine or feces may result in SHOCK and multiple organ failure. Loss of blood circulation may lead to gangrene and death of affected tissue. Ultimately, kidney failure (see KIDNEY DISEASE) causes death.

Diagnosis is sometimes difficult to make, but Rocky Mountain spotted fever should be suspected when these signs appear in a tick-infested dog during spring to fall. The diagnosis is best confirmed with tests, which are available in veterinary laboratories or schools.

When the disease is suspected, dogs should be treated immediately with doxycycline or tetracycline even before blood tests confirm the diagnosis. Dogs suffering from acute disease will respond with a reversal of symptoms within only a day or two of antibiotic therapy, which should be continued for two to three weeks. Dogs may also require other supportive therapy, such as fluid replacement to combat SHOCK and clotting disorders. Dogs that recover from infection appear to become resistant to reinfection.

To prevent the disease, practice tick control with appropriate insecticides. In most instances, the tick vector must be attached and feeding for twelve to forty-eight hours before a rickettsial agent can be transmitted. Therefore, prompt removal of any ticks found on your dog will virtually eliminate chance of the disease.

However, the crushed tick that contaminates your skin may result in infection. To protect yourself from exposure, wear gloves and/or use tweezers to remove ticks from your pet. Human signs of the disease include flulike symptoms, and a rash on the hands, wrists, ankles, and feet. *See your doctor immediately if you suspect you've been exposed, because the disease causes death in 15 to 20 percent of untreated cases* (see also ZOONOSIS and TICKS).

Dogs enjoy rolling in scent *(Photo credit: Betsy Stowe)*

Rolling

Dogs tend to live through their noses, and certain pungent scents prompt rolling behavior in some dogs. This scent ecstasy is similar to what cats experience when exposed to catnip; however, the canine indulgence is a good bit more noxious and tends toward offal.

When a dog finds what he considers an attractive odor, he rolls to rub his shoulders, back, and neck into the offering. He spreads the scent over himself as though it's doggy cologne. Nobody knows for sure why dogs roll in nasty things like rotting garbage, dead animals, or feces. Experts theorize that perfuming themselves with such scents may allow the dog to carry the smelly message home, so other dogs can "read" all about it.

Roundworms

Roundworms are intestinal parasites, a kind of ascaridoid nematode found in almost all puppies at birth. The species *Toxocara canis* most commonly affects dogs. Roundworms are passed in the stool or are vomited, and they look like masses of spaghetti.

Dogs can become infected in four different ways. Puppies may be infected before they are born when immature worms the BITCH harbors migrate to the uterus. Puppies may also contract roundworms from nursing the mother's milk. The parasite can also be contracted when a dog swallows infective larvae found in the environment, or by eating an infected host like a mouse or bird.

When a puppy swallows infective eggs, the larvae that hatch in the intestines subsequently migrate to the liver and lungs. They are coughed up and swallowed again, and then mature once they return to the intestines. The parasites grow into one- to seven-inch-long adults. Mature females can lay two hundred thousand hard-shell eggs in a single day, which pass with the stool and can live in the environment for months to years. Eggs hatch into infective larvae, completing the cycle.

Older dogs that swallow infective larvae are more resistant to the worms, and their immune system tends to arrest the worms' development. Such larvae simply stop developing and remain wherever they happen to alight—muscles, kidneys, brain, or even the eye. In male dogs, and females that are spayed or never bred, the larvae remain permanently frozen in time. But when a bitch becomes pregnant, the same hormones that promote the unborn puppies' development also stimulate the worms. They begin again to migrate and typically cross into the placenta or the mammary glands to infect the puppies before or shortly after birth.

Roundworms are rarely life-threatening, but massive infestations may cause intestinal damage or, rarely, bowel obstruction or even rupture. More

ROUNDWORMS

SYMPTOMS
Puppies with potbellied appearance, dull coat, diarrhea, or mucus in the stool; "spaghetti worms" in stool or vomit; adult dogs rarely show signs when infected

HOME CARE
None (CONTAGIOUS TO PEOPLE IF STOOL IS INGESTED—USE CAUTION WITH SMALL CHILDREN)

VET CARE
Oral worm medication

PREVENTION
Preventative worm medication in puppies; routine sanitation—pick up feces from yard

commonly, roundworms interfere with absorption of food, resulting in a pot-bellied appearance, a dull coat, DIARRHEA, or mucus in the stool. Seeing the worms coiled in the feces or vomit is diagnostic. Eggs identified by your veterinarian's microscopic examination of a stool sample confirm that worms are present.

Children may be at risk for infection with *Toxocara canis*, primarily from accidentally ingesting infective stages from contaminated environment (most often by eating dirt). The parasite causes a disease in humans called *visceral larva migrans* in which immature worms never reach maturity, but simply migrate throughout the body; symptoms include fever, anemia, liver enlargement, pneumonia, and other problems. Because of this human risk, the Centers for Disease Control (CDC) recommends that all puppies and their mothers undergo deworming treatments, whether diagnosed with the parasite or not (see ZOONOSIS).

Liquid oral medication given at age two, four, six, and eight weeks is the current CDC recommendation. Pyrantel pamoate (Nemex), fenbendazole, and febantel are all extremely effective and are considered safe enough to use in young puppies. Many current HEARTWORM preventatives also protect against HOOKWORMS and roundworms.

These precautions, along with simple sanitation procedures, will protect both canine and human family members from roundworms. Clean up feces from the dog's yard at least once a week, and prevent young children from playing in the dog's "toilet area."

Salivary Mucocele

This is the infection and rupture of a salivary gland. The condition is not common. Dogs have four pairs of salivary glands that produce and feed saliva into the mouth. Saliva is a fluid that lubricates and helps digest food.

Any of the salivary ducts may become blocked from food particles or other foreign matter, like grass seeds, or simply by thick secretions. Most commonly, the gland beneath the jaw in the floor of the mouth is involved. Blockage causes fluid to back up and rupture the duct, which then forms a CYST in the gland (mucocele). The cyst swells with thick, honey-colored material. The swelling is on the side of the neck, or in the dog's mouth usually on one side of the tongue.

SALIVARY MUCOCELE

SYMPTOMS
Swelling on the side of the neck, or in the mouth on one side of the tongue

HOME CARE
None

VET CARE
Drain cyst with syringe; more often, surgical correction

PREVENTION
None

A salivary mucocele may swell to the point that it interferes with eating or breathing. Occasionally, simply draining the cyst with a syringe will cure the problem. Most times, though, surgery is required.

Salmonella

Salmonella is a bacteria that can cause illness in people and dogs. There are nearly two thousand kinds of salmonella bacteria; most are found naturally in the environment and can remain alive for months or years in manure or soil. Some types are normal inhabitants of animals and don't cause problems. Others prompt a variety of illnesses from diarrheal disease to life-threatening illness.

Puppies, young dogs, and those that are stressed by other illness, poor kenneling conditions, or inadequate nutrition are most commonly affected. Dogs contract the bacteria by drinking infected water, by eating raw food or commercial rations contaminated with infected droppings, or by eating manure.

Most infected dogs never show signs of illness, but may harbor the bacteria and spread the disease to other animals and people. When illness develops, signs include bloody, foul-smelling DIARRHEA, fever, VOMITING, loss of appetite, stomach PAIN (a "hunching" posture), and depression. The bacteria may be carried in the bloodstream to the liver, lungs, kidneys, or uterus. Signs of disease typically last four to ten days, but diarrhea may continue for a month or longer.

The condition is diagnosed from signs of illness and from finding the bacteria in the blood or tissues of the affected dog. When ENTERITIS is the

SALMONELLA

SYMPTOMS
Bloody, foul-smelling diarrhea; fever; vomiting; loss of appetite; hunching posture from pain; depression

HOME CARE
None

VET CARE
Fluid therapy; antibiotics

PREVENTION
Don't feed raw or undercooked meats; prevent dog from eating wildlife; keep yard clean by promptly picking up feces

S

primary problem, treatment usually consists of fluid therapy to help correct DEHYDRATION. A culture of the stool sample will identify the strain of salmonella, so that the most effective antibiotic can be given. However, antibiotic therapy is indicated only in instances of severe systemic disease, to avoid the possibility of prompting the development of a drug-resistant strain of the bacteria.

Protect your dog from salmonella by curtailing his hunting; dogs that eat rodents or other wildlife are at much greater risk. Don't feed the dog raw or undercooked meat. Pick up the yard and dispose of fecal material promptly. Protect yourself by religiously washing your hands after dealing with feces or handling an ill dog. Use a dilute chlorine-bleach-and-water solution (one-to-thirty-two ratio) to disinfect your hands, dog bowls, toys, and areas where the dog sleeps.

Salmon Poisoning

This disease is an acute, frequently fatal gastrointestinal disease contracted from eating raw salmon or trout infected with the rickettsial bacteria *Neorickettsia helminthoeca*. This disease is limited to the Pacific Northwest region of the United States.

The prevalence of the disease corresponds to the natural home range of a snail that lives in the streams of Washington, Oregon, and northern California. These snails are host to a FLUKE called *Nanophyetus salmincola*, which later leaves the snail to parasitize salmon and trout. When a dog eats the raw fish infested with flukes carrying *Neorickettsia helminthoeca*, salmon poisoning

S

SALMON POISONING
SYMPTOMS
Loss of appetite; depression; runny eyes and nose; weight loss; severe vomiting; bloody diarrhea; subnormal temperature
HOME CARE
None; VET CARE NEEDED IF DOG IS TO SURVIVE
VET CARE
Supportive therapy, including fluids, blood transfusion, and antibiotics
PREVENTION
Keep dog from eating raw or undercooked fish

is the result. (Humans may also contract the fluke by eating infested raw fish, but aren't affected by salmon poisoning.) The fluke rarely causes problems by itself.

Dogs typically become ill within five days of eating the tainted fish. The agent infects the lymphatic system and spreads throughout the body, causing a persistent high fever. The signs of illness resemble those of CANINE PARVOVIRUS and include loss of appetite, depression, runny eyes and nose, weight loss, severe VOMITING, and bloody DIARRHEA. After several days, the fever drops to subnormal levels. Untreated dogs die within five to seven days of infection.

Diagnosis is based on signs of illness and confirmed by finding either fluke eggs in the stool or the rickettsiae in a blood sample. Treatment is supportive and similar to that for parvovirus; fluid therapy to combat dehydration is extremely important. Blood transfusions may also be required. Antibiotics like tetracycline eliminate the parasite.

Dogs in endemic regions should be prevented from eating any raw fish. Keep dogs under your direct supervision when they are outside, or confine them to a safe area. Feed only cooked fish, or fish that has been frozen for at least twenty-four hours.

Seborrhea

This term is commonly used to describe symptoms of scaling, flaking skin (dandruff) that may be characterized by dry, waxy skin and fur (seborrhea sicca), or greasy, oily skin and fur (seborrhea oleosa). Most commonly, seborrhea is a sign of any number of unrelated disorders of the skin, including MANGE, flea ALLERGY, and HYPOTHYROIDISM. The skin condition is treated appropriate to the underlying cause.

However, a condition called *primary seborrhea* is an inherited skin disorder that interferes with the normal processes of skin cell generation and development. Dogs suffering from the condition will develop, in addition to skin crusting and dandruff, a waxy OTITIS along with a rancid body odor. Weeping sores and hair loss develop in some cases, in part due to itchiness and trauma from scratching. Dogs may suffer secondary bacterial infections of the skin. There is a genetic predisposition to primary seborrhea in the Basset Hound, Chinese Shar-Pei, Cocker and Springer Spaniel, Doberman Pinscher, German Shepherd Dog, and Irish Setter.

Diagnosis is based on symptoms, breed risk, and microscopic examination of a skin sample (biopsy) that shows characteristic changes. Treatment may involve a combination of medications to slow down the symptoms, including antiseborrheic shampoos.

S

SEBORRHEA
SYMPTOMS
Dandruff and either dry, waxy skin or greasy, oily skin; sometimes waxy ear discharge and rancid body odor, with weeping sores and hair loss over the body
HOME CARE
Medicated shampoos as prescribed by vet
VET CARE
Treat underlying cause; antibiotics; sometimes steroid-type drugs to control itching; antiseborrheic shampoos
PREVENTION
Control fleas

Shedding

The seasonal loss of HAIR is a normal function of dog fur. Hair does not grow all the time, but is continuously renewed in a cycle of growth, rest, and loss. New hair pushes out the old resting ones, and this fur loss is called *shedding*.

Light exposure, either to sun or artificial light, determines the amount and timetable of canine shedding. Environmental temperature has a lesser influence. More hair is shed during the greatest exposure to light, which typically coincides with the summer months. In fact, house dogs under constant exposure to artificial light may shed all year long. Outdoor dogs living in the northeastern United States tend to experience seasonal sheds, with the most fur flying in late spring for the several weeks during which daylight increases.

In North America, the growing season for fur begins in the early spring, heralded by shedding when the new incoming growth pushes out the old dead hairs. Fur grows unevenly and is shed in an irregular pattern that leaves double-coated dogs looking decidedly ragged.

The fur continues to grow throughout the summer, then rests during the winter months when the least amount of daylight is present. During this resting phase, fur tends to be most easily pulled out, because the hair root loosens in preparation for the spring shed.

All dogs shed, but some breeds shed more than others. In general, breeds with curly coats, like Poodles and Soft-Coated Wheaten Terriers, have much longer fur-growing seasons, in which hair continuously grows for years at a time; they tend not to lose huge amounts of hair all at once. These "nonshedding" breeds also tend to have curly coats, so that any lost hairs are caught and held in the coat and are not more obviously left on the furniture. Those breeds that have heavy double coats, like German Shepherd Dogs and Chow Chows, are more obvious in their fur loss. The hair reaches a certain length, stops growing, and is shed en masse, with dogs typically leaving clumps of undercoat in their path during seasonal sheds.

Thickly furred and curly-coated dogs may also suffer from painful mats when shed fur is caught and trapped by remaining fur next to the skin. To help prevent skin problems like HOT SPOTS, pay particular attention to GROOMING your dog during shedding season (see also HAIR).

Shock

Shock is a common condition that results from injury or illness. It is defined as a collapse of the circulatory system often secondary to trauma associated with BURNS, crushing injuries, or profound DEHYDRATION. Common causes of shock include hit-by-car injuries, HYPERTHERMIA, severe VOMITING or DIARRHEA, BLEEDING disorders, and HEART DISEASE.

A decrease in blood volume, compromised heart function, or a collapse of the vessels means blood can't adequately be distributed to oxygenate the body; tissues become starved for oxygen. The body attempts to compensate by shutting down normal blood flow to nonvital areas. The compensation mechanism also produces toxic by-products that further compromise circulation. And as the organs become more and more oxygen starved, they start to

SHOCK
SYMPTOMS
Depression; loss of consciousness; below-normal temperature (feels cold to touch); weakness; shivering; pale gums; shallow, rapid breathing; faint, rapid pulse
HOME CARE
Warm dog in blanket; if unconscious, place head lower than body; when not breathing, provide artificial respiration; SEE VET IMMEDIATELY!
VET CARE
Intravenous fluid therapy; other supportive care
PREVENTION
Avoid trauma; treat illness promptly

S

fail. This vicious cycle intensifies the shock, and without treatment, the dog will die.

Signs include mental depression or loss of consciousness; body temperature that feels cold to the touch; weakness; shivering; pale gums; shallow, rapid breathing; and faint, weak PULSE. *Shock is an emergency that must be treated as soon as possible by the veterinarian.*

First aid involves keeping your dog warm and as calm as possible. Wrap her in a blanket, and if she's conscious, allow her to find a comfortable position. If she's unconscious, place her head below her body to improve circulation to the brain. Determine whether she's breathing, and pull her tongue clear to keep the airway open.

When the dog has no heartbeat or is not breathing, begin ARTIFICIAL RESPIRATION or CARDIOPULMONARY RESUSCITATION. When possible, apply pressure to stop copious BLEEDING, immobilize obvious FRACTURES, then get your dog veterinary attention as soon as possible. The ideal treatment is efficiently and quickly rehydrating the dog using intravenous fluids and/or blood transfusions.

Sinusitis

Sinusitis is the inflammation of one or more of the sinus cavities. A sinus is an open area in the skull that communicates with the nasal passage. Human sinusitis typically results from an allergy.

However, the most common cause of acute sinusitis in dogs is a viral infection, such as CANINE DISTEMPER, or fungal infections. Sometimes a foreign body, such as a grass awn, may be sniffed up inside the nose and cause inflammation. Dogs may also develop sinusitis secondary to a tooth abscess or to a tumor.

Signs include a nasal discharge that initially is clear and later becomes thick and cloudy as infection sets in. When the cause is due to systemic disease, both nostrils are affected; foreign bodies or tooth abscesses more typically affect only one side, in which case the dog may paw at that side of his nose. In addition, dogs suffering sinusitis may breathe with the mouth open, or exhibit a "reverse sneeze" in an attempt to clear breathing passages.

Diagnosis is based on physical signs and sometimes X RAYS. Treatment attempts to address the underlying cause. Because a runny nose may be a sign of deadly viral infection, a veterinarian's expertise is particularly important in these instances. Symptoms may be relieved by keeping the dog's nose clean using a damp cloth, and by using a vaporizer to open up swollen sinuses. Try running the shower with hot water, then placing your stopped-up dog in the steamy bathroom to help him breathe.

SINUSITIS

SYMPTOMS
Clear nasal discharge that turns thick and cloudy; mouth-breathing (not panting); reverse sneeze

HOME CARE
Keep dog's nose clean with dampened cloth; use vaporizer or humidifier (or steamy shower) to help dog breathe

VET CARE
Treat underlying cause

PREVENTION
Vaccinate dog against systemic illnesses like distemper

Skin

The skin is the largest organ of the body and serves as a protective barrier between the dog and the outside world. Skin insulates the dog from extremes of temperature, controls moisture loss, and shields the body from foreign agents like toxins or bacteria.

Dogs have three primary layers of skin. The outermost is called the *epidermis* and provides external protection. It contains special pigment-producing cells that color your dog's body and fur, and screens her from the harmful rays of the sun.

The dermis is the middle, thickest layer found immediately beneath the epidermis. The dermis defines the skin's shape and also contains the elastic connective tissue that gives skin flexibility. The nerves are also found here, along with specialized cells of the immune system. HAIR follicles that produce the root of each hair are found in this layer, along with SWEAT GLANDS. Hair grows from the follicles, and each follicle is adjacent to a pressure-sensitive pad that responds to TOUCH.

The subcutis is the final and innermost layer. It's composed of fat cells and connective tissues, which divide the outer surface of the body from the inside open cavities that contain the organs.

Skunk Encounters

Curious dogs allowed outdoors in rural areas may stick their noses where they don't belong, and end up on the receiving end of a skunk. The skunk is simply telling the dog to "back off!" the only way it knows how, and consequently sprays its pungent defense on the nosy canine.

A skunked dog needs a bath—usually several baths, in fact. Perseverance is the key to eliminating the odor; a single dunking rarely does the job. A regular pet-grooming shampoo may do the trick, but there are other, more effective options.

Commercial products available from pet stores, like Skunk Kleen (G. G. Bean Products), are designed to help neutralize skunk odor. A tried-and-true home remedy is a tomato-juice soak; wash the dog first with pet shampoo, towel him dry, then douse him with the juice and let it soak for ten or fifteen minutes. Then rinse him off and suds again with the regular shampoo. Alternate the tomato-juice soak with the shampoo bath until he's less pungent. Another option is to use a rinse of one part ammonia in ten parts water (avoid the eyes); follow the rinse with a soapy bath.

Massengill douche is recommended by some professional groomers as an effective odor-absorbing soak. Mix two ounces of the douche to a gallon of water, pour over the washed dog, and let soak for at least fifteen minutes. Then bathe with normal shampoo once more.

Avoid the problem altogether by preventing skunk encounters. Confine your dog to a fenced yard that's secure against critters, or supervise outdoor ex-

SKUNK ENCOUNTERS	
SYMPTOMS	
Pungent odor	
HOME CARE	
Bathe; alternate pet shampoo with tomato juice, Massengill soak, or one-to-ten ratio of ammonia and water (keep out of eyes), or use commercial product	
VET CARE	
Same; sometimes ointment to soothe eyes	
PREVENTION	
Keep dogs indoors at night; supervise outdoor treks; make pet doors inaccessible to wildlife	

S

cursions. Skunks tend to be nocturnal, so try not to let your dog roam about at night. If you have a pet door, investigate those that allow only your dog access so that varmints don't come into your home. Staywell doors, sized for small dogs, feature a coded collar that "keys" access to the door.

Snakebite

Dogs living in rural areas may encounter snakes in their outdoor exploration. When the dog is too curious—or too hardheaded—to leave a snake alone, she may be bitten.

Most snakes in the United States are not poisonous, and such bites may at most be painful and risk secondary infection. Thick fur helps protect the dog from body injuries, and bites most often occur on the face or neck when the dog tries to catch the snake. A nonpoisonous snakebite will leave tiny horseshoe-shaped teeth marks. Clean the wound with soapy, warm water and see a veterinarian if you notice any swelling. An antibiotic is usually sufficient.

There are four poisonous snakes endemic to the United States: copperheads, cottonmouths (water moccasins), and rattlesnakes—all of which are pit vipers—and the tiny coral snake. Pit vipers have slit-eyed pupils like a cat (compared to round pupils in nonpoisonous snakes), pits beneath their eyes, big arrow-shaped heads, rough scales, and a pair of fangs in the upper jaw. The coral snake is recognized by its small black-nosed head and vivid-banded body,

SNAKEBITE
SYMPTOMS
Usually profound pain and swelling at bite site; sometimes agitation; excessive panting and drooling; weakness; vomiting; diarrhea; collapse; seizures; shock; sometimes paralysis and coma
HOME CARE
EMERGENCY! SEE VET IMMEDIATELY! If help is more than half an hour away, apply a tight bandage between dog's heart and wound (not around the neck) and loosen for five minutes once an hour; keep dog quiet
VET CARE
Supportive care; sometimes antitoxin; medications to counter symptoms
PREVENTION
Discourage dog's interest in snakes; supervise outdoor exploration in snake habitat

S

colored red, yellow, white, and black (red and yellow bands are always next to each other).

If you suspect your dog has been bitten by a poisonous snake, kill the snake if possible and bring it to your veterinarian for positive identification. At the very least, take note of what it looks like—but be aware that the snake is also venomous to you, and even a scratch or an accidental puncture from a dead snake can kill or harm you. *Get veterinary help immediately; this is an emergency.* Bites are diagnosed by identification of the snake, characteristics of the wound, and behavior of the dog.

A poisonous snakebite results in fang marks and usually rapid and severe swelling of the wound, which is extremely painful. There may be redness or bleeding. The dog's behavior varies depending on the size of the dog and snake, species of snake, and location of the wound. First signs of poisoning usually include agitation, excessive PANTING, DROOLING, and weakness. VOM-ITING, DIARRHEA, collapse, seizures, SHOCK, and sometimes paralysis (with coral snake bites), leading to coma and potentially death, may follow.

If help is more than a half hour away, apply a tight bandage between the dog's heart and leg wounds (but *not* on the neck), and loosen for five minutes once every hour. *Don't wash the wound, cut it to suction out poison, or apply ice,* as these procedures may actually increase venom absorption and/or cause further damage to the tissue.

Soiling

Soiling is a break in HOUSE-TRAINING in which the dog eliminates inappropriately in the house. In some instances, the accidents are simply due to inadequate housebreaking, which a refresher in training should cure.

However, dogs that suddenly begin leaving puddles or piles about the house may have an underlying health problem. Inappropriate urination may signal problems like CYSTITIS, DIABETES MELLITUS, KIDNEY DISEASE, or urinary-tract problems, like BLADDER STONES or obstruction. Loss of bowel control is associated with DIARRHEA, which can be a sign of dangerous viral infection, like CANINE PARVOVIRUS or DISTEMPER, or simply result from raiding the garbage. Elderly dogs may lose control due to age-related problems (see GERI-ATRIC DOG). Check with your veterinarian to rule out a medical cause.

Soiling is often confused with territorial MARKING, which is a DOMINANCE display usually of intact male dogs. STRESS may prompt increased marking behavior. Changes such as the addition of a pet, moving to a new home, or a change in the owner's work schedule may exacerbate the problem. Stress-related marking is a way for the dog to try to bring his world back under control.

Accidents in the house, if not adequately cleaned, can inspire a return to the scene of the crime and repeat offense. Clean soiled areas with a commercial product designed for that purpose. Avoid ammonia-containing cleaners, which tend to intensify the smell of urine.

Dogs dislike eliminating in the same area where they eat, so moving a bowl of food to a canine target area may help dissuade him. Some dogs prefer privacy and refuse to do their duty when under scrutiny, instead hiding their deposits beneath the piano when you're not looking. A pet door that allows the dog access to a fenced backyard may be the answer for some dogs, particularly if he's having trouble containing himself for scheduled bathroom breaks.

It may be necessary to confine the dog when you can't watch his every move. Review the section on house-training, and remember that patience is key. Some hardcase dogs will need days to weeks of convincing before they'll become reliable.

Spaying

Spaying is the surgical sterilization (ovariohysterectomy) of a female dog in which her uterus and ovaries are removed. This prevents the birth of unwanted puppies and eliminates or reduces the chances of health problems like PYOMETRA and mammary CANCER. It also curtails obnoxious heat-related behaviors. When she's in season, your dog's bloody vaginal discharge may stain your carpet and furniture. Spaying also curbs the attentions of doggy Romeos who tend to stake out your front yard.

To gain the greatest benefits, dogs should be spayed before reaching sexual maturity. Individual dogs and breeds mature at different rates, but most are able to become pregnant by six months of age. The American Veterinary Medical Association (AVMA) currently recommends that pet dogs be spayed at four months of age.

It's better to perform the surgery when your dog is not in heat; during estrus, the uterus becomes engorged with blood, and this slightly increases the risk of BLEEDING. And if accidentally bred, she can still be spayed within about two weeks of pregnancy without increased risk. However, most veterinarians prefer waiting until the mother dog has stopped nursing before spaying, because the milk may interfere with healing of the incision line. Consult with your veterinarian to determine the best schedule for your dog.

The ovariohysterectomy is performed while the dog is under general

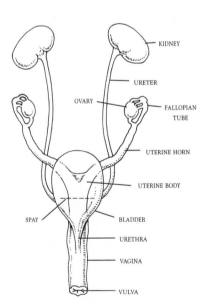

KIDNEY

URETER

OVARY

FALLOPIAN TUBE

UTERINE HORN

UTERINE BODY

SPAY

BLADDER

URETHRA

VAGINA

VULVA

Female Urogenital Tract

ANESTHESIA. In most cases, veterinarians recommend you withhold food and water from your dog for a period prior to surgery so the dog's stomach is empty; this reduces the risk of inhaling vomit while she's asleep. Should your dog sneak an unauthorized snack prior to surgery, be sure to inform the veterinarian so that appropriate precautions can be taken.

A variety of anesthetics may be used, alone or in combination. Many times, preanesthetic blood analysis is performed to help determine the best anesthetic for a particular dog. The spay procedure is major abdominal surgery and takes a bit longer than castrating a male dog. Often, an injectable sedative is first given, followed by inhalant anesthesia usually administered by an endotracheal tube inserted into the mouth, down the throat, and into the lungs. Some practices may use a mask that fits over the dog's face to administer the anesthesia. Inhaled anesthesia is preferred, because the dosage can be adjusted during surgery, and the dog awakens quickly after the anesthesia is stopped.

The sleeping dog is placed on a towel or heating pad to keep her warm during the procedure, then positioned on her back. Her tummy is shaved and disinfected with antiseptic soap solutions to keep the surgical field sterile. For some dogs, respiratory and cardiac monitors or even EKG machines may be used.

A small slit in a sterile paper or cloth drape is positioned over the prepared abdomen. Surgery is performed through this shielding drape, which helps keep fur out of the way and the incision sterile.

The surgeon makes an incision in the skin of the dog's tummy, usually just

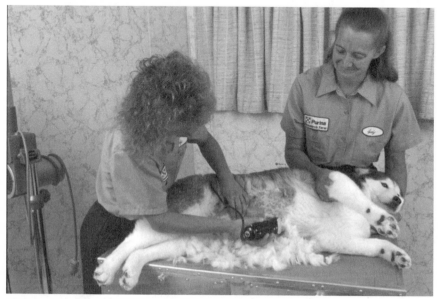

Shaving a dog's tummy to spay *(Photo credit: Ralston Purina Company)*

below the belly button and along the midline. Depending on the size of the dog, the incision is an inch to two inches long. The veterinarian uses a razor-sharp scalpel to incise first the skin, then a thin layer of fat, and finally the abdominal wall. Special instruments hold the incision open so the surgeon can see into the abdomen.

The canine uterus is shaped like a Y with an ovary attached to the top of each "horn." An ovarian artery, vein, and nerve are attached to each ovary. The spay hook, a long, smooth metal instrument with a crook on the end, is inserted into the abdomen to retrieve the uterus. The ovarian ligament that attaches ovaries to the wall of the abdomen is detached, to allow the ovaries and uterine horns to be brought further out. Each ovary is ligated, or tied off, with absorbable suture or secured with stainless-steel Hemoclips to prevent bleeding. Each is then cut free. The stumps containing the artery, vein, and nerve recede into the abdomen. Finally, the uterus is ligated just beyond the cervix, then cut free. The uterus and ovaries are discarded. Once the surgeon ensures there is no bleeding, the uterine stump is allowed to fall back into the abdomen.

The dog's abdomen is stitched closed in three layers, using absorbable suture material or even metal sutures or staples for the internal layers. The surface skin is the last layer stitched closed, using a curved needle and placing individual loops that are separately knotted. Other times, a continuous pattern with absorbable suture material may be used. A routine spay is completed in about twenty-five to forty-five minutes, depending on the size of the dog and other factors.

The type of anesthesia influences how quickly the dog will awaken. Usually, the dog is moved from the surgery table to a recovery area, and she is kept warm and monitored as she recovers. Typically, the drugs cause drunken behavior until they fully leave the body; your dog may not be steady on her feet for several hours. Sometimes the dog is kept overnight, while other times she's sent home the same afternoon. Occasionally, the veterinarian will prescribe medication for pain; however, most times slight discomfort is necessary to keep the dog from overdoing until healing can take place.

Dogs generally don't interfere with their stitches, but always keep an eye on the incision to be sure your dog isn't a problem licker. Fitting the dog with an ELIZABETHAN COLLAR prevents any damage.

Limit your dog's activities for the first two or three days following the procedure. Stitches are removed in a week to ten days after the surgery, and outdoor dogs should be confined indoors and not allowed to sleep in the dirt or grass until after the stitches are out.

Complications resulting from a spay procedure are rare. Occasionally, dogs develop nominal puffiness or redness at the incision site. See your veterinarian if there's bleeding or severe swelling, or if your dog acts depressed or refuses to eat for more than twenty-four hours.

Stray

A stray is an owned dog separated from his home who must fend for himself. Stray dogs that have experienced kindness from former owners may seek out people. But those that have been mistreated or are suffering from illness, injury, or emotional trauma often exhibit extreme shyness.

Dogs may stray when allowed to roam unattended. In particular, hunting breeds, like Beagles, may become carried away by the chase and inadvertently become lost. Other times, a dog may leap from a car or escape a confined yard and wander away. A few dogs may be able to find their way home (see NAVIGATION).

Unfortunately, some strays are purposefully created by owner abandonment. Perhaps the dog has outgrown the cute "puppy stage," or the owner must move and is unable to take the dog along. Some people mistakenly believe that such dogs have a better chance on their own than if they're relinquished to a shelter. However, the vast majority of dogs have lived a sheltered life and aren't able to survive for long on the streets. Strays are at high risk for disease and injury from other animals and lethal encounters with traffic.

Although a large percentage of cats are adopted off the street as strays, dogs for the most part tend to be "chosen" from local animal welfare agencies, friends, or reputable breeders. A stray dog can become an excellent pet; the reality is, however, that few do.

Should you undertake the rewarding goal of rehabilitating a stray dog, be aware that he may exhibit AGGRESSION, aloofness, or even FEARFUL behavior. If you already have pets, the resident animals' health and feelings must be addressed by providing safe QUARANTINE and proper INTRODUCTIONS. Strays that are ill or injured will need special veterinary attention.

Finding a stray should first prompt you to try to find his owner. Friendly strays are the easiest to help, but remember that you don't really know the dog, so be cautious. Look for a collar, tags, or other IDENTIFICATION. Decide

S

FINDING YOUR LOST DOG OR THE STRAY'S OWNER

1. Monitor local lost-and-found advertisements for not less than a month
2. Contact area shelters and give them a description of the dog
3. Take area shelters a photo of the dog
4. Distribute posters around the neighborhood (with or without photo)
5. Check veterinary offices, pet stores, the post office, and community bulletin boards for lost-and-found notices; leave a notice on each location

what you'll do with this furry waif: relinquish him to a shelter, temporarily hold him until you find his old owner or a new one, or adopt him yourself.

Shelters may be public or private, but all are essentially warehouses for unwanted pets. They do their best with limited funds to help animals in their care. When the stray is wearing identification, it is held until every effort to find the owner is exhausted. Pets without identification are kept only a short time, and if not adopted, they are put to sleep—a sad end, but better than a slow death on the street.

Your other choices mean you assume responsibility for the stray's life. If this is the case, the dog should first be evaluated by a veterinarian.

A friendly, healthy stray indicates only recent separation from owners. Advertise your find in the local paper and at the shelter, which are the first places an owner should look for a lost dog. If after a diligent search his owner can't be found, seek an adoptive home by advertising his availability in the same places. Promote his handsome looks and affectionate nature, and mention if he's a healthy, neutered animal. Ask friends for names of people who may want a dog.

Don't give him to just anyone; interview prospective owners with pointed questions. You don't want him to be abandoned again, so seek a responsible, loving—and permanent—home for your adoptee. Chances are good you will fall in love with the stray before a new owner can be found, and will decide to keep him yourself.

Stress

Stress is an emotional state that physically and/or mentally impacts the health of the dog. Dogs most commonly suffer stress as a result of change to the dynamics of their social group, especially as it relates to the owner.

Introduction of a new family member, like a pet, baby, or spouse, or conversely, the loss of a close family member, often results in stress. Change in work habits that alter the amount or quality of the time spent with the dog is also a common stress inducer. Dogs in overcrowded conditions, such as kennels, or with compromised health are subject to stress-related behaviors. Even a STRAY cat in the neighborhood or moving to a new home may cause stress to some dogs.

The most common signs of stress in dogs are increased behavior problems, such as leg-lifting in the house (see MARKING) or inappropriate elimination. Dogs may demand more attention, whine and stay underfoot, or destroy a loved one's property (like shoes or a purse) to feel closer to that person. Separation anxiety may lead the dog to refuse food when the owner is gone any length of time. Stress and insecurity may also result in AGGRESSIVE behaviors toward other pets or the owner, while SUBMISSIVE dogs may hide.

Stress-related behavior problems are best resolved by identifying and eliminating the cause, when possible. PLAY therapy is also a great stress-reliever; it offers aggressive dogs an outlet and helps build the shy dog's self-confidence. Interactive games are best, such as fetch and tug-of-war games (tug games for shy dogs only!).

A small percentage of dogs suffering psychological stress react by excessively licking themselves, which can result in hair loss. Excessive licking, biting, and pulling at the fur can become a habit and even lead to self-mutilation if the stressful conditions are not addressed. Dogs may worry an isolated area and cause an ongoing sore, usually on one leg, the flank, or feet (see LICK SORES).

Removing the cause of the stress is helpful, but often these behaviors develop into habits that are hard to break. Veterinary diagnosis followed by anti-anxiety drug therapy and/or a behaviorist's intervention is probably necessary to break the cycle (see Appendix C, "Veterinary Resources").

Stud

The term *stud* refers to an intact male dog used in arranged breedings to sire, or father, exceptional puppies. A stud dog is generally considered by professional breeders to be of outstanding conformation and quality for his particular breed. Stud dogs are used in the hope that puppies they father will inherit these fine qualities.

Submission

S

Submission is ritualized behavior that communicates deference to another individual. Low-ranking dogs within a social group are submissive and give way to the more forceful personalities within the family (see DOMINANCE).

The canine social system is based on a stair-step ranking of individuals, with the most dominant at the top and lesser-ranking individuals below. Submissive dogs yield to those in power, be that another dog or pet, or the owner. However, submission is not necessarily expressed as FEAR, but is more a matter of compliance to those that are perceived to be in authority.

Submissive behavior is expressed in a variety of ways (see COMMUNICATION). Submissive dogs avert their eyes from a dominant dog or owner. They may whine, whimper, or yelp, or offer a distinctive doggy grin as a way to appease a more dominant individual. Such vocalizations, as well as licking of the owner's hands or face, or raising a paw, may be directed at a dominant individual to solicit attention or food, or to go in or out. Wide, loose wags of the tail that include the whole body are characteristic of a submissive dog.

A submissive dog both figuratively and literally assumes a low position. He crouches humbly before his superiors and wags his tail in a low position—even tucked tightly between the legs—and looks almost apologetic. The ultimate sign of submission is rolling onto the back to expose the throat and belly. The submissive dog will urinate in a crouched position, or while on his back to show his deference.

A submissive dog isn't necessarily tiny, either. Big dogs, like Golden Retrievers or Great Danes, may be dominated by an assertive Chihuahua or child. But it's important that within the household the human owner be the most dominant member of the family.

In its best sense, the submissive dog is one that is biddable—that is, willingly follows the directives of the owner and yearns to please. These are the dogs that are most easily trained and are the best choice for most pet owners. (See also INTRODUCTIONS and TRAINING.)

Sunburn

Sunburn is an inflammation of the skin caused by exposure to the sun's radiation. Certain breeds are more prone to a condition previously called *solar nasal dermatitis* (see LUPUS ERYTHEMATOSUS COMPLEX).

SUNBURN
SYMPTOMS
Redness, crusting, or curling of ear tips or nose; hair loss; itchiness
HOME CARE
Apply cool, damp cloth; mist burns with water; apply moisturizing cream, like nonmedicated Vaseline, aloe vera, or jojoba several times a day
VET CARE
Topical steroid preparations; sometimes amputation of damaged skin
PREVENTION
Keep dogs inside during prime sunburn hours, especially white or sparsely furred dogs; apply SPF 15 or higher-rated sunscreen to ears and nose of at-risk dogs

Too much sun can burn your pet *(Photo credit: Amy D. Shojai)*

Sunburn most commonly affects short-haired, white or light-colored dogs, especially on the sparsely furred bridge of the nose and tips of the ears. White Bull Terriers and Dalmatians seem particularly prone, and dogs that enjoy lying on their backs, like Basset Hounds, risk sunburning their tummies. But any dog that is clipped close for summer weather loses furry protection and can suffer a painful burn. Pets living in particularly sunny regions or in the mountains at higher elevations tend to burn more quickly.

The first signs are redness that leads to hair loss in the affected areas, followed by crustiness and itching. In some cases, the ear margins may curl and turn brittle. The problem tends to go away during cool weather and returns in sunny summer months. Sunburn is painful for your dog and can lead to disfiguring loss of tissue requiring veterinary amputation, or even to sun-induced CANCER.

Prevent sunburn by restricting your dog's outside activities during the most dangerous hours of the day—from ten A.M. to four P.M. When she must endure the sun, apply topical sunscreens containing PABA and a high sun-protection factor (SPF) of 15 or higher. Your veterinarian may provide steroid creams or pills to control the inflammation of existing burns. Aloe vera or jojoba moisturizing creams are helpful to rehydrate the area, and a cool, damp cloth applied two or three times a day will help soothe the burn.

Swallowed Objects

Dogs are incredibly mouth-oriented creatures, designed to use their jaws and teeth the way people use hands. Dogs explore their world in the same way small children and infants do, by putting everything in their mouths. They stick their pointy or pushed-in noses into everything, and bite, chew, and taste to learn about it. Just about anything that doesn't move faster than the dog is fair game—so consequently, they often swallow inedible objects.

Whole toys or parts of toys, jewelry, coins, pins, erasers, and paper clips are often swallowed. String, thread (with or without the needle), fishing hooks and lines, Christmas tree tinsel, and yarn are extremely dangerous. And for dogs able to crunch up the object, pieces of wood or bone prove hazardous. Dogs may even eat rocks.

Objects small enough may pass through the digestive system and be eliminated with the feces and cause no problems. But any object, even a tiny one, potentially may lodge in and block the intestinal tract.

Specific signs depend on where the blockage is located. An object caught in the stomach or intestines causes VOMITING, which may come and go for days or weeks if the blockage is not complete and food can pass around it. *Complete blockage is a medical emergency that results in a bloated, painful stomach with sudden, constant vomiting.* The dog refuses food and immediately throws up anything she drinks.

Dogs may paw at their mouth when objects catch between teeth or stick to

---

SWALLOWED OBJECTS

S

SYMPTOMS
Pawing at mouth; choking or gagging; vomiting; diarrhea; swollen stomach; painful abdomen (hunched posture); constipation

HOME CARE
If possible, remove small objects caught in mouth; DON'T PULL STRING ITEMS, which risks killing the dog; see vet for evaluation if object is not removable or if blockage continues

VET CARE
Diagnostic X rays; often surgery to remove object

PREVENTION
Supervise play with toys; keep swallowable objects out of reach; DON'T GIVE DOG SWALLOWABLE BONES!

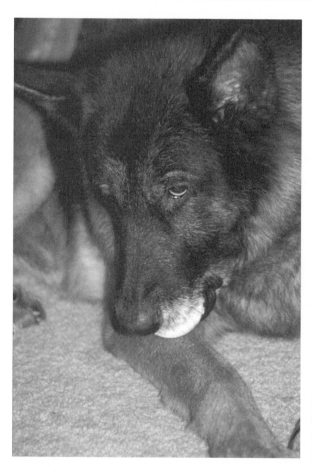

**Supervise a dog when
he plays with any toys**
(*Photo credit: Amy D.
Shojai*)

the palate. If something catches in the throat, the dog typically gags, coughs, or even retches in an attempt to move it. Use extreme caution when investigating such cases. A dog upset by the experience may object to your attempts to open her mouth, and you could be bitten. (This sign may also indicate RABIES.)

You could injure your dog by trying to remove the object. String-type articles may be caught between the teeth in the mouth, with the rest swallowed. *Never pull on this visible end, because string and thread are often attached to a needle or fishhook that's embedded in tissue further down the digestive tract.* Pulling the string at your end could further injure the intestines and kill the dog.

Intestines propel food using muscle contractions called *peristalsis* that move through the entire length of the intestine to help push the contents through. But when a foreign object like string is caught at one end, the intestine literally "gathers" itself like fabric on a thread, resulting in a kind of accordion formation. The result is sudden severe vomiting and DIARRHEA, and

S

rapid DEHYDRATION. Your veterinarian should evaluate any blockage situation to determine the best course of treatment. Surgery is often necessary to remove the obstruction.

If blockage is not promptly addressed, the resulting damage may become irreparable. Sharp objects may slice or puncture the bowel, and obstruction may interfere with blood flow to the organs and cause bowel tissue to die. PERITONITIS is the end result in either case and usually kills the victim.

Often, the owner witnesses the dog chewing or swallowing the object. Other times, diagnosis can be based on symptoms. However, X RAYS usually are necessary to determine the exact location and size of the blockage and sometimes to identify the object itself. When the obstruction is caused by a non-metal object, which isn't visible on X rays, barium is used to better define the situation. Barium is given either orally or as an enema to help provide a positive contrast that outlines the foreign object during X rays.

Once located, the object is surgically removed, and when possible, any internal damage is repaired. If surgery can correct the problem before peritonitis sets in, most dogs fully recover. Should tissue die, the damaged sections of the intestine may be removed and the living portions of bowel reattached; these dogs typically have a good prognosis.

The best course is preventing your dog from swallowing dangerous items. Choose dog-safe toys that can't be chewed into tiny pieces, and supervise object play. Anything a child would put in his mouth is fair game for dogs, especially puppies. Real bones should be forbidden, and rawhide chews offered only with supervision. Better choices are Nylabone or Gumabone toys that are too large to swallow and can't be chewed apart. Puppy-proof your home by thinking like your dog, so that you won't be caught off guard when your dog eats the rubber bumpers off the door stops.

Sweat Glands

Sweat glands are saclike structures in the skin that open to the air and secrete fluid. Dogs have two kinds of sweat glands, the *apocrine glands* and the *eccrine glands*.

Apocrine glands are found throughout the body and empty secretions into the adjacent hair follicles. The scented fluid they produce is thought to play a role in reproduction as a sexual attractant. Eccrine glands are limited to the dog's footpads and nasal pad. They are like human sweat glands that open to the surface and secrete watery fluid as a means of cooling the body.

But sweat glands in dogs are not particularly effective and do little to regulate the pet's TEMPERATURE. Instead, a dog pants to cool off, lolling her wet tongue out of her mouth and breathing across it to produce an evaporative cooling effect. Dog SKIN also helps regulate body temperature when blood vessels in the skin dilate to dissipate heat, and constrict to retain warmth. The exception to this rule is the hairless variety of the Chinese Crested breed, which, in addition to PANTING, also sweats.

S

Tapeworms

Tapeworms (cestodes) are a ribbonlike flat worm that parasitizes the intestines of pets. There are several varieties, but *Dipylidium caninum* is seen most often in cats and dogs.

Immature worms must spend developmental time inside an intermediary host before being able to infest a dog. The FLEA serves this purpose. Dogs that are infested with fleas are highly likely to also have tapeworms. That's why incidence of tapeworms closely parallels the summer months of flea season.

Tapeworm eggs are eaten by the flea larvae, which then develop as the flea itself matures. When a dog nibbles to relieve the flea's itch, he often swallows the flea and infects himself with tapeworms.

The head of the tapeworm, called the *scolex* or *holdfast*, is equipped with hooks and suckers that are used to anchor itself to the wall of the small intestine. There is no mouth as such; in fact, tapeworms don't even have a digestive system. Instead, nutrients are absorbed through their segmented body. Called *proglottids*, these segments are linked together like a chain. The parasite continuously grows new segments that are added from the neck down. Adult worms continue to add segments as long as they live, until tapeworms sometimes attain lengths of two feet or more composed of hundreds of segments.

Each proglottid contains both male and female reproductive organs. When mature, the segment produces up to two hundred eggs. Segments furthest from the scolex are most mature, and once "ripe," they are shed from the worm's body and passed in the dog's feces.

Once outside the body, each segment can move independently like tiny inchworms, but when dry they look like grains of rice. Infested dogs typically have segments stuck to the hair surrounding the anal area, or in their bedding.

TAPEWORMS
SYMPTOMS
Ricelike debris or moving segments stuck to dog's anal area or in feces
HOME CARE
None
VET CARE
Antitapeworm medication, either injection or pill
PREVENTION
Flea control; prevent dogs from eating wild game

Eventually, the segments dry and rupture, releasing the eggs they contain into the dog's environment. The life cycle is complete in two to four weeks.

Tapeworm eggs are passed and shed so sporadically that examining the dog's stool for telltale evidence is usually inconclusive. It's considered diagnostic to find the segments on the pet.

Tapeworms are rarely a medical problem; usually they are considered an unpleasant annoyance. The moving proglottids may cause irritation to the anal region, which may prompt dogs to excessively lick themselves or "scoot" their rear against the floor or ground. Without treatment, however, massive tapeworm infestations potentially interfere with digestion and/or elimination. Puppies may suffer intestinal blockage should too many worms become suspended along the length of the intestinal tract. Also, the hooks of the holdfast can damage the intestinal wall. DIARRHEA with mucus and occasionally blood may be signs of tapeworm infestation. Long-term infestation can result in an unkempt, dry-looking coat, a generally unhealthy appearance, and reduced energy.

Flea tapeworms are the most common kind of cestodes affecting dogs. However, other species may be contracted if the dog eats wild animals like mice or rabbits. There's a human health risk associated with two species of tapeworms, which dogs may expose people to if they eat the host animal. *Echinococcus granulosis* has a sheep host and is found in Utah, California, Arizona, and New Mexico; *Echinococcus multilocularis* affects foxes and rodents indigenous to Alaska, the Dakotas, and surrounding north-central states. Both of these species cause deadly cyst growths in the liver and lungs of infected people. The Centers for Disease Control recommends pets living in these areas, particularly those with access to host animals, be treated every month for tapeworms as a precaution.

There are several safe and highly effective treatments for tapeworms, which may be administered either as a pill or an injection. Unless the dog is constantly exposed to reinfestation by fleas, a one-dose treatment will eliminate the tapeworms. Controlling fleas is the best way to prevent tapeworm infestation.

Teeth

The bony growths on the jaw found inside the mouth are called *teeth*. They are used to capture, kill, and prepare food for eating, and as tools for defense.

Almost without exception, puppies are born without teeth. Deciduous teeth, or "milk teeth," begin to appear at about three weeks of age. By six to eight weeks of age, the puppy will have a full set of twenty-eight baby teeth. A puppy's age can be estimated by which teeth have erupted.

The incisors are the first to appear, at about two to three weeks of age. Puppies have six incisors on both the top and bottom jaw at the front of the mouth. Four needlelike canines appear at age four weeks; they frame the incisors, one on each side, top and bottom. Premolars and molars begin to grow behind the canines at three to six weeks of age; there are three on the top and three on the bottom on each side. The last molars appear by six to eight weeks of age.

At about the same time, permanent teeth begin pushing out the milk teeth. The roots of the baby teeth are absorbed by the body, and in most cases, milk teeth simply fall out. Permanent teeth replace the milk teeth tooth for tooth, but in addition add four premolars and ten molars. Forty-two permanent teeth are in place by about seven months of age.

Dogs use their incisors to rip and scrape meat from bone and, secondarily, as a grooming tool to nibble matter from their fur. Stabbing canine teeth are used to capture and hold objects and prey. The premolars and molars in the rear of the jaw are sharp, triangular teeth and include the carnassial teeth that are characteristic of meat eaters. They work like scissors to shear flesh and crush bone. The flattened molars are designed to crush vegetable foods and bone.

When deciduous teeth don't fall out on time, the dog may appear to have a double set of teeth. Retained baby teeth should be extracted so that permanent teeth will have room to grow. Sometimes, a crowded mouth pushes teeth out of alignment, resulting in difficulty eating or poor dental hygiene (see also PERIODONTAL DISEASE).

When the mouth is closed, the lower canine teeth are normally situated in front of the upper canines, the upper incisors overlap the lower, the upper premolar points fit into the spaces between lower premolars, and the upper carnassials overlap the lower. *Malocclusion* refers to the abnormal "bite" or fitting of these teeth. Malocclusion can be normal for certain dog breeds due to

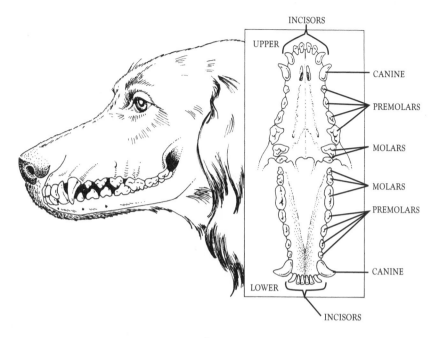

Teeth

differences in the shape of the jaw and mouth. For instance, the flat-faced (brachycephalic) dog breeds, like Bulldogs, have a normal malocclusion because their lower jaw is longer than the upper.

Temperature

Temperature refers to the body's warmth as measured by a thermometer. The adult dog's normal body temperature ranges from 100.5 to 102.5 degrees, while a newborn puppy's temperature is considerably lower at 92 to 97 degrees (see PUPPY). A body temperature outside the normal range is an indication of illness.

Temperatures higher than normal are referred to as a *fever* and can be a sign of infection related to a wide variety of illnesses or a sign of heatstroke (see HYPERTHERMIA). A drop in body temperature may indicate SHOCK as a result of trauma, or loss of body heat from extreme cold (see HYPOTHERMIA). Treatment addresses the cause.

Use a rectal thermometer, either digital or bulb, to take your dog's temperature. Most dogs don't mind the procedure, but if yours protests, be gentle and firm to get the job done (see RESTRAINT). First shake down the thermometer

t

until it reads about 96 degrees. Use baby oil, mineral oil, or petroleum jelly to lubricate the tip. Your dog will need to remain still for at least one minute, so allow her to choose a comfortable standing or reclining position.

Use one hand to firmly grasp and lift her tail to expose the anus. Your other hand gently inserts the greased end of the thermometer about one inch into the dog's rectum (Note: do not release the thermometer while taking the temperature). Speak calmly to your dog, so the thermometer will remain in place for the specified time, then remove and wipe clean, and read the temperature. After each use, clean and disinfect the thermometer with alcohol or a comparable disinfectant.

Tetanus

Tetanus is caused by a bacterial neurotoxin called *Clostridium tetani*. Almost all mammals are susceptible to tetanus, which is also referred to as *lockjaw*. Dogs can be affected, but generally are resistant to the infection.

The bacterium is a common inhabitant of the soil. Also, many animals naturally harbor the bacteria in their intestines without its causing illness. In most cases, the infectious agent is introduced into tissue through a deep puncture wound.

Signs may take only two days to develop following injury or may take several weeks; generally, illness appears within two weeks. The bacterium grows best in low-oxygen locations, such as a sealed-over flesh wound. As

t

TETANUS

SYMPTOMS
Muscle spasms, especially in face and jaw; rigid extension of rear legs; difficulty breathing

HOME CARE
None; EMERGENCY! SEE VET IMMEDIATELY if you suspect your dog has tetanus

VET CARE
Tetanus antitoxin injection; antibiotics; fluid therapy; sedatives

PREVENTION
Remain vigilant to wounds and treat promptly; sometimes vaccination as recommended by vet

THREADWORMS   413

the agent grows, it manufactures a toxin that affects the central nervous system.

The toxicity causes severe muscle spasms, particularly of the face and jaw, and rigid extension of the rear legs. These spasms may be triggered by nearly anything—a loud noise, bright light. The dog typically will stiffly extend his tail, wrinkle his forehead (which pushes the ears erect), and pull his lips back in a grin. The poison also interferes with blood circulation and respiration; about 80 percent of untreated dogs will die, usually of suffocation.

Diagnosis is based on signs and the history of a wound. It is imperative that the wound be thoroughly cleaned of infected tissue to help eliminate the bacterium. Treatment includes tetanus antitoxin, antibiotics, fluid therapy to fight DEHYDRATION, and sedatives to control spasms. The sooner signs appear following the injury, the more guarded the prognosis.

Once treatment is begun, dogs may not show improvement for several days, and it may take six weeks or longer to fully recover. Because most dogs are resistant to tetanus, preventative VACCINATION is rarely recommended, and the disease can be prevented by reducing opportunities for wounds. Dogs that are exposed to livestock, such as herding dogs, may benefit from preventative vaccines.

Threadworms

Threadworms (*Strongyloides stercoralis*) are tiny, round intestinal parasites that aren't particularly common. The infective larvae penetrate the dog's skin either from contact with infected soil through the footpads, or through the mouth or esophageal structures when the larvae are swallowed.

From point of contact, larvae enter the dog's bloodstream and are carried to the heart and lungs. To reach the dog's intestines, the worms must be coughed up and swallowed. The mature worms live in the surface tissues of the small intestine, where they produce eggs that hatch into larvae. These larvae are passed in the dog's stool, where they develop further in the soil. The worms either become free-living adults that spend their entire life in the soil, where they mate and reproduce; or they develop into the parasitic form that affects dogs. Only female worms infect dogs, and they are able to reproduce in the dog's body without need of a male worm's fertilization.

Infections are most common in warm climates and cause more problems in young puppies than in adult dogs. Typically, the first signs are coughing prompted by the worms in the lungs. This is followed by large amounts of watery DIARRHEA or bloody, mucus-filled diarrhea. Dogs may also suffer characteristic changes in their footpads from the penetration of

THREADWORMS	
SYMPTOMS	
Coughing; watery diarrhea or bloody, mucus-filled diarrhea; cracked, bleeding footpads	
HOME CARE	
None	
VET CARE	
Supportive care; fluid therapy; medication to kill the parasite	
PREVENTION	
None	

the worm similar to the pododermatitis seen in some cases of HOOKWORMS. Diagnosis is based on signs of disease and by finding the larvae in a stool sample.

The recommended treatment involves supportive care and sometimes fluid therapy to combat DEHYDRATION. The medication thiabendazole (Mintezol) is given daily for five days, and then monthly until the stool test is negative.

Tick Paralysis

This is a progressive paralysis that most commonly affects dogs, sheep, and, rarely, humans. It's caused by a neurotoxin found in the saliva of some TICKS (*Dermacentor*, *Ixodes*, and *Amblyomma* species). The disease has a worldwide distribution, but the species responsible have not been identified in all countries.

Usually, the affected dog has a heavy load of ticks; however, it may take only one tick to cause clinical signs. Paralysis usually doesn't develop until ticks have been attached and feeding for about six days.

The dog typically feels no particular discomfort, but over a forty-eight- to seventy-two-hour period, affected dogs become progressively weaker. First signs may be an elevated temperature, sometimes VOMITING, an altered bark, or difficulty swallowing. But you may not notice anything is wrong until the dog displays incoordination of the hind legs characterized by an unsteady gait. This progresses to forelimb paralysis. Reflexes are lost, but the dog retains sen-

TICK PARALYSIS
SYMPTOMS
Presence of one too many ticks on dog; progressive weakness; fever; vomiting; strange-sounding bark; trouble swallowing; incoordination of hind limbs that progresses to complete paralysis; respiratory failure
HOME CARE
REMOVE TICKS IMMEDIATELY! Then see vet as soon as possible
VET CARE
Same; sometimes antiserum is necessary, along with supportive therapy
PREVENTION
Prevent ticks

sation and consciousness as the paralysis worsens. She's able to feel your touch or a needle prick, but can't move or respond. Eventually, the dog is totally immobilized and unable to stand, walk, or even raise her head. If the clinical signs are not arrested, they will lead ultimately to respiratory failure and death.

Diagnosis is based on characteristic signs, as well as the presence of the parasite. Treatment is simple; remove all the ticks, and paralysis will normally disappear within a few hours. Use an approved insecticide and/or mechanically remove all visible ticks. When the signs have progressed to a great degree, antiserum may be necessary to save the dog's life. Prognosis for recovery is usually good, and dogs typically suffer no permanent damage.

Dogs that have suffered a bout of tick paralysis develop only short-term immunity and can suffer another episode should they again be exposed to a toxic tick bite within as little as two weeks of recovery. Protect your pet by using appropriate TICK preventatives.

Ticks

t

Ticks are an extremely common skin parasite of dogs. These spider relatives have eight legs and live off blood. They typically are gray to brown with oval-shaped, leathery bodies or hard, flat bodies that inflate as the tick feeds. Ticks come in a vast array of species and vary from pinhead size to as large as a lima bean when fully engorged.

The ticks that usually afflict dogs spend up to 90 percent of their time off the host. Ticks typically are a three-host parasite; that is, they target a different kind of animal during each stage of development. Should a preferred host (like a deer or rat) be unavailable, ticks will feed from what's handy, including cats, dogs, or people.

Tick eggs hatch into tiny seed ticks, six-legged larvae that live in vegetation until they can board a passing host animal. Seed ticks feed for several days, then drop off and molt into eight-legged nymphs, which again seek an appropriate host. After another blood meal, nymphs drop off and molt into adults. Adults must again feed before mating. Once fertilized, females drop off the host to lay a thousand to four thousand eggs. The entire life cycle of a tick can take as long as two years.

Ticks bury their heads beneath the victim's skin to feed, and can cause infected sores and prompt skin disease such as HOT SPOTS. Massive infections cause ANEMIA. Ticks are also the vectors, or transmitters, of many devastating illnesses that affect dogs or even people (see BABESIOSIS, EHRLICHIOSIS, LYME DISEASE, ROCKY MOUNTAIN SPOTTED FEVER, and TICK PARALYSIS).

The best way to avoid tick infestation and potential disease is to use effective tick control. There are collars made to kill ticks only. But a number of canine FLEA preventative preparations can be very effective against ticks. Ticks frequent high grass and vegetation. Inspect your dog after field excursions and remove ticks before they have a chance to attach themselves. Simply combing or brushing your dog will eliminate a number of them from his fur before they have a chance to burrow into place.

Wear gloves to remove ticks from your pet to avoid exposing yourself to a tickborne disease agent. Ticks are usually found on the head, the back of the

TICKS	
SYMPTOMS	
Small pinhead- to lima-bean-size bugs attached by the head to the skin, usually on dog's head, neck, and behind or inside the ears	
HOME CARE	
Wear gloves to remove ticks crawling on dog; when tick is attached, grasp tick with tweezers flush to the skin and pull with even pressure to dislodge its head; daub alcohol on exit wound	
VET CARE	
Same as home care	
PREVENTION	
Tick repellents and insecticides	

neck, and inside the ears where the dog has trouble reaching to scratch. Use tweezers to grasp the tick right at the skin level, and pull firmly straight out.

Toad Poisoning

Toads are a kind of amphibian that typically live on land (as opposed to in water, like frogs). Most toads secrete a nasty-tasting but harmless fluid as a defense, and dogs that play with toads and taste this noxious substance may slobber and drool as a result.

The South is home to a tropical toad *(Bufo marinus)* that secretes a toxin in this fluid. The toxin can affect a dog's heart and circulation and cause death in as little as fifteen minutes. Signs of toad poisoning vary from mild DROOL-ING to seizures and sudden death. *If you suspect your dog has had contact with such a toad, get her to your veterinarian immediately.* Prognosis depends on the amount of POISON the dog absorbs.

If help is more than half an hour away, and your dog is conscious, flush her mouth with running water. Use a turkey baster, the spray nozzle attachment from your sink, or the garden hose, but take care she doesn't inhale the fluid. Also attempt to induce vomiting. Be aware that you may need to perform AR-TIFICIAL RESPIRATION.

TOAD POISONING
SYMPTOMS
Drooling; seizures; sudden death
HOME CARE
EMERGENCY! SEE VET IMMEDIATELY! If help is a half hour or more away, flush dog's mouth with water and induce vomiting; provide artificial respiration if necessary
VET CARE
Supportive care; medication to control seizures; fluid therapy to combat shock
PREVENTION
Don't allow dog to play with toads, particularly if poisonous varieties live in your region

t

Toenails

Toenails, or claws, are found at the ends of each toe. Most dogs have five toes on the front feet and four on the back. The fifth toe, called a *dewclaw*, doesn't touch the ground and may be present on either front or hind legs, but often appears on the hind feet of large-breed dogs. Dewclaws are sometimes surgically removed by a veterinarian shortly after a puppy is born, to prevent their catching on objects and causing the dog injury. (However, the Briard and Great Pyrenees standards call for dewclaws to remain intact.) Dewclaws are thought to be a throwback to an archaic ancestral form, since the extra toes serve no functional purpose.

The claw itself is made of hard, nonliving protein that is usually white to clear, and sometimes black. The quick deep inside feeds the rigid structure with a network of blood vessels and nerves. Claws grow from the quick, and in dogs, the nails are rather blunt and wear down through normal activity when they make contact with the ground.

The dog's footpads are very thick and calloused and are the strongest area of the body. Canine claws protect the toes, are used as back scratchers, and serve as tools for digging. Toenails that don't wear down through normal activity may overgrow, split, or tear and cause the dog PAIN and lead to infection. Address your dog's toenail needs in routine GROOMING.

Tongue

The tongue contains the sensory organs that provide dogs with their sense of taste. The long, mobile organ is rooted in the floor of the mouth. The tongue also acts as a tool for self-grooming, EATING, and drinking, and serves as the dog's primary cooling mechanism (see GROOMING, PANTING, and TEMPERATURE).

Not everything is known about the dog's sense of taste. We know that a facial nerve is "wired" to the taste buds on the front two-thirds of the tongue only, leaving the remainder somewhat of a mystery. Most of the dog's taste buds are circular structures located on the upper forward surface of the tongue and in four to six large cup-shaped bumpy papillae at the rear of the tongue.

The majority of canine taste buds respond to sugar, which can get them in trouble (see ANTIFREEZE and CHOCOLATE TOXICITY). This is most likely a reflection of their omnivorous evolution. Dogs needed to eat seasonal fruits and vegetables to survive, so they evolved a sweet tooth because sweetness is a mechanism in plants that signals optimum ripeness. And like people, dogs are able to detect a kind of "fruity-sweet" flavor that attracts us—and them—to the calorie-rich ripeness of fruits and vegetables.

The second greatest number of canine taste buds respond to acidic tastes, which correspond to sour and bitter in people. However, dogs don't appear to have a specific response to salt. Odor coupled with taste tends to impact what the dog will eat.

Touch

Touch refers to the sensation produced when contact is made with the skin. The sense of touch arises from countless temperature- and pressure-sensitive nerve endings found in the SKIN.

Touch serves as a protective mechanism that prompts feelings of pleasure or discomfort in response to external stimulation. When something is too hot or too cold, feels good or causes pain, the nerves tell the dog to react appropriately. Direct contact with the skin isn't necessary, because each HAIR on the dog's body acts like an antenna that feeds sensation down to nerves called *mechanoreceptors* found near the base of each hair in the skin.

Nerves in the paw pads react to vibration. Sense of touch is most sensitive in the area surrounding the MUZZLE, which also contains the sensitive WHISKERS. Temperature is detected by specialized thermoreceptor nerves scattered over the body. Some react to cold, while others respond to heat. Dogs even have a special cold receptor on the lips, the purpose for which remains unknown.

Nociceptor nerves are sensitive to PAIN; some respond to mechanical stimulation like crushing or squeezing, and others are sensitive to temperature extremes.

Touch is also a pleasurable sensation, which is why petting feels so good to both you and your dog. It is this sensation that newborn puppies experience as their mothers wash them. Contact with other creatures provides an emotional link between them and is also thought to be a component of COMMUNICATION.

Toxoplasmosis

Toxoplasmosis is a disease caused by the single-cell organism *Toxoplasma gondii*, a parasitic protozoan. Infection with this agent is quite common in people and many animals, but illness is relatively uncommon. Domestic and wild-

TOXOPLASMOSIS

SYMPTOMS
Rarely, dog develops breathing problems, coughing, fever, diarrhea, or neurological signs

HOME CARE
None

VET CARE
Rarely needed; supportive therapy, such as fluid therapy, and medication to control diarrhea and respiratory signs

PREVENTION
Prevent dogs from hunting; don't feed rare or raw meat; keep yard clean

cats are the only animals in which toxoplasmosis can reproduce. Clinical disease in dogs is rare.

The protozoans multiply in the wall of the small intestine and produce egglike oocysts. Only infected cats are able to pass these immature forms of the organism, which are shed in the cat's stool. Oocysts can survive in moist or shady soil or sand for many months.

The disease is spread when an animal or a person swallows these infective oocysts. Toxoplasmosis can be contracted by ingesting infected animals, eating raw or undercooked meat, or through contact with infective soil or cat feces.

Once inside the bird, rodent, dog, or person, the protozoan continues to mature, causing pockets of disease throughout the body. In most cases of canine infection, the dog's IMMUNE SYSTEM renders the organism dormant at this point so it causes no illness. If the dog's immune system is suppressed due to other illness, however, the dormant infestation may become active and cause clinical disease.

Signs, when they occur, include difficulty breathing, with coughing, fever, neurological signs, gastrointestinal problems, and/or sudden death. Diagnosis is based on clinical signs and blood tests showing elevated antibody levels, which indicate that exposure has taken place. Sometimes the parasite can be found in body tissues.

Healthy adult humans rarely get sick, even when infected. The most common sign is swollen lymph glands. However, the disease can cause life-threatening illness in immune-suppressed people and can severely injure or kill unborn babies. *You cannot contract toxoplasmosis from your dog;* and the chance of contracting toxoplasmosis from a well-cared-for pet cat is extremely low (see TOXOPLASMOSIS in *The Purina Encyclopedia of Cat Care*).

The most common infection source in people in the United States is undercooked or raw meat, especially pork. Protect yourself and your dog by avoiding undercooked or raw meat, and never feed pork to your dog. Prevent your dog from eating wild game and from drinking from potentially infected mud puddles. Wash your hands after handling raw meat, wear gloves when working in the garden to prevent contracting the agent from the soil, and keep your dog out of the cat box. Prompt disposal of cat feces will virtually eliminate the chance of exposure (see also zoonosis).

Training

Training is teaching. Dogs have been bred to be highly trainable, and many are eager to learn because it pleases their owners. Dogs are able to learn a wide range of simple to complicated commands, depending on the individual animal, the breed, and the competence of the trainer.

Specialized training educates dogs to serve in traditional roles as hunters, herders, and protectors, or as surrogate eyes, ears, or extra hands for people requiring such assistance. But all dogs benefit from a basic knowledge of obedience. This helps dogs understand the difference between acceptable and unacceptable behavior and promotes more suitable canine companions.

Principles of effective training involve positive and negative reinforcement, which basically mean rewarding the dog for doing the right thing, and correcting for inappropriate performance. Most dogs respond enthusiastically to praise—"Good boy, King!"—or to treat and toy rewards. Conversely, verbal shaming from the beloved owner—"Bad boy!"—or being shut away in a room by himself is often enough to keep a dog in line.

Punishment in the form of pain has no place in training—ever. Dogs trained in this way may react with extreme shyness or AGGRESSION, which can in fact endanger the trainer or others. Dogs that are hit or slapped with objects or hands learn to associate hands with PAIN rather than petting.

Negative reinforcement is anything the dog considers unpleasant. At its best, it interrupts or makes the inappropriate behavior undesirable so the dog makes the correction himself. The word *no!* spoken in a commanding tone, along with water squirted from a distance, clapping your hands, shaking a tin can filled with marbles, hot-tasting or foul-smelling sprays judiciously applied to forbidden objects, or even a tossed toy all work as corrections. When the dog corrects the behavior, reward him with a "Good boy, King!"

The best training methods use consistency, patience, and positive reinforcement. Commands are linked to short, single-syllable words like *sit* or *come*, and correct performance is rewarded with verbal praise or another strong motivator such as a treat or favorite toy. Bad behavior is corrected with the word *no!*, either alone or in combination with a physical interruption (i.e., noisemaker), and when the dog does the right thing, he is immediately rewarded.

Training is best begun during puppyhood, but can be implemented at any age. Short sessions several times a day work better than a single marathon session. You must act confident, or your dog will try to buffalo you and cut corners. Use the dog's own language of erect posture, unflinching eyes, and a low, compelling voice (not high, loud, or strident) to assume command so your dog will listen to you and be eager to do your bidding.

Entire books are written on the subject of dog training. However, detailed step-by-step instruction is best received through demonstration in a class in which both owner and dog participate. Classes are often sponsored locally by animal welfare organizations or dog clubs. Ask your veterinarian for a recommendation.

It's not necessary for your dog to be an obedience champion (see TRIALS) to be a wonderful companion; however, it helps, and it will promote a more rewarding relationship.

Without exception, all dogs benefit from basic training. At a minimum, your dog should respond to his name, understand and obey the meaning of the word *no*, come on command, and accept a leash. This basic education goes beyond having a well-behaved dog; it's a safety issue that protects you both from liability and injury. The dog that understands these basic commands may be prevented from dashing into traffic or eating a poisonous substance. And leash

This dog is trained to hand signals *(Photo credit: Ralston Purina Company)*

training not only keeps a dog under the owner's safe control, but gives you both freedom to explore the world beyond your house and property.

Your dog's name should be linked with praise as well as an action command whenever possible. Say, "Good boy, King!" and "King, come!" Conversely, whenever he must be shamed or corrected, do *not* use his name, but only the word *no* and "shame on you, bad dog." You want your dog to associate his name with only good, positive things.

Dogs should wear a collar with appropriate IDENTIFICATION at all times. Use one sized appropriately to your dog; a flat leather or woven nylon collar works well. Avoid all electronic/shock, slip, and so-called choke training styles of collar *unless and only if* you have an expert available to show you the proper technique. Misuse of these training tools risks injury to the dog, may promote behavior problems, and can damage a positive pet relationship. Some of the best and most humane training tools currently available are the halter products like Gentle Leader.

Train your dog to accept the leash by first simply clipping the leash to the collar to let him get used to the idea. Some pets throw a fit, and others couldn't care less. Give him lots of positive reinforcement for putting up with the contraption. Next, just pick up your end of the leash. Give short tug-release instructions while calling your dog's name, or use his favorite toy or treat to prompt him to follow you at the leash's direction. Praise him when he stays by your side.

Use the leash to train your dog to come. Again, use short tug-release instructions as you command "come!" and perhaps tempt him with his favorite toy or treat. Praise him when he responds appropriately. Use mealtimes as a training tool as well. If you know the sound of kibble hitting the bowl always brings your dog running, then couple that trigger with the "come" command; reward him with his food. Make sure he knows you think he's the smartest dog in the world, and he'll do his best to prove you right!

Be careful, however, that you *never* call your dog to come in order to punish him for some infraction. That will undermine all your training. If your dog must be corrected, or you need to perform some unpleasantness upon his person (i.e., trim his toenails), then don't command him to come; simply go get him.

Training sessions should be fun for you both. The one-on-one attention is glorious for your dog, so make the most of each session. Be sure to always end on an up note; you want your dog to remember he did well and was praised for doing well, so finish with an exercise he's already mastered. (See also HOUSE-TRAINING and TRIALS.)

Traveling

All dogs travel during their lives, if only during an annual trek to the veterinarian's office. But many dogs routinely make trips to the groomer or a boarding facility, and show dogs travel a great deal.

All dogs should travel in the safety of a confined carrier, even for relatively short trips. Upset tummies and nervous behavior are better controlled in a confined, easily cleaned area. However, large- and giant-breed dogs may be more difficult to accommodate, and often are better confined in the backseat.

Don't allow your dog to ride in your lap. Even dogs accustomed to car rides may be startled by something unexpected, leap from an open window, or interfere with control of the car. During a car accident, an unrestrained dog becomes a furry projectile that not only suffers injury himself, but could severely injure others. Your dog could escape the car and become lost when rescuers seek to help you, or conversely, could try to attack and prevent rescuers from offering you aid.

Additionally, don't let your dog hang her head out the window in a moving vehicle. This will prevent eye injuries, as well as keep your dog inside the car in case he decides he wants to try to leap out.

Commercial carriers, from elaborate to simple, are available for your dog's

Confine dogs in crates to travel (*Photo credit: Ralston Purina Company*)

comfort. The best are big enough for the adult dog without being cramped; cardboard pet totes available from pet-supply stores or the veterinarian's office are fine for short trips. But long trips or repeated outings require better accommodations, so plan on getting a more substantial crate. Bigger dogs benefit from harnesses that can be secured to a seat belt. Grilles that screen the rear of the car are also helpful to give a big dog room while keeping her out of your lap.

Airlines, buses, and trains that allow pets have various rules regarding fees and pet accommodations. Health certificates signed by your veterinarian are an absolute must; your dog won't be allowed to travel these public transportation systems without one. Such certificates are good for only ten days, so call in advance to be sure you're prepared. Solid plastic carriers must be airline approved if you are transporting the dog with cargo. Only a few small animals sized to fit beneath the seat as "carry-on luggage" are allowed on certain flights, so call ahead and reserve space if this is your intention. Airline carriers are usually box-shaped hard plastic with a grille opening in one side or the top. Canvas bags or duffel-type carriers with zipper openings are also popular for smaller dogs. Several travel books list hotels, campsites, and parks that welcome your dog, so be certain you choose canine-friendly accommodations.

Traveling is often stressful for pets, especially if your dog associates car rides with a visit to the vet. Train your dog to better accept car rides by turning the crate or carrier into a play area or even a bed. Take your dog for short car rides that end at a canine playmate's house or a park for play (and a healthy treat or two?), so she'll associate the car with good things. In some cases, your veterinarian may prescribe a tranquilizer for you to give to your dog to reduce her anxiety during trips (see CAR SICKNESS).

If your dog is traveling with you for extended periods (particularly across state lines), you are required to carry with you a vaccination and health certificate, and copies of your dog's medical records. Out-of-country travelers should call the local embassy or consulate of the country of destination at least a month in advance to get necessary information on pet travel. Some countries require only health and vaccination certificates, while others may impose a six-month QUARANTINE. Request a free copy of the pamphlet "What You Should Know about Traveling with Your Pet" by sending a self-addressed stamped envelope to the American Veterinary Medical Association (see Appendix C, "Veterinary Resources").

Should you decide to leave your dog at home when you travel, investigate the services of a pet sitter or boarding kennel (see Appendix C, "Pet Services"). Some states license kennels and inspect them on a regular basis, and pet sitters may also be regulated by various associations. Ask your veterinarian and other pet owners for a recommendation.

Trials

Trials are competitive events established to test the performance and/or appearance of dogs against an established standard of excellence. There are three basic categories of dog sport competition: dog shows, field trials, and obedience trials. These may be formal "licensed" events that earn participating dogs points or credits toward titles and championships, or they may be informal "fun matches" that offer practice to participating dogs and their handlers.

Dog shows are essentially beauty contests in which registered purebred dogs are judged on *conformation*—that is, how closely they meet their breed's standard. Dogs are judged on general appearance; size; coat; color; how they move; and even their temperament. Specialty conformation shows are limited to dogs of a single breed or grouping of breeds; for instance, the Pekingese Club of America Specialty is for Pekingese only. An all-breed conformation show includes dogs of all breeds. Competition is fierce, with various classes competing in a process of elimination with only the winners advancing to the finals. A separate category, called Junior Showmanship, judges youthful dog handlers ages ten through sixteen on their ability to show dogs in conformation trials.

Obedience trials test both the dog and handler on how well they perform preestablished exercises: heeling on and off the leash, standing for examination, coming when called, staying in a sitting and down position, fetching an object, leaping a high jump and broad jump, scent discrimination, etc. While conformation trials require participants to be a recognized breed and intact (able to produce puppies), any dog breed or combination of breed, neutered or intact, may compete in obedience trials. Three levels of progressively difficult competition—Novice, Open, and Utility trials—earn the dog points toward titles, and ultimately championship.

The Canine Good Citizen Program encourages all dog owners to train their dogs in basic obedience. Dogs are tested in a pass/fail system on such things as walking naturally on a loose leash, walking through a crowd, accepting a stranger's approach, and containing themselves during the unexpected, such as a door slamming. Dogs that pass earn a Canine Good Citizen title (CGC).

Tracking trials test the dog's scenting ability. Again, increasingly difficult tests are set up; the dog able to follow the trail by scent and pass the first level earns a Tracking Dog title (TD); passing a more advanced test earns the dog TDX for Tracking Dog Excellent.

Field trials and hunting tests demonstrate the hunting dog's ability to perform those functions for which he was developed. Pointers, retrievers, spaniels,

Conformation show (Westminster) *(Photo credit: Amy D. Shojai)*

Hunting trial *(Photo credit: Ralston Purina Company)*

Beagles, Basset Hounds, and Dachshunds compete in various events, according to their breed's purpose. Dogs earn the ultimate titles of Field Champion and Master Hunter.

Herding trials measure these dogs' ability to herd and control livestock.

Herding tests measure a dog's inherent ability and training potential, while the trials themselves earn points toward titles and championships. The ultimate title here is Herding Champion (HCH).

Lure-coursing events test the sight-hound breeds (i.e., Greyhound, Saluki, Afghan Hound) in the same way field trials challenge scent hounds and sporting dog breeds. Dogs are challenged to run down "prey" (in this case, air-filled plastic bags) as they were bred to do. Field Champion (FC) is the ultimate title.

There are a number of other dog sports available as well. Earth dog events test the terrier's ability to "go to ground" in tunneling and digging trials. Dogsledding is a favorite of northern breeds such as Siberian Huskies, Alaskan Malamutes, and Samoyeds. Weight-pulling events measure a dog's strength; American Staffordshire Terriers are standouts in this event. And agility trials wed a number of performance skills into an all-around package of dogs able to leap, climb, run, and do all manner of skills over (and under) obstacle courses. For dogs (and owners) with a sense of humor and creative spirit, the newest event, called freestyle, may be appealing; here, nearly anything goes as long as dog(s) and handler(s) are choreographed appropriately to the music (with props and sometimes costumes). (For contact information on the various dog sporting events, see Appendix A, "Dog Associations.")

Tuberculosis

Tuberculosis is a devastating respiratory infection that affects people. It's so named for the characteristic *tubercles* that form in the lungs as a result of the infection.

Human tuberculosis is caused by one of three bacterium: *Mycobacterium tuberculosis* (the primary agent of people), *Mycobacterium bovis* (also affects cows and other livestock), and *Mycobacterium avium* (affects birds), collectively referred to as the *tubercle bacillus*. M. *tuberculosis* and M. *bovis* can also infect dogs.

For a while it was thought this disease of antiquity was on the decline; however, in recent years the scourge has made a comeback, due to a combination of emerging antibiotic-resistant strains and an increase in human immunodeficiency virus (HIV) infections. Currently, it's estimated that as many as twenty-five thousand new human cases each year are being diagnosed in the United States.

Dogs typically contract the disease by contact with an infected human. In most cases, the infection causes no signs of disease in a dog with a healthy immune system. When the dog does become ill, respiratory signs such as coughing, labored breathing, retching, weight loss, fever, ANOREXIA, and enlargement

TUBERCULOSIS

SYMPTOMS
Coughing; labored breathing; retching; weight loss; fever; anemia; enlarged lymph nodes; bloody sputum

HOME CARE
None; EXTREMELY CONTAGIOUS TO HUMANS. SEE VET IMMEDIATELY!

VET CARE
None; due to human health risk, euthanasia is recommended

PREVENTION
Prevent your dog's exposure to human tuberculosis sufferers

of the lymph nodes may be seen. The dog may cough up bloody sputum. Such dogs are extremely contagious and pose a health risk to other dogs and people.

Diagnosis of canine tuberculosis is extremely difficult. Skin testing and blood tests that detect antibodies (both used successfully in people) are not reliable in dogs. Other methods, such as finding the agent in tissue samples (biopsy), are involved and take a long time to accomplish. An X RAY that shows lung changes may be helpful.

Human antituberculosis medications have been used experimentally in infected dogs. However, successful treatment requires weeks to months of therapy, and because of the potential zoonotic risk, therapy is not recommended in dogs. Sadly, dogs confirmed to have tuberculosis are usually euthanized to protect other pets and people. Fortunately, the disease is considered rare in dogs. (See also ZOONOSIS.)

t

Ulcer

An ulcer is a slow-to-heal open sore that may be located anywhere on the body. An ulcer can cause progressive tissue damage and loss, particularly if infection becomes involved. Dogs may suffer an EYE ulcer from injury or anatomical conditions (see ECTROPION/ENTROPION). They may suffer ulcers on the skin secondary to insect bites or trauma, or due to other problems like LICK SORES. Any sore that is slow to heal should be addressed by a veterinarian.

Ultrasound

An ultrasound is a noninvasive diagnostic instrument that employs sound waves to penetrate various structures of the body. These waves pass over or through tissue in various ways depending on its density. The echo reflection of these waves provides a two-dimensional image that offers veterinarians an accurate picture of the soft areas of the body that X RAYS aren't able to discern.

Uveitis

Uveitis refers to an inflammation of the iris (the colored portion of the eye) and the ciliary body that supports the lens and produces fluid to the front portion of the eye. The condition is common in dogs and may affect only

UVEITIS

SYMPTOMS

Change of eye color in one or both eyes; clouding of cornea; rough eye surface; squinting and watering eye; soft eyeball; small pupil that reacts slowly to light

HOME CARE

None

VET CARE

Treat cause if possible; steroids to relieve inflammation; atropine to dilate pupil; medication to buffer pain

PREVENTION

Avoid exposure to systemic illness, parasites, and trauma

one eye or both. Unless diagnosed and treated, the dog may lose her sight in that eye.

When both eyes are affected, the condition is likely a result of systemic illness. Parasites, fungus, and bacterial or viral disease including TOXOPLASMO-SIS may cause uveitis. Trauma and CANCER are other causes, and corneal ULCER often precedes the condition.

Signs of the condition vary depending on the cause. Dogs may squint, suffer watery eyes, clouding of the cornea, or even a change in eye color. Often, the affected eye feels abnormally soft, and the pupil is small and reacts slowly to light. Without treatment, the condition may progress to blindness as a result of underlying GLAUCOMA or CATARACTS.

Some cases of uveitis are diagnosed with blood tests and evaluation of the fluid within the eye itself. ULTRASOUND or X RAYS may also be required. Treatment depends on the underlying cause; antibiotics, antifungal treatments, and parasite-killing medications address these causes. Treatment almost always involves high doses of anti-inflammatory drugs such as corticosteroids.

U

Vaccinations

Vaccinations are medical preventatives, often injections, designed to stimulate the IMMUNE SYSTEM to mount a protective defense against disease. Vaccines essentially program the dog's body to recognize alien substances, such as viruses and bacteria, as dangerous and to mount an attack to neutralize them.

Vaccinations prompt immunity by exposing the dog to a non-disease-producing form of the foreign agent. Such exposure stimulates the production of protective cells and antibodies designed to seek and destroy pathogens before they cause illness.

Dogs should be vaccinated against those diseases for which they are at risk. Risk factors vary depending on the individual dog's immune competence, exposure, and stress levels. Very young and very old dogs typically have less effective immune systems and so are at higher risk for disease. Risk of disease is increased in dogs exposed to other dogs, such as kenneled dogs, show dogs, and dogs being boarded. Dogs in overcrowded conditions, such as shelters, and show dogs or working dogs that travel a lot have increased exposure. This also causes higher STRESS levels, which can make a dog more susceptible to illness. And dogs that are allowed to roam, particularly intact animals, have increased exposure to other dogs and disease. The geographic region in which a dog lives also influences risk, because the incidence for some canine diseases is higher in certain areas than in others. An "only" dog that is a healthy neutered or spayed house dog is probably at lowest risk for exposure to disease (see NEUTERING and SPAYING).

Due to these many variables, a single vaccination program may not be appropriate for all dogs. Your veterinarian can best design an appropriate regimen for your particular pet.

Almost without exception a dog should be given vaccinations that protect

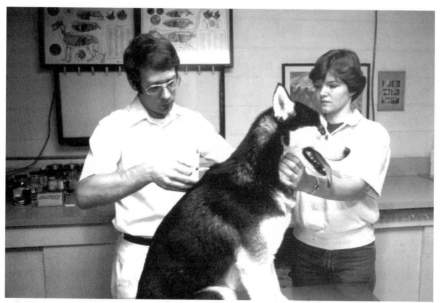

Vaccinate to prevent disease *(Photo credit: Ralston Purina Company)*

against CANINE DISTEMPER VIRUS, INFECTIOUS CANINE HEPATITIS, LEPTOSPIROSIS, canine parainfluenza virus (see KENNEL COUGH), and CANINE PARVOVIRUS. These vaccinations are often given as a single five-in-one injection termed a DHLPP. In addition, vaccination against RABIES is required by law in all states.

A mother dog that has a healthy immune system passes her immunity on to her PUPPIES when they drink the first milk, called *colostrum*. This passive immunity fades over a few weeks as the babies' own immune systems mature and take over. Unfortunately, this borrowed immunity also interferes with the vaccines. The protective agents in the vaccines are identified as foreign and are attacked and destroyed just like the virus or bacteria would be. That's why a single vaccination given at six weeks of age won't protect puppies from becoming sick.

Your dog's immune system isn't completely mature until about six to eight weeks of age—but Mom's immunity won't stop neutralizing the vaccinations until the babies are about fourteen weeks of age (timing is different from puppy to puppy). The window when Mom's immunity has faded and Junior's is finally mature is quite narrow. Therefore, a series of vaccinations is given so that active immunity is stimulated just as maternal protection fades away.

The majority of vaccinations are given by injection beneath the skin. Those for canine parainfluenza virus, or kennel cough, can be given under the skin or as drops in the nose to stimulate local protection in cells first exposed to these viruses. Maternal antibodies don't block cell-mediated immunity, which means protection can be administered before six weeks of age if the puppy is at risk for exposure. However, the vaccination for kennel cough isn't recommended until nine weeks of age.

Schedules vary, but first vaccinations are typically given between six to nine weeks of age. Follow-up booster shots are given every three to four weeks thereafter until the puppy reaches fourteen to sixteen weeks of age when the rabies vaccine is first given.

Other vaccinations are useful for certain dogs. Outdoor dogs in endemic regions may benefit from a vaccination designed to protect against LYME DISEASE. Dogs with multidog exposure, such as field-trial or show dogs or those regularly boarded, may benefit from vaccinations against kennel cough or CANINE CORONA-VIRUS. And in certain instances, puppies less than six weeks of age are given vaccination against human measles, which is very similar to and will stimulate immunity against canine distemper; the measles vaccination is better at overcoming interference from maternal immunity than is the distemper vaccine.

Some vaccinations are designed to reduce or treat the symptoms of disease but not necessarily to prevent illness. A vaccination against the bacterial agent that causes leptospirosis helps reduce the severity of disease, but does not prevent the infection.

No vaccine is 100 percent protective. Individual immune competence, exposure incidence, the virulence of the disease-causing agent, and the type of vaccine all influence the effectiveness of a vaccine's protection.

Most canine vaccinations are either modified live vaccines or "killed" (inactivated) vaccines. The type of vaccine depends on the infectious agent. For instance, an inactivated vaccine against canine distemper virus isn't effective, so all those used today are modified live vaccines.

Vaccines are modified to reduce or eliminate their ability to cause disease, but when left "alive" they are able to multiply inside the body the way a normal virus would. Modified live vaccines more closely imitate natural infections, so the immune system is better stimulated. They also negate maternal immunity more easily to provide a better and quicker protection for puppies than killed vaccines do.

However, some extremely virulent agents, like rabies and canine parvovirus, may prove difficult to inactivate enough to ensure they won't cause the disease they are trying to prevent. Modified live vaccines can cause problems in pets with suppressed immune systems, or result in birth defects in unborn puppies when the vaccine is given to the DAM during pregnancy.

A safer alternative is killed vaccines. They can be given to pregnant dogs and will not cause disease. They are usually more expensive because they must contain an additive (adjuvant) that stimulates the immune response. While a modified live vaccine may be effective after only one dose, a series of at least two vaccinations is generally required to ensure the best protection when using killed vaccines. Some experts are concerned that adjuvants used in the leptospirosis vaccine may cause adverse reactions in susceptible toy dog breeds.

Occasionally a dog responds adversely to a vaccination. The most serious, an ANAPHYLACTIC reaction, occurs within ten to fifteen minutes following the injection. Signs vary from relatively minor problems like facial swelling or hives, to severe respiratory distress along with VOMITING, DIARRHEA, and collapse. *These are emergencies that require immediate veterinary help.* If your pet has previously had an allergic reaction to vaccination, medications can be given prior to vaccinations to prevent or lessen the symptoms of future reactions.

Moderate lethargy and/or slight fever is the most common type of vaccine reaction and rarely lasts longer than a day. Signs usually go away without treatment. Local reactions of tenderness or swelling at the injection site also generally fade away in a few days.

Nobody really knows how long vaccination protection lasts. Studies have proven that the three-year rabies vaccination does protect for that period of time—perhaps even longer. We do know protection longevity varies depending on the type of infectious agent that's being prevented and the type of vaccine being used.

Immunity against viruses generally lasts longer than bacterial immunity. But killed vaccines don't protect nearly as long as modified live, and local immunity in the nose or eyes doesn't last as long as systemic protection that includes the whole body. In fact, the canine measles vaccine offers only temporary protection for puppies and isn't intended for use in adult dogs. The vaccine for leptospirosis offers partial protection for only three to six months.

In the past, vaccinations were recommended to be given on an annual basis to healthy adult dogs. However, studies are under way to determine the actual duration of vaccination protection and the optimum revaccination schedule. Until then, rely on your local veterinarian's recommendation to best protect your dog. He or she best knows your area's disease incidence and your dog's situation.

Vomiting

Vomiting is the forcible expulsion of the stomach's contents up the dog's throat and out of the mouth. Dogs tend to vomit more readily than almost all other animals. When the "vomit center" of the brain is stimulated, the dog begins to salivate and swallow repeatedly. Your dog may seek attention or look anxious. Then the stomach and abdominal muscles forcibly and repeatedly contract, while at the same time the esophagus relaxes. The dog extends her neck, opens her mouth, and makes a strained, gagging sound as the stomach empties. When a dog has eaten something she shouldn't, vomiting should usually be induced by the owner or veterinarian (see POISON).

V

Most cases of canine vomiting result from gastric irritation due to swallowing grass, eating inedible objects, eating spoiled or rich food (raiding the garbage, table scraps), or simply eating too much too fast. The most common cause of vomiting in dogs is gluttony. Dogs that gorge their food tend to lose it as quickly as it's swallowed, particularly if they exercise shortly after finishing a meal. This type of vomiting isn't particularly dangerous, but is annoying. Slowing down the rate of consumption will go a long way toward relieving mealtime vomiting. Feed dogs in separate bowls to cut down on "competition" eating, or place a large, nonswallowable ball in the dish so the dog is forced to eat around it. Meal-feeding several times a day rather than once will also alleviate overeating. A few dogs vomit when they're excited or fearful (see STRESS, FEAR, and CAR SICKNESS).

Vomiting is different from regurgitation, which is a passive process without strong muscle contractions. Regurgitation can occur minutes to hours after eating, and the expelled material is undigested and may even be tube-shaped like the throat. Occasional regurgitation isn't a cause for concern unless it interferes with NUTRITION. Chronic regurgitation typically is seen in a young dog that as a result grows very slowly (see MEGAESOPHAGUS).

Vomiting that happens only once or twice isn't a cause for concern as long as the dog acts normal before and after. Resting the digestive tract by withholding food and water for twelve to twenty-four hours or so will usually resolve the gastric irritation (see ENTERITIS).

Repeated vomiting, unproductive vomiting, vomiting not associated with eating, and/or the dog acting as though she feels bad before or after the event is a cause for alarm. Vomiting can be a sign of CANINE DISTEMPER VIRUS, CANINE PARVOVIRUS, SWALLOWED OBJECTS, or LIVER or KIDNEY DISEASE. If the vomit contains blood or fecal material, if vomiting lasts longer than twenty-four hours, or if other signs such as DIARRHEA accompany the vomiting, contact your veterinarian immediately.

Von Willebrand's Disease

Von Willebrand's disease is an inherited bleeding disorder caused by a defect in the clotting factors of the blood. It has been found in many breeds, but is most common in Doberman Pinschers and German Shepherd Dogs. It's also commonly reported in the Miniature Schnauzer and Golden Retriever.

Most cases are mild, and some even lessen as the dog grows older. Signs include nosebleeds, blood in the stool or urine, BLEEDING into the joints or beneath the skin, and slow-to-clot wounds that ooze blood for a prolonged period of time (see also HEMOPHILIA).

W

Wart

A wart is a small, horny protrusion of the skin. Canine warts are actually benign tumors of the upper layers of the skin and are caused by a variety of papillomaviruses.

Warts are much more common in people, who are usually affected on their hands or feet. GERIATRIC DOGS may develop warts anywhere on their body. Warts are often hidden by fur and don't cause any problem, but should be removed if they become irritated or bleed.

Young dogs may develop a condition called *papillomatosis* in which warts develop in their mouths or sometimes on the eyelids, cornea, conjunctiva, or skin in other locations. Clusters of warts typically appear on the gum surfaces

PAPILLOMATOSIS (WARTS)

SYMPTOMS

Single to multiple small, horny protrusions of skin; they often appear rashlike in the mouths or eyes of young dogs

HOME CARE

None

VET CARE

Usually goes away without treatment; sometimes surgery when severe

PREVENTION

Avoid contact with dogs suffering the condition

or lips. The condition may be spread to another dog by close contact with an infected dog.

Papillomatosis is almost always a transient condition, which is cured by itself within a few months. It can be unsightly and uncomfortable for the affected dog, however. If the condition is extreme or is slow to resolve, a veterinarian may intervene with surgery. Cryosurgery (freezing) or electrosurgery (cautery, or burning) are options. Once the dog recovers, he's usually immune to the virus and will have no further problem.

Whipworms

Whipworms (*Trichuris vulpis*) are thin, two- to three-inch-long, threadlike worms that narrow at one end like a whip. All dogs are at risk, but puppies may be more profoundly affected.

Dogs contract the parasite by ingesting eggs found in the soil. Eggs can live for five years in the soil of cold climates. Consequently, whipworms may cause more problems in northern states than in southern climes where the eggs are more readily killed. The eggs hatch and mature in the dog's large intestine in about seventy to ninety days.

The parasite feeds on blood by burrowing into the wall of the intestine. In small numbers, whipworms cause few problems. The female worm produces fewer offspring than many other kinds of intestinal parasites do, so typically the infestation is light. However, a heavy worm load may cause DIARRHEA, VOMITING, ANEMIA, and weight loss, and such dogs typically have a rough coat or "unthrifty" appearance.

WHIPWORMS	
SYMPTOMS	
Diarrhea; vomiting; anemia; weight loss; rough coat	
HOME CARE	
None	
VET CARE	
Treatment with medication to kill parasite	
PREVENTION	
Practice good hygiene by picking up feces promptly from the yard; some heartworm preventatives also protect against whipworms	

W

Diagnosis is made by finding eggs during microscopic examination of the stool. But dogs may show clinical signs for several weeks before worm eggs will be shed in the stool. Later, eggs may be shed only intermittently, continuing to make diagnosis difficult.

Effective medications are available, but once whipworms are in the environment, infestations can be hard to contain since dogs are often reinfected from egg-contaminated soil. Treatment for three months or longer may be necessary to totally eliminate the infestation.

Good hygiene is the only way to reduce the chance of your dog contracting whipworms. Pick up the yard after your dog at least weekly. Some monthly HEARTWORM preventatives, such as Interceptor or Sentinel (which also control fleas), can control whipworm-related illness.

Whiskers

Whiskers are the thick, long, wirelike hairs that protrude from the dog's face. Also called *vibrissae*, whiskers are specialized hairs that are long, supple, and

W

Whiskers are a sensory tool for dogs (*Photo credit: Amy D. Shojai*)

thick, or groupings of short, stiff bristles. Whiskers are much more developed in animals that hunt during the night or low-light times. They act as feelers and are seated deep in the SKIN, where they trigger nerve receptors at the slightest touch.

Dogs have whiskers in four places on each side of the head and in two places on the lower jaw. The most obvious are those on each side of the dog's MUZZLE, where whiskers grow in four rows; they provide information when the dog is sticking his nose in and around objects. Bristles of four or five whiskers above each eye act like extended eyelashes that prompt a protective blink reflex when brushed. A clump of whiskers is located on each cheek, and there is a smaller clump near each corner of the mouth. Finally, the dog has a tuft beneath the chin, which probably serves to keep his head from scraping the ground during tracking behavior, or may even help in food-burying activities. (See also HAIR.)

Wobbler's Syndrome

More accurately termed *cervical spondylopathy*, wobbler's syndrome is a malformation and/or misalignment of the lower cervical (neck) vertebrae, which results in varying degrees of spinal-cord compression. The pressure on the spinal cord causes progressive degeneration of rear-limb function with a resulting "wobbly" gait.

The condition is seen in several breeds of dogs, but most commonly affects Great Danes less than a year old and Doberman Pinschers older than five. Initial signs are loss of coordination of the rear limbs, along with a peculiar unsteady gait. As the disease progresses, paralysis advances from rear limbs to the forelimbs, with neck movements becoming more and more painful and stiff.

The cause remains a mystery. Experts speculate that genetics, rapid growth, and nutrition, alone or in combination, are influencing factors. Because the syndrome may have an inherited basis, dogs diagnosed with wobbler's syndrome should not be bred. Diagnosis is based on signs, breed predisposition, and X RAYS. Prognosis is guarded, depending on the severity of the condition and the age of the dog. Some dogs are helped with corticosteroid therapy, which helps relieve accompanying inflammation. In others, surgical intervention may be necessary to relieve the pressure on the spinal cord and to stabilize the cervical disks to prevent further damage.

W

X ray

X rays, also called *radiographs*, are a kind of wavelike electromagnetic radiation that's invisible and is similar to but shorter than visible light.

The unique radiation that's produced can penetrate different body structures in varying degrees, and the result is recorded on photographic film. A negative film image results in areas of the body where radiation is able to fully

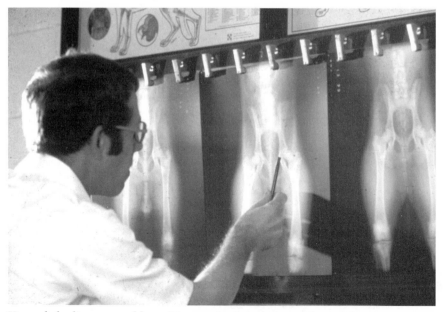

X rays help diagnose problems (*Photo credit: Ralston Purina Company*)

penetrate. The more waves that pass through, the darker will be the image; the fewer waves there are, the lighter the picture on the film.

Empty space allows the greatest penetration, so air-filled spaces like the lungs look black on the film. Fat is next, and it is dark gray. Fluid or soft tissue are recorded in varying degrees of medium to light gray. The radiation can't penetrate bone or teeth, which are extremely complex, dense structures; these areas will appear white on the film.

X rays provide significant diagnostic information in both human and veterinary medicine. Because of radiographs, it's possible to see and diagnose kidney or BLADDER STONES, FRACTURES, and SWALLOWED OBJECTS without the need for exploratory surgery. Often, this ensures timely treatment that otherwise might come too late.

Diagnostic X rays employ a safe radiation level that's carefully regulated. When used therapeutically as a treatment for CANCER, radiation is increased to specific levels and targeted to precise areas (see CANCER, Radiation therapy).

X

Zinc-Responsive Dermatosis

This is a skin disorder caused by a deficiency of zinc in the diet. Zinc is required in tiny amounts and helps promote healthy skin and hair growth.

Alaskan Malamutes, Bull Terriers, Samoyeds, and Siberian Huskies may inherit a genetic defect that interferes with the proper absorption of zinc. The condition can be prompted in any dog fed generic foods or other poor-quality rations low in zinc, or in dogs whose diets are oversupplemented with minerals, such as calcium.

Signs of zinc deficiency include thinning of the fur and a scaly DERMATI-TIS, especially on the face. The dog's feet also typically develop thick calluses and crack and bleed.

ZINC-RESPONSIVE DERMATOSIS
SYMPTOMS
Thinning fur; scaly facial dermatitis; thick footpads that crack and bleed
HOME CARE
Feed complete and balanced diet
VET CARE
Supplement the diet with zinc; sometimes zinc supplement for rest of dog's life
PREVENTION
Feed complete and balanced diet

The condition is diagnosed by the signs and based on the dog's diet history. Correcting the diet to a complete and balanced ration, along with short-term zinc supplementation, will reverse the signs of disease. Most dogs show rapid improvement in as little as one week. Dogs suffering an inherent absorption problem typically require veterinary-supervised zinc supplementation for the rest of their lives. (See also FOOD, FOOD SUPPLEMENTS, NUTRITION, and READING FOOD LABELS.)

Zoonosis

Zoonosis refers to a disease that a person can contract from an animal under ordinary circumstances. Humans are vulnerable to many viral and bacterial diseases, fungi, and parasitic conditions that more commonly affect animals.

Of the two-hundred-plus known zoonoses, only a few are associated with pets. Of these, most cause only transient disease and can be easily treated and resolved, with incidence of such cases remaining low. Still, the potential danger of zoonotic disease mustn't be dismissed, because a few do actually cause severe human illness or even death.

Without exception, the most common zoonoses associated with dogs can be avoided. Routine hygiene and conventional prevention protect your dog and yourself from potential illness. (See also BRUCELLOSIS, CANINE SCABIES, GIARDIASIS, HOOKWORMS, LEPTOSPIROSIS, PLAGUE, RABIES, RINGWORM, ROUNDWORMS, TAPEWORMS, TOXOPLASMOSIS, and TUBERCULOSIS.)

Appendix A

Dog Associations and Breeds

A dog association is a national organization that registers dogs, keeps records of their ancestry in pedigrees, publishes breed standards, sponsors dog shows and events, and determines who will judge them. Kennels are individual establishments that strive to produce the "ideal" dog of a given breed. These dogs then compete in conformation and performance trials sanctioned by the dog association in which that dog is registered. The goal is to determine which dog is closest to the standard of perfection in looks, temperament, and/or performance.

Kennels, and sometimes individuals, hold membership in local or national dog clubs, which in turn are members of one or more dog associations. There are several kinds of dog clubs: all-breed clubs, specialty breed clubs (a single breed), and performance clubs, which test obedience, tracking, fielding, hunting, herding, coonhounding ("treeing" varmints), and lure coursing. There are also a number of dog associations. Breed standards may vary from association to association, and not all dog associations recognize the same dog breeds. Be aware that registration does not guarantee quality of a dog, only that both parents were the same breed. However, registered dogs can prove their quality by earning titles, and dog parents with titles usually produce high-quality puppies. If you are interested in learning more about dog show opportunities for you and your dog, contact one or more of the following organizations.

American Kennel Club
5580 Centerview Drive
Raleigh, NC 27606
(919) 233-9767
http://www.akc.org

American Mixed Breed
Obedience Registration
10236 Topanga Boulevard,
Suite 205
Chatsworth, CA 91311
(818) 887-3300
http://www.amborusa.org

American Rare Breed Association
9921 Frank Tippett Road
Cheltenham, MD 20623
(301) 868-5718
http://www.arba.org

Australian National Kennel Council
Royal Showgrounds
Ascot Vale 3032
Victoria 3032
Australia

Canadian Kennel Club
Commerce Park
89 Skyway Avenue, Suite 100
Etobicoke, ON M9W 6R4
Canada
(416) 675-5511

Fédération Cynologique Internationale
13 Place Albert I
B6530 Thuin
Belgium

Kennel Union of Southern Africa
P.O. Box 2659
Cape Town 8000
South Africa

Mixed Breed Dog Club of America
1937 Seven Pines Drive
St. Louis, MO 63146-3717

New Zealand Kennel Club
Private Bag 50903
Porirua 6220
New Zealand

States Kennel Club
P.O. Box 389
Hattiesburg, MS 39403-0389
(601) 583-8345

The Indian National Kennel Club
Belvedere Court, 2nd Floor
148 N. Karve Road
Bombay, 400 020
India
telephone: +91 22 2029106

The Kennel Club
1–5 Clarges Street
Picadilly
London W1Y 8AB
United Kingdom
http://www.the-kennel-club.org.uk

United Kennel Club
100 East Kilgore Road
Kalamazoo, MI 49002-5584
(616) 343-9020
http://www.ukcdogs.com

DOG BREEDS

AFFENPINSCHER

The name means *monkey-dog*, and this ancient toy with the simian face is from central Europe, where tiny mouse-catching pet dogs were developed during the seventeenth century. The stiff, wiry coat, facial tufts, and docked tail and ears give him the look of a terrier. In France, the breed is described as "the mustached little devil," which describes both his appearance and temperament. He is smart but resistant to training, which must be firm and consistent. Usually a quiet, inquisitive companion, he likes to dig, and he can become a noisy and fearless defender if threatened. He gets along well with older kids.

AFGHAN HOUND

The Afghan Hound was unveiled to western eyes in the nineteenth century, and brought from Afghanistan to England later that century. Her origins remain shrouded in mystery, but her forebears likely existed in Egypt thousands of years ago. Afghans served in various capacities in their native region, from guards and herders to hunters of everything, from hares and deer to wolves and snow leopards. She is an agile, swift coursing hound that hunts by sight. A tall, deep-chested but lithe dog, she has distinctive silky fur in almost any color combination except white markings. Aloof and dignified—especially with strangers—she enjoys relaxing, but needs room for running. Afghans prefer a quiet home and need privacy; this is not the best choice for young children or homes with other small pets. Training is slow and rather difficult with the Afghan.

AIREDALE TERRIER

This is the largest of the terriers. He is most likely descended from early terriers crossed with Otter Hounds, and he became recognized in the late 1800s in England as a separate terrier breed adept at hunting larger game. The Airedale was one of the first breeds employed in Great Britain's police dog force.

This large, wire-haired dog's black-and-tan coat is close-fitting and crinkly. Airedales love water, and they have a sweet disposition with those they know, but are aloof with strangers and can be aggressive with other dogs. They have a strong prey drive toward small animals and pets. Smart and trainable, and good with older kids, the Airedale won't tolerate the unpredictable behavior of very small children.

AKITA

This is the national dog of Japan. It is a northern spitz-type dog with prick ears, dense coat, and curled tail. In Japan the Akita signifies health, happiness, and long life; small statues of the Akita are often given as lucky gifts to a newborn child, or as a get-well gift for those feeling under the weather. The Akita is thought to have been developed in the seventeenth century; his thick fur helped him hunt deer, bear, and boar even in the deepest snow.

The breed was nearly lost to extinction several times over the centuries, but today is one of the world's most popular breeds. The Akita is a large, powerful, bearlike dog that comes in many colors. He is friendly and affectionate with family, but quite protective and wary of strangers, and aggressive toward other dogs. The Akita tends toward dominance, which can turn to aggression. He is smart but learns slowly, and he may throw tantrums during training. A firm, knowledgeable owner is best equipped to deal with the Akita, and homes with small children should choose another breed.

ALASKAN MALAMUTE

The quintessential northern-type dog, the Malamute is a large, densely furred, prick-eared dog with a gracefully curling plumelike tail. She is the largest, and one of the oldest, sled dogs, named for the native Inuit tribe (Mahlemuts) of the upper-western part of Alaska. The Malamute comes in the gray to black wolf colors, with a characteristic dark "cap" over the white face, or a dark "mask" surrounding brown (never blue!) eyes.

The Malamute was a worker and draft dog in her native land (like her cousins the Samoyed and Siberian Husky) and today retains a fiercely loyal and independent nature. She is a dignified and powerful dog and is friendly and devoted. Highly trainable, she is nonetheless a freethinker who likes to do things her own way. She may be aggressive toward other dogs, tends to howl and bark, and loves to dig and pockmark your yard.

AMERICAN ESKIMO DOG

This white northern breed looks like a small Samoyed and comes in three sizes: Standard is fifteen to eighteen inches tall at the shoulder; Miniature stands twelve to fifteen inches; and the Toy is under twelve inches. He is an energetic and independent dog that's reserved with strangers and devoted to those he knows. The Eskimo Dog is a playful, happy dog that likes to bark, and can be a handful to train due to his somewhat stubborn nature. He does well with older children, but may not put up with very young kids.

AMERICAN STAFFORDSHIRE TERRIER

This massive dog arose from combining the early Bulldogs and terriers reared for bull baiting, and was originally called the Bull-and-Terrier Dog or Half-and-Half Dog. Today, this striking, lovable breed (often erroneously called a Pit Bull) is known for her strength, courage, and heart.

Am Staffs have characteristically massive heads with naturally prick or closely cropped ears, a close-fitting short coat in nearly any color, and an air of unmistakable power. She is highly trainable, usually docile, and very affectionate when well socialized. However, she can be aggressive and hard to handle for those who aren't knowledgeable and firm. This breed tends toward dominance and is dangerous in the wrong hands. Consult an expert to help you choose an Am Staff right for you, or pick a different breed.

AMERICAN WATER SPANIEL

This medium-size dog is an all-around hunter equally adept at retrieving in water or land. He's an enthusiastic worker, and like most spaniels, he lives to please. Rather than "pointing" game, he "springs" it—makes the rabbit or quail spring from cover—so a hunter can bring it down for him to retrieve.

His coat is solid liver, brown, or dark chocolate. It is wavy (marcelled) to tightly curled everywhere, like that on a Poodle, except on his forehead and tail, where it is smooth. The Water Spaniel loves to swim and is a high-energy pet that can be suspicious of strangers. He'll enjoy older children and can make a good family dog.

AUSTRALIAN CATTLE DOG

This herding dog is a medium-size prick-eared and short-haired dog developed during the colonization of Australia in the early 1800s. The Australian Cattle Dog was produced by first crossing blue merle Collies with Dingoes (the native wild dog), then crossing the resulting pups with Dalmatian, and their pups with a sheepdog called the Black and Tan Kelpie. The result was a heavier Dingo-type dog with a distinctive blue or red speckled short coat, initially called the Blue Heeler or Queensland Heeler.

He is suspicious of strangers, which makes him a loyal, intelligent, and courageous watchdog. He's an outstanding worker, but is not a good choice for children or for those wanting an easygoing pet. Both dog and owner are happiest when he's working livestock.

AUSTRALIAN SHEPHERD

The Aussie was developed for herding cattle and sheep in the harsh environment of the Australian outback. She is an active dog with a medium-length, wavy to straight coat colored blue merle, red merle, red, or black. She is a medium-size tailless dog, highly intelligent, and happiest when she has a job to do.

The Aussie tends to be high-strung and needs an outlet for her energy. She is so smart, she can be a standout at nearly any task she's given. The breed is affectionate with her family, but suspicious of strangers and can be a bit noisy. The Aussie enjoys older children.

AUSTRALIAN TERRIER

This small, sturdy fellow has a long, low body, docked tail, erect ears, and medium-length harsh coat in blue, red, or blue and tan. He is a working terrier developed to be a watchdog and to control rodents and snakes in the Australian outback.

This fearless little dog is devoted to his people. His weather-resistant coat and intrinsic toughness allow him to stand the rigors of outdoors, while his stature and biddability make him a welcome addition to the home. He tends to be aggressive toward small animals and will do well with older children, but may become aggravated by noisy or rambunctious young children.

BASENJI

This "barkless" dog can actually be quite noisy, for she uses expressive yodels and chortles. One of the oldest breeds, she arose in central Africa, where Basenji were given as gifts to the pharaohs of ancient Egypt. As in ancient times, this relatively small dog is prized today for her hunting ability, speed, and intelligence.

The Basenji has large prick ears, a forehead that wrinkles quizzically, a curling tail, and a shiny silky coat in chestnut red, pure black, tricolor, or brindle. She's a happy dog that's quite stubborn and can be hard to train. The Basenji has been characterized by trainers as the "brat" dog because she'll throw tantrums to get her way. This proud, elegant dog needs a firm hand from the beginning, so that her dominant personality doesn't become a problem.

BASSET HOUND

The Basset is an old, noble breed of French-Belgian origin where he was used as a slow, patient tracker of rabbits, deer, and other game. He is distinguished by his short legs and long body; long, floppy ears; easy-care short coat; exquisite sense of smell; and loud, distinctive, baying voice. In tracking, his nose is second only to the Bloodhound's.

The Basset is a gentle, medium-size but heavy dog, who is endearing for his clownish looks. He's loyal and devoted to family and friends. Any recognized "hound" coloring is acceptable on this dog—typically, combinations of brown, black, tan, and white. He tends to be noisy—baying, barking, and snoring—and can be a challenge to train because he's so easily distracted by scent. Bassets can be pretty dominant and probably aren't the best choice for families with small children.

BEAGLE

Beagles of various sizes have been popular for centuries. Modern Beagles come in thirteen-inch and fifteen-inch varieties, are worked singly or in packs, and are tireless hunters born to sniff and run. Beagles have short, hard coats of medium length that come in hound colors, and they make gentle, fun-loving pets. If anything, Beagles are too friendly and willingly run to friend or stranger with a happy wag.

Beagles are barkers by nature; don't expect him to be a quiet dog, or to stay at home unless leashed or fenced. Like many hounds, scent rules this dog's life; he'll ignore anything (even training and food) for a really good sniff.

BEARDED COLLIE

This old British breed is also known as the Highland Collie. She was the herdsman's dog, a companion, friend, and talented working partner. This average-size dog has shaggy, long fur in either black, blue, brown, or fawn. The Beardie is an active, hardworking dog that's a devoted and intelligent pet. She tends to be good with children, but may try to herd them by nipping their heels. Like many of the herding dogs, the Beardie likes to chase, and she may run after joggers, bikes, or cars. She needs regular exercise and, though a bit stubborn, can be trained to excel at herding, agility, and obedience trials.

BEDLINGTON TERRIER

This medium-size lamb look-alike was developed as a hunter of badgers, foxes, otters, and other vermin. The mild, gentle expression hides the courage of a tiger; this is one of the most dog-aggressive breeds, and she will take on opponents much bigger than herself.

Bedlingtons are lovable, devoted pets, but may not be trustworthy around small animals. They come in a variety of colors, including blue, sandy, liver, blue and tan, sandy and tan, and liver and tan. Be aware that like many terriers, this dog likes to bark and dig. This breed makes a fine companion for adults, or responsible older children who treat him with respect.

BELGIAN MALINOIS
The Malinois is a large, short-coated fawn shepherd with a black mask, and looks similar to the German Shepherd Dog. This is a confident, intelligent dog, reserved with strangers but affectionate and protective with his own people. He is easily trained and does best when given a job to do. Cars, joggers, and bikers may become targets for this dog that loves to chase, and he may try to herd children by nipping at their feet.

BELGIAN SHEEPDOG
Also known as the Groenendael, this is a longer-furred version of the Malinois, but with a solid black coat. She has been used as a herder, police dog, messenger dog during war, guard dog, and companion. She is an elegant, intelligent dog easily trained to a wide variety of tasks and devoted to and even possessive of her people. She may target cars, joggers, and bikers to chase, and herd children by nipping at their feet.

BELGIAN TERVUREN
This is the most profusely coated of the Belgian dogs, similar in type to the Belgian Sheepdog, but colored a rich mahogany with black overlays. The Tervuren was developed as a guardian and herder of stock, and today continues to excel as a herder, obedience dog, and even sled dog. Cars, joggers, and bikers may become targets for this dog that loves to chase, and children may be herded by an industrious Tervuren nipping at their heels. His intelligence and devotion make him a wonderful companion.

BERNESE MOUNTAIN DOG
The Bernese Mountain Dog comes from the highlands of Switzerland, where she served as drover, draft animal, and watchdog. This mastiff-type breed is always tricolored—predominantly black, with rich rust and clear white markings—and with fur that's thick, long, and slightly wavy or straight. The Bernese is a hardy, confident dog that does well in cold weather, thrives on human companionship, and is a good-natured, loyal pet. She may be aloof with strangers, and some trainers have noticed a tendency toward timidity that can prompt fear-biting. The Bernese generally is a stubborn, headstrong dog but, with patience and a firm hand, can be trained. This large, active breed is best in a rural environment with plenty of exercise and in a home without small children.

BICHON FRISE
The Bichon originated in the Mediterranean and is descended from the Water Spaniel. She became a great favorite of the French aristocracy during the

Renaissance and today retains that popularity. The Bichon is a small powder puff on legs, her curly white coat setting off her dark eyes and nose. The Bichon rates high on the "cute" factor and is a gentle, playful, and cheerful companion that excels at obedience training. She tends to do better with older children, but is a great family pet.

BLACK AND TAN COONHOUND

This is an old breed, probably descended from the Talbot Hound of eleventh-century England. He was developed specifically for his characteristic color and proficiency in hunting possum and raccoon. The Black and Tan is a big, active, muscular dog with short, sleek hair and a friendly but businesslike attitude. He hunts by scent, then "barks up" or gives voice the moment his quarry is treed, and he is happiest when working. This breed does not tolerate children well and does best in the home of a hunter who understands and can give him the firm direction he needs.

BLOODHOUND

This is easily the best scenting dog in the world and one of the oldest breeds, with similar dogs known to exist long before the onset of the Christian Era. The Bloodhound is a large, short-haired dog with drooping jowls and long, floppy ears. He carries a perpetually worried expression on his noble face, due to wrinkles in the loose folds of skin beneath his neck and jowls. He is absolutely ruled by his nose, which is used in hunting both man (by the police) and beast.

The Bloodhound is single-minded when on the trail and does best in a working environment. He is not meant to be a family pet and may bite children who tease or provoke him.

BORDER COLLIE

Arguably the smartest breed of all, the Border Collie is a result of the combined bloodlines of several herding dogs and was developed during the nineteenth century in England and Scotland. This dog is a magician with sheep, able to control them with a simple stare. She is sized midway between the Collie and the Shetland Sheepdog and in type looks similar. Her medium-length coat comes in black and white, gray and white, or blue merle.

The Border Collie is affectionate with family, but reserved with or even shy of strangers. Her extreme intelligence can make her a challenge to train, but she often is a standout in obedience, herding, and agility trials. Like most herders, she loves to chase cars, bikes, and other moving objects (like kids); instead, offer her a ball to fetch, and she'll play until she drops. Families with young children should consider another breed. A Border Collie is best given a job to do; otherwise, she will find something to do herself, and potentially get into all kinds of trouble.

BORDER TERRIER

This is one of the oldest kinds of terrier from Great Britain. He was developed to counter the attacks of foxes upon stock animals. Long legs allow him to easily follow a horse, and he's sized to easily follow prey to ground (into its below-ground den). The Border Terrier is an active, tireless, and plucky dog.

He comes in a red, grizzle and tan, blue and tan, or a wheaten short coat that's harsh and weather resistant, and he carries his short, thick tail high. He is one of the most affectionate of the terriers and tends to be a good-tempered dog that makes a fine pet. He will pockmark your yard by digging if given half a chance.

BORZOI

Previously known as the Russian Wolfhound, this large coursing hound is little changed from its Russian ancestors of the thirteenth century. The Borzoi comes in any color, with long, silky fur that's either flat, wavy, or curly—except the head, ears, and leg fronts, where it's short and smooth.

This is an elegant dog that needs room to run. Dignified and quiet, he is a typical sight hound. Reserved with strangers, he's affectionate with family members, but can be unpredictable around children and may attack smaller pets. The Borzoi is a dog that likes privacy and alone time and is not an "in-your-face" breed.

BOSTON TERRIER

The Boston is an American breed developed by crossing an English Bulldog with a white English Terrier in the mid to late 1800s. This "Boston Gentleman" today has the characteristic pushed-in Bulldog nose and is a compactly built, well-proportioned, little, short-haired dog that comes in black, seal, or brindle with distinctive white markings. His expressive face gives an air of determination, and he is a friendly dog that has a great deal of nervous energy. The Boston is suspicious of strangers and may be aggressive toward other dogs or smaller pets; very young children will drive this dog nuts, but he'll enjoy interacting with older children. Training goes slowly (some dogs throw tantrums!), and the Boston can be a digger and barker. But he is also a lively, loyal pet that adapts well to apartment living.

BOUVIER DES FLANDRES

The Bouvier is a working dog similar in looks to large terriers, with a harsh, tousled double coat, erect ears, and docked tail. He was developed as a herder and a draft dog and has also served as a police, defense, and army dog. This is a rough-looking dog that is bold and fearless. He comes in any color except chocolate, white, or parti-color.

The Bouvier tends to be an easygoing dog that may be moody or aloof from time to time and suspicious of strangers. His dominant nature can be a challenge for training, and though intelligent, the breed tends to learn slowly. He likes to chase—other dogs, cars, runners, strange children—although he is normally quite good with his own family's children. Regular exercise gives the Bouvier an outlet for his energy.

BOXER

The German-born Boxer is a medium-size, refined, mastiff-type dog, with short, satiny fur in either fawn or brindle with white markings, and a broad muzzle with a slightly undershot jaw. His tail is docked short, and his natural drop ears are cropped long so that they stand erect. He is a cousin to Bulldog breeds and is a courageous character historically used in bull-baiting and dogfighting matches. His name comes from his characteristic manner of using his front paws much as a boxer would. The Boxer was one of the first breeds selected in Germany for police dog training.

The modern Boxer is intelligent, fearless, agile, and strong, playful and loyal to family and friends, but suspicious of strangers, and thus is a great guard dog. He is a dignified, self-assured dog. Friendly and headstrong, he is easily distracted. He is quite good with children. With firm guidance and daily exercise, he is an outstanding companion.

BRIARD

This is an old French working breed used from the eighth century to herd and defend the flock against the attacks of poachers and wolves. She is a medium-size dog with a long, flowing, straight coat in any uniform color except white. She has a long, low-held tail with a crook on its end, high-held ears from which fur cascades, and a fur-covered face and beard.

The Briard is reserved with strangers and is an intelligent, readily trained dog that does best with a job such as herding trials or obedience competition. She likes to chase cars, bikes, and joggers, and she may try to herd running children by nipping at their feet. A firm hand and lots of exercise can mold this dog into a fine companion.

BRITTANY

Formerly known as the Brittany Spaniel, this medium-size, leggy bird dog is named for the French province in which he originated. Dogs similar to the modern Brittany appear in seventeenth-century tapestries.

The Brittany has a characteristic dense, flat or wavy, medium-length coat that's usually colored either liver and white, or orange and white. He is either born tailless, or the tail is docked. The Brittany is a happy, alert dog that's neither mean nor shy. He likes other dogs and children and makes an excellent hunter and family pet.

BRUSSELS GRIFFON

This toy breed has lots of personality and comes in either a wiry, rough or a short, smooth coat in red, beige, black and tan, or black. Her cropped ears and tail, thickset, short body, and expressive, pushed-in face were developed by combining the Affenpinscher and Belgian street dogs sometime in the seventeenth century.

This is an intelligent, sensitive dog that has the terrier attitude of stubbornness and reticence around strangers. She likes to dig and bark and needs slow, careful training. The Brussels Griffon is a busy, happy little dog that makes a good apartment pet.

BULLDOG

This old breed was developed to promote the cruel sport of bull-baiting, and the original dog must have been ferocious; the modern version only looks the part.

Today's Bulldog is extreme in nearly every way, from his pushed-in nose and wrinkled face, undershot jaw, massive head and shoulders, and small pelvis, to his distinctive "screw" tail. The Bulldog is a massive yet compact dog of small but impressive and dignified stature, with a fierce expression that belies the breed's kind and affectionate nature. The breed comes in various colors, including red, brindle, white, fawn, and piebald.

The Bulldog is an extremely lovable and friendly dog that doesn't know his own strength and can bowl over the unprepared with his enthusiastic greeting. He's not particularly aggressive, but tends to resist training. He is good with children, but may inadvertently knock them down with his body. Because of his facial structure, the Bulldog makes all kinds of unbecoming noises; the most polite are described as snores.

BULLMASTIFF

The Bullmastiff is likely a centuries-old breed, but detailed records are not available. He is a hybrid probably from Mastiff and Bulldog crosses, which produced a massive, courageous, and powerful yet quiet dog that gamekeepers used to apprehend poachers. These dogs were trained to attack on command, and throw and hold the miscreant, but without mauling.

The modern Bullmastiff looks like a Boxer on steroids (but with natural drop ears and long, uncropped tail) and weighs up to 130 pounds. The short coat comes in red, fawn, or brindle. For those who have the room to keep him, and are aware of his propensity to snore and drool, the Bullmastiff makes a confident, fearless, yet docile pet willing to please his family and be their protector. He tends to be good with his own family and children, but is an extremely territorial dog that can be unpredictable with strangers.

BULL TERRIER

This breed dates to about 1835 and comes in two colors: white and "colored," which is any color (solid or with white), brindle being preferred. He also comes in two sizes, separated as two breeds; the Bull Terrier is the larger, while the Miniature Bull Terrier should not exceed fourteen inches at the shoulder. He has fine, short fur; a distinctive egg-shaped head; small, dark, sunken eyes; erect ears; and a tapered tail. This powerful gladiator was developed when dogfights were legal and popular, and was trained to be a "gentleman's companion" that didn't provoke a fight, but only defended master and self. Spuds MacKenzie is the best-known modern example of the breed.

The Bull Terrier is a very friendly dog that loves affection and is ready to play or fight at the drop of a hat. However, he is quite reserved with strangers. These dogs are often stubborn and tend to be slow learners. They may also be aggressive toward small pets or small children.

CAIRN TERRIER

The Cairn is a small, short-legged terrier developed to hunt the "cairns" or rocky hills of Scotland. Her shaggy, medium-length coat comes in any color but white, and she holds her prick ears and docked tail erect.

This is a working terrier, ready and eager to go after small prey. She tends to be a barker and may be a reluctant learner that's suspicious of strangers. The Cairn is a smart, sassy little dog with a bright-eyed, happy expression, and makes a good apartment pet. You'll recognize the Cairn as Toto from *The Wizard of Oz*.

CANAAN DOG

This is an ancient pariah dog that arose more than 2200 years ago in the region today known as Israel. These dogs roamed the deserts freely and sometimes were used as flock guardians or herders. In the 1930s, efforts were made to preserve and domesticate this unusual, heat-tolerant breed.

Today's Canaan is a medium-size, short-haired dog with prick ears and curled tail. He comes in any color except solid white, gray, or brindle, and in two color patterns: solid with or without white trim; and white with a mask, with or without patches of color on the body. He retains the traits that made the earliest pariah dogs natural watchdogs and is affectionate with those he knows. This breed is reserved with strangers and very territorial, and can be dog-aggressive.

CAVALIER KING CHARLES SPANIEL

This small dog looks like a larger version of the English Toy Spaniel but with a long, straight coat. Colors are black and tan, tricolor (red, black, and white), Ruby (red), or Blenheim (white and red).

The Cavalier was the companion of kings and was developed specifically as a pet. This sweet, gentle dog is affectionate to family and strangers alike and loves children. The size (about twelve inches tall at the shoulder) makes her an ideal indoor pet, and she learns quickly with gentle instruction. This is a great family dog that doesn't require lots of exercise, but she can't withstand a lot of roughhousing.

CHESAPEAKE BAY RETRIEVER

These water-loving dogs were developed to retrieve birds from the icy waters of the Chesapeake Bay—sometimes two hundred ducks a day. The modern Chessie is still a standout retriever, as well as a tracking and obedience competition dog. In shape, he looks a bit like the Labrador, but the thick, short coat has a wooly, dense undercoat, and the coat may be wavy on his shoulders and back. The Chessie colors are solids, from dark brown to light tan.

The Chessie tends to be a pushy, dominant dog that requires strong leadership to train. He's affectionate with owners, but will walk all over (even snap at) those he doesn't respect, especially children. He makes a great watchdog and can make a fine pet for a firm leader.

CHIHUAHUA

The ancient Toltec civilization of ninth-century Central America kept a small, heavy-boned, long-coated, mute dog. Called the Techichi, it was important to the religious life of the Toltec and later the Aztec peoples. The Techichi is the founding father of our modern Chihuahua, which is the smallest of the dog breeds.

She comes in any color and two coat lengths, smooth and short, or long and silky. Despite her stature, the Chihuahua truly believes she is a big dog and acts accordingly. She doesn't care for other dogs (although she may accept other Chihuahuas) and is an alert, boisterous character that makes a good watchdog— although she can become yappy. She's smart, but tends to resist training (even housebreaking), and needs firm, patient teaching to keep her from becoming nippy. Most problems can be avoided simply by remembering not to spoil her. Homes with boisterous children need to find another breed.

CHINESE CRESTED

It is believed that this unique breed was developed by the Chinese from the African hairless dogs and was carried around the world with sailors to fight the rats on the ships. Spanish explorers found these dogs in Mexico as early as the 1500s.

This toy breed comes coated—powder-puff variety, with double, silky, all-over fur—or hairless, with only tufts of fur on the head and face, feet, and tail tip. This is an elegant, graceful dog. A playful and devoted pet, he is cheerful and alert. Like many small dogs, he tends to resist training and can become nippy and noisy if spoiled. Older children who respect his delicate build are appreciated.

CHINESE SHAR-PEI

This ancient, unique breed arose as early as the Han dynasty (200 B.C.) in China and is known as the "wrinkled dog." Like many Chinese dogs, the breed nearly became extinct during the ascent of communism in that country, when most dogs were eliminated. The few remaining outside of China (Hong Kong, Taiwan, etc.) gave rise to the breed we know today.

The Shar-Pei is a medium to large dog with a characteristic hippopotamus face, black tongue, small ears and eyes, a curled tail, and masses of loose skin covered in bristly, short fur that comes in nearly any solid color. He is a loyal, devoted dog to those he loves, but has an independent nature and acts the dignified and regal snob with strangers. His recent popularity has prompted poor breeding practices that produce dangerous dogs that are biters of both strangers and owners. This is an extremely dominant and dog-aggressive animal that doesn't belong anywhere near other pets or young children. Training must begin during puppyhood if an owner is ever to establish control. Choose your dog wisely by consulting with an expert—or get another breed.

CHOW CHOW

This is a Chinese hunting dog traceable to the Han dynasty (150 B.C.), but likely was developed even before that. She is a massively built, large dog with a profuse, thick, standoff coat, curled tail, erect ears, and blue-black tongue. She may have common ancestors with other northern breeds like the Samoyed, Norwegian Elkhound, and Pomeranian.

The Chow may be colored red, black, blue, cinnamon, or cream. She is an independent, intelligent dog that's loyal to and protective of owners. The Chow tends to bond with only one or two people and is suspicious and often aggressive toward strangers and other dogs. She is very stubborn and resistant to training. The Chow is a dominant dog that needs a firm hand from puppyhood on; she'll constantly challenge your authority and does best in a predictable environment. Families with children should consider another breed.

CLUMBER SPANIEL

This short-legged breed differs widely from other spaniels. His long, low body is likely due to early crosses with the Basset Hound, and he has a distinctive haw visible. The Clumber moves with a characteristic rolling gait. He is a quiet and slow worker, but a tenacious hunter.

He looks small, but is solid and weighs up to eighty pounds. The Clumber is a white dog with lemon or orange markings and a medium-length, dense, straight coat with a longer neck frill. Clumbers tend to be possessive of food and toys and are hard to train because they're easily scent-distracted. A loyal, affectionate dog, he's reserved with strangers and won't appreciate small children.

COCKER SPANIEL

Spaniels are mentioned as far back as 1368 in the canine written record, with "cockers" named for their expertise in flushing and retrieving woodcock. The modern American Cocker Spaniel is quite different from her English counterpart. Although her breeding allows her to be trained to serve in the field as a hunter, American Cockers are better known as pets. Energetic, merry tail-waggers, Cockers have a profuse medium to long, silky or slightly wavy coat (short and fine over the head), docked tail, and pendulous ears. They may be solid black (sometimes with tan points), any solid color other than black (sometimes with tan points), and parti-color.

Sadly, the high popularity of this breed has created some very poor dogs that have myriad health and behavior problems, including viciousness; Cockers tend to bite. They don't bark too much, but may scream when thwarted. This beautiful, smart dog can make a wonderful pet, if bred correctly (seek an expert's advice!) and trained with a firm hand. Families with children should choose another breed.

COLLIE

Known to most as the "Lassie dog," this is an old sheepherding breed native to Scotland and England. He is a large, solid dog that comes in two coat varieties: The Rough is the better known, with a profuse, straight, double coat, plume tail, and characteristic white mane; the Smooth coat has hair that's very short and close to the body. Coat color can be sable and white, tricolor, blue merle, and white.

Modern Collies are not often called upon as herders, but primarily are treasured companions. However, Collies love to bark and can be very noisy and, like other herding dogs, like to chase cars, bikes, and joggers. Collies are smart but sensitive dogs that need calm environments and readily accept training. They are affectionate, loyal, and protective pets that have a great love of children.

CURLY-COATED RETRIEVER

This is one of the oldest of the retrievers, thought to be descended from sixteenth-century spaniels and setters. His tightly curled, solid black or liver-colored coat is likely due to the influence of the Poodle (the onetime retrieving dog of France).

These dogs love the water and are affectionate pets that can be wary of strangers. They don't appreciate the roughhousing of young children and tend to be stubborn, slow learners. They are standouts as retrieving dogs for hunters, though, and thrive on this work.

DACHSHUND

This distinctive breed was developed to hunt badgers (*Dachs* means *badger*; *hund* means *dog*), and her short legs and svelte, long, low-slung body is admirably suited to following prey into narrow dens beneath the earth. Dogs similar to the modern Dachshund were around as early as the fifteenth century. Today's Dachshund comes in two sizes and three hair coats. Miniatures are eleven pounds and under; standards, twelve to thirty-two pounds. Smooth varieties have short, smooth, and shiny fur; Long-haired Dachshunds have slightly longer fur with feathering on the ears, tail, and legs; and Wirehaired varieties sport short, thick, rough, wiry coats with a longer "beard" on the jaw and smooth fur on the ears. Colors are all-over red or cream, or predominantly black, chocolate, gray, or fawn with tan markings.

The Dachshund is a courageous, affectionate, high-energy dog that loves to play, romp, and bark. She can be stubborn and somewhat resistant to training, or pushy and hardheaded. Dachshunds are the perfect size for a house dog and are personable little dogs that are good with children.

DALMATIAN

This is a distinctive pointer-type dog known for his short, white, polka-dot coat. Known in England as the Coach Dog or Firehouse Dog, the Dalmatian's origin is shrouded in mystery. He's served as a ratter, draft dog, shepherd, bird dog and retriever, and pack hound—and as a guardian of the coach and horse.

The Dalmatian is a quiet dog that needs to run and is quite protective of family and property. He is born pure white and develops black or liver-colored spots as he matures. He tends to be suspicious of strangers and, when worried or unhappy about instruction, may bite. This is not a good dog for young children. Dalmatians bond very closely with their owner, but are stubborn and difficult to train. He excels as a hunting dog and makes a great jogging partner.

DANDIE DINMONT TERRIER

The Dandie looks like a wirehaired Dachshund on steroids. Low to the ground, she has a hard, wiry coat in mustard or pepper color, and her clipped ears and fluffy topknot and beard give the Dandie her distinct look. She was first listed as a breed about 1700 as a hunter of badger and otter.

Today, the Dandie is a treasured house dog. Smart but stubborn, she likes kids and may test an owner's will by obstinately doing what she pleases. Spoiling a Dandie may turn her into a brat, and she tends to be aggressive toward small pets.

DOBERMAN PINSCHER

This is a relatively new breed by canine standards, developed in Germany about 1890 by breeder Louis Dobermann. These earliest Dobermans were hybrids composed of the best qualities of indigenous short-haired shepherds, Rottweiler, Black and Tan Terrier, and smooth-haired German Pinscher. The modern breed is a large, elegant, short-haired dog, traditionally with tail docked short and ears cropped long and held erect. Colors are black, red, blue, or fawn with rust markings.

The Doberman is an agile, muscular, intelligent dog used today in police and protection work. These are energetic, excitable, yet fearless dogs that may be slow to accept strangers and often aggressive toward other dogs. A bored Doberman tends to be destructive and may dig and bark. They are highly trainable, but tend toward stubbornness, and are good with older children. They make fine pets when properly trained and socialized.

ENGLISH COCKER SPANIEL

The longer muzzle and less distinctive "break" in profile of the English Cocker distinguishes her from her American cousin. Less well known in this country (except to hunters), the English Cocker is a standout in the field. She is more even-tempered than the American Cocker, but has as much energy, enthusiasm, and tail-wagging exuberance.

Like her American cousin, she has a docked tail, pendulous ears, and a silky coat not quite as profuse; parti-colors are white in combination with black, liver, or shades of red; solids are black, liver, or shades of red. She can be a stubborn dog that's slow to learn, but is affectionate to family and friends, loves kids, and makes a good pet.

ENGLISH SETTER

This hunting dog looks a bit like an Irish Setter, but is white with darker (orange, lemon, blue, or black) flecking throughout the coat.

The English Setter has a mild, sweet disposition and is an intelligent, very active dog that needs lots of exercise and running room. Her great scenting ability is a distraction during training, and she may become an incorrigible barker. She typically is a very affectionate dog that makes friends easily and loves kids. With patient training, the English Setter makes a fine family pet.

ENGLISH SPRINGER SPANIEL

Before the seventeenth century, all spaniels were lumped together until size variance made smaller ones more adept at flushing woodcock (Cockers), while larger spaniels were "springers" of game. Size alone was the only difference between the English Cocker and English Springer Spaniel, with both types sometimes born in the same litter. Later (the 1920s) the two were categorized as separate breeds, and the Springer became more distinctive as time passed.

Today, the Springer remains a medium-size dog with a moderate coat nicely fringed on the ears, chest, legs, and belly. His coat is colored in black or liver with white markings; white with black or liver markings; tricolor; and blue or liver roan. He is an eager-to-please dog, quick to learn, highly intelligent, and biddable. Overbreeding has caused aggression problems in some dogs, though, so choose carefully with an expert's help; *pick a different breed for children.*

ENGLISH TOY SPANIEL

Like her full-size namesakes, the English Toy Spaniel has the silky long coat, drop ears, docked tail, and happy temperament characteristic of spaniels. But she's much smaller and has a short, pushed-in nose. This breed has been known at least since the sixteenth century and was a favorite of royalty, from which she takes her "color" names. The Blenheim variety is a white dog with deep red or chestnut markings; the Prince Charles is tricolor—white, black, and tan; the King Charles is black with tan markings; and the Ruby is a self-colored rich mahogany red.

Though small, the English Toy Spaniel retains many of the hunting instincts that make her larger cousins standouts in the field, but she is primarily a house and apartment dog. She is good with children and is an affectionate and biddable dog that may be shy at first but usually warms up quickly to strangers.

FIELD SPANIEL

The Field Spaniel is a dog suited to hunting, having agility, speed, and endurance; he looks like a worker and performs admirably. He is the product of Springer and Cocker crosses combined with a Sussex Spaniel and Welsh Cocker hybrid. His usually black, single, moderately long, flat coat is dense and water-repellent, with feathering on the legs and chest similar to that on a setter. He also may be liver, golden liver, roan, or any of these colors with tan points. The Field Spaniel is typically a docile, sensitive dog, independent and intelligent, and often reserved with strangers. This breed accepts older, considerate children.

FINNISH SPITZ

This is a red, foxy-looking dog with a thick, medium-length coat, curled tail, and erect ears. She is the national dog of Finland, where she still serves as a hunting dog that trees game, then alerts the hunter by barking and pointing. The Finnish Spitz is a brave, eager, and friendly companion, cautious of strangers, and typically fond of older children. Because she was developed to think for herself, this highly intelligent dog can be stubborn and hard to train. She can be dog-aggressive and tends to be a noisy barker.

FLAT-COATED RETRIEVER

This delightful breed, hugely popular in the late 1800s, is making a comeback after being overshadowed by the Labrador and Golden Retrievers and nearly becoming extinct during the world wars. The Flat-Coated Retriever is similar to these breeds in temperament, being an energetic, intelligent, tail-wagging, eager-to-please dog that excels in hunting trials. His moderate-length coat is shiny, dense, and full, but straight and flat. In fact, this dog looks and acts like a dark Golden Retriever and is colored liver or black only. He is a wonderful hunter and family dog.

FOXHOUND (AMERICAN and ENGLISH)

The Foxhound very generally looks like a larger version of the Beagle, with the English Foxhound a bit more refined-looking than the American breed. Both breeds have short, close coats, drop ears, and high-held tails, with voices described as "bell-like" when the dog calls as she hunts. Both breeds have been around for several centuries and are high-speed, energetic hunters that run singly or in packs against fox and other small game.

Foxhounds are ideal for the outdoorswoman/man, but not for the average dog lover. This is not a house dog, although she'll probably get along well with older children. She tends to be suspicious of strangers, can be dog-aggressive, and makes a good watchdog—but unless given an outlet, she can drive her owner crazy with her high energy.

FOX TERRIER

The Smooth and Wire varieties are now recognized as separate breeds, but are essentially the same except for the coat. The Fox Terrier is an old English breed that appeared as early as the late 1700s. This is a medium-size, white dog with dark patches, V-shaped drop ears, and a high-held, short, thick tail. The Smooth Fox Terrier has very short, close fur, showing a clean tapering head; the Wire Fox Terrier has a wiry, broken, twisty or crinkly coat fitting closely to the body and a bit longer on the legs and muzzle. This is a gay, active dog that seems always ready for a run or a romp.

These dogs are very independent, suspicious of strangers, and smart but defiant of the rules. They have high prey drives that make them dangerous when around smaller pets and very small children; they are fine around older kids. Fox Terriers like to dig and bark and enjoy games of fetch.

FRENCH BULLDOG

This is essentially a toy Bulldog, similar in look to the Boston Terrier, but with large bat ears. She is a medium-size, short-coated dog that's very muscular for her size. Alert, curious, and interested, she wants to be in on everything. The easy-care coat comes in brindle, fawn, white, and brindle and white.

The Frenchie is a happy, gregarious breed that makes friends easily. She is a quiet dog that requires minimal exercise and is an ideal apartment dog. She tolerates polite children well.

GERMAN SHEPHERD DOG

This breed is a German dog descended from a variety of working farm and herding dogs and was initially a herder and protector of sheep. He is known for his loyalty, courage, and intelligence, and today serves in a variety of capacities, including police dog, search-and-rescue dog, guide dog, and guard dog. He has a medium-length, double coat that comes in nearly any color. The German Shepherd Dog is extremely intelligent and not always easy to train, because *he* always knows a *better* way to do things. But this elegant and powerful dog is incredibly devoted to his family (kids, too!) and, when properly socialized, is an outstanding family pet.

He typically is aloof with strangers, may be dog-aggressive, and likes to chase cars, bikes, and strangers. German Shepherds are very sensitive to an owner's mood and emotion, which may provoke unexpected aggression or fear in certain circumstances. Give this dog productive work to do, and he'll be your devoted friend for life.

GERMAN SHORTHAIRED POINTER

This extraordinary all-purpose hunter has been making a name for himself since before 1870, when the first records were kept. His webbed feet and short, water-resistant coat make him a standout field and water retriever, and he is equally adept as a bird, rabbit, or varmint dog.

He is similar in look to the Pointer, but with a more tapered muzzle and a tail docked long. His short, close coat comes in solid silver or any combination of liver and white (ticked, roan, or spotted). He is a good watchdog that's accepting of approved strangers and gets along well with children and other dogs. But this is not an easygoing house dog; he's stubborn and hard to train and may become noisy and destructive without constructive work (hunting!) to do.

GERMAN WIREHAIRED POINTER

This hunter combines the ideals of the Pointer, Foxhound, and Poodle to create a versatile dog able to point and retrieve equally well on land or water. His all-weather, wiry coat is straight, harsh, and about two inches long to protect him from brambles of the field. The coat is liver and white (spotted, roan, ticked, or solid liver), with the head solid liver.

This is another breed that should be a working dog, not a pet. She is aloof with strangers and can be stubborn, with terrierlike obstinacy. This breed is a busy, high-energy dog that isn't particularly good with children, but is ideal for hunting or field-trial work.

GIANT SCHNAUZER

This is the largest of the three distinct Schnauzer breeds (see also Miniature and Standard). Schnauzers were the farmers' attempt to develop a terrier-type dog able to drive different-size livestock to market. The Giant Schnauzer's home is Bavaria, where he was a cattlemen's drover and guard dog.

Modern Giant Schnauzers also serve as police dogs in Germany. He looks like a bigger, enhanced version of the Standard Schnauzer, with a black or salt-and-pepper, wiry terrier coat and harsh beard and eyebrows. The tail is docked short, and the ears are V-shaped drop ears when natural, or sometimes cropped and held erect. He is a robust, alert, courageous dog easily trained, loyal, and playful. The Giant Schnauzer is stubborn, though, and may be selective in obeying commands.

He may be dog-aggressive, with a high prey drive toward smaller pets. Homes with small children should choose another breed.

GOLDEN RETRIEVER
Arguably one of the most popular breeds, the Golden Retriever is both an outstanding hunting dog and family companion due to her winning personality, desire to please, and high intelligence. The Golden is a large dog with medium-length, dense fur in various shades of gold, from dark red-gold to pale yellow.

Goldens are one of the most devoted and eager-to-please breeds, which makes them standouts for training. They are in-your-face dogs that want constant attention; training will help with this pushy attitude. They love kids—all ages, come one, come all—and make friends easily with strangers. They don't make particularly good guard dogs and may adopt a burglar as one of the family. Goldens need lots of exercise, so plan accordingly.

GORDON SETTER
The Gordon looks a bit like the Irish Setter, but is smaller and colored solid black with tan markings. She dates to seventeenth-century Scotland and was developed as a bird dog.

The Gordon has a loyal, almost fanatical devotion to family members, but is wary of strangers. She is an alert, gay, and interested dog that's not quite so goofy as the Irish Setter. She needs lots of exercise and is good with older children. The Gordon is smart and fearless and tends to be willing but slow to learn.

GREAT DANE
This is a giant of a dog, an elegant mastiff-type that was developed in Germany. However, dogs remarkably similar to today's Dane appear on Egyptian monuments dating from 3000 B.C., so the type has been around since antiquity. It's believed our modern dogs likely arose from influences of the Irish Wolfhound and English Mastiff breeds. The breeders wanted a "superdog" capable of hunting boar, and they got a noble, powerful canine ideally suited to the job.

Despite their imposing appearance, Danes are friendly, dependable dogs, spirited and slow to learn, but willing to please. The short, easy-care coat comes in brindle, fawn, blue, and harlequin. The Dane loves the children in his own family, but may be suspicious of neighborhood kids and other strangers and can be dog-aggressive. The biggest drawback is that Danes tend to be short-lived, reaching geriatrics by age six or so.

GREAT PYRENEES
Also known as the Pyrenean Mountain Dog, this breed originated on the slopes of the Pyrenees Mountains in France as the working man's dog as early as 1800 B.C. She may have come from Siberia originally and is likely descended from the Mastiff dogs depicted in Babylonian art of the third millennium B.C.

She is a large, massive dog, snow white with a profuse, heavy coat suited to cold climates. The Pyrenees is a guardian, bred to vanquish wolves and bears (which she resembles), and a protector of those she considers her friends. She is confident, gentle, and affectionate, but very territorial of family and flock. The Pyrenees is a reserved and independent freethinker that's hard to train. She is dog-aggressive, an inbred trait born of defending the flock from wolves. The best home for this dog is a ranch, where she can guard stock.

GREATER SWISS MOUNTAIN DOG
This mastiff-type dog is a giant, standing twenty-eight inches tall at the shoulder and weighing up to 130 pounds. In temperament and looks, this breed closely resembles the Bernese Mountain Dog, except he has shorter fur.

GREYHOUND
This ancient coursing breed is depicted in Egyptian tomb carvings dating from 2900 to 2751 B.C. The large, fleet "gray dog" has been a favorite of royalty for centuries, used to run down deer, hare, foxes, and other game. Despite her aristocratic heritage and bearing, the Greyhound is a lovable, easygoing, sensitive, short-haired dog that makes a great pet. Like most sight hounds, Greyhounds tend to be reserved with strangers, and they learn best with patient, slow training. She adapts well even to apartment life—as long as she has a good outlet for running—but she may prove hazardous to smaller, "prey-size" pets. She'll do well with older children, but may not appreciate the attentions of very young children.

HARRIER
This essentially is a smaller version of the Foxhound breeds and was developed to run in packs after hares and foxes. He is an outgoing, friendly dog that gets along well with other dogs. His high energy level makes him a difficult house pet; he needs to run and hunt. Though trainable, the Harrier is easily distracted by interesting smells. He gets along well with older children, but if left alone when confined outside, he tends to be a barker and digger.

IBIZAN HOUND
This is another ancient sight hound, a coursing breed traceable to approximately 3400 B.C., during which time the Egyptian deity Anubis (Watchdog of the Dead) in fact was identical to our modern Ibizan. The dog somehow made her way to an island now known as Ibiza (now belonging to Spain), where she hunted a variety of prey and was given her name. The moderately sized Ibizan may have either a short, smooth coat, or a wire-haired coat one to three inches in length with a mustache. She is a strong, remarkably healthy breed that makes a good pet, hunter, and watchdog.

The Ibizan does best in a predictable and quiet environment and is a quiet, reserved, but friendly breed that won't be all over you but likes her own space. She tends to be a slower learner. This is not the best choice for a home with very small children or other pets.

IRISH SETTER

This big, red dog became popular in the early 1800s and today remains a favorite of hunters and families. His handsome, moderately long coat is solid mahogany to rich chestnut red and is straight and flat with fringes on the legs, belly, and tail. Described as clownlike for his love of play, he's a gay, outgoing, happy dog that tends to take longer to mature. Slower to learn than some, the Irish remains devoted to his people and makes a fine family pet.

IRISH TERRIER

This medium-size, red dog is one of the oldest of the terrier breeds and claims Ireland as her home. Her shape has been described as a miniature of the old-style Irish Wolfhound, but in attitude she is a true terrier, ready to take on the world. She has been a successful hunter of small game and vermin, loves the water, and some say matches the hunting expertise of the Chesapeake Bay Retriever. During World War I, she even served as a messenger dog.

The Irish Terrier is an elegant dog, faithful to family, an eager playmate of older children, and a born guard dog. Like many terriers, she likes to bark and dig and needs a firm hand during training. She is plucky and has a fiery temperament that prompts some to call her the daredevil of terriers.

IRISH WATER SPANIEL

This breed is quite ancient, with similar types traced to the seventh or eighth century A.D. Yet some might mistake him for a Poodle due to his curly, crisp, water-resistant, liver-colored coat. The curled fur covers his body but is smooth and short on the front of the throat, face, whiplike tail, and rear legs below the hocks.

He's called the "clown of the spaniels" because of his distinctive topknot and peak of curly fur between the eyes and his precocious personality. The Irish Water Spaniel is loyal to those he knows, forbidding to strangers, and loves the water. He can be a stubborn dog to train and needs to be kept busy (hunting is his preferred activity). He likes children.

IRISH WOLFHOUND

This is a giant of a dog, sized at thirty-two inches at the shoulders and 120 pounds. The Wolfhound is a coursing sight hound that's been known since at least A.D. 391. He is similar to but more robust than a Greyhound and has a rough, weatherproof coat. Developed to hunt giant Irish elk and wolves, the Wolfhound has an intimidating appearance—but in fact is a mild-mannered dog that matures slowly and may be timid.

Wolfhounds need room to run—but be aware that he can leap over a six-foot fence. He may be aggressive toward smaller pets and tends to be suspicious of strangers. His quiet manner and gentle nature make him a good pet for those who understand his needs.

ITALIAN GREYHOUND

This toy sight hound is thought to have originated nearly two thousand years ago in the region now known as Greece and Turkey. The Italian Greyhound is the smallest of her kind (from five to fifteen pounds) and in fact is identical—except in stature—to the Greyhound. She may have been developed to hunt small prey, but today is primarily a pet. She tends to be a shy, high-strung dog, but usually warms up to strangers pretty quickly. This on-the-go, affectionate, and somewhat fragile little dog may not appreciate the roughhousing of small children.

JACK RUSSELL TERRIER

This is a small but bold dog that comes in either a smooth or "broken" coat that's predominantly white, with black or tan markings usually confined to the head. The Jack Russell is a high-energy, happy little dog developed in the 1800s to trail hounds and bolt foxes from their dens. She has become quite popular since television stardom on such shows as *Wishbone* and *Frazier*. This clever dog is a barker and digger, like most terriers, and can be aggressive toward small animals. Though exceedingly affectionate, she can be a stubborn, independent, and hardheaded dog that's not easy to train. She needs lots of regular exercise to diffuse all her energy and keep her out of trouble.

JAPANESE CHIN

The Chin is an ancient toy known for centuries in Japan, where he was the chosen companion of emperors. Most are black and white, or red and white. The coat is profuse, long, and straight; the tail twists over the back to one side; and the muzzle is short and broad. He is a bright, affectionate dog that has strong opinions of himself and others.

The Chin is a playful dog that tends toward shyness upon first meeting. He can be a stubborn character, but patient training will generally win the day. The short face of this breed makes him prone to snoring.

KEESHOND

This Dutch breed is the national dog of Holland, known for centuries there as a barge dog that guarded the ships and barges of the rivers. The Keeshond is a spitz-type northern dog that probably has ancestors in common with the Finnish Spitz, Samoyed, and Chow Chow breeds. He is a medium-size, profusely furred dog with prick ears, a foxy face, and a curled tail. The standout coat is a mixture of black, gray, and cream.

The Keeshond is a lively, alert, and intelligent dog, friendly with strangers and other dogs. With the right training, he is a standout in the obedience competition. He'll adapt well to apartment living, but can be a barker and needs daily exercise.

KERRY BLUE TERRIER

This medium-size terrier arose in the mountainous region of County Kerry in Ireland several hundred years ago. She is a jack-of-all-trades, used as hunter, retriever, and herder of cattle and sheep. She has even been used as a police dog in England. Her distinctive, dense, soft, wavy coat, always in blue-gray, gives the breed its name. This is a lovable, intelligent dog that does not get along well with other dogs or small pets and can be a challenge to train. Homes with small children should choose another breed.

KOMONDOR

The Komondor is a large Hungarian breed set apart by a distinctive long, white, corded coat. The Komondor is a guard dog and protector of livestock. He has been bred for centuries to rely on his own wits and to defend the flocks against all manner of beast; his distinctive coat offers protection from fang and claw.

This dog is wary of strangers and can make a fine watchdog, but is best suited to working. He is wary, independent, and very territorial and may show aggression even toward owners. The Komondor must be well socialized from an early age by an owner with a firm hand. This is not the best choice for a family pet.

KUVASZ

Similar in looks to the Great Pyrenees (though larger), this is a white, mastiff-type dog that hails from Hungary but was known over much of the ancient world. The name comes from the Turkish word *kawasz*, which means *armed guard of nobility*, and the breed became particularly popular during the fifteenth century.

The Kuvasz is courageous and curious, intelligent and sensitive, and not particularly demonstrative. Incredibly protective but slow to make new friends, she is an ideal guard dog. She is often suspicious and aggressive toward strangers and other dogs, and sometimes her own human family. An ideal home is a ranch where she can guard stock; choose another breed for a family pet.

LABRADOR RETRIEVER

The Labrador actually came from Newfoundland and was developed as a hunting dog. Today, their high intelligence and willingness to please puts these dogs in the field as hunters; in the home as companions; as service dogs that guide the blind; or as search-and-rescue dogs.

This is a short-coated dog with a distinctive "otter" tail—broad-based and tapering—that is always wagging. Labs come in three solid colors: black, yellow, and chocolate. Gregarious dogs that love the whole world—kids, adults, strangers, and burglars (labs aren't great watchdogs)—they are highly trainable but sometimes pushy in terms of demanding affection. Labs need lots of exercise.

LAKELAND TERRIER

In the past known as the Patterdale Terrier, the Lakeland was bred to work in the lake districts of England as exterminators of raiding foxes. The dogs are known for their "gameness," or willingness to go after prey with courage and fervor; they even travel dozens of feet below ground to rout the quarry!

This is a quiet, well-behaved dog with a hard, wiry coat that comes in a variety of colors. He's a square, long-legged, self-confident dog that's not too aggressive, but he may have a high prey drive toward small animals. He is a slow learner that needs patience during training. He'll enjoy older children and, like many terriers, likes to dig.

LHASA APSO

Tibet is the home of this distinctive small dog, which served as an, indoor guard dog. He has a profuse, heavy coat that falls straight from a middle part on his back to the ground, and a curled tail held high over the back. Today the Lhasa Apso is a pet, but retains the watchfulness and loyalty that made the breed outstanding guards.

He is an intelligent dog, but can be willful and independent, and nasty to people he dislikes. He may bond with one family member over another and make life miserable for the less-preferred person. This can make the Lhasa difficult to train, so begin when he's a puppy, and be firm. A home without children is best. Remember to treat a Lhasa Apso like a dog, or he'll act like a tyrant and treat you like a peon.

MALTESE

This ancient toy breed of Malta has been around for twenty-eight centuries and, from the beginning, was prized as a pampered pet. She is covered in cascades of white, silky fur that reach to the ground, her tail is carried plumelike over her back to one side, and she has heavily feathered drop ears. Her hair is often tied into a topknot to reveal striking dark eyes and a black nose.

The Maltese is a clean and engaging dog, with a friendly yet spirited temperament similar to other spaniels. She is a quiet, gentle dog that is smart, but doesn't respond well to overbearing training methods; slow and patient is best. The Maltese thrives on the status quo, so the unpredictability of small children isn't the best environment for her.

MANCHESTER TERRIER

This sleek, short-haired dog looks something like a scaled-down long-tailed Doberman Pinscher. He is the quintessential rat terrier bred since the mid 1500s, and is thought to have Whippet, Greyhound, or Italian Greyhound in his background. Manchesters come in two sizes: the Toy variety doesn't exceed twelve pounds, while the Standard is over twelve pounds but under twenty-two pounds. He is always solid black with mahogany markings.

The Manchester is a smart, quick little dog and a great companion. He's a devoted, sometimes bossy but personable character that needs firm training from the beginning. He may act aggressively toward small pets or young children, but gets along well with older kids. He also likes to dig.

MASTIFF

The Mastiff has been bred in England for over two thousand years as a watchdog, and similar dogs appear in Egyptian artifacts dating from 3000 B.C. Today's Mastiff has a heavy head and short muzzle; short fur in fawn, apricot, or brindle with dark (black) ears and muzzle; natural drop ears; and a long, supple tail. She is a giant among dogs, weighing up to two hundred pounds, and is massive and powerful, with a nobility that's hard to miss.

Despite her courage and rough appearance, the Mastiff is a good-natured, laid-back, docile dog that has a perpetual air of dignity. She is very protective and, though affectionate with the family children, may be suspicious of their friends. She can be aggressive toward other dogs or small pets. Confidently lead and train her from puppyhood on.

MINIATURE PINSCHER

Here's a toy breed with the look of the Doberman Pinscher. Native to Germany, the Minpin has been a fixture for several centuries. Despite a small stature, this toy has a "big-dog" attitude and takes her watchdog duties very seriously. Her short coat comes in red, black with rust markings, or chocolate with rust markings.

Some trainers describe the Minpin as a high-strung, noisy little imp and characterize her as much tougher than the comparatively sensitive Doberman. She is a lively, intelligent dog that is stubborn and difficult to train because she's so smart. Typically she bonds to only one or two people, and to them shows total devotion. Because of her dominant, difficult attitude and tendency to nip to get her way, families with small children should choose another breed.

MINIATURE SCHNAUZER

This breed was derived from mixing small Standard Schnauzers with Poodles and Affenpinschers. Essentially, he looks very much like his larger namesakes, the Standard and Giant Schnauzers, but all three are distinct breeds. He is distinguished by his wiry coat, abundant whiskers, and leg furnishings, usually in salt-and-pepper color. He is fond of kids, intelligent, and hardy, with a heritage as a farm dog and ratter.

This feisty terrier may become pushy if spoiled, and may bark and dig when bored. His curiosity and personality make him one of the most popular of the terriers.

NEWFOUNDLAND

The Newfie is another giant mastiff dog, similar in looks to the Great Pyrenees, but instead of solid white he comes in solid black, brown, or gray, or in white with black markings (Landseer color). He originated in Newfoundland, probably from dogs brought to that country by fishermen. He is a superior water dog, used at times to help fishermen with their nets or even to rescue drowning victims. He also was used as a draft dog, pulling carts and carrying packs like a horse.

The Newfie is a powerful dog that is loyal, intelligent, and above all, sweet of temper. He is the quintessential child's playmate and guardian and an excellent family pet. Exercise is important—especially swimming, which the Newfie loves.

NORFOLK TERRIER

This small, harsh-coated dog is a sturdy, fearless ratter characterized by her drop ears and erect docked tail. The coat comes in shades of red, wheaten, black and tan, or grizzle. She is a hardy working terrier, developed to go to ground and tackle or dispatch small vermin either alone or with a pack.

The Norfolk is a gregarious charmer, affectionate, fearless, and loyal, but only as obedient as she wants to be. Active and versatile, she's reserved with strangers and, though trainable, tends to be easily distracted. She does best with older children, particularly if they take a hand in her training.

NORWEGIAN ELKHOUND

The Elkhound dates to 5000–4000 B.C. and was the companion of Vikings, acting as guardian, herder, and hunter of big game. He is a compact, medium-size dog of the northern (spitz) type—that is, curled tail, prick ears, and dense, weather-resistant, standout coat. His thick, gray fur is striking and offers protection as well from attack.

The Elkhound is an agile, intelligent, and devoted dog, a versatile hunter adept at capturing a variety of game from raccoon and fox, to lynx, mountain lion, and elk. He is an eager companion, but barks a lot. A high-energy dog, he does not adapt easily to apartment living. He gets along well with older children and is best trained from an early age to defuse a tendency toward dominance.

NORWICH TERRIER

Until 1964, this dog was registered as the prick-ear variety of Norfolk Terrier. Since that date, she has been registered as a separate breed and called the Norwich Terrier. She is a happy-go-lucky, gregarious dog that likes kids and is a loyal companion similar in temperament to the Norfolk.

OLD ENGLISH SHEEPDOG

This shaggy, big breed is at least 150 years old and was developed to drive sheep and cattle to market. Because drovers' dogs were exempt from taxes, their tails were docked to identify their owner's occupation. He is characterized by lots of long, straight fur all over his body, usually in shades of gray, grizzle, blue, or blue merle with or without white markings. Modern dogs are rarely asked to herd, but are welcomed as companions.

The Old English is a homebody that makes a good house dog and is an intelligent, affectionate pet that's not particularly boisterous but can be moody and suspicious of strangers. Like most herding dogs, the Old English likes to chase cars, kids, and other moving objects.

OTTER HOUND

In the early 1300s, these dogs hunted otters in great packs to control their predation on fish. This breed has been described as looking like a cross between a hound and a giant terrier, with the floppy ears of the hound and the rough, coarse coat of the terrier. An Otter Hound may weigh up to 115 pounds, and her oily, water-repellent blue-and-white (or black-and-tan) fur and webbed feet make her an extraordinary swimmer.

This boisterous, amiable dog needs lots of exercise (she loves swimming!) and is eager to show her devotion to a worthy master. The Otter Hound is not a laid-back pet; she wants to work and will get into trouble if the owner doesn't offer her good direction.

PAPILLON
Known in the sixteenth century as the Dwarf Spaniel, the Papillon is a toy breed named for her distinctive erect, fringed ears that look similar to butterfly wings (*papillon* is French for *butterfly*). She also appears in a drop-ear variety, known as the Phalene. She is a delicate-looking, fine-boned, and dainty dog with long, fine, silky hair that flows about the body and off the tail, which is held high and arched over the back. She is always parti-color, or white with patches of color.

The Papillon is a happy and alert dog, a friendly, elegant dynamo that accepts training quite readily and is a standout in the obedience ring. However, she tends to bark, and her small size makes her rather delicate for rambunctious kids (or bigger dogs) to play with, although she'll get on well with cats and small dogs.

PEKINGESE
The earliest record of this toy breed's existence is traced to the Tang Dynasty of eighth-century China. The earliest Pekingese were alternately called Lion Dogs (for their massive manes), Sun Dogs (for their gold-red color), or Sleeve Dogs (for their tiny size and favorite perch). Pekingese were introduced to the Western world by the British after the looting of the Imperial Palace at Peking in 1860.

The Pekingese is a heavy-fronted, short-muzzled dog with rather short, bowed legs, a tail carried over the back, and profuse, long, thick, straight fur in any color. Today, this dog still retains his dignified personality and stubbornness and expects to be treated like royalty. He is suspicious of strangers and other dogs and not particularly cooperative during training. Yet he is a good choice for a single person or older owner because he has low exercise needs and tends to bond closely to one or two people.

PETIT BASSET GRIFFON VENDEEN
This is one of the many small and ancient French hounds, and a PBGV looks somewhat like a rough, wirehaired Basset. The name is quite descriptive: *Petit* means *small*; *Basset* means *low to the ground*; *Griffon* means *rough* or *wire-coated*; and *Vendeen* refers to the location of origin.

PBGVs are scent hounds historically used to find and drive small game like rabbits or hares. Most PBGVs are stubborn, tend toward independence, and may be hard to train due to scent distraction and high energy. But this breed can be a good family pet, as a PBGV is a happy extrovert willing to please an understanding master.

PHARAOH HOUND
This dog is one of the oldest of domesticated dogs, tracing her ancestry to at least 3000 B.C., where she was a favorite of the ancient Egyptians. This is a rather large

sight hound, with a tan to chestnut (red) short, smooth coat, amber eyes, long whiplike tail, and prick ears. When excited or happy, the Pharaoh "blushes": her nose and ears turn a deep rosy color. This elegant, striking dog is at once graceful and powerful, and loves to run.

Like most sight hounds, the Pharaoh Hound learns slowly and can't be rushed; she may also develop a "head in the sand" attitude and simply ignore your commands. Very active (she's able to jump a six-foot fence), she is an affectionate and playful dog, friendly with family but suspicious of strangers, and is easily distracted by the thrill of the chase. She should not live with smaller pets, which may prove too tempting for her hunting instinct. She will tolerate older children, but won't appreciate fawning from smaller kids—or adults; respect her need for privacy, or she may snap in protest. If you want to hug, adopt a Golden Retriever.

POINTER

The first reliable record of the Pointer appeared in England in 1650, and it's likely the Foxhound, Greyhound, and Bloodhound share in his ancestry. The modern Pointer is a short-haired "gun dog," a specialist that's most at home in the fields hunting. The breed is named for his talent of finding, and then "pointing" out, game.

The Pointer has a short, white coat with color (liver, lemon, black, or orange) speckled over the body, and solid patches of color on the head or tail. This is a medium to large dignified dog that may seem aloof, but he's single-minded and focused when it comes to hunting. He gets along well with kids and other dogs, but as a high-octane dog, he's best suited to a hunting home.

POMERANIAN

This toy dog is actually a miniaturized spitz descended from the sled dogs of Iceland and probably reduced in size in Pomerania. He has a heavy, standout, double coat that comes in red, orange, black, and a variety of other colors, a curled tail, and a foxlike face. Tiny yet sturdy, this delicate-looking smart and sassy dog is a wonderful pet and a good watchdog. He needs consistent training and often becomes a good obedience dog.

POODLE

One of the most popular breeds, the Poodle comes in three sizes: The Toy is ten inches or under (at the shoulder); the Miniature is ten to fifteen inches; and the Standard is over fifteen inches tall. The Poodle type arose in a number of countries, but most experts credit Germany as her homeland, where she was employed as a water retriever. The Standard is the oldest variety, with the two smaller dogs developed from their big cousin. Apart from size, all three are identical.

The Poodle's distinctive double coat comes in a variety of colors and is a cascade of profuse, wiry curls with a wooly undercoat. Left to its own devices, the coat forms ropelike cords similar to the Puli or Komondor coat. More commonly, the coat is clipped in traditional forms based on old hunting styles. Poodles are extremely intelligent, friendly, and high-energy dogs that get along well with strangers and children; in particular, the Standard is one of the best family dogs to be found. However, all varieties are smart enough to train an owner rather than the other way around!

PORTUGUESE WATER DOG

This breed was developed to aid fishermen in their work and actually herds fish into nets, retrieves lost tackle, and carries messages through the water from ship to ship. It's theorized that the breed was native to the Chinese-Russian border, where they worked as herders about 700 B.C., but were captured by invaders and eventually made their way to Portugal in the eighth century. The Portuguese looks somewhat like a Poodle, but in fact has two accepted coat types, either curly or wavy. Typically he's clipped short all over. He can also be clipped in a "lion clip" that leaves the coat long on his front half and tail tip and clips his muzzle and back half short. Fur comes in black, white, or brown.

The Portuguese needs direction and is a spirited, self-willed dog that bends his will only to those he respects. He loves the water and needs regular exercise. As he dislikes hectic activity, families with young children should look toward other breeds.

PUG

The Pug has a short, dense coat and curled tail. This toy breed has been around since before 400 B.C. and is a miniature of the mastiff-type dog.

His expressive, short-muzzled face endears him to most all who meet him. The Pug is a playful, charming, yet dignified dog that gets a great kick out of life. Training may take time, because he tends toward stubbornness. He loves kids, gets along well with other pets, and is easily adapted to apartment living.

PULI

This Hungarian breed is a medium-size, rusty-black dog with a distinctive corded coat and curled tail. She has been around for at least a thousand years and was developed as a drover that herded sheep. Her natural coat falls in cords from the middle of her back to the ground; when groomed, the fur takes on a wirehaired appearance.

Today, the Puli is more often a watchdog and companion than a working dog. The Puli's suspicion of strangers still makes her an excellent watchdog; however, she may resort to biting when thwarted. She is an affectionate and intelligent companion, but tends to bond closely to only one or two people. The Puli can be dog-aggressive, likes to bark and chase, and may not appreciate children.

RHODESIAN RIDGEBACK

Sometimes referred to as the African Lion Dog, this large breed is a hybrid developed with the influence of Great Danes, Mastiffs, Greyhounds, Bloodhounds, Terriers, and a native ridgeback hunting dog of the indigenous Hottentot people of South Africa. The result was a versatile dog able to flush birds, pull down large game (even lions), and protect farms from marauders. His short, wheat-colored hair, stamina, and endurance suited him to the rigors of the African bush, while his devotion endeared him to the settlers.

Today he remains a courageous, devoted dog that's clean, likes older children, and tends to accept obedience training. Some dogs are pushy with owners, and they all need firm guidance or they can become aggressive if they feel threatened. Pairs of Ridgebacks may opt for clan loyalty and collectively disobey the human owner, so keep only one at a time. A home without small children is best.

ROTTWEILER

This is a medium-size, mastiff-type, short-haired dog with black fur highlighted with rust markings. It's believed she is descended from the ancient Roman drover dogs, but her type was firmly established in Rottweil (Germany) about A.D. 700. The Rottweiler drove cattle and pulled carts; more recently, she's a police dog.

The Rottie is a calm, courageous, and confident dog, with an aloof attitude that is off-putting to strangers. She's an intelligent and extremely protective dog that needs a strong, firm hand. High demand for this breed has created poorly bred specimens that tend toward aggression and fear-biting. Dogs properly socialized and bred have the potential for outstanding obedience work and make wonderful family dogs. Be sure you choose wisely; get expert help, or choose a different breed.

SAINT BERNARD

This breed is another of the giant mastiff dogs, introduced to Switzerland by Roman armies during the first century A.D. There, he became a guard, herding, and draft dog and was well known by A.D. 1050 when he became intrinsic to safe passage through the mountainous, snowy regions between Switzerland and Italy.

The breed comes in both smooth short-haired and medium-length wavy-coated varieties, usually in combinations of red and white. This powerful, stern-looking dog actually tends to be quite mellow and makes a great family pet, but as he's so big, he may inadvertently hurt a small child simply by sitting on him! The Saint Bernard tends to be a slow learner easily distracted by scent. Be aware that the Saint is also a snorer and drooler.

SALUKI

The Saluki is probably the oldest known domesticated dog, with carvings of them from the Sumerian empire from 7000 B.C. looking identical to the appearance of modern dogs. She is a large sight hound with a Greyhound's body and short coat, but long, feathered fur on the ears, tail, and legs. She has extraordinary sight, loves to run, and is easily distracted by moving prey. This elegant, aristocratic dog comes in a variety of coat colors.

The Saluki is affectionate with owners, but not clingy or demonstrative, and needs her own space. She tends to be obstinate and a slow learner. She does best in a quiet home without very small children or other pets.

SAMOYED

This snow-white dog is a true ancient northern type, with profuse, thick fur, prick ears, and a curled tail. She is probably as close to a primitive dog as any can be, and served early on as a guardian of reindeer and, later, as a sled dog.

The Samoyed personality is described as happy and childlike, with an independent nature and a natural "smile" that wins hearts. Despite her friendliness, she can be a challenge to train and may bark, bite, and throw tantrums to get her way. The Samoyed is easily bored and, left alone, may become an annoying barker and digger. She gets along better with older children rather than younger ones.

SCHIPPERKE

The breed dates from the 1800s and originated in the Flemish provinces of Belgium, probably from herd-dog types like the Groenendael. This small, black dog has a foxlike face with prick ears and is a thickset, cobby dog either born tailless or docked. He is an agile rat hunter and takes watchdog duties seriously.

The Schipperke is a curious, devoted dog that's reserved with strangers. Training this independent, intelligent breed can be difficult, but persistence without harshness will win the day. The Schipperke tends to be a barker.

SCOTTISH DEERHOUND

This giant of a dog looks remarkably similar to the Irish Wolfhound, but is a bit smaller, with the upper weight ranges reaching about 110 pounds. The rough, harsh, wiry coat is three or four inches long and is typically a dark blue-gray color. The breed can readily be traced to the sixteenth century. Dogs were used to scent-find, run down, and kill the large (250-pound) Scottish deer.

The modern Deerhound is a wonderful companion, loyal and devoted, although suspicious of strangers and not particularly gregarious. He tends to be aggressive toward other dogs, particularly smaller pets, and may bite if scared or annoyed; a house with young children won't be well tolerated. He needs slow and patient training, a quiet place to laze away the day, and lots of running room for daily exercise.

SCOTTISH TERRIER

The Scottie is arguably the oldest of the terriers from Scotland. Her dense, wiry coat is rather short on the body, but is longer elsewhere to form a beard and bushy eyebrows and leggings. She is often colored black to dark gray. Her prick ears and short, tapered tail are always upright. This powerful, small dog tends to bond closely with only one or two people and remain suspicious of the rest.

Scotties typically are curmudgeons and don't appreciate small children or new experiences. Her suspicious nature makes her a good watchdog. Early socialization is important. Scotties are intelligent, but may choose to simply ignore training if it's not to their liking.

SEALYHAM TERRIER

The Sealyham was developed as a game little dog eager to go to ground after badger, otter, and fox. In shape, this Welsh Terrier somewhat resembles a light-colored Scottie with drop ears.

Today's dog is most often a pet, but still retains the terrier instinct toward prey. She makes a great watchdog and has a "big-dog" attitude despite her small size. The Sealyham is trainable but has a mind of her own. She can be moody like the Scottie, but usually is an outgoing, friendly pet.

SHETLAND SHEEPDOG
This is a miniature working Collie that grew small due to the environment of the Shetland Islands. Sheltie colors are black, blue merle, and sable, with white or tan markings.

These beautiful dogs are highly intelligent and easily trained; they are standouts in obedience. Their small size makes them great house dogs and companions, and they are also excellent guard dogs. They like to bark, chase cars, bikes, and joggers, and may nip a child's feet trying to herd him. Some tend toward extreme shyness, and early socialization is very important.

SHIBA INU
This small spitz-type dog from Japan has a curled tail, erect ears, and a short, thick coat that comes in all colors, with red, red sesame, and black and tan preferred. She was developed as a hunting dog and remains a very active dog with a strong hunting instinct that can be dangerous to small pets.

The Shiba is an independent character that's stubborn to train, and she can be aggressive with other dogs and aloof with strangers. But she's a clean, lively dog that will adapt well to apartment living and is very affectionate with her people.

SHIH TZU
This Chinese toy dog dates from A.D. 624, when it was known as the Lion (which is the translation of *Shih Tzu*). The breed was also called "the chrysanthemum-faced dog" because of the profuse hair that grows from the face in all directions, like the petals of the flower. They are known for their long, flowing hair, which comes in any color.

Shih Tzus were selectively bred to be small, smart, and very tame. Today's dogs retain these features and exhibit an outgoing, affectionate nature. They are stubborn, but are more easily trained than the Lhasa Apso or Pekingese. This active, curious dog may not appreciate very young children, but does fine with older children.

SIBERIAN HUSKY
The Husky is a northern-type sled dog that originated with the Chukchi people of northeastern Asia. Thick, dense fur, prick ears, and curled tail proclaim her as the spitz type, with the medium-length coat coming in any color imaginable. The eyes may be brown or blue, or even one of each color.

This dog is alert and outgoing, and friendly to a fault, although somewhat reserved with strangers. She is not particularly territorial; she may show burglars where you hid the silver! The Husky is extremely intelligent, so much so that she may think you're nuts when you try to train her. She tends to be a vocal dog, yodeling and howling similarly to wolves, and may be prey-aggressive toward smaller dogs. Huskies make great family dogs and get along well with children.

SILKY TERRIER

This toy was developed in Australia by crossing Australian Terriers with Yorkshire Terriers, producing a dog with the best qualities of both breeds. He is a low-set dog a bit longer than tall, with long, silky, blue-and-tan hair parted down the middle of his back, docked tail, and erect ears.

This curious, quick little dog has the same temperament as the "big" terriers— that is, he is aggressive toward other dogs, has a high prey drive toward smaller pets, and likes to bark and dig. He tends to be resistant to training, but can learn when exposed to patient consistency.

SKYE TERRIER

The Skye has been known for nearly four hundred years and hails from the Isle of Skye in Scotland. She was developed to hunt the rocky dens and cairns of the region. This long-bodied, low-slung dog has a distinctive long, silky coat that reaches the ground, with fur flowing down both cheeks from her erect ears. She should measure twice as long as she is tall—i.e., twenty inches by ten inches.

Today she's most treasured as a companion dog. The Skye is a fearless, gay dog loyal to friends yet cautious with strangers. Slow, consistent training is key with this breed, which may bite to get her own way. Homes with young children should consider another breed.

SOFT-COATED WHEATEN TERRIER

The Wheaten has been known for at least two hundred years in Ireland, and some believe it to be an ancestor of the Kerry Blue Terrier. He is a medium-size dog with soft, medium-length, wheat-colored fur.

He has a mild manner for a terrier. He tends to be a worrier, and so needs early socialization to improve his confidence level. Training needs to be slow and patient—not overbearing or demanding—to avoid turning timidity into fear-biting. The Wheaten is a sensitive dog, but can be self-confident and gay with those he knows.

STAFFORDSHIRE BULL TERRIER

This short-coated, medium-size dog is a Hercules for his size. Agile and active, he was developed early in the nineteenth century when dogfighting was the vogue, and arose from mixing early Bulldogs with smaller terriers to create the Old Pit Bull Terrier, now renamed Staffordshire Bull Terrier.

This is a courageous dog, intelligent and strong, and affectionate with family and friends. However, the breed can be aggressive toward small animals and tends toward dominance. In the wrong hands, this dog can be dangerous; once he bites, he won't let go. Ask an expert to help you choose, or pick a different breed.

STANDARD SCHNAUZER

The Standard is the prototype for the other sizes (Miniature and Giant) and is an ancient German breed. It's believed she was developed by crossing a black German Poodle and gray wolf spitz with wirehaired Pinscher dogs; this prompted the characteristic salt-and-pepper color, terrier look, and wirehaired coat. She worked as a rat catcher, yard dog, and guard.

Today, she's prized as a house companion. Typically her tail is docked, and ears cropped to stand erect; her natural ears are drop. She is a fearless protector, intelligent and high-spirited. Though affectionate, she's not especially eager to please, as she always has her own agenda. She may be aggressive toward smaller pets and can be noisy if not given enough to do, but she gets along well with older children.

SUSSEX SPANIEL

The rich golden liver color characteristic of this breed was developed by a founding breeder from Sussex, England, which gave the dog its name. The Sussex is a short-legged, long-bodied, medium-size dog with an exceptionally fine nose. He makes a determined, somewhat slow, but patient and sometimes noisy hunter who bays when on the scent.

The breed can be obstinate and hard to train because they're easily distracted by scent. The Sussex needs room to run and gets along well with children but won't tolerate roughhousing. He does best when offered the opportunity to hunt.

TIBETAN SPANIEL

This dog arose in the same place and time as the Lhasa Apso and, in fact, looks a bit like a short-haired Lhasa Apso. It's believed the Tibetan Spaniel had common ancestors with the Japanese Chin, Pekingese, and other Oriental dog breeds. She is a short-legged, long-bodied dog with curled tail, drop spaniel ears, and short face. In Tibet, she perched on the tops of monastery walls as a lookout, alerting her masters with shrill barks to approaching wolves or strangers.

The modern dog has a moderately long, straight coat that comes in any color. She's a highly intelligent, sweet, and affectionate dog. Suspicious of strangers, she tolerates other pets well. The Tibetan barks a lot and is a great watchdog, but needs consistent training from puppyhood to combat her stubborn attitude. Older children are fine, but this breed may not appreciate unpredictable small children.

TIBETAN TERRIER

The Lhasa Apso, Tibetan Spaniel, and Tibetan Terrier all arose about two thousand years ago through the lamas' careful breeding in the monasteries of this region. He is a medium-size dog that carries his tail over his back and has a profuse, soft, double coat that comes in any color and falls over the face. Unlike the other two breeds, the Terrier is rather square and not particularly low to the ground.

He was developed purely as a companion and today remains an affectionate, intelligent pet. The Tibetan Terrier is decidedly unterrierlike; he's not bossy, not dominant, and is a quiet, happy, and friendly companion that will make friends with strangers quite readily. As he also gets along well with children and other pets, he's a wonderful choice for the family dog.

VIZSLA

This breed is also referred to as the Hungarian Pointer. Stone etchings from the tenth century portray dogs very similar to the Vizsla. Pointer in type, this breed has a slightly more tapered muzzle, tail docked long, and a short, smooth, solid golden-rust coat.

The Vizsla is a medium to large elegant-looking dog. A hunter, she's easily trained to tasks involving hunting, but can be distracted from other tasks by an interesting scent. She's lively and gentle with those she knows, but protective and fearless with strangers.

WEIMARANER

He was developed to hunt the large game of Germany, including wolves, wildcats, mountain lions, and bears. Once the big game was gone, the Weimaraner made the transition to bird dog. This is a big, ghostly looking dog similar in type but larger than the Vizsla and with a distinctive silvery, short, satin coat and amber or light gray eyes. The photography of William Wegman has made this dog famous.

He thrives on human interaction and is an outstanding hunter, but not always an ideal family pet. The Weimaraner needs to stay busy and can be suspicious of strangers and too rough with small children.

WELSH CORGI

The Corgi has been around for more than three thousand years, and today the two varieties are designated as separate breeds. The Pembroke Welsh Corgi has no tail, while the Cardigan Welsh Corgi (the older of the two varieties) has a full-length tail. Both are low-to-the-ground, short-legged, prick-eared herding dogs that resemble sawed-off German Shepherds. Corgies worked by nipping the heels of the cattle to drive them where needed.

Strong-willed pets with a sassy attitude, Corgies often are suspicious of strangers. However, they are loyal and even-tempered with family and those they know. They are extremely agile dogs and can be outstanding obedience and herding dogs. They'll do best when given a job to do to use up some of their energy.

WELSH SPRINGER SPANIEL

This is one of the most ancient of hunting breeds, traceable back to 250 B.C. The red-and-white Welsh Springer Spaniel is an excellent water dog with a sensitive nose. He is larger and stronger than the Cocker Spaniel but smaller than the English Springer. He's known to be gentle and affectionate with children and other dogs, but is reserved with strangers and will act as a guard dog should the occasion arise.

WELSH TERRIER

In shape and size, this dog looks remarkably like a small Airedale. This medium-size terrier is likely a very old breed. Similar dogs are portrayed in paintings of the 1800s and earlier as the Black and Tan Terrier.

The Welsh is an alert and spirited dog, friendly with family but reserved around strangers. She tends to be aggressive with other dogs and small animals and may be timid when young. She is a stubborn dog that learns slowly, likes to dig and bark, and doesn't relish small children.

WEST HIGHLAND WHITE TERRIER

This snow-white terrier is an old Scottish breed and packs big-dog attitude in a small, compact body. He's a spunky, devoted pet, eager to play, but hardy and able to handle the outdoors. The two-inch-long white coat is left longer on the legs and around the face to frame expressive, black, shoe-button eyes. The Westie makes a good watchdog due to his suspicion of strangers and may be a challenge to train due to his stubborn nature. For those who enjoy an active, impetuous dog, the Westie makes a wonderful pet.

WHIPPET

This medium-size sight hound is, in fact, a miniature version of the Greyhound. He is a charming, affectionate, and intelligent pet whose twenty-pound size makes him an ideal house or apartment dog. He is clean and quiet, and though probably the friendliest of the sight hounds, he can be timid of strangers.

He can be trained with patience, but tends toward information overload if given too much to think about at once. He needs daily exercise—he's a runner, after all—and may be aggressive toward smaller pets. He appreciates children who respect his space.

WIREHAIRED POINTING GRIFFON

This is a medium-size general-purpose hunting dog known for his distinctive harsh, wiry, double coat. He's believed to have in his ancestry various setter, spaniel, and Otter Hound blood. The color typically is steel gray with brown markings. The coat fits it admirably to wet hunting, and the dog is a strong swimmer and excellent water retriever.

Unlike many hunting dogs, the intelligent Griffon is quick to learn and wants to please. He makes a great family dog as well as hunting companion.

YORKSHIRE TERRIER

The Yorkie was developed as a ratter in the nineteenth century and, despite her small size, has a big-dog attitude. She has beautiful, unique steel-blue-and-golden-tan silky fur that parts down the back and hangs straight down both sides. The tail is docked to medium length, her head is held high, and her ears are small and carried erect.

Like all terriers, Yorkies have an attitude of self-importance and like to bark and dig. She tends to be timid of strangers, but is a highly intelligent dog that responds to patient, consistent training. The Yorkie is a very affectionate dog devoted to her special people.

Appendix B

Symptoms at a Glance: The Quick Reference Guide for Home Diagnosis

SIGNS AND SYMPTOMS	DISEASE OR CONDITION
abortion, stillbirth	brucellosis
aggression, toward people/ other pets	dominance, fear, hyperthyroidism, rabies, rage syndrome
appetite, increased	Cushing's disease, diabetes mellitus, hyperthyroidism, megaesophagus
appetite, loss of (anorexia)	abscess, Addison's disease, anemia, babesiosis, blastomycosis (fungus), cancer, canine coronavirus, canine distemper virus, canine parvovirus, coccidiosis, copper poisoning, dehydration, diabetes, ehrlichiosis, enteritis, fever, hyperparathyroidism, hypoparathyroidism, infectious canine hepatitis, insect bites, kennel cough, kidney disease, lead poisoning, leptospirosis, liver disease, lungworms, mastitis, pain, pancreatitis, periodontal disease, peritonitis, prostatitis, pyometra, rabies, Rocky Mountain spotted fever, salmon poisoning, salmonella, stomatitis, swallowed objects, valley fever (fungus)

SIGNS AND SYMPTOMS	DISEASE OR CONDITION
barking, voice changes	laryngeal paralysis, laryngitis, tick paralysis, tumor
blackheads/pimples, on chin and mouth	acne
bleeding	aspirin toxicity, blood disorders, cancer, ehrlichiosis, heatstroke, hemophilia, infectious canine hepatitis, leptospirosis, poison, trauma, Von Willebrand's disease
blood, coughing up	cancer, heartworms, infectious canine hepatitis, poison, tuberculosis
blood, in bitch's milk	mastitis
blood, in stool	aspirin toxicity, blood disorder, cancer, canine parvovirus, coccidiosis, colitis, copper poisoning, histoplasmosis (fungus), hookworms, infectious canine hepatitis, inflammatory bowel disease, kidney disease, liver disease, poison, Rocky Mountain spotted fever, salmon poisoning, salmonella, threadworms, whipworms
blood, in urine	babesiosis, bladder stones, cancer, copper poisoning, cystitis, ehrlichiosis, infectious canine hepatitis, liver disease, poison, Rocky Mountain spotted fever
blood, in vomit	aspirin toxicity, cancer, canine parvovirus, kidney disease, NSAIDs poisoning (Tylenol), other poison, ulcer
bloody nose	cancer, ehrlichiosis, head trauma, hemophilia, hyperthermia, infectious canine hepatitis, poison, Rocky Mountain spotted fever, Von Willebrand's disease
blindness	cataract, diabetes, epilepsy, glaucoma, liver disease, poison, progressive retinal atrophy, proptosis of eyeball, PRA
breathing, choking/gagging	anaphylaxis, bloat, cancer, insect bites, poison, swallowed/inhaled objects, tuberculosis
breathing, gasping/wheezing	anaphylaxis, asthma, collapsed trachea, heart disease, heartworms, insect bites, kennel cough, laryngeal paralysis, laryngitis, pneumonia, poison, tetanus

SIGNS AND SYMPTOMS	DISEASE OR CONDITION
breathing, labored	anaphylaxis, anemia, asthma, blastomycosis (fungus), bloat, cancer, canine distemper virus, collapsed trachea, electrical shock, heart disease, heartworms, hernia, insect bites, internal bleeding, lungworms, pneumonia, poison, Rocky Mountain spotted fever, trauma, tuberculosis, vaccine or drug reaction
breathing, panting excessively	antifreeze poisoning, asthma, bloat, hyperthermia, hypoparathyroidism, laryngeal paralysis, pain, poison, snakebite
breathing, rapid	anemia, bloat, eclampsia, electrical shock, pneumonia, poison, shock, snakebite
breathing, shallow	bloat, electrical shock, hernia, pain
breathing, stopped	anaphylaxis, drowning, electrical shock, hypothermia, poison, tick paralysis, trauma
bruising	hematoma, hemophilia, poisoning
bumps	abscess, atopy, cancer, cuterebra, cyst, insect bite, papillomatosis (warts), vaccination reaction
chewing, of coat or skin	allergy, canine scabies, insect bite, lice
chewing, grinding teeth	babesiosis, canine distemper virus, epilepsy, lead poisoning, poison, rabies
choking, gagging	bloat, collapsed trachea, flukes, swallowed objects
circling	bloat, cryptococcosis (fungus), Cushing's disease, head trauma, otitis
coat condition, dandruff	cheyletiellosis, seborrhea
coat condition, dry	giardiasis, malabsorption syndrome, roundworms, tapeworms, whipworms
coat condition, oily	malabsorption syndrome, seborrhea
coat condition, ricelike debris	tapeworms
collapse	Addison's disease, anaphylaxis, antifreeze poisoning, babesiosis, bloat, cancer, canine parvovirus, disk disease, eclampsia, epilepsy, heart disease, heartworms, insect bites, poison, snakebite

SIGNS AND SYMPTOMS	*DISEASE OR CONDITION*
constipation	bloat, cancer, diabetes, kidney disease, lead poisoning, swallowed objects
coughing	blastomycosis (fungus), bronchitis, collapsed trachea, flukes, heart disease, heartworms, histoplasmosis (fungus), kennel cough, laryngeal paralysis, laryngitis, lungworms, pneumonia, Rocky Mountain spotted fever, threadworms, tuberculosis, valley fever (fungus)
crying, whining, yelping	bladder stones, bloat, car sickness, disk disease, dominance display, fear, fractures, hip dysplasia, insect sting, pain
defecation, large volume	malabsorption syndrome
defecation, strained or unproductive	colitis, constipation, inflammatory bowel disease, prostatitis, swallowed object
depression	abscess, Addison's disease, anemia, cancer, canine coronavirus, canine parvovirus, dehydration, ehrlichiosis, fever, hemophilia, histoplasmosis (fungus), hypothyroidism, kidney disease, lead poisoning, liver disease, peritonitis, pneumonia, prostatitis, pyometra, rabies, salmon poisoning, salmonella, shock, snakebite, stress
diarrhea	Addison's disease, antifreeze poisoning, canine coronavirus, canine distemper virus, canine herpesvirus, canine parvovirus, changing diet, chocolate poisoning, coccidiosis, colitis, copper poisoning, enteritis, feeding milk, flukes, food allergy, giardiasis, histoplasmosis (fungus), hookworms, hyperthermia, infectious canine hepatitis, inflammatory bowel disease, lead poisoning, leptospirosis, liver disease, pancreatitis, poison, Rocky Mountain spotted fever, roundworms, salmon poisoning, salmonella, snakebite, swallowed objects, threadworms, whipworms
discharge, from penis	balanoposthitis, candidiasis (fungus), cystitis, prostatitis
discharge, from vagina	candidiasis (fungus), cystitis, imminent birth, pyometra

SIGNS AND SYMPTOMS	DISEASE OR CONDITION
drinking, difficulty or refusal	cancer, canine parvovirus, foreign object in mouth, oral burns, rabies, tetanus
drinking, increased thirst	antifreeze poisoning, chocolate poisoning, Cushing's disease, diabetes mellitus, hyperparathyroidism, hyperthyroidism, infectious canine hepatitis, kidney disease, leptospirosis, pyometra
drooling	car sickness, chocolate poisoning, eclampsia, foreign body, hyperthermia, insect bites, insecticide toxicity, oral burns, pain, periodontal disease, poison, rabies, snakebite, stomatitis, toad poisoning
drunk, incoordination	antifreeze poisoning, babesiosis, canine distemper virus, carbon monoxide poisoning, Cushing's disease, disk disease, eclampsia, epilepsy, head trauma, hypoparathyroidism, insect bites, otitis, poison, tick paralysis
ears, dark crumbly debris	ear mites, insect bites
ears, discharge and/or odor	otitis
ears, red or raw	allergy, otitis
eyes, change of color	corneal ulcer, infectious canine hepatitis, uveitis
eyes, cloudy	cataract, glaucoma, infectious canine hepatitis, keratitis, uveitis
eyes, dilated/nonresponsive pupil	glaucoma
eyes, discharge/runny	canine distemper virus, cherry eye, dry eye, ectropion/entropion, ehrlichiosis, glaucoma, infectious canine hepatitis, Rocky Mountain spotted fever, salmon poisoning, ulcer, uveitis
eyes, glazed/staring	epilepsy, hyperthermia, rabies
eyes, hard	glaucoma, tumor
eyes, out of socket	proptosis of eyeball
eyes, pawing at	cherry eye, dry eye, foreign object, glaucoma, pain, ulcer, uveitis

SIGNS AND SYMPTOMS	DISEASE OR CONDITION
eyes, rough surface	uveitis
eyes, soft	uveitis
eyes, sores/ulcers	dry eye, ectropion/entropion, keratitis
eyes, squinting	allergy, dry eye, ectropion/entropion, glaucoma, infectious canine hepatitis, keratitis, leptospirosis, otitis, pain, ulcer, uveitis
eyes, sunken	dehydration
eyes, swelling	allergy, cherry eye, glaucoma, tumor
face rubbing	hypoparathyroidism, inhalant allergy, insect sting, periodontal disease, porcupine quills
fading puppies	brucellosis, canine herpesvirus, hypoglycemia
fainting, especially during exercise	anemia, asthma, bloat, heart disease, histoplasmosis (fungus)
flinching	arthritis, disk disease, fear, fractures, hip dysplasia, pain
footpads, thickened/cracked/ bleeding/swollen	canine distemper virus, demodicosis, hookworms, lupus erythematosus complex, threadworms, zinc-responsive dermatosis
growling, snarling	aggression, dominance, epilepsy, fear, pain, stress
hair loss	allergy, Cushing's disease, fleas, hot spots, hypothyroidism, mange, ringworm, seborrhea, shedding, stress, sunburn, zinc-responsive dermatosis
head tilt	cryptococcosis (fungus), disk disease, head trauma, otitis, tumor
hiding	fear, pain, rabies, stress
hunching (painful abdomen/ back)	bladder stones/obstruction, bloat, botulism, brucellosis, cystitis, disk disease, infectious canine hepatitis, kidney disease, lead poisoning, leptospirosis, pancreatitis, peritonitis, poison, prostatitis, Rocky Mountain spotted fever, salmonella, swallowed object, trauma

SIGNS AND SYMPTOMS	*DISEASE OR CONDITION*
hyperactivity, agitation	chocolate poisoning, hyperthyroidism, insecticide poisoning, lead poisoning, other poison, snakebite
itching, all over	flea allergy, food allergy, insect sting, mange, vaccination reaction
itching, of back and tail	fleas
itching, of chest, armpits, and feet	inhalant allergy
itching, of chin and face	inhalant allergy, demodicosis
itching, of ears	ear mites, fly bites, otitis, sunburn, ticks
itching, localized	demodicosis, hot spots, insect bites, sunburn
itching, self-mutilation	canine scabies, demodicosis, hot spots, lick dermatitis, obsessive-compulsive disorders
lethargy, listlessness	anemia, dehydration, fever, hypoglycemia, shock
licking, anal region	anal gland problem, constipation, swallowed object
licking, coat or skin	abscess, allergy, fleas, hookworms, insect bites, lice, lick sores, mange
licking, feet	inhalant allergy
licking, genitals	balanoposthitis, bladder stones, brucellosis, cystitis, estrus, labor, mating, pyometra, trauma
limping, lameness	arthritis, cancer, demodicosis, ehrlichiosis, fractures, hemophilia, hip dysplasia, Lyme disease, Rocky Mountain spotted fever, slipping kneecap, valley fever (fungus)
loss of consciousness	antifreeze poisoning, asthma, carbon monoxide poisoning, chocolate poisoning, dehydration, drowning, electrical shock, heart disease, hyperthermia, hypoglycemia, hypothermia, shock, snakebite, trauma
lumps	abscess, allergy, cancer, cuterebra, vaccination reaction
milk, yellow/blood-streaked	mastitis

SIGNS AND SYMPTOMS	*DISEASE OR CONDITION*
mouth, blue-tinged tongue/gums	asthma, heart disease, pneumonia, poison, respiratory distress
mouth, bright red gums	carbon monoxide poisoning, gingivitis, hyperthermia, leptospirosis, poison, stomatitis
mouth, brown tongue	kidney disease, leptospirosis
mouth, burns	caustic poisons, electrical shock
mouth, difficulty chewing/ swallowing	botulism, burns, cancer, foreign body, insect bites, poison, porcupine quills, rabies, tetanus, tick paralysis
mouth, dry/tacky gums	dehydration, kidney disease
mouth, jaw paralysis	abscess, fracture, rabies, tetanus
mouth, loose/broken teeth	gingivitis, periodontal disease, trauma
mouth, pale	anemia, canine coronavirus, canine parvovirus, coccidiosis, dehydration, eclampsia, fleas, hemangiosarcoma, hemophilia, hookworms, shock, trauma
mouth, pawing at	abscess, cancer, caustic poison, periodontal disease, porcupine quills, swallowed objects
mouth, sores/ulcers	caustic poison, kidney disease
mouth, stringy saliva	dehydration
mouth, swollen/bleeding	gingivitis, insect bites, periodontal disease, salivary mucoceles, snakebite, trauma
mouth, yellow/brown tooth debris	periodontal disease
muscle tremors, twitches	brain tumor, chocolate poisoning, dehydration, eclampsia, ehrlichiosis, epilepsy, hyperthermia, hypoparathyroidism, insecticide toxicity, poison, tetanus
nose, bloody	cancer, ehrlichiosis, hemophilia, infectious canine hepatitis, poison, Rocky Mountain spotted fever, shock, trauma, Von Willebrand's disease
nose, discharge/runny	cancer, canine distemper virus, canine herpesvirus, ehrlichiosis, foreign object, infectious canine hepatitis, kennel cough, rhinitis, sinusitis

SIGNS AND SYMPTOMS	DISEASE OR CONDITION
nose, eroding	lupus erythematosus complex
odor, ammonia breath	dehydration, kidney disease
odor, ammonia urine	bladder stones, cystitis
odor, anal area	anal glands, flatulence, poor grooming
odor, bad breath	cancer, periodontal disease
odor, of body	abscess, cancer, demodicosis, dermatitis, skunk
odor, from ears	cancer, otitis
odor, mousy	acanthosis nigricans, demodicosis, seborrhea
pacing	bloat, car sickness, chocolate toxicity, Cushing's disease, eclampsia, fear, pain, poison
paddling, with feet	dreaming, seizure (epilepsy)
pale: ears, nose, toes, tail tip, scrotum	frostbite
pale: lips, tongue, gums	anemia, babesiosis, eclampsia, electrical shock, fleas, hemophilia, histoplasmosis (fungus), hookworms, poison, shock, snakebite, trauma
paralysis	botulism, cancer, disk disease, trauma, tick paralysis
pulse, too fast	anemia, dehydration, heart disease, hyperthermia, hyperthyroidism, shock
pulse, too slow	Addison's disease, dehydration, heart disease, hypothermia, poison
rolling	head trauma, otitis, pain, poison, submission display
salivation	anaphylaxis, car sickness, chocolate poisoning, eclampsia, foreign body, hyperthermia, insect bites, pain, periodontal disease, poison, rabies, snakebite, toad poisoning
scooting (on bottom)	allergy, anal gland problems, tapeworms

SIGNS AND SYMPTOMS	*DISEASE OR CONDITION*
seizures	antifreeze poisoning, brain tumor, canine distemper virus, canine parvovirus, chocolate poisoning, cryptococcosis (fungus), Cushing's disease, electrical shock, epilepsy, head trauma, hypoparathyroidism, kidney disease, lead poisoning, liver disease, low blood sugar, poison, snakebite, toad poisoning
shivering	car sickness, disk disease, eclampsia, electrical shock, fear, fractures, hypothermia, insecticide toxicity, pain, poison, shock, snakebite
skin, black (or color change)	acanthosis nigricans, chronic dermatitis, lupus erythematosus complex, mange
skin, blisters/charred	caustic poison, frostbite, sunburn
skin, greasy	acanthosis nigricans, seborrhea
skin, loss of elasticity	Addison's disease, dehydration, kidney disease
skin, lumpy/bumpy	cancer, insect bites, papillomatosis (warts), vaccination reaction
skin, moist sores	candidiasis (fungus), frostbite, hot spots, seborrhea, sunburn
skin, painful	abscess, burns, frostbite, ulcers
skin, pepperlike debris especially at tail root	fleas
skin, red and peeling	burns, frostbite, lupus erythematosus complex, sunburn
skin, scabby/crusty	fleas, lice, mange, ringworm, sunburn
skin, scaly/dandruff	lice, mange, seborrhea, zinc-responsive dermatosis
skin, sores/ulcers	burns, candidiasis (fungus), lick sores, lupus erythematosus complex, mange, sunburn, tumor, valley fever (fungus)
skin, swelling	abscess, anal glands, balanoposthitis, burns, cancer, frostbite, hypothyroidism, tumor
skin, thickened	acanthosis nigricans, canine scabies, chronic dermatitis, hypothyroidism, sunburn

SIGNS AND SYMPTOMS	*DISEASE OR CONDITION*
skin, waxy debris	seborrhea
skin, yellow tinge (jaundice)	babesiosis, copper poisoning, hemolytic anemia, leptospirosis, liver disease
sleeping too much	anemia, carbon monoxide poisoning, disk disease, fever, hypoglycemia, hypothyroidism, obesity, pain, stress
sneezing	abscessed tooth, foreign body, lungworms, rhinitis, sinusitis
sores, draining	abscess, anal glands, cancer, cysts, ulcers
sores, slow healing	abscess, cancer, lick granuloma, ulcer
stiffness, of joints	arthritis, cancer, disk disease, fractures, hip dysplasia, Lyme disease
stiffness, odd gait	arthritis, cancer, disk disease, eclampsia, hip dysplasia, poison, tetanus
stiffness, paralysis	botulism, cryptococcosis (fungus), disk disease, fractures, poison, snakebite, tetanus, tick paralysis
sterility, loss of libido	brucellosis, prostatitis
swelling, of abdomen (no pain)	copper poisoning, Cushing's disease, heart disease, heartworms, obesity, pregnancy, roundworms
swelling, of abdomen (painful)	bloat, cancer, canine herpesvirus, constipation, hemangiosarcoma, infectious canine hepatitis, liver disease, pancreatitis, peritonitis, pyometra, swallowed objects, urethral obstruction
swelling, of breast	cancer, false pregnancy, mastitis, pregnancy
swelling, of ear flap	hematoma
swelling, of ear tips, nose, tail, toes	frostbite
swelling, of face/head	abscess, anaphylaxis, hypothyroidism, infectious canine hepatitis, insect bites, Rocky Mountain spotted fever, salivary mucoceles, snakebite
swelling, of joints	arthritis, ehrlichiosis, Lyme disease

SIGNS AND SYMPTOMS	*DISEASE OR CONDITION*
swelling, of legs	cancer, ehrlichiosis, heart disease, heartworms, liver disease, Rocky Mountain spotted fever
swelling, of lymph nodes	brucellosis, cancer, plague, tuberculosis
swelling, of penis	balanoposthitis, foreign object
swelling, of scrotum	brucellosis, postneutering
swelling, of skin	abscess, cancer, cuterebra, fracture, hematoma, hernia, insect bites, trauma
temperature, fever	abscess, babesiosis, canine coronavirus, canine distemper virus, canine parvovirus, eclampsia, ehrlichiosis, heatstroke, histoplasmosis (fungus), infectious canine hepatitis, leptospirosis, Lyme disease, mastitis, metritis, pancreatitis, peritonitis, plague, pneumonia, prostatitis, pyometra, Rocky Mountain spotted fever, salmonella, seizures, tick paralysis, tuberculosis, valley fever (fungus)
temperature, too cold	anemia, dehydration, hypothermia, hypothyroidism, kidney disease, salmon poisoning, shock, snakebite
urination, blocked	bladder stones, cancer
urination, excessive	antifreeze poisoning, chocolate poisoning, Cushing's disease, diabetes mellitus, hyperparathyroidism, hyperthyroidism, kidney disease, leptospirosis, pyometra
urination, frequent/ small amounts	bladder stones, cystitis
urination, in odd places	bladder stones, cystitis, diabetes mellitus, kidney disease
urination, straining, splattery stream	bladder stones, cancer, cystitis
urination, with blood	bladder stones, cancer, cystitis, hemolytic anemia, hemophilia, poison, prostatitis, Von Willebrand's disease

SIGNS AND SYMPTOMS	DISEASE OR CONDITION
vomiting	Addison's disease, anaphylaxis, antifreeze poisoning, botulism, canine coronavirus, canine parvovirus, carbon monoxide poisoning, car sickness, chocolate poisoning, copper poisoning, eclampsia, enteritis, food allergy, hookworms, hyperparathyroidism, hyperthermia, inner ear infection, insect bites, kidney disease, lead poisoning, leptospirosis, liver disease, megaesophagus, NSAIDs poisoning (Tylenol), overeating, pancreatitis, poison, Rocky Mountain spotted fever, salmon poisoning, salmonella, snakebite, swallowed objects, tick paralysis, whipworms
vomiting, unproductive (or prolonged)	bloat, poison
weakness	Addison's disease, anemia, aspirin toxicity, babesiosis, botulism, cancer, canine distemper virus, disk disease, heart disease, hemophilia, hookworms, hyperthermia, hypoglycemia, hypoparathyroidism, insulin reaction, kidney disease, liver disease, poison, shock, snakebite, tick paralysis
weight gain	diabetes mellitus, hypothyroidism, obesity
weight loss	anemia, anorexia, arthritis, aspirin toxicity, babesiosis, blastomycosis (fungus), brucellosis, cancer, coccidiosis, copper poisoning, diabetes mellitus, diarrhea, ehrlichiosis, heart disease, heartworms, histoplasmosis (fungus), hookworms, hyperthyroidism, kidney disease, liver disease, lungworms, malabsorption syndrome, malnutrition, megaesophagus, NSAIDs poisoning (Tylenol), pain, pancreatitis, roundworms, salmon poisoning, tuberculosis, valley fever (fungus), whipworms
weight, unable to maintain	cancer, giardiasis, malabsorption syndrome, megaesophagus, poor nutrition

Appendix C

Resources

ANIMAL WELFARE AND INFORMATION SOURCES

AKC Gazette
51 Madison Avenue
New York, NY 10010
http://www.akc.org

American Humane Association
Animal Protection Division
63 Inverness Drive East
Englewood, CO 80112-5117
(303) 792-9900
http://www.americanhumane.org

American Society for the Prevention
of Cruelty to Animals
424 East 92nd Street
New York, NY 10128-6804
(212) 876-7700
http://www.aspca.org

Bloodlines Magazine
United Kennel Club
100 East Kilgore Road
Kalamazoo, MI 49002-5584
http://www.ukcdogs.com/publications.htm

Delta Society
289 Perimeter Road East
Renton, WA 98055-1329
(800) 869-6898
http://www.petsforum.com/deltasociety

Dog Fancy Magazine
P.O. Box 6050
Mission Viejo, CA 92690
http://www.dogfancy.com

Dog World
500 North Dearborn
Suite 1100
Chicago, IL 60610
(312) 396-0600
http://www.dogworldmag.com

Friends of Animals
777 Post Road, Suite 205
Darien, CT 06820
(low-cost neutering)
(800) 631-2212
http://arrs.envirolink.org/foa

National Animal Control Association
P.O. Box 480851
Kansas City, MO 64148-0851
(800) 828-6474

National Animal Interest Alliance
P.O. Box 66579
Portland, OR 97290-6579
(503) 761-1139
http://www.naiaonline.org

PetLife Magazine
1227 West Magnolia Avenue
Fort Worth, TX 76104
http://www.petlifeweb.com

Tree House Animal Foundation
1212 West Carmen Avenue
Chicago, IL 60640-2999
(773) 784-5488
http://www.treehouseanimals.org

PET SERVICES

American Boarding Kennels
Association
4575 Galley Road, Suite 400 A
Colorado Springs, CO 80915
(719) 591-1113

American Dog Owner Association
1654 Columbia Turnpike
Castleton, NY 12033
(518) 477-8469
http://www.adog.org

Animal Blood Bank
P.O. Box 1118
Dixon, CA 95620
(800) 243-5759
http://www.io.com/~tradew/abb

ASPCA National Animal Poison
Control Center
(800) 548-2423
(900) 680-0000
htpp://www.napcc.aspca.org

Association of Pet Dog Trainers
P.O. Box 385
Davis, CA 95617
(800) 783-3647
http://www.puppyworks.com

AVID Identification Systems, Inc.
3179 Hamner Avenue
Norco, CA 91760
(800) 336-2843
(microchip ID)
http://www.avidid.com

Eastern Veterinary Blood Bank
2138-B Generals Highway
Annapolis, MD 21401
(800) 949-3822
http://evbb.com

Hemopet (blood bank)
17672-A Cowan, Suite 300
Irvine, CA 92614
(714) 252-8455

HomeAgain Companion Animal
Retrieval System
1095 Morris Avenue
P.O. Box 3182
Union, NJ 07083-1982
(800) 2FIND-PET
(microchip ID)
http://www.sp-animalhealth.com/
homeagain/ha.htm

IdentIchip
4894 Lone Mountain Road, Suite 169
Las Vegas, NV 89130
(800) 926-1313
http://www.identichip.com

InfoPet Identification Systems
415 West Travelers Trail
Burnsville, MN 55337
(800) 463-6738
(microchip ID)

Pet Loss Support Hot Line
University of California at Davis
(503) 752-4200

Pet Loss Support Hot Line
University of Florida at Gainesville
(904) 392-4700 ext. 4080

Pet Sitters International referrals
(800) 268-SITS

Tattoo-A-Pet
(800) TATTOOS
Once enrolled in program, this
hot line is free

VETERINARY RESOURCES

American Animal Hospital
Association
P.O. Box 150899
Denver, CO 80215-0899
(800) 883-6305
http://www.healthypet.com

American Holistic Veterinary
Association
2214 Old Emmorton Road
Bel Air, MD 21015

American Veterinary Chiropractic
Association
P.O. Box 249
Port Byron, IL 61275

American Veterinary Dental Society
530 Church Street, Suite 700
Nashville, TN 37219
(800) 332-AVDS

American Veterinary Medical
Association
1931 North Meacham Road Suite 100
Schaumburg, IL 60173-0805
http://www.avma.org

American Veterinary Society of
Animal Behaviorists
Dr. Wayne Hunthausen, President
Westwood Animal Clinic
4820 Rainbow Boulevard
Westwood KS 66205
(913) 362-2512

Animal Behavior Society
2611 East 10th Street
Office 170
Indiana University
Bloomington, IN 47408-2603
http://www.cigab.indiana.edu.ABS

Association of American
Veterinary Medical Colleges
1101 Vermont Avenue NW
Suite 710
Washington, DC 20005-3521
http://www.aavmc.org

International Veterinary
Acupuncture Society
P.O. Box 1478
Longmont, CO 80502
(303) 682-1167

CANINE RESEARCH FOUNDATIONS

AKC Canine Health Foundation
51 Madison Avenue
New York, NY 10010
(212) 696-8236
http://www.akc.org/found.htm

American Veterinary Medical
Association
1931 North Meacham Road
Suite 100
Schaumburg, IL 60173-0805
http://www.avma.org

Canine Eye Registration Foundation
(CERF)
SCC-A
Purdue University
West Lafayette, IN 47907
(317) 494-8179
(317) 494-9981 fax
http://www.cheta.net/connect/
canine/health/cerf.htm

Morris Animal Foundation
45 Inverness Drive East
Englewood, CO 80112-5480
(800) 243-2345
http://www.petgalaxy.com/
wildlife/morris/main.html

Orthopedic Foundation for Animals
2300 East Nifong Boulevard
Columbia, MO 65201-3856
(573) 442-0418
http://www.offa.org

VetGen
3728 Plaza Drive, Suite 1
Ann Arbor, MI 48108
(800) 4-VETGEN
(734) 669-8440
(734) 669-8441 fax
http://www.vetgen.com/research.html
(DNA-based genetic disease
detection service)

CREDITS

Grateful thanks to the following breeders, owners, or handlers who allowed their dogs to be photographed privately and/or during the Texas Kennel Club 100th Annual All-Breed Dog Show and Obedience Trial in Dallas, the Trinity Valley Kennel Club 30th Anniversary Show in Fort Worth, the Westminster Kennel Club 122nd and 123rd Annual Show in New York, and the Fort Worth Kennel Club Show in Fort Worth.

Affenpinscher
Ch Yarrow's Lucy in the Sky
Owner: Jacqueline Stacy, Beth Swergart,
    and Letisha Webbell

Afghan Hound
Molie're du Menuel Galopin
Owner: Victoria Spencer

Airedale Terrier
Ch Serendipity's Highlander
Owner: Vera Marie and Russell J. Hammond

Akita
Ch Carousel's Never Surrender
Owner: Sandra Pretari and S. Gignilliat

Alaskan Malamute
Malaworth I'll Take My Chances
Owner: Hal and Stephanie Shaffer

American Eskimo, standard
Ch Yoshi's Racer-X
Owner/Breeder: Andrew and Nancy
    Heister

American Staffordshire Terrier
Mithril Habenero
Owner: Brenda Lilly

American Water Spaniel
Ch California Regal Rex, CDX, CGC
Owner: Linda Ford

Australian Cattle Dog
Ch Shalimars Renegade N Disguise
Owner: Joyce Rowland and Chris Ann
    Vohsen

Australian Terrier
Ch Yaralla's Dunn Deal
Owner: Sheila Dunn

Basenji
Ch Signet Unforgetable O'Bedlam
Owner: Brenda J. Cassell and Phyleen
    Steward Ramage MD

Basset Hound
Mabest's Scarlet Letter
Owner: Joe Greenland and Mary E.
    Stover

Bedlington Terrier
Ch Chelsea's Blue Cameo
Owner: Mary Jo Dunn

Belgian Malinois
Ch Crocs Blancs' Daktari Turick
Owner: Carolyn and Leonard Bain

Belgian Sheepdog
Ch Nordost's Amulett
Owner: Delphine Johnsen and Rita
    Thatcher

Belgian Tervuren
Ch Sidekick's Aviatrix
Owner: Karen and Jeffrey Simchak

Bernese Mountain Dog Int.
Ch/German Ch/VDH-Ch Berri
    v.d. Horlache

Bichon Frise
Ch Heights Illustrious Illusion
Owner: Michele L. Nelson and Tamara
    Roth

Black and Tan Coonhound
PR Canyon Creek Birdman
Owner: Janet Kosnik

Bloodhound
Ch Bloomoon's James Thurber
Owner: Walt Partin, B. Howard, and
    A. Taylor

Border Collie
Rosaltess Bob B Sox
Owner: Ronnie Waddell

Border Terrier
Ch Double Take Torn Curtain
Owner: Gary and Paula Wolf

Boston Terrier
Rivermist Ready to Rumble
Owner: Rachel Stoyanova

Boxer
Ch Mid-Dea's Table Talk
Owner: George McGrath

Borzoi
Am. Ch Midknight Mmardi Gras
Owner: Donna R. Maharan

Bouvier des Flandres
Silver Magic Von Blouche
Owner: Gene and Theresa D. Geyer

Briard
Ch Kaliphi Jadzia Dax
Owner: Tommy and Merry Jeanne
    Millner

Brittany
Ch Jump Up Bhabalu
Owner: Sandra and David H. Bolin

Brussels Griffon
Ch Bo-Mar's Pocket Rocket
Owner: Mamie Gregory and Evalyn
    Gregory-Haag

Bulldog
Ch Shrink A Bull White Label
Owner: Rachael Earl and
    Christopher O'Reilly

Bulldog
Ironstone's Bud
Owner: Jack and Dianna Holmes

Bullmastiff
Ch Semper Fi Truly Impressive
Owner: Maggi Ahrens

Bull Terrier (miniature)
Ch Torringford's Red Storm Rising
Owner: M. and E. Bettigole and James
    Gaignet

Cairn Terrier
Ch Zomerhof's Top of the Liszt
Owner: Julie M. Ross

Canaan Dog
Ch Catalina's Felix to the Max,
C.D.C.A.-H.C., C.G.C.
Owner: Leal and Cynthia Grupp

Cavalier King Charles Spaniel
Ch Corneel V.H. Lamslag
Owner: Janet York

Chesapeake Bay Retriever
Ch Sand Bar's Last Laugh
Owner: Diane Kiester

Chihuahua, smooth coat
Ch Ouachitah Rialto
Owner: Dan Greenwald and Bill Andrews

Chihuahua, longhair
Ch Charming Chi's Cheyenne
Owner: Mary Lou Brown

Chinese Crested, powderpuff
Mariah's Windstorm
Owner: Dottie Thompson

Chinese Crested
Ch Razzmatazz Spectacular
Owner: Janice Chaffin-Bell and Amy
    Fernandez

Chinese Crested
Ch Gingery's Krimson 'N' Clover
Owner: Arlene Butterklee

Chinese Shar-Pei
Grayland's Little Wyoming Bear
Owner: Dorothy Schuerman

Chow Chow
Ch Sitze-Gou's Dust Devil
Owner: Yvette Freguson and Bill Buell

Clumber Spaniel
Ch Clussexx Billy Goat's Gruff
Owner: A. Kalter and C. Lezotte and
    J. Haverick and D. Johnson

Cocker Spaniel
Ch Larmaro's Handsome Dancer
Owner: Nancy Foley and Ken Feller

Collie, rough
Briarwood's Silver Signature
Owner: Sondra Myers, Judith Charlton,
  and Alice and Noel Abert

Collie, smooth
Ch Mystery's Intrepid
Owner: Diane Hall and Van W. Hall Jr.

Curly Coated Retriever
Ch Black Jack of Alamar, TT, WC, JH
Owner: Marilyn Smith

Dachshund, longhaired
Ironstone's Dijac Cece
Owner: Jack and Dianna Holmes

Dachshund, smooth
Gen Tari Jesse Ann CD
Owner: Eugene I. Morris MD
  and Ann C. Arnold MD

Dachshund, wirehaired
Ch Brazos Ski Whistle Stop
Owner: Kellie Williams

Dalmatian
Ch Gresemenalli's Rolando
Owner: John Meggitt, Deborah Nagle, and
  Maria D. Zink

Dandie Dinmont Terrier
Ch Montizard King's Mtn Kricket
Owner: Dr. M. and P. Parker, and D. and
  J. Young

Doberman Pinscher
Ch Dadlus Mark My Word Elisaton
Owner: Devona Downing

English Cocker Spaniel
Ch Whitfield's Crescent Moon
Owner: Jane Gray Doty

English Setter
Ch Sevenoaks Golden Garters
Owner: R. Foster DVM, M. Smith DVM,
  and P. Ziebart

English Springer Spaniel
Morning Star's Regal Splendor
Owner: Dawn D'Amato

English Toy Spaniel
Ch Tudorhurst Thespian
Owner: Jo Ann Johnston

Field Spaniel
Ch Whicksford's Tigerlily
Owner: Jane Linden

Finnish Spitz
Ch Finkkila's Tikko
Owner: Tom T. and Marg G. Walker

Flat-Coated Retriever
Ch Torlum Dalziel
Owner: Helen Eley and Dorothy Mottram

Flat-Coated Retriever
Ch Hardscrabble's Blacsatin Sheen, CD
Owner: Susan D. Cooper

Foxhound, American
Ch Kelly Mt Prime Big Boy
Owner: Judy G. Rea

Fox Terrier, Wire
Dalriada's Six Shooter
Owner: Jackie Thatcher

French Bulldog
Little Brooks-Roshire's Susie Q
Owner: Margaret Brooks and DeAnne B.
  Little

German Shorthaired Pointer
Lyndon's Luck Be A Lady
Owner: Dr. Henry Clair

German Wirehaired Pointer
Ch Ebbtied Summer Heat
Owner: Theodore J. Magness Jr., Cindy
  Kelly, and G. Persinger

Giant Schnauzer
Ch Rodvins Pirate Looks at Forty
Owner: Paige McCarver

Golden Retriever
Eldorado's Deep River Hot and Spicy
Owner: Dottie Ann and Bob VonSuskil

Gordon Setter
Temmoku's Untamed Heart
Owner: Cindy L. Partridge

Great Dane
Ch Haltmeier's I.Z. Spots
Owner: Pat Haltmeier

Great Pyrenees
Ch Pyragon's Eternal Portrait CD
Owner: Rhonda Dalton and Laurie Scarpa

Greater Swiss Mountain Dog
Shadetree-Brushcreek Klausen
Owner: Gail and Gene Kasson

Greyhound
Ch Gala Tailor Maid
Owner: Laurie and Walt Goodell and
    Judie Treuschel

Ibizan Hound
Ch Bramblewood Husn Sharib Hawa JC
Owner: Carol Dickerson Kauffman

Irish Setter
Jessica of Tanor on Harbor Lights
Owner: Loren Schwartz

Irish Terrier
Ch Bally Riche Cave Canem
Owner: Robert F. Wynne and Joyce Wilson

Irish Water Spaniel
Ch Poole's Ide O'Regon Rain
Owner: Cathy and Robert K. Shelby

Irish Wolfhound
Ch Gooseberry's Wilde Magnolia C.G.C.
Owners: Ricki Gies and Steve McCrossan

Italian Greyhound
Donmar Viva's Chardonnay
Owner: Deborah Roddy and Edwina Martin

Japanese Chin
Ch Kikichans Bagheera
Owner: L. Ward and R. Millican and
    S. Werner and B. Naidorf

Jack Russell Terrier
Vagabond Voodoo of Little Eden
Owner: Michelle Ward

Keeshond
Ch KJ's Purrcolator
Owner: Kristen Jackson

Kerry Blue Terrier
Ch Blue Chip's Petal's Thunder
Owner: Albert Prinz and Edith Prinz

Komondor
Ch Lajosmegyi Far and Away
Owner: P. Turner, A. Quigley, and
    R. Halmi

Kuvasz
Ch Highlanders Enchanted Szlena
Owner: Stephen H. and Alice C.
    Kovacs

Labrador Retriever
Briarglen's Un-Finnished Business
Owner: Kim Livingston

Lhasa Apso
Bearnger Partial Eclipse MBA
Owner: N. and D. Greene and
    M. and L. Brockway

Lhasa Apso
Bay Wind Listen to Your Heart
Owner: Gina Pastrana

Lakeland Terrier
Ch Revelry's Awesome Blossom
Owner: Jean L. Heath and William H.
    Cosby Jr.

Maltese
Anoria's Ramblin' Rose
Owner: Anne Staudt

Manchester Terrier, standard
Ch Salutaire Foolish Pleasure
Owner: Barbara Odell and
    Colleen Jaehnig

Mastiff
NK Valiant Knight
Owner: Roger and Karen Smith

Miniature Pinscher
NHL's Jumping Jack Flash
Owner: Linda Anthony

Newfoundland
Ch Blue Heaven's Guardian Angel
Owners: Joseph and Dana Molloy and
    Rhoda Lerman

Norfolk Terrier
Ch Elve Nick RedThorn at Belleville
Owner: John F. Beale, Pamela G. Beale,
  and Cathy Thompson

Norwegian Elkhound
Ch Arjess Sit'N On a Gold Mine
Owner: Roberta Jean Sladeck and Sandi
  Peterson

Old English Sheepdog
Ch Merrimoppet Mood Indigo
Owner: Jim and Beverly Coleman and
  Karen and Joe Riley

Otter Hound
Ch Aberdeen's Caveman
Owner: Betsy Maxton and Jack and
  Andrea McIlwaine

Pekingese
Ch Morningstar Festival Music
Linley's Dance with Mandy
Owner: Herbert Holcomb and Erna
  Holcombe

Pharaoh Hound
Kamaraj Amon-Maya
Owner: Robin M. Lutwinas

Pointer
Ch Marjetta Moonshadow
Owner: Marjetta Kennel

Pomeranian
Ch Dimonde's Wicked Wenona
Owner: Diana M. Downey

Poodle, miniature
Clarion Bar King Clarabelle
Owner: Brian and Arlie Townley

Portuguese Water Dog
Ch Sete Mares Windward Breeze
Owner: Robin Zaremba, Lorraine
  Carver, and Virginia Murray

Pug
Winleigh's Moon of Xanadu
Owner: Cynthia Getchell

Puli
Ch Prydain Kodi
Owner: Christine Davidson and Barbara
  Edwards

Rhodesian Ridgeback
Ch Southridge Kimby Ladysmith
Owner: Grace Granberry

Rottweiler
Ch Hobson's Choice Froxanne
Owner: Jane Hobson and
  Kris Dunnebacke

Saluki
Raszuli Avicenna Omega
Owner: Jack Seelye/John Zimmerman

Samoyed
Iceway's Sox It to 'Em Hn'p
Owner: Robert Chaffin, Robin
  Cohen, and Bobbie L. Smith

Schipperke
Ch Kebrill's Mercurial Argonaut
Owner: Melanie Coronetz and Bruce
  Miller

Scottish Terrier
Belfyre Say It Again
Owner: Mike and Polly O'Neal

Sealyham Terrier
Ch Fanfare's Goodfellow
Owner: Carl and Laurie Prather

Shetland Sheepdog
Show Down's Blue Skye
Owner: Phil and Mary Monteith

Shetland Sheepdog
Ch Edgemont's Blue Rembrant
Owner: Pat, Chuck, and Ashley Albro

Shiba Inu
Ch Steelcrest's Magic Potion
Owner: Catherine and Brooke Browne

Shih Tzu
Ch Ming Dynasty's Devil's Play
Owner: Gloria and Jim Blackburn

Silky Terrier
Ch Wyncrest Born to Be Wild
Owner: Betty Pomeroy and Barbara A.
   Heckerman

Skye Terrier
Ch Gleanntan Gotheriteonebaby
Owner: Donna Dale

Soft-Coated Wheaten Terrier
Ch Aslan's Bach Star
Owner: Roger Weyersberg

Staffordshire Bull Terrier
Ch Knowbull's Dylan the Daring
Owner: Jose Rodriguez and Joan E. Dishion

Standard Schnauzer
Ch Charisma Jailhouse Rock
Owner: Constance Adel

Sussex Spaniel
Ch Three D. Stonecroft Endeavor
Owner: E. Miller and D. Horn and
   D. Johnson and M. Curtis

Tibetan Terrier
Ch Atisha Kimik's Magic Masquerade
Owner: Sheryl Rutledge and Mikki
   DeMers

Welsh Corgi (Cardigan)
Ch Rhydowen Noteworthy Allegro
Owner: Steve and Linda Donaldson and
   Pat Santi

Welsh Corgi (Pembroke)
Ch Heronsway Tybrenin B the Day
Owner: Anne H. Bowes and Douglas and
   Kathleen Sanders

Welsh Springer Spaniel
Am/Finn/Intl. Ch Rwyn Madrigal
Owner: Dawn C.

Vizsla
Ch Russet Leather Anasazi OA
Owner: Carol Dostal

Weimaraner
Ch Aldemar's Loose Levi's
Owner: Veronica and Chris Valentine and
   Amanda Nusbaum

Whippet
Edinburgh's Ceili
Owner: Scott Marlow

Wirehaired Pointing Griffon
Ch Wet Acres Blaze of Glory
Owner: Wendy and Robert Gerity

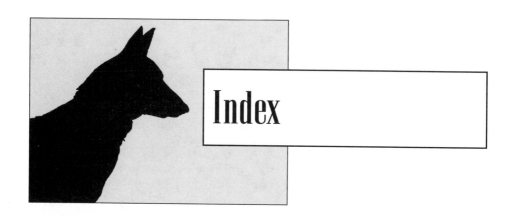

Index

About the Author

AMY D. SHOJAI is a nationally known authority on pet care and behavior who began her career as a veterinary technician. She is the author of eleven nonfiction pet books and more than 300 published articles and columns, and is the spokesperson for Purina brand pet foods.

Ms. Shojai has written widely in the pet field on training, behavior, health care, and the human/companion animal bond. She is a professional member of the Dog Writers' Association and the Association of Pet Dog Trainers, and has won numerous awards for her books and articles.

Ms. Shojai frequently speaks to groups on a variety of pet-related issues and regularly appears on national radio and television in connection with her work. She is also the author of *The Purina™ Encyclopedia of Cat Care* and is the founder and president of the Cat Writers' Association. She lives with her husband, Mahmoud, at Rosemont, their thirteen-acre "spread" located north of Dallas, which they share with assorted critters.